SLAYING EXCEL DRAGONS

Slaying Excel Dragons

A Beginners Guide to Conquering Excel's
Frustrations and Making Excel Fun

Mike "excelisfun" Girvin

Holy Macro! Books

PO Box 82, Uniontown, OH 44685

Slaying Excel Dragons

ISBN: 978-1-61547-000-6

Library of Congress Control Number: 2010904992

Printed in USA by: Edwards Brothers

First Printing: February, 2011. Printed with corrections: May 2013

Author: Mike Girvin

Technical Editor: Bob Umlas

Copy Editor: Keith Cline

Cover Design: Shannon Mattiza, 6Ft4 Productions

Illustrations: Timm Joy

More Graphics: Scott "Scottie P" Pierson

Image Processing: Fine Grains, India

Layout: Mary Ellen Jelen

Additional Production: Zeke Jelen

InDesign Consultant: Anne Marie Concepcion

Publisher: Bill Jelen

Published by: Holy Macro! Books, PO Box 82, Uniontown OH 44685

Distributed by: Independent Publishers Group, Chicago, IL

TABLE OF CONTENTS

Dedication...xiii

About the Author..xv

Acknowledgments xvii

Foreword xix

Introduction i

How to Use This Book xxiii

    A Note from the Author About Stepped Procedures xxiv

    A Note from the Publisher About Figures in the Print Edition xxiii

Working Along With This Book xxvi

1 HOW EXCEL IS SET UP 1

2 KEYBOARD SHORTCUTS 5

Ctrl Key Shortcuts (and a few others) 5

    Moving Data 5

    Highlighting the Current Region 6

    Copying Data 7

    Amazing Excel 2010 Ctrl Key Smart Tags 8

    Transposing a Range of Cells 11

    Highlighting a Column of Data 13

    Ctrl + Enter Keyboard Magic 16

Alt Shortcuts 22

3 DATA IN EXCEL 25

Raw Data Versus Information...25

SUMIFS Function 26

Verifying Formula Results (and tracking down bad data) 30

PivotTables 34

Table Format Structure 40

Sorting 42

Excel Table Feature (Excel as a database) 43

    Convert the table format structure to an Excel Table 44

    Dynamic ranges.. 45

    Adding a New Record in a Table 47

    AutoComplete 48

    Trouble with AutoComplete 49

    Table Names and Table Formula Nomenclature 51

Number Formatting as Façade 57

    Decimal Number Formatting 57

    Date Number Formatting 61

    Time Number Formatting 65

    Percentage Number Formatting 70

    Questions.. 71

Answers 71
Data Alignment (types of data Excel recognizes) 78
  Numbers Stored as Text 79

4 STYLE FORMATTING AND PAGE SETUP 89
Applying Style Formatting 90
Understanding Page Setup 98
  Printing and Print Preview 99
  Printing an Entire Workbook 104
  Page Setup for More Than One Page 105
  Set Print Area 106
  Page Break View 107
  Page Setup for Large Spreadsheets 108
Built-in Styles 111
  Table Styles 111
  Cell Styles 114

5 FORMULAS AND FUNCTIONS 119
Formulas Defined 119
  Five Types of Formulas 120
  Creating Formulas 120
  Formula Elements 120
Order of Operations 144
  Cost of Goods Sold Formula 144
  TRUE/FALSE Formula 146
  IF Function 148
Putting Cell References in a Formula 151
Cell References 155
  Relative Cell References 158
  Absolute Cell References 160
  Mixed with Row Locked Cell References 167
  Mixed with Column Locked Cell References 169
  Three Types of Cell References in One Formula 171
  Assumption Tables / Formula Input Area 185
  Efficient Formula Creation 188
  What-If Analysis 188
  Worksheet Cell References (sheet references) 191
  Workbook Cell References 195
  3D Cell References 198
Entering Formulas into Cells 202
Efficient Formulas That Use Ranges 203
Built-in Functions 207
  Finding Functions with the Insert Function Dialog Box 208
  FV Function for Investment Value 208
  Figuring Out How a Function Works 217
  Average Without Zeros Using Find 218

Average Without Zeros Using the AVERAGEIF Function..............................219
PMT Function for Loan Payment Amount 221
Defined Names Feature..224
MAX for Finding the Largest Value 225
Defined Name Manager...226
Create Names from Selection..227
MIN for Finding the Smallest Value 228
COUNTA for Counting the Total Number of Words.............................229
SUMIFS for Adding with Two Criteria 231
COUNTIFS for Counting with Two Criteria....................................234
COUNTIF Function to Create a Small Report.................................236
AVERAGEIFS for Averaging with Two Criteria................................238
Logical Tests (and/or)..238
SUMPRODUCT (to multiply and then add in succession) 240
Multiple Criteria Counting and Summing for Excel Versions Before 2007 ...244
IF Function (for putting one of two items in a cell or formula)...........248
  IF Function (to check whether two columns are in balance) 254
  OR Function..255
  Nesting Functions 256
  AND Function...258
  IF Function (to analyze customer creditworthiness).....................260
  IF Function (for commission calculation)...............................261
  Nesting IF Functions...263
Lookup Functions..268
  VLOOKUP (for looking up values) 268
  VLOOKUP Function (to assign a category to a sales number)..............271
  VLOOKUP Function (to help calculate commissions earned) 275
  VLOOKUP Function (to assign a grade)...................................278
  Data Validation and VLOOKUP (to complete an invoice) 278
  MATCH Function with VLOOKUP (to do a two-way lookup) 286
  VLOOKUP (to retrieve customer information from a different sheet)......291
  Defined Name for Data Validation List and VLOOKUP and MATCH Functions.....292
  MATCH Function (to check whether item is in master list)...............300
  INDEX and MATCH Functions (for two-way lookup).........................302
  INDEX and MATCH (for one-way lookup to the left) 306
  INDEX and MATCH (for one-way lookup above) 307
ROUND Function..308
Averaging with AVERAGE, MEDIAN, and MODE Functions 311
  AVERAGE Function...312
  MEDIAN Function 312
  MODE Function..314
New Excel 2010 Functions (RANK.EQ and RANK.AVE) 316
  RANK.EQ Function...316
  RANK.AVE Function 317
Goal Seek...318
Array Formulas..320
  Array Formulas Use Less Spreadsheet Real Estate 320
  SUMPRODUCT (to avoid Ctrl + Shift + Enter).............................324
  Array Formulas as the Only Efficient Option...........................326

Array Functions...332
Transposing a Range of Cells with the TRANSPOSE Array Function......................336
Errors **339**

6 DATA ANALYSIS FEATURES..341
Sort Feature 343
Sorting Numbers in a Single Column A to Z (smallest to biggest) 344
Sorting Numbers in a Data Set with More Than One Column A to Z...........344
Sorting Z to A by Using Right-Click 345
Sorting Words A to Z...346
Hierarchy for Sort When the Column Has Mixed Data 346
Sorting Blanks to Bottom to Remove Unwanted Records (A to Z)................348
Sorting #N/A Errors to the Top 350
Sorting with Keyboard Shortcuts...351
Using the Sort Dialog Box When Field Names Are Accidentally Sorted........352
Randomly Sort a Data Set..353
Sorting Left to Right 355
Sorting by Color 355
Sorting on More Than One Field...357
Using Icon Sort Buttons, Sort the Major Sort Field Last 358
Using the Sort Dialog Box, Select the Major Sort Field as the First Level 358
Rules for Sorting More Than One Field 359
Subtotal Feature 360
Subtotals to Summarize Data by Region (sum calculation) 361
Selecting Visible Cells Only (copy, paste)...364
Subtotals to Summarize Data by Region (average calculation) 368
Removing Subtotals 369
Subtotal to Count Words 370
Subtotals Within Subtotals 371
PivotTable Feature...374
PivotTables Are Easy to Make! 374
Creating a PivotTable in Four Clicks. 376
Changing the Report Layout to Show Field Names.......................................381
Style Formatting..382
Number Formatting...383
Changing the Calculation from Adding to Averaging....................................384
Pivoting the PivotTable 385
Listing Two Fields in Row Labels Area (similar to the Subtotal feature)......387
Collapsing PivotTable Row Labels...388
Filtering a Field in a PivotTable 388
Listing Three or More Fields in the PivotTable 390
Removing Fields from PivotTables 390
PivotChart Feature..391
Pivoting PivotTables and PivotCharts...395
Grouping Dates 396
Blanks in Data Sets 402

Words in Date Field 403
Amazing Report Filter Area 405
Creating 5 Reports with 1 Click Using Show Report Filter Pages Feature ... 408
Slicer Feature in Excel 2010 409
Frequency Distribution Reports... 412
   Creating Product Frequency Tables..413
   Creating Sales Frequency Tables 413
Percentage of Total to Show Employee Performance.......................... 414
   Creating Percentage of Total Reports 414
   Creating Running Total Reports 416
Showing Three Calculations for the Same Field: AVERAGE, MAX, MIN 416
   Creating AVERAGE, MAX, MIN Reports...417
When Source Data Changes, PivotTables Update Only *After* You Refresh ... 418
Filter Feature 420
Turning on the Filter Feature 421
Filtering with One Criterion 421
Filtering with "And" Criteria 422
Filtering with "Or" Criteria.. 423
Filtering to Extract Records from Data Sets...................................... 424
Removing Applied Filters 424
Right-Click Filtering.. 425
Filtering on Cell Fill Color 425
Filtering Below Average Values... 426
Filtering Top Five Sales 427
Filtering Words/Text... 429
Filtering Dates 430
Filtering Records to Add or Average with Multiple Criteria................ 432
Advanced Filter Feature 434
Extracting Records with One Criterion 435
Extracting Records with Two Criteria (*and* criteria is on one line)................ 436
Extracting Records with Two Criteria (*or* criteria is on two lines) 438
Extracting Records with "And" and "Or" Criteria................................ 439
Extracting Records with "Between" Criteria.. 440
Extracting Records with Date Criteria... 441
Extracting Records to a New Sheet 442
Extracting Unique Records/Items to a New Location (removing duplicates). 445
Text to Columns Feature 448
Separating First and Last Name from One Cell into Two Cells 449
Separating First and Last Name from 1 Cell into 2 Cells (formula) 453
Separating Full Address from One Cell into Four Cells....................... 454
Importing Data..457
Importing Data from a Different Excel Workbook............................... 457
   Copy and Paste 457
   Using the Get External Data Feature..457
Importing Comma-Separated or Tab-Separated Data.......................... 460
Importing Data from Access... 460
Using the Stock Quote Web Query 461

7 CHARTS 465

Categories and Series 466
Chart Types 468
  Pie Charts 468
  Histograms 469
  Bar Charts 469
  Stacked Bar or Column Charts 470
  Line Charts 470
  X-Y Scatter Charts 471
Creating and Formatting Charts 471
  Pie Charts 472
    Linking Chart Labels to Cells 474
    Adding Chart Data Labels 475
    Moving Charts 478
    Printing Charts 478
    Changing Chart Styles 479
    Saving Chart Templates 480
    Keyboard Shortcuts to Create Complete Charts 481
  Column Charts 481
  Histograms 483
  Bar Charts 489
  Stacked Bar or Column Charts 491
  Line Charts 492
  X-Y Scatter Charts 494
    Trendlines 496
    Break-Even Analysis 500
  Two Chart Types in One Chart 501
  Selecting/Editing Source Data for a Chart 501
  Sparklines 505

8 CONDITIONAL FORMATTING 507

Built-in Conditional Formatting 508
  Highlighting Duplicates 509
  Highlighting Values That Are Greater Than the Average 510
  Highlighting Values That Are in the Top 10% 510
  Icons 511
  Data Bars 511
Logical Formulas 512
  Highlighting a Cell Based on Another Cell's Value 512
  Highlighting a Whole Row for an Exact Value 517
  Highlighting a Whole Row for an Approximate Value 519
  Highlighting Weekends or Holidays 520

9 FIND AND REPLACE AND GO TO FEATURES 523

APPENDIX EXCEL EFFICIENCY-ROBUST RULES 527

INDEX 533

DEDICATION

Dedicated to:

Dennis Big D Ho (14 year old son) who like to read a lot

Isaac Viet Girvin (4 year old son) who likes to go on adventures a lot

ABOUT THE AUTHOR

My name is Michael Gel Girvin. From 1984 to 1997 I was a world class boomerang thrower who won multiple world titles. From 1988 to 1998 I ran a boomerang manufacturing company called Gel Boomerangs and the boomerangs earned numerous awards. During the early years of running the company I was computer illiterate and did not know how to use a database or spreadsheet. After I hired a consultant to teach me how to build a database and how to use a spreadsheet, my business life was transformed. My ability to create financial reports, do taxes and perform cost accounting was dramatically improved because I was starting to become computer literate. In particular, it was my growing ability to use Excel that allowed me to make better business decisions. As I learned more about what Excel could do it dawned on me that knowing how to use Excel to efficiently build robust solutions was one of the most important skills that any working human should possess. Why isn't this taught in the schools, I thought?

This led me into teaching. From 2002 to current I taught (and still teach) accounting, finance, statistics and math classes at Highline Community College. My primary goal as a teacher is to teach all my classes in a computer lab using only Excel - no paper and handheld calculators are allowed. In about 2004 I found Bill MrExcel Jelen's web site: www.mrexcel.com. This site had three amazing things: a message board where anyone could ask questions, a daily Excel PodCast (Excel TV) and easy to understand books. As a business person and an educator who was like a dry Excel sponge, I soaked up all I could from the MrExcel site and brought it to my classes. In addition, I appropriated MrExcel's idea of Excel TV by posting over 1000 Excel how to videos at YouTube (www.youtube.com/user/excelisfun). About 15,000 videos are watched every day at the excelisfun channel at YouTube site.

It is from my insights as a once-computer illiterate business person, an Excel-Business teacher and an avid fan of the MrExcel web site that I write this book.

ACKNOWLEDGMENTS

Thanks to Bill MrExcel Jelen for doing more than any other person on the earth to bring Excel to the world with his Message Board, Excel TV Podcasts and his amazing books! If it were not for him, I would not be writing this book. Thanks to Bob Umlas for an amazing technical editing job! Thanks to Keith Cline for the stellar "paying attention in English class" editing. Thanks to my two bosses at Highline Jeff Ward and Joy Smucker for bending over backwards to allow me time for writing this book.

FOREWORD

I remember the day like it was yesterday. I was on the phone with a fruit-and-nut guy, a potential client who was interested in hiring me to write some VBA macros to automate the recipe calculations for the various trail mixes that he sold. He started off with a line that I had heard a few times before:

"I love your Learn Excel podcasts on YouTube..."

I was about to thank him for the compliment, when I realized that it wasn't a compliment at all. He finished his sentence:

"...you are almost as good as that ExcelisFun guy."

Huh? What was he talking about??? I, MrExcel, was the Excel podcast guy on YouTube. Thanks to my former gig on TechTV, I had monthly access to podcasting pioneers such as Leo Laporte and Amber MacArthur. They were both a few months into their podcasting career when I jumped aboard and was producing video podcasts every weekday back in 2006. I had been pretty sure that I had the corner on the Excel podcast market.

Soon thereafter, I met Mike Girvin. Our "Dueling Excel" podcasts each Friday show that there are many different ways to solve a problem in Excel.

I love the fact that Mike builds his college classes around Excel. Whether he is teaching Excel, Statistics, Accounting, or Math, his students do 100% of their school work in Excel. This is, quite frankly, how the world should work. You should do everything in Excel.

I've written quite a few intermediate to advanced books about Excel. In my world, the accountants in my seminars use Excel 40 hours a week. The questions that I get all the time are the fairly advanced. I am too far removed from the people who are brand new to Excel. Mike, through his students, has contact every school day with dozens of people who might be struggling through their first experiences with worksheets. Because of this, Mike has a unique perspective into the "dragons" that make Excel seem so intimidating. I wanted to add a beginning Excel book to my publishing line-up and I am thrilled that Mike offered to write the book that you are holding.

—*Bill "MrExcel" Jelen*

INTRODUCTION

Have you ever used Excel and been frustrated that you couldn't get it to do what you want? Like trying to enter 2% into a cell, but it shows up as 200%, or trying to create a month report from daily transactional data, but you don't know how to add sales for each month, or adding a column of numbers, but the total is a few pennies off. If you have encountered problems such as these, this book can help you to overcome these problems and become an Excel Master!

Being an Excel Master is important because Excel is the default program on the planet, and we humans must know how to use it. Because most people aren't "fluent" in Excel, knowing how to use Excel efficiently is an easy way to impress the boss, look good in a job interview, or transform your ability to run your own business.

This book is intended for anyone who wants to master Excel: beginners, intermediate users, and even advanced users. The fact is that most of us intermediate and advanced users learned Excel in bits and pieces and have "holes in what we know". This book tells the story of how to master Excel without holes. In this way, this book can be useful for anyone who reads it.

This book will teach you two things:
- How to avoid the everyday frustration that most people encounter
- How to efficiently build robust Excel solutions

Efficient, in this scenario, means that you build your solutions quickly. Robust means that the solutions will not break easily and your Excel solutions are adaptable to change. This book will not teach you the rudimentary basics of Excel, such as opening a file, saving, printing, minimizing, and so on. Instead, this book assumes that you have opened Excel before and used it a little bit.

Before learning what you can do with Excel, you need to understand what Excel can actually do. Generally speaking, Excel does three things:
- Data storage: Stores raw data (like a database)
- Calculations: Makes calculations (math, retrieves data, text manipulation, or more)
- Data analysis: Turns raw data into useful information

This book covers the following broad topics:

- How Excel is set up
- Keyboard shortcuts
- Data storage in Excel
- Style formatting and page setup
- Calculations via formulas, functions, pivot tables, and other features
- Excel's powerful data analysis features
- Charts to visualize quantitative data
- Conditional formatting to visualize data

Guide to the Dragons in the Margins

A dragon in the margin indicates a particularly troublesome or amazing issue. You will notice these dragons:

 The fire-breathing dragon indicates things that you should never do. Stay away from these items

 The "uh-oh" dragon appears near things that can and frequently do go wrong in Excel.

 The question dragon appears next to confusing topics.

 The "note this" dragon appears next to things you should note.

 The "thumbs up" dragon appears near our favorite Excel tips.

HOW TO USE THIS BOOK

Every book is unique and this one is no exception.

The first time that a term is defined, it will appear in **bold**. Words or formulas that you are supposed to type will also appear in **bold**.

> *There are 43 Excel Efficiency Rules that appear in this book. You should cut these out and hang them up by your computer. We've even reprinted all of the Excel Efficiency Rules in the appendix to make this easier. The Excel Efficiency Rules appear in italics like this paragraph.*

Notes about the "why" you are doing something will appear in a grey box.

Sidebars Appear in a Box Like This

Sometimes, in the middle of a set of steps, there will be an opportunity to summarize some points. This summary is not part of the steps, but it seems like a good time to offer the summary. This discussion will appear in a box like this one.

A Note from the Author About Stepped Procedures

I must mention an unusual convention that I am using in this book. Most books that have step-by-step instructions limit the steps to 7 to 10 steps. I did not do that in this book. Some of the step–by–step instructions have more than 20 steps, and in some of the sequencing of steps I have injected large blocks of text in between the steps. What I am trying to do with this unusual approach is to simulate how I teach. When I teach, I do a project in class, and the students follow along. I do step 1 and step 2, then I stop and explain the significance of what we just did, then I do step 3 and step 4, then I stop and explain the significance of what we just did, and so on. The idea is that if I explain the 'whys" as close to the "hows" as possible, what you're learning sticks in the brain more firmly because the glue is stronger.

A Note from the Publisher About Figures in the Print Edition

I want to thank you for holding this antique in your hands. Someday, your children or grandchildren will experience a world where 100% of their reading happens on an e-Reader. However, you, the person holding *this* book, is one of the last to get to experience the look and feel of holding a printed book in your hands.

A printed book is a unique opportunity for the publisher to present to you a series of two-page spreads. We have 14.75 inches of paper extending from the left edge of this page over to the right edge of the facing page. The person who is doing the book layout is well aware that these words are appearing on the a left-hand page and that I have about 1.7 more pages to get my point across before you turn the page and these words disappear from view.

A decade ago, before I was writing books or publishing books on Excel, I was a customer of books about Excel. I had a certain author who was my favorite Excel author and I would buy every book that he wrote, as soon as it came out. Then, a book arrived that was a little annoying. The text on the right side of the page would be referring to a figure that was on the next two-page spread. I found myself flipping back and forth, over and over, for almost 80 straight pages. I couldn't believe that they would let this happen. If someone would have just inserted about half a blank page, then all of those figures would have appeared on the same page as the text.

Thus, I often have an almost manaical desire to have the figure and the text appear somewhere on the same printed two-page spread. If you are reading some words about a figure, I want you to be seeing the figure. We went through a lot of adjustments to get the words and figures on the same two-page spread.

As this book was running very late, awaiting layout from a guy half way around the world, Mike Girvin sent me a note that awoke something in me. Mike said, "This layout guy cares a lot more about saving paper than getting figures on the same page as text. This layout is going to annoy the reader".

I love the fact that Mike, a first-time author, pointed this out. Customers from Amazon to Wal-Mart were cancelling their orders because the book was late (due to no fault of Mike). I fired the layout guy, took a step back, and started over. To paraphrase Bruce Springsteen, a 1970's rock and roll star, "The release date is only a day, the book will exist forever." In other words, a year from now, no one will remember if the book came out on time. They will definitely hate us if the figures and the text are not together.

In the interest of getting the words and figures together, you will notice three things that "break the rules" of traditional publishers:

- Sometimes, we will cram a lot of words and figures on a two-page spread. You will see words that appear next to a figure. We went with figures close to the spine and words wrapping around the outside. When you see words wrapping around a figure, it is because we were trying to finish a topic on this particular two-page spread. Less times, when we needed to fit just another line or two on a page, we would throw out the rule of putting one-quarter of a pica of white space between paragraphs and jam everything a little closer together.

- Rarely, you will see the same figure twice. Sometimes there would be several paragraphs talking about the same figure. If we couldn't decide if that figure belonged on the bottom of the right-hand page or the top of the next left-hand page, we would put it on both pages. I've never seen any other book do this, but again, we're driven by the manaical need to have the figures and words on the same page.

- Frequently, we simply just punted and left a huge amount of white space at the bottom of a right-hand page. We aren't trying to pad the page count; when you see the big gap on the right, it is because the next words were going to describe a figure that really needed to be on the next page. If we had time, we would find someone to draw cute little cartoons to fill that white space. For now, it is just white space.

Hey look...here is some white space at the bottom of a right-hand page. This is a great place to jump to the next page, so that the very important information about downloading files is right next to the first page of chapter 1. Doodle your first dragon image here:

WORKING ALONG WITH THIS BOOK

This book comes with two main Excel workbook files, as follows:
- excelisfun-Start.xlsm
- excelisfun-Finished.xlsm

Download these files from either of these sites:
- http://www.mrexcel.com/slayingfiles.html.
- https://people.highline.edu/mgirvin/ExcelIsFun.htm

The Start file has the blank templates and worksheets so that you can try everything that you see in the book. As you read this book, prompts will tell you what worksheet in the workbook you must use to follow along with the examples in the book. The Finished file has all the finished examples from the book. There is also one zipped folder named Products that contains some files for Chapter 3, "Data in Excel," and a third workbook titled "May NetIncome.xlsm" for the "Workbook References" section in Chapter 5, "Formulas and Functions."

In addition, because this book is set up to enable people to learn Excel from beginning to end, teachers may want to use this book in the classroom. To this end, there is a zipped folder named Homework available that has homework files and solutions for each chapter in the book.

You can download these files from the URLs above.

Alright, now it's time to get started learning about the power of Excel!

HOW EXCEL IS SET UP

As we get started, we must look at how Excel is set up. The essence of Excel is that it has a rectangular shape that has two directions.

The left-to-right direction is represented by letters that indicate columns. The letters are called **column headers**. In Figure 1, you can see the vertical column C. As we move to the left from column C, the letters go backward, and as we move to the right, the columns advance through the alphabet. (When you get to Z, the next columns are AA, AB, AC, and continue to the last column, which is XFD, which is the 16,384th column.)

The up-and-down direction is represented by numbers that indicate rows. The numbers are called **row headers**. In Figure 1, you can see the horizontal row 5. As we move down from row 5, the row numbers increase (the last row is 1,048,576), and as we move up, the row numbers decrease.

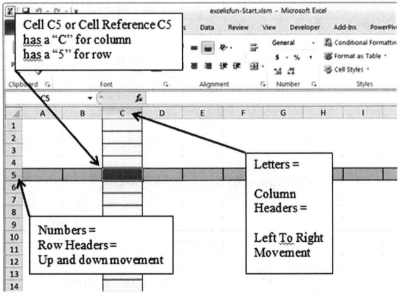

Figure 1

The intersection of a row and column is called a **cell** or a **cell reference**. In Figure 1, you can see that the cell C5 is the intersection of column C and row 5.

All the cells together are called the **worksheet** or **spreadsheet** or simply **sheet**. There can be many sheets in an Excel file. The name of the sheet is shown in the **sheet tab**. In Figure 1, the sheets tabs are a dark color, and the **active sheet tab** (sheet showing) is a light color. The default names for the sheets are sheet1, sheet2, and so on.

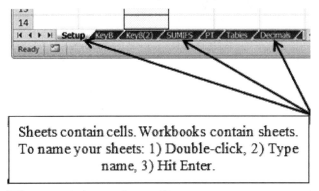

Sheets contain cells. Workbooks contain sheets.
To name your sheets: 1) Double-click, 2) Type
name, 3) Hit Enter.

Figure 1 (continued)

Because the default names hinder efficient and robust formula creation and navigation through a workbook, you should always give the sheet a logical name. For example, if the sheet has sales data, name it something like SalesData. This way, when you look at the sheet or make a formula with a sheet reference (more later), you have a good idea about what the sheet contains. To name the sheets, just double-click the sheet tab, type a name, and press Enter. To select a sheet, simply click the sheet tab with your cursor. All the worksheets in an Excel file are together called the **workbook**. You can see the workbook name in the **title bar** at the very top of the window (excelisfun-Start.xlsm).

Because there are more than 150 sheets in the Excel workbook file named excelisfun-Start.xlsm that came with this book, we need to be sure that you know how to navigate through this large workbook to any particular sheet that we may be working with. In Figure 2, the active sheet is named Setup, and it is colored white to indicate that the cells from this sheet can be seen and worked with. To select a sheet, simply use your cursor (white diagonal arrow) to click the sheet tab. In Figure 2, the last sheet that we can see is named Decimals. But there are many more sheets beyond (to the right). There are three ways to access sheets that cannot be seen:

- Use the keyboard shortcuts Ctrl + Page Down to move to the next sheet in a workbook (thus making it the active sheet) or Ctrl + Page Up to move to the previous sheet in a workbook (again, making it the active sheet).
- Use the sheet navigation arrows. The arrows without vertical lines move the view of the sheets without changing the active sheet, and the

arrows with the vertical lines jump all the way to the end or beginning of the sheets.

- Right-click any of the sheet navigation arrows, click More Sheets, and then navigate to whichever sheet you would like.

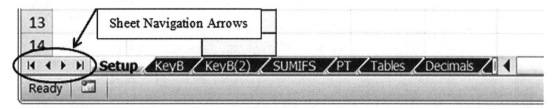

Figure 2

If you are not familiar with navigating in workbooks with a large number of sheets, try all three methods before reading further in this book. Doing so will help you to follow along with the more than 150 sheets in the Excel examples in this book.

Now we can state our first two Excel Efficiency-Robust Rules:

Rule 1: Excel sheets are rectangles with columns (letters) that move left to right and rows (numbers) that move up and down. A firm understanding of this will help us later to build formulas that are efficient and robust.

Rule 2: Always name sheets (double-click the sheet tab, type the name, press Enter) with an easy-to-understand name so that navigation through the workbook and formulas with sheet references are easy to understand.

Figure 3 shows a few more Excel elements that this book assumes you are familiar with, or at least have seen before.

> **Note:** Your ribbon might look slightly different. This is because the groups in the ribbon will expand and collapse depending on two things:
>
> - Whether your window is maximized or restored down
> - The display resolution for your computer (Control Panel settings)

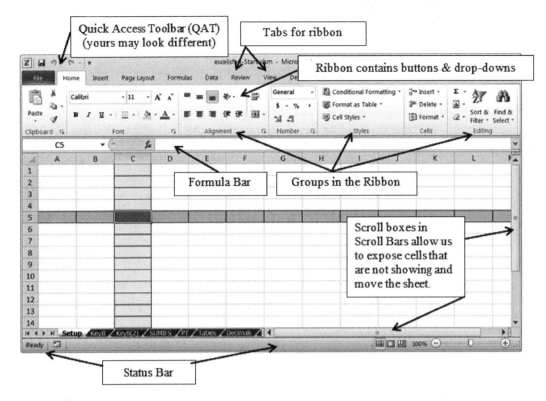

Figure 3

Note: There is one ribbon that has many tabs. The standard seven tabs are Home, Insert, Page Layout, Formulas, Data, Review, and View. There are many context-sensitive ribbon tabs that will show up when we use certain features. For example, when we make charts or pivot tables, specific ribbon tabs will appear when we work with the charts or pivot tables. In this book, when we want to get to the Insert or Page Layout part of the ribbon, I write, "Click the Insert tab or Page Layout tab."

Note: Because the ribbons take up a lot of space, you can hide and un-hide them with the keyboard shortcut Ctrl + F1.

Note: You can add buttons that you see in the ribbons to the Quick Access Toolbar (QAT) by right-clicking a button in the ribbon and pointing to Add to Quick Access Toolbar. The advantage to this is that the QAT is always visible no matter what ribbon tab you have selected.

Now it's time to take a look at keyboard shortcuts.

2

KEYBOARD SHORTCUTS

Now we are about to learn the best trick in all of Excel! Yes, this is the one trick that will guarantee you extra vacation time and instant success in the eyes of your bosses and co-workers. The one trick is... well it's not just one trick, it is many. Are you ready for this?

Learn keyboard shortcuts!

Keyboard shortcuts are one of the best ways to save time and become efficient. Let's look at a few examples here, and then throughout the rest of the book, you will see many more keyboard shortcuts.

To follow along, open the file named excelisfun-Start.xlsm and navigate to the KeyB sheet.

Ctrl Key Shortcuts (and a few others)

Figure 4 shows a summary sales report for January sales summed by product and sales representative. We would like to move this summary sales report from the cell range A1:F7 to H1:M7.

Moving Data

When you move something, there are four steps:
1. Highlight the current region (cell range with data) (Ctrl + *).
2. Cut the cell range (Ctrl + X).
3. Select the upper-left corner of the destination cell range. For example, select cell H1 if you are pasting the cut cell range into the range H1:M7.
4. Paste the cut cell range (Ctrl + V).

Highlighting the Current Region

In Excel, if a cell is selected, the term **current region** refers to the cells surrounding the selected cells that contain data. For example, in Figure 4 if cell A1 is selected, the current region is the range A1:F7 because the cells around the parameter of cell A1 contain data and because the data stops before the G column and the eighth row. This term is important because there is a great keyboard shortcut to select the current region. Now, Let's try an example.

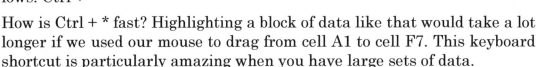

	A	B	C	D	E	F	G
1	January Sales	Sales Rep1	Sales Rep2	Sales Rep3	Sales Rep4	Totals	
2	Pro1	$415.00	$244.00	$248.00	$417.00	$1,324.00	
3	Pro2	279.00	223.00	321.00	191.00	1,014.00	
4	Pro3	379.00	382.00	215.00	304.00	1,280.00	
5	Pro4	181.00	227.00	150.00	260.00	818.00	
6	Pro5	290.00	440.00	212.00	368.00	1,310.00	
7	Totals	$1,544.00	$1,516.00	$1,146.00	$1,540.00	$5,746.00	
8							

Figure 4

1. Click the sheet named KeyB and then click cell A1.
2. To select the whole report use Ctrl + * (the * on the number pad).

The way most Ctrl keyboard shortcuts work is that you hold the Ctrl key (and keep it held), and then tap the second key. For example, our Ctrl + * would involve holding the Ctrl key and then "tapping" the * key, just as you would tap someone on the shoulder. We write this keyboard shortcut as follows: Ctrl + *

How is Ctrl + * fast? Highlighting a block of data like that would take a lot longer if we used our mouse to drag from cell A1 to cell F7. This keyboard shortcut is particularly amazing when you have large sets of data.

3. To cut the range of cells, press Ctrl + X.

In Figure 5, after pressing Ctrl + X, you should see "**dancing ants**" around the outside of the cut area. The dancing ants tell you that the range has been cut.

	A	B	C	D	E	F
1	January Sales	Sales Rep1	Sales Rep2	Sales Rep3	Sales Rep4	Totals
2	Pro1	$415.00	$244.00	$248.00	$417.00	$1,324.00
3	Pro2	279.00	223.00	321.00	191.00	1,014.00
4	Pro3	379.00	382.00	215.00	304.00	1,280.00
5	Pro4	181.00	227.00	150.00	260.00	818.00
6	Pro5	290.00	440.00	212.00	368.00	1,310.00
7	Totals	$1,544.00	$1,516.00	$1,146.00	$1,540.00	$5,746.00

Figure 5

To paste the cut cell range:
    4. Click in cell H1.
    5. Press Ctrl + V.

You should see that your range has been moved to a new location. Notice that when you copy a range and paste it into just one cell, the range is pasted to the right and down.

January Sales	Sales Rep1	Sales Rep2	Sales Rep3	Sales Rep4	Totals
Pro1	$415.00	$244.00	$248.00	$417.00	$1,324.00
Pro2	279.00	223.00	321.00	191.00	1,014.00
Pro3	379.00	382.00	215.00	304.00	1,280.00
Pro4	181.00	227.00	150.00	260.00	818.00
Pro5	290.00	440.00	212.00	368.00	1,310.00
Totals	$1,544.00	$1,516.00	$1,146.00	$1,540.00	$5,746.00

Figure 6

How is that faster? Because you avoid moving your mouse up to the Home tab to copy and paste. Most of the time, using the mouse and the ribbon is much slower than using keyboard shortcuts.

Copying Data

In Figure 6, we see a summary sales report (range of cells). We would like to copy this report and paste it into a new sheet. To copy something, you must complete four steps:
    1. Highlight the current region (Ctrl + *).
    2. Copy the cell range (Ctrl + C).
    3. Select the upper-left corner of the destination cell range.
    4. Paste the copied cell range (Ctrl + V).

The complete list of steps follows:
    1. To copy the range of cells, press Ctrl + C.

January Sales	Sales Rep1	Sales Rep2	Sales Rep3	Sales Rep4	Totals
Pro1	$415.00	$244.00	$248.00	$417.00	$1,324.00
Pro2	279.00	223.00	321.00	191.00	1,014.00
Pro3	379.00	382.00	215.00	304.00	1,280.00
Pro4	181.00	227.00	150.00	260.00	818.00
Pro5	290.00	440.00	212.00	368.00	1,310.00
Totals	$1,544.00	$1,516.00	$1,146.00	$1,540.00	$5,746.00

Figure 7

Before we can paste, we need to insert a new sheet to the left of the sheet named KeyB.

2. To insert a new sheet to the left of the sheet named KeyB, press Shift + F11.

3. A new sheet tab will appear. (It might have a different name from the one shown.)

Figure 8

4. To name the sheet, double-click the sheet tab.
5. Type **CopiedTable**.
6. Press Enter.

Figure 9

7. After inserting the new sheet, A1 is selected; so to paste the copied range, press Ctrl + V.

Amazing Excel 2010 Ctrl Key Smart Tags

In Figure 10, we can see that after we paste, a bunch of **pound signs** (#####) appear. Pound signs mean that the columns are not wide enough to allow the data to be seen. Also notice in Figure 10 that there is a **Ctrl key smart tag** that has the Paste icon and the word *Ctrl.*

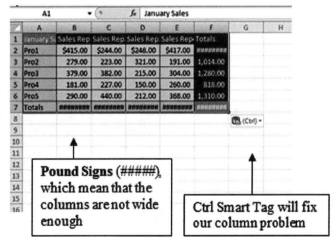

Figure 10

This is a new keyboard shortcut in Excel 2010, and it is one of the most amazing new features in Excel 2010. In older versions of Excel, fixing the column width problem was more difficult than it is with this new Ctrl Key smart tag. Let's see how this works.

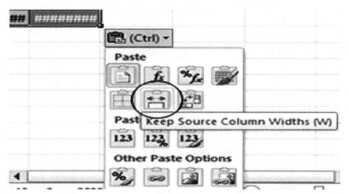

8. Press the Ctrl key to open the smart tag.
9. Tap the W key to apply the Keep Source Column Width option.

Figure 12 shows the end result.

Figure 11

	A	B	C	D	E	F
1	January Sales	Sales Rep1	Sales Rep2	Sales Rep3	Sales Rep4	Totals
2	Pro1	$415.00	$244.00	$248.00	$417.00	$1,324.00
3	Pro2	279.00	223.00	321.00	191.00	1,014.00
4	Pro3	379.00	382.00	215.00	304.00	1,280.00
5	Pro4	181.00	227.00	150.00	260.00	818.00
6	Pro5	290.00	440.00	212.00	368.00	1,310.00
7	Totals	$1,544.00	$1,516.00	$1,146.00	$1,540.00	$5,746.00

Figure 12

Keep Source Column Width means that we can keep the original, copied cell range's column width. Figure 11 shows that when the Ctrl key smart tag opens it shows icons. Microsoft put these there for people who like to use the mouse. If you hover your cursor (using your mouse) over the icons without clicking them, however, a screen tip pops up that has the keyboard shortcut in parentheses. In Figure 11, we can see that the letter *W* is the letter keyboard shortcut for applying the Keep Source Column Widths option.

So in total, the new Ctrl key smart tag keyboard shortcut for "paste everything we copied including the source column width" is as follows:
1. Press Ctrl + V.
2. Tap Ctrl.
3. Tap W.

This is much faster than how it was done in earlier versions of Excel. Also notice that the second part of the keyboard shortcut requires that we *not* hold Ctrl and press the second key. To keep source column widths, we had to use the original Ctrl keyboard method (pre-Excel 2010) of hold Ctrl and press V to paste, and then we had to use the new Excel 2010 Ctrl keyboard method of tap Ctrl and then tap W. By *tap*, I mean press Ctrl and then the W key in succession.

Going forward in this book, to help us distinguish between holding a key and tapping two keys in succession, we will use this convention:

- Plus sign (+) means "hold"
- Comma (,) means to tap in succession.

With this new convention, the keyboard shortcut for "paste everything we copied including the source column width" is as follows: Ctrl + V, Ctrl, W.

Figure 13 shows a list of the Ctrl key smart tag keyboard shortcuts. Learning the shortcuts for the operations that you use most often in your job will save you a lot of time.

Paste Formulas Only	=	Ctrl + V, tap Ctrl, tap F
Paste Formulas and Number Formatting	=	Ctrl + V, tap Ctrl, tap O
Keep Source Formatting	=	Ctrl + V, tap Ctrl, tap K
Do Not Paste Borders	=	Ctrl + V, tap Ctrl, tap B
Keep Source Column Widths	=	Ctrl + V, tap Ctrl, tap W
Transpose Columns and Rows	=	Ctrl + V, tap Ctrl, tap T
Paste Values Only (Convert Formulas to Values)	=	Ctrl + V, tap Ctrl, tap V
Paste Values and Number Formatting	=	Ctrl + V, tap Ctrl, tap A
Paste Values and Source Formatting	=	Ctrl + V, tap Ctrl, tap E
Paste Formatting	=	Ctrl + V, tap Ctrl, tap R
Paste Link	=	Ctrl + V, tap Ctrl, tap N
Paste Picture (Converts Cells to an actual picture)	=	Ctrl + V, tap Ctrl, tap U
Paste Linked Picture	=	Ctrl + V, tap Ctrl, tap I

Figure 13

Another option to the keyboard shortcuts in Figure 13 involves using the right-click key (in-between the Ctrl key and Window key on the right side of the keypad). Although I do not illustrate this method in this book, Figure 14 shows a list of these keyboard shortcuts that you can use after you have copied data using Ctrl + C.

Paste Values Only (Convert Formulas to Values)	=	Right-click key, tap V
Paste Formulas Only	=	Right-click key, tap F, Enter
Transpose Columns and Rows	=	Right-click key, tap T, Enter
Paste Formatting Only	=	Right-click key, tap R
Paste Link	=	Right-click key, tap N, Enter

Figure 14

Now let's look at a brilliant use of the Ctrl key smart tags for flipping a summary sales report of data on its side (transposing a range of cells).

Transposing a Range of Cells

Row Headers →

January Sales	Sales Rep1	Sales Rep2	Sales Rep3	Sales Rep4	Totals
Pro1	$415.00	$244.00	$248.00	$417.00	$1,324.00
Pro2	279.00	223.00	321.00	191.00	1,014.00
Pro3	379.00	382.00	215.00	304.00	1,280.00
Pro4	181.00	227.00	150.00	260.00	818.00
Pro5	290.00	440.00	212.00	368.00	1,310.00
Totals	$1,544.00	$1,516.00	$1,146.00	$1,540.00	$5,746.00

Figure 15

In Figure 15, you can see we have a cell range of data. Our goal is to flip our range so that the row headers in Figure 15 become the column headers in Figure 16 and the column headers in Figure 15 become the row headers in Figure 16.

Become Column Headers ↓

Figure 16

January Sales	Pro1	Pro2	Pro3	Pro4	Pro5	Totals
Sales Rep1	$415.00	279.00	379.00	181.00	290.00	$1,544.00
Sales Rep2	$244.00	223.00	382.00	227.00	440.00	$1,516.00
Sales Rep3	$248.00	321.00	215.00	150.00	212.00	$1,146.00
Sales Rep4	$417.00	191.00	304.00	260.00	368.00	$1,540.00
Totals	$1,324.00	1,014.00	1,280.00	818.00	1,310.00	$5,746.00

Figure 16

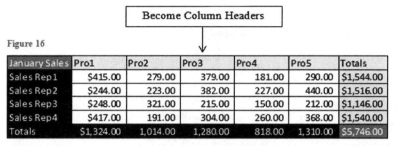

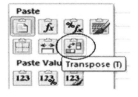

Figure 17

The process of flipping the row and column headers so that they become column and row headers, respectively, is called **transposition**. In Figure 17, you can see that the letter *T* will execute the transpose operation. Let's try this and see whether we can get it to work with keyboard shortcuts.

Figure 18

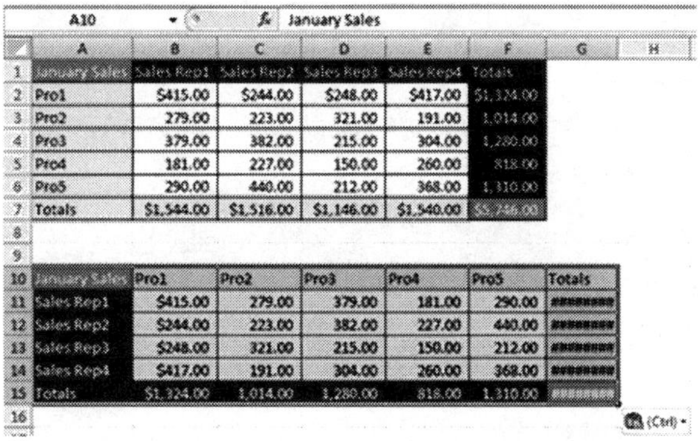

1. Select the range A1:F7.
2. Press Ctrl + C.
3. Select cell A10.
4. Press Ctrl + V.
5. Tap the Ctrl key.
6. Tap the T key.
7. Notice that the G column is not wide enough.

8. To make column G wider, hover your cursor in-between the G and H columns, and when you see the vertical black line and horizontal-arrow cursor, double-click.

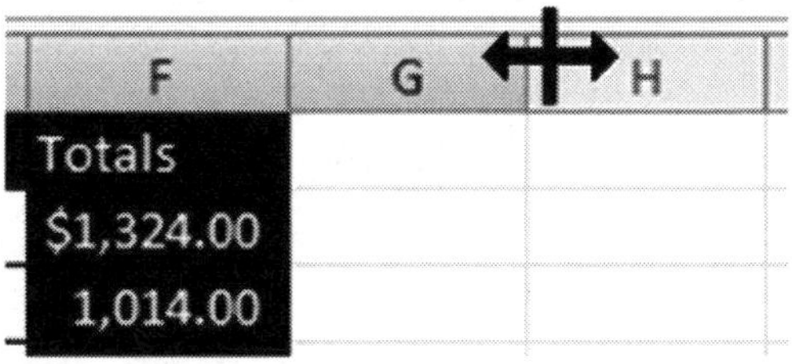

Figure 19

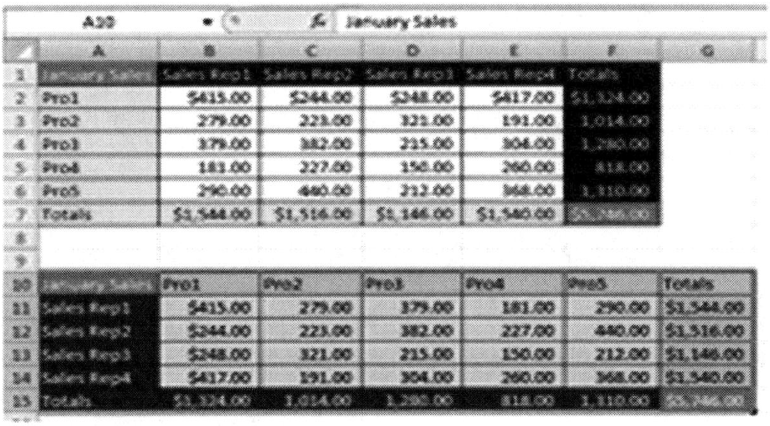

Figure 20

Double-click between columns to change the column width to the largest item in the column (called **best fit**).

Figure 21 and Figure 22 show two alternatives for transposing a range of cells

After you copy, transposing can be done by going to the Paste drop-down arrow in the Clipboard group in the Home tab.

This method is particularly useful because it will give you a Live Preview! Live Preview is great if you are doing this operation for the first time. However, if it is a task you do regularly, the Ctrl keyboard method is significantly faster.

Figure 21

Figure 22

After you copy, paste and press Ctrl to open the Ctrl key smart tag, then transposing can be done by using your arrow keys to move through the icons. When you get to the Transpose icon and you see an orange highlight, press Enter.

This method is still faster than using the mouse to go to the Home tab.

Highlighting a Column of Data

Next we want to look at a keyboard shortcut that is a huge time saver. This keyboard shortcut involves the Ctrl key and the arrow keys (Up, Down, Left, Right). Let's take a look.

10		Dec Total
11	Dec Sales	
12	563	
13	719	
14	477	
15	601	
16	773	

Figure 23

In Figure 23, the content of cell A11 is the column label Dec Sales. But how far down do the numbers go? You could use the scrollbar to scroll down and find out, but that would take a long time. Instead, we will use the keyboard shortcut to jump to the bottom of a column: Ctrl + Down Arrow.

This keyboard shortcut will jump to the bottom of the column of data. How does it know to stop? It will know to stop when it sees the first blank cell. This sort of keyboard shortcut is called a **navigation keyboard shortcut**.

70	860
71	872
72	967
73	860
74	321
75	925
76	914
77	979
78	

Figure 24

Let's see how to do this.
1. Select cell A11 on Sheet KeyB.
2. To jump to the bottom of the column of data, press Ctrl + Down-Arrow.
3. To jump back to the top of the column press, Ctrl + Up Arrow.

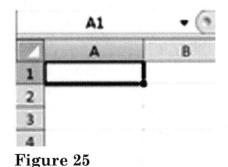

Figure 25

4. To jump to cell A1, use Ctrl + Home-key.

5. To move to cell B1, press the Right-Arrow key.
6. The entire B Column has no data. So if we press Ctrl + Down arrow, we will jump to the last cell in the column.
7. To jump to B1048576, use Ctrl + Down Arrow.

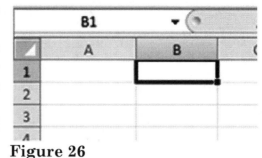

Figure 26

8. To jump back to cell A1 , press Ctrl + Home key.

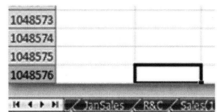

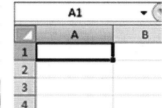

Figure 27

In the last few navigation keyboard shortcuts, you saw how to jump the cursor to a new location. In all those actions, if we had held the Ctrl key and Shift key together (instead of just the Ctrl key), it would have highlighted, or selected, the regions instead of just jumping the cursor. To see how adding the Shift key will work, let's create a formula that requires that we highlight a column of numbers. Our goal with this next formula is to use the SUM function to add the Dec Sales numbers.

1. Click in cell C11.
2. Then use the Alt + = keyboard shortcut for the SUM function. (Tap the equal sign key while holding the Alt key.)

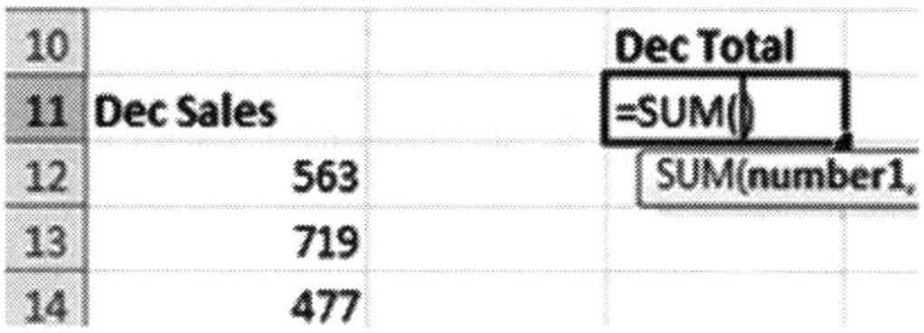

Figure 28

3. Select cell A12. You can do this with the keystrokes Left Arrow, Left Arrow, Down Arrow. Dancing ants will appear around the selected cell.

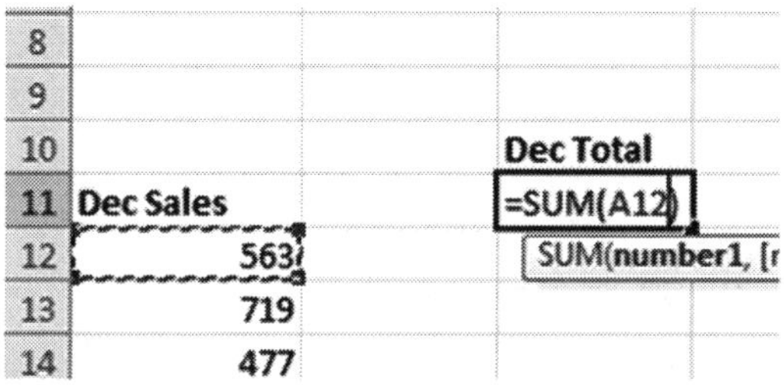

Figure 29

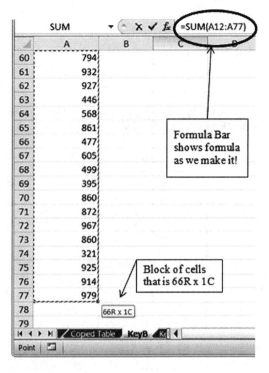

Figure 30

4. To highlight to the bottom of the column, press Ctrl + Shift + Down Arrow.
5. After you press Ctrl + Shift + Down Arrow, the screen will jump down to show you that all the numbers are highlighted, and the formula bar will show you that the SUM function is looking at the correct range of cells. The screen tip shows us that we have a block of cells that is 66R x 1C.
6. Now that we are finished making the formula, we need to put the formula in the cell and jump back up. To do this, instead of pressing the Enter key to put the formula in the cell, we press Shift + Enter.

Shift + Enter puts the formula in the cell and jumps the cursor up, one cell above cell C11 (where the formula is located). This is advantageous here because you will immediately be able to see the label and formula result.

	A	B	C	D	E
C10			*fx* Dec Total		
10			Dec Total		
11	Dec Sales		44164		
12		563			
13		719			
14		477			

7. After we use Shift + Enter, you should see the total 44164.

Figure 31

Altogether, the keyboard shortcuts for adding the Dec Sales in cell C11 were as follows:

1. Alt + = (SUM function).
2. Select cell A12. You can do this with the keystrokes Left Arrow, Left Arrow, Down Arrow.
3. Ctrl + Shift + Down Arrow (highlight data below selected cell).
4. Shift + Enter (entering the formula and moving the cursor up).

This series of keyboard shortcuts is dramatically faster than the alternative of using the mouse to get the SUM function from the Home tab and then selecting the cells by dragging the mouse. But more important, this is

the sort of keyboard shortcut that when done in an interview can help you to get the job. The interviewer will probably fall out of character and say, "Wow, I like that one!"

The following table summarizes the navigation and highlighting (selecting) keyboard shortcuts.

Navigation Keyboard Shortcuts		
Jump to the bottom of the column of data	=	Ctrl + Down Arrow
Jump to the top of the column of data	=	Ctrl + Up Arrow
Jump to the left end of a row of data	=	Ctrl + Left Arrow
Jump to the right end of a row of data	=	Ctrl + Right Arrow
Jump to cell A1	=	Ctrl + Home
Jump to last cell used	=	Ctrl + End

Highlighting or Selection Keyboard Shortcuts		
Highlight or select the column of data below the selected cell	=	Ctrl + Shift + Down Arrow
Highlight or select the column of data above the selected cell	=	Ctrl + Shift + Up Arrow
Highlight or select the row of data to the left of the selected cell	=	Ctrl + Shift + Left Arrow
Highlight or select the row of data to the right of the selected cell	=	Ctrl + Shift + Right Arrow
Highlight Current Region	=	Ctrl + * (on Number Pad)

Ctrl + Enter Keyboard Magic

Another time-saving Ctrl keyboard shortcut is Ctrl + Enter. (Hold the Ctrl key and then and tap the Enter key.) When putting something into a cell, such as a word or a formula, most people just press Enter. Enter puts the thing in the cell and selects the cell below. Many times this is exactly what you want. But if your goal is to put the thing in the cell and then do something to the cell like format it or copy it, it saves you an extra click if you use Ctrl + Enter. Ctrl + Enter will put the thing in the cell and keep the cell selected. Although it does not seem like a lot of time saved, over the long run it does save substantial time. Let's see an example.

In Figure 32, you see sales numbers in the range A2:A7. We need to add a column header and format the column header so the viewer can tell what the numbers represent. We also need to add a total at the bottom and format the total so that the viewer knows that it is a total.

To follow along, open the file named excelisfun-Start.xlsm and navigate to the sheet named KeyB(2).

	A	B
1		
2	10	
3	22	
4	50	
5	35	
6	14	
7	52	
8		

Figure 32

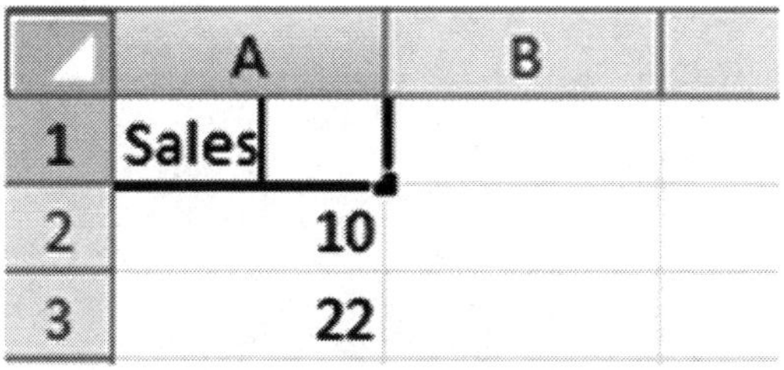

Figure 33

Figure 34

Figure 35

Figure 36

1. Click in cell A1 and type **Sales**.
2. Don't press Enter!

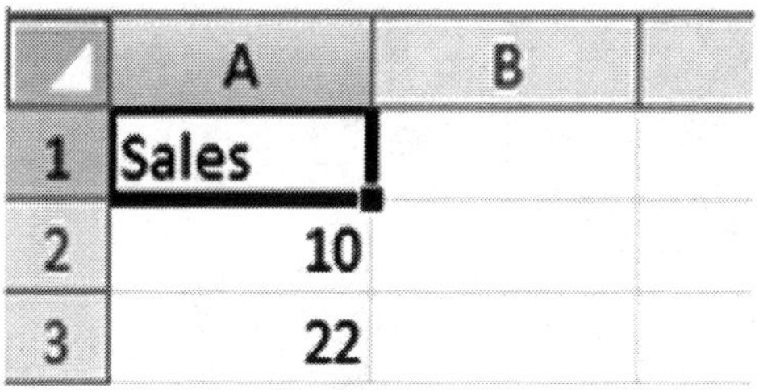

3. Because our goal is to put the word in the cell and then immediately add the bold format to the cell, press Ctrl + Enter.
4. The word "*Sales*" is entered into cell A1, and A1 is selected.

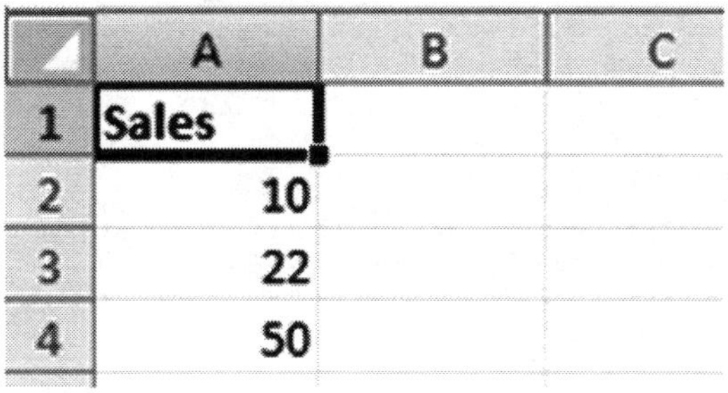

5. To make the word *Sales* bold, use the keyboard shortcut for bold: Ctrl + B.

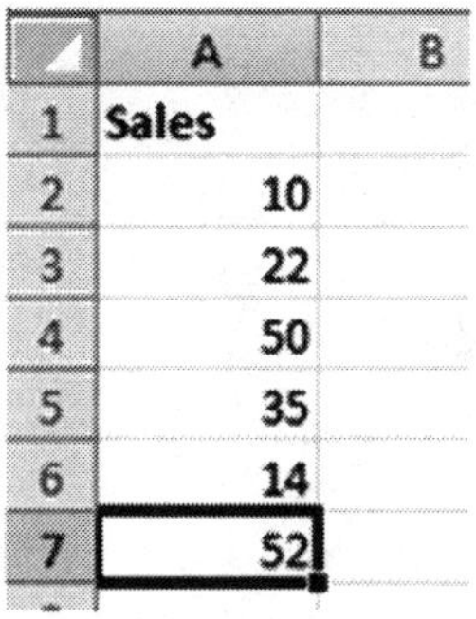

6. To jump down to the bottom of the column of data, press Ctrl + Down Arrow.
7. To move to the cell where we want to add a formula for adding, press the Down Arrow.

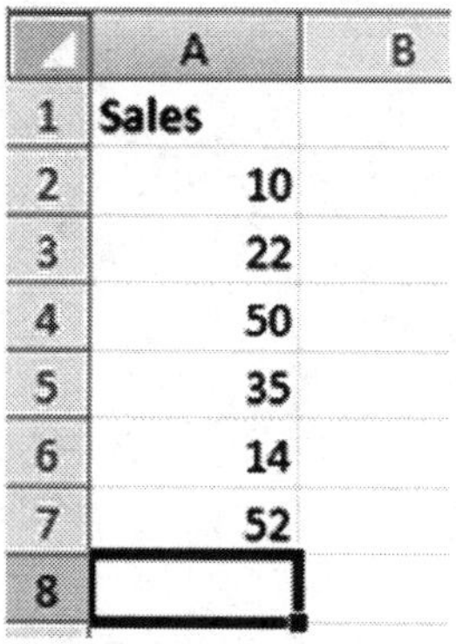

Figure 37

8. To add the SUM function, press Alt + =.
9. Verify that the cell range is the correct one (A2:A7).

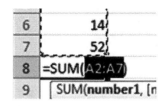

Figure 38

10. Tap the equal sign a second time.

Note: When your goal is to create a total with the SUM function and you will accept the default range, the complete keyboard shortcut is Alt + = + = (with a pause between the two equal signs to check whether the range is correct).

	A	B
1	Sales	
2	10	
3	22	
4	50	
5	35	
6	14	
7	52	
8	183	
9		

Figure 39

11. On the Home tab from the Font group, click the arrow next to the Borders button.
12. Click Top and Double Bottom Border.
13. Press Enter twice to move the cursor down so that you can see the Border stylistic formatting
14. You should see what is shown in Figure 41.

Figure 40

	A	
1	Sales	
2	10	
3	22	
4	50	
5	35	
6	14	
7	52	
8	183	
9		

Figure 41

D	E	F	G	H
	Jan	Feb	Mar	Apr
Revenue	$10,000	$20,000	$18,500	$21,550
Expenses	6,600	13,800	12,025	15,947
Net Income				

Figure 42

Look at Figure 42. Our goal here is to subtract expenses from revenue. We will use Ctrl + Enter along with other keystrokes to do this as quickly as possible.

1. Click in cell E4 so that you can create a Net Income formula.

D	E	F	G	H
	Jan	Feb	Mar	Apr
Revenue	$10,000	$20,000	$18,500	$21,550
Expenses	6,600	13,800	12,025	15,947
Net Income	=E2			

Figure 43

2. Type the equal sign to start your formula (complete story on formulas in Chapter 5, "Formulas and Functions.").
3. Press the Up Arrow key twice to insert the cell reference for revenue into the formula.

Note: Using an arrow key to insert a cell reference into a formula can be much faster than using your mouse if the cell reference is close to the cell that houses the formula.

D	E	F	G	H
	Jan	Feb	Mar	Apr
Revenue	$10,000	$20,000	$18,500	$21,550
Expenses	6,600	13,800	12,025	15,947
Net Income	=E2-E3			

Figure 44

4. Press the minus sign on the number keypad.
5. Press the Up Arrow once.

In Figure 44, the E2 and E3 cell references are called "relative cell references" because relative to the formula, the revenue cell is two cells above the cell with the formula and the expenses cell is one cell above. This is convenient because when we copy the formula to the Net Income cells for Feb, Mar, and April, the cell references will adjust perfectly. We examine cell references in more detail later in this book.

Because we want to enter the formula in the cell and then immediately format the cell, we will use Ctrl + Enter to put the formula in the cell and keep the cell selected.

6. To put the formula in the cell and keep the cell selected, press Ctrl + Enter.

D	E	F	G	H
	Jan	Feb	Mar	Apr
Revenue	$10,000	$20,000	$18,500	$21,550
Expenses	6,600	13,800	12,025	15,947
Net Income	$ 3,400			

7. With cell E4 selected, notice the black border surrounding the cell. This black border means that "this cell is selected."

Figure 45

8. Notice the Fill Handle, which is the little black box in the lower-right corner. It will enable us to copy formulas, formatting, numbers, or text quickly.

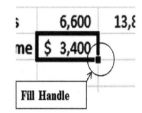

Fill Handle

Figure 46

Note: If you do not see the fill handle, click the File tab, Options, the Advanced tab on the left, and then check Enable Fill Handle and Cell Drag-and-Drop check box.

Look at Figure 47. Our goal is to copy the formula for Net Income from cell E4 all the way to cell H4. To do this, you must move your cursor slowly toward the fill handle and watch carefully as the cursor turns from the "thick" white cross **selection cursor** (Figure 47) to a "thin" black **crosshair cursor** (Figure 48).

D	E	F	G	H
	Jan	Feb	Mar	Apr
Revenue	$10,000	$20,000	$18,500	$21,550
Expenses	6,600	13,800	12,025	15,947
Net Income	$ 3,400			

Figure 47

9. Move your cursor toward the fill handle and you will see the selection cursor.

D	E	F	G	H
	Jan	Feb	Mar	Apr
Revenue	$10,000	$20,000	$18,500	$21,550
Expenses	6,600	13,800	12,025	15,947
Net Income	$ 3,400			

10. When your cursor is on top of the fill handle, you will see the crosshair.

Figure 48

11. When you see the crosshair, click and drag your mouse to the right.

D	E	F	G	H
	Jan	Feb	Mar	Apr
Revenue	$10,000	$20,000	$18,500	$21,550
Expenses	6,600	13,800	12,025	15,947
Net Income	$ 3,400			

Figure 49

As you drag to the right, a gray rectangle will appear. The gray rectangle is showing you where the formula will be copied (Figure 49).

D	E	F	G	H
	Jan	Feb	Mar	Apr
Revenue	$10,000	$20,000	$18,500	$21,550
Expenses	6,600	13,800	12,025	15,947
Net Income	$ 3,400	$ 6,200	$ 6,475	$ 5,603

Figure 50

12. When the right edge of the gray box gets to the cell H4, let go of your mouse.

You can see that the range E4:H4 is selected and that the formula has been copied.

13. Before we verify that our formula is correct, add Top and Double Bottom Border to the selected range. (Look back to Figure 40 if you can't remember where the button is located.)

Now we want to check to see whether our formula copied correctly. The F2 key will put a cell into Edit mode (the lower-left status bar will confirm this) so that we can check if our formulas are correct.

fx	=E2-E3			
D	E	F	G	H
	Jan	Feb	Mar	Apr
Revenue	$10,000	$20,000	$18,500	$21,550
Expenses	6,600	13,800	12,025	15,947
Net Income	=E2-E3	$ 6,200	$ 6,475	$ 5,603

Figure 51

14. To put the active cell into Edit mode use, press F2.

Edit mode gives us a rainbow color coding of the cells being used in the formula. This color coding helps us to visually track which cells are being used. This color coding is called the **range finder**. This black-and-white picture does not show the color, but the relative cell reference E2 is shown in blue, and the cell E2 is shown in green. Checking the formula, we see that it is correct. Now we need to check the other three formulas, too. When we do this, we should notice that the relative cell references in our formula copied over perfectly. Let's check the remaining three.

15. Press Tab to move to the right.
16. Press the F2 key to put the cell in Edit mode.

The formula looks correct.

f_x	=F2-F3			
D	**E**	**F**	**G**	**H**
	Jan	Feb	Mar	Apr
Revenue	$10,000	$20,000	$18,500	$21,550
Expenses	6,600	13,800	12,025	15,947
Net Income	$ 3,400	=F2-F3	$ 6,475	$ 5,603

Figure 52

17. Press Tab.
18. Press F2.

The formula looks correct.

f_x	=G2-G3			
D	**E**	**F**	**G**	**H**
	Jan	Feb	Mar	Apr
Revenue	$10,000	$20,000	$18,500	$21,550
Expenses	6,600	13,800	12,025	15,947
Net Income	$ 3,400	$ 6,200	=G2-G3	$ 5,603

Figure 53

19. Press Tab.
20. Press F2.

The formula looks correct.

Click the Esc key to exit Edit mode.

f_x	=H2-H3			
D	**E**	**F**	**G**	**H**
	Jan	Feb	Mar	Apr
Revenue	$10,000	$20,000	$18,500	$21,550
Expenses	6,600	13,800	12,025	15,947
Net Income	$ 3,400	$ 6,200	$ 6,475	=H2-H3

Figure 54

You are probably starting to see why keyboard shortcuts and the fill handle with the mouse can save a lot of time. Next we want to look at the keyboard shortcuts using the Alt key.

Alt Shortcuts

The Alt key is a special keyboard shortcut key because when you tap the Alt key, the ribbon tabs and the QAT show little messages called **screen tips** or **ToolTips**.

Unlike the Ctrl keyboard shortcuts, where you have to hold the Ctrl key and tap the next key, most Alt keyboard shortcuts do not require that you hold the Alt key down while pressing the next key. For most Alt keyboard shortcuts, you will tap each key in succession without holding the Alt key.

To illustrate how the Alt keyboard shortcuts work, we will open the Page Setup dialog box using an Alt keyboard shortcut.

1. Tap the Alt key once and you should see the ToolTips appear.

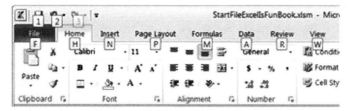

Figure 55

Notice that P stands for the Page Layout tab.

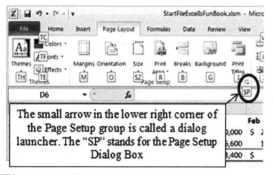

Figure 56

2. Tap the P key and you will see the Page Layout tab appear and that a second level of ToolTips appears.
3. To open the Page Setup dialog box, tap the S key, and then tap the P key.

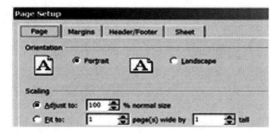

Figure 57

4. You should see the Page Setup dialog box. We discuss this in great detail in Chapter 4, "Style Formatting and Page Setup."
5. Press the Esc key to close the Page Setup dialog box.

The rule for Alt keyboard shortcuts is to learn the ones for the features that you use most often. For example, the Page Setup dialog is something that Excel users use all the time. So knowing Alt, P, S, P (Press Alt, tap P, tab S, tab P in succession) will save you a lot of time (as compared to using the mouse). You will see many Alt keyboard shortcuts throughout this textbook.

Our next Excel Efficiency-Robust Rule is the following:

Rule 3: Learn keyboard shortcuts because they are fast!

Next we want to talk about the different types of data in Excel.

DATA IN EXCEL

To make calculations (such as adding) or perform data analysis (converting data to information), you first need raw data. So, you need to learn about how Excel deals with raw data. In order that you understand how Excel sees data, this chapter covers the following six important points:

- The difference between raw data and information
- The table format structure and the Excel Table feature
- Entering data into Excel
- Number formatting as façade (i.e., number formatting sits on top of data)
- How data is aligned

Raw Data Versus Information

What is raw data? **Raw data** is data in small bits. For example, the number of units a sales representative sold in one day is a piece of raw data. **Information** is made from raw data and is used to make decisions. For example, if you need to decide whether a sales representative met the sales quota for the week, you must first look at the raw data, add all the sales for just that one sales representative, and then decide "yes, the sales quota was met" or "no, the sales quota was not met." The process is as follows:

	A	B	C
1	Date	SalesRep	UnitsSold
2	8/9/2010	Sioux	10
3	8/9/2010	Tina	9
4	8/10/2010	Sioux	4
5	8/10/2010	Tina	8
6	8/11/2010	Sioux	1
7	8/11/2010	Tina	3
8			
9	Sales Period	SalesRep	UnitsSold
10	Week	Sioux	

Figure 58

1. Take raw data.
2. Create information.
3. Make decision.

Figure 58 shows a raw data set. We can see that on 8/9/2010, the number of units Sioux sold was 10. The number 10 is an example of a piece of raw data. To make information from all the bits of raw data, we need to organize it in a way that will allow us to make decisions based on that information.

The information we need is "Sioux's total weekly units sold." The decision we need to make is "did Sioux make the weekly quota of 20 units?" We can create this information by using the SUMIFS function. Let's take a look at how to do this.

SUMIFS Function

The goal is to add with the single condition (criteria) Sioux. The SUMIFS function is perfect for this because it will sum units sold "if the units sold belong to Sioux." The name of the SUMIFS function means this:

- The SUM part means to add.
- The IF part means there is a condition or criteria.
- The S part means that you can have more than one condition or criteria. (We have only one condition here: Sioux).

In this first example, we will do both calculating and data analysis in Excel. The calculating part is the adding of the sales numbers, and the data analysis part is the taking raw data and converting it into information.

To follow along, open the file named excelisfun-Start.xlsm and navigate to the sheet named SUMIFS.

1. Click the sheet tab (sheet) named SUMIFS.
2. Notice that the raw data we have is Units Sold and the information we need is Sioux's total units sold for the week.

The SUMIFS functions will be part of a formula that we will put into cell C10. A **formula** is simply a calculation that we make in a cell, and a **function** is a built-in formula element that will do the "heavy lifting" for us (do the math or analysis for us). Formulas and functions always start with an equal sign as the first character in the cell. You'll learn more about these in Chapter 5, "Formulas and Functions."

3. Click in cell C10. And type an equal sign (=) and then type the letter **s**.

In Figure 59, a drop-down list of built-in functions appears with a list of functions that start with **Figure 59** the letter s.

This drop-down is Excel's way of trying to be polite. Excel is reminding us of functions we might want to use. Notice that an fx icon appears next to each function name. (Later we will see other formula elements show up on this list.) We don't see the SUMIFS functions, so we have to type the next letter, u.

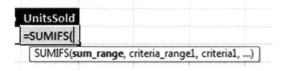

Figure 60

Figure 61

4. Type the letter **u** and you should see the SUMIFS function as the fifth function in the list.
5. Using your Down Arrow key, arrow down until the SUMIFS function is highlighted, and then press the Tab key to insert the SUMIFS function into cell C10.
6. After you insert the SUMIFS function, a screen tip prompts you to enter the sum_range, criteria_range1, and criteria1.

In Figure 61, we can see our formula take shape. The equal sign tells Excel that this is a formula that requires some sort of calculation. The SUMIFS function has built-in code that will do the hard work for us. **The open parenthesis** tells us that we need to provide some details for the SUMIFS function. The text box below is called a **screen tip** or a **ToolTip** and tells us what arguments the SUMIFS function requires to do the adding.

Argument? What is an argument? An **argument** is a word from math that means "element that is needed for the function to make the calculation." The **sum_range** argument is just asking for the range of cells with the numbers to add. For us, it will be the UnitsSold range. The **criteria_range1** argument is the range of cells with all the criteria. For us, it will be the SalesRep range. The **criteria1** argument is the criteria for adding. For us, it will be cell B10 because that cell holds the criteria, Sioux. Also, the word SUMIFS in the screen tip is a hot-link to Excel Help for the SUMIFS function. If you click the hot-link for this or any other function, a window opens with help for the function. In addition, after you inserted your SUMIFS function with the Tab key, the cursor became a flashing vertical bar. The **flashing vertical bar** tells you that this part of the formula can be edited. Finally, notice that the sum_range argument in the screen tip is bold. The fact that it is bold means that the SUMIFS function is waiting for that argument. Let's not keep it waiting any longer.

7. With the cursor flashing in the sum_range argument, select the range C2:C7 by clicking in cell C2 and dragging the cursor to cell C7. You can tell that you have selected the cells correctly by the dancing ants that surround the range of cells.

| SUM | ▼ | X ✓ ƒx | =SUMIFS(C2:C7 |

	A	B	C	D	E
1	Date	SalesRep	UnitsSold		
2	8/9/2010	Sioux	10		
3	8/9/2010	Tina	9		
4	8/10/2010	Sioux	4		
5	8/10/2010	Tina	8		
6	8/11/2010	Sioux	1		
7	8/11/2010	Tina	3		
8					
9	Sales Period	SalesRep	UnitsSold		
10	Week	Sioux	=SUMIFS(C2:C7		
11			SUMIFS(sum_range, criteria_range)		

Figure 62

In Figure 62, you can see that the dancing ants surround the cell range C2:C7 and the range C2:C7 is inserted into the sum_range argument of the SUMIFS function. Notice that the cell range C2:C7 is the formula notation to indicate that the cells C2, C3, C4, C5, C6, and C7 are being referred to. For this book, cell ranges like C2:C7 can be referred to as a **cell range**, or a **range of cells**, or simply as a **range**.

Note: Don't worry if you make a mistake when selecting the range. As long as the ants are still dancing, just reselect the correct range and the formula will automatically update to the correct range!

8. Notice the word *Point* in the lower-left corner (location in the status bar). **Point mode** means that you are selecting cells for a formula or function.

Figure 63

9. After the range C2:C7 is inserted into the formula, type a comma (,) to get to the next argument.

	A	B	C	D	E	F
1	Date	SalesRep	UnitsSold			
2	8/9/2010	Sioux	10			
3	8/9/2010	Tina	9			
4	8/10/2010	Sioux	4			
5	8/10/2010	Tina	8			
6	8/11/2010	Sioux	1			
7	8/11/2010	Tina	3			
8						
9	Sales Period	SalesRep	UnitsSold			
10	Week	Sioux	=SUMIFS(C2:C7,			
11			SUMIFS(sum_range, **criteria_range1**, criteria1,			

Figure 64

When you type a comma, two things happen:
- The dancing ants stop dancing, which means the range is no longer editable by simply dragging your selection cursor.
- The next argument in the screen tip becomes bold. When Excel bolds the criteria_range1 argument, this is Excel's way of politely saying, "Hey, what I need next is the cell range with the criteria."

	A	B	C	D	E	F
1	Date	SalesRep	UnitsSold			
2	8/9/2010	Sioux	10			
3	8/9/2010	Tina	9			
4	8/10/2010	Sioux	4			
5	8/10/2010	Tina	8			
6	8/11/2010	Sioux	1			
7	8/11/2010	Tina	3			
8						
9	Sales Period	SalesRep	UnitsSold			
10	Week	Sioux	=SUMIFS(C2:C7,B2:B7			
11			SUMIFS(sum_range, **criteria_range1**, criteria1,			

10. To put the range into the criteria_ range1 argument, select the range B2:B7.

Figure 65

The criteria_range1 is the range that the SUMIFS function will look to determine which numbers should be added. From the SalesRep column, whenever it sees the word Sioux, it then knows to go over to the UnitsSold column and use the corresponding number of units sold for adding.

9	Sales Period	SalesRep	UnitsSold
10	Week	Sioux	=SUMIFS(C2:C7,B2:B7,
11			SUMIFS(sum_range, criteria_range1, **criteria1**,

Figure 66

11. Type a comma and you will see that the screen tip is asking for criteria1.

9	Sales Period	SalesRep	UnitsSold
10	Week	Sioux	=SUMIFS(C2:C7,B2:B7,B10
11			SUMIFS(sum_range, criteria_range1, **criteria1**,

Figure 67

12. Because our criteria is Sioux, we click cell B10.

9	Sales Period	SalesRep	UnitsSold
10	Week	Sioux	=SUMIFS(C2:C7,B2:B7,B10)
11			

Figure 68

13. Type a close parenthesis to tell the SUMIFS function that we have entered all the arguments. Notice that the screen tip goes away.

14. Press Enter to put the formula in the cell and tell Excel to create our information from our SUMIFS calculation.

With this information we can now determine whether Sioux met the sales quota of 20. Sioux didn't; 15 is less than 20. Notice that we used Excel to do two things:

- Calculate a total by adding with the criteria Sioux
- Perform data analysis (that is, convert raw data into useful information)

	A	B	C
1	Date	SalesRep	UnitsSold
2	8/9/2010	Sioux	10
3	8/9/2010	Tina	9
4	8/10/2010	Sioux	4
5	8/10/2010	Tina	8
6	8/11/2010	Sioux	1
7	8/11/2010	Tina	3
8			
9	Sales Period	SalesRep	UnitsSold
10	Week	Sioux	15

Figure 69

Note: Suppose you want to share your workbook with someone who does not have Excel 2007 or 2010. Because the SUMIFS function does not exist in earlier versions, this formula would show a #NAME! error and would not work. In this scenario, however, you can use the following alternative formula:

=SUMIF(B2:B7,B10,C2:C7)

Even so, if you can avoid using the SUMIF function and instead use the SUMIFS function, you'll realize two big advantages:

The SUMIFS function allows more than one criterion. In our case, we had just one criterion, but in many cases you will have more than one.

SUMIFS argument names are much easier to understand, and therefore inexperienced users of the functions will make fewer mistakes.

We discuss the SUMIFS function in more detail in Chapter 5.

Verifying Formula Results (and tracking down bad data)

So, what did we just do with the SUMIFS function? We converted raw data to information and made a decision. But, is 15 units sold for the week correct? If we are the ones designing the spreadsheet, we always want a way to double-check to determine whether our calculation or data analysis is correct. In this case, the data set is small enough that we can do it manually, as follows:

	A	B	C
1	Date	SalesRep	UnitsSold
2	8/9/2010	Sioux	10
3	8/9/2010	Tina	9
4	8/10/2010	Sioux	4
5	8/10/2010	Tina	8
6	8/11/2010	Sioux	1
7	8/11/2010	Tina	3
8			
9	Sales Period	SalesRep	UnitsSold
10	Week	Sioux	15
11			

Figure 70

1. Click in cell C2.
2. Then, holding the Ctrl key, click cell C4 and then C6.
3. When you do this, notice that the three cells are highlighted even though they are not next to each other. (This is called a **noncontiguous range**.)

Figure 70 shows what is called the noncontiguous range selection trick.

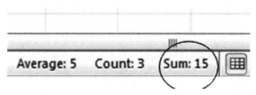

Figure 71

After highlighting C2, C4, and C6, look at the right side of the status bar. You will see that Excel has given us a preview of the sum. Because it says 15, we can assume that our calculation is correct.

And that leads to our next Excel Efficiency-Robust Rule:

> *Rule 4: If we are the ones designing the spreadsheet, we always want a way to double-check to determine whether our calculation or data analysis is correct.*

B11			f_x
	A	B	C
1	Date	SalesRep	UnitsSold
2	8/9/2010	Sioux	10
3	8/9/2010	Tina	9
4	8/10/2010	Sioux	4
5	8/10/2010	Tina	8
6	8/11/2010	Sioux	1
7	8/11/2010	Tina	3
8			
9	Sales Period	SalesRep	UnitsSold
10	Week	Tina	11

Figure 72

Now, what about Tina? Did Tina meet the sales quota of 20 units sold? To determine the answer, do we have to create the whole formula over again? No way! Because of Excel's updateability, we can just change the word Sioux in cell B10 to Tina and the formula will calculate the total units sold for Tina. This is called changing a **formula input**. A formula input is simply the raw data in a cell.

1. Click in cell B10.
2. Type **Tina**.
3. Press Enter.

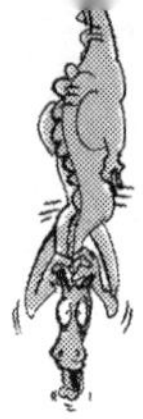

That is amazing! Our formula updated. But wait... Is 11 units sold for Tina correct? Using our noncontiguous range selection trick, we want to determine whether we got the right answer for Tina. Figure 73 shows the sum of 20 in the status bar. So, we have a problem.

The 20 in the status bar is correct because we have the correct cells selected and Excel does not make math errors. This means that we must investigate further. When investigating a problem with a formula, it is efficient to check the formula first to determine whether we created it correctly, and then to work backward through the formula's inputs to determine whether any of the raw data is creating the problem. To check the cells with formulas or raw data, you can use a keyboard shortcut, the F2 key, to put the cell into Edit mode. (The status bar will indicate when you are in Edit mode.)

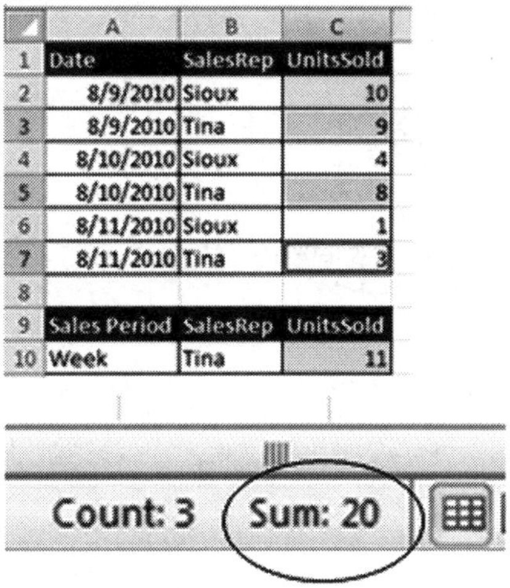

Figure 73

1. Click in the cell with the formula, cell C10.
2. Press the F2 key.
3. Look at the color-coded ranges to determine whether they are correct.

Figure 74

They are correct

Next we must look in the actual cells to determine whether we can find a problem with the formula inputs.

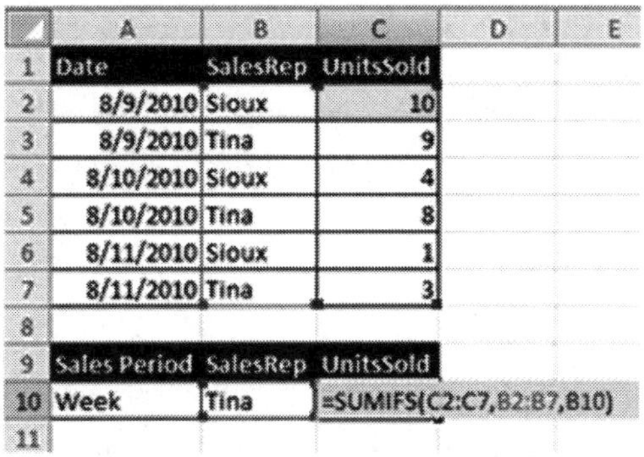

We will work backward from B10 and look at the content of each cell.

1. To get out of Edit mode in cell C10, press the Esc key.
2. Click in cell B10.
3. Press F2.

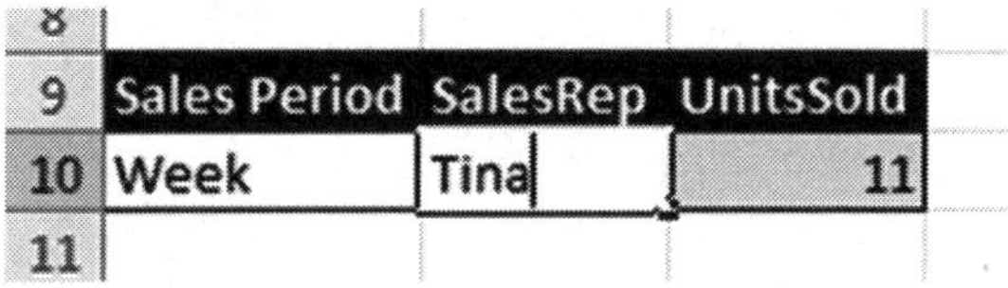

Figure 75

This looks okay because there are only four characters: T, I, N, A.

5	8/10/2010	Tina	8
6	8/11/2010	Sioux	1
7	8/11/2010	Tina|	3
8			

Figure 76

1. Click in cell B7.
2. Press F2.

This looks okay because there are only four characters: T, I, N, A.

3	8/9/2010	Tina	9
4	8/10/2010	Sioux	4
5	8/10/2010	Tina|	8

Figure 77

1. Click in cell B5.
2. Press F2.

This looks okay because there are only four characters: T, I, N, A.

	A	B	C
1	Date	SalesRep	UnitsSold
2	8/9/2010	Sioux	10
3	8/9/2010	Tina	9

Figure 78

1. Click in cell B3.
2. Press F2.

We found the problem! There are five characters: T, I, N, A, space.

Date	SalesRep	UnitsSold
8/9/2010	Sioux	10
8/9/2010	Tina	9
8/10/2010	Sioux	4
8/10/2010	Tina	8
8/11/2010	Sioux	1
8/11/2010	Tina	3

Sales Period	SalesRep	UnitsSold
Week	Tina	20

Figure 79

To fix this problem, press the Backspace key and then press Enter.

After you remove the space, the formula updates.

Excel sees "Tina" and "Tina " as different things. This is a very common problem with data in Excel. Later when we look at examples with larger data sets, we will see a nonmanual way to remedy this problem.

Our next two Excel Efficiency-Robust Rule are as follows:

Rule 5: Excel is literal about how it sees data. Spaces matter in Excel. "Tina" is different from "Tina ".

Rule 6: When investigating a problem with a formula, it is efficient to check the formula first to determine whether the formula is correct, and then to work backward through the formula's inputs to determine whether any of the raw data is creating the problem. The keyboard shortcut F2 puts a cell into Edit mode and places the cursor at the end of the formula.

In the preceding example, we used the SUMIFS function to perform a calculation that converted raw data into information. Next we want to use a PivotTable to perform data analysis to convert raw data into information.

PivotTables

The PivotTable feature is one of Excel's most powerful data analysis features. (You'll learn more about Excel's data analysis features in Chapter 6, "Data Analysis Features.") PivotTables can quickly summarize data and create reports that can be used for decision making. Our goal in the next example is to summarize the raw data shown in Figure 80 into the report shown Figure 81 in just seven clicks. Before we make our report, we have to look at how the raw data is set up and how we want our resultant report to look.

Figure 80 shows us a raw data set. The raw data set has the following **column headers** or **field names**: Date, SalesRep, and UnitsSold. These field names tell the user of the raw data what sort of data will be in the column. Dates are in the Date column, names are in the SalesRep column, and numbers of units sold are in the UnitsSold column.

	A	B	C
1	Date	SalesRep	UnitsSold
2	8/9/2010	Sioux	10
3	8/9/2010	Tina	9
4	8/10/2010	Sioux	4
5	8/10/2010	Tina	8
6	8/11/2010	Sioux	1
7	8/11/2010	Tina	3
8	8/12/2010	Chin	4
9	8/12/2010	Sioux	5
10	8/12/2010	Tina	3
11	8/13/2010	Chin	6
12	8/13/2010	Sioux	5
13	8/13/2010	Tina	8
14	8/14/2010	Chin	14

Figure 80

Figure 81

Row Labels

SalesRep	Sum of UnitsSold
Chin	24
Sioux	25
Tina	31
Grand Total	**80**

Figure 81

Each row in the data set represents a transactional record that contains one date, one sales representative name, and the number of units sold for that date. Each transactional **record** is an individual recording of a sales event.

Before you create a PivotTable, it is helpful to visualize how you want your report to look. In Figure 81, we can visualize how we want the report to look. You can create such a visualization by sketching with a pen and paper or by typing out a "sketch" in Excel. This is important because if you sketch it out, creating the PivotTable will be easier than if you do not. In the working world, you often hear people say that PivotTables are hard. They are not hard if you make a sketch first, or at least visualize the end result in your head. In Figure 81, the sales representatives' names (each name listed one time, creating a **unique** list) are called **row labels** because each name sits at the beginning of the row and is the label for that row. The total number of units sold for each sales rep is called a **value**. The terms field, row labels, and value are important to remember when using the PivotTable feature. Notice also that the final report shows that the PivotTable can add with one condition: Don't add all the units sold, just the ones for each sales representative.

To follow along, open the file named excelisfun-Start.xlsm and navigate to the sheet named PT.

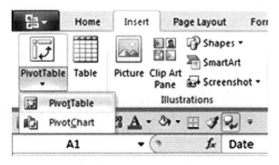

1. On the PT sheet, select just the single cell A1.
2. With only cell A1 selected, click the Insert Tab.
3. In the Tables group, click the PivotTable drop-down arrow.
4. Click PivotTable

Figure 82

If you create a lot of PivotTables, use the Alt keyboard shortcut: Alt, N, V, T. This keyboard shortcut (and all Alt keyboard shortcuts) is performed by tapping these keys in succession. You do not have to hold them all down together.

When you create a PivotTable, the Create PivotTable dialog box will pop up (see Figure 83).

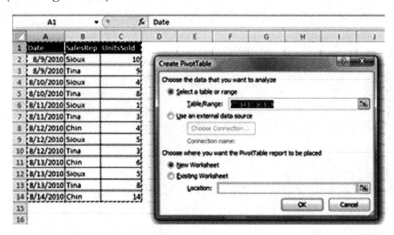

Figure 83

5. The Table/Range text box already has the correct range because we did not have any blank rows or columns in our table; in essence, it guessed correctly. If it had not guessed correctly, we would simply correct it by highlighting the correct range.

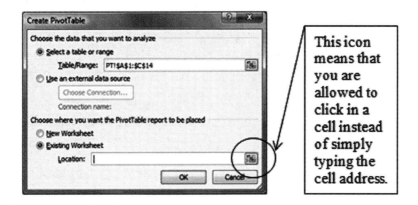

Figure 84

6. Click the Existing Worksheet button.
7. Click in the Location text box. The cursor will flash to indicate that you should click the cell where you want the Pivot-Table to go.
8. Click in cell F1.

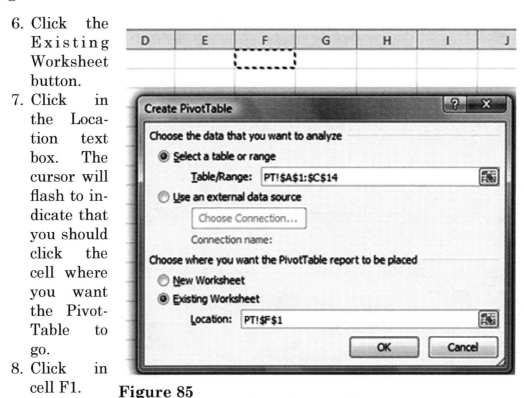

Figure 85

Notice that the name box shows F1 and that the cell F1 has dancing ants around it.

9. Click OK.

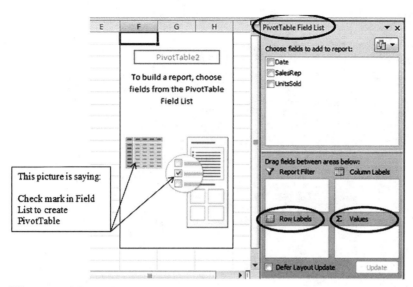

Figure 86

Figure 86 shows the Create PivotTable user interface. At the top right is the PivotTable Field List. Notice it has a list of the original table's field names. At the lower right, you have the four areas of the

potential PivotTables. Look back to Figure 81 and see that the two things we need are row labels (SalesRep) and a value (UnitsSold).

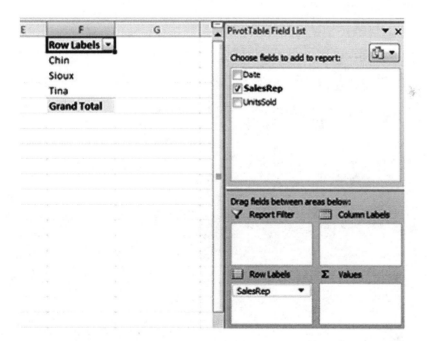

Figure 87

10. In the PivotTable Field List, click the SalesRep field to put a check mark next to it.
11. Look at the cell range F1:F5 and notice that each sales rep name appears only once. (This is called a unique list.)

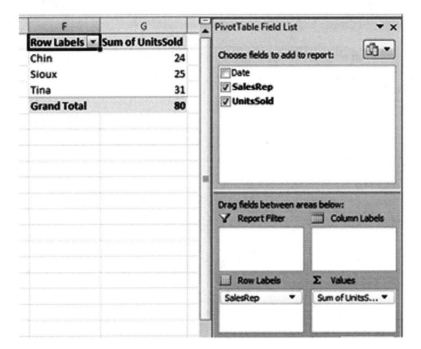

Figure 88

> 12. In the PivotTable Field List, click the UnitsSold field to put a check mark next to it.

The PivotTable is almost done.

Figure 89

With the PivotTable still selected, do the following:
> 13. Click the context-sensitive PivotTable Tools Design tab.
> 14. Go to Layout group.
> 15. Click the drop-down arrow on the Report Layout button.
> 16. Click Show in Tabular Form.

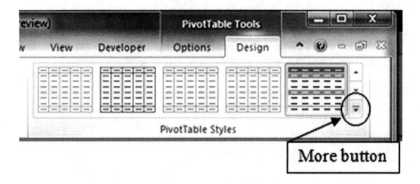

Figure 90

17. Click the PivotTable Tools Design tab.
18. Go to PivotTable Styles group.
19. Click the More button to reveal more styles.
20. Select a style that you like.

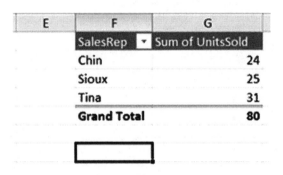

21. Click in cell F7. (Doing so hides the Field List and the PivotTable Tools tab).

Figure 91

When you click in a cell that is outside of the PivotTable, the Field List and the PivotTable Tools tabs are hidden. If you want to see the PivotTable Tools tab, click back inside the PivotTable (for example, cell F1). If you click inside the PivotTable and you don't see the Field List, right-click the Pivot-Table and point to Show Field List.

It is important to notice two things about our PivotTable in Figure 91:

- We had Excel make a calculation when we added with one condition (add only the sales representative's units sold).
- We had Excel perform data analysis when we created a summary report (useful information) from the raw data.

Now what about creating a PivotTable is seven clicks? Let's do this same example again, but instead of putting the PivotTable on the same sheet as the data, let's put it on a different sheet. Figure 92 shows the list of seven clicks and the finished result. (It isn't actually seven clicks, it's seven actions, but seven clicks sounds better.)

1. With cell A1 selected, press Alt, N, V, T. (Tap each key in succession.)
2. Press Enter.
3. Click to check mark the Sales-Rep field in Field List.
4. Click to check mark the Units-Sold field in Field List.
5. Double-click the new sheet.
6. Type PT2.
7. Press Enter.

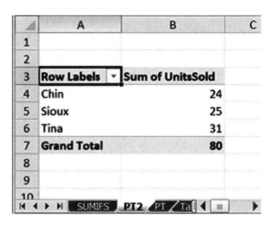

A summary report in seven clicks? PivotTables are amazing! You will learn much more about PivotTables in Chapter 6.

Figure 92

Our next Excel Efficiency-Robust Rule is as follows:

Rule 7: PivotTables are amazing for summarizing data. As long as you can visualize the summary table and see the row labels or column labels before you begin creating the PivotTable, PivotTables are not hard to do!

You just saw how to convert raw data into information using the SUMIFS function and the PivotTable feature. In both examples (Figure 79 and Figure 80), the raw data was set up similarly. In each case, the data was set up in a table format structure. We want to take a look at the importance of this table format structure next.

Table Format Structure

You just saw an example of how quickly a PivotTable could take raw data and convert it into useful information. This would not be possible if the data was not set up properly. To set up raw data properly in Excel, we must use what is called the **table format structure** (also called **table** or **table format** or **database** or **list**). When the data is in a table format, you can use Excel data analysis features such as sorting, filtering, PivotTables, database functions, and more.

The table format structure has these characteristics:

- **Field** names (also called column headers):
  - Placed at the top of each column
  - Formatted differently from the raw data
  - No blank field names
- Rows contain **records** or transactions with a single entry for each field.
- Blank cells/row headers/column headers must surround the whole table. There can't be any data in any of the cells around the outside edge of the table.
- No completely blank rows or columns inside the table (and try not to have any blank cells anywhere inside the table).

You can harness Excel's true power only when your data is set up with this table format. Let's take a look at an example of this table format and see how to harness Excel's power to sort a data set quickly in our workbook named excelisfun-Start.xlsm.

	A	B	C	D	E	F
1	Date	SalesRep	ProductSold	Units Sold	Total Sales	
2	1/1/2010	Bob	Boom 11	26	492.7	
3	1/2/2010	Bob	Boom 5	24	336	
4	1/3/2010	Shelia	Boom 15	20	873.8	
5	1/3/2010	Shelia	Boom 8	10	159.5	
6	1/5/2010	Donita	Boom 6	18	269.1	
7	1/6/2010	Tina	Boom 14	23	757.85	
8	1/6/2010	Chin	Boom 2	10	120	
9	1/6/2010	Chin	Boom 5	13	182	
10	1/6/2010	Tina	Boom 5	25	350	
11	1/6/2010	Shelia	Boom 8	8	127.6	
12	1/7/2010	Tina	Boom 10	13	234	
13	1/7/2010	Donita	Boom 11	14	265.3	
14	1/7/2010	Shelia	Boom 13	6	153.3	
15	1/8/2010	Tina	Boom 15	27	1179.63	
16	1/8/2010	Sioux	Boom 6	23	343.85	
17	1/8/2010	Bob	Boom 10	14	252	
18						

Figure 93

1. Click the Tables sheet.
2. This data set has field names at the top of each column, and sales transaction records are in each row.

We already saw how this sort of data setup allowed us to use a PivotTable. Now let's see how sorting the whole table to show the largest sales numbers at the top works with this table format.

Sorting

When you use the table format, you can simply sort the sales column and the entire table (all fields and all records) will become sorted; nothing will be mixed up (which is often the fear when sorting). The trick to sorting is to select only one cell in the field you want to sort before you click the Sort button.

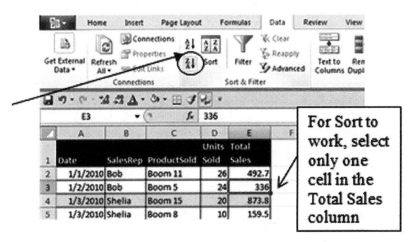

Figure 94

Notice the third record (Shelia on Jan 3) is colored yellow.

3. Click in cell E3.
4. Click the Data tab.
5. In the Sort & Filter group, click the Z – A button.

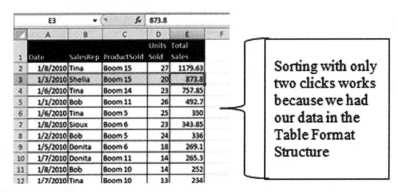

Figure 95

You can see that after you sorted, all the records remain intact. Nothing is mixed up. You can see that Shelia's Jan 3 yellow record is ranked second and that her record remains intact.

In Figure 95, we can see that our goal of sorting the whole table on the Total Sales field worked perfectly. How many clicks did that take? Two clicks. You will learn much more about data analysis and the table format in Chapter 6.

Our next Excel Efficiency-Robust Rule is as follows:

> *Rule 8: To use Excel's data analysis features, such as Sorting and Pivot-Tables, you have to store your raw data with a table format structure, which requires that you have: 1) field names in first row, 2) records in rows, 3) blank cells surround outside edge of table, 4) no blank cells, columns, or rows inside table.*

Next we want to look at how you can store data in Excel efficiently using the Excel Table feature.

Excel Table Feature (Excel as a database)

As we just saw in the preceding section, if you are storing raw data in Excel, it is efficient to use the table format structure because then you have access to Excel's data analysis features such as Sort and PivotTables. However, we can achieve even more efficiencies if we take our table format structure and convert it to an "official" Excel table using the Excel Table feature. The Excel Table feature retains the table format structure, adds some helpful formatting, and adds a number of behind-the-scenes features that will make our data analysis more robust. Really, what the Excel Table feature does is to convert our data set to a database. What's a database? A **database** is a program (such as Access, QuickBooks, or custom SAP database) that is specifically created for storing raw data and creating useful information. If you have a lot of data, it is usually most efficient to store your raw data in a database. However, in the working world, many Excel users use Excel to store raw data. Therefore, it is great that Excel added this Excel Table feature, which has some of the features of a real database program.

Benefits of converting your table of data to an Excel table include the following:
- Cell ranges are dynamic. This means that when you add new data to the table, any formulas, PivotTables, or charts that are looking at your table automatically update (just like in a database program).
- New data can be added to the bottom of the table and the new data will automatically be considered part of the table.

- To add a new record, we simple use the Tab key in the lower right of our table.
- Sorting and filtering can be done without clicking up onto the Data tab; instead, we just use the drop-down arrows next to each field name.
- Formatting field names and records differently with a table style can be done with a single click.

Note: The Excel Table feature first appeared in Excel 2007. In Excel 2003 it was called Excel List feature. In versions before Excel 2003 this feature was not available.

Now we want to learn how to:
- Convert our data in a table format structure to an Excel Table.
- Take advantage of the dynamic ranges that the Excel Table features provides us.
- Add records to the bottom of the table.
- Learn about benefits and drawbacks of AutoComplete.

Convert the table format structure to an Excel Table

To take our raw data in a table format and convert it to an Excel Table using the Excel Table feature, select only one cell in the table and then use the keyboard shortcut Ctrl + T. (You could also go to the Insert tab, Tables group, and click the Table button.) Let's take a look at how to do this:

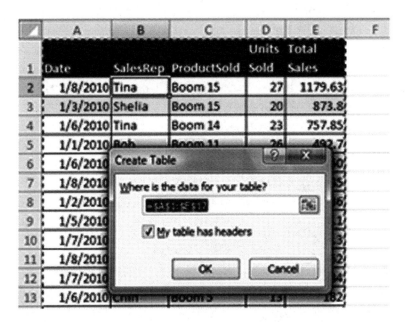

Figure 96

1. On the Tables sheet, click in cell B2 (any one cell will do).

2. To create an Excel Table from our data with the table format, press Ctrl + T.
3. Click OK.

	A	B	C	D	E	F
1	Date	SalesRep	ProductSold	UnitsSold	Total Sales	
2	1/8/2010	Tina	Boom 15	27	1179.63	
3	1/3/2010	Shelia	Boom 15	20	873.8	
4	1/6/2010	Tina	Boom 14	23	757.85	
5	1/1/2010	Bob	Boom 11	26	492.7	
6	1/6/2010	Tina	Boom 5	25	350	
7	1/8/2010	Sioux	Boom 6	23	343.85	
8	1/2/2010	Bob	Boom 5	24	336	
9	1/5/2010	Donita	Boom 6	18	269.1	
10	1/7/2010	Donita	Boom 11	14	265.3	
11	1/8/2010	Bob	Boom 10	14	252	
12	1/7/2010	Tina	Boom 10	13	234	
13	1/6/2010	Chin	Boom 5	13	182	
14	1/3/2010	Shelia	Boom 8	10	159.5	
15	1/7/2010	Shelia	Boom 13	6	153.3	
16	1/6/2010	Shelia	Boom 8	8	127.6	
17	1/6/2010	Chin	Boom 2	10	120	
18						

Figure 97

The table should automatically get banded-row formatting (table style) and drop-down arrows next to each filed name for sorting/filtering.

Notice that our original formatting is still there and the new formatting is added in addition to the original formatting.

Dynamic ranges

The biggest advantage that the Excel Table provides us is that the Excel Table creates behind-the-scenes dynamic ranges. A dynamic range simple means that if a formula is looking at the range E2:E17 and we add one new record to the table, the range will change to E2:E18 – the ranges will expand!. This is an efficient feature to use because any formula, PivotTable, or chart that is using a range of cells from an Excel Table automatically updates when new raw data is added. In the working world this feature is a huge time saver because it is common that people have data sets where they are continually adding new data. If we did not have dynamic ranges, every time we added new records to a data set, we would have to remake our existing formulas. This would take a lot of time. The fact that dynamic ranges will allow our formulas (PivotTables and charts also) to update makes dynamic ranges efficient (save time).

Let's look at how dynamic ranges work in an Excel Table.

E	F	G	H	I	J	K	L
Sales ▾		Criteria	Tina	Sales	=SUMIFS(E2:E17,B2:B17,H1)		
1179.63							
873.8							
757.85							
492.7							

Figure 98

1. On the Tables sheet in the cell G1, type **Criteria**.
2. In H1, type **Tina**.
3. In I1, type **Sales**.
4. In J1, type the formula. (Type the cell references this time. Do not click and drag. If you click and drag, you will get table formula nomenclature in your formula, which we have not talked about yet, but will later.) =SUMIFS(E2:E17,B2:B17,H1)

When you type a formula such as this, you type the characters: equal sign, S, U, M, I, F, S, (, E, 2, colon, E, 1, 7, comma , B, 2, colon, B, 1, 7, comma, H, 1,).

5. Press Ctrl + Enter. (Ctrl + Enter is a great keyboard shortcut that puts a formula in the cell and keeps the cell selected, instead of moving down as Enter does.)

For more information about the SUMIFS function, see Figures 61 to 79.

*f*x	=SUMIFS(E2:E17,B2:B17,H1)			←				Formula Bar	
C	D	E	F	G	H	I	J		
ctSold ▾	UnitsSold ▾	Total Sales ▾		Criteria	Tina	Sales	2521.48		
15	27	1179.63							
15	20	873.8							
14	23	757.85							
11	26	492.7							

Figure 99

Tina's sales should be $2,521.48.

Notice that the formula bar shows that the SUMIFS function is using the cell range E2:E17. Be aware of this because this range will automatically update when we add more data to the table.

Next we need to add some new data (add a record) to determine whether the formula will update.

Adding a New Record in a Table

As mentioned earlier, it is common task to have to add new data (new records) to an existing data set. With Excel tables it is easy to do. Let's see how to do this.

14	1/3/2010	Shelia	Boom 8		10	159.5
15	1/7/2010	Shelia	Boom 13		6	153.3
16	1/6/2010	Shelia	Boom 8		8	127.6
17	1/6/2010	Chin	Boom 2		10	120
18						
19						

Figure 100

1. Click in cell E17.

14	1/3/2010	Shelia	Boom 8		10	159.5
15	1/7/2010	Shelia	Boom 13		6	153.3
16	1/6/2010	Shelia	Boom 8		8	127.6
17	1/6/2010	Chin	Boom 2		10	120
18						
19						

Figure 101

2. Press Tab to add a new record (row) to the table.

In Figure 101, the newly inserted blank row is called a record. To enter data in each field in our record, type the data and then press the Tab key. The Tab key enters the data and moves the cursor to the next field in the table. When all the fields in the record are filled with data and the cursor is in the last field, the Tab key will add a new blank record.

14	1/3/2010	Shelia	Boom 8
15	1/7/2010	Shelia	Boom 13
16	1/6/2010	Shelia	Boom 8
17	1/6/2010	Chin	Boom 2
18	1/8/2010		
19			
20			

Figure 102

To enter the date in the date field, complete these steps:

3. In cell A18, type **1/8/2010**.
4. Press Tab.

AutoComplete

To enter the sales rep's name in the SalesRep field, complete these steps:

5. In cell B18, type the letter **t**.
6. Look at cell B18.
7. Notice that Tina's name has been automatically filled in. This is called AutoComplete.

14	1/3/2010	Shelia	Boom 8
15	1/7/2010	Shelia	Boom 13
16	1/6/2010	Shelia	Boom 8
17	1/6/2010	Chin	Boom 2
18	1/8/2010	tina	
19			
20			

Figure 103

In Figure 103, when we type the letter t, Excel tries to help us by filling in the word Tina. This is called AutoComplete. After you type a lower- or uppercase T, Excel searches the column for all the words that start with the letter T. Because Tina is the only word that starts with T, Excel fills in the word for you. If you press the Tab key, the highlighted part (in our case "ina") is automatically filled in. More on AutoComplete later.

8. Press the Tab key to accept the AutoComplete suggestion.

| 17 | 1/6/2010 | Chin | Boom 2 |
| 18 | 1/8/2010 | Tina | |

Figure 104

9. Type the word **Boom** and notice that AutoComplete does not appear.

| 17 | 1/6/2010 | Chin | Boom 2 |
| 18 | 1/8/2010 | Tina | Boom |

Figure 105

In Figure 105, when we type the word Boom, Excel finds many Booms in the column above and so it does not know which one to fill in.

Enter the rest of the data for this record:

10. For ProductSold, type **Boom 1**.
11. Press Tab.
12. Type the number **12**.
13. Press Tab.
14. Type the number **120**.
15. Press Enter.

8	1/2/2010	Bob	Boom 5	24	336
9	1/5/2010	Donita	Boom 6	18	269.1
10	1/7/2010	Donita	Boom 11	14	265.3
11	1/8/2010	Bob	Boom 10	14	252
12	1/7/2010	Tina	Boom 10	13	234
13	1/6/2010	Chin	Boom 5	13	182
14	1/3/2010	Shelia	Boom 8	10	159.5
15	1/7/2010	Shelia	Boom 13	6	153.3
16	1/6/2010	Shelia	Boom 8	8	127.6
17	1/6/2010	Chin	Boom 2	10	120
18	1/8/2010	Tina	Boom 1	12	120
19					
20					

Figure 106

By using the Enter key rather than the Tab key when we get to the last cell, we avoid adding a new row (record) to our table.

Now we want to determine whether our dynamic range worked. We can do this by putting the cell with the formula into Edit mode using the F2 key.

=SUMIFS(E2:E18,B2:B18,H1)

D	E	F	G	H	I	J	K	L
UnitsSold	Total Sales		Criteria	Tina	Sales	=SUMIFS(E2:E18,B2:B18,H1)		
27	1179.63							
20	873.8							

Figure 107

16. Click in cell J1 and press the F2 key to put the cell into Edit mode.
17. Notice that the range has updated to include the newly added record.

In Figure 98, we saw the SUMIFS function use the range B2:B17 and E2:E17. In Figure 107, we can see that the SUMIFS function updated and is now showing the range B2:B18 and E2:E18. I still remember the first time I saw an Excel Table do this. I was amazed then, and I am still amazed now. This saves a huge amount of time because you do not have to edit and change the formula when new data is added!

Our next Excel Efficiency-Robust Rule is as follows:

Rule 9: The Excel Table feature converts a table of data stored with the table format structure into an Excel-like database that has advantages such as dynamic ranges.

Trouble with AutoComplete

Now we want to take one more look at the AutoComplete feature by adding a new record to our Excel Table for the sales rep Don. Because we already have a sales rep named Donita, when we enter a new record for a new sales rep named Don, the AutoComplete feature will cause us some trouble.

17	1/6/2010	Chin	Boom 2	
18	1/8/2010	Tina	Boom 1	
19				
20				

1. Click in cell E18.
2. Press Tab.

Figure 108

17	1/6/2010	Chin	Boom 2	
18	1/8/2010	Tina	Boom 1	
19	1/9/2010	donita		
20				

3. Type the date **1/9/2010**.
4. Press Tab.
5. Type **d**.

Figure 109

Notice that AutoComplete is trying to fill in the name Donita. If we are not paying attention this can cause big trouble.

6. Type the letter **o**.
7. Type the letter **n**.

18	1/8/2010	Tina	Boom 1
19	1/9/2010	don**ita**	
20			

Figure 110

In Figure 110, notice that as you type more letters, AutoComplete does not turn off; instead, if you are typing the same letters as the ones that are already highlighted, the highlighting simply gets smaller.

8. After you type **don**, press the Tab key.

18	1/8/2010	Tina	Boom 1
19	1/9/2010	Donita	
20			

Figure 111

As you can see in Figure 111, this is a disaster! Don made the sale, but we are giving Donita credit because we are not paying attention to Auto-Complete.

To fix it, we have to reenter the data for that field.

9. With your cursor still in cell C19, use Shift + Tab to move your cursor to the left (or click in cell B18).
10. Type **Don**. Notice that "ita" is highlighted.

18	1/8/2010	Tina	Boom 1
19	1/9/2010	Don**ita**	
20			

Figure 112

11. Press the Delete key to get rid of the "ita" AutoComplete text that you do not want.

18	1/8/2010	Tina	Boom 1
19	1/9/2010	Don	
20			

Figure 113

12. Press Tab to put **Don** in the field and move to the next field.

18	1/8/2010	Tina	Boom 1
19	1/9/2010	Don	
20			

Figure 114

17	1/6/2010	Chin	Boom 2	10	120
18	1/8/2010	Tina	Boom 1	12	120
19	1/9/2010	Don	Boom 10	1	29
20					

Figure 115

18. Type the number **29**.

13. For ProductSold, type **Boom 10**.
14. Press Tab.
15. Type the number **1**.
16. Press **Tab**.

19. Press Enter. (This moves cursor out of table to D20.)

This means that you must be careful when entering data in a column. Auto-Complete can save a lot of time as long as you keep a watchful eye out when entering new elements in a field.

Next we want to look at something that was mentioned earlier: table formula nomenclature.

Table Names and Table Formula Nomenclature

Table formula nomenclature is an automatic feature that occurs when you convert a table of data to an Excel Table using the Excel Table feature. When you create an Excel Table, the columns of data (fields), the field names, and the table itself all are given **table names** so that you can use the names as a substitute for cell references in formulas. Not everyone likes to use this feature (especially since the dynamic range feature works regardless of whether you use the table names), so I will show you how to use them, and then I will show you how to turn the feature off if you do not like them. Let's first look at the name that was given to the Excel Table when we created it, and then you'll learn how to change that name.

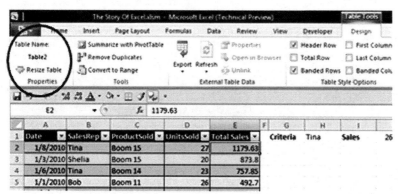

Figure 116

1. Click in one cell in the table.
2. Click the Table Tools tab.

Notice the table name: Table2. (Your table number may differ.)

3. Click in the Table Name text box. Doing so highlights the whole name.

Table Name:
Table2
Resize Table
Properties

Figure 117

4. Type the table name **BoomSales.**
5. Press Enter.

Now that we have a table name, let's see how to use this table name and the table formula nomenclature in a formula.

Table Name:
BoomSales
Resize Table
Properties

Figure 118

6. Click in cell J2 and type the start of our formula: **=SUMIFS(**

Notice that the sum_range argument in the screen tip is bold. This is Excel's way of asking you to put the cell range for summing into the function as the first argument.

H	I	J	K
Tina	Sales	2641.48	
Bob	Sales	=SUMIFS(	

SUMIFS(**sum_range**, criteria_range1, criteria1,

Figure 119

7. Click in cell E2 and drag your cursor to cell E18 to select the Total Sales column.

=SUMIFS(BoomSales[Total Sales]

Figure 120

Notice that our Table Name shows up, followed by our field name enclosed in square brackets.

In Figure 120, we can see what is called table formula nomenclature: Table names always come first followed by field names enclosed in square brackets. If you are familiar with Access database query formulas, you should recognize the field names in square brackets.

=SUMIFS(BoomSales[Total Sales],BoomSales[SalesRep],H2)
      SUMIFS(sum_range, criteria_range1, **criteria1**,

Figure 121

8. Type a comma.
9. Select the SalesRep column.
10. Type a comma.
11. Click cell H2.
12. Type a close parenthesis.
13. Press Enter.

In Figure 121, we can see how to use table formula nomenclature by select ranges in an Excel table. Next, let's see how to type out this table formula nomenclature in a formula.

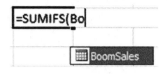

Figure 122

14. Click in cell J3 and type the start of our formula: **=SUMIFS(bo**

Notice that as soon as we type bo our table name appears highlighted in blue in a drop-down list.

Notice that unlike functions that use an fx icon in the drop-down list that appears, an Excel Table uses an table icon.

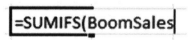

Figure 123

15. Once the Table Name is high-lighted in blue, press Tab to enter the name into our formula.

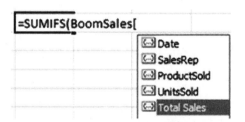

Figure 124

16. Type an open square bracket (below Backspace key and to left).

Notice a drop-down with the list of field names appears. Unlike functions that use an fx icon or Excel Tables that use a table icon, field names use a gold-rectangle icon in the drop-down list that appears.

Figure 125

17. Press the Down Arrow key four times to select the Total Sales field.

18. Once the field name is highlighted in blue, press Tab to enter the name into our formula.

Notice that the names are not blue.

19. Type a close square bracket and the reference becomes blue again.

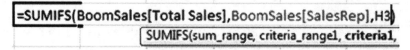

Figure 126

20. Using this typing convention, complete the formula so that it looks like Figure 126.
21. Press Enter.

One of the main advantages of this table formula nomenclature is that once you have an Excel Table in a workbook, you can use this table formula nomenclature typing convention on any sheet in the workbook. You just start typing your formula and the drop-down lists with the names just pops up! People who have a large data set and are referring to that data set often in formulas find this table formula nomenclature fast and easy.

However, other people would rather see cell references in their formulas. Therefore, learning how to turn this table formula nomenclature off is important. Let's take a look at how to do this.

1. To turn off the table formula nomenclature, click the green File tab.
2. Click the Options button (near the bottom left).
3. On the left, click the Formulas category.

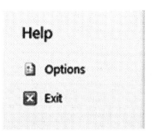

Figure 127

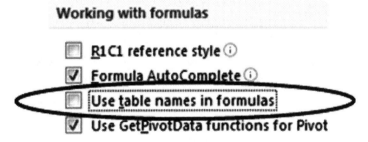

Figure 128

4. On the right in the Working with Formulas area, uncheck the Use Table Names in Formulas option.
5. Click OK.

The table name and table formula nomenclature is convenient because we can use names in formulas as a substitute for cell ranges. In the "Built-in Functions" section, later in this book, we look at the Excel name feature that is a great alternative to table names.

Now we want to take a look at the appearance of the table. In particular, look at the Total Sales column. It might be better to show these numbers as dollar amounts. Not only that: Some numbers have two decimals showing, whereas some have no decimals showing. This is an inconsistent look that you can fix easily with formatting. Let's take a look at how to apply the Accounting number formatting for the whole column with just one click. Before we apply the Accounting number formatting, let's look at the data in cell E6 in Figure 129. On the surface of the cell, E6, you can see the number 350, and in the formula bar you can see the number 350. What we see in the cell is the same as what we see in the formula bar. Now, let's add dollar signs to the whole column of data.

Figure 129

1. Click in cell E6.

Notice that E6 and the formula bar both show the number 350.

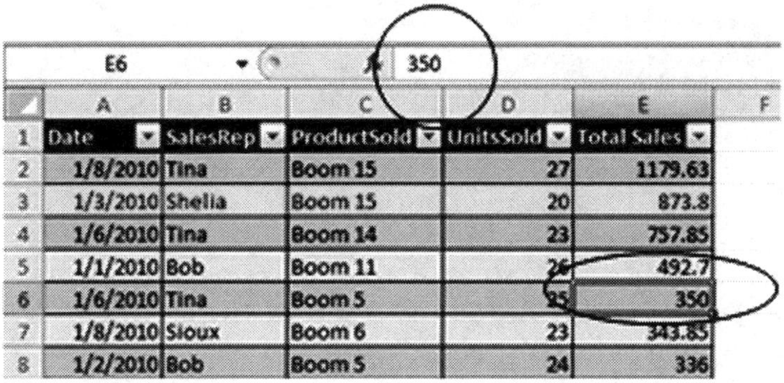

Before we can add formatting, we need to highlight the range E2:E19.

Figure 130

2. Click in cell E2, and then use the keyboard shortcut Ctrl + Shift + Down Arrow. (While holding down Ctrl and Shift simultaneously, tap the Down Arrow key.)

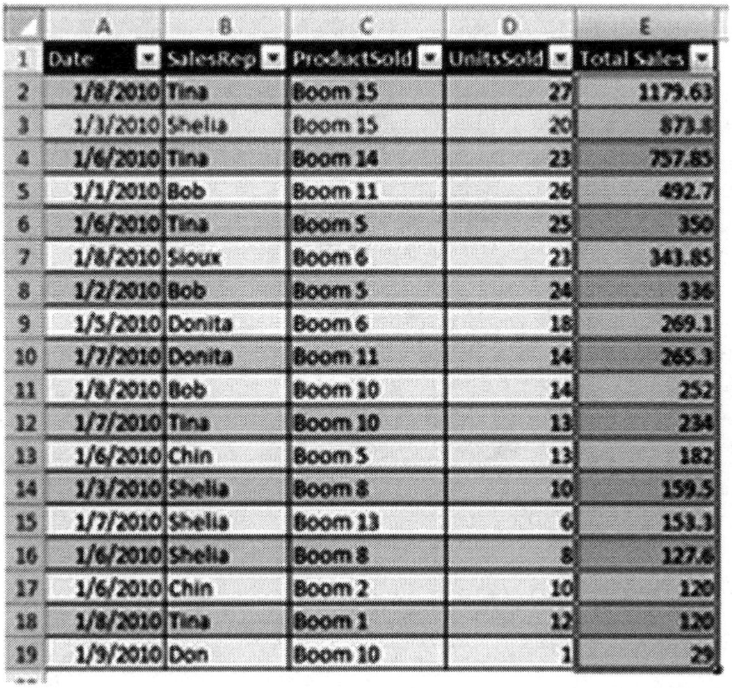

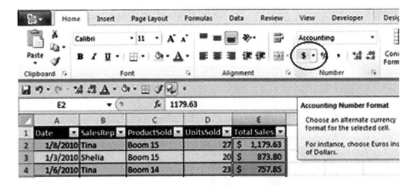

Figure 131

3. Click the Accounting number formatting button in the Number group in the Home tab to apply our Accounting Number format.

With one click of a button, the whole column of numbers is formatted with dollar signs and two decimal places are showing. The whole column has a consistent look.

Now, let's take a closer look at what the Accounting number formatting did to the raw data.

E6		f_x	350	
A	B	C	D	E
	SalesRep	ProductSold	UnitsSold	Total Sales
3/2010	Tina	Boom 15	27	$ 1,179.63
3/2010	Shelia	Boom 15	20	$ 873.80
5/2010	Tina	Boom 14	23	$ 757.85
1/2010	Bob	Boom 11	26	$ 492.70
5/2010	Tina	Boom 5	25	$ 350.00
3/2010	Sioux	Boom 6	23	$ 343.85

Figure 132

4. Click in cell E6.

On the surface of the spreadsheet in cell E6, we can see seven characters: $, 3, 5, 0, decimal, 0, 0.

But if you look in the formula bar, you can see that what is actually stored in the cell is the number 350, just three characters.

Figure 132 shows an amazing time-saving feature in Excel: number formatting. In this example, we had to type only three characters, and then Excel formatted that number to make it appear as if there were seven characters. If you are entering raw data into an Excel spreadsheet, this is a profound time saver. The following section covers some even more amazing aspects of number formatting. In fact, you will see how number formatting is like the paint on the outside of your house!

Number Formatting as Façade

If the paint on the outside surface of your house is chipped and old, but the inside of the house is immaculate and beautiful, the façade of the house looks much different from what is under it. It is often the same with number formatting and data in Excel. What you see on the surface of the spreadsheet is often much different from what is underneath, inside the cells. Number formatting can be like the façade of the house. We will call this idea "formatting as façade." Let's look at an example.

To follow along, open the file named excelisfun-Start.xlsm and navigate to the sheet named Decimals.

Decimal Number Formatting

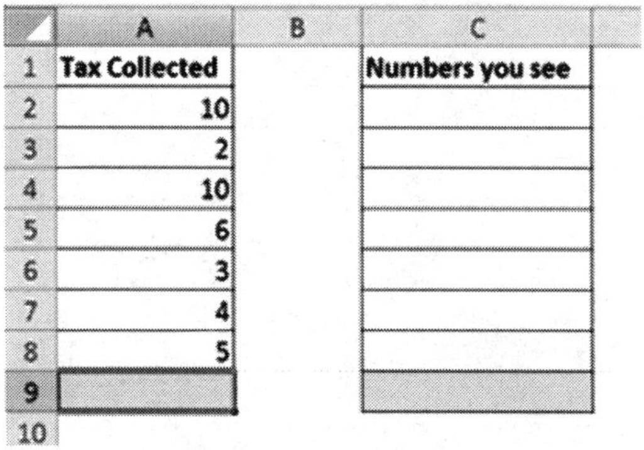

Figure 133

1. Select the Decimals sheet and look in the range A2:A8.

What do you see?

It looks like the numbers 10, 2, 10, 6, 3, 4, 5 are in the cells.

We want to add the column of taxes collected and see what sum we will get.

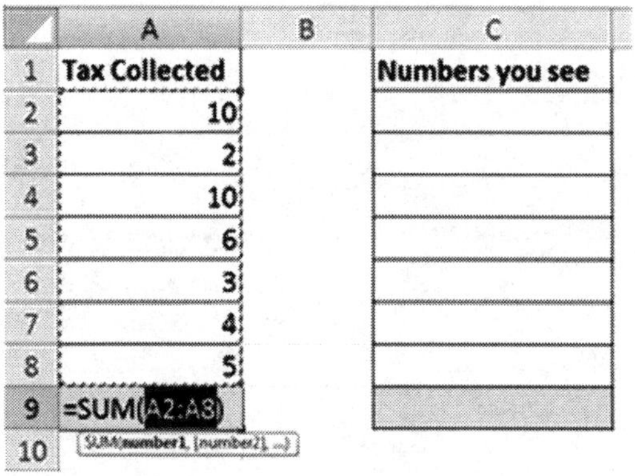

Figure 134

2. Click in cell A9.
3. To insert the SUM function, use the keyboard shortcut Alt + =, then hit Enter

4. It looks like the total is 41.

Type the numbers you see in the range A2:A8 into the new cell range C2:C8. The idea is to type what you see.

	A	B	C
C2		X ✓ fx 10	
1	Tax Collected		Numbers you see
2	10		10
3	2		
4	10		
5	6		
6	3		
7	4		
8	5		
9	41		

Figure 135

5. You see the numbers 10, 2, 10, 6, 3, 4, 5 in column A, and you type them in column C.

After typing the numbers you see in the range A2:A8 into the new cell range C2:C8, you should appear to have the same numbers in both columns.

6. Click in cell C9.

	A	B	C
C9		fx	
1	Tax Collected		Numbers you see
2	10		10
3	2		2
4	10		10
5	6		6
6	3		3
7	4		4
8	5		5
9	41		

Figure 136

7. Use the keyboard shortcut to add the SUM function (Alt + =).

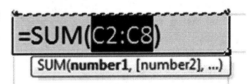

Figure 137

8. Press the Enter key; the total should be 40.

What is going on in Figure 138? 10 + 2 + 10 + 6 + 3 + 4 + 5 cannot be equal to both 40 and 41!

	A	B	C
1	Tax Collected		Numbers you see
2	10		10
3	2		2
4	10		10
5	6		6
6	3		3
7	4		4
8	5		5
9	41		40

Figure 138

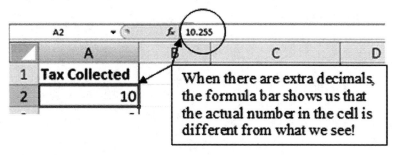

Figure 139

9. Click in A2. Look at A2. A2 shows 10.

Look at the formula bar. It shows the number 10.255. What is going on here?

In Figure 139, we see an example of a common error that people make when using Excel. What is happening is that cell A2 shows us the "formatted version of the number" and the formula bar shows us the "actual number" that is really in the cell A2. Do you get this? Here it is, one of the most important things to know about Excel:

- Number formatting is on the surface of the cell; it is what we "see."
- The actual number is underneath, inside the cell; sometimes we cannot "see" this number.
- To make the number formatting and actual number in the cell the same, change the number formatting.

Let's take a look at how to change the number formatting.

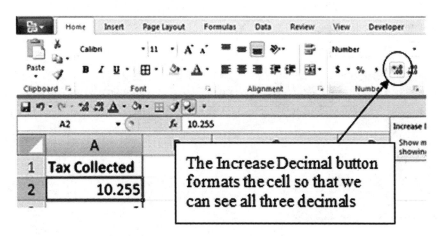

Figure 140

10. To format the number in cell A2 to match the actual number in the cell, click the Increase Decimal button in the Number group on the Home tab.

11. Select the range A2:C9 and increase the decimals to show four decimals.

In Figure 141, we can see that 10 + 2 + 10 + 6 + 3 + 4 + 5 is equal to 40 and the numbers we typed differ from the original numbers. We were tricked by formatting! What happened here is common. The numbers were originally entered in with all the decimals, and then they were formatted to show no decimals.

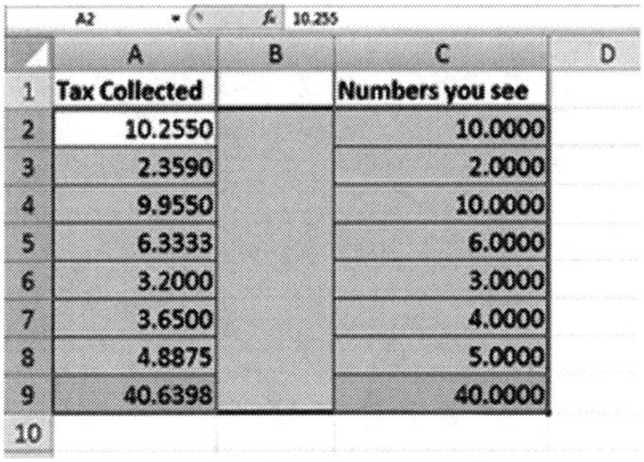

	A	B	C	D
	A2		fx 10.255	
1	Tax Collected		Numbers you see	
2	10.2550		10.0000	
3	2.3590		2.0000	
4	9.9550		10.0000	
5	6.3333		6.0000	
6	3.2000		3.0000	
7	3.6500		4.0000	
8	4.8875		5.0000	
9	40.6398		40.0000	
10				

Figure 141

	A	B	C
	A2		fx 10.255
1	Tax Collected		Numbers you see
2	10		10
3	2		2
4	10		10
5	6		6
6	3		3
7	4		4
8	5		5
9	41		40

When we decrease the decimals, the decimals are not actually removed

It just looks like they are removed!

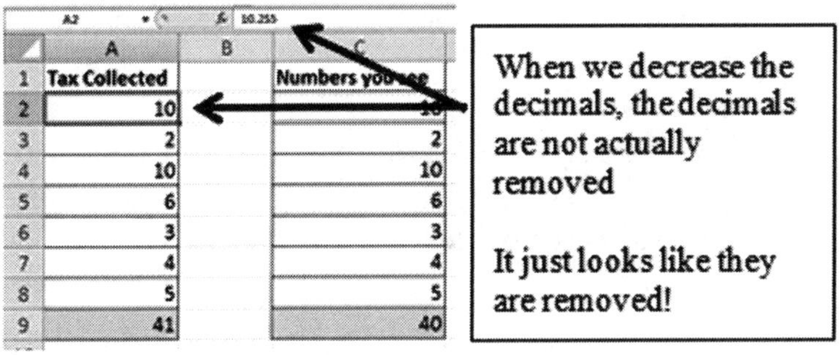

Figure 142

12. To prove this to yourself, click the Decrease Decimal button four times to see how number formatting can make the surface of the spreadsheet look different from the actual numbers in the cells. Our next Excel Efficiency-Robust Rule is this:

Rule 10: Number formatting can make the surface of the spreadsheet look different from what is actually there, in the cells. For example, you can format the number 10.255 to look like it is the number 10.

13. Click in cell A9.

The SUM function is not adding the formatted numbers; it is adding all the decimals not showing. This is why we get an answer of 41, even though it looks like we should get an answer of 40.

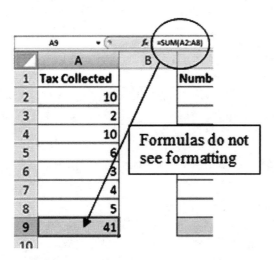

Figure 143

In Figure 143, we can see that our formatted formula result is 41 because it adds all the decimals not showing. This means that even though we may change the format, the formula will always calculate the answer from the actual numbers that sit in the cells. If formulas could see formatting, the formula result would be 40, but formulas do not see formatting.

Note: There is an option (File tab, Options, Advanced category) to set Precision as Displayed. This feature would permanently remove all decimals that are not showing due to number formatting. It is not advised that you use this option because it can cause data to lose accuracy. It is mentioned here just in case you encounter it in someone else's spreadsheet.

Our next Excel Efficiency-Robust Rule is this:

Rule 11: Formulas do not "see" formatting. When formulas calculate, they do not look at the formatted numbers, but instead they look at the actual number that sits in the cell. In terms of our house metaphor, formulas do not look at the façade of the house; they look at the inside of the house. The lone dreaded exception to this rule is if someone has enabled the Precision as Displayed option.

Date Number Formatting

Another example of formatting as façade is **Date number formatting**. When we type a date such as 4/26/2009 into a cell, we see the date, but Excel sees a number. Excel sees 1/1/1900 as the number one, 1/2/1900 as the number two, and so on up to dates such as 4/26/2009, which Excel sees as the number 39929. Officially, they are called **serial numbers**, and the series would be 1, 2, 3, 4, …, 39929.…

A date in Excel is formatted to look like a date on the surface of the spreadsheet, but underneath the date format is a number that we can use for **date math.** We can easily figure out things like "how many days is the invoice past due?" or "what is the maturity date for the loan?"

Why did they start with 1/1/1900? Mostly because there aren't many invoices or loans that are still around that were issued before 1/1/1900.

When you enter a date into a cell, you have to be careful to follow the proper convention. You must type month, forward slash, day, forward slash, and year. This is the default setting. You can change this, however, in the Regional and Language Settings in the Control Panel. Let's take a look at some examples.

To follow along, open the file named excelisfun-Start.xlsm and navigate to the DateMath sheet.

1. Select cell B1 on the DateMath sheet.
2. Type **1/1/1900**.
3. Press Enter.

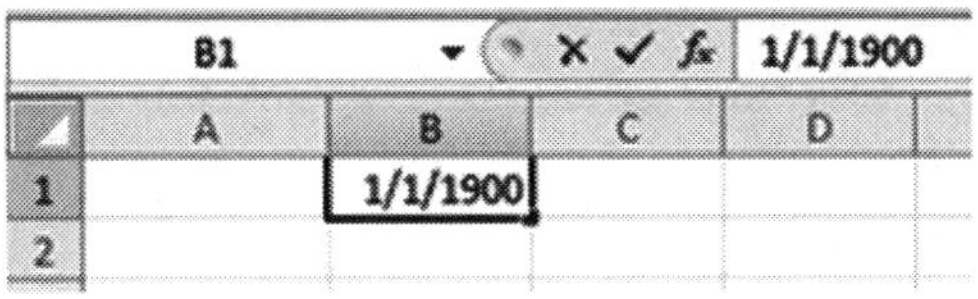

Figure 144

4. Type **1/2/1900**.
5. Press Enter.
6. Type **4/26/2009**.
7. Press Enter.
8. Type **5/12/2009**.
9. Press Ctrl + Enter (to put the date in cell and keep the cell selected).

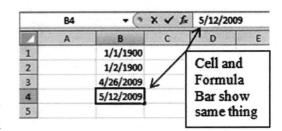

Figure 145

Notice that each time you type a date that the content of the cell and the formula bar look the same.

10. Type **Due Date** in cell A3.
11. Type **Today** in cell A4.
12. Click in cell B5.
13. Type an equal sign (to start your formula).
14. Press the Up Arrow key to insert the cell reference B4 into the formula.
15. Press the minus sign key on **Figure 146** the number keypad.
16. Press the Up Arrow key two times to insert the cell reference B3 into the formula.

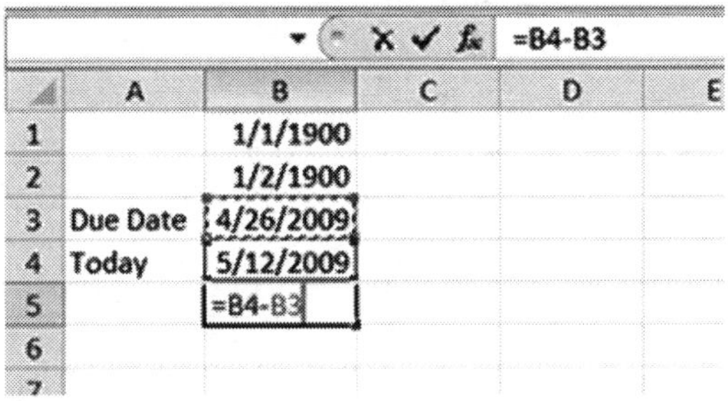

Figure 146 shows the formula for calculating the number of days between two dates. In general terms, the formula will always be Number of Days Between Two Dates = Later Date – Earlier Date.

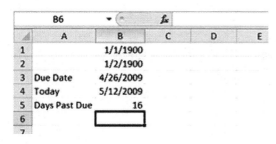

Figure 147

17. Press Enter.
18. Type **Days Past Due** in cell A5.

Our date math calculation shows us that the invoice is 16 days past due. Why did our formula work? How did it know that there were 16 days between 5/12/2009 and 4/26/2009?.

Let's take a closer look at the Date number formatting to see why our formula worked.

	A	B	C
1		1/1/1900	
2		1/2/1900	
3	Due Date	4/26/2009	
4	Today	5/12/2009	
5	Days Past Due	16	
6			

Figure 148

19. Select the range B3:B4.
20. Open the Format Cells dialog box with the keyboard shortcut Ctrl + 1. (You can also open the Format Cells dialog box by right-clicking and pointing to Format Cells, or you can use the Dialog Launcher in the Number group in the Home tab.)

21. Click the Number tab.

On the left, you can see that Date number formatting is highlighted. This means it was automatically applied when we typed in our dates.

Figure 149

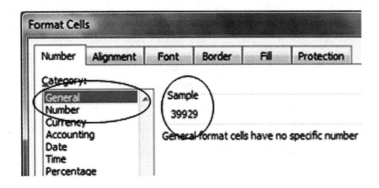

Figure 150

22. In the Category list, click the General number formatting. Notice that a sample of the formatted number is given.

23. Click OK.

When you click OK, you will see the serial numbers without the Date number formatting.

In Figure 151, we can see that by applying the General number formatting we have wiped away the Date number format: There is no more number formatting façade!

	A	B	C
1		1/1/1900	
2		1/2/1900	
3	Due Date	39929	
4	Today	39945	
5	Days Past Due	16	
6			

Figure 151

Now we can see how Excel can calculate the number of days between any two dates because we can see that 39,945 − 39,929 = 16. However, dates without Date number format would be very confusing. So let's use the Undo command to undo the application of the General number format.

Use the keyboard shortcut for Undo: Ctrl + Z. (There is also an Undo button on the Quick Access Toolbar).

Notice that we go back one step to the Date format that was applied before we applied the General number format.

	A	B	C
1		1/1/1900	
2		1/2/1900	
3	Due Date	4/26/2009	
4	Today	5/12/2009	
5	Days Past Due	16	
6			

Figure 152

It is important to note that when you type the date 4/26/2009 into a cell, Excel is doing two things at once:
- Applying the Date number formatting so that you see 4/26/2009
- Putting the number 39,929 in the cell so that you can do date math

Now we want to look at another great use for Date number formatting and date math. Figure 153 shows that we can take the loan issue date in cell G1 and add the length of the loan in cell G2. By adding the number 45 to the loan issue date, we get a date that is 45 days in the future. (You can see this example on the DateMath sheet.)

G3	▾	f_x	=G1+G2

	E	F	G	H
1		Loan Issue Date	1/1/2010	
2		Term	45	days
3		Maturity Date	2/15/2010	
4				

Figure 153

Date math is amazing. In the past people had to look at calendars and count, add, and subtract dates, but it was very time-consuming. Excel changes all that with its Date number formatting and date math.

Our next Excel Efficiency-Robust Rule is as follows:

Rule 12: When entering dates, Excel uses Date number formatting for the surface of the spreadsheet, but underneath is a serial number that enables us to do date math. Examples of serial numbers are 1 for 1/1/1900, 2 for 1/2/1900, and so on. Examples of date math are "Days Between Two Dates = Later Date – Earlier Date" and "Loan Maturity Date = Loan Issue Date + Number of Days Loan Is Outstanding."

Time Number Formatting

Similar to Date number formatting and date math is Time number formatting and time math. Whereas when you type a date into a cell and a serial number that represents that number of days since December 31, 1899 gets put into the cell, when you type a time into a cell, a serial number that represents the proportion of one 24-hour day gets put into the cell. If you type 6:00 AM in a cell, the serial number 1/4 or 0.25 gets put in the cell because 6/24 = 1/4 = 0.25. At 6:00 AM, 1/4 of the day has gone by.

When you enter time into a cell, you have to be careful to follow the proper convention. You must type hour, colon, minutes, colon, seconds (if there are any), colon, space, AM if it is before noon and PM if it is noon or later. Let's take a look at some examples.

To follow along, open the file named excelisfun-Start.xlsm and navigate to the TimeMath sheet.

1. On the TimeMath sheet, click in the cell B1.
2. Type the number 6, then a colon (:), a 0, a second 0, a space, and AM.

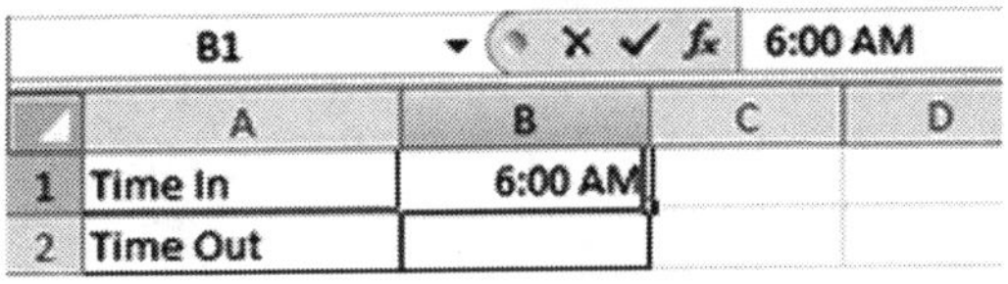

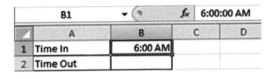

Figure 154

> **Note**: If you do not have the colon, space, and AM or PM in the correct place, the time will not be entered correctly.

3. Press Ctrl + Enter (to put time in cell and keep cell selected).

After we enter the time in the cell, look in the formula bar and see that Excel put an extra colon and two 0s for the seconds.

Figure 155

1. To see how time works in Excel, enter the number 0.25 into the cell C1.

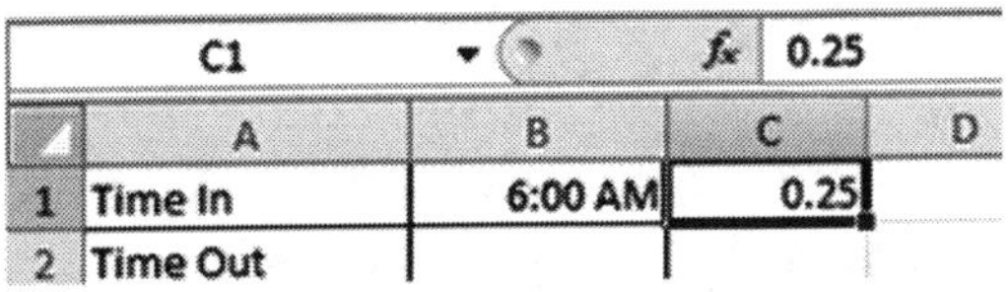

Figure 156

2. Use the keyboard shortcut Ctrl + 1 to bring up the Format Cells dialog box.
3. Click the Number tab and notice that the General format is applied.

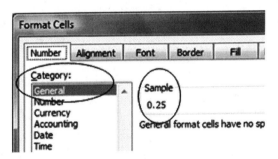

Figure 157

4. In the Category list on the left, click Time.
5. In the Type list on the right, click 1:30 PM.
6. Click OK.

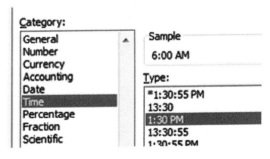

Figure 158

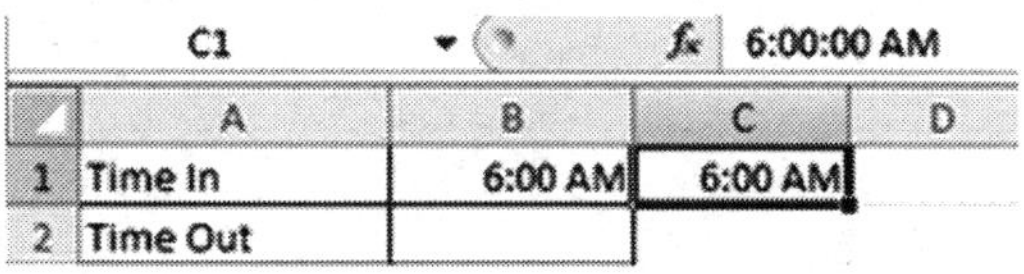

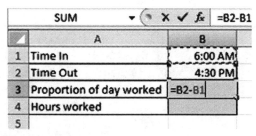

After you click OK, you can see that if you apply Time number formatting to the number 0.25, you get 6:00 AM.

Figure 159

In Figure 159, the number 0.25 represents 1/4 of the way through the day, and when we apply the Time number format, it shows 6:00 AM. Why? Because the serial number $0.25 = 1/4 = 6/24 = 6$ hours / 24 hours.

This helps to illustrate the connection between the number in the cell and the formatting that sits on top of the number. Or said a different way, this helps to illustrate how formatting is on the surface of the spreadsheet and a number is underneath that formatting.

Now you're going to learn how to use this Time number formatting and time math to calculate the time worked in a day by an employee.

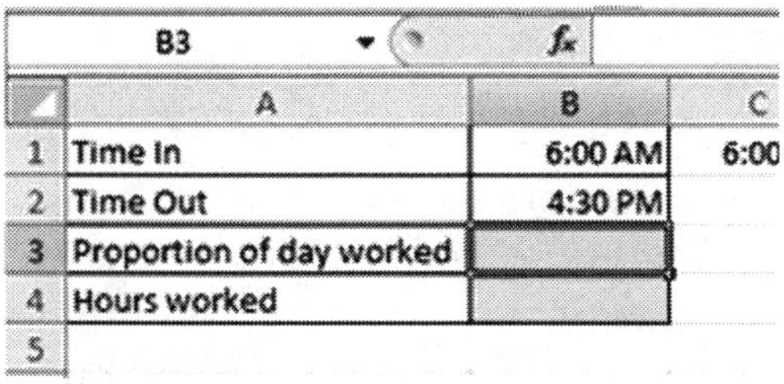

1. Type the time 4:30 PM into cell B2 and press Enter.

Figure 160

2. Click in cell B3.
3. Create the formula that will take the later time and subtract the earlier time: =B2-B1

Figure 161

In Figure 161, we can see that just as with date math, where we took the later date and subtracted the earlier date, time takes the later time and subtracts the earlier time. In general terms, the formula will always be "Proportions of 24 Hour Day = Later Time – Earlier Time."

Note: If you subtract the later date from the earlier date, you will see an error that looks like a railroad track. Delete formula and reenter the correct formula using "Later Time – Earlier Time." See Figure 162.

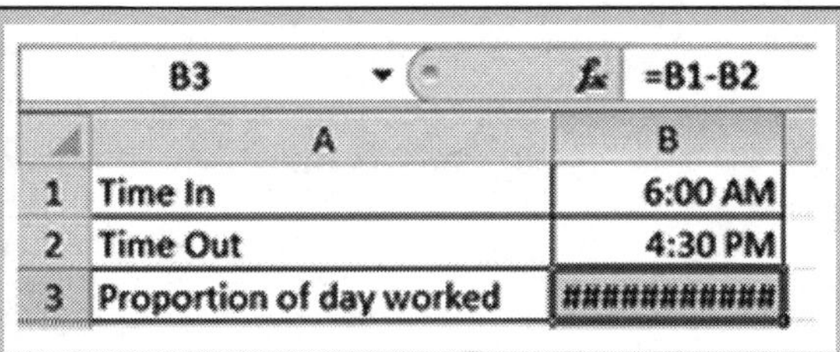

Figure 162

4. To put our correct formula into cell B3, press Ctrl + Enter.

You should see 10:30 AM in cell B3. You should see the formula in the formula bar.

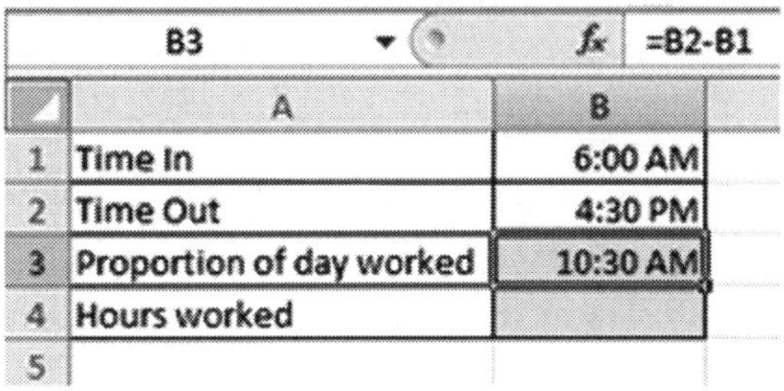

Figure 163

Why do we see 10:30 AM in cell B3 in Figure 163? Because the formula "pulled" the Time number formatting from the cells B1 and B2. The cells B1 and B2 have Time number format. When we used the cell references B1 and B2 in our formula, the Time number formatting from those cells automatically gets applied to the cell with the formula. Because this is not what we want, we need to get rid of the Time number formatting by applying the General number formatting. We could apply the General number formatting with the Format Cells dialog box, but instead, let's use the keyboard shortcut for General number format:

Ctrl + Shift + ~

The ~ key, or tilde key, is directly to the left of the number 1 key on the standard U.S. keypad. Although there are other ways to apply the General number formatting, applying the General number formatting with the keyboard shortcut Ctrl + Shift + ~ is convenient when you do a lot of date or time math.

Note: In Figure 163, we can see that the formula pulled the Time number formatting from the formula input cells, but the formula itself still calculates off the actual number that sits in the cell (in our case, the proportion of one 24-hour day).

	A	B
1	Time In	6:00 AM
2	Time Out	4:30 PM
3	Proportion of day worked	0.4375
4	Hours worked	
5		

5. With B3 still selected, apply the General number formatting with the Ctrl + Shift + ~ keyboard shortcut.

Figure 164

Applying the General number formatting wipes away all number formatting and reverts back to the default setting. When the General number formatting is applied, it supersedes all other number formats.

In Figure 164, we can see that this employee worked .4375 of one 24-hour day. That is (10.5 hours) / (24 hours) = 0.4375. The number 0.4375 is not too helpful when what we really want is hours. To convert the decimal to hours, we will multiply the decimal by 24.

3	Proportion of day worked	0.4375
4	Hours worked	=B3*24

6. To get the proportion into hours, multiply cell B3 by 24 hours with this formula: =B3*24

Figure 165

In Figure 165, why didn't we put the number 24 in a cell and refer to it with a cell reference? Because the number of hours in one day, 24 hours, will never change! It would be a waste of time and spreadsheet real estate if you were to put numbers that never change into cells and refer to them with cell references.

Our next Excel Efficiency-Robust Rule is this:

> *Rule 13: If a formula input will never change, just type the number into the formula; otherwise, if a formula input will change, put it in a cell and refer to it in a formula with a cell reference. This leads to efficient formula creation.*

B4			fx	=B3*24	
	A		B	C	
1	Time In		6:00 AM	6:00 AM	
2	Time Out		4:30 PM		
3	Proportion of day worked		0.4375		
4	Hours worked		10.5		
5					

7. Press Ctrl + Enter.

Notice that the time worked is 10.5 hours.

Figure 166

Time math is quite helpful if you understand that each time entered into a cell is the proportion of one 24-hour day. With Time number formatting, we see 6:00 AM, but what is in the cell is 6/24 or 0.25, which is the proportion of the 24-hour day that has elapsed. What is awesome about this is that we get to see the 6:00 AM on the surface, which is easy to understand, but underneath, the number 0.25 does the hard work for us; it can do the time math.

When you type the time 6:00 AM into a cell, Excel is doing two things simultaneously:

- Applying the Time number formatting so that you see 6:00 AM
- Putting the number 0.25 in the cell so that you can do time math

Figure 167 shows some examples of numbers between 0 and 1 and what they look like with Time number formatting applied.

Number	Time
0	12:00:00 AM
0.25	6:00:00 AM
0.333333333	8:00:00 AM
0.5	12:00:00 PM
0.75	6:00:00 PM
0.999988426	11:59:59 PM
1	12:00:00 AM

Figure 167

Our next Excel Efficiency-Robust Rule is this:

*Rule 14: When you enter time into Excel, enter hour, minutes, seconds separated by colons, then a space, then AM or PM. Excel uses Time number formatting for the surface of the spreadsheet, but underneath is a serial number that allows us to do time math. Time serial numbers are between 0 and 1 and represent the proportion of one 24-hour day. For example, the time 6:00 AM represents the number 0.25 or 6/24. Two useful time formulas are "Proportions of 24 Hour Day = Later Time – Earlier Time" and "Hours Worked = 24 * (Later Time – Earlier Time)."*

Next we want to talk about another common number formatting: the Percentage number formatting.

Percentage Number Formatting

Before we talk about Percentage number formatting, we need to review the concept of percentages.

We all understand what a percentage is if we say your sales tax rate is 8.8%. That means for every $1, the government wants 8.8 cents, or 8.8 pennies for every 100 pennies. (Back when kings did this, the king would ask for 8.8 sheep for every 100 sheep, and then they would take 9 sheep).

So the government does this:

8.8 / 100 = 0.088.

The number 0.088 is hard to visually understand, and so they came up with a formatting solution that makes it easier to look at. The steps to format the number are as follows:

1. Multiply the number by 100:
2. 0.088 * 100 = 8.8
3. Add a percentage symbol:
4. 8.8 and the symbol % → 8.8%

8.8% is symbolic. 8.8% means that for every 100 items give us 8.8 of those items, (in our case pennies, in the king's case sheep).

Okay that's fine, but let me ask you two questions:

Questions
1. What is 0.088?
2. What is 8.8%?

Answers
1. 1. 0.088 is a number.
2. 8.8% is not a number. 8.8% is a formatted symbolic representation of the number 0.088.

What? 8.8% is not a number, but instead it is a formatted symbolic representation of a number? I can just here some accounting and math teachers saying, "What? Of course, 8.8% is a number!"

Okay

Does 0.088 = 8.8?

No.

In step 2 of converting 0.088 into 8.8%, we took the number 0.088 and multiplied it by 100 to get 8.8. As soon as you do that, you have exited the realm of math and entered the realm of symbolism or simply formatting because 0.088 does not equal 8.8.

Our next Excel Efficiency-Robust Rule is as follows:

Rule 15: 8.8% is not a number. 8.8% is a formatted symbolic representation of the number 0.088.

Now, let's see that Excel does that same thing: Excel takes the number 0.088 and formats it as 8.8%.

To follow along, open the file named excelisfun-Start.xlsm and navigate to the Percentage(1) sheet.

1. Click the Percentage(1) sheet.
2. Enter the number 0.088 in cell A2.

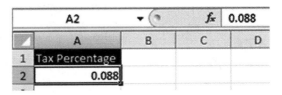

Notice that what is in the cell is the number 0.088, and notice that the formula bar and the cell show the same thing.

Figure 168

3. With cell A2 selected, press Ctrl + 1 to open the Format Cells Dialog box.
4. Click the Number tab.
5. On the left, select Percentage format.
6. On the right, click the down-up arrow (spin button) so you will show only one decimal place.
7. Click OK.

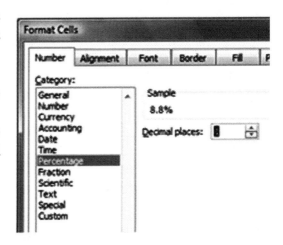

Figure 169

Notice that the formula bar and the cell show the same thing. (This is the same as Date and Time number formatting.)

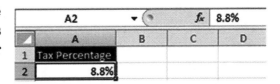

Figure 170

In Figure 170, what we did was to apply Percentage number formatting on top of the number 0.088. We did this because it is easier for us to understand what 8.8% means. But underneath that Percentage number formatting is the number 0.088. To prove to ourselves that the number 0.088 sits underneath the formatted 8.8%, let's switch to Formula Auditing mode. You can think of Formula Auditing mode as looking behind the scenes to see what is really going on, or think of it as looking underneath or below the surface of the spreadsheet. The keyboard shortcut for looking underneath the surface of the spreadsheet is Ctrl + `. The `, or grave accent key, is directly to the left of the number 1 key on the standard U.S. keypad. This keyboard shortcut is a toggle, which means you can go into this mode and then out of this mode by using the same keyboard shortcut. Instead of using the keyboard shortcut, you could go to the Formulas tab, Formula Auditing group, and click the Show Formulas button (see Figure 171).

Figure 171

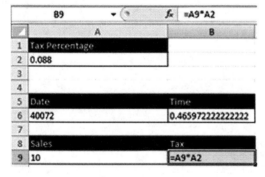

Figure 172

Let's look at an example.

Figure 172 shows the formatting that we see on the surface of the Percentage(1) sheet.

Notice that there is a formula in cell B9. Also notice that we can see the formula result of $0.88 in the cell, and we can see the actual formula in the formula bar.

Press Ctrl + ~ to look underneath the surface of the spreadsheet.

Formula Auditing mode shows you what is actually in the cell, not the formatted surface.

In Figure 173, you can see a whole different world that lives underneath the surface of the spreadsheet. In Figure 172 and Figure 173, we can clearly see what is meant by "formatting as façade":

Figure 173

- Cell A2 has the number 0.088 in the cell and has Percentage number formatting on the surface.
- Cell A6 has 40,072 days since Dec 31, 1899 in the cell and Date number formatting on the surface.
- Cell B6 has 0.465972222222222 of the way through one 24-hour day in the cell and Time number formatting on the surface.
- Why did the number 0.465972222222222 stop when it got to the 10th 2? Because the maximum number of digits that Excel can display is 15, that is why the repeating 2 stopped when it got to the 15th digit.
- Cell A9 has the number 10 in the cell and Currency number formatting on the surface.
- Cell B9 has a formula in the cell and Currency number formatting on the surface.

8. Press Ctrl + ` to toggle out of Formula Auditing mode.

In Figure 174, the formula result in cell B9 is correct because Excel used the number 0.088 when it made the calculation, not the 8.8 that we see on the surface.

B9			fx	=A9*A2
	A	B	C	D
1	Tax Percentage			
2	8.8%			
3				
4				
5	Date	Time		
6	9/16/2009	11:11 AM		
7				
8	Sales	Tax		
9	$10.00	$0.88		

Figure 174

Next we want to look at six common situations that people run into when using percentage in Excel. Let's get started.

1. Click the Percentage(2) sheet.
2. In cell C1, type the number 0.03.
3. Press Ctrl + Enter to enter the number and keep the cell selected.

C1		fx	0.03
	A	B	C
1	Situation 1:	Type .03 in cell, then add % format	0.03
2	Situation 2:	Type 3 in cell, then add % format	
3	Situation 3:	Add % format, then type 3, Enter	
4	Situation 4:	Add % format, then type .03, Enter	
5	Situation 5:	Add % format as you type	
6	Situation 6:	Type .025, then add % from ribbon	
7			

Figure 175

4. Press Ctrl + 1 to open the Format Cells dialog box.
5. On the Number tab, choose Percentage format showing one decimal.
6. Click OK.

C1		fx	3%
	A	B	C
1	Situation 1:	Type .03 in cell, then add % format	3.0%
2	Situation 2:	Type 3 in cell, then add % format	
3	Situation 3:	Add % format, then type 3, Enter	
4	Situation 4:	Add % format, then type .03, Enter	
5	Situation 5:	Add % format as you type	

Figure 176

Our next Excel Efficiency-Robust Rule is as follows:

Rule 16: If you type .03 in cell, and then apply the Percentage number formatting, you get 3.0%.

7. Press Enter.
8. Type 3.
9. Press Ctrl + Enter.

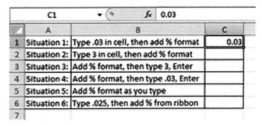

C2		fx	3
	A	B	C
1	Situation 1:	Type .03 in cell, then add % format	3.0%
2	Situation 2:	Type 3 in cell, then add % format	3
3	Situation 3:	Add % format, then type 3, Enter	
4	Situation 4:	Add % format, then type .03, Enter	
5	Situation 5:	Add % format as you type	
6	Situation 6:	Type .025, then add % from ribbon	
7			

Figure 177

	C2		*fx*	300%
	A	B		C
1	Situation 1:	Type .03 in cell, then add % format		3.0%
2	Situation 2:	Type 3 in cell, then add % format		300.0%
3	Situation 3:	Add % format, then type 3, Enter		
4	Situation 4:	Add % format, then type .03, Enter		
5	Situation 5:	Add % format as you type		

10. Press Ctrl + 1 to open the Format Cells dialog box.
11. On the Number tab, choose Percentage format showing one decimal.
12. Click OK.

Figure 178

Note: Typing the number 3 and then applying the Percentage number formatting and expecting to get 3.0% is one of the most common errors that people make in Excel. If you know how to avoid this error, your fellow co-workers will love you at any job you may have. Admiration and job security can be yours if you know that formatting is a façade.

Our next Excel Efficiency-Robust Rule is this:

Rule 17: If you type 3 in a cell, and then apply the Percentage number format, you get 300.0%.

Now let's look at what preformatting a cell will do.

	C3		*fx*	
	A	B		C
1	Situation 1:	Type .03 in cell, then add % format		3.0%
2	Situation 2:	Type 3 in cell, then add % format		300.0%
3	Situation 3:	Add % format, then type 3, Enter		
4	Situation 4:	Add % format, then type .03, Enter		
5	Situation 5:	Add % format as you type		
6	Situation 6:	Type .025, then add % from ribbon		

1. Highlight the range C3:C4.
2. Apply the Percentage number formatting with one decimal showing before you type any numbers.

Figure 179

	C3	X ✓ *fx*	3%	
	A	B		C
1	Situation 1:	Type .03 in cell, then add % format		3.0%
2	Situation 2:	Type 3 in cell, then add % format		300.0%
3	Situation 3:	Add % format, then type 3, Enter		3%
4	Situation 4:	Add % format, then type .03, Enter		
5	Situation 5:	Add % format as you type		
6	Situation 6:	Type .025, then add % from ribbon		

3. Click in cell C3 and type the number 3.
Notice that immediately the percent symbol (%) pops up. This tells you that the cell is preformatted.
4. Press Enter.

Figure 180

	C4		*fx*	
	A	B		C
1	Situation 1:	Type .03 in cell, then add % format		3.0%
2	Situation 2:	Type 3 in cell, then add % format		300.0%
3	Situation 3:	Add % format, then type 3, Enter		3.0%
4	Situation 4:	Add % format, then type .03, Enter		
5	Situation 5:	Add % format as you type		
6	Situation 6:	Type .025, then add % from ribbon		

When you preformat the cell with Percentage number formatting, you can type the number 3 and it will know that you want 3.0%.

Figure 181

5. Type the number .03.

Notice that even though this cell is pre-formatted with Percentage Number format, % does not pop up.

C4	▾	ⓧ ✗ ✓ *fx*	.03

	A	B	C
1	Situation 1:	Type .03 in cell, then add % format	3.0%
2	Situation 2:	Type 3 in cell, then add % format	300.0%
3	Situation 3:	Add % format, then type 3, Enter	3.0%
4	Situation 4:	Add % format, then type .03, Enter	.03
5	Situation 5:	Add % format as you type	
6	Situation 6:	Type .025, then add % from ribbon	
7			

Figure 182

6. Press Enter.

When you preformat the cell with Percentage number formatting, you can type the number .03 and it will know you want 3.0%.

C5	▾	ⓘ	*fx*	

	A	B	C
1	Situation 1:	Type .03 in cell, then add % format	3.0%
2	Situation 2:	Type 3 in cell, then add % format	300.0%
3	Situation 3:	Add % format, then type 3, Enter	3.0%
4	Situation 4:	Add % format, then type .03, Enter	3.0%
5	Situation 5:	Add % format as you type	
6	Situation 6:	Type .025, then add % from ribbon	
7			

Figure 183

Our next Excel Efficiency-Robust Rule is as follows:

Rule 18: If you preformat the cells with Percentage number formatting and type a .03 or a 3 into a cell, you get 3.0%.

1. To enter data and format as you type, add a percentage symbol to the end of your number (without a space).
2. In the unformatted cell C5, type 3.0%.
3. Press Enter.

C5	▾	ⓘ ⓧ ✗ ✓ *fx*	3.0%

	A	B	C
1	Situation 1:	Type .03 in cell, then add % format	3.0%
2	Situation 2:	Type 3 in cell, then add % format	300.0%
3	Situation 3:	Add % format, then type 3, Enter	3.0%
4	Situation 4:	Add % format, then type .03, Enter	3.0%
5	Situation 5:	Add % format as you type	3.0%
6	Situation 6:	Type .025, then add % from ribbon	
7			

Figure 184

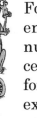

Formatting as you type is convenient if you just have a few numbers to enter. Typing 3.0% puts the number 0.03 in the cell and adds a Percentage number format. Similarly, typing $4.00 in a cell puts the number 4 in the cell and applies the Currency number format. But be careful, percentage formatting as you type always shows two decimal places by default. For example, typing 3.999% in a cell would put the number 0.03999 in the cell and add the Percentage number formatting that shows 4.00%.

Next we want to see how the Percentage number formatting button in the Number group in the Home tab adds the format with zero decimals showing.

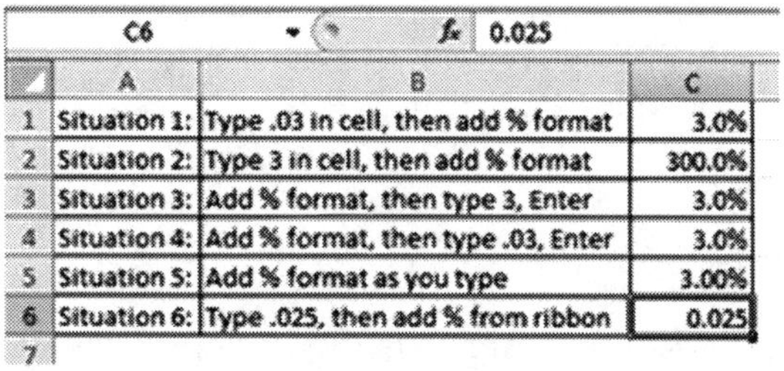

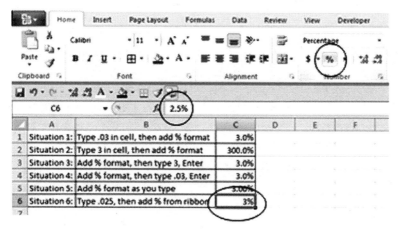

1. To see the trouble that the ribbon button for the Percentage number formatting can cause, type 0.025 in cell C6.
2. Press Ctrl + Enter.

Figure 185

Figure 186

3. Click the % button in the Number group in the Home tab.

Notice that 3% is showing in the cell and that 2.5% is showing in the formula bar.

    4. To fix this, we must use the "increase decimal" button in the Number group in the Home tab.

In Figure 186, we can see that the button in the ribbon for the Percentage number formatting can lead to trouble if you are not paying attention. This is another common mistake that people make. It is a good idea to always determine whether you have enough decimals showing when you are using the Percentage number formatting.

Our next Excel Efficiency-Robust Rule is this:

    Rule 19: Always be sure to determine whether you have enough decimals showing when you are using Percentage number formatting.

You have now seen Decimal number formatting, Date number formatting, Time number formatting, and Percentage number formatting and how the formatting sits on top of the cell and how the numbers sit underneath the formatting. Formatting as façade is a very important concept in Excel. Without understanding that Number formatting is on the surface of the spreadsheet and the numbers are underneath, you cannot become proficient in making calculations or doing data analysis. For us, though, we will become proficient because we know that formatting is like the paint on the outside of the house.

Our next Excel Efficiency-Robust Rule is this:

Rule 20: Number formatting is on top (what you see), and the numbers are underneath (what Excel uses for calculations).

Let's take look at how data is aligned in Excel and what sort of data Excel recognizes.

Data Alignment (types of data Excel recognizes)

Excel recognizes three types of data: numbers, text (words), and logical values (true or false). By default, Excel aligns numbers to the right, words to the left, and logical values in the center. This default alignment comes from the Normal style, which all cells have when you open a new workbook. This is important because if the numbers, text, or logical values are not aligned in this way, it gives us a hint that something might be wrong with the data.

Let's take a look at an example of how data is aligned.

To follow along, open the file named excelisfun-Start.xlsm and navigate to the Align(1) sheet.

1. Click the Align(1) sheet.
Notice the cells A2, A4 and A6 are empty.
2. These cells have the default cell formatting called "Normal style."

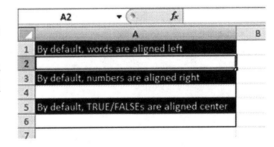

Figure 187

3. Type Excel in cell A2.
4. Type 43 in cell A4.
5. Type true in cell A6.

In Figure 188, we can see the default behavior in action. Text is aligned left, numbers right, and the word true is centered and also in uppercase letters.

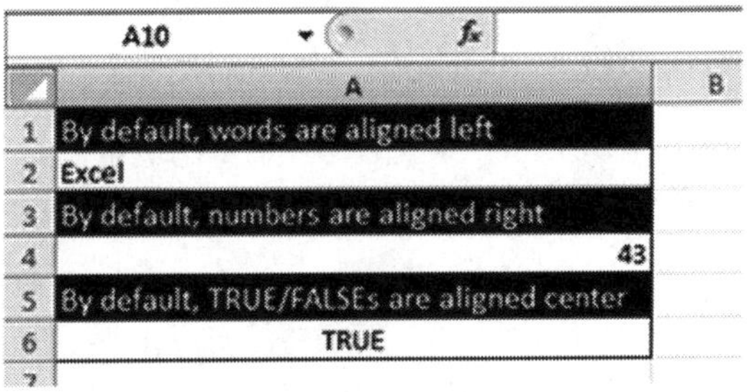

Figure 188

This default alignment can be changed, but it is not a good idea (as you will see in a bit). Nevertheless, let's see how to change this default alignment.

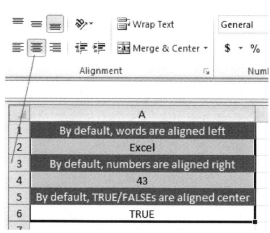

Figure 189

1. Highlight the range A1:A6.
2. Click the Align Center button in the Alignment group in the Home tab.

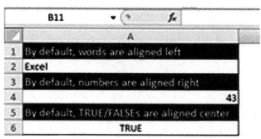

Figure 190

3. Press Ctrl + Z to undo the center alignment.

So, it is possible to change this default behavior. However, when you change the default alignment, you lose the visual ability to determine whether Excel thinks the data is a number, text, or true/false.

Let's take a look at how to use our knowledge of the default alignment in Excel to help us track down problems. To follow along, open the file named excelisfun-Start.xlsm and navigate to the Align(2) sheet.

Numbers Stored as Text

	A	B	C	D
1	Sales Data Imported as Text		Dates	
2	$15.00		9/23/2009	
3	$25.00		9/25/2009	
4	$62.00		9/28/2009	
5	$52.00		9/30/2009	
6	$25.00			
7	$62.00			
8	$32.00			

Figure 191

1. Click the Align(2) sheet.
2. Click in cell A9.

Notice the column header in column A. This sales data was imported from an external source as text (importing numbers as text is a common mistake).

In Figure 191, we can see that the numbers are aligned to the left. Left-aligned numbers are a visual cue that lets us know that there could be a problem. Let's try to add these numbers.

3. In cell A9, create this formula:
   =SUM(A2:A8)

> **Note**: If you use the keyboard shortcut for the SUM function, a default range will not appear because the numbers are stored as text. You will have to manually select the range, A2:A8.

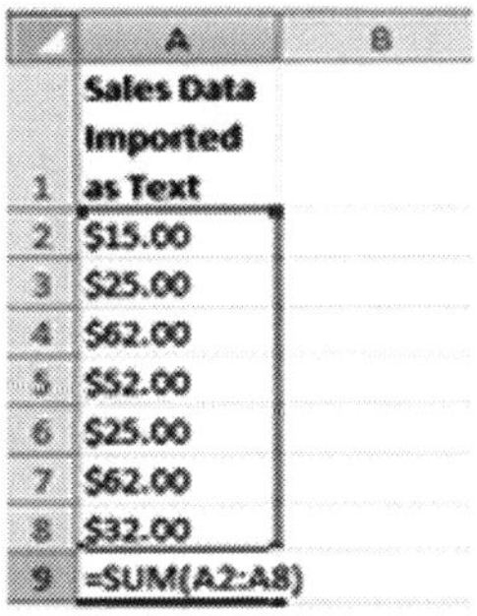

Figure 192

> **Note**: This cell was not part of the data import and therefore has the default General number formatting before we add the SUM function.

4. Press Ctrl + Enter.

Immediately we see the calculated result is zero because the SUM function ignores text. We see a zero because the cell had the default General number formatting before we entered our SUM function.

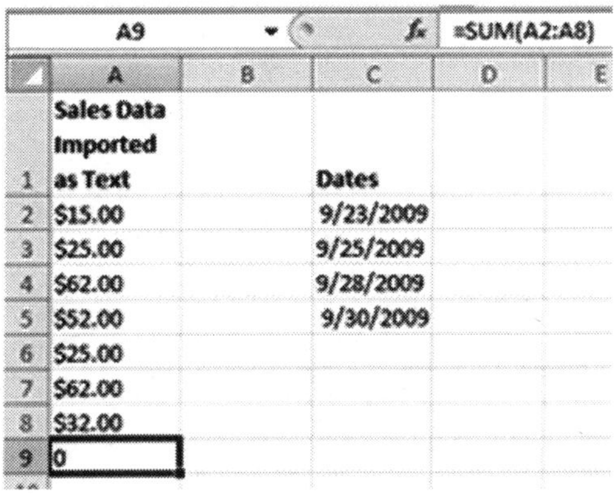

Figure 193

> **Note**: After we enter the formula, the cell A9 adopts the Text number formatting. If cell A9 had been preformatted with Text number formatting, we would not see zero, but instead we would see the formula itself.

In Figure 193, the cell A9 is showing a sum of zero because the SUM function is programmed to ignore text. (You can prove this to yourself by pressing the Help key, F1, and searching for "SUM function.") When the data was originally imported into Excel, it was imported as text (a common mistake). And here's the catch: If you do not pick up on the visual cue that the numbers are aligned left, it might take you a long time to figure out what the problem is. So, to avoid this sort of frustration, always keep an eye out for how your data is aligned. Now, before we fix it, let's prove to ourselves that Excel really sees those numbers as text.

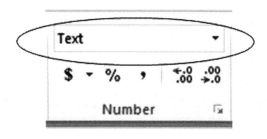

Figure 194

5. To prove to yourself that the Excel really thinks that the numbers are text, highlight the range A2:A8.
6. Look at the Number formatting text box in the Number group in the Home tab. You can see that the Number formatting is Text.

The solution for the "numbers stored as text" problem is to change the number formatting to General number formatting, Currency number formatting, or some other preferable number formatting. However, this can get tedious because we would have to change each cell's formatting, put it into Edit mode, and reenter the number. Luckily, there is a well-known trick for solving this common data import error. Let's take a look at how it works.

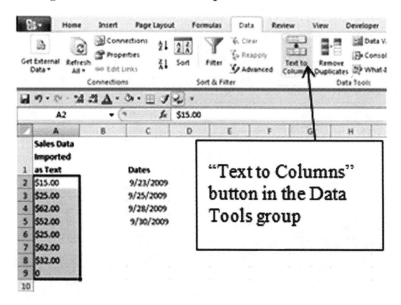

Figure 195

7. Select the range A2:A8.
8. Click the Data tab.
9. Click the Text to Columns button in the Data Tools group.

10. Click the Finish button in the Convert Text to Columns Wizard dialog box. (We talk more about text to columns later.)

Figure 196

After you click the Finish button, all the numbers stored as text will become numbers stored as numbers with the Currency number formatting.

In Figure 197, we can see that the SUM function can now add correctly because Excel considers the column of numbers not text, but instead numbers that can be added.

It was the Text number formatting that caused the problem. When data is imported as text (common mistake), it brings the data into Excel with the Text number formatting.

	A
1	**Sales Data Imported as Text**
2	$15.00
3	$25.00
4	$62.00
5	$52.00
6	$25.00
7	$62.00
8	$32.00
9	$273.00

Figure 197

The Text number formatting can cause problems such as this and other problems, too. Avoid the Text number formatting whenever possible.

You might be thinking, "But wait a second! I thought you already stated earlier in this book that formulas do not see formatting? In fact, we have already seen date math and time math formulas that were not affected by the formatting (Figure 147 and Figure 164). So why won't the SUM function see through the Text number format?" It is simply because the SUM function is specifically programmed to ignore text.

	Sales Data Imported as Text
12	
13	$15.00
14	$25.00
15	$62.00
16	$52.00
17	$25.00
18	$62.00
19	$32.00
20	=A13+A14+A15+A16+A17+A18+A19

Figure 198

If you look at Figure 198, you can see an example of a formula that will calculate the sum even though the Text number formatting is applied. This formula can add text because it is not preprogrammed like the SUM function. Does that mean that we should use a formula like we see in Figure 198? No way! The formula in Figure 198 takes too long to make. Imagine if you had a column of 30 numbers to add.

Nevertheless, people who deal with a lot of imported data do sometimes use these type of formulas. We won't make this mistake, however, because as soon as we see numbers aligned to the left, we will have a good cue that we are dealing with text rather than numbers. Let's look at another example of how the default alignment can help us to track down the cause of a problem.

	A	B	C	D
1	Sales Data Imported as Text		Dates	
2	$15.00		9/23/2009	
3	$25.00		9/25/2009	
4	$62.00		9/28/2009	
5	$52.00		9/30/2009	
6	$25.00		=COUNT(C2:C5)	
7	$62.00			

Figure 199

Our goal is to create a formula in cell C6 that will count how many dates there are.

1. Click in cell C6 and create this formula: **=COUNT(C2:C5)**

The COUNT function counts numbers.

2. Press Ctrl + Enter.

Notice that the formula can be seen in the formula bar and the number 1 can be seen in cell A6.

The COUNT function counts numbers. Because dates are serial numbers, if we want to count dates, this is the correct function to use. But our formula result should be 4, not 1. Look at Figure 200, we have a visual cue that three of the numbers are being stored as text. Let's examine further.

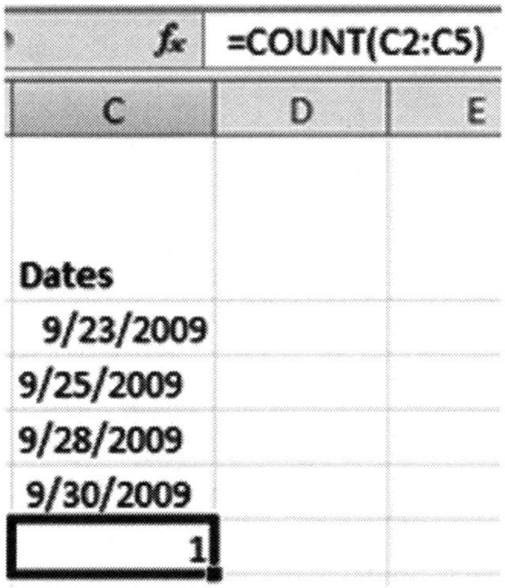

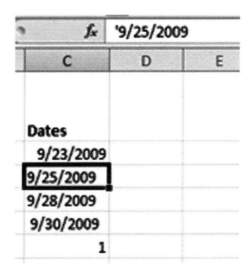

Figure 200

3. Click in cell C3 and look in the formula bar.

Notice that this date was entered with a lead apostrophe.

In Figure 201, we can see the lead apostrophe. A lead apostrophe tells Excel to treat the item as if it were text. We want to remove this lead apostrophe.

Figure 201

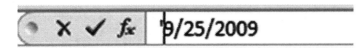

Figure 202

4. Move your mouse into the formula bar and when you see the I-beam cursor click in-between the apostrophe and the number 9.
5. Then press the Backspace key and press Enter.

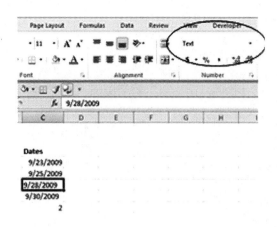

Figure 203

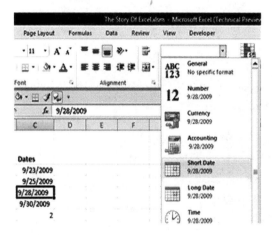

Figure 204

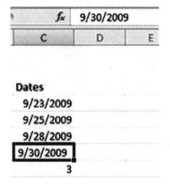

Figure 205

Notice that the COUNT function updated to show 2 after we removed the apostrophe.

6. Select cell C4 and notice that the number formatting is Text.

7. With cell C4 selected, go to the Home tab, Number group, and select the drop-down arrow for number formatting.
8. Select Short Date.

After formatting it, the problem will not be fixed until you reenter the data.

9. With cell C4 selected, press the F2 key (Edit mode).
10. Press Enter.

11. With cell C5 selected, look in the formula bar and you can see that there appears to be a lead space before the 9.
12. Using the formula bar, remove the space and press Enter.

An apostrophe, the Text number formatting, and a leading space caused our COUNT function to count only one date. Our knowledge of default alignment in Excel helped us to quickly track down the problem.

Dates
9/23/2009
9/25/2009
9/28/2009
9/30/2009
4

Figure 206

What happens if you use the Alignment cell formatting to align numbers to the left? Nothing really, except that you lose your ability to quickly find data problems with your knowledge of default alignment. Let's take a look at an example.

1. Click the Align(3) sheet.
Notice that SUM function in cell A9 was able to add a column of numbers

2. Highlight the range A2:A8.

3. Look at the Alignment group in the Home tab; you will see that the cells have Horizontal Alignment Left.

Although the SUM function works correctly in the situation, try to avoid formatting numbers in this way.

Figure 207

In Figure 208, notice the green triangles in the upper-left corner of each cell in the range C2:C8. The green triangles are from Excel's Error Checking feature. (If you do not see this, open the File tab, click the Options button, choose the Formulas category, and check the Enable Background Error Checking check box.) Although this feature does not work very well for formulas, it is great for finding numbers stored as text.

	A	B	C	D
1	Sales Data Imported as Text		Sales Data Formatted as Text	
2	$15.00	◈	$15.00	
3	$25.00		$25.00	
4	$62.00		$62.00	
5	$52.00		$52.00	
6	$25.00		$25.00	
7	$62.00		$62.00	
8	$32.00		$32.00	
9	$273.00		0	

Figure 208

The range C2:C8 was formatted with Text number formatting. However, these numbers are not numbers from a data import, like back in Figure 191; these are numbers that have been formatted with the Text number formatting by the spreadsheet author. Let's take a look at how to use the Error Checking feature to quickly change the format.

1. Select the range C2:C8.

Notice the error check "smart tag" that pops up.

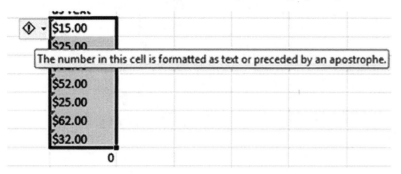

Figure 209

2. Hover your cursor over the error check smart tag.

The screen tip gives its best guess as to what is causing the problem.

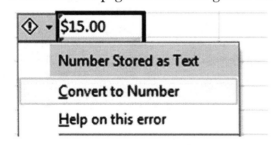

3. Click the error check smart tag drop-down error.
4. Click Convert to Number.
5. Look at the formula result in cell C9; you should see the correct formula result.

Figure 210

So you have seen how knowledge of the default alignment can help you track down the cause of problems with data. That leads to our next rule.

Our next Excel Efficiency-Robust Rule is as follows:

> *Rule 21: Avoid adding alignment formatting to data because the default alignment (numbers = right, text = left, logical values = centered) can help us to quickly track down data problems.*

The next chapter shows you how to take data that is summarized into information or a report and format it in a professional way.

4

STYLE FORMATTING AND PAGE SETUP

Style formatting and page setup are important skills to have if you want people to be able to read and interpret the reports that you create in Excel. **Style formatting** (such as bold and font color) is applied directly in the cells in the spreadsheet and shows while the spreadsheet is in use and in the printed-out report. **Page setup** is just a set of guidelines you define (such as landscape/portrait or headers/footers) that determine how the spreadsheet will look on the page when it is printed out. In Figure 211, we can see our unformatted report, and in Figure 212, we can see our final printed report. The headers and footers that you see in Figure 212 are an example of page setup, and the centered title, Wind Sport Inc., is an example of style formatting. Now let's see how to create this report by applying style formatting and page setup.

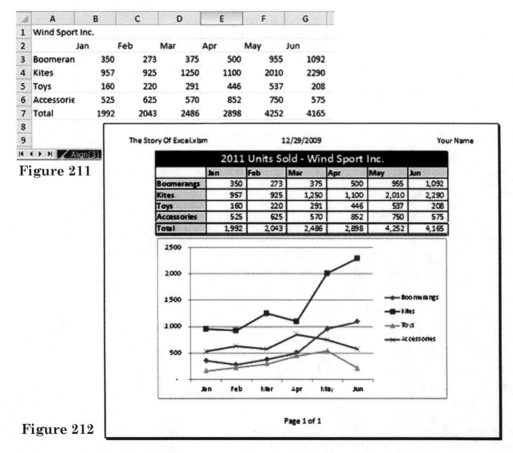

Figure 211

Figure 212

Applying Style Formatting

To follow along, open the file named excelisfun-Start.xlsm and navigate to the sheet named Store 1.

1. Click the Store1 sheet.
2. Click in cell A1.
3. Use the keyboard shortcut Ctrl + * (the asterisk on the number keypad) to highlight the current range.

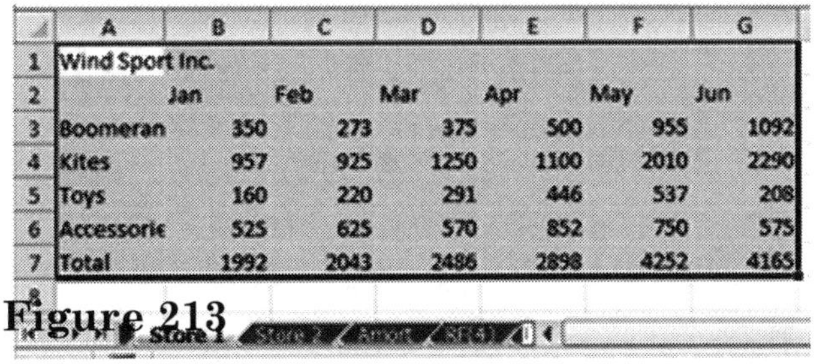

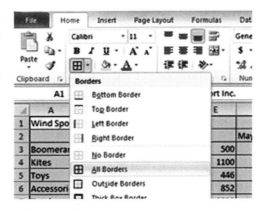

Figure 213

(The current range consists of all the contiguous cells; that is, cells touching each other.)

4. Go to the Home tab, Font group, and click the drop-down arrow next to the Borders button.
5. Click All Borders.

In Figure 214, notice that we can apply style formatting (as well as number formatting) using the Home tab.

Figure 214

In the next example, we use the Format Cells dialog box to apply formatting. Although the Home tab has many of the most popular formatting features, the Format Cells dialog box has all the features that you can find in the Home tab plus many more.

6. Highlight the range A1:G1.
7. Press Ctrl + 1 to open the i4-05Format Cells dialog box.
8. i4-On the Alignment tab, click the drop-down arrow for the Horizontal text alignment and select Center Across Selection.

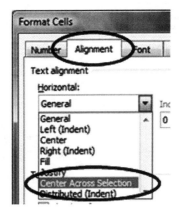

Figure 215

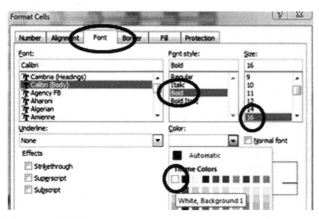

Figure 216

9. Click the Font tab.
10. From the drop-down arrow in the Color box, select the first color, white.
11. Select Size 16.
12. Select Font Style: Bold.

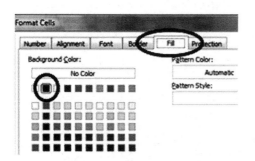

Figure 217

13. Click the Fill tab.
14. From the drop-down arrow in the Background Color box, select the second color, black.
15. Click the OK button.

Figure 218

The title for the report should look like what is shown in Figure 218. In that figure, you can see the title for the report is centered across the selection A1:G1. An alternative for centering titles is called Merge and Center (see Figure 219). Most spreadsheets that you will encounter in the working world use Merge and Center. However, several drawbacks to Merge and Center make the Center Across Selection feature a better way to center titles. The drawbacks of Merge and Center include the following:

- Moving the report may require that you unmerge the cells.
- Inserting columns may not be possible.
- Formulas that use the cell references in the merged area may not work properly.

The Center Across Selection feature has none of these problems. The only caveat when using Center Across Selection is that when you want to edit the title, you must click in the first cell in the range (in our example, cell A1).

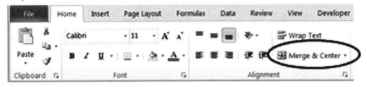

Figure 219

Our next Excel Efficiency-Robust Rule is as follows:

> *Rule 22: Center Across Selection is a good alternative to the commonly used Merge and Center because it has fewer drawbacks (like cut and paste problems with Merge and Center). You can apply Center Across Selection from the Horizontal option on the Alignment tab in the Format Cells dialog box.*

16. Highlight the range A3:A7.
17. Hold the Ctrl key.
18. Highlight the range B2:G2.

	A	B	C	D	E	F	G
1				Wind Sport Inc.			
2		Jan	Feb	Mar	Apr	May	Jun
3	Boomeran	350	273	375	500	955	1092
4	Kites	957	925	1250	1100	2010	2290
5	Toys	160	220	291	446	537	208
6	Accessorie	525	625	570	852	750	575
7	Total	1992	2043	2486	2898	4252	4165
8							

Figure 220

Notice that by holding the Ctrl key when selecting you can highlight non-contiguous ranges (cells not next to each other).

19. To add bold, press the Ctrl + B keyboard shortcut.
20. Go to the Home tab, Font group, and click the drop-down arrow next to the Fill Color button and select a light gray.

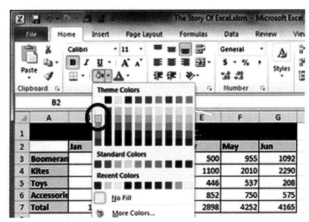

Figure 221

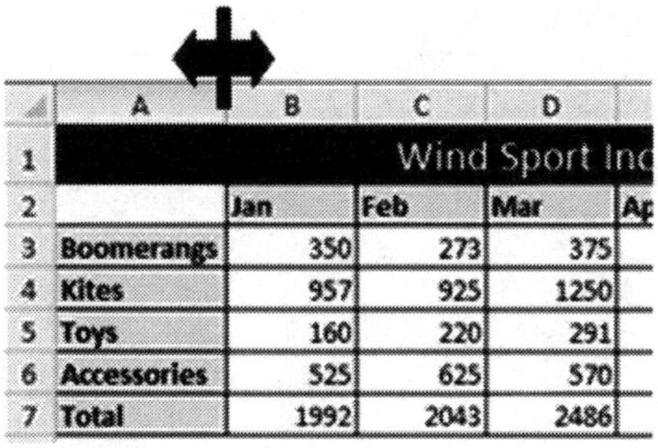

Figure 222

21. To expand the width of column A so that the labels can be seen, point your cursor in between the column headers A and B (directly over the thin line) and double-click. Be sure to double-click only when you see the cursor with a thin black vertical line and a black horizontal double-arrow line.

Here are two important notes about style formatting for labels in reports:

- It is helpful to format labels differently than you format numbers. A different format will help you to quickly differentiate visually between the labels and other data.
- The value difference (dark vs. light) between the cell Fill Color ("paint bucket tipped on its side" icon) and the Font Color must be large. (This seems obvious, but many printed reports do not follow this rule, and therefore the labels are hard to read.)

The way to tell for sure if the value difference is large is to squint your eyes and look at the labels. If the labels are hard to read, the value different is not big enough. A simple rule to follow is this: If the Font Color is dark, the Fill Color must be light; if the Fill Color is dark, the Font Color must be light.

Figure 223

22. Highlight the range B3:G7.
23. Go to the Home tab, Number group, and click the Comma Style.
24. Comma Style is the Accounting number formatting without a dollar sign.

The keyboard shortcut for Comma Style is Ctrl + Shift + 1.

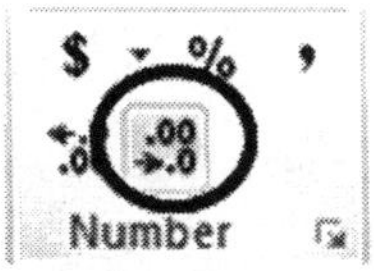

Figure 224

25. Because this report shows units sold, we do not need to show decimals.
26. Go to the Home tab, Number group, and click the Decrease Decimal button twice. (Getting rid of unnecessary decimals makes the report less cluttered.)

27. Click in cell A1 to access the report title text.

28. Click in the formula bar and change the title to **2011 Units Sold - Wind Sport Inc.**

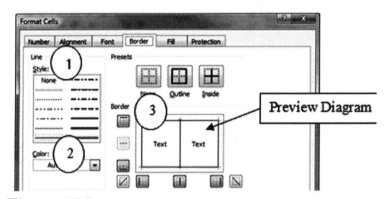

A1		▼	f_x	2011 Units Sold - Wind Sport Inc.		
	A	B	C	D	E	F
1			2011 Units Sold - Wind Sport Inc.			
2		Jan	Feb	Mar	Apr	May	Ju
3	Boomerangs	350	273	375	500	955	
4	Kites	957	925	1,250	1,100	2,010	

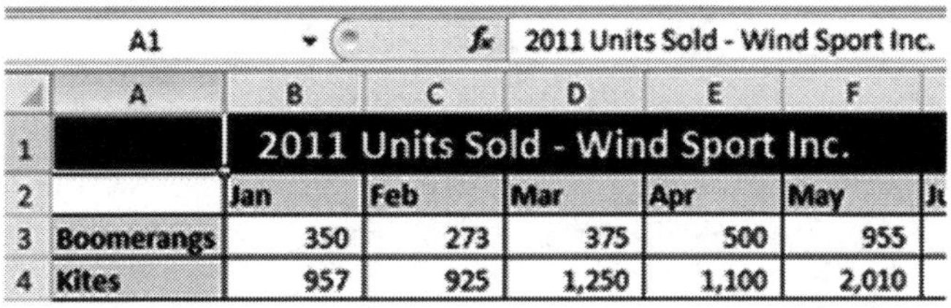

Figure 225

In Figure 225, notice that to edit a title that uses Center Across Selection, we had to select the first cell in the range (in our case, cell A1).

Next we want to use borders to emphasize the totals at the bottom of the report.

29. Select the range A7:G7.

30. Press Ctrl + 1 to open the Format Cells dialog box.

31. Select the Border tab.

Figure 226

Figure 226 shows the Border tab in the Format Cells dialog box. You must apply borders in the correct sequence; otherwise, borders might not appear as you intended. The correct order is as follows:

- 1 Click a line style to select it.
- 2 Select a line color.
- 3 Click a preset, one of the border buttons, or click to preview the diagram.

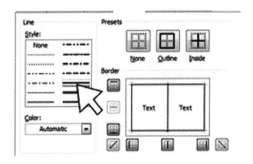

32. With your white diagonal-pointing cursor, click the medium-thick border style (fifth down in second column of styles).

We do not need to change the line color.

Figure 227

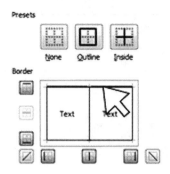

Figure 228

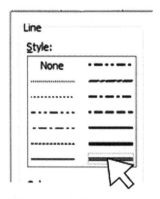

Figure 229

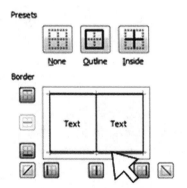

Figure 230

33. Click the top border in the preview diagram.

34. To add a second line style, click the double-line border style (seventh down in second column of styles).

35. Click the bottom border in the preview diagram.
36. Click the OK button.
37. Select cell A1 to see the borders that you just added. To get a clear preview, you must select a cell *not* in the range that has the applied borders.

In Figures 227 to 230, notice that we had to click back and forth between the line styles and the preview diagram when applying borders with different line styles. This is an example of why the sequence of applying borders is so important.

◢	A	B	C	D	E	F	G
1		2011 Units Sold - Wind Sport Inc.					
2		Jan	Feb	Mar	Apr	May	Jun
3	**Boomerangs**	350	273	375	500	955	1,092
4	**Kites**	957	925	1,250	1,100	2,010	2,290
5	**Toys**	160	220	291	446	537	208
6	**Accessories**	525	625	570	852	750	575
7	**Total**	1,992	2,043	2,486	2,898	4,252	4,165
8							

Figure 231

The bottom border should now look like Figure 231.

For many reports that summarize numeric data, it is customary to have a double line below the last number and a single thick dark line above the last number. This is to visually indicate that this is the "bottom-line" number (or the final number) that the report is trying to present. Technically, the double line means that this is the bottom line (the goal of the report), and the single think dark line means that "some calculation has been made on the numbers above to get to the 'bottom line' number." Calculations that the single bottom line imply include the following:

- Adding a column of numbers for a Total Units Sold report (as in the earlier example)
- Multiplying to calculate an inventory value for an Inventory report
- Subtracting to calculate net income for an Income Statement report
- Doing a net present value calculation for an Asset Value report

Our next Excel Efficiency-Robust Rule is this:

Rule 23: Borders must be applied in the proper sequence: 1) style, 2) color, 3) preview diagram. A single line above and a double line below the last number in a report is a visual indicator that the number is the "bottom line."

Next we want to add a chart to this report. Charts are great because they visually portray numeric data in a more immediate way as compared to simply showing the numbers alone. With charts, you can more quickly spot trends and patterns. Later, in Chapter 7, "Charts," we discuss them in more detail.

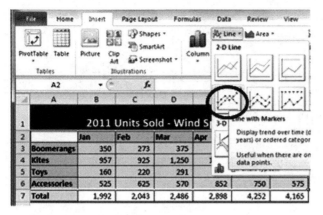

Figure 232

1. Highlight the range A2:G6. Do not include the Totals row (row 7) or the title (row 1).
2. Go to the Insert tab, Charts group, and click the drop-down arrow next to the Line Chart icon and select Line with Markers (the first item in the second row).

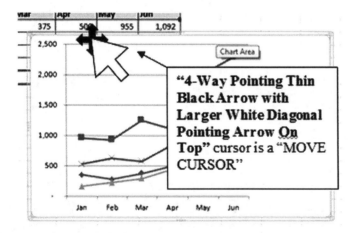

Figure 233

3. After the chart appears, point to the translucent edge of the chart. When you see "four-way-pointing thin black arrow with a larger white diagonal-pointing arrow on top" cursor (as shown in Figure 233), click and drag the chart under the report.

4. After moving the chart, it should be below the report, not covering the double borders at the bottom of the report, and it should not be wider than the report. If it is wider, point to the edge of the chart and click and drag inward when you see the black diagonal-pointing double arrow.

5. The line chart shows one numeric variable of the vertical axis and a category on the horizontal axis. (You'll learn more about this type of chart in Chapter 7.)

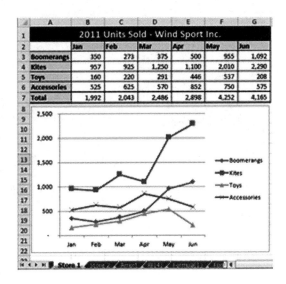

Figure 234

As you can see in Figure 234, the line chart adds an immediate visual portrayal of the data. For example, we can clearly see that in April the kite and boomerang sales started to increase and that the toys and accessories started to decrease.

Next we want to put the finishing touches on this report by applying page setup.

Understanding Page Setup

Page setup determines how the report will look on the page when it is printed. Page setup will allow us to orient the page, set margins, add headers and footers, and more. Page setup can be done from the Page Layout tab or the Page Setup dialog box. The advantage of the Page Layout tab is that many buttons are visible at one time. The advantage of the Page Setup dialog box is that it has a more complete listing of page setup features than the Page Layout tab, and it is sometimes faster to use than the Page Layout tab.

Before you do page setup, it is always important to view the report in Print Preview. In earlier versions of Excel, the Print Preview feature and the Print feature were different features. In Excel 2010, they are the two older features rolled into one. As a result, the keyboard shortcut Ctrl + P will open the Print dialog box and show us Print Preview.

To follow along, open the file named excelisfun-Start.xlsm and navigate to the Store 1 sheet. In this section, we are building on what we did in the last section (style formatting).

Printing and Print Preview

Figure 235

1. Press Ctrl + P to see Print Preview and the printing options.
2. When you have finished with Print Preview, press the Esc key to close Print Preview. Do *not* click the red X in the upper-right corner. The red X button is the close file button. If you click it, you close the file.

We do Print Preview before page setup so that we can see what needs to be done in page setup. From Figure 235, we can see that we need to do the following:

- Use landscape orientation because the report is longer than it is tall.
- Scale the report up to about 150% to fill the page and make it easier to read.
- Center the margins horizontally so that the report looks neat and balanced.
- Add dynamic headers and footers that automatically update when the date or sheet name changes.

Our next Excel Efficiency-Robust Rule is as follows:

Rule 24: Always use Print Preview before you print so that you can determine what page setup must be done to create a professional-looking report.

We will use the Page Setup dialog box to do our page setup. In Figure 236, you can see what is called a **dialog launcher** (a small right-pointing, diagonal-downward arrow) in the lower-right corner of the Page Setup group in the Page Layout tab. The Page Setup dialog launcher opens the Page Setup dialog box. Because page setup is such a common task, it is worthwhile to learn the Alt keyboard shortcut to open the Page Setup dialog box:

Alt, P, S, P (Tap Alt, then tap P, then tap S, then tap P in succession.)

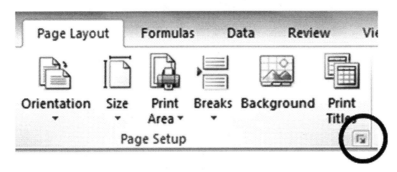

Figure 236

3. Press Alt, P, S, P to open the Page Setup dialog box.
4. In the Orientation options, click the Landscape button.
5. Use the Up Arrow key to adjust scaling to 150%.

Figure 237

6. Click the Margins tab.
7. Check the Center on Page Horizontally check box in the lower-left corner.

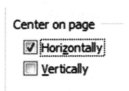

Figure 238

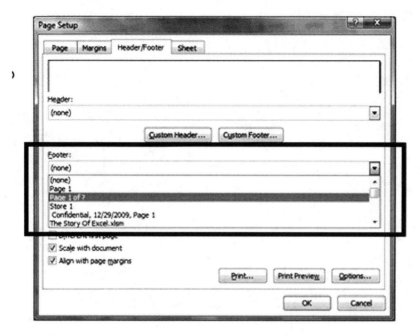

Figure 239

8. Click the Header/Footer tab.
9. In the Footer box, use the drop-down arrow to select Page 1 of ?.

Page 1 of ? is a useful footer for two reasons:
- If you have 10 pages, the pages will show 1 of 10, 2 of 10, and so on.
- It helps people to know how many pages the report contains (and so, the number they should have, even if it is just one page).

Figure 240

10. To add a custom header, click the Custom Header button.

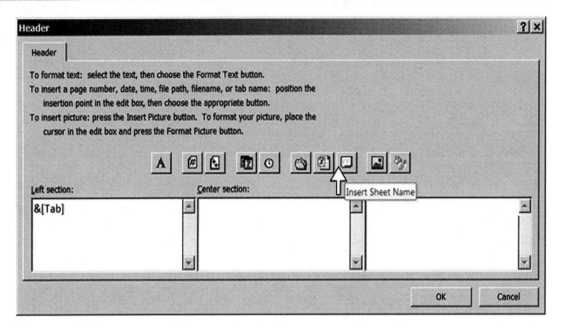

Figure 241

11. With your cursor flashing in the Left section, click the Insert Sheet Name button.

In Figure 241, you can see that the Insert Sheet Name button inserts the code &[Tab] into the Left section of the header. This allows the header to be dynamically linked to the sheet name. If you change the sheet name, the header will automatically update. This sort of efficient header/footer trick is great for budget templates and other similar reports that have sheet names such as Jan – 2009, Feb – 2009, and so on. You can do the page setup once and it will work for more than one report!

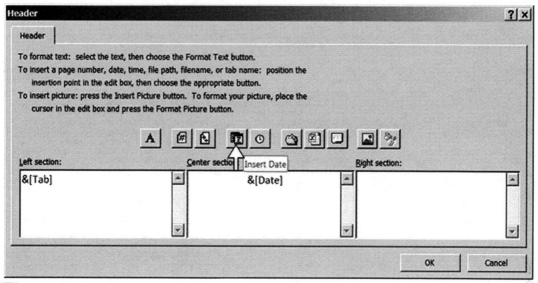

Figure 242

> 12. Press the Tab key to move to the Center section.
> 13. Click the Insert Date button to insert the code for a dynamic date.

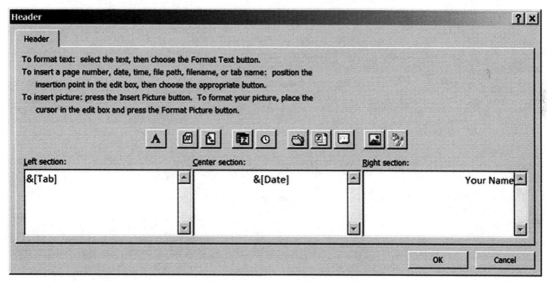

Figure 243

> 14. Press the Tab key to move to the Right section.
> 15. Type your name.
> 16. Click the OK button on the Header dialog box.
> 17. Click the OK button on the Page Setup dialog box.

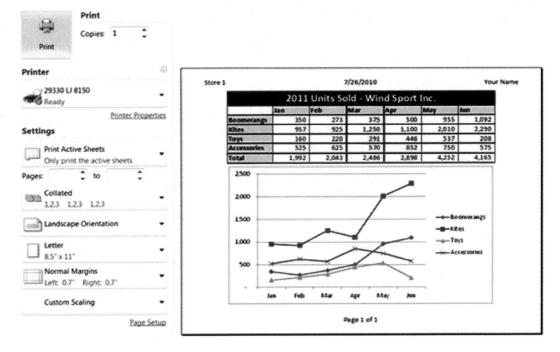

Figure 244

18. To see Print Preview and the Printing options press Ctrl + P.
19. Check to determine whether the report looks correct.
20. Click the Print button to print (or simply press Enter if the Print button is highlighted orange).

Printing an Entire Workbook

To print an entire workbook (all the sheets) or a highlighted area in a particular sheet, press Ctrl + P, and then select the desired item from the Settings drop-down (see Figure 245).

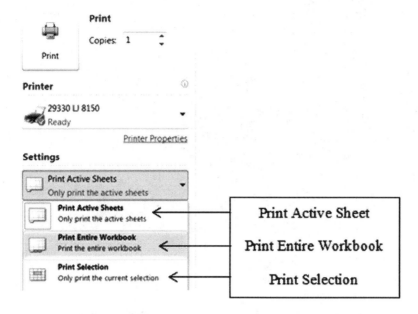

Figure 245

Page Setup for More Than One Page

You might sometimes have two reports on one sheet and need to print out each one on a separate sheet. In Figure 246, you can see two reports that need to be printed. The report that must be printed on page 1 is in the range A9:G15, and the report that must be printed on page 2 is in the range A1:G7. To solve this problem, just use the Set Print Area feature after highlighting the noncontiguous ranges (ranges not next to each other) in the correct order.

	A	B	C	D	E	F	G
1	Wind Sport Inc.						
2		Jul	Aug	Sep	Oct	Nov	Dec
3	Boomerangs	376	293	403	538	1,027	1,174
4	Kites	1,029	994	1,344	1,183	2,161	2,462
5	Toys	172	237	313	479	577	224
6	Accessories	564	672	613	916	806	618
7	Total	2,141	2,196	2,672	3,115	4,571	4,477
8							
9	Wind Sport Inc.						
10		Jan	Feb	Mar	Apr	May	Jun
11	Boomerangs	350	273	375	500	955	1,092
12	Kites	957	925	1,250	1,100	2,010	2,290
13	Toys	160	220	291	446	537	208
14	Accessories	525	625	570	852	750	575
15	Total	1,992	2,043	2,486	2,898	4,252	4,165
16							

Store 1   Store 2   Amort

Figure 246

To follow along, open the file named excelisfun-Start.xlsm and navigate to the Store 2 sheet.

1. Click the Store 2 sheet.
2. Highlight the range A9:G15.

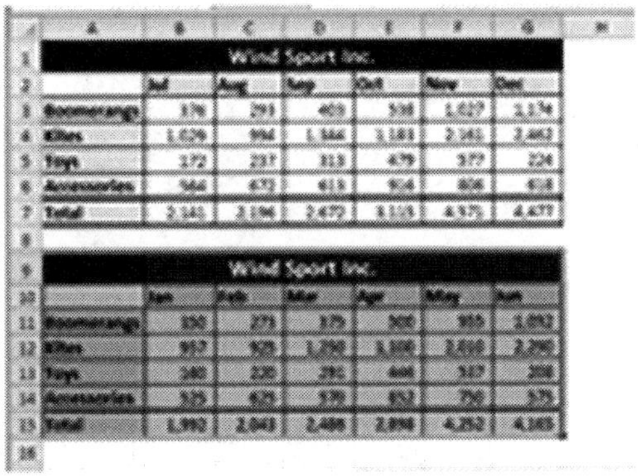

Figure 247

3. To select a second range that is noncontiguous, hold the Ctrl key while selecting the second range, A1:G7.

In Figure 247 and Figure 248, you can see that we highlighted the report that will go on page 1, first, then we highlighted the report that will go on page 2, second.

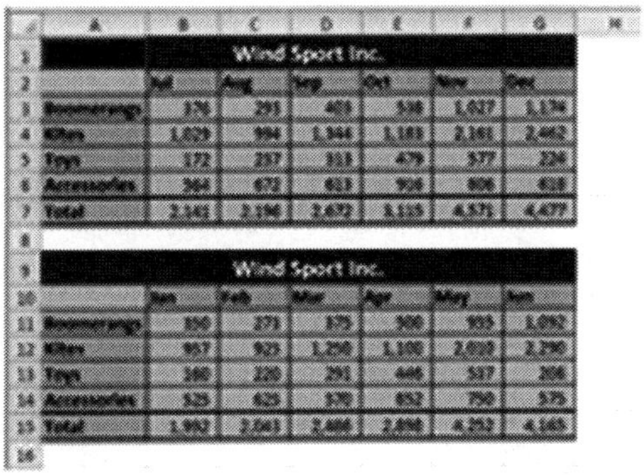

Figure 248

The order in which you highlight the ranges before applying Set Print Area determines the page numbers that the report sits on. You can extend this trick to any number of reports that you might have.

Set Print Area

4. With the two noncontiguous ranges still highlighted, go to the Page Layout tab, Page Setup group, and click the drop-down arrow next to the Print Area icon and select the Set Print Area.

5. Now when you print, the Jan-Jun report will be on page 1, and the Jul-Dec report will be on page 2.

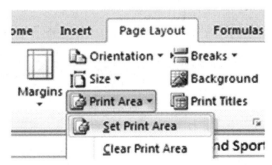

Figure 249

Advantages of Set Print Area include the following
- Allows you to highlight noncontiguous ranges in a particular order and have each area printed on a separate page in that order.
- Areas that are not within the Set Print Area will not print. This means that notes or calculations that are not part of the report can be placed on the sheet with the report and they will not be printed. This can be a useful trick when there are many calculations that go into the reports final numbers but the calculations themselves are superfluous to the report.

Before we leave this discussion, let me leave with two notes about page setup and printing for reports with more than one page:
- If you have completed the page setup on one sheet (say, for example, a template), if you copy the sheet all the page setup will also be copied. To copy a sheet, right-click the sheet and point to Move or Copy.
- If you have many sheets that all should get the same page setup, you can highlight all the sheets by clicking the first sheet, holding the Shift key, and clicking the last sheet (or use Ctrl to select noncontiguous sheets) and then apply your page setup. After you have completed page setup across multiple sheets, right-click one of the selected sheets and point to Ungroup Sheets. If you do not "ungroup sheets," any action that you do will occur to all sheets, which can prove very damaging.

Page Break View

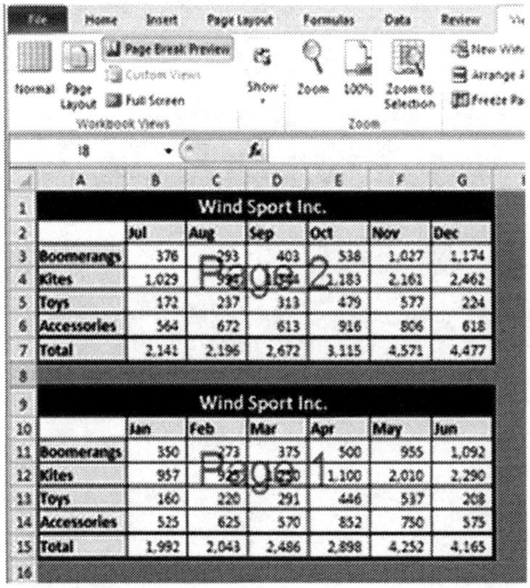

6. Go to the View tab, Workbook Views group, and select Page Break Preview.

In Figure 250, we can see Page Break view.

Advantages of Page Break view include the following:
- The gray areas indicate the parts of the report that will not print.
- The areas inside the blue borders are the areas that will print.
- Page numbers can be seen within the blue-bordered areas.

Figure 250
- If necessary, the blue borders can be dragged (point to the blue border, click and drag) to extend or retract the printing area.

So far, we have seen how to do basic page setup for a report and how to print two reports on separate pages. But, what if we have one huge report that spans multiple pages. Let's take a look at how to deal with this next.

Page Setup for Large Spreadsheets

To follow along, open the file named excelisfun-Start.xlsm and navigate to the Jones - Amortization Table sheet.

Figure 251 shows an amortization table report as it would look on the sheet. We would have four problems if we were to print it out without applying any page setup, as follows:

Figure 251

- Because the report is too wide to fit on a page, the Lump Sum column would not print on the same page as the rest of the columns (see Figure 252).

- The report would not be centered on the page.

- There would be no informative footers, especially page numbers to help organize this long report.

Figure 252

- Only the first printed page would have column headers (Figure 252); for subsequent pages, the column headers would not appear (see Figure 253).

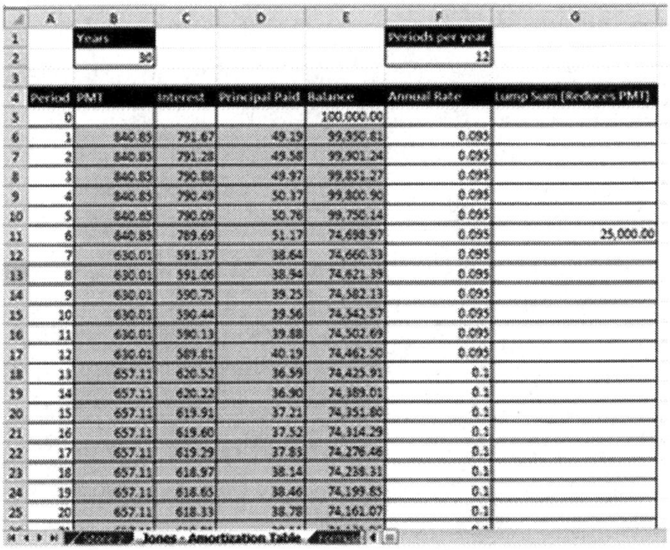

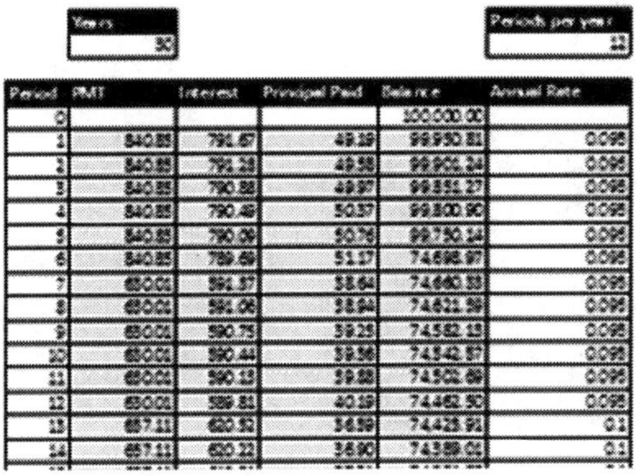

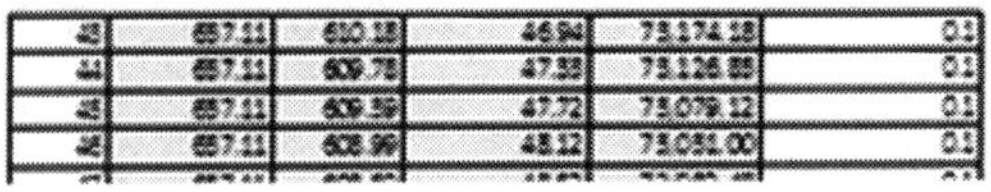

Figure 253

You can confirm that these problems would occur by pressing Ctrl + P to view Print Preview and then scrolling through the preview of all 16 pages. Be sure to press the Esc key when you have finished with Print Preview; again, don't click the red X.

In the following steps, we solve these four problems by applying page setup.

1. Click the Jones - Amortization sheet.
2. With the sheet selected, use the keyboard shortcut Alt, P, S, P to open the Page Setup dialog box.

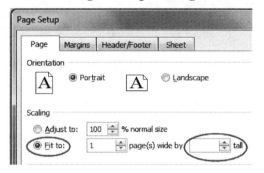

Figure 254

3. Click the Page tab.
4. Click the Fit To dialog button.
5. Highlight the number 1 in the tall text box and press the Delete key. This tall text box tells us how many pages the report will have. The reason we leave the tall text box blank is because we don't know how many pages tall the report is.

Excel will interpret the "blank" correctly and always print the correct number of pages regardless of how far down the table extends.

Figure 254 shows that we need our scaling to be Fit to 1 Page Wide by "Blank" Pages Tall to squeeze the report to one page wide and accommodate as many pages as are needed tall (solving the first problem above). If we leave the tall text box blank, Excel knows to print as many pages as necessary (not too many, not too few).

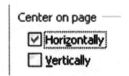

Figure 255

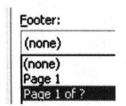

Figure 256

6. Click the Margins tab.
7. Check the Center on Page Horizontally check box. (Applying Center on Page Horizontally solves the second problem above).

8. Click the Header/Footer tab.
9. From the Footer drop-down, select Page 1 of ?.

10. Click the Custom Footer button.

Figure 257

11. With the cursor flashing in the Left section, click the Insert Sheet Name button.

Figure 258

12. With the cursor flashing in the Right section, click the Date button.

Figure 259

Left section:	Center section:	Right section:
&[Tab]	Page &[Page] of &[Pages]	&[Date]

Figure 260

13. The Custom Footer dialog box should look like Figure 260.
14. Click OK on the Custom Footer dialog box.

Adding informative footers solves the third problem above.

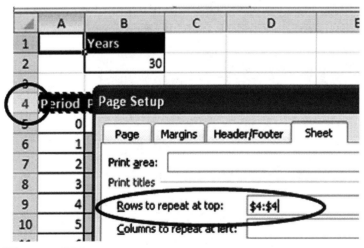

Figure 261

15. Click the Sheet tab.
16. Click in the Rows to Repeat at Top field, and then click the fourth row header for the spreadsheet. This puts the row reference $4:$4 into the field.

17. Click OK in the Page Setup dialog box to apply all the page setup settings.

Adding row reference $4:$4 to the Rows to Repeat at Top text box solves the fourth, and final, problem above.

Figure 262 shows page 1 of the report, and Figure 263 shows page 2. In both cases, all four of our problems have been solved by using page setup wisely. Never underestimate the power of page setup to help a report deliver useful and easy-to-understand information.

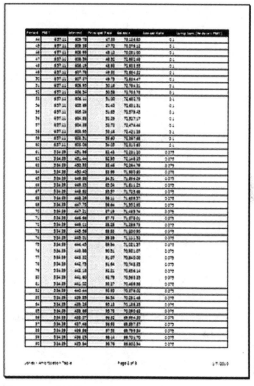

Figure 262   **Figure 263**

Next we want to look at built-in styles and how they can save time when we have the same sorts of styles used in many different reports.

Built-in Styles

If you use the same style for your reports often, knowing how to apply a table style or cell style can save time.

Table Styles

Back in Figure 93 to Figure 97 (in Chapter 3, "Data in Excel"), we saw how to use the Excel Table feature. The Excel Table feature is great for properly setup data sets because it will do the following:
- Add a Table Style
- Add automatic filtering/sorting
- Create dynamic ranges
- Allow you to add new records to the bottom of the table

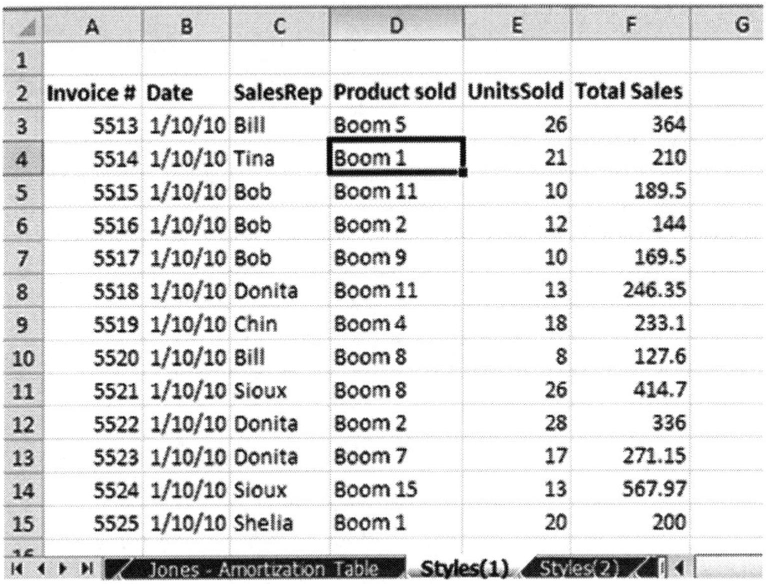

	A	B	C	D	E	F	G
1							
2	Invoice #	Date	SalesRep	Product sold	UnitsSold	Total Sales	
3	5513	1/10/10	Bill	Boom 5	26	364	
4	5514	1/10/10	Tina	Boom 1	21	210	
5	5515	1/10/10	Bob	Boom 11	10	189.5	
6	5516	1/10/10	Bob	Boom 2	12	144	
7	5517	1/10/10	Bob	Boom 9	10	169.5	
8	5518	1/10/10	Donita	Boom 11	13	246.35	
9	5519	1/10/10	Chin	Boom 4	18	233.1	
10	5520	1/10/10	Bill	Boom 8	8	127.6	
11	5521	1/10/10	Sioux	Boom 8	26	414.7	
12	5522	1/10/10	Donita	Boom 2	28	336	
13	5523	1/10/10	Donita	Boom 7	17	271.15	
14	5524	1/10/10	Sioux	Boom 15	13	567.97	
15	5525	1/10/10	Shelia	Boom 1	20	200	

H ◀ ▶ H / Jones - Amortization Table / Styles(1) / Styles(2) /

Figure 264

Figure 264 shows a properly setup data set:
- Field names (column headers) are in first row of the data set.
- Records are in remaining rows.
- No blanks are inside the data set.
- The data is surrounded by either blank cells or column/row headers.

In this section, we are talking about styles, and so we'll take a look at how to convert the properly setup data set to an Excel Table and then change the table style to match our formatting requirements. It is important to note that before converting a data set into an Excel Table, you must have only *one cell selected* in the data set. Technically, the rule is that one cell or all the cells must be selected, but selecting all the cells is a waste of time.

To follow along, open the file named excelisfun-Start.xlsm and navigate to the Styles(1) sheet.

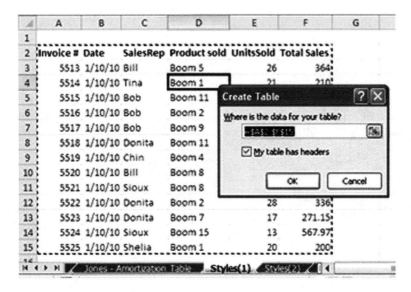

Figure 265

1. With D4 selected, use the Create Table keyboard shortcut Ctrl + T. Notice that only one cell is selected before we create the table.
Notice that because the data set is surrounded by either blank cells or column/row headers, the Excel Table feature highlights the correct range.
2. Click OK.

	A	B	C	D	E	F	G
1							
2	Invoice #	Date	SalesRep	Product sold	UnitsSold	Total Sales	
3	5513	1/10/10	Bill	Boom 5	26	364	
4	5514	1/10/10	Tina	Boom 1	21	210	
5	5515	1/10/10	Bob	Boom 11	10	189.5	
6	5516	1/10/10	Bob	Boom 2	12	144	
7	5517	1/10/10	Bob	Boom 9	10	169.5	

Figure 266

The table should look like Figure 266. In that figure, you can see that with a click of a button we have formatted our report. The banded rows help to distinguish each record as a unique entry. The report even looks good when printed without any further formatting modification. Notice that the drop-down arrows for sorting/filtering appear at the top of each column. These will not appear when you print the report. However, if you do not want to see them on the spreadsheet, you can toggle them off and on with the keyboard shortcut Ctrl + Shift + L.

Next, let's see how to change the table style.

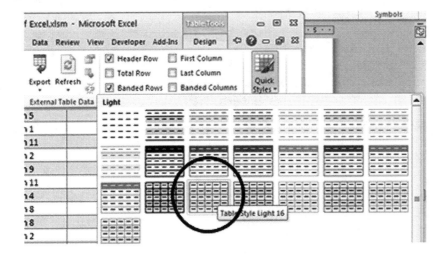

Figure 267

1. To change the table style, make sure that a cell in the table is selected to display the TableTools Design tab (context-sensitive ribbon tab).
2. Click the Design tab, and then click the Quick Styles button in the Tables Styles group.
3. Click the style that you like.

Depending on the style you select, other formatting features in the Design tab may be of interest. Next we want to look at cell styles.

Cell Styles

If you use the same style formatting over and over, cell styles can save you time.

To create a cell style, just complete the following steps:
1. Add whatever style formatting you want to a cell.
2. Select that cell.
3. Go to the Home tab, Styles group, and click the Cell Styles drop-down arrow.
4. Click New Cell Style (all the way at the bottom).
5. Click a style name in the Style Name text box.
6. Click OK.

To apply the cell style, complete these steps:
1. Select the cell/cells that you want to apply the cell style to.
2. Go to the Home tab, Styles group, click the Cell Styles drop-down arrow, click the style name.

To follow along, open the file named excelisfun-Start.xlsm and navigate to the Styles(2) sheet.

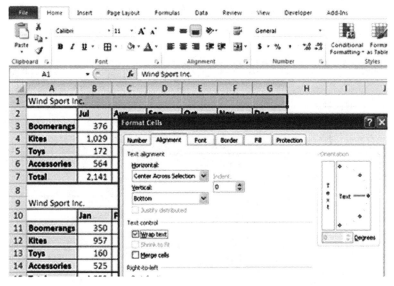

Figure 268

1. On the Sheet(2) sheet, select the range A1:G1.
2. To open the Format Cells dialog box, press Ctrl + 1.
3. Select the Alignment tab.
4. From the Horizontal drop-down, select Center Across Selection.
5. Check the Text Control Wrap Text check box.

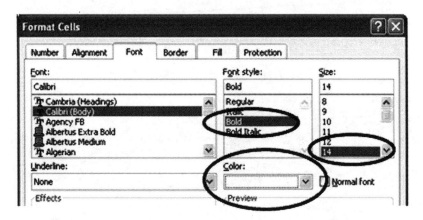

Figure 269

6. Select the Font tab.
7. For font style, click Bold.
8. For size, click 14.
9. For color, select white.

10. Select the Border tab.
11. Click Outline.

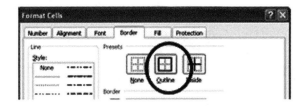

Figure 270

12. Select the Fill tab.
13. Select a dark fill color such as dark blue (to match our white font color).
14. Click OK.

That completes our cell formatting.

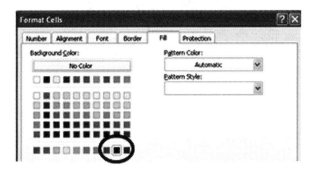

Figure 271

15. Make sure the formatted range A1:G1 is still selected.

16. To create the cell style, go to the Home tab, Styles group, and click the Cell Styles drop-down arrow.
17. Click New Cell Style (all the way at the bottom).

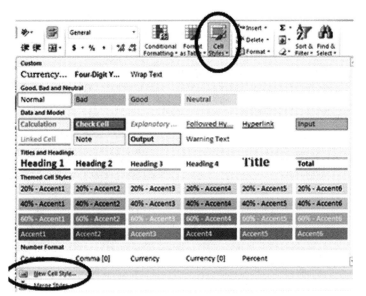

Figure 272

Figure 273

18. When the Styles dialog box pops up, click in the Style Name text box and type **BlueTitle**.
19. Click OK.

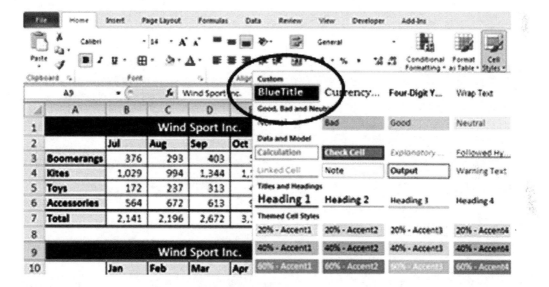

Figure 274

20. To apply the BlueTitle style, highlight range A9:G9.
21. Click the Cells Styles button.
22. Click the BlueTitle style.

In Figure 274, we applied the cell style to nine cells. That is the same size as the original cells that we formatted by hand. You are not limited to just nine cells. You can apply this style to more or fewer cells. Let's take a look at how to apply it to fewer cells.

23. With the cells A17:E17 selected, apply the BlueTitle cell style.

It should look like Figure 275.

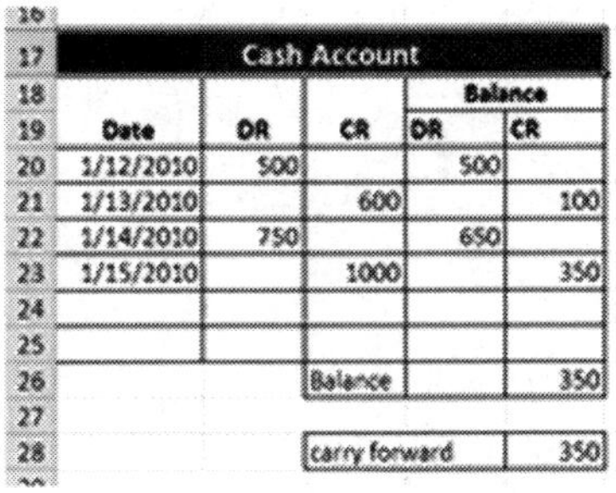

17	Cash Account				
18				Balance	
19	Date	DR	CR	DR	CR
20	1/12/2010	500		500	
21	1/13/2010		600		100
22	1/14/2010	750		650	
23	1/15/2010		1000		350
24					
25					
26			Balance		350
27					
28			carry forward		350

Figure 275

You just learned how to use style formatting, complete page setup, and use styles to apply formatting quickly. In the next chapter, we take a detailed look at formulas and functions.

◇◇

FORMULAS AND FUNCTIONS

So far in this book, we have created a few formulas; for example, to add with one condition, to calculate the number of days an invoice is overdue, and even to calculate the number hours worked. In this chapter, you'll learn more about formulas and functions. The discussion here of all the different aspects of formulas will empower you to accomplish any calculating or data analysis goal you set. In particular, this rather long chapter covers the following topics:
- Formulas defined
  - Types of formulas
  - Creating formulas
  - Formula elements
- Order of operations
- Three ways to put a cell reference into a formula
- Cell references
- Formula input setup (assumption tables)
- Five ways to enter formulas
- Efficient formulas that use ranges
- Built-in functions
- Defined names

Formulas Defined

What is a formula? Formulas do things for us such as add numbers, calculate the number of hours worked, look up a product price, create a label for a report, or tell us whether two accounts are in balance (examples of all coming up later). Those are things that formulas can do, but let's get more specific about what makes a formula a formula by considering the following:
- Types of formulas
- Creating formulas
- Formula elements (what can go into a formula)

Five Types of Formulas

In general, we can create five types of formulas:
- **Calculating formulas** that calculate a number answer (like adding)
- **Lookup formulas** that look up an item in a table (like looking up a tax rate or customer phone number).
- **Text formulas** that deliver a word to a cell or create labels for reports (like an income statement label).
- **Logical formulas** that give you a logical value, either TRUE or FALSE (like formulas that say whether two accounts are in balance)
- **Array formulas** are advanced formulas that act on arrays (ranges) instead of individual cell references.

Creating Formulas

When creating formulas, you must follow these guidelines:
- Most of the time, you put formulas in cells. But you can also build a formula in the Name Manager – New Name dialog box or the Conditional Formatting dialog box (examples later).
- You must enter an equal sign as the first character in the cell (or dialog box) to signal to Excel that what you are creating is a formula and not simply typing a number or word.
- If you have a space before the equal sign, the formula won't calculate.
- If a cell is preformatted with the Text number formatting, the formula will not calculate.
- Formulas deliver a single item to a cell (or dialog box), such as a number, word, or logical value. Here we are referring to nonarray formulas; later we will discuss how array formulas can act on more than a single item.

Formula Elements

Here is a list of the different sorts of things that we can put into formulas:
- Equal sign (starts all formulas)
- Cell references (also defined names, sheet references, workbook references)
- Math operators (plus, subtract, multiply, and so on)
- Numbers (if the number will not change; for example, 12 months, 24 hours)
- Built-in functions (AVERAGE, SUM, COUNTIF, DOLLAR, PMT, and so forth)
- Comparative operators (=, >, >=, <, <=, <>)
- The ampersand join symbol (&) (Shift + 7)
- Text within quotation marks (for example, "For the Month Ended")
- Array constants (for example, {1,2,3})

In this section, we take a look at 10 examples that will help to illustrate how to use the previously mentioned formula elements.

In our first example, we look at the equal sign and see how it must always be the first character in a cell in order for a formula to calculate correctly.

To follow along, open the file named excelisfun-Start.xlsm and navigate to the Formula(1) sheet.

	A	B
	B4 ▾ (fx	=B2-B3
1	Cell B4 contains a formula because the 1st character in the cell is an equal sign and the cell does not have Text Number format	
2	Sales	100
3	Expenses	91.25
4	Net Income	8.75

Figure 276

This is a formula because the first character in the cell is an equal sign and the cell does not have Text number formatting (Figure 276). The equal sign tells Excel to look in cell B2 and then subtract from it whatever is in cell B3. The equal sign is the trigger that tells Excel to make the calculation. Notice that this is a calculating formula.

	A	B
	B9 ▾ (fx	=B7-B8
6	Cell B9 does NOT contain a formula because the 1st character in the cell is a space	
7	Sales	100
8	Expenses	91.25
9	Net Income	=B7-B8

Figure 277

This is *not* a formula because the first character in the cell is a space (Figure 277). If a space is the first character in the cell, Excel has no idea that you want to make a calculation.

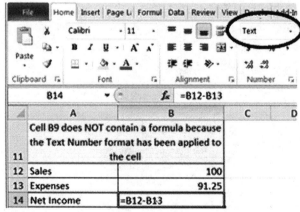

Figure 278

This is *not* a formula because the Text number formatting has been applied to the cell (Figure 278). Back in Figure 208, we saw how Text number formatting caused numbers to appear as text. It is the same with formulas. If the Text number formatting is applied, when you enter a formula, it will not calculate, but instead, it will show the formula without calculating.

There are almost no good reasons to use the Text number format. The few reasons that you might want to use it are if you have a column of credit card numbers or Social Security numbers without dashes.

As shown in Figure 276, once an equal sign is the first character in the cell, Excel knows you want to make a calculation. But what can come after the equal sign? We have already seen how a cell reference or the SUM function can come after the equal sign, but many other formula elements can help us do exactly what we want to do. Let's take a look at some more examples.

To follow along, open the file named excelisfun-Start.xlsm and navigate to the Formula(2) sheet. In our second example, we're going to look at a quantity times price formula with the following formula elements: equal sign, cell references, and a math operator. Our goal with this formula is to multiply quantity times price and get the subtotal before tax. People use this common formula every day for invoicing-type situations.

1. Navigate to the Formula(2) sheet.
2. Click in cell B5.
3. Type an equal sign.
4. Click cell B4.
5. Type multiplication symbol (Shift + 8, or use the number pad *).
6. Click cell B3.
7. Press Ctrl + Enter.

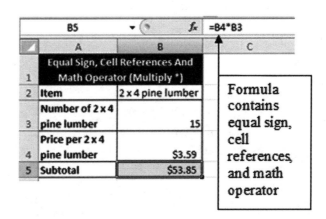

Figure 279

Notice that this is a calculating formula. Figure 279 shows an example of a calculating formula. Notice that our formula used the numbers 15 and 3.59 to make the calculation, and notice that we put the quantity and price in cells and referred to them with cell references. This is so that if we need to make a change, we can do it quickly. If our quantity sold changed to 20, it is easy for us to update our formula.

8. Click in cell B3.
9. Type **20**.
10. Press Ctrl + Enter.

Notice that the Subtotal updates and shows $71.80.

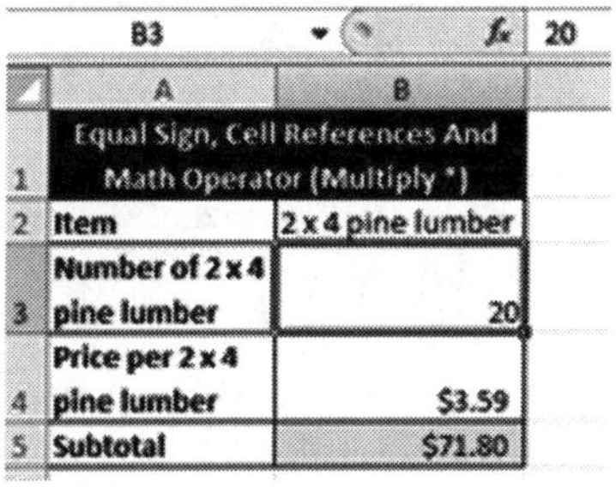

Figure 280

In Figure 280, the number of items and the price per item are called **formula inputs**. Because these formula inputs can change, we don't type those numbers into our formula, but instead we put them in cells and refer to them with cell references when building formulas. This is important because it allows us to update our spreadsheets quickly. Without this technique, you might find it difficult to find the cell where you put your formula (if you want to edit the formula, for example). Look at Figure 281 and notice that the formula has the numbers hard-coded into the formula. Imagine if all your formulas were like this and you had to hunt through all the cells to find the formula to change the quantity sold.

2	Item	2 x 4 pine lumber
3	Number of 2 x 4 pine lumber	15
4	Price per 2 x 4 pine lumber	$3.59
5	Subtotal	=3.59*15

Figure 281

Do not ever build formulas like what is shown in Figure 281.

When we put all data that can vary into cells and use cell references in formulas we gain the power of "efficient formula creation." Efficient formula creation simply means that we can create and edit the maximum number formulas for a spreadsheet with the minimal amount of effort and time.

This leads us to one of the important rules for efficient formula creation and our next Excel Efficiency-Robust Rule:

> *Rule 25: When building formulas, if the formula input can change, put it into a cell and refer to it with a cell reference in all formulas. Said a different way: If the formula input can change, don't type it into a formula. This leads to efficient formula creation.*

In our last example, we used the math operator multiplication. The symbol for multiplication in Excel is the asterisk, *. Figure 282 shows a complete list of the math operators used in Excel.

Math Operators
( ) represents Parentheses
^ represents Exponents (powers and roots)
* represents Multiplication
/ represents Division
+ represents Addition
− represents Subtraction

Figure 282

In our third example, we want to look at an allocation formula with the following formula elements: equal sign, cell reference, math operator, and number. Our goal with this formula is to calculate the monthly insurance allocation given an annual amount. This type of formula is commonly used for budgeting and accounting reports.

1. On the Formula(2) sheet and click in cell B9.
2. Type an equal sign (=).
3. Click B8.
4. Type the division symbol, /.
5. Type 12.
6. Press Enter.

7	Equal Sign, Cell Reference, Math Operator, Number	
8	Annual Insurance	$5,250.00
9	Monthly Allocation	=B8/12

Figure 283

Notice that this formula contains an equal sign, a cell reference, a division symbol, and a number.

Notice also that is a calculating formula.

In Figure 283, we can see that we typed a number into a formula. But I thought we just established that this is not a good practice! Hold on, though. This is different. The number 12 represents the number of months in a year. This is a number that does not change. A formula input that does not change can be typed right into the formula. This means that the formula in Figure 283 is perfectly fine with a 12 typed in for the number of months.

Our next Excel Efficiency-Robust Rule is this:

Rule 26: Numbers that don't change (for example, 12 months or 24 hours) can be type directly into a formula.

In our fourth example, we're going to look at an averaging formula with the following formula elements: equal sign, AVERAGE function, and cell range. Our goal with this formula is to calculate the average student score for a test.

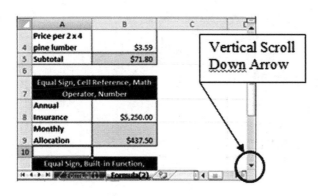

Figure 284

1. On the Formula(2) sheet, click in cell A10 and find the vertical scroll-down arrow.

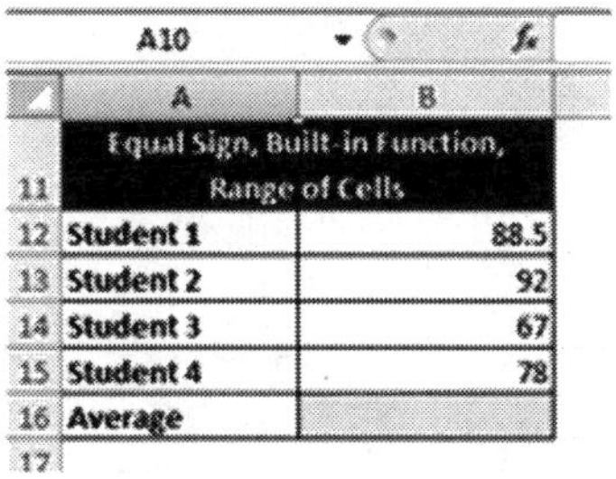

Figure 285

2. Click the vertical scroll-down arrow 10 times.

Notice that the Name box shows that cell A10 is selected, but we do not see cell A10 on the screen.

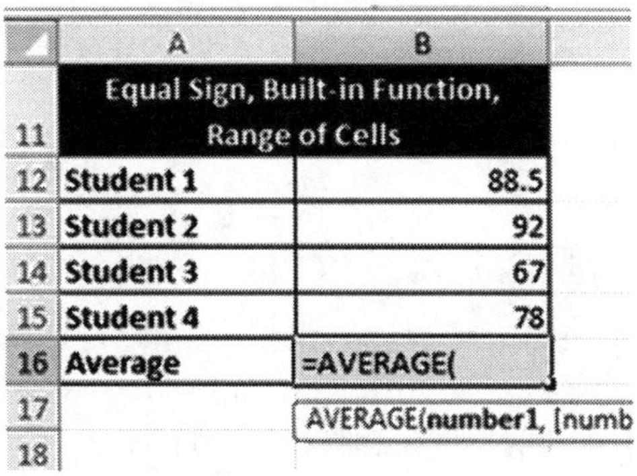

	A	B
11	Equal Sign, Built-in Function, Range of Cells	
12	Student 1	88.5
13	Student 2	92
14	Student 3	67
15	Student 4	78
16	Average	=AVERAGE(
17		AVERAGE(**number1**, [numb
18		

Figure 286

3. Click in cell B16.
4. Type an equal sign.
5. Type the word AVERAGE.
6. Type an open parenthesis.

7. With your selection cursor, click in cell B12 and hold the click while dragging to cell B15.

Notice that the dancing ants indicate that the AVERAGE function will look at cell range B12:B15.

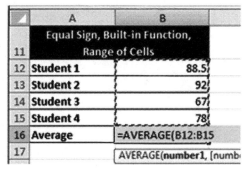

Figure 287

8. Press Ctrl + Enter.

Notice that the formula result is shown in the cell. The average student test score is 81.375.

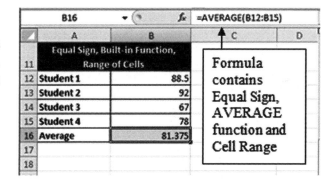

Figure 288

Notice that we did not need to type a closing parenthesis. Excel put one in for us.

Notice that this formula contains an equal sign, the AVERAGE function and a cell range.

Like the first two formulas, this is also a calculating formula.

In our fifth example, we want to look at a net income formula with the following formula elements: equal sign, cell reference, math operator, SUM function, and cell range. Our goal with this formula is to calculate net income (total revenue minus total expenses) without a separate cell for adding all the expenses. Net income formulas show the profit or earnings for a given period.

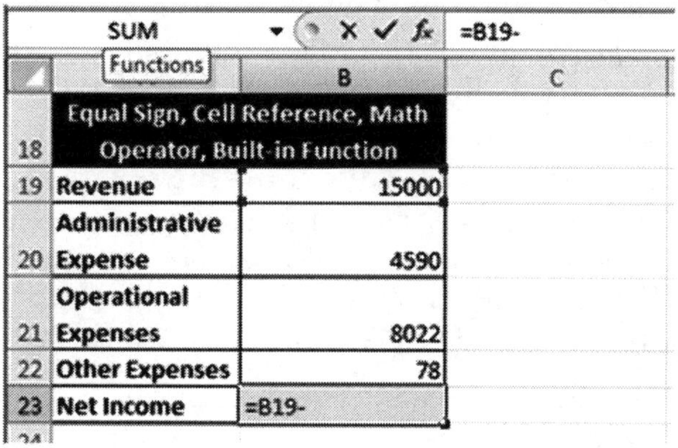

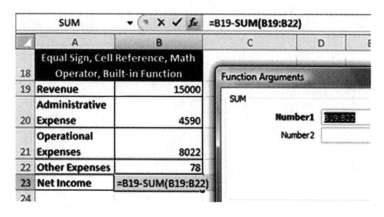

Figure 289

1. On the Formula(2) sheet, use the vertical scroll-down arrow to scroll down so that the first row showing is row 18 (as shown in Figure 289).
2. Click in cell B23.
3. Type an equal sign.
4. Click cell B19.
5. Type a minus sign.

Notice the Name box is now called Functions (if you hover your cursor over the Name box). In Figure 289, we can see that when you are in the middle of creating a formula (as soon as you type an equal sign as the first character in a cell) the Name box becomes an Insert Function box with a drop-down arrow. In Figure 289, the Insert Function box shows the SUM function. This Insert Function box will always show the last function used. It is showing SUM this time because the SUM function was the last function that I used.

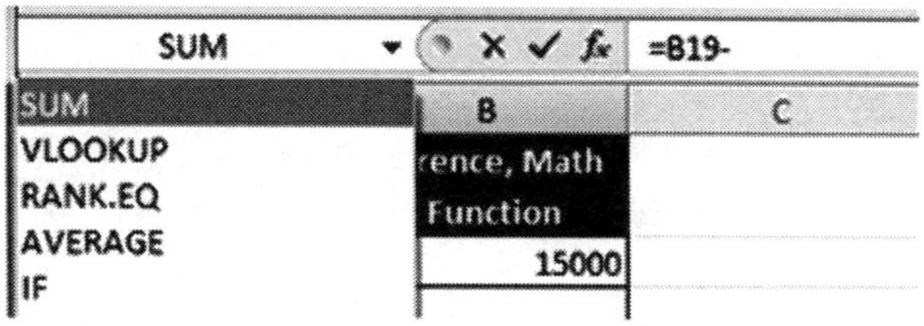

Figure 290

6. Click the drop-down arrow in the Insert Function box.
7. Point to and then click SUM.

Figure 291

8. After the SUM Function Arguments dialog box pops up, look at the range that Excel put in by default. This is *not* the correct range!

In Figure 291, Excel is trying to be polite and help you by putting the range in for you. But Excel got it wrong. This is often the case when you use the built-in functions. So, you must always double-check when Excel tries to guess what range you want for a function. For our formula, we want to take the revenue in cell B19 and subtract from it the sum of all the expense in the cell range B20:B22. The range B19:B22 is already highlighted, so to replace it with the correct range, just drag your cursor over the correct range.

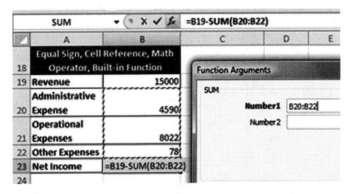

Figure 292

9. With your selection cursor, drag through the range B20:B22.
10. Press Ctrl + Enter.

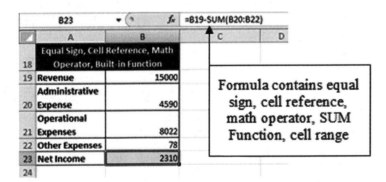

Figure 293

Notice that this formula contains an equal sign, a cell reference, a minus sign, the SUM function, and a cell range.

This is another example of a calculating formula.

In our sixth example, we're going to look at three separate formulas with the following formula elements: an equal sign, SUM function, cell range, cell reference, and equal sign as comparative operator. We will take a look at two adding formulas and a formula that can verify whether two numbers are equal. Our goal with these three formulas is to add two separate columns of numbers and then have a formula verify that the two totals are equal. People who are in charge of balancing the books like to have formulas that will double-check their work and make sure that things are in balance.

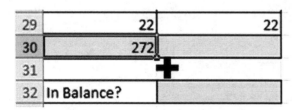

Figure 294

1. On the Formula(2) sheet, use the vertical scroll-down arrow to scroll down.
2. Select cell A30.
3. To add a total to the bottom of the DR column, use the keyboard shortcut Alt, =, = for the SUM function. (Be sure to pause before the second equal sign to verify that the default range is correct.)

Notice that this calculating formula contains an equal sign, the SUM function and a cell range.

Notice that the formula in the formula bar uses the relative cell reference range A27:A29, which can be read as "please always look at the three cells above." This means that we can copy the formula over to the CR column and it will add the corresponding three cells above in the CR column.

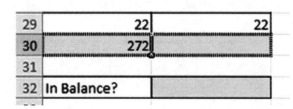

Figure 295

4. To copy the SUM function, point to the fill handle with your crosshair cursor and then click, hold the click, and drag your mouse to the right.

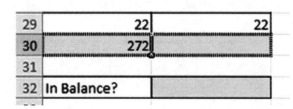

Figure 296

Notice that when you drag your mouse to the right, you will see a gray rectangle.

5. When the gray rectangle surrounds the cell B30, let go of the held click. If you drag too far, keep holding

the click firmly and drag back until the gray rectangle surrounds B30.

Notice that it looks like the column totals are equal.

But you want the power of Excel to verify that they are equal, especially if your boss put you in charge of balancing the books.

26	DR	CR
27	200	200
28	50	50
29	22	22
30	272	272
31		
32	In Balance?	

Figure 297

1. Click in cell B32.
2. Type an equal sign.
3. Click cell A30.
4. Type the comparative operator equal sign.
5. Click cell B30.

	A	B
25	Equal Sign, Cell Reference,	Comparative Operators
26	DR	CR
27	200	200
28	50	50
29	22	22
30	272	272
31		
32	In Balance?	=A30=B30

Figure 298

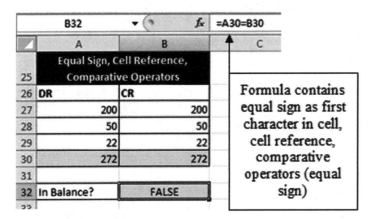

Figure 299

6. Press Ctrl + Enter

Notice that the formula result is FALSE

Notice that this formula contains an equal sign as the first character in the cell, two cell references, and the comparative operator (equal sign).

This type of formula is called a logical formula.

In Figure 299, we can see our "balance checking formula" in the formula bar. The equal sign as the first character in the cell tells Excel that it is a formula, but the second equal sign is a comparative operator that asks "are the two things equal?" A formula using a comparative operator like this is called a **logical formula**. (There are also logical built-in functions, which we will talk about later.) Logical formulas can only result in TRUE or FALSE. From our study of how data is aligned in Excel, we know that TRUE and FALSE data is always aligned in the center and is always uppercase. But why is the answer FALSE when we can clearly see that 272 is equal to 272?

Specifically, our formula is asking this: Is the data in cell A30 equal to the data in cell B30? If the formula result says FALSE, that means that the data in cell A30 is *not* equal to the data in cell B30. We had better investigate.

	A	B
	Equal Sign, Cell Reference,	
25	Comparative Operators	
26	DR	CR
27	200.00	200.00
28	50.01	50.01
29	22.10	22.10
30	272.11	272.11
31		
32	In Balance?	FALSE

Figure 300

7. Highlight the range A27:B30, and using the Increase Decimal button show two decimal places.

Notice that this still look in balance, but our logical formula still says FALSE.

	A	B
	Equal Sign, Cell Reference,	
25	Comparative Operators	
26	DR	CR
27	200.000	200.000
28	50.010	50.010
29	22.101	22.100
30	272.111	272.110
31		
32	In Balance?	FALSE

Figure 301

8. Increase the decimals to show three decimal places.

One of the numbers in cells A29 or B29 is causing the problem.

In Figure 301, we can see that when we increased the decimals to three places, we found the problem!

But it was not us; it was Excel that found the problem. This sort of logical formula is very common among people who are in charge of getting the books to balance. Because Excel does not make math or logic errors, we love formulas like this that can help us to find mistakes. But how does a number like 22.101 get there in the first place. Possible reasons include data entry error, data was imported with the extra digit or copied from a different section of the workbook, and the extra decimal was not obvious.

Figure 302 shows a list of the comparative operators that you can use in Excel formulas.

Comparative Operators
> Greater Than
>= Greater Than Or Equal To
< Less Than
<= Less Than Or Equal To
= Equal To
<> Not Equal To

Figure 302

In our seventh example, we want to look at a join or concatenation formula with the following formula elements: equal sign, cell reference, join symbol, and text in quotes. Our goal with this formula is to take a first name in column A and a last name in column B and join them together in column C. The process of joining content from two cells is called **concatenation**. We will use the ampersand, &, using Shift + 7 to join the first and last name into one cell. This sort of formula can be a lifesaver if your job is to combine first and last names into a new column because it will let you avoid a lot of copying and pasting.

1. On the Formula(2) sheet, use the vertical scroll-down arrow to scroll down.
2. Select cell C36.
3. Type an equal sign.
4. Click cell A36.
5. Type & (Shift + 7).
6. Click cell B36.

	A	B	C
34		Equal Sign, Cell Reference, Join Symbol (Ampersand = Shift + 7 = &), Text in Quotes	
35	First	Last	First & Last
36	Bill	Masters	=A36&B36
37	Tina	Smith	
38	Sioux	Lim	
39	Sue	Chin	
40	Luong	Pham	

Figure 303

The ampersand, &, is the join symbol. The & tells Excel to take two separate, different things and join them to make one item.

C36	▼	f_x	=A36&B36	
	A	B	C	
34		Equal Sign, Cell Reference, Join Symbol (Ampersand = Shift + 7 = &), Text in Quotes		
35	First	Last	First & Last	
36	Bill	Masters	BillMasters	
37	Tina	Smith		

Figure 304

7. To enter our join formula into cell C36, press Ctrl + Enter.

Notice we joined two things in cell C36: the content in cell A36 and B36.

Notice that we really needed to join three things, not just two things in cell C36. We need first name, a space, and last name.

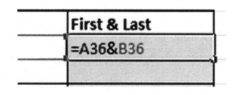

Figure 305

8. With cell C36 selected, press the F2 key to put the cell in Edit mode.

Notice that there is one ampersand joining two cells. Because we need to add a third thing (a space) to our formula, we need a second ampersand.

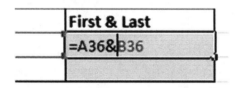

Figure 306

9. Move your cursor over the formula and when your cursor turns to an I-beam cursor, click after the ampersand and before the green B.

Notice that a vertical line flashes on and off. This is Excel telling you that it is ready for you to edit the formula.

10. Type a double quote.
11. Type a space.
12. Type a double quote.
13. Type &.
14. Press Enter.

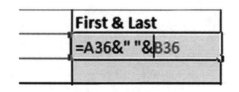

Figure 307

15. Click in cell B36.
16. Type **Droke**.
17. Press Enter.

C36	▼ (•	fx	=A36&" "&B36
	A	B	C
34	Equal Sign, Cell Reference, Join Symbol (Ampersand = Shift + 7 = &), Text in Quotes		
35	First	Last	First & Last
36	Bill	Droke	Bill Droke
37	Tina	Smith	

Figure 308

Notice that our formula updates. Notice that this formula contains an equal sign, two cell references, two ampersands, and text in quotes; our text is a single space. Notice that this is a text formula.

The formula in Figure 308 is called a **text formula** because the formula result is considered text by Excel. This is not a calculating formula that gives us a number result or a logical formula that gives us a TRUE or FALSE. It is a text formula that gives us two words (text). Look back at Figure 293 and Figure 301 and Figure 308 and notice that the default alignment applies for our formula results also. Formula results that are numbers are aligned right, formula results that are TRUE/FALSE are aligned center, and formula results that are text are aligned left. As always, noticing this pattern will help us find problems more quickly.

Now we need to copy the text formula down. In Figure 308, notice that the cell references are A36 and B36, which Excel sees as a relative cell references. This means that the formula will always look at the two cells directly to the left of the cell that houses the formula. This is good because when we copy the formula down the formula result will be Tina Smith and then Sioux Lim and so forth. When we copy the formula down the column, we will use our fill handle and crosshair trick, but this time we will learn a special double-click the fill handle trick that will make our copy process even faster than before!

18. Point to the fill handle.
19. When you see your crosshair cursor, double-click the fill handle.

Last	First & Last
Droke	Bill Droke
Smith	
Lim	
Chin	
Pham	

Figure 309

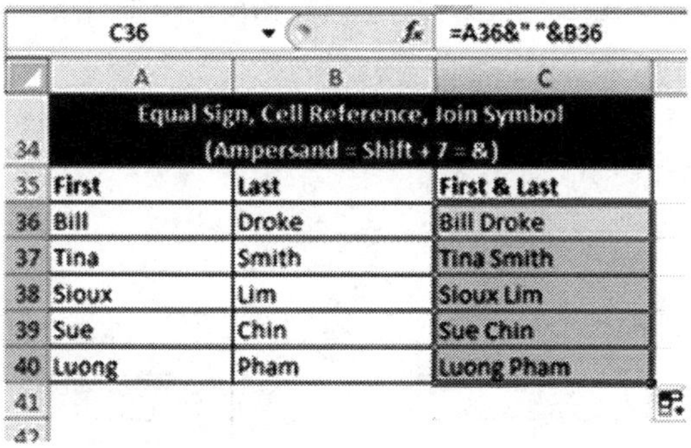

C36	▼	fx	=A36&" "&B36

	A	B	C
34	Equal Sign, Cell Reference, Join Symbol (Ampersand = Shift + 7 = &)		
35	First	Last	First & Last
36	Bill	Droke	Bill Droke
37	Tina	Smith	Tina Smith
38	Sioux	Lim	Sioux Lim
39	Sue	Chin	Sue Chin
40	Luong	Pham	Luong Pham
41			
42			

Figure 310

Because there is data in the column to the left, double-clicking the fill-handle will copy the formula down the column automatically.

This sort of text formula using the ampersand is quite common and saves a lot of time. Imagine if you had to cut and paste a whole column of names like this.

> **Note**: Double-clicking the fill handle with the crosshair cursor to copy content down a column will work when there is cell content below the cell you are copying, to the left of the cell, or to the right of the cell. In our example, there was cell content to the left. If there is cell content to the left, right, and below the cell you are copying, the content will be copied as far down as there is content below the cell being copied. If there is content to the left and right of the cell, but none below, whichever column is longer determines how far down the cell content is copied.

In our eighth example, we're going to look at a "count with one condition" formula with the following formula elements: equal sign, COUNTIF function, cell range, comparative operator in quotes, join symbol, and cell reference. Our goal is to create a formula that will count the number of sales over $500. Our condition or criteria for counting is sales greater than $500.

1. On the Formula(2) sheet, use the vertical scroll-down arrow to scroll down.
2. Select cell C45.
3. Type **=COUNTIF(**.

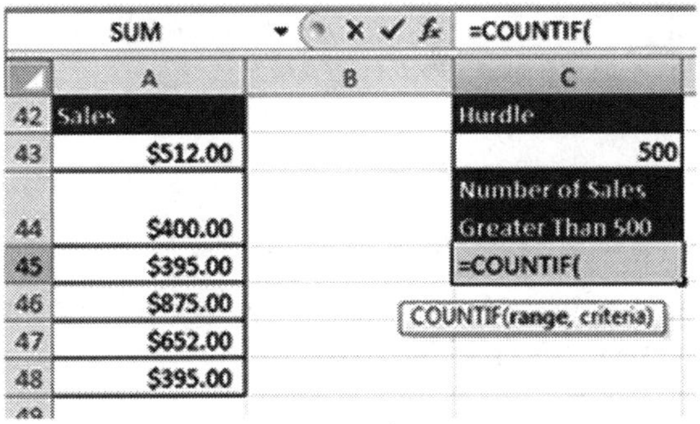

Figure 311

In Figure 311, we see the COUNTIF function. This function requires that you tell it the range of value to look through and what criteria it should use for counting. Notice that the two function arguments are named wisely: range and criteria. The range for us will be the cell range A43:A48, and our criteria will be >500. This will allow the COUNTIF function to count the numbers in the range A43:A48 that are greater than 500. However, we do not want to type >500, but instead we want the COUNTIF function to look at the 500 in cell C43. The way we will accomplish this is to join the > symbol with the cell C43 using the join symbol (ampersand, &).

4. Using your selection cursor, select the range A43:A48.
5. Type a comma.
6. Type a double quote.
7. Type a greater than symbol.
8. Type a double quote.
9. Type ampersand, **&** (Shift + 7).
10. Click cell C43.
11. Type a close parenthesis.

Your formula should look like this figure.

Notice that what we entered into the criteria argument is ">"&C43.

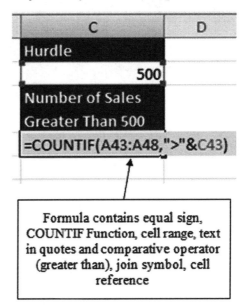

Formula contains equal sign, COUNTIF Function, cell range, text in quotes and comparative operator (greater than), join symbol, cell reference

Figure 312

What we have done is to join the comparative operator > and the cell C43. It is efficient and robust to construct our criteria with this technique because if we change the value in cell C43, the formula count will update.

> **Note**: Later in Figure 505 and Figure 506 you will see an alternative method for creating the criteria for the COUNTIF function.

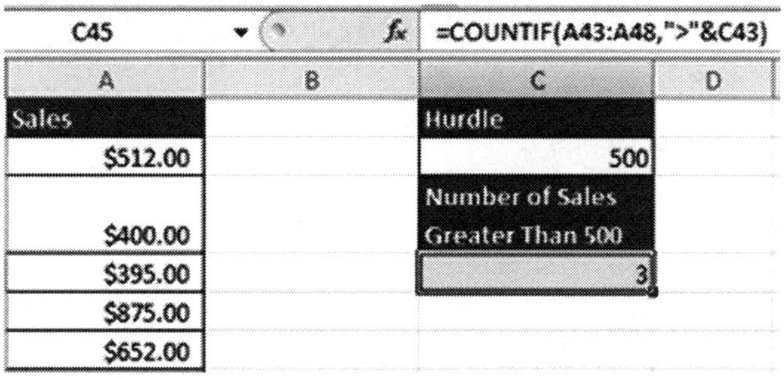

C45	▼	f_x	=COUNTIF(A43:A48,">"&C43)	
	A	B	C	D
Sales			Hurdle	
	$512.00		500	
			Number of Sales	
	$400.00		Greater Than 500	
	$395.00		3	
	$875.00			
	$652.00			

Figure 313

12. Press Ctrl + Enter.

You should get a count of 3.

Notice that this formula contains an equal sign, the COUNTIF function, a cell range, comparative operator in double quotes (COUNTIF requires this), an ampersand, and a cell reference.

Notice that this is a calculating formula.

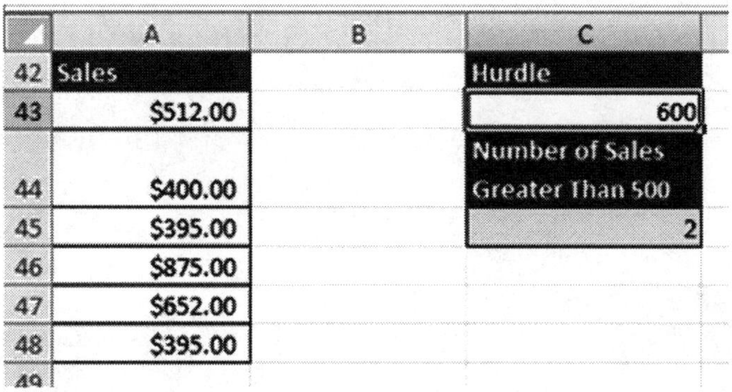

	A	B	C
42	Sales		Hurdle
43	$512.00		600
			Number of Sales
44	$400.00		Greater Than 500
45	$395.00		2
46	$875.00		
47	$652.00		
48	$395.00		
49			

Figure 314

13. Click in cell C43 and change the hurdle to 600.

Our formula for counting updates the count to two, but what about our label? It still shows the number 500. We need to fix this.

In our ninth example, we look at a label formula with the following formula elements: equal sign, text in quotes, join symbol, cell references, and a DOLLAR function. Our goal with this formula is to create a "variable label" next to a formula that counts the number of sales over $600. Our variable label should say Number of Sales Greater Than $600. However, if we change the hurdle from $600 to $700, we want our label to update so that it says Number of Sales Greater Than $700. Informative labels such as this are as important as the formulas doing the calculations because labels help the spreadsheet user to understand what is going on.

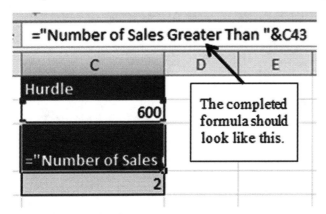

Figure 315

1. Click in cell C44.
2. Press the Delete key to delete the contents of the cell.
3. Click in the formula bar.
4. Type an equal sign.
5. Type **"Number of Sales Greater Than "** (including a space before the last double quote). Remember, whenever you put text or words into a formula you must enclose the text in double quotes.
6. Type ampersand, **& (Shift + 7)**.
7. Click cell C43.
8. Press Enter.

C43			f_x	700	
	A	B		C	D
42	Sales			Hurdle	
43	$512.00			700	
44	$400.00			Number of Sales Greater Than 700	
45	$395.00			1	
46	$875.00				
47	$652.00				
48	$395.00				

Figure 316

9. Change the value in cell C43 to **700**.

Notice that both of the formulas update: the calculating formula and the text formula.

Notice that the label shows 700 rather than $700.00.

="Number of Sales Greater Than "&C43			
C	**D**	**E**	**F**
Hurdle			
700			

Figure 317

10. Click in cell C44.
11. Press the F2 key to put the cell in Edit mode.
12. Click in the formula bar between the ampersand (&) and the cell reference, C43.

In Figure 317, we can see that our formula is looking at a number in cell C43. But how do we format a number in a formula? If it is the Currency number formatting that you would like to apply to whatever number we type into cell C43, we can use the DOLLAR function. What!? There is a built-in function that applies the Currency number formatting in a formula? Yes, that is exactly right. The **DOLLAR function** takes a number (for us it is whatever number is in cell C43) and applies the Currency number formatting and converts the number to text. This is what we want because we are creating a text formula. Let's take a look at how this works.

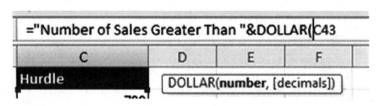

="Number of Sales Greater Than "&DOLLAR(C43			
C	**D**	**E**	**F**
Hurdle	DOLLAR(number, [decimals])		

Figure 318

13. Type **DOLLAR(**.

In Figure 318, we can see the screen tip for the DOLLAR function. The **number** argument can be a number or reference to a number, and the **decimals** argument is for specifying how many digits you want to show. If we put a 2 as the decimals argument, DOLLAR will show two decimals; If we put a 0 as the decimals argument, DOLLAR will show no decimals. Notice that the decimals argument has square brackets around it. This is a visual cue that means this argument has a default setting and is therefore optional. (This information is in the Help menu under DOLLAR function.) The default setting for the decimal argument is 2. Because we want two decimals showing, we do not need to type a 2 for the decimals argument. Let's take a look at this how this works.

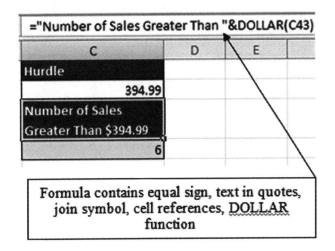

Figure 319

14. With your I-beam cursor, click at the end of the formula in the formula bar.
15. Type a close parenthesis (Shift + 0).
16. Press Enter.
17. Change the value in cell C43 to **394.99**.

Notice that this formula contains an equal sign, text in quotes, ampersand, the DOLLAR function, and a cell reference.

Notice that this is a text function.

Figure 319 shows a spreadsheet that is easy to use because both the calculating formula and the text formula update when we change the value in cell C43. It is like magic. Your boss or co-workers will love it when you make spreadsheets that work like this.

In our tenth example, we look at a "add two largest values" formula with the following formula elements: equal sign, SUM function, LARGE function, cell range, and array constant. Our goal with this formula is to look through a list of numbers and add only the two largest values. This sort of formula is used for scoring systems, like in the Maximum Time Aloft Boomerang event where you are given three throws; for scoring, however, you add the two longest times. This sort of example is also common in the sales or marketing department where you want to add the top 10 sales figures for a certain sales period. Let's take a look at how to make a formula like this.

	A	B	C	D	E
	SUM	▾ ⊙ X ✓ fx	=SUM(LARGE(B53:D53,{1,2}))		
50	Equal Sign, SUM function, LARGE function, Cell Range, Array				
51	MAXIMUM Time Aloft Score Sheet				
52	Thrower	Throw 1	Throw 2	Throw 3	SUM of Best Two
53	Daniel	45.99	23.78	51.02	=SUM(LARGE(B53:D53,{1,2}))
54	Richard	40.22	42.32	43.69	86.01
55	Matt	37.55	34.2	31.5	71.75
56	Stevie	69.43	0	56.11	125.54

Figure 320

1. On the Formula(2) sheet, use the vertical scroll-down arrow to scroll down.
2. Select cell E53.
3. Type the **=SUM(LARGE(B53:D53,{1,2}))** formula.
4. Press Ctrl + Enter.
5. Double-click the fill handle to copy the formula down.

Notice that this formula contains an equal sign, two built-in functions, a cell range, and an array constant with the numbers 1 and 2.

Figure 320 shows that our formula for adding the two longest times contains two built-in functions. The LARGE function is finding the two largest values and the SUM function is adding the two values. We can also see that we typed the array constant formula element, {1,2}. This array is what told the LARGE function to find the first and second largest values in the cell range B53:D53. An array constant always starts and ends with curly brackets. The elements in the array are separated by commas (columns) or semicolons (rows). In our example, it does not matter whether we use commas or semicolons. Also, in our example, we gave the LARGE function a 1 and a 2. You can put a single number or many numbers in the second argument of the LARGE function. You could ask the LARGE to find the fifth largest by putting the number 5 in the second argument, or you could ask it to find the five largest values by putting the array {1,2,3,4,5}. If Excel has a LARGE function, do you think it has a SMALL function, too? Yes! And the SMALL function works the same way as the LARGE function does. The SMALL function is used for finding things such as the three fastest times to make a product, or the two fastest times in the Fast Catch event in the sport of boomeranging.

The process we just saw of having one function inside of another function is called **nesting functions**. Nesting functions simply means that we have a function inside another function. We will see more of this later on.

Next, we want to look at how Excel calculates the formula we just created. We want to see the step-by-step process that Excel uses to come to the formula result. We can use an Excel feature called **Evaluate Formula**.

Figure 321

1. Click in cell E53.
2. Click Formula tab.
3. Click the Evaluate Formula button in the Formula Auditing group.

The keyboard shortcut is Alt, T, U, F.

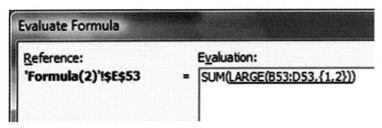

Figure 322

The Evaluate Formula dialog box displays the Reference (which cell the formula is in) and Evaluation (shows the formula).

Notice that part of the formula is underlined. When you press the Enter key, the underlined part will be calculated.

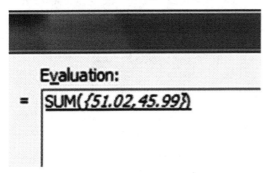

Figure 323

4. Press Enter.

Notice that the LARGE function did exactly what we wanted it to do: It found the two largest values.

Notice that the two largest values are listed in curly brackets and separated by a comma. This is because we used the array constant {1,2} to tell it to find the two biggest values.

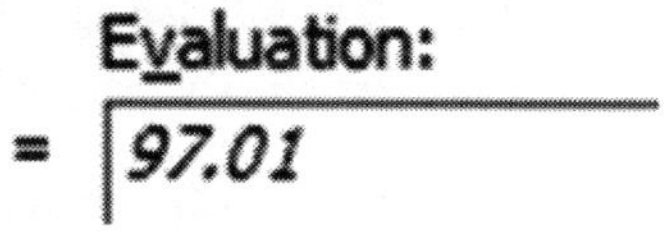

Evaluation:

= 97.01

Figure 324

   5. Press Enter.

Notice it shows the final calculation.

That is the first time we have seen the Evaluate Formula feature. We will come back to this later because this feature is also useful for tracking down formula errors and seeing how Excel interprets the order of operations in calculating formulas (math).

Wow, that is amazing. We just saw examples of all the different formula elements! With knowledge of all the formula elements, we now have the power to build any type of formula that we want!

Next we want to look at the order of operations for math. Math!? You mean you have to know math if you want to use Excel? Yes, but you only have to learn four basic rules, and then doing any basic math problem (arithmetic) will be a snap!

Order of Operations

A common question that I hear is this: Why isn't Excel calculating correctly? What they really mean to say is this: I've forgotten my math order of operations, can you help me? A common "order of operations" mistake that people make is with a cost of goods sold (COGS) calculation.

To follow along, open the file named excelisfun-Start.xlsm and navigate to the OrderOfOperations sheet.

In the COGS formula in Figure 325, we can see that we are trying to make the calculation 10 − 3 * $5. We want the 7 units sold times $5 equals $35 for the cost of the goods sold. The problem is that Excel knows the order of operations. Excel knows that multiplying is done before subtraction. So in Figure 326, we can see that the answer for this particular formula is -$5. We know that this is not the answer.

Cost of Goods Sold Formula

F	G	H	I	J
Beg Qty	End Qty	Value Each	COGS	
10	3	$5	=F2-G2*H2	

Figure 325

=F2-G2*H2			
F	G	H	I
Beg Qty	End Qty	Value Each	COGS
10	3	$5	-$5.00

Figure 326

If we know our order of operations, we will not make this sort of mistake.

Figure 327 provides a list of math operators. (These tables are also shown on the MathOperations sheet.)

Math Operators	
( ) represents Parentheses	Shift + 9 and Shift + 0
^ represents Exponents (powers and roots)	Shift + 6
* represents Multiplication	* on Number pad
/ represents Division	/ on Number pad
+ represents Addition	+ on Number pad
− represents Subtraction	- on Number pad

Figure 327

Figure 328 lists the order of operations.

		Order of Operations	
1	Please	Parenthesis	( )
2	Excuse	Exponents	^
3	My Dear	Multiply & Divide (Left to Right)	* , /
4	Aunt Sally	Adding & Suntracting (Left To Right)	+ , -

Figure 328

- Now, let's see how Excel calculated the formula that we saw in Figure 325. Figure 329 shows how Excel calculated it.

Cost Of Goods Sold
10 - 3 * 5 = -5
10 - 15 = -5
-5 = -5

Figure 329

Figure 329 shows us that Excel did the multiplying before the subtracting. So to fix this, we must tell Excel to do the subtracting before the multiplying by placing parentheses around the subtraction (see Figure 330 and Figure 331).

=(F4-G4)*H4

F	G	H	I	J
Beg Qty	End Qty	Value Each	COGS	
10	3	$5	-$5.00	
Beg Qty	End Qty	Value Each	COGS	
10	3	$5	=(F4-G4)*H4	

Figure 330

=(F4-G4)*H4

F	G	H	I	J
Beg Qty	End Qty	Value Each	COGS	
10	3	$5	-$5.00	
Beg Qty	End Qty	Value Each	COGS	
10	3	$5	$35.00	

Figure 331

But how do I remember the order of operations? You can use the memorization trick "Please Excuse My Dear Aunt Sally." The first letter of each word is P, E, M, D, A, S. PEMDAS stands for "Parenthesis Exponents Multiply Divide Add Subtract."

But really, it is only four things you need to remember, and then all your formula creating days will be much happier.

All we have to remember are the four things, but Excel has to remember a lot more than that. Figure 332 shows a list of what Excel goes through when calculating.

Excel's Order of Operations:
Parenthesis ( )
Ranges use of colon symbol ":"
Example: =SUM(A1:A4)
Evaluate intersections with spaces
Example: =E12:G12 F10:F15 (retrieve what is in F12)
Evaluate unions (,)
Example: =SUM(E10:G10,E14:G14)
Negation (-)
Example: =-2^4 ➜ 16
Example: =-(2^4) ➜ -16
Converts % (1% ➜ .01)
Exponents (^)
Example: 4^(1/2) = 2
Example: 3^2 = 9
Multiplication (*) and division (/), left to right
Adding (+) and subtracting (-), left to right
Ampersand (&)
Comparative symbols: =, <>, >=, <=, <, >
If anything is still left, then left to right

Figure 332

Figure 332 shows us a complete list of the order of operations when Excel calculates a formula. (I originally saw this list in the great Excel book *Managing Data with Microsoft Excel* by Conrad Carlberg.) We do not need to remember all this, but we do need to remember to come and look this up when we are having trouble with a complicated formula. Nevertheless, we do want to look at one example that involves comparative operators.

TRUE/FALSE Formula

To follow along, open the file named excelisfun-Start.xlsm and navigate to the OOO sheet.

	A	B	C	D	E
1	Sales	Expenses	Profit Hurdle	Question	Pass Hurdle = Bonus
2	$500	$392	$100	Is 500-392 > 100 TRUE or FALSE?	=A2-B2>C2
3	$500	$392	$100	Is 500-392 > 100, Yes or No?	
4	$500	$392	$100	Is 500-392 > 100, 10 or 0?	

Figure 333

1. Click in cell E2.
2. Enter the **=A2-B2>C2** formula.

In Figure 333, notice that there is a subtraction sign and a greater than symbol in our formula. Which one will Excel evaluate first? According to our list in Figure 332, Excel should calculate the subtraction first and then the greater than symbol. Figure 334 shows how Excel calculates this logical formula. Notice that the math operator is evaluated before the comparative operator. This is always the case.

$$500 - 392 > 100$$
$$108 > 100$$
$$\text{TRUE}$$

Figure 334

E2				f_x =A2-B2>C2	
	A	B	C	D	E
1	Sales	Expenses	Profit Hurdle	Question	Pass Hurdle = Bonus
2	$500	$392	$100	Is 500-392 > 100 TRUE or FALSE?	TRUE
3	$500	$392	$100	Is 500-392 > 100, Yes or No?	
4	$500	$392	$100	Is 500-392 > 100, 10 or 0?	

Figure 335

In Figure 335, we see the formula result TRUE. But what if we do not want TRUE but instead want the word Yes? In essence, what we want is this:

IF 500 - 392 > 100 is TRUE, then give me the word Yes; otherwise, IF 500 - 392 > 100 is FALSE, give me the word No.

We can easily do this with Excel's built-in IF function. The IF function is great because it will take our logical formula, called a logical_test, and then ask us what to put in the cell if it comes out TRUE and what to put in the cell if it comes out FALSE. The arguments of the IF function look like this:

IF(logical_test,value_if_true,value_if_false)

Let's take a look at how to make this formula work.

IF Function

1. On the OOO sheet, click in cell E3 and type **=IF(**.

Notice that the screen tip is polite. The logical_test argument is bold, which means it is waiting for you to enter a logical_test that will either deliver a TRUE or a FALSE.

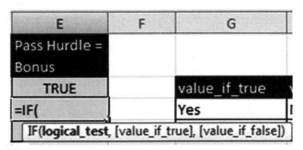

Figure 336

<table>
<tr><td></td><td>A</td><td>B</td><td>C</td><td>D</td><td>E</td></tr>
<tr><td></td><td colspan="3">Profit</td><td></td><td>Pass Hurdle =</td></tr>
<tr><td>1</td><td>Sales</td><td>Expenses</td><td>Hurdle</td><td>Question</td><td>Bonus</td></tr>
<tr><td>2</td><td>$500</td><td>$392</td><td>$100</td><td>Is 500-392 > 100 TRUE or FALSE?</td><td>TRUE</td></tr>
<tr><td>3</td><td>$500</td><td>$392</td><td>$100</td><td>Is 500-392 > 100, Yes or No?</td><td>=IF(A3-B3>C3</td></tr>
<tr><td>4</td><td>$500</td><td>$392</td><td>$100</td><td>Is 500-392 > 100, 10 or 0?</td><td>IF(logical_test, [va</td></tr>
</table>

Figure 337

2. Enter the **A3-B3>C3** logical_test.

3. Type a comma and notice that the screen tip bolds the next argument. The value_if_true argument is what you want to put in the cell if the logical_test comes out TRUE.

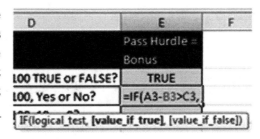

Figure 338

4. Click cell G3.
5. Type a comma and notice that the screen tip bolds the next argument. The value_if_false argument is what you want to put in the cell if the logical test comes out FALSE.

Figure 339

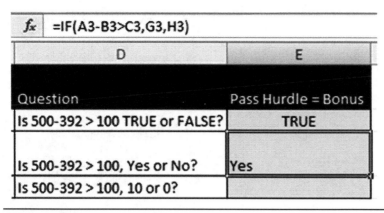

6. Click H3.
7. Type a close parenthesis.
8. Press Ctrl + Enter.

D	E
Question	Pass Hurdle = Bonus
Is 500-392 > 100 TRUE or FALSE?	TRUE
Is 500-392 > 100, Yes or No?	Yes
Is 500-392 > 100, 10 or 0?	

Figure 340

In Figure 340 we can see our fantastic IF function that will put a Yes or No rather than a TRUE or FALSE. Now let's use the Evaluate Formula feature to see how Excel uses its order of operations to calculate this formula.

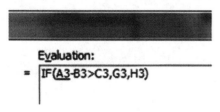

Figure 341

1. With E3 selected, use the Alt, T, U, F keyboard shortcut for Evaluate Formula.

Notice that inside the first argument of the IF function there is a subtraction sign and a greater than comparative operator.

Notice that A3 is underlined. The underline says that Excel will calculate this first.

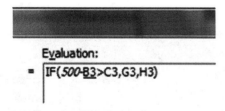

Figure 342

2. Press Enter.

Notice that the A3 changed to 500 in it.

3. Press Enter.

Notice that B3 changed to 392.

Notice that the underline is showing that it will calculate the subtraction before the comparative operator (greater than symbol).

Figure 343

4. Press Enter.
5. Press Enter again.

Notice that the underline is showing it will evaluate the comparative operator after the subtraction.

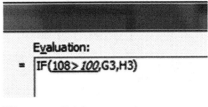

Figure 344

6. Press Enter.

Notice that the word TRUE is the result from the logical_test. Because the logical_ test is TRUE, the value from G3 will be put into the cell.

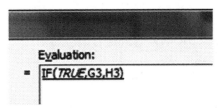

Figure 345

7. Press Enter.
8. Press Esc to close the Evaluate Formula dialog box.

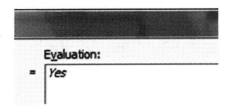

Figure 346

Let's look at another use for the IF function. In Figure 347, we can see the IF function is going to test to determine whether the profit hurdle has been met. If it has been met, a bonus of $10 will be given; otherwise, a bonus of $0 will be given.

	A	B	C	D	E	F	G	H
1	Sales	Expenses	Profit Hurdle	Question	Pass Hurdle = Bonus			
2	$500	$392	$100	Is 500-392 > 100 TRUE or FALSE?	TRUE		value_if_true	value_if_false
3	$500	$392	$100	Is 500-392 > 100, Yes or No?	Yes		Yes	No
4	$500	$392	$100	Is 500-392 > 100, 10 or 0?	=IF(A4-B4>C4,G4,H4)		$10.00	$0.00

Figure 347

Finally, the real magic of the IF function can be seen if you change the input values. If you change the input value in column B (Figure 348), you can see that the logical formula delivers a FALSE, the first IF delivers a No, and the second IF delivers a 0 (zero). As you may recall from the "How Data Is Aligned in Excel" section, in chapter 3, the FALSE is properly aligned center, the No is aligned left, and the number is aligned right.

	A	B	C	D	E	F	G	H
1	Sales	Expenses	Profit Hurdle	Question	Pass Hurdle = Bonus			
2	$500	$700	$100	Is 500-700 > 100 TRUE or FALSE?	FALSE		value_if_true	value_if_false
3	$500	$700	$100	Is 500-700 > 100, Yes or No?	No		Yes	No
4	$500	$700	$100	Is 500-700 > 100, 10 or 0?	0		$10.00	$0.00

Figure 348

The IF function is one of the most commonly used function in Excel. We will come back and talk more about the IF function in the "Built-in Functions" section, later in this chapter.

In this section, we just saw how knowing our order of operations helps us to create formulas that calculate the correct answer.

Our next Excel Efficiency-Robust Rule is as follows:

Rule 27: Learn the math order of operations so that you can create accurate formulas.

Next we want to look at three different methods for entering cell references into formulas.

Putting Cell References in a Formula

There are three ways to enter a cell reference into a formula:
- **Using the arrow keys to get the cell reference**: This method is the fastest method if the cell references are close to the cell that houses the formula.
- **Using the mouse and selection cursor to click a cell**: This method is good when the cell reference is a long way from the cell with the formula.
- **Typing the cell reference into the formula**: If you type accurately and you know exactly what the cell reference address is, this can be a good method.

Let's take a look at an example of these three methods as we create a formula for COGS (Sales * COGS%) and gross profit (Sales – COGS).

To follow along, open the file named excelisfun-Start.xlsm and navigate to the 3WaysToGetCR sheet.

1. Click in cell C5.
2. Type an equal sign.

Notice that the lower-left corner of the status bar shows Enter. This means that you can use your arrow keys or mouse to insert cell references into formulas.

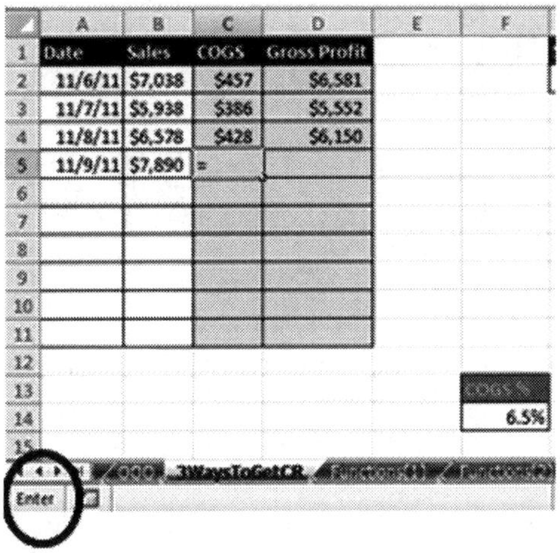

Figure 349

3. Press the Left Arrow key once.

Notice that the cell reference, B5, has been entered into our formula by using an arrow key.

Notice that the lower-left corner of the status bar shows Point. This means that you are in the middle of inserting cell references into formulas.

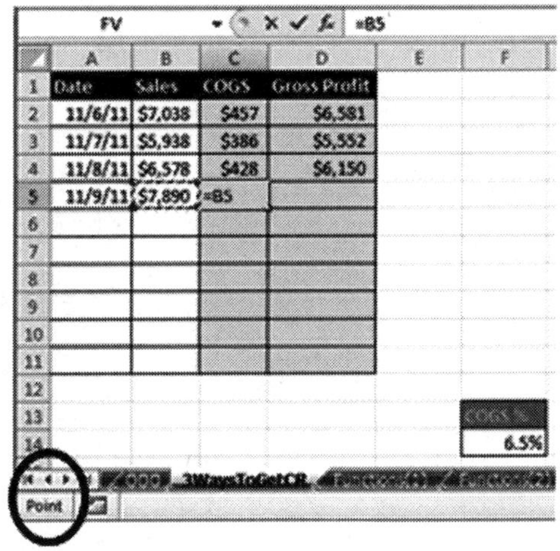

An arrow key can be used to enter a cell reference into a formula anytime you are creating a formula and the left side of the status bar says Enter.

Figure 350

If your status bar does not show Enter, you can use the F2 key to toggle back into Enter mode. The F2 key works in this manner when you are creating a formula.

Arrow keys are a fast and accurate method of entering cell references into a formula. It is preferable to use the arrow keys rather than the mouse to put cell references into formula because it can be so much faster. If you make a mistake and arrow too far so that the incorrect cell reference is in your formula, you can simply arrow back to the correct cell reference. (This is true as long as the dancing ants are dancing or you see the word Point in the status bar.)

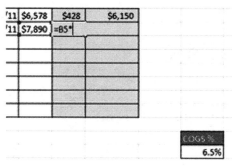

Figure 351

4. Type a multiplication symbol.

Notice that the cell reference F14 is a long way away from the cell C5, which houses our formula. In this case, it may be faster to use your mouse rather than the arrow keys to enter the cell reference into the formula. Also notice that the insertion point in the formula is flashing.

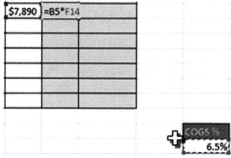

Figure 352

5. With the insertion point after the multiplication symbol, click cell F14 with the selection cursor.

Notice that the cell F14 is inserted into your formula exactly where the insertion point was flashing.

If you are creating a formula and the insertion point is flashing in the formula location here you want a cell reference to go, you can click the cell with your selection cursor to insert the cell references into your formula. This method can be faster than using the arrow keys if the cell reference is a long way from the cell that houses the formula. If you make a mistake by clicking in the wrong cell, just change it by clicking the correct cell. (This is true as long as the dancing ants are dancing or you see the word Point in the status bar.)

	A	B	C	D
1	Date	Sales	COGS	Gross Profit
2	11/6/11	$7,038	$457	$6,581
3	11/7/11	$5,938	$386	$5,552
4	11/8/11	$6,578	$428	$6,150
5	11/9/11	$7,890	$513	=b5-c5
6				

Figure 353

6. To enter the COGS formula into cell C5 and move to D5, press the Tab key.
7. Type the =b5-c5 formula.

Notice that the cell references are highlighted in blue and green to help you identify whether you typed the correct cell references.

8. To Enter the formula and keep the cell selected, press Ctrl + Enter.

Notice that b5-c5 becomes B5-C5.

D5				f_x	=B5-C5	
	A	B	C	D		E
1	Date	Sales	COGS	Gross Profit		
2	11/6/11	$7,038	$457	$6,581		
3	11/7/11	$5,938	$386	$5,552		
4	11/8/11	$6,578	$428	$6,150		
5	11/9/11	$7,890	$513	$7,377		

Figure 354

Typing cell references into formulas can be fast if you are a fast typist and can type accurately. However, this method can lead to errors if you type the wrong cell addresses. For example, 09 (zero, nine) will be interpreted as a number, whereas O9 (capital letter O, nine) will be interpreted as a cell reference.

Another important point about putting cell references into formulas is this: Sometimes a formula will cover up a cell and you cannot use your mouse and selection cursor to put a cell reference into a formula. In this case, you must use either the arrow keys or type your cell reference. Let's take a look at an example of this.

Our goal in Figure 355 is to create a formula that calculates the bonus on sales of $15,000. Our formula inputs are in cells G2, I2, and J2. And we want to put a formula in cell H2.

1. Our goal with this formula is to calculate the bonus earned on sales of $15,000.

f_x			
G	H	I	J
Sales	Earned Bonus		Hurdle
$15,000		$500	$10,000

Figure 355

2. In cell H2, begin the formula by typing the following:
   =IF(G2>=J2,

When we create our formula using the IF function, to enter the cell reference I2 into the value_if_true argument we have to use our arrow keys or type the cell reference because the formula is covering up cell I2 and we cannot use our mouse.

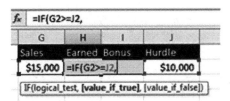

f_x	=IF(G2>=J2,		
G	H	I	J
Sales	Earned Bonus		Hurdle
$15,000	=IF(G2>=J2,		$10,000

IF(logical_test, [value_if_true], [value_if_false])

Figure 356

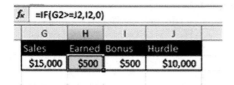

Figure 357

3. Press the Right Arrow once.
4. Type a comma.
5. Type a zero (**0**).
6. Press Ctrl + Enter.

In this section, you saw how to use the arrow keys, the mouse and selection cursor, even your own typing to put cell references into formulas. However, up to this point in the book, we have discussed only relative cell references. This is just one of seven different types of cell references that can be put into formulas. The following section describes all seven types of cell references.

Cell References

In Excel, we put our raw data in cells. We can then make formulas (or use other Excel features) that look at that raw data using cell references. We then can change the raw data and the formulas update. That is the efficient part of setting up formulas that look at formula inputs through cell references. So far in this book, we have seen some great examples of this, but all the examples (except for Figure 295 and Figure 309), were single-cell formulas that we did not need to copy. What happens if we are required to create a whole column of formulas and we don't want to create each formula individually, but instead we want to create the formula one time and then copy it down the column? To do this, we need to learn about the different types of cell references. When we learn about cell references in formulas, we gain the power of "efficient formula creation." Efficient formula creation simply means that we can create and edit the maximum number formulas for a spreadsheet with the minimal amount of effort and time.

As an example, suppose you have to create a budget formula for 12 months and there are 12 expense categories. If you do not know how to use cell references, you would have to enter 144 individual formulas. If you know the tricks of the trade when it comes to cell references, you can create all 144 formulas by just entering one formula and copying it to the rest of the cells! 144 times faster! You will see an example like this later (see Figure 413).

Of all the topics we cover in this book, the topic of cell references is among the most important because of the huge time savings that this knowledge can bring. And because not many people in the Excel working world know that there are seven different types of cell references, if you do know, you can get all your Excel jobs done quickly and people will tend to see you as an Excel magician!

The seven types of cell references are as follows:

- Relative cell reference
- Absolute cell reference
- Mixed with row locked cell reference (also known as row absolute, column relative)
- Mixed with column locked cell reference (also known as column absolute, row relative)
- Worksheet cell reference
- Workbook cell reference
- 3D cell reference

Note: There is actually an eighth type of cell reference called table formula nomenclature. This topic was covered back in Chapter 3, "Data in Excel."

The first four cell references in this list (relative, absolute, mixed with row locked, and mixed with column locked) are the four universal cell references. The last three (worksheet, workbook, and 3D) are specific types of the first four.

Before we get started with examples, let's quickly take a look at the important points about cell references. You can skip this information and come back to it later after you have gone through the examples, but for those of you who like the conclusion first (to see where we are going), I have put this information up front.

Relative Cell References – Example: A1

- No dollar signs
- Moves relatively throughout the copy action.
- *Relatively* means that if the formula is looking at a cell reference that is three cells to the left, when you copy the formula to any other cell, the cell reference will still be looking three cells to the left.

Absolute Cell References – Example: $A$1

- Dollar signs before both:
  - Column reference = A
  - Row reference = 1
- *Absolute* means that if the formula is looking at a particular cell reference, when you copy the formula to any other cell, the cell reference will still be looking at that particular cell reference.
- If the absolute cell reference is $A$1, the formula will always look at cell A1. It is as if the formula is locked on the cell A1 throughout copy action.
- Locks cell reference when copying it horizontally (side to side or across the columns) and vertically (up and down or across the rows).

Mixed Cell References with Row Locked – Example: A$1

- Dollar sign before row reference only.
- Remains absolute or locked when copying vertically (up and down or across the rows).
- Remains relative when copying horizontally (side to side or across the columns).

Mixed Cell References with Column Locked – Example: $A1

- Dollar sign before column reference only.
- Remains absolute or locked when copying horizontally (side to side or across the columns).
- Remains relative when copying vertically (up and down or across the rows).

Keyboard shortcut F4 key: Toggles between the four types of cell references.

When creating formulas with cell references that you will copy to other cells, ask two questions of every cell reference in your formula to figure out which of the four cell references you need:

Q1: What do you want the cell reference to do when you copy it across the columns or horizontally?

Should the cell reference move relatively? Or, should the cell reference be locked or absolute?

Q2: What do you want it to do when you copy it across the rows or vertically?

Should the cell reference move relatively? Or, should the cell reference be locked or absolute?

If your formula will never be copied to another cell, you do not need to worry about which of the four cell references you need. Cell references without any dollar signs will work just fine. It is only when we copy the formula that it matters what type of cell reference it is.

Relative Cell References

To follow along, open the file named excelisfun-Start.xlsm and navigate to the CR(1) sheet.

In Figure 358, we can see a formula sitting in cell D2. This formula will be copied down the column so that we can avoid having to create six separate formulas. That formula is using the cell reference B2. However, from the point of view of the formula, the formula does not see a B2 cell reference, but instead it sees the relative position "two cells to the left of whatever cell the formula is sitting in (housed in)." Similarly, the cell reference C2 is not really C2, it is "one cell to the left of whatever cell the formula is sitting in (housed in)." Even though we see the cell reference B2 with our eyes, that is not what the formula sees. Now, let's prove that when you copy the formula down the formula does not really see "B2 minus C2" but instead it sees "two cells to the left minus one cell to the left."

1. On the CR(1) sheet, click in cell D2 and create the **=B2-C2** formula.
2. Enter the formula and copy the formula down to cell D3.

	A	B	C	D
1	Month	Total Revenue	Total Expenses	Net Income
2	Jan	20,000.00	13,050.00	=B2-C2
3	Feb	20,300.00	13,245.75	
4	Mar	20,604.50	13,444.45	
5	Apr	20,913.57	13,646.11	
6	May	21,227.27	13,850.81	
7	Jun	21,545.68	14,058.54	

Figure 358

3. Put the formula in cell D3 into Edit mode with the F2 key.

In Figure 359 we have proved that when you copy the formula the formula does not really see "B2 minus C2" but instead sees "two cells to the left minus one cell to the

	A	B	C	D
1	Month	Total Revenue	Total Expenses	Net Income
2	Jan	20,000.00	13,050.00	6,950.00
3	Feb	20,300.00	13,245.75	=B3-C3
4	Mar	20,604.50	13,444.45	
5	Apr	20,913.57	13,646.11	
6	May	21,227.27	13,850.81	
7	Jun	21,545.68	14,058.54	

left minus one cell to the left."   **Figure 359**

The formula in cell D3 does not have a B2 or a C2 cell reference. When we copied the formula down, the row reference 2 changed to 3. We can see with our own eyes that =B2-C2 changes to =B3-C3. This further proves that the original formula was not B2 minus C2 because if it were, when we copied it down, it would still say B2 minus C2. If you are to become great with formulas, you must read formulas just as Excel reads them. The formula =B3-C3 that sits in cell D3 is read as "two cells to the left minus one cell to the left." Now let's copy the formula down the whole column.

	A	B	C	D
1	Month	Total Revenue	Total Expenses	Net Income
2	Jan	20,000.00	13,050.00	6,950.00
3	Feb	20,300.00	13,245.75	7,054.25
4	Mar	20,604.50	13,444.45	7,160.05
5	Apr	20,913.57	13,646.11	7,267.46
6	May	21,227.27	13,850.81	7,376.46
7	Jun	21,545.68	14,058.54	=B7-C7

4. Select cell D3.
5. Double-click the fill handle with your crosshair cursor (as discussed back in Figure 309) to copy the formula down.
6. Put cell D7 into Edit mode.

Figure 360

In Figure 360, we can see the formula =B7-C7, but we know that because these are relative cell references and we are copying the formula, the proper way to read this formula is "two cells to the left minus one cell to the left."

Next we want to look at absolute cell references. Before we do, however, let's brush up on our math for formulas that involve percentage or proportional increases.

Percentage or Proportion Increase (or decrease)

In the following section, we will have to build a formula that increases an amount by a proportion or percent. For example, we may want to start with $1,000 and say something like "increase $1,000 by 10%." Our calculation would be as follows:

$1,000 + $1,000 * 10% = $1,000 + $1,000 * 0.10 = $1,000 + $100 = $1,100

But it would be equally correct to write it this way:

$1,000 * (1 + 10%) = $1,000 * (1 + 0.10) = $1,000 * (1.1) = $1,100

In finance and economics, it is common to see the calculation "increase $1,000 by 10%" written as follows:

$1,000 * 1.1

Similarly we may see the calculation "decrease $1,000 by 10%" written as follows:

$1,000 * 0.9

The mathematical reason that we can use these formulas comes from the math concept of factoring. In our example, it would look like this:

$1,000 + $1,000 * 0.10 = $1,000 * (1 + 0.10) = $1,000 * 1.1.

In Excel, using this convention is handy because it can reduce the size of our formulas. The next two examples will use this idea, first in an "increasing the price" formula, and then in an "increasing the revenue" formula.

Absolute Cell References

Figure 361 shows that we have 18 item prices in the range B3:D8. Our goal in the range E3 to G8 is to increase all the prices by 5%. This means we need to create 18 formulas, one for each price. In cell E3, you can see we have started to create our formula. Currently, we see relative cell references in our formula that would be read as "three cells to the left *times* three cells to the left and eight cells below." But is that really the formula we want? To find out, let's see what happens when we copy this formula.

To follow along, open the file named excelisfun-Start.xlsm and navigate to the CR(2) sheet.

	A	B	C	D	E	F	G
1		Retail Selling Price by Margin					
2	Items	45%	50%	55%	New Price	New Price	New Price
3	Sofa	$1,087.27	$1,196.00	$1,328.89	=B3*B11		
4	Head Lamp	154.55	170.00	188.89			
5	Table	276.36	304.00	337.78			
6	Chair	180.00	198.00	220.00			
7	Dining Set	1,045.45	1,150.00	1,277.78			
8	Picture	45.45	50.00	55.56			
9							
10	Assumption Table						
11	Increase in Price	1.05					

Figure 361

1. Click in cell E3 and create the following formula:
   =B3*B11
2. Enter the formula and then copy it down to cell E4.

	A	B	C	D	E	F	G
1		Retail Selling Price by Margin					
2	Items	45%	50%	55%	New Price	New Price	New Price
3	Sofa	$1,087.27	$1,196.00	$1,328.89	$1,141.64		
4	Head Lamp	154.55	170.00	188.89	=B4*B12		
5	Table	276.36	304.00	337.78			
6	Chair	180.00	198.00	220.00			
7	Dining Set	1,045.45	1,150.00	1,277.78			
8	Picture	45.45	50.00	55.56			
9							
10	Assumption Table						
11	Increase in Price	1.05					
12	Sofa	598					

Figure 362

3. With cell E4 selected, use the F2 key to put the cell in Edit mode.

The F2 key not only puts a formula into Edit mode, it also gives us a "color-coded cell reference map" called Range Finder. Range Finder helps us to audit our formula and track down errors.

In Figure 362, we can see that the formula is not correct. The formula we really need to calculate the new price for the Head Lamp based on the 45% margin is not =B4*B12 but instead =B4*B11. The relative cell reference, B4, which is "three cells to the left," is correct. But the B12 should be B11! What happened is that the row reference, 11, moved to 12 even though we did not want it to move. We can see that the green Range Finder rectangle is highlighting one cell below our "Increase in Price Number, 1.05." This is not correct. We really want our formula to always be looking at the number in cell B11. We do not want the B11 part of our formula to be a relative cell reference. We need the B11 to be "locked" or "absolute" because we copy the formula to the rest of the cells. Before we see how to lock a cell reference, let's see what happens when we copy the formula, not down, but to the right.

	A	B	C	D	E	F	G
1		Retail Selling Price by Margin					
2	Items	45%	58%	55%	New Price	New Price	New Price
3	Sofa	$1,087.27	$1,196.00	$1,328.89	$1,141.64	=C3*C11	
4	Head Lamp	154.55	170.00	188.89			
5	Table	276.36	304.00	337.78			
6	Chair	180.00	198.00	220.00			
7	Dining Set	1,045.45	1,150.00	1,277.78			
8	Picture	45.45	50.00	55.56			
9							
10	Assumption Table						
11	Increase in Price	1.05					

Figure 363

4. Click the Esc key to get out of Edit mode.
5. Press the Delete key to remove the formula from cell E4.
6. Click in E3 and copy the formula over to cell F3.
7. Click in cell F3 and press the F2 key to show the formula in Edit mode.

In Figure 363, we can see that the formula is not correct. The formula we really need to calculate the new price for the sofa based on the 50% margin is not =C3*C11 but instead =C3*B11. The relative cell reference, C3, which is "three cells to the left," is correct. But the C11 should be B11! What happened is that the column reference, B, moved to C even though we did not want it to move. We can see that the green Range Finder rectangle is highlighting one cell to the right of our Increase in Price Number, 1.05. This is not correct. We really want our formula to always be looking at the number in cell B11. We do not want the B11 part of our formula to be a relative cell reference. We need the B11 to be locked or absolute as we copy the formula to the rest of the cells. Let's take a look at how to lock our cell reference to make an absolute cell reference.

	A	B	C	D	E	F	G
1		Retail Selling Price by Margin					
2	Items	45%	50%	55%	New Price	New Price	New Price
3	Sofa	$1,087.27	$1,196.00	$1,328.89	=B3*B11		
4	Head Lamp	154.55	170.00	188.89			
5	Table	276.36	304.00	337.78			
6	Chair	180.00	198.00	220.00			
7	Dining Set	1,045.45	1,150.00	1,277.78			
8	Picture	45.45	50.00	55.56			
9							
10	Assumption Table						
11	Increase in Price	1.05					
12	Sofa	598					

Figure 364

8. Click the Esc key to get out of Edit mode.
9. Press the Delete key to remove the formula from cell F3.
10. Click in E3 and create the following formula:
   =B3*B11

In Figure 364, we can see that we have a formula that uses two cell references. We already saw that the relative cell reference, B3, which is "three cells to my left," will work perfectly. When we copy the formula down one row, the 3 will move to a 4 to give us B4; and when we copy the formula to the right one column, the B will move to a C to give us C3. So that relative cell reference will work perfectly. But the B11 needs to be locked on B11 when we copy it down across the rows and to the right across the columns. We can lock cell references in formulas by placing $ signs (dollar signs) in front of either the row or column reference. For us, we need the cell reference, B11, to be locked in both directions when we copy the formula across the rows and across the columns, so we need our formula to look like this:

   =B3*$B$11

When you have a $ sign in front of both the letter (column reference) and number (row reference), this is called an absolute cell reference.

Why a dollar sign? No reason; they just picked a symbol and used it to designate that either the row or column should be "locked" or absolute throughout the copy action.

When putting $ into your cell references, instead of typing them in, you can use the F4 key. When the insertion point in a formula is touching a cell reference, the F4 key will add the $ to the cell reference. Let's take a look at how this works.

	A	B	C	D	E
1		Retail Selling Price by Margin			
2	Items	45%	50%	55%	New Price Ne
3	Sofa	$1,087.27	$1,196.00	$1,328.89	=B3*$B$11
4	Head Lamp	154.55	170.00	188.89	
5	Table	276.36	304.00	337.78	
6	Chair	180.00	198.00	220.00	
7	Dining Set	1,045.45	1,150.00	1,277.78	
8	Picture	45.45	50.00	55.56	
9					
10	Assumption Table				
11	Increase in Price	1.05			

Figure 365

11. With the insertion point in a formula touching B11, press the F4 key.

Notice the F4 key puts in two $ signs, one for column B column and one row 11.

Next we need to copy the formula to the entire range E3: G8. This means we need to copy the formula down and then over. This is a two-step process. Let's take a look at how to do it.

E	F	G
New Price	New Price	New Price
$1,141.64		

Figure 366

12. To put the formula in cell E3 and keep the cell selected, press Ctrl + Enter.
13. The first copy step is to double-click the fill handle with the crosshair cursor to copy the formula down across the rows.

E	F	G
New Price	New Price	New Price
$1,141.64		
$162.27		
$290.18		
$189.00		
$1,097.73		
$47.73		

Figure 367

A smart tag may appear after the first copy step, but you can ignore it.
14. The second copy step is to click the fill handle with the crosshair cursor and drag to the right across the columns.

Notice that we are copying a whole column of formulas with our fill handle and crosshair trick.

15. When you drag your cross-hair cursor to the right, you will see a gray rectangle. When the gray rectangle surrounds the F and G column, let go of the mouse.

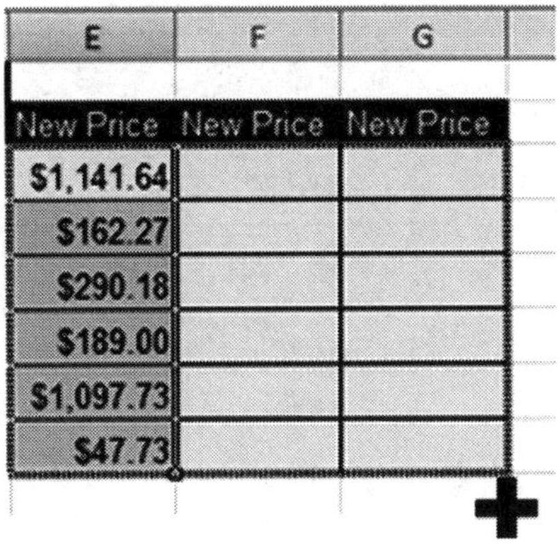

Figure 368

16. Click in Cell G8 and press the F2 key to put the cell in Edit mode.

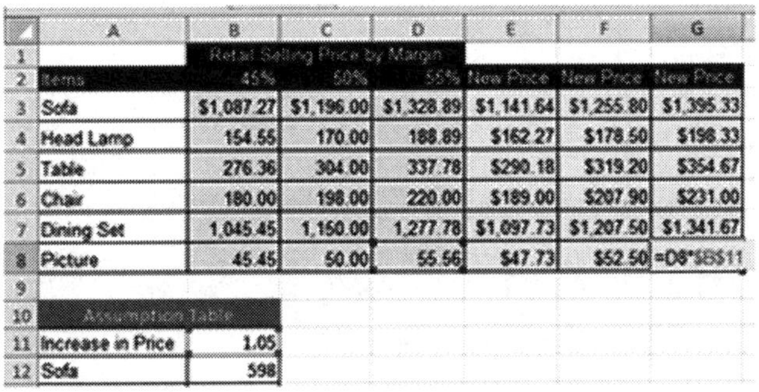

Figure 369

In Figure 369, we can see that our formula works perfectly. The relative cell reference, D8, is looking "three cells to the left" and the absolute cell references is looking at cell B11. With our knowledge of cell references and our two-step copy process, we made 18 calculations with one formula! That is 18 times faster than doing it individually!

Before we move on to the next type of cell reference, we want to see how to apply the Ctrl + Enter keyboard trick to enter (or populate) an entire range of cells with formulas. This trick will allow us to enter the formula into all the cells (E3:G8) at one time and enable us to avoid having to use the two-step copy process that we used in Figure 366 to Figure 368. Avoiding the two-step copy process can save time!

A key idea to remember is this: This trick is a substitute for our two-step copy process.

	A	B	C	D	E	F	G
1		Retail Selling Price by Margin					
2	Items	45%	50%	55%	New Price	New Price	New Price
3	Sofa	$1,087.27	$1,196.00	$1,328.89			
4	Head Lamp	154.55	170.00	188.89			
5	Table	276.36	304.00	337.78			
6	Chair	180.00	198.00	220.00			
7	Dining Set	1,045.45	1,150.00	1,277.78			
8	Picture	45.45	50.00	55.56			
9							
10	Assumption Table						
11	Increase in Price	1.05					

Figure 370

1. Highlight the range E3:G8.
2. Press the Delete key to delete all the formulas.

Notice that the upper-left cell is light colored and the rest of the highlighted cells are a darker color. The light-colored cell is called the active cell.

In Figure 370, we have highlighted the range E3:G8: all of these cells will get the same formula. Because all the cells get the same formula, we can create our formula in the active cell (light-colored cell, namely E3) and use the keyboard shortcut Ctrl + Enter to populate all the cells with the formula.

	A	B	C	D	E	F	G
1		Retail Selling Price by Margin					
2	Items	45%	50%	55%	New Price	New Price	New Price
3	Sofa	$1,087.27	$1,196.00	$1,328.89	=B3*$B$11		
4	Head Lamp	154.55	170.00	188.89			
5	Table	276.36	304.00	337.78			
6	Chair	180.00	198.00	220.00			
7	Dining Set	1,045.45	1,150.00	1,277.78			
8	Picture	45.45	50.00	55.56			
9							
10	Assumption Table						
11	Increase in Price	1.05					

Figure 371

3. In cell E3 create the following formula:
   Three cells to the left times B11

The description I just gave of the formula is the "idea" or "concept" of the formula. This is the way you should think of it when you create formulas such as this. Explicitly, here is the formula: =B3*$B$11

In Figure 371, it is important to note that we must build the formula from the point of view of the active cell, E3. This means that if the formula has a relative cell reference that is "three cells to the left," the relative cell reference you put in the formula must be "three cells to the left" of the active cell.

4. To populate all the cells with the formula from the active cell, press Ctrl + Enter.

In Figure 372, we can see that the keyboard shortcut Ctrl + Enter populated all the highlighted cells with the formula.

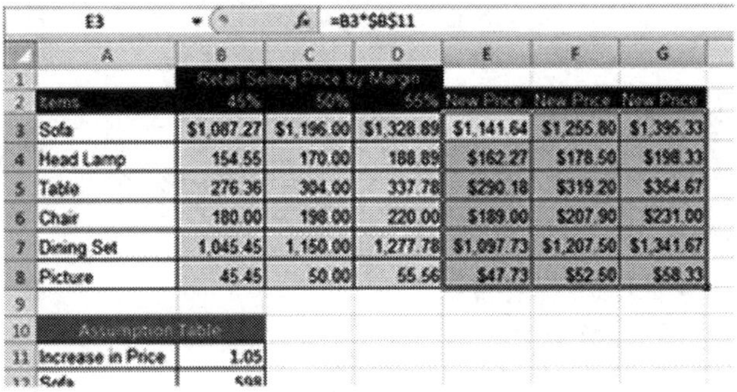

Figure 372

Anytime you have a range of cells that will get the same formula, number, or word, you can use this method for entering the same item into a range of cells. When you use the Ctrl + Enter method to enter a formula into a range of cells, you want to verify that you actually entered the correct formula. To do this, check the lower-right corner to determine whether that formula is correct. If that one is correct, you can infer that all the rest are correct also. One fast way to more from corner to corner in a highlight range is to use the keyboard shortcut Ctrl + period.

5. With the active cell in the upper-left corner, to move to the lower corner, press and hold Ctrl and tap the period key two times.

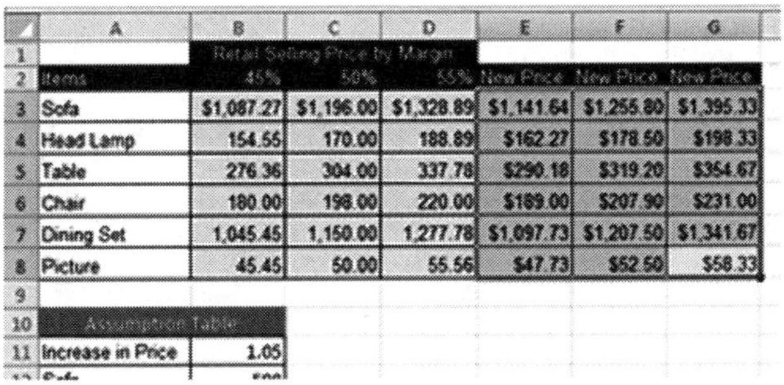

Figure 373

6. To verify that the formula is correct, press the F2 key to put the formula into Edit mode.

The formula looks correct.

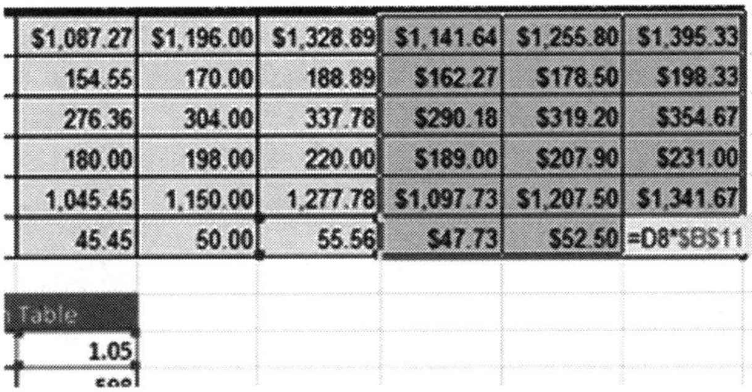

Figure 374

When learning how to use this Ctrl + Enter trick to populate a range of cells with a formula, remember this: It is a substitute for copying. So before using Ctrl + Enter, it is always important, when you are creating the formula to think about what cell references are required for the "copying" action.

Next we want to look at mixed cell references. With these, we can increase the speed with which we make formulas much more than if we just know relative and absolute cell references.

Mixed with Row Locked Cell References

Figure 375

In Figure 375, we can see that our sales reps are in column A, the sales amounts for each sales rep are in column B, and the earned commission formula will be in column C. Our goal is to create one formula in cell C5 that we can copy from cell C5 all the way down to cell C52. If we can create one formula that will do all 48 earned commission calculations, we will have saved a lot of time.

Looking at Figure 375, will our formula =B5*B2 work when we copy it down? To determine whether it will work, let's try it.

To follow along, open the file named excelisfun-Start.xlsm and navigate to the CR(3) sheet.
1.   On the CR(3) sheet, click in cell C5 and create the **=B5*B2** formula.

2. Press Ctrl + Enter.
3. Copy the formula to cell C6.
4. Using the F2 key, put cell C6 into Edit mode.

B6 is a relative cell reference that is correctly looking one cell to the left.

B3 is incorrectly looking at the empty cell B3 when it is supposed to be looking at cell B2, which contains the commission rate.

Figure 376

Notice that we want B2, but the 2 (row reference) moved to a 3 and we got B3. To fix this we will edit our original formula and put a $ sign in front of the number 2 to prevent the 2 from moving to a 3.

Also notice that the column reference B did not change because as we copied the formula down, column C is still the same relative distance away from column B.

5. To get out of Edit mode, click Esc.
6. To delete the formula in cell C6, press the Delete key.
7. Using the F2 key put cell C5 into Edit mode.
8. With the section cursor touching cell B2, press the F4 key twice to put the $ in front of the number 2.

Figure 377

In Figure 377, the reason we put a $ in front of the row reference, 2, is because we want to prevent the 2 from changing to a 3. The $ in front of the row reference, 2, will lock the cell reference on row 2 as we copy it down across the rows. As we copy the formula down, B$2 will be locked and the formula will always be looking at the 0.04 commission rate.

9. To enter the formula, press Ctrl + Enter.
10. To copy the formula down, double-click the fill handle with the crosshair cursor.

			Earned Commision
4	SalesRep	Sales	
5	Abraham	$1,161.00	$46.440
6	Hironobu	$1,321.00	$52.840
7	Daniel	$1,039.00	$41.560
8	Dante	$1,761.00	$70.440
9	Sarah B	$1,561.00	$62.440
10	Tonya	$1,868.00	$74.720
11	Janita	$2,787.00	$111.480
12	Debra	$1,849.00	$73.960

Figure 378

50	Ewelina	$2,833.00	$113.320
51	Jori	$1,604.00	$64.160
52	Abdullahi	$2,588.00	=B52*B$2

Figure 379

11. To jump to the bottom of the column, use the Ctrl + Down Arrow keyboard shortcut.
12. To verify that the formula is correct, press the F2 key.

In Figure 379 We can see that our formula is correct: one cell to the left times B2. Notice that there is no $ in front of the column reference, B. This means that if we were to copy this formula left or right, the column reference 2 would move; it would act like a relative cell reference. That is why this cell reference is called "mixed," because it is part relative and part absolute. But that does not come into play here because we were only copying the formula down across the rows and therefore only needed to lock the row reference, 2. You will see how the mixed cell reference can be used both as a relative and absolute cell reference in an upcoming example.

Using the Minimum Number of $ Signs for Cell References

Now let's think about this. We entered the formula =B5*B$2 into cell C5 and copied our formula down the column. Many people would say, "Yes but why can't we use the formula =B5*$B$2 instead?" Although the formula =B5*$B$2 will work in this situation, here are two reasons to not use it:

- Because we are only copying our formula down across the rows, we do not need the extra $ in front of the column reference.
- If you always use the minimum number of $ signs for cell references when you create your formulas, when you get the formulas where mixed cell references are mandatory, you are already trained to use them automatically.

We will talk much more about this throughout the rest of the book.

Next we need to look at the other type of mixed cell reference, when only the column reference is locked.

Mixed with Column Locked Cell References

In Figure 380, you can see that January revenues are assumed to be $20,000 and we expect a 0.015 (1.5%) increase in revenues each month. The formula in cell C2 is properly looking at the previous month's revenue (one cell to the left) times the assumed increase in cell B4. But what will happen to the formula when we copy it to column D or then column E? Let's copy the formula from cell C2 to D2 and determine whether it works.

	A	B	C	D	
1		January	February	March	
2	Revenue	20,000.00	=B2*B4		
3					
4	Increase each month	1.015			

Figure 380

To follow along, open the file named excelisfun-Start.xlsm and navigate to the CR(4) sheet.
1. Click in cell C2 and create the =B2*B4 formula.
2. Press Ctrl + Enter.
3. Copy the formula to cell D2.

4. With cell D2 selected, press the F2 key to put it into Edit mode.

Notice that the "one cell to my left" is perfect because we always want our formula to be looking at last month's revenue.

Notice that the original B4 incorrectly changed to C4.

	A	B	C	D	
1		January	February	March	A
2	Revenue	20,000.00	20,300.00	=C2*C4	
3					
4	Increase each month	1.015			
5					

Figure 381

In Figure 381, we can see that our technique of copying the formula on cell to the right is helpful because we can visually see the colored rectangles (called Range Finder) that indicate which cell references are being used by the formula. It is clear that the green rectangle is looking at an empty cell. We wanted cell B4 in our formula, not C4. How do we prevent the column reference B from changing to a C? The answer is to lock down the column reference in the original formula with a $ sign. A $ in front of the B will lock the cell reference on the B column whenever we copy the formula across the columns. Let's take a look at how to do this.

5. Delete the formula in cell D2.
6. Put cell C2 in Edit mode.
7. With your cursor touching B4, press the F4 key three times to put the $ sign in front of the B.
8. Press Ctrl + Enter.
9. Copy formula from C2 to G2.

	A	B	C	
1		January	February	Marc
2	Revenue	20,000.00	=B2*$B4	
3				
4	Increase each month	1.015		

Figure 382

	A	B	C	D	E	F	G
1		January	February	March	April	May	June
2	Revenue	20,000.00	20,300.00	20,604.50	20,913.57	21,227.27	=F2*$B4
3							
4	Increase each month	1.015					

Figure 383

10. Put cell G2 in Edit mode.

Your formula should be read "one cell to the left times B4."

Some of you reading this are saying, "I do not get this!" Just stop, and practice a lot. There is no great solace in you reading "practice a lot," but because it is true, I must write it. In all my years of teaching, this is the hardest topic for people to get, but, it is one of the most useful concepts to learn.

In our next example, we will get to see how to apply our knowledge of cell references to create a rectangular range of formulas 54 times faster than most people. Remember, 54 times faster can be your incentive to make you practice and learn this; 54 times faster means more vacation time and bosses and co-workers who love you!

Three Types of Cell References in One Formula

In Figure 384, you can see a range of pension values given an assumed rate earned per year and an assumed length in years for investment. For example, in cell E8 you can see that you will have $153,480.36 if you deposit $3,000 at the end of each year, make deposits for 20 years, and assume a 9% interest rate earned per year. (That's pretty good given that the total amount put in is 20 * $3,000 = $60,000.) But imagine having to make all these calculations by hand. Fifty-four "future value of the pension" calculations would take forever! Luckily, there is a built-in FV (Future Value) function that can do the math for us, and with our knowledge of the four types of cell references, we will be able to do all 54 calculations with one formula! Let's take a look at how.

	A	B	C	D	E	F	G
1	Yearly PMT	$3,000.00					
2							
3			What will your Pension be worth when you retire?				
4	Years/Rate	6.0%	7.0%	8.0%	9.0%	10.0%	11.0%
5	5	$16,911.28	$17,252.22	$17,599.80	$17,954.13	$18,315.30	$18,683.40
6	10	$39,542.38	$41,449.34	$43,459.69	$45,578.79	$47,812.27	$50,166.03
7	15	$69,827.91	$75,387.07	$81,456.34	$88,082.75	$95,317.45	$103,216.08
8	20	$110,356.77	$122,986.48	$137,285.89	$153,480.36	$171,825.00	$192,608.50
9	25	$164,593.54	$189,747.11	$219,317.82	$254,102.69	$295,041.18	$343,239.92
10	30	$237,174.56	$283,382.36	$339,849.63	$408,922.62	$493,482.07	$597,062.63
11	35	$334,304.34	$414,710.64	$516,950.41	$647,132.26	$813,073.11	$1,024,768.66
12	40	$464,285.90	$598,905.34	$777,169.56	$1,013,647.34	$1,327,777.67	$1,745,478.20
13	45	$638,230.54	$857,247.93	$1,159,516.85	$1,577,576.20	$2,156,714.51	$2,959,915.68

Figure 384

Note: In this section, we will not talk in full detail about the FV function; we will save the discussion for later in this chapter. For now, let's concentrate on cell references.

To follow along, open the file named excelisfun-Start.xlsm and navigate to the CR(5) sheet.

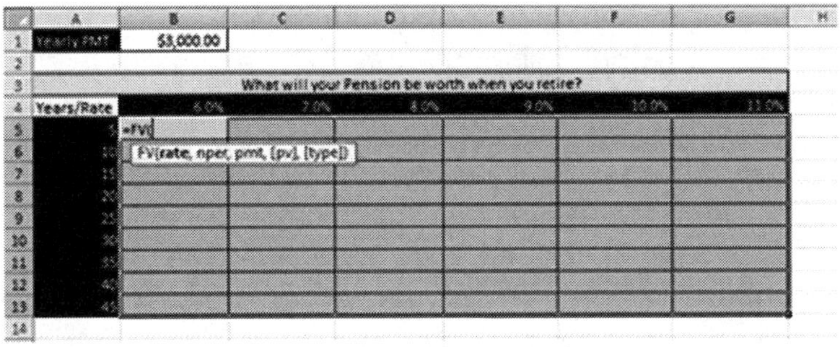

Figure 385

1. In the CR(5) sheet, select the range B5:G13. Because we want cell B5 to be the active cell after we select our range, select the range by clicking in cell B5 and dragging to G13.
2. In the active cell, B5, type **=FV(**.

3. The first argument in the FV functions is the rate, so click cell B4.

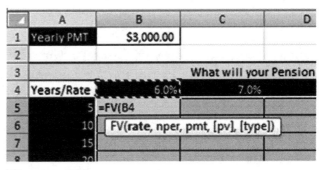

Figure 386

In Figure 386, we can see that we selected cell B4 for the rate argument. But which of the four types of cell references do we need? To get the answer, we will ask two questions:

Q1: When we copy our formula from the 6% column to the 7% column (column B to C or copying horizontally), do we want the cell reference to move relatively or do we want the cell reference to be locked on cell B4?

Answer: We want our cell reference to move relatively; we want the cell reference, B4, to move to C4. This means that we do not put a $ sign in front of the B. We want the 6% value in column B, but when we copy the formula to the C column, we need the 7% value, and therefore we want our cell reference to move relatively.

Q2: When we copy our formula from the 5 year row to the 10 year row (row 5 to 6 or copying vertically), do we want the cell reference to move relatively or do we want the cell reference to be locked on cell B4?

Answer: We want the cell reference to be locked on cell B4. This means that we want to put a $ in front of the row reference, 4. We want to use the 6% value in all the cells in the B column, and therefore we want our cell reference to be locked as we copy the formula vertically, across the rows.

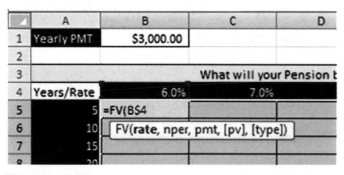

Figure 387

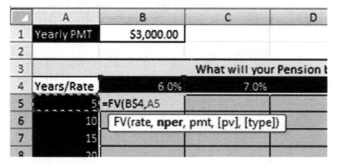

Figure 388

4. To lock the cell reference when copying up and down, across the rows, but not lock it when copying side to side, across the columns, press the F4 key twice to get the B$4 cell reference.

5. Type a comma

6. Enter the cell reference A5 for the nper argument. The nper argument is for total number of years for the pension.

In Figure 388, we can see that we selected cell A5 for the nper argument. But which of the four types of cell references do we need? To get the answer, we will ask two questions:

Q1: When we copy our formula from the 6% column to the 7% column (column B to C or copying horizontally), do we want the cell reference to move relatively or do we want the cell reference to be locked on cell A5?

    Answer: We want the cell reference to be locked on cell A5. This means that we want to put a $ in front of the column reference, A. We want to use the 5 year value in all the cells in row 5 or 5 year row, and therefore we want our cell reference to be locked as we copy the formula horizontally, across the columns.

Q2: When we copy our formula from the 5 year row to the 10 year row (row 5 to 6 or copying vertically), do we want the cell reference to move relatively or do we want the cell reference to be locked on cell A5?

    Answer: We want our cell reference to move relatively; we want the cell reference, A5 to move to A6. This means that we do not put a $ in front of the 5. We want the 5 year value in row 5 or 5 year row, but when we copy the formula to the row 6 or 10 year row, we need the 10 year value, and therefore we want our cell reference to move relatively.

7. To lock the cell reference when copying side to side, across the columns, but not lock it when copying up and down, across the rows, press the F4 key three times to get the $A5 cell reference.

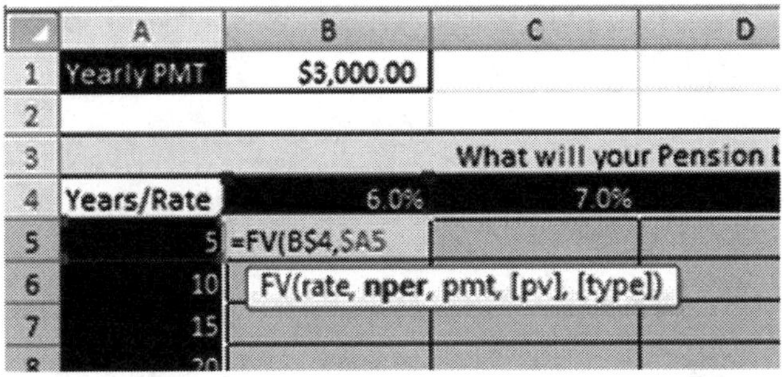

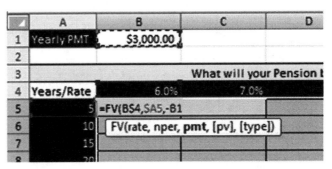

Figure 389

8. Type a comma
9. Enter a minus sign. (Payments are negative.)
10. Enter the cell reference B1 for the pmt argument.

Figure 390

The pmt argument is for yearly payment into the pension, and the minus sign is because you pay it out each year (more later on the FV function).

In Figure 390, we can see that we selected cell B1 for the pmt argument. But which of the four types of cell references do we need? To get the answer, we will ask two questions:

Q1: When we copy our formula from the 6% column to the 7% column (column B to C or copying horizontally), do we want the cell reference to move relatively or do we want the cell reference to be locked on cell B1?

Answer: We want the cell reference to be locked on cell B1. This means that we want to put a $ in front of the column reference, B. We want to use the $3,000 contribution amount in all the cells in row 5, and therefore we want our cell reference to be locked as we copy the formula horizontally, across the columns.

Q2: When we copy our formula from the 5 year row to the 10 year row (row 5 to 6 or copying vertically), do we want the cell reference to move relatively or do we want the cell reference to be locked on cell B1?

Answer: We want the cell reference to be locked on cell B1. This means that we want to put a $ in front of the row reference, 1. We want to use the $3,000 contribution amount in all the cells in column B, and therefore we want our cell reference to be locked as we copy the formula vertically, across the rows.

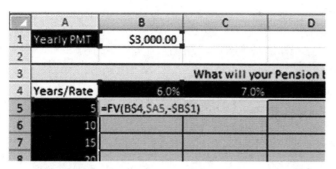

Figure 391

11. To lock the cell reference when copying side to side, across the columns, and when copying up and down, across the rows, press the F4 key one time, to get the $B$1 cell reference.

12. Type a close parenthesis.

	A	B	C	D	E	F	G	H
1	Yearly PMT	$3,000.00						
2								
3			What will your Pension be worth when you retire?					
4	Years/Rate	6.0%	7.0%	8.0%	9.0%	10.0%	11.0%	
5	5	$16,911.28	$17,252.22	$17,599.80	$17,954.13	$18,315.30	$18,683.40	
6	10	$39,542.38	$41,449.34	$43,459.69	$45,578.79	$47,812.27	$50,166.03	
7	15	$69,827.91	$75,387.07	$81,456.34	$88,082.75	$95,317.45	$103,216.08	
8	20	$110,356.77	$122,986.48	$137,285.89	$153,480.36	$171,825.00	$192,608.50	
9	25	$164,593.54	$189,747.11	$219,317.82	$254,102.69	$295,041.18	$343,239.92	
10	30	$237,174.56	$283,382.36	$339,849.63	$408,922.62	$493,482.07	$597,062.63	
11	35	$334,304.94	$414,710.64	$516,950.41	$647,132.26	$813,073.11	$1,024,768.66	
12	40	$464,285.90	$598,905.34	$777,169.56	$1,013,647.34	$1,327,777.67	$1,745,478.20	
13	45	$638,230.54	$857,247.93	$1,159,516.85	$1,577,576.20	$2,156,714.51	$2,959,915.68	
14								

Figure 392

13. To populate all the cells in the highlighted region with the formula, press Ctrl + Enter.

Remember, Ctrl + Enter to populate all the cells with a formula is a substitute for the two-step copy process.

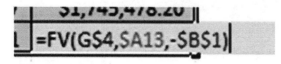

Figure 393

To verify that the formula is correct, put cell G13 into Edit mode.

Figure 392 is proof that "knowing when to use the right cell reference saves time in formula creation." If you can create a range of formulas that quickly, people will stop and notice. But how do you get proficient with knowing which cell reference to use and when? Practice a lot and remember to ask the two questions of each cell reference in your formula. If you do that, you will always know which cell reference to use.

Our next Excel Efficiency-Robust Rule is this:

Rule 28: The four types of cell references are relative, absolute, mixed with column locked, and mixed with row locked. When creating formulas with cell references that you will copy to other cells, ask two questions of every cell reference in your formula to figure out which of the four cell references you need. Q1: What do you want the cell reference to do when you copy it across the columns or horizontally? Q2: What do you want the cell reference to do when you copy it across the rows or vertically? This leads to efficient formula creation.

Because learning how to apply the concept of mixed cell references is not easy, we now want to look at a simple example that you can quickly duplicate anytime you forget how to use mixed cell reference. Our goal with this example is to make a 12 x 12 multiplication table (Figure 394) with just one formula. (The word *table* in the phrase *multiplication table* does not refer to table format structure or Excel table.) The nice thing about this example is that we all know the mechanics of how a multiplication table works: For any cell in the multiplication table, we need to multiply the column header and the row header. In Figure 394, you can see the formula in cell H8 takes 6 times 5 and calculates the result. Now let's see how to create the whole multiplication table with just one formula using mixed cell references.

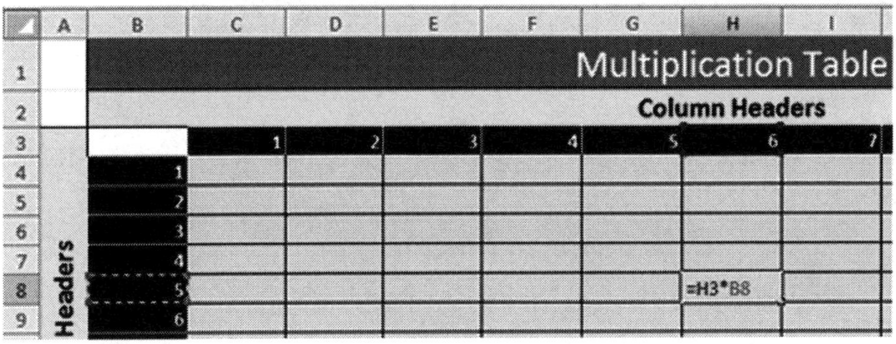

Figure 394

To follow along, open the file named excelisfun-Start.xlsm and navigate to the CR(6) sheet.

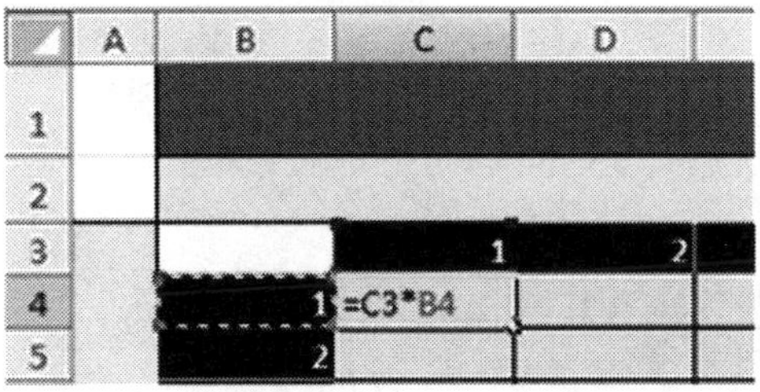

Figure 395

   1. Click in cell C4 and create the base formula:
      =C3*B4

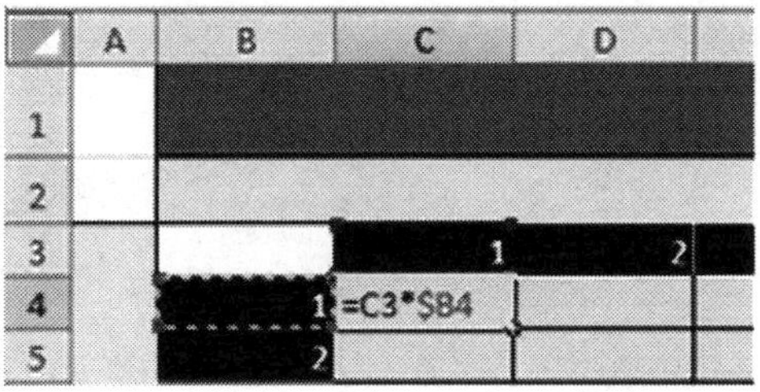

Figure 396

   2. With your insertion point touching the cell reference B4, press the F4 key three times so that you lock the column reference, but not the row.

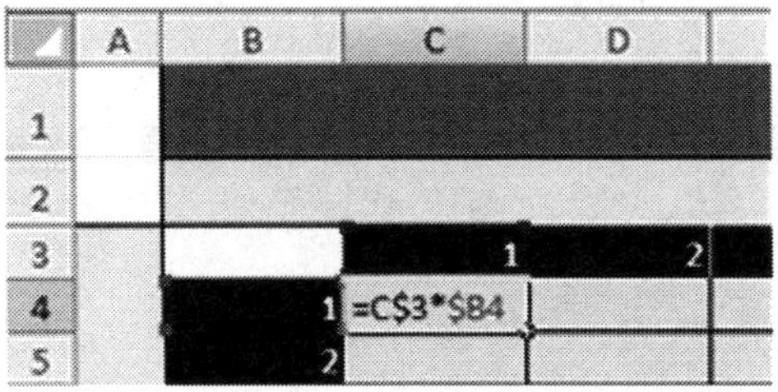

Figure 397

   3. With your insertion point touching the cell reference C3, press the F4 key twice so that you lock the row reference, but not the column.
   4. Press Ctrl + Enter.
   5. Copy the formula in cell C4 down one row to cell C5.
   6. Click back in cell C4.
   7. Copy the formula in cell C4 across one column to cell D4.

After you have the formula to the cells C4, C5, and D4, put each cell in Edit mode and take a look at how the Mixed Cell References change throughout the copy action.

In Figure 398, we can see the reference C$3, and when we copy it down the rows (vertically), it remains locked on C$3 (Figure 399) because the $ is in front of the row reference. Lesson learned: *The $ sign in front of row reference means it is locked or absolute when copied across the rows (vertically).*

In Figure 398 we can see the reference C$3, and when we copy it across the columns (horizontally), it changes to D$3 (Figure 400) because there is no $ in front of the column reference. Lesson learned: *No $ sign in front of column reference means it is relative when copied across the columns (horizontally).*

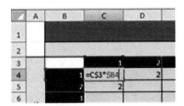 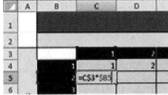 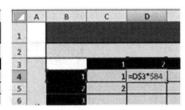

Figure 398   **Figure 399**   **Figure 400**

In Figure 398, we can see the reference $B4 and when we copy it across the columns (horizontally), it remains locked on $B4 (see Figure 400) because the $ sign is in front of the column reference. Lesson learned: *The $ sign in front of column reference means it is locked or absolute when copied across the columns (horizontally).*

In Figure 398 we can see the reference $B4, and when we copy it down the rows (vertically), it changes to $B5 (see Figure 399) because there is no $ in front of the row reference. Lesson learned: *No $ sign in front of row reference means it is relative when copied across the rows (vertically).*

 To understand how a mixed cell reference moves throughout the copy action is one of the more important Excel skills to have. In my opinion, it is one of the dividing lines between ordinary Excel users and Excel power users.

Now we want to copy our formula to the whole multiplication table.

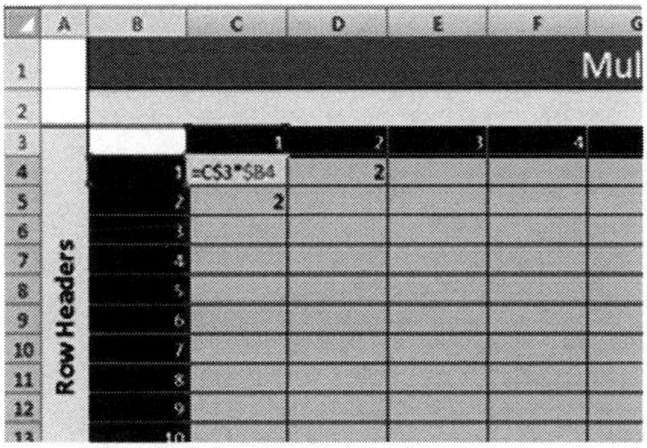

Figure 401

8. Highlight the range C4:N15.
9. Make sure C4 is the active cell.
10. Press F2.

It does not matter that there are some formulas in some of the cells, because they will all be replaced when we populate all the cells with the formula from the active cell.

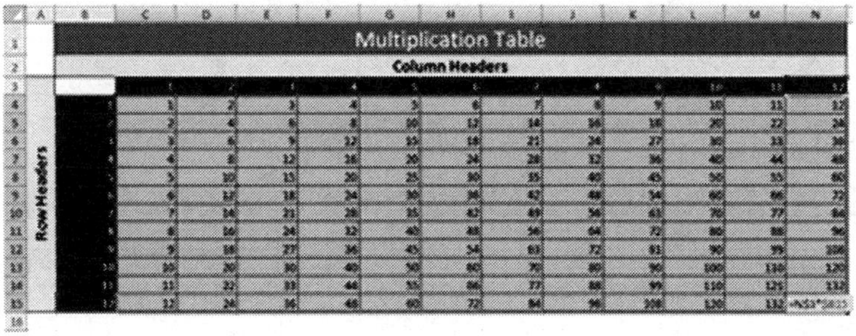

Figure 402

11. Use Ctrl + Enter to populate all the cells with the formula from the active cell.
12. Be sure to verify that all the formulas are correct.

When I was learning how to use mixed cell references and I would forget how they worked, I would quickly create this multiplication table to remind myself. This multiplication table exercise is good practice for learning mixed cell references.

So far we have only talked about single-cell references. But what about a whole range of cells? The same concepts we have seen so far apply to ranges of values. Let's take a look at an example.

To follow along, open the file named excelisfun-Start.xlsm and navigate to the CR(7) sheet.

In Figure 403, you can see in the range G2:G8 we have the sales rep's names and in the range H2:H8 we would like to create a formula that will add all the sales from the data set for each sales rep. Our goal is to create one formula using the SUMIFS function (talked about in detail in Chapter 3) in cell H2 and then copy it down. This formula is an illustration of adding with one criterion or one condition. So for example, in cell H2 we need to add all the cells in the E columns that correspond to all the Tinas found in column B. Tina is the criterion used to determine which records to add.

	A	B	C	D	E	F	G	H	I
1	Date	SalesRep	ProductSold	UnitsSold	Sales		SalesRep	Total Sales	
2	1/8/2010	Tina	Boom 15	27	$1,179.63		Tina		
3	1/3/2010	Shelia	Boom 15	20	$873.80		Shelia		
4	1/6/2010	Tina	Boom 14	23	$757.85		Bob		
5	1/1/2010	Bob	Boom 11	26	$492.70		Sioux		
6	1/6/2010	Tina	Boom 5	25	$350.00		Donita		
7	1/8/2010	Sioux	Boom 6	23	$343.85		Chin		
8	1/2/2010	Bob	Boom 5	24	$336.00		Don		
9	1/5/2010	Donita	Boom 6	18	$269.10				

Figure 403

1. On the workCR(7) sheet, select cell H2.
2. In H2 create the following formula:
   =SUMIFS(E2:E19

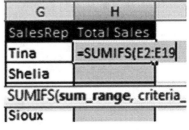

Figure 404

If you think about it, the sum_range argument for the SUMIFS, E2:E19, has to remain E2:E19 as we copy the formula down from Tina to Shelia. Why? Because each formula in each cell will have to look at the same sum_range to get the correct total. This means that because we are only copying down across the rows, we only need the dollar signs in front of the row references 2 and 19.

3. To lock the row references 2 and 19, press the F4 key twice.

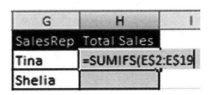

Figure 405

B	C	D	E	F	G	H	I	J
SalesRep	ProductSold	UnitsSold	Sales		SalesRep	Total Sales		
Tina	Boom 15	27	$1,179.63		Tina	=SUMIFS(E$2:E$19,B$2:B$19		
Shelia	Boom 15	20	$873.80		Shelia			
Tina	Boom 14	23	$757.85		SUMIFS(sum_range, criteria_range1, cri			
Bob	Boom 11	26	$492.70		Sioux			
Tina	Boom 5	25	$350.00		Donita			
Sioux	Boom 6	23	$343.85		Chin			
Bob	Boom 5	24	$336.00		Don			
Donita	Boom 6	18	$269.10					

Figure 406

4. Type a comma.
5. Select the range B2:B19. This range has all the criteria to determine which sales numbers to add.
6. Press the F4 key twice.

In Figure 406, we can see we locked the sum_range (numbers for adding) and the criteria_range1 (all criteria used to determine which numbers to add) so that when we copy the formula down each formula in each cell will be looking at the same range.

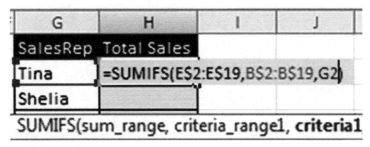

Figure 407

7. Type a comma.
8. Click one cell to the left.
9. Type a close parenthesis.

In Figure 407, the content of cell G2 (one cell to the left) is the criterion for adding. Each time the SUMIFS function finds a Tina in column B, it will jump over to the corresponding sales number in column E and use it for adding. The fact that this criterion is a relative cell reference is perfect, because when we copy the formula down it will move relatively and properly point to Shelia, then Bob, and so on.

	E		F	G	H	I	J	
	old	Sales		SalesRep	Total Sales			
27		$1,179.63		Tina	$2,641.48			
20		$873.80		Shelia	$1,314.20			
23		$757.85		Bob	$1,080.70			
26		$492.70		Sioux	$343.85			
25		$350.00		Donita	$534.40			
23		$343.85		Chin	$302.00			
24		$336.00		Don	=SUMIFS(E$2:E$19,B$2:B$19,G8)			
18		$269.10						

Figure 408

10. Press Ctrl + Enter to put the formula in the cell and keep the cell selected.

11. Double-click the fill handle with your crosshair cursor to copy the formula down.

12. Check the last cell to verify that the formula works.

In Figure 408, you can see that the last formula in our range is still looking at the locked sum_range E$2:E$19, the locked criteria_range1, B$2:B$19, and the relative reference, G8. Seven formulas for the time-price of one!

> **Note**: If you have to share your workbook with someone who does not have Excel 2007 or 2010, the SUMIFS function will not work because it does not exist in earlier versions. In that case you would use a formula like this:
>
>   =SUMIF(B$2:B$19,G2,E$2:E$19)
>
> See the CR(7) sheet for an example of this Excel 2003 formula.

In the next example, you will see how to use your knowledge of cell references to build a cross-tabulation summary report. You will also see how to use the SUMIFS function for adding with two criteria rather than one criterion like in our preceding example.

In Figure 409, you can see the data set and the end result for our cross-tabulated summary report. The range B22:H127 holds the raw data, and the range J22:N27 holds the cross-tabulated summary report where the products are listed as row headers and the regions are listed as column headers. This report requires that we add with two criteria. For example, in cell L24, we need to add all the sales from the Sales field (column) for the Carlota products sold in the MidWest region. Our formula will have to simultaneously look through three fields: 1) the Product field (looking for Carlota), 2) the Region field (looking for MidWest), and 3) the Sales field (to find the numbers for adding). This would be a hard report to create with formulas if we did not know how to use the four different types of cell references, but luckily we do, so we can create all 20 calculations with just one formula. Let's take a look at how to do this.

L24			fx	=SUMIFS($G$23:$G$127,$B$23:$B$127,$J24,$C$23:$C$127,L$22)								
	B	C	D	E	F	G	H	I	J	K	L	M	N
21													
22	Product	Region	SalesRep	Customer	Units	Sales	COGS		Product/Region	East	MidWest	West	South
23	Sunshine	East	Franks	KBTB	58	$1,102.00	$464.00		Sunshine	$4,313	$3,933	$5,415	$2,812
24	Sunshine	MidWest	Sioux	MNGD	17	$323.00	$136.00		Carlota	$2,530	$7,981	$4,485	$4,876
25	Sunshine	West	Franks	JAQ	59	$1,121.00	$472.00		Sunset	$420	$6,216	$2,058	$3,486
26	Carlota	MidWest	Chin	FRED	55	$1,265.00	$605.00		Quad	$5,805	$7,749	$5,454	$3,078
27	Sunset	MidWest	Franks	WFMI	44	$924.00	$407.00		Bellen	$3,586	$1,276	$4,400	$2,090
28	Quad	MidWest	Smith	TTT	61	$1,647.00	$884.50						
29	Quad	MidWest	Franks	ET	50	$1,350.00	$725.00						

Figure 409

To follow along, open the file named excelisfun-Start.xlsm and navigate to the CR(7) sheet.

J	K	L	M	N	O
SUMIFS(sum_range, criteria_range1, criteria1, [criteria_range2, **criteria2**],					
Product/Region	East	MidWest	West	South	
Sunshine	=SUMIFS($G$23:$G$127,$B$23:$B$127,$J23,				
Carlota	$C$23:$C$127,K$22)				
Sunset					
Quad					
Bellen					

Figure 410

1. On the CR(7) sheet, scroll down so you can see our data and template.
2. In cell K23 create the following formula:

=SUMIFS($G$23:$G$127,$B$23:$B$127,$J23,$C$23:$C$127,K$22)

Let's take a close look at our SUMIFS function and the five arguments that we used, as shown in Figure 410. The first argument is sum_range. We used an absolute reference that points to the Sales field because we need that range in all 20 cells. The second argument is criteria_range1. We used an absolute reference that points to the Product field because we need that range in all 20 cells. The third argument is criteria1. This is the argument where we must list the product name. Because the product names are listed as row headers in the report, we need to lock the column reference, but not the row reference. This way when we copy it to the right it will be locked on the product name, but when it is copied down it will move relatively to the next product name. The fourth argument is criteria_range2. We used an absolute reference that points to the Region field because we need that range in all 20 cells. The fifth argument is criteria2. This is the argument where we must list the region name. Because the region names are listed as column headers in the report, we need to lock the row reference, but not the column reference. This way when we copy it to the right it will move relatively to the next region name, but when it is copied down it will be locked on the region name.

J	K	L	M	N	O	P	Q
Product/Region	East	MidWest	West	South			
Sunshine	$4,313	$3,933	$5,415	$2,812			
Carlota	$2,530	$7,981	$4,485	$4,876			
Sunset	$420	$6,216	$2,058	$3,486			
Quad	$5,805	$7,749	$5,454	$3,078			
Bellen	$3,586	$1,276	$4,400	=SUMIFS($G$23:$G$127,$B$23:$B$127, $J27,$C$23:$C$127,N$22)			

Figure 411

3. Enter the formula and then copy it to the rest of the 20 cells.
4. Verify that the formula is correct by checking the last formula with the F2 key.

In Figure 411, we can see that the absolute ranges for the Sales field, Product field, and Region field remain correct after our copy action, and the criteria1 and criteria2 cell references are correctly looking at the last row header and column header, respectively.

Note: If you have to share your workbook with someone who does not have Excel 2007 or 2010, the SUMIFS function will not work because it does not exist in earlier versions. In that case, you would use a formula like this (example on CR(7) sheet):

=SUMPRODUCT($G$23:$G$127,--($B$23:$B$127=$J35),--($C$23:$C$127=K$34))

Note: This sort of cross-tabulation summary report can be done much more easily with a PivotTable. However, one of the advantages of this sort of formula method is that the formulas immediately update when any of the following occur:
- The raw data changes.
- You change the criteria listed in the cells.
- You use the Excel Table feature that allows dynamic ranges (as discussed earlier in this book).

Throughout the rest of the book, you will see many other examples of how to use the four universal cell references (relative, absolute, mixed with row locked, and mixed with column locked). Next we want to look at how the setup of the spreadsheet can profoundly affect the efficiency with which we can create formulas.

Assumption Tables / Formula Input Area

Now that we have talked about the awesome power of using formula inputs and cell references, we want to see that the setup for the formula inputs can help to reduce formula creation time and lead to efficient formula creation (creating and editing the maximum number formulas with the minimal amount of effort and time). In Figure 412, we can see a budget worksheet. The revenues for January through June are listed in row 3, and we need to create a formula in the range B4:G9 that will calculate the expenses based on our assumptions, or formula inputs. But which formula inputs should we use? Should we use the percentages in the range B14:B19 (vertical orientation), or should we use the percentages in the range A23:F23 (horizontal orientation)? If you do not know how to use mixed cell references, it does not matter which one you use. However you would have to create six individual formulas rather than just one formula. If you know how to use mixed cell references, you would use the percentages in the range B14:B19 and you would have to create only one formula.

	A	B	C	D	E	F	G	H
1					Budget			
2		Jan	Feb	Mar	Apr	May	Jun	Total
3	Revenue	1,000.00	1,250.00	1,370.00	1,250.00	2,000.00	2,215.00	9,085.00
4	Expense1							-
5	Expense2							-
6	Expense3							-
7	Expense4							-
8	Expense5							-
9	Expense6							-
10	Total Expenses	-	-	-	-	-	-	-
11	Net Income	1,000.00	1,250.00	1,370.00	1,250.00	2,000.00	2,215.00	9,085.00
12								
13	Assumptions - Formula Inputs							
14	Expense1	5.00%						
15	Expense2	7.50%						
16	Expense3	15.50%						
17	Expense4	22.50%						
18	Expense5	4.50%						
19	Expense6	12.00%						
20								
21	Assumptions - Formula Inputs							
22	Expense1	Expense2	Expense3	Expense4	Expense5	Expense6		
23	5.00%	7.50%	15.50%	22.50%	4.50%	12.00%		

Figure 412

This means that if you know how to use mixed cell references, you can finish the expense formulas six times faster than other people who do not know how to use mixed cell references. The rule of thumb for remembering which direction to orient your formula inputs (assumption table) is to keep the labels in the assumption table parallel to the labels in the formula range. (The word *table* in the phrase *assumption table* does not refer to table format structure or Excel table.) In our example, because the labels in the formula range are oriented vertically (Expense1 to Expense6), we must create an assumption table that also has the labels oriented vertically (Expense1 to Expense6). If our formula range were oriented horizontally, we would make our assumption table with a horizontal orientation. Let's take a look at how to create the formula.

To follow along, open the file named excelisfun-Start.xlsm and navigate to the Assumptions sheet.

◢	A	B	C	D	E	F	G	
1				Budget				
2		Jan	Feb	Mar	Apr	May	Jun	To
3	Revenue	1,000.00	1,250.00	1,370.00	1,250.00	2,000.00	2,215.00	
4	Expense1	=B$3*$B14						
5	Expense2							
6	Expense3							
7	Expense4							
8	Expense5							
9	Expense6							
10	Total Expenses	-	-	-	-	-	-	
11	Net Income	1,000.00	1,250.00	1,370.00	1,250.00	2,000.00	2,215.00	
12								
13	Assumptions - Formula Inputs							
14	Expense1	5.00%						
15	Expense2	7.50%						
16	Expense3	15.50%						
17	Expense4	22.50%						
18	Expense5	4.50%						
19	Expense6	12.00%						

Figure 413

1. Highlight range B4:G9.
2. Make sure that the active cell is B4.
3. Create the following formula: **=B$3*$B14**
4. Use Ctrl + Enter to populate all the cells with the formula.

	A	B	C	D	E	F	G	H
1				Budget				
2		Jan	Feb	Mar	Apr	May	Jun	Total
3	Revenue	1,000.00	1,250.00	1,370.00	1,250.00	2,000.00	2,215.00	9,085.00
4	Expense1	50.00	62.50	68.50	62.50	100.00	110.75	454.25
5	Expense2	75.00	93.75	102.75	93.75	150.00	166.13	681.38
6	Expense3	155.00	193.75	212.35	193.75	310.00	343.33	1,408.18
7	Expense4	225.00	281.25	308.25	281.25	450.00	498.38	2,044.13
8	Expense5	45.00	56.25	61.65	56.25	90.00	99.68	408.83
9	Expense6	120.00	150.00	164.40	150.00	240.00	=G$3*$B19	
10	Total Expenses	670.00	837.50	917.90	837.50	1,340.00	1,484.05	6,086.95
11	Net Income	330.00	412.50	452.10	412.50	660.00	730.95	2,998.05
12								
13	Assumptions Formula Inputs							
14	Expense1	5.00%						
15	Expense2	7.50%						
16	Expense3	15.50%						
17	Expense4	22.50%						
18	Expense5	4.50%						
19	Expense6	12.00%						

Figure 414

5. Verify that the formula is correct.

In Figure 413 and Figure 414, you can see that the cell reference that points to the monthly revenue is locked on the row reference so that as we copy it down, across the rows, it will remain locked on the month revenue, but when it is copied to the right, across the columns, the cell reference will move relatively to the next monthly revenue. Similarly, the cell reference that points to the percentage will move relatively when it is copied down across the rows and locked as it is copied across the columns.

Our rules for efficient assumption table creation are below.

Efficient Assumption Table – Formula Input Rules

Labels in formula range and assumption table must be parallel to use mixed cell references to reduce formula creation time.

The assumption table should be placed away from the formula range and have formatting that is different from the formula range. This helps to distinguish formula inputs from formulas.

The assumption table should be clearly labeled so that each formula input is unambiguous and can be easily understood by the user of the spreadsheet.

Our next Excel Efficiency-Robust Rule is as follows:

Rule 29: To save time in formula creation and to create spreadsheets that are easy to use, formula inputs should be put into an assumption table created with these rules in mind: 1) Labels in the formula range and assumption table are parallel, 2) the assumption table is set off to the side and distinctly formatted, and 3) formula inputs are unambiguously labeled.

Efficient Formula Creation

You have already been exposed to the term *efficient formula creation* a few times in this book. Efficient formula creation means creating and editing the maximum number formulas with the minimal amount of effort and time.

Our next Excel Efficiency-Robust Rule is as follows:

Rule 30: The rules for efficient formula creation are: 1) If a formula input can vary, put it into a cell and refer to it in your formula with a cell reference; 2) label all formula inputs; 3) if a formula input does not vary, type it directly into the formula; 4) learn how to use all four types a cell references effectively; 5) orient your assumption table so that the labels in the formula range and assumption table are parallel.

Next we want to talk about the Scenario feature, which is great for what-if analysis when you have assumption tables with multiple scenarios.

What-If Analysis

What-if analysis is when you ask a question like, what if the expenses go up by 10%? In Figure 415, we can see two sets of assumptions for a budget. The one on the right is 10% more than the one on the left. If you goal is to be able to switch back and forth between these two scenarios and have your formulas update, we can save each scenario and access whichever one that we want using the Scenario Manager. This saves us time because we do not have to retype the numbers when we want to switch between scenarios.

Assumptions - Formula Inputs	
Expense1	5.00%
Expense2	7.50%
Expense3	15.50%
Expense4	22.50%
Expense5	4.50%
Expense6	12.00%

Assumptions - Formula Inputs	
Expense1	5.50%
Expense2	8.25%
Expense3	17.05%
Expense4	24.75%
Expense5	4.95%
Expense6	13.20%

Figure 415

Let's take a look at how to save and then retrieve these scenarios.

To follow along, open the file named excelisfun-Start.xlsm and navigate to the Scenarios sheet.

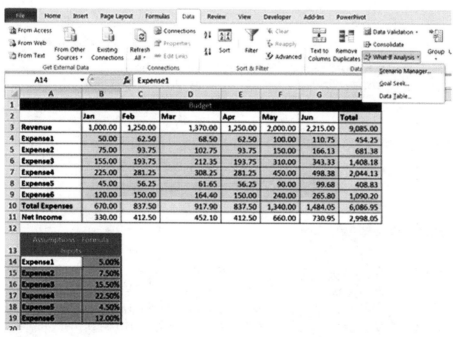

Figure 416

1. Select the range A14:B19.
2. Go to the Data tab, DataTools group, and click the drop-down arrow next to the What-if Analysis button, and then click Scenario Manager.

3. When the Scenario Manager dialog box appears, click the Add button

4. In the Scenario name field, type **Set 1**.

5. Click OK on the Add Scenario dialog box.

6. Click OK on the Scenario Value dialog box.

7. Click the Close button on the Scenario Manager dialog box.

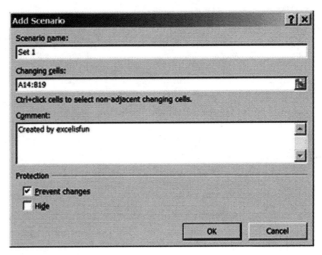

Figure 417

8. In the range B14:B19, enter the new percentages as shown in Figure 418.

9. Repeat steps 1 to 7 to add this second scenario with the name **Set 2**.

Assumptions - Formula Inputs	
Expense1	5.50%
Expense2	8.25%
Expense3	17.05%
Expense4	24.75%
Expense5	4.95%
Expense6	13.20%

Figure 418

In Figure 419, you can see that we have two scenario sets. Any time you want to show the one of your scenarios, you just open the Scenario Manager dialog box, select the scenario that you want, and click the Show button; all the formulas will update. You can store many scenarios and access them at any time.

Figure 419

Now we need to discuss the remaining three types of cell references. Next we will look at a worksheet cell reference.

Worksheet Cell References (sheet references)

Worksheet cell references, called sheet references, are cell references in a formula that come from a different sheet than the one that houses the formula. This is convenient because it means that you can store your assumption table (formula inputs) on any sheet in your workbook. In Figure 420, you can see two worksheets. The sheet on the left is named CR(8), and the sheet on the right is named CAR (for Controlling Accounts Receivable). On the CR(8) sheet, we need to create a formula that will check to determine whether the total for the schedule of accounts receivable in cell B11 is equal to the total for the controlling AR account on CAR in cell A5. This will require that we make a formula with a sheet reference. Let's take a look at how to do this.

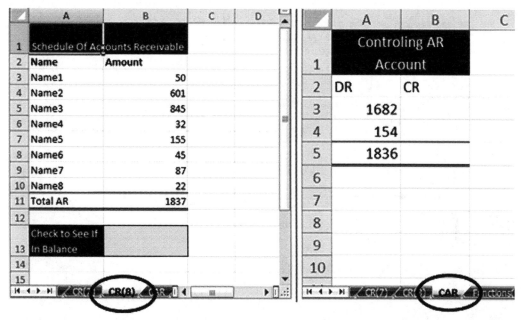

Figure 420

To follow along, open the file named excelisfun-Start.xlsm and navigate to the CR(8) sheet.

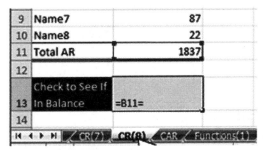

Figure 421

1. Click the CR(8) sheet.
2. Click in cell B13.
3. Type an equal sign.
4. Click the cell B11.
5. Type the comparative operator = (equal sign).

In Figure 421, you can see that we are building a logical formula. The first equal sign tells Excel that this is a formula, but the second equal sign is a comparative operator that will check to determine whether two things are equal. Because we need to check B11 on this sheet against A5 on the CAR, we need to add a sheet reference to our formula.

9	Name7	87
10	Name8	22
11	Total AR	1837
12		
13	Check to See If In Balance	=B11=
14		

Figure 422

6. To add a sheet reference to our formula, click the sheet with the name CAR with your white diagonal cursor.

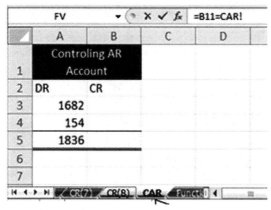

Figure 423

7. After you click the CAR sheet with your white diagonal cursor, the CAR sheet becomes the active sheet.
8. Notice in the formula bar we can see the sheet name and an exclamation point in the formula.
9. Also notice that the CR(8) sheet is highlighted in white to indicate that the formula is housed in CR(8) sheet.

In Figure 423 you can see that the formula bar shows us the sheet reference: CAR!

CAR is the name of the sheet, and the exclamation point is the symbol that Excel uses in formulas to indicate that this is a sheet name and not "text" or a defined name.

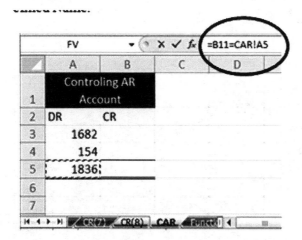

Figure 424

10. Click cell A5.

You can see the full sheet reference in the formula bar.

11. To enter the formula back in CR(8), press Enter.

Be careful. If you click back on the original sheet instead of pressing Enter, the sheet reference will not work.

Notice the formula in the formula bar.

In Figure 425, the formula result is FALSE.

B13			*f*ₓ	=B11=CAR!A5

	A	B	C	D
7	Name5	155		
8	Name6	45		
9	Name7	87		
10	Name8	22		
11	Total AR	1837		
12				
13	Check to See If In Balance	FALSE		
14				

Figure 425

The FALSE indicates that the two numbers are not equal. The schedule of accounts receivable and the controlling AR accounts are not in balance. The accountant in charge would then search for the cause of the problem. This sort of TRUE / FALSE logical formula can be very helpful in finding errors. Alternatively, you could use the IF function in this situation. (An example is presented later in the "Built-in Functions" section, later in this chapter.)

Note: In Figure 425, we can see the sheet reference, CAR!, and the cell reference, A5. By default, the cell reference is relative. You can change this easily to any one of the four universal references by using the F4 key to place the $ signs where you want them.

Note: If you are working between two worksheets and doing a lot of sheet references and cell references, it is helpful to open a second view of the workbook. To open a second view of the workbook and display two different tabs complete these steps:

1. On the View tab in the Window group, click the New Window button.

2. On the View tab in the Window group, click the Arrange All button.

3. Click the Vertical (or other) dialog button. This will cause two windows of the same workbook to appear.

4. In each of the duplicate windows, select a different sheet by clicking the sheet tabs.

Now when you create formulas, you can easily click back and forth between windows.

Notice that one of the windows shows a :1 in the title bar and the other shows :2.

To close the one of the duplicate windows, just use the red X to close one of the windows.

Note: If you have spaces in the sheet name, single apostrophes will appear in the formula. Figure 426 shows an example of what the formula would look like if the worksheet were named C AR rather than CAR.

=B11='C AR'!A5

Figure 426

Next we want to look at a workbook reference.

Workbook Cell References

A workbook reference is similar to a sheet reference, except when you build the formula, you don't click a cell in a different sheet, but instead you click a cell in a different workbook. When you make a workbook reference, the two workbooks become linked. As a result, you have to be careful not to delete or move the workbooks if you want them to remain linked. Let's take a look at how to do this.

To follow along, open the file named excelisfun-Start.xlsm and navigate to the CR(9) sheet. You will also need to open a second workbook named May Net Income.xlsm.

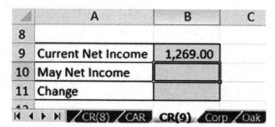

	A	B	C
8			
9	Current Net Income	1,269.00	
10	May Net Income		
11	Change		

CR(8) / CAR / **CR(9)** / Corp / Oak

Figure 427

  1. Click in cell B10 on the CR(9) sheet.

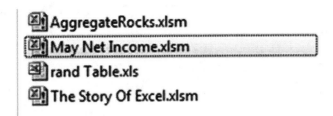

Figure 428

2. Open the second workbook using the Ctrl + O keyboard shortcut.
3. Double-click the file May Net Income.xlsm.

Figure 429

4. In cell B10 in the workbook where the formula will be housed, type an equal sign.
5. To jump to the other workbook, click the workbook icon on the taskbar with your white diagonal cursor (or you can use the keyboard shortcut Alt + Tab).

FV		='[May Net Income.xlsm]May'!$B$8
	A	B	C	D
1	Rev	10,000.00		
2	E1	900.00		
3	E2	654.00		
4	E3	85.00		
5	E4	958.00		
6	E5	6,522.00		
7	E6	12.00		
8	May Net Income	869.00		

Figure 430

6. After the new workbook opens, click cell B8.

Notice the workbook name in square brackets, the sheet reference syntax, and the fact that the B8 cell references are absolute by default.

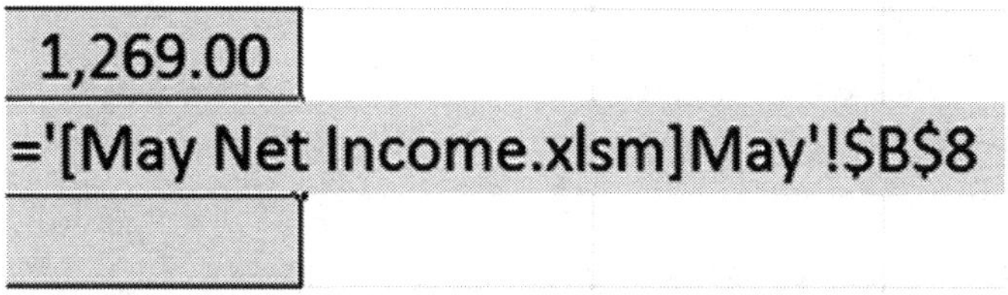

1,269.00

='[May Net Income.xlsm]May'!$B$8

Figure 431

7. To enter the workbook reference into cell B10 in the original workbook, press Ctrl + Enter (or Enter).
8. With B10 selected, press the F2 key to put cell in Edit mode.

In Figure 431 you can see the syntax used in workbook references:
- The workbook name appears in square brackets. Because square brackets are used in table formula nomenclature, there are single quotes around the workbook name (also sheet name).
- The syntax for sheet references is present (sheet name, exclamation point).
- Absolute cell reference. This is the default setting.
- If you close the workbook (in our example, the May Net Income.xlsm workbook), the file path will appear in the formula (see Figure 432).

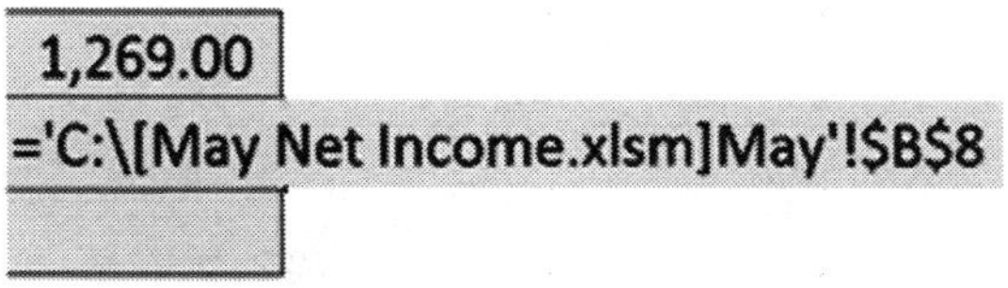

1,269.00

='C:\[May Net Income.xlsm]May'!$B$8

Figure 432

Note the file path appears in formula when the workbook is closed.

The fact that a workbook references is set up as an absolute cell reference by default is annoying. Often, you do not want an absolute cell references. In Figure 433, you can see that it is easy to change by putting the insertion point next to the cell reference and then using the F4 key to select the cell reference that you want.

1,269.00

='C:\[May Net Income.xlsm]May'!B$8

Figure 433

After you close the workbook with the workbook reference, the next time you open it you are asked if you want to update the link. Figure 434 shows the dialog box that you will see when opening a workbook with a workbook reference.

Figure 434

One last point about workbook references: If you move the workbook and need to reconnect the workbook reference to the workbook in the new location, you can do so by following these steps:

1. Click the File menu, then click the Edit Links to Files button in the lower-right corner. Or, go to the Data tab, Connections group, and click the Edit Links button.
2. Select the link in the list of links that you want to update.
3. Click the Change Source button.

In the next section, we will look at the final type of reference, the 3D cell reference.

3D Cell References

A 3D cell reference is a type of worksheet reference or workbook reference that spans more than one sheet. In Figure 435, you can see four different sheets with the names Corp, Oak, Sea, and Tac. On the Corp sheet, we need to add the totals from the other three sheets. For example, in cell B3 on the Corp sheet, we need to tally the Jan/Pro1 totals from the other three sheets. Doing it by hand we would get $14 + 9 + 8 = 31$.

Because the layout is the same on each sheet and the number to add is in cell B3 on each sheet, we can use a 3D cell reference. Our formula will look like this:

=SUM(Oak:Tac!B3)

This formula says, "Please add up all the B3s from Oak to Tac." The colon between the sheets indicates that if we were to insert any sheets between the two "bookend sheets" Oak and Tac the formula would update by including the new sheet in the calculation. The exclamation point (as mentioned previously) indicates that the formula is using a sheet reference. The fact that there is more than one B3 cell reference is the reason it is called a 3D cell reference; it is as if the B3s are stacked on top of each other in three dimensions. Now, let's see how to do this with the SUM function and a 3D cell reference.

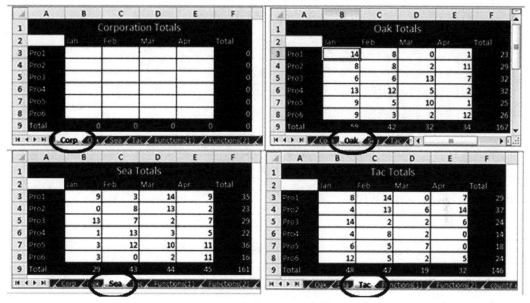

Figure 435

To follow along, open the file named excelisfun-Start.xlsm and navigate to the Corp sheet.

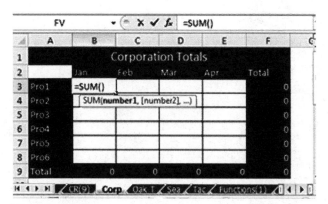

Figure 436

1. On the Corp sheet, click in cell B3.
2. Use the Alt + = keyboard shortcut for the SUM function.

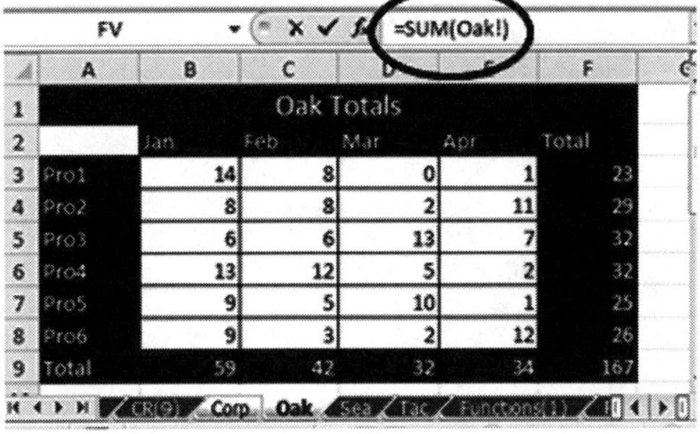

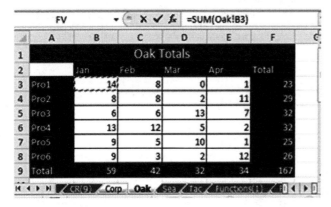

Figure 437

3. Click the Oak sheet (first sheet in sequence).

Notice that the sheets become a white color to indicate that they are being used in the formula.

Notice the sheet reference beginning to emerge in the formula bar.

Figure 438

4. Click cell B3.

Notice the B3 appear in the formula in the formula bar.

FV				=SUM(Oak:Tac!B3)		
	A	B	C	D	E	F
1			Oak Totals			
2		Jan	Feb	Mar	Apr	Total
3	Pro1	14	8	0	1	23
4	Pro2	8	8	2	11	29
5	Pro3	6	6	13	7	32
6	Pro4	13	12	5	2	32
7	Pro5	9	5	10	1	25
8	Pro6	9	3	2	12	26
9	Total	59	42	32	34	167

Figure 439

5. Hold Shift, and then click the last sheet, Tac.

Notice that the formula is complete in the formula bar.

Notice that all the sheets are now a white color to indicate that they are all being used in the formula.

6. Press Ctrl + Enter to put the formula in cell B3 on the Corp sheet.

FV				=SUM(Oak:Tac!E8)		
	A	B	C	D	E	F
1			Corporation Totals			
2		Jan	Feb	Mar	Apr	Total
3	Pro1	31	25	14	17	87
4	Pro2	12	29	21	27	89
5	Pro3	33	15	17	20	85
6	Pro4	18	33	10	7	68
7	Pro5	18	22	27	12	79
8	Pro6	24	8	6	=SUM(Oak:Tac!E8)	
9	Total	136	132	95	111	474

Figure 440

7. Copy the formula throughout the range B3:E8.
8. Verify that the formula is correct.

The beautiful thing about 3D cell references is that if you change the numbers on any of the sheets, or even insert a new sheet with a new template with the same layout between the Oak and Tac sheets, the formula on the Corp sheet will update perfectly!

In summary, to use a 3D cell reference, templates on each sheet need to have the same layout, and then you just complete these steps:
1. Add a SUM function on the summary sheet.
2. Click the first sheet in the sequence.
3. Click the cell address you want in the first sheet.
4. Hold Shift and then click the last sheet in the sequence.
5. Press Ctrl + Enter.

Next, we want to turn our attention to different methods of entering formulas into a cell.

Entering Formulas into Cells

Five different keystrokes will allow you to enter a formula into a cell, and depending on the situation, it can be more efficient to use one method over the other. Because you have already seen examples of all of these methods except Shift + Tab, we will just list the methods and potential advantages here. In addition, we will list one potentially dangerous method that can wreck formulas. The five methods for entering formulas and the one dangerous method are listed here:

- **Enter** will put the formula in the cell and select the cell below. It is most efficient to use this method if you are entering formulas vertically into a column. For example, if you are entering a formula into cell A1 and the next cell to get a formula is cell A2, then using Enter can save time.
- **Tab** will put the formula in the cell and select the cell to the right. It is most efficient to use this method if you are entering formulas horizontally into a row, moving from left to right. For example, if you are entering a formula into cell A1 and the next cell to get a formula is cell B1, using Tab can save time.
- **Ctrl + Enter** does two beneficial things:
    - If a single cell is selected, Ctrl + Enter will put the formula in the cell and keep the cell selected. It is most efficient to use this method if your goal is to put the formula into the cell and then immediately do something to the cell like copy it or format it. For example, if you are entering a formula into cell A1 and you immediately want to format the cell, Ctrl + Enter can save time.
    - If a range of cells is selected, Ctrl + Enter will populate all the cells with the formula from the active cell and keep the active cell selected. It is most efficient to use this method if you have one formula that will go into a block of cells or you are editing a block of cells. For example, if you are entering the same formula into all the cells in the range A1:D10, using this method can save time. This method will work on noncontiguous selected cells (cells that are not next to each other).
- **Shift + Tab** will put the formula in the cell and select the cell to the left. It is most efficient to use this method if you are entering formulas horizontally into a row, moving from right to left. For example, if you are entering a formula into cell D1 and the next cell to get a formula is cell C1, using Shift + Tab can save time.
- **Shift + Enter** will put the formula in the cell and select the cell above. It is most efficient to use this method if you are entering formulas into a column one on top of the other. For example, if you are entering a

formula into cell A5 and the next cell to get a formula is cell A4, using Shift + Enter can save time.

- *Never* use the mouse to enter a formula into a cell. The reason is that as soon as you type an equal sign into a cell, the mouse is programmed to insert cell references into the formula. As a result, if you try to click in a cell (not the cell with the formula) to enter the formula, you may insert the incorrect cell reference and wreck your formula.

Note: The default behavior for the Enter key is to go down. You can change this to go left or right by going to the File tab, Options button, Advanced category on left, Editing Options section.

Note: The default behavior for the Tab key is to move to the right. However, if you have a range like A1:B2 selected and the active cell (light-colored cell) A1 selected, pressing the Tab key four times will move the selected cell from A1 to B1 to A2 to B2 to A1.

Next we want to talk about how cell ranges can be more efficient than individual cells in formulas.

Efficient Formulas That Use Ranges

If you have a choice between the formula =A2+A3+A4+A5+A6+A7 and =SUM(A2:A7), it is more efficient to use =SUM(A2:A7) for these four reasons:

- It is faster to enter the formula =SUM(A2:A7) than it is to enter the formula =A2+A3+A4+A5+A6+A7.
- The formula =SUM(A2:A7) will accommodate structural updates like inserting rows, but the formula =A2+A3+A4+A5+A6+A7 will not.
- The formula =SUM(A2:A7) will accommodate structural like deleting cells, but the formula =A2+A3+A4+A5+A6+A7 will not.
- The formula =SUM(A2:A7) will accommodate inconsistent data (like numbers and words in the same column), but the formula =A2+A3+A4+A5+A6+A7 will not.

For example, in Figure 441 you can see that the cells D1, D2, and D3 have the same formula result from adding the numbers in column A, but three different formulas. (Formulas used in the D column can be seen in column E.) The first thing to notice is that the formula in cell D3 was the fastest to create. Using the SUM function and the cell range A2:A7 saves time when compared to the other three formulas.

	A	B	C	D	E
1	Sales		Inefficient formula because formula will not update when structural changes like inserting rows are made	$176.00	=A2+A3+A4+A5+A6+A7
2	$12.00		Inefficient formula because formula will not update when structural changes like inserting rows are made	$176.00	=SUM(A2,A3,A4,A5,A6,A7)
3	$45.00		Efficient formula because formula will update when structural changes like inserting rows are made	$176.00	=SUM(A2:A7)
4	$32.00				
5	$25.00				
6	$10.00				
7	$52.00				
8					
9					

H ◀ ▶ H / CR(9) / Corp / Oak / Sea / Tac **Ranges** / Functions(1) / Functions(2)

Figure 441

The second thing to notice is that if we were to insert a row at row 5, the =SUM(A2:A7) formula would update to include any new values, but the other two formulas would not update. Now, most people ask, "Yes, but my formula works, why should I worry about details like this?" The reason we all should worry about details like this is because formula creation time-saving tips like this add up over the long haul. The second reason is that structural updates are common for all spreadsheet users. And building formulas to accommodate updates is fundamental to Excel efficiency. Now, let's see what happens when we insert a row at row 5.

To follow along, open the file named excelisfun-Start.xlsm and navigate to the Ranges sheet.

	A	B	C	D	E
1	Sales		Inefficient formula because formula will not update when structural changes like inserting rows are made	$176.00	=A2+A3+A4+A6+A7+A8
2	$12.00		Inefficient formula because formula will not update when structural changes like inserting rows are made	$176.00	=SUM(A2,A3,A4,A6,A7,A8)
3	$45.00		Efficient formula because formula will update when structural changes like inserting rows are made	$176.00	=SUM(A2:A8)
4	$32.00				
5					
6	$25.00				
7	$10.00				
8	$52.00				

Figure 442

1. On the Ranges sheet, right-click the row header 5 (not cell A5), and on the drop-down menu click Insert.

Notice that a row is inserted and the numbers that were in row 5 and below get pushed down.

	A	B	C	D	E
1	Sales		Inefficient formula because formula will not update when structural changes like inserting rows are made	$176.00	=A2+A3+A4+A6+A7+A8
2	$12.00		Inefficient formula because formula will not update when structural changes like inserting rows are made	$176.00	=SUM(A2,A3,A4,A6,A7,A8)
3	$45.00		Efficient formula because formula will update when structural changes like inserting rows are made	$196.00	=SUM(A2:A8)
4	$32.00				
5	$20.00				
6	$25.00				
7	$10.00				
8	$52.00				

Figure 443

2. Enter the number **20** into cell A5.

Notice that the formulas in cells D1 and D2 do not include the cell A5. Notice that the formula in cell D3 does include the cell D5.

In Figure 443, we can see that when we insert a row and add a new number, the formula that uses a SUM function and a cell range rather than a list of individual cells, updates to show the correct total. This is because the original formula, =SUM(A2:A7), changes to =SUM(A2:A8). Using any function with a range such as this will update when you insert a row (or column) between the two end cells in the original range. Notice that the other two formulas in Figure 443 do not list the cell reference A5.

The third thing to take notice of is that if we deleted cell A2 (select cell A2, go to Home tab, Cells group, click the Delete button), the SUM function with the cell range will update perfectly. The other two formulas in Figure 444 will yield a #REF! error. A #REF! error means that a cell reference in a formula has been deleted or does not exist. When this happens, quickly undo the action with the keyboard shortcut Ctrl + Z, and then fix your formula or the data.

	A	B	C	D	E
1	Sales		Inefficient formula because formula will not update when structural changes like inserting rows are made	#REF!	=#REF!+A2+A3+A5+A6+A7
2	$45.00		Inefficient formula because formula will not update when structural changes like inserting rows are made	#REF!	=SUM(#REF!,A2,A3,A5,A6,A7)
3	$32.00		Efficient formula because formula will update when structural changes like inserting rows are made	$184.00	=SUM(A2:A7)
4	$20.00				
5	$25.00				
6	$10.00				
7	$52.00				

Figure 444

The fourth thing note is that if we were to add the word *none* (for no sales on that day) in cell A1, the SUM function with the cell range will update perfectly. The other two formulas in Figure 445 will yield a #VALUE! error. A #VALUE! error means that you put the wrong thing into a formula (wrong argument, operator, or data type). In our example, we used the wrong data type. Excel knows that it is not possible to add words and numbers.

	A	B	C	D	E
1	Sales		Inefficient formula because formula will not update when structural changes like inserting rows are made	#VALUE!	=A2+A3+A4+A6+A7+A8
2	none		Inefficient formula because formula will not update when structural changes like inserting rows are made	$164.00	=SUM(A2,A3,A4,A6,A7,A8)
3	$45.00		Efficient formula because formula will update when structural changes like inserting rows are made	$184.00	=SUM(A2:A8)
4	$32.00				
5	$20.00				
6	$25.00				
7	$10.00				
8	$52.00				

Figure 445

Our next Excel Efficiency-Robust Rule is as follows:

Rule 31: Use cell ranges in formulas whenever possible. For example, use the formula =SUM(A2:A7) rather than =A2+A3+A4+A5+A6+A7 because it is faster to create, it allows structural updates (like inserting rows or deleting cells), and it can handle inconsistent data (like numbers and words in same column).

Next we want to look more closely at Excel built-in functions.

Built-in Functions

Built-in functions (such as SUM and COUNTIF), are predefined formula elements that can help us complete tasks quickly. Examples of what functions can do include adding, counting, or looking up a value in a tax table. Each function is programmed to complete a specific task (such as adding or counting with one condition), and each function requires arguments, which are just the parts you put into the function like numbers for adding or the criteria for counting. The word *arguments* comes from math, but we will think of arguments simply as the required parts that the function needs to make the calculation. For example, the COUNTIF function needs two arguments: 1) the cell range with the elements that need to be counted, and 2) the criteria for counting.

We have already seen some of the amazing things that Excel's built-in functions can do:
- The SUM function can add numbers.
- The SUMIFS function can add only certain numbers in a list if we tell it what the criteria is for adding.

- The COUNT function will count the numbers in a list.
- The AVERAGE function will add up the values and divide by the count to give us an average (typical value that represents all the data points).
- The COUNTIF function can count only certain items in a list if we tell it what the criteria is for counting.
- The DOLLAR function will take a number and convert it to text with the Currency number format.
- The LARGE function can find a single large number or a group of large numbers among a list of numbers.
- The SMALL function can find a single small number or a group of small numbers among a list of numbers.
- The IF function uses a TRUE / FALSE test to put one of two things in a cell (one thing if the test yields TRUE, and the other thing if the test yields FALSE).

That is only 9 of the more than 400 functions that Excel offers! If we don't have all the function names memorized, how can we find the function that we want? Lucky for us, Excel's Insert Function dialog box can help us to find exactly the function we want. Let's take a look at how this works.

To follow along, open the file named excelisfun-Start.xlsm and navigate to the Functions(1) sheet.

Finding Functions with the Insert Function Dialog Box

So here is the situation: Suppose you get a lump sum of money ($14,000) that you don't need to use for five years. The CD contract says it will pay 5.5% annual interest compounded quarterly. Our goal is to find a built-in function that will calculate what this CD will be worth when we withdraw it.

FV Function for Investment Value

Although we briefly talked about the FV function earlier in this chapter, we will assume that you are unfamiliar with the function to help illustrate how to search for a function.

	A	B
2	Yearly Contribution	$14,000.00
3	Assumed Annual Rate	4.00%
4	Years Invested	5
5	Number of periods per year	4
6	Period Rate	=B3/B5
7	Total Periods	
8	Investment Worth	

Figure 446

1. Click the Functions(1) sheet.
2. Click in cell B6.

Notice that we are given an annual rate of 5.5%, but we earn interest four times a year (that is what *compounded quarterly* means).

3. Because we can't use an annual rate in our calculation if we are given interest compounded quarterly, we must create the formula for period rate (Annual Rate / Number of Periods). So we must create the following formula:

   =B3/B5

4. Press Enter.

Anytime you are given an annual rate that is compounded more than one time a year, you should be happy! You will earn more interest during any given year when you earn an annual interest rate compounded quarterly than you would if it were compounded just once (even more if they give you interest compounded 365 times a year). Compounding just means how many times per year they add interest to your account. However, if they do compounding, you can't use the annual rate in your calculation, but instead you must use the period rate. The period rate is just the annual rate divided by the number of compounding periods in the year. Similarly, if we are compounding, we must calculate the total number of periods. The total number of periods equals years times compounding periods per year.

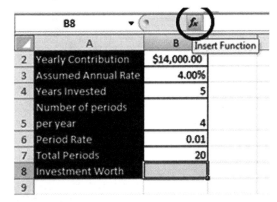

	A	B
2	Yearly Contribution	$14,000.00
3	Assumed Annual Rate	4.00%
4	Years Invested	5
5	Number of periods per year	4
6	Period Rate	0.01
7	Total Periods	=B4*B5
8	Investment Worth	
9		

Figure 447

> 5. In cell B7, calculate the Total Periods with the following formula:
>   **=B4*B5**
> 6. Press Enter.

Now we need to find a way to calculate investments worth when the CD is withdrawn. To do this, we will search the Insert Functions dialog box for the right built-in Excel function.

B8	▼	f_x

	A	B	Insert Function
2	Yearly Contribution	$14,000.00	
3	Assumed Annual Rate	4.00%	
4	Years Invested	5	
5	Number of periods per year	4	
6	Period Rate	0.01	
7	Total Periods	20	
8	Investment Worth		
9			

Figure 448

> 7. With cell B8 selected, click the Insert Function button on the formula bar (keyboard shortcut is Shift + F3).

Notice the button looks like function notation from algebra (fx)

Figure 449

After you click the Insert Function button, the Insert Function dialog box will pop up.

    8. In the Search for a Function field, type **investment**.

    9. Press Enter.

Notice that a list of functions such as NPV, NPER, and FV show up in the Select a Function field.

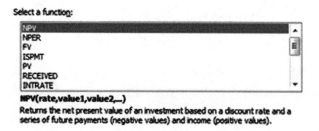

Figure 450

Notice that the NPV function gives a description of what the function does and in bold it shows the arguments requires for the function.

    10. The NPV description does not fit our needs, so let's, click the next function, NPER.

11. When you click the next function, NPER, you can see that the description does not fit our needs.

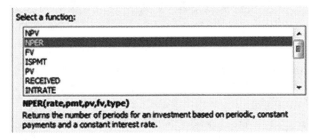

Figure 451

12. When you click the next function, FV, you can see that the description seems to fit our needs. We have a constant payment (one lump sum) and we have a constant rate.

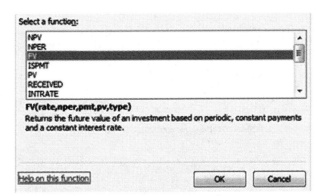

Figure 452

13. Click the OK button to insert the function into cell B8.

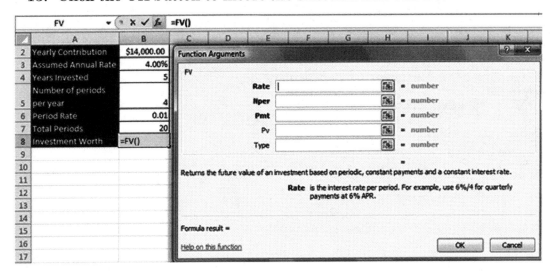

Figure 453

In Figure 453, we can see the Functions Arguments dialog box. In cell B8 and the formula bar, you can see the beginnings of our FV (Future Value) function formula. In the dialog box on the left, you can see the five arguments for the FV function listed vertically on the left with a field for each argument input. In addition, as you select each field, the description of the function argument will give you hints about what is required for each argument in the middle of the dialog box. Let's take a look at how this works.

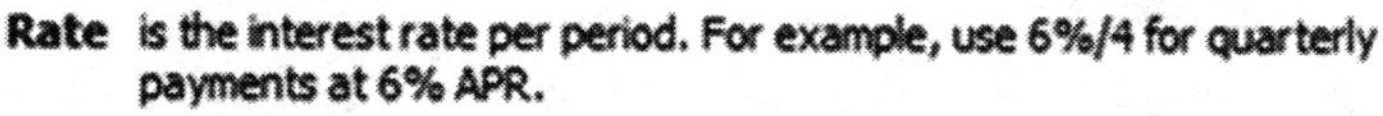

Rate is the interest rate per period. For example, use 6%/4 for quarterly payments at 6% APR.

Figure 454

14. With you cursor flashing in the Rate Argument field, read the description of the rate argument.

=FV(B6)
B
C
D
E
F
G
H
I
$14,000.00
4.00%
5
4
0.01
20
=FV(B6)
Function Arguments
FV
Rate
B6
= 0.01
Nper
= number
Pmt
= number
Pv
= number
Type
= number

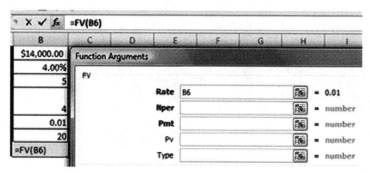

Figure 455

15. With you cursor flashing in the Rate Argument field, click in cell B6.

Notice that B6 is inserted into the Rate Argument field and the formula in cell B6 and in the formula bar.

Notice that the Rate field is followed by an equal sign and it shows the number result from cell B6, which in our case is 0.01. This preview of what the functions sees in the cell can be helpful for tracking down errors.

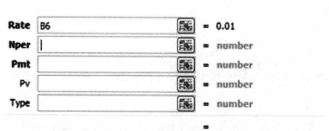

16. Press Tab to move to the next Function Argument dialog box.

Rate
B6
= 0.01
Nper
= number
Pmt
= number
Pv
= number
Type
= number
e of an investment based on periodic, constant payments and a constant interes
Nper is the total number of payment periods in the investment.

Figure 456

Because the function argument, Nper, does not have a name that helps us figure out what should go in this argument, we will read the description of the function argument in the middle of the Functions Arguments dialog box (Figure 456).

17. Because the Nper argument requires the total number of periods, click B7.
18. Press Tab

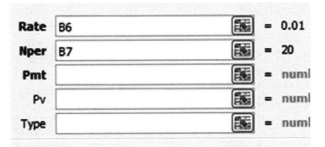

Figure 457

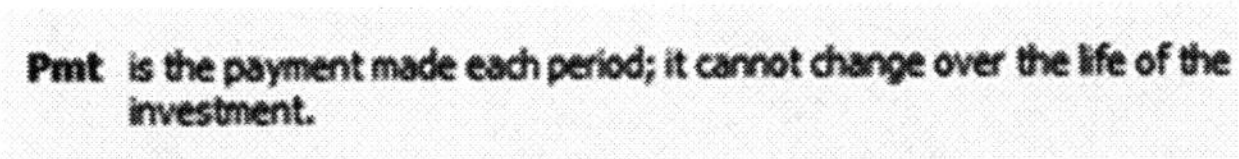

Pmt is the payment made each period; it cannot change over the life of the investment.

Figure 458

19. Read the description of the Pmt argument.

We are not making periodic payments, we are depositing one lump sum amount and so we need to leave this argument empty (If you looked in Help, you would see that it says to leave this empty.)

20. To leave the Pmt argument empty, press Tab.

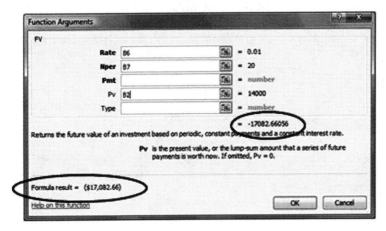

Figure 459

21. After reading the description of the Pv argument, we realize that we do have a lump sum amount and so we must click cell B2.

Notice that the preview of the number in cell B2 is 14000. Notice that you can see the formula result (both formatted and unformatted). Notice that the formula result is negative. This can't be right!

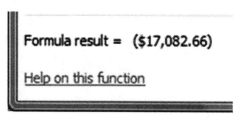

Formula result = ($17,082.66)

Help on this function

22. -$17,082.66 could not possibly be the right number. So we will click the blue Help on this function link.

Figure 460

In Figure 460, we see a Help on This Function link. The help that this link provides is simply amazing. Anytime you find a great new function, or you are having a hard time with a function that you use often, this help link will usually provide great help. There are descriptions of the arguments, remarks, and examples. In Figure 461, you can see that we have scrolled down to the remarks and the first example. Notice that the remarks and the example show that deposits into savings are represented by negative numbers. This is true because the direction of the cash flows are out of your wallet and into the bank. Financial functions like the FV understand cash coming in to your wallet as a positive and cash coming out of your wallet as a negative. So now we need to go back and change the $14,000 into the CD to a -$14,000.

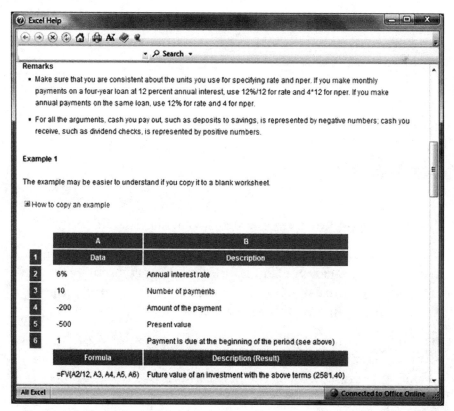

Figure 461

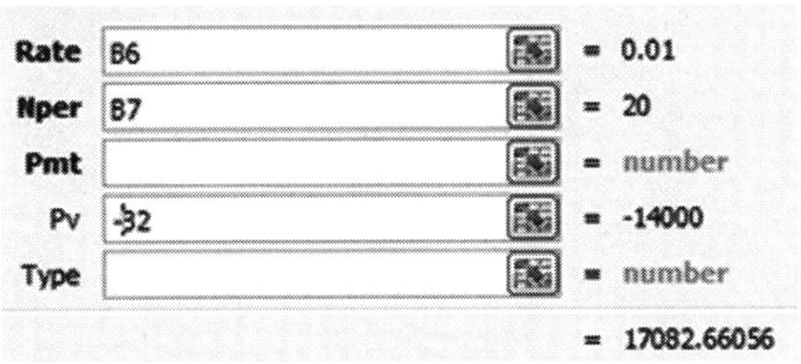

Rate	B6		=	0.01
Nper	B7		=	20
Pmt			=	number
Pv	-B2		=	-14000
Type			=	number
			=	17082.66056

Figure 462

23. Click the red X in the upper-right corner of the Help window.
24. Click in the Pv argument field and type a negative sign (minus) in front of B2.

Notice that the preview of this argument shows -14000 and the preview of the answer has changed to 17,082.66.

25. Press Tab

The Type argument is for the payment, not the lump sum amount, and so we can leave this argument blank.

26. Click OK

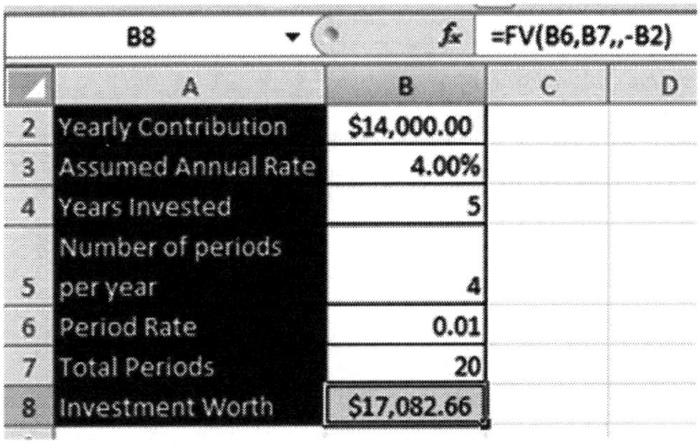

	B8 ▼	f_x	=FV(B6,B7,,-B2)	
	A	B	C	D
2	Yearly Contribution	$14,000.00		
3	Assumed Annual Rate	4.00%		
4	Years Invested	5		
5	Number of periods per year	4		
6	Period Rate	0.01		
7	Total Periods	20		
8	Investment Worth	$17,082.66		

Figure 463

Notice that the formula bar shows the formula with the FV function.

Notice that the arguments we did not use show commas with nothing entered for that argument. This convention is important to remember because it is often the case that you must skip an argument. If you forget to put a comma in for a skipped argument, the answer will not be correct.

As you just saw, the FV function is convenient for calculating an investment's worth at maturity (when you withdraw the funds). If you had never done any finance calculations before, the FV Functions Arguments dialog box and the Help might not make much sense (with positive and negative cash flows and all else), but if you did know a little finance, then the Functions Arguments dialog box and the Help are very useful. This just means that whatever field you are in (financial, statistical, engineering, or whatever), when you look up the functions you need, it should be quite easy to figure out how to use them. You can teach yourself many of Excel's built-in functions just by reading the help and trying the examples that are given in the Help menu.

Our next Excel Efficiency-Robust Rule is this:

Rule 32: Use the Insert Functions dialog box to find functions and use the function Help to learn how to use a specific function.

Now, let's see another example of the Functions Arguments dialog box and the Help.

Figuring Out How a Function Works

If you calculate an average using the AVERAGE function and some of your values are zeros, but you don't want to have the zeros included in the calculation, the AVERAGE function will give you the wrong answer. But how would you know this? When you are using a function and you are not getting the answer you want, look in Help. Let's take a look at how to do this after we have already entered our formula into a cell.

To follow along, open the file named excelisfun-Start.xlsm and navigate to the Functions(1) sheet.

B29		fx	=AVERAGE(B11:B28)
	A	B	C	D
10	Names	Scores		
11	Student 1	88.5		
12	Student 2	52		
13	Student 3	0		
14	Student 4	68		
15	Student 5	78		
16	Student 6	81		
17	Student 7	82		
18	Student 8	0		
19	Student 9	55		
20	Student 10	85		
21	Student 11	79		
22	Student 12	74		
23	Student 13	91		
24	Student 14	0		
25	Student 15	0		
26	Student 16	0		
27	Student 17	67		
28	Student 18	78		
29	Average	54.36111111		

Figure 464

1. On the Functions(1) sheet, use the vertical scroll-down arrow to scroll down so that you can see the range A10:B29.
2. Click in cell B29.

Notice the AVERAGE function in the formula bar.

3. Click the Insert Function button (fx) on the formula bar.
4. Click the Help on This Function link.

5. Scroll down until you can see the Remarks.

The third button gives us the information we need: Cells with the value zero are included.

The sixth bullet gives us a hint about what we can do if we want to show the zeros, but not include them in the calculation.

Remarks

- Arguments can either be numbers or names, ranges, or cell references that contain numbers.
- Logical values and text representations of numbers that you type directly into the list of arguments are counted.
- If a range or cell reference argument contains text, logical values, or empty cells, those values are ignored; however, cells with the value zero are included.
- Arguments that are error values or text that cannot be translated into numbers cause errors.
- If you want to include logical values and text representations of numbers in a reference as part of the calculation, use the **AVERAGEA** function.
- If you want to calculate the average of only the values that meet certain criteria, use the **AVERAGEIF** function or the **AVERAGEIFS** function.

Figure 465

In Figure 465, we see that we can get help with a function. Bullet three suggests that if we don't want the zeros in our AVERAGE function calculation, we must get rid of the zeros. This is good if you don't mind the cells being blank. Bullet number six suggests a second method and this method will allow us to keep the zeros in the cells, but not include them in the calculation. This is great that Help gives us two methods to deal with zeros and the AVERAGE function! Why? Because some people like to show blanks in the cells when they are calculating an average and others like to show zeros in the cells (but not include them in the calculation) when they are calculating an average. Let's take a look at how to implement both of these methods.

Average Without Zeros Using Find

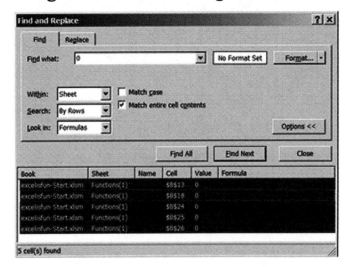

Figure 466

If our goal is to remove all the zeros from our data set without doing it manually, we can use the Find feature.

1. On the Functions(1), sheet, use the selection cursor to select the range B11:B28.
2. Use the Ctrl + F keyboard shortcut for Find.
3. Type a zero (**0**) in the Find What field.

4. Click the Options button.
5. Check the Match Entire Cell Contents check box.
6. Click the Find All button.
7. Use the Ctrl + A keyboard shortcut for Select All.

Notice that when we used Ctrl + A, all the cells listed in the Find and Replace dialog box are highlighted.

8. Click Close.

	A	B
10	Names	Scores
11	Student 1	88.5
12	Student 2	52
13	Student 3	
14	Student 4	68
15	Student 5	78
16	Student 6	81
17	Student 7	82
18	Student 8	
19	Student 9	55
20	Student 10	85
21	Student 11	79
22	Student 12	74
23	Student 13	91
24	Student 14	
25	Student 15	
26	Student 16	
27	Student 17	67
28	Student 18	78
29	Average	75.26923077

Figure 467

When you click Close, all the cells that contained zeros in the selected range are selected.

9. Press the Delete key.

Notice that all the selected cells do not have zeros, but instead they are blank.

Notice that the AVERAGE function now gives us the answer that we want.

Average Without Zeros Using the AVERAGEIF Function

If our goal is to keep all the zeros in our data set but not include them in the calculation, we can use the AVERAGEIF function. The AVERAGEIF function was a new function in Excel 2007 and did not exist in earlier versions. So if you were to open a spreadsheet that uses the AVERAGEIF is earlier versions, you would get a #NAME! error. A #NAME! error means that the formula sees the word AVERAGEIF in the formula, but it does not understand what it means.

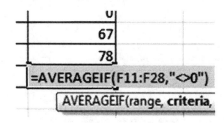

Figure 468

To follow along, open the file named excelisfun-Start.xlsm and navigate to the Functions(1) sheet.

1. On the Functions(1) sheet, click in cell F29 and create the following formula:

=AVERAGEIF(F11:F28,"<>0")

Just as we saw before with the COUNTIF function (Figure 312), you include the cell range with the numbers in the range argument and the criteria is enclosed in double quotes for the criteria argument.

2. Press Enter.

Notice that the average calculation is the same as back in Figure 467 when we removed the blanks.

F29		fx =AVERAGEIF(F11:F28,"<>0")				
	A	B	C	D	E	F
10	Names	Scores			Names	Scores
11	Student 1	88.5			Student 1	88.5
12	Student 2	52			Student 2	52
13	Student 3				Student 3	0
14	Student 4	68			Student 4	68
15	Student 5	78			Student 5	78
16	Student 6	81			Student 6	81
17	Student 7	82			Student 7	82
18	Student 8				Student 8	0
19	Student 9	55			Student 9	55
20	Student 10	85			Student 10	85
21	Student 11	79			Student 11	79
22	Student 12	74			Student 12	74
23	Student 13	91			Student 13	91
24	Student 14				Student 14	0
25	Student 15				Student 15	0
26	Student 16				Student 16	0
27	Student 17	67			Student 17	67
28	Student 18	78			Student 18	78
29	Average	75.26923077			Average	75.26923077

Figure 469

Note: If you have to share your spreadsheet with someone who is using Excel 2003 or earlier, the AVERAGEIF function will not work, but instead give you a #NAME? error. Here is an alternative formula that will work in versions of Excel 2003 or earlier:

=SUMIF(F11:F28,"<>0")/COUNTIF(F11:F28,"<>0")

You can see an example of this formula on the Functions(1) sheet.

Next we want to use the Insert Functions dialog box to see a list of all the available functions. This is a great trick if you just want to hunt around for potential functions that are available in Excel.

1. Click in cell B37 (or any cell).
2. To open the Insert Function dialog box, press Shift + F3.
3. Using the drop-down arrow next to the Or Select a Category field, select the All category.

Figure 470

If you select the first function in the list, you can use your down arrow to scroll through the list.

Notice that as you scroll through the list a description of each function appears.

Looking through this list is a great way to familiarize yourself with various functions that Excel offers.

4. Click the Esc key to close the Insert Function dialog box

Next we want to take a look at some of the most common functions that people use in Excel. We will look at functions like PMT for calculating a loan payment, MAX for finding the largest value, MIN for finding the smallest value, COUNTA for counting the total number of words, SUMIFS for adding with two criteria, COUNTIFS for counting with two criteria, AVERAGEIFS for averaging with two criteria, VLOOKUP for looking up values, and SUMPRODUCT for when you have to multiply and then add in succession.

PMT Function for Loan Payment Amount

If you are shopping around for a loan, the Excel PMT function will enable you to calculate a monthly loan payment on various loans so that you can compare and choose the best one. Let's take a look at how to use the PMT function.

To follow along, open the file named excelisfun-Start.xlsm and navigate to the Functions(1) sheet.

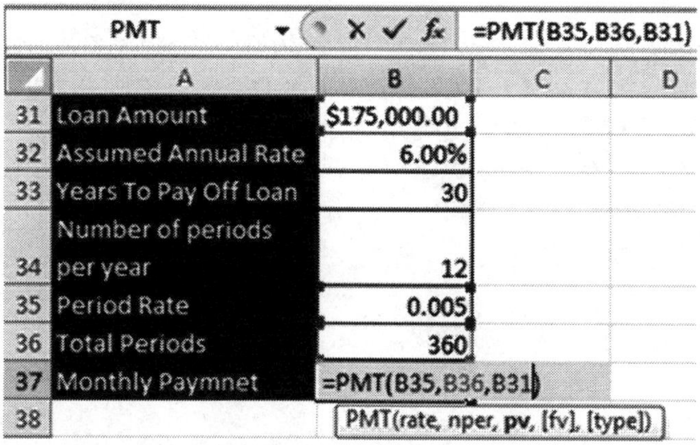

Figure 471

1. On the Functions(1) sheet, use the vertical scroll-down arrow to scroll down so you can see the range A31:B37.
2. Click in cell B37.

3. Create the following formula:
   =PMT(B35,B36,B31)
4. Press Enter.

Notice that your answer is -$1,049.21. Because this is a payment that comes out of your wallet (purse) each month, it shows as a negative.

In Figure 471, you can see that we use the rate, nper, and pv arguments. These arguments have the same names as the arguments we saw in the FV function (see Figure 459). This is because these financial functions are interrelated. Notice that one of the arguments in the PMT function is fv (just like the FV function), and if you look back to Figure 459, you will see that the FV function has an argument named pmt. This is convenient because if you know how to use the arguments for one, you know how to use them for the other financial functions. For example, the rate argument for our PMT function, just like the FV function, requires a period rate and not the annual rate. Our nper argument must have the total number of payments that we will make over the life of the loan. The pv argument means "present value" or value of the loan on the day it is issued. The screen tip shows the fv and type arguments in square brackets. This is a visual cue that these arguments can be left out of the formula if they are not required. The fv argument is used when you make an extra lump sum payment at the end of 30 years. Because we do not have a lump sum payment at the end in our contract, we will not use this argument. The type argument uses a 0 if the payment is made at the end of the month (like most consumer loans), and a 1 if the payment is made at the beginning of the month (like most leases). However, if you use the PMT Function Argument dialog box (or Help), it says that if you have a loan with payments at the end of the period we can leave that argument blank and by default it will assume that payments are made at the end of the period. Because our payments are made at the end of each month, we will leave the type argument blank. Remember also that because these financial functions understand cash flows, the payment is shown as a negative (out of your wallet or purse). Let's change some of the formula inputs and see how the PMT function will update.

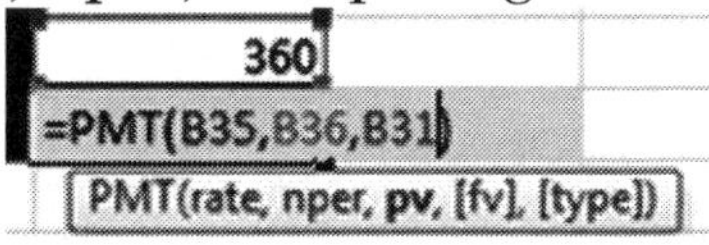

Figure 471

	A	B
31	Loan Amount	$175,000.00
32	Assumed Annual Rate	5.75%
33	Years To Pay Off Loan	25
34	Number of periods per year	12
35	Period Rate	0.004791667
36	Total Periods	300
37	Monthly Paymnet	-$1,100.94
38		

Figure 472

5. Change the annual rate to 5.75% and the Years to 25.

This loan contact indicates that we could pay off the loan five years earlier with an increase of about $50 per month.

Notice the power of Excel can help us to compare loan contacts and come to an informed decision.

Next we want to see how to use the functions MAX, MIN, COUNTA, SUMIFS, COUNTIFS, and AVERAGEIFS on a large data set (Figure 473). We are going to make calculations like "find the largest value in the Sales column," "find the smallest value in the Sales column," and "count the number of sales made between $1,000 and $1,500 in the Sales column." In each case, we will have to highlight the Sales column cell range, G2:G106. Because more than one formula will refer to the same range, over and over, we can instead assign the cell range an Excel defined name and use that defined name in our formula rather than the actual cell range. In our example, we will assign the defined name Sales to the cell range G2:G106, and then we can use the Sales name in all our formulas. The two big advantages of using defined names as a substitute for cell references in formulas is that 1) it saves time when you create many formulas that use the same range of cells, and 2) it will help reduce errors when selecting ranges (for example, selecting too many or too few cells for your range).

	A	B	C	D	E	F	G	H	I	J	
1	Date	Product	Region	SalesRep	Customer	Units	Sales	COGS		MAX	
2	1/26/11	Bellen	West	Pham	FRED	61	$5,000.00	$610.00		MIN	
3	1/10/11	Bellen	MidWest	Gault	FM	7	$154.00	$70.00		COUNTA	
4	1/3/11	Sunshine	South	Sioux	PCC	6	$114.00	$48.00		SUMIFS	
5	1/7/11	Sunset	West	Pham	T	61	$1,281.00	$564.25		Criteria 1	C
6	1/18/11	Sunshine	West	Sioux	AST	8	$152.00	$64.00		Criteria 2	P
7	1/20/11	Carlota	East	Chin	ET	59	$1,357.00	$649.00		COUNTIFS	
8	1/26/11	Bellen	MidWest	Gault	PSA	23	$462.00	$210.00		Criteria 1	>
9	1/7/11	Carlota	MidWest	Franks	HHH	12	$276.00	$132.00		Criteria 2	<
10	1/5/11	Carlota	West	Franks	ITTW	60	$1,380.00	$660.00		COUNTIFS	
11	1/17/11	Quad	East	Franks	HII	62	$1,674.00	$899.00		Criteria 1	
12	1/28/11	Sunshine	South	Smith	FRED	51	$969.00	$408.00		Criteria 2	
13	1/17/11	Quad	East	Gault	SFWK	43	$1,161.00	$623.50		AVERAGEIFS	
14	1/16/11	Bellen	MidWest	Sioux	YTR	56	$1,232.00	$560.00		Criteria 1	B
15	1/15/11	Sunshine	MidWest	Chin	YTR	11	$209.00	$88.00		Criteria 2	W
16	1/12/11	Bellen	South	Chin	WT	7	$154.00	$70.00		SUMIFS	
17	1/3/11	Sunset	South	Pham	WSD	23	$483.00	$212.75		OR Criteria 1	W
18	1/22/11	Carlota	South	Smith	KBTB	29	$667.00	$319.00		OR Criteria 2	N

Figure 473

You already saw an example of table names and table formula nomenclature in Chapter 3, in the section "Table Names and Table Formula Nomenclature." In that section, you saw how converting a range to an Excel table allowed us to use table names that were dynamic: When we added new records, the formula dynamically updated. If you do not require that your names are dynamic, the Excel Defined Name feature (not table names) is a great formula efficiency trick. Let's take a look at how to use the Excel Defined Name feature.

Defined Names Feature

Our goal is to name the Sales column (field) Sales and use it as a substitute for the range of cells in the Sales column. Let's take a look at how to do this.

To follow along, open the file named excelisfun-Start.xlsm and navigate to the Functions(2) sheet.

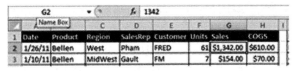

Figure 474

1. Click the Functions(2) sheet, and then click in cell G2.

Figure 475

2. To highlight the column, use the Ctrl + Shift + Down Arrow keyboard shortcut.

Notice that the keyboard shortcut Ctrl + Shift + Down Arrow is *much* faster than clicking in a cell and then dragging with the mouse.

Figure 476

3. Point to the Name box, and when your cursor turns to an I-beam cursor, click in the Name box.

Notice the cell reference, G2, is highlighted.

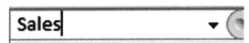

Figure 477

4. Type **Sales**.

5. Press the Enter key to register the name.

Figure 478

6. To test to determine whether the name registered, click in cell A4.

7. Point to the drop-down arrow next to the Name box.

8. Click the Sales defined name in the drop-down list.

When you select the name from the drop-down, the newly named range will highlight the Sales column.

Now that we have created this named range, let's use it in a formula to find the biggest value in the Sales column.

MAX for Finding the Largest Value

If our goal is to find the biggest number in a cell range that contains numbers, we can use the MAX function.

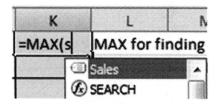

Figure 479

1. Click in cell K1 and type the following:
       =MAX(s

Notice that our defined name appears in our drop-down list and the icon for defined names looks like a name tag icon.

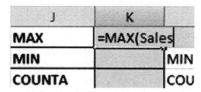

Figure 480

2. After your defined name is highlighted in blue, press Tab to insert the Sales name into the formula.

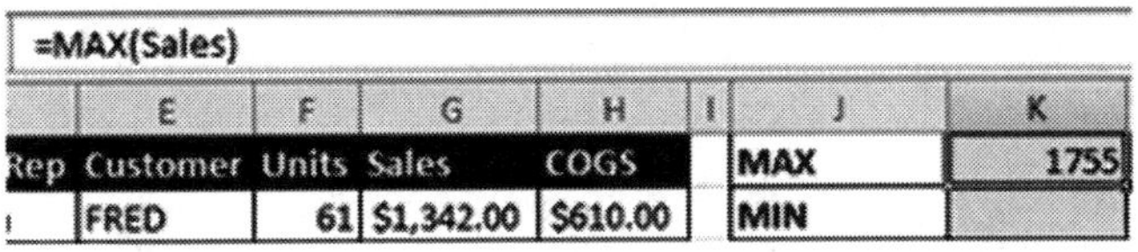

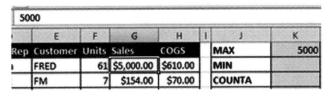

Figure 481

3. Without typing a close parenthesis, Press Ctrl + Enter.

Notice that the closing parenthesis is automatically added. (This is true for functions with only a few arguments.)

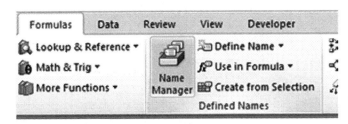

Figure 482

4. To test our MAX function and determine whether it works, click in cell G2.
5. Type **5000**.

Notice that the MAX function updates.

6. To undo the entering of 5000, press Ctrl + Z.

Defined Name Manager

Next, we want to check to determine whether our sales name is looking at the correct range. If it isn't, we may have formula mistakes. To verify, edit, delete, or create names, we can go to the Name Manager.

Figure 483

1. Click the formula tab.
2. Click the Name Manager button in the Defined Names group.

The keyboard shortcut to get to the Name Manager is Ctrl + F3.

Figure 484

3. Click the Sales defined name.

Notice that there is an Edit button and a Delete button so that you can edit and delete names that are not correct.

Notice that it shows the range G2:G106.

Even though G2:G106 is the correct range, we want to delete this name so that we can see what happens.

4. Click Delete.
5. Click OK.
6. Click Close.

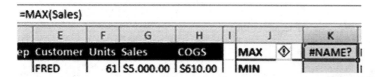

Figure 485

Notice in this figure that you can see the word *Sales* in the formula bar. If you put a word into a formula that is not a defined name or a function name, you will get this #NAME? error.

Create Names from Selection

As you can see in Figure 485, we have a problem. We actually have to name the Sales column again. But this time, we want to name all the columns with a single keyboard shortcut. This action is called create names from selection. You can do it two ways: 1) Click the formula tab, and then click the Create from Selection button in the Defined Names group, or 2) use the keyboard shortcut Ctrl + Shift + F3. Let's take a look at how to do this.

Figure 486

1. Click in cell A1.
2. To highlight the whole table use the **Ctrl + *** (* on number pad) keyboard shortcut.
3. To create names from selection press Ctrl + Shift + F3.
4. Uncheck the Left Column check box.
5. Click OK.

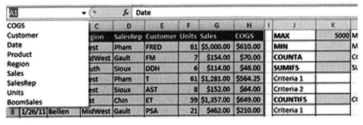

Figure 487

1. To verify that the names were created, click the drop-down arrow in the Name Box.
2. Notice that the MAX formula with the Sales name in cell K1 is no longer showing a #NAME? error.

Now let's use our names in formulas.

MIN for Finding the Smallest Value

If our goal is to find the smallest value in a range of values, we can use the MIN function.

To follow along, open the file named excelisfun-Start.xlsm and navigate to the Functions(2) sheet.

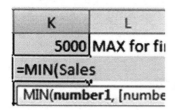

1. Click in cell K2.
2. Type =**MIN(**s.
3. Press Tab.
4. Press Enter.

Figure 488

Notice how fast you can create formulas when you are using defined names.

The minimum value should be 114.

Next, we want to count how many transactions, or records, that we have. Let's take a look at how to do this using the COUNTA function.

COUNTA for Counting the Total Number of Words

Back in Figure 199, we saw how to use the COUNT function. The COUNT function counts numbers. In our data set we have four columns with numbers: Date (remember that dates are serial numbers), Units, Sales, and COGS. We could use the COUNT function on one of these columns and it would tell us how many transactions we have; this is given that we have no blanks. But sometimes you want to count records and all you have are words or text. The COUNTA function can count text entries. Technically, the COUNTA function counts nonempty cells. (*Nonempty* means the cell could have numbers, TRUE, FALSE, words, formula errors, or even blanks delivered by a formula, as discussed later.) Our columns have only text entries, so the COUNTA function will work just fine. Let's take a look at how to use the Products column to count the total number of transactions in our data set.

1. Click in cell K3.
2. Type =**COUNTA(**pro.

Notice the drop-down list shows a gold name tag icon with the name Product and an fx icon with the function name PRODUCT.

Figure 489

3. Click the Down Arrow key one time to select the named range Product.

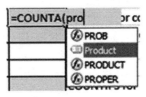

Figure 490

4. Press Tab to insert the name into the COUNTA function.

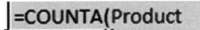

Figure 491

5. Press Enter. (You don't have to type the close parenthesis.)

You can see that there are 105 transactions in this data set.

	J	K
	MAX	5000
	MIN	114
	COUNTA	105

Figure 492

In the last few examples, you saw how defined names make referring to the columns in a data set fast and easy.

Next we want to take a look at how to use the SUMIFS function to add all the sales made by the sales rep, Sioux, to the customer, PCC. This means that we need a function that will look through the SalesRep column and find all the Sioux entries *and* look through the Customer column and find all the PCC entries, and then when a record has both Sioux *and* PCC, use the sales number from the Sales column in the adding calculation. The SUMIFS function can do just that. Let's take a look at how this works.

	A	B	C	D	E	F	G	H
1	Date	Product	Region	SalesRep	Customer	Units	Sales	COGS
2	1/26/11	Bellen	West	Pham	FRED	61	$5,000.00	$610.00
3	1/10/11	Bellen	MidWest	Gault	FM	7	$154.00	$70.00
4	1/3/11	Sunshine	South	Sioux	PCC	6	$114.00	$48.00
5	1/7/11	Sunset	West	Pham	T	61	$1,281.00	$564.25
23	1/6/11	Quad	West	Sioux	PCC	64	$1,728.00	$928.00
24	1/26/11	Sunset	South	Sioux	DFGH	44	$924.00	$407.00
29	1/7/11	Sunset	MidWest	Sioux	PCC	22	$462.00	$203.50
30	1/29/11	Bellen	East	Chin	AST	50	$1,100.00	$500.00
54	1/10/11	Quad	East	Smith	DFR	17	$459.00	$246.50
55	1/17/11	Bellen	MidWest	Smith	PCC	16	$352.00	$160.00
101	1/18/11	Sunshine	MidWest	Chin	PCC	62	$1,178.00	$496.00
102	1/28/11	Quad	South	Franks	YTR	44	$1,188.00	$638.00
103	1/17/11	Carlota	East	Sioux	PCC	39	$897.00	$429.00
104	1/18/11	Sunshine	East	Franks	AA	24	$456.00	$192.00

Figure 493

SUMIFS for Adding with Two Criteria

The **SUMIFS function** will add with two criteria; this just means that instead of adding all the sales, we will add only the sales that meet two conditions. (THE SUMIFS function can handle 1 to 127 criteria.) Back in Figure 59 to Figure 69 we saw how to use the SUMIFS function to add with one criterion. In those figures, we saw how to add just the sales numbers that belonged to Sioux. If you look in Figure 493, rows 4, 23, 29 and 103, all show transactional records where the sales rep, Sioux, made sales to the customer, PCC. (Some of the rows are hidden in Figure 493.) Our goal is to add these sales without having to do it manually. We have two criteria: The sales rep must be Sioux in the SalesRep column, *and* the customer must be PCC in the Customer column. If both of the criteria are met (both are TRUE), we must use the sales number in the Sales column for adding. In general terms, when both criteria say TRUE, we can use that record in our calculation. Let's take a look at how to do this next.

To follow along, open the file named excelisfun-Start.xlsm and navigate to the Functions(2) sheet.

SUMIFS	=SUMIFS(Sales	
SUMIFS(**sum_range**, criteria_range1, criteria1, ...)		
Criteria 2	PCC	

Figure 494

1. Click in cell K4.
2. Type **=SUMIFS(s**.
3. Press Tab.

The Sales name is the column the SUMIFS function will look in to find the numbers for adding. Notice that the name of this argument is sum_range.

SUMIFS	=SUMIFS(Sales,SalesRep	
Criteria 1	SUMIFS(sum_range, **criteria_range1**, criteria1, [cri	
Criteria 2	PCC	

Figure 495

4. Type a comma to get the next argument.

Notice that the next argument becomes bold indicating you should enter this argument.

Notice that the name of this argument is criteria_range1.

5. Type **s**.
6. Press the Down Arrow key one time.
7. Press Tab.

The SUMIFS function will use the named range, SalesRep in the criteria_range1 argument to look for the word Sioux.

SUMIFS	=SUMIFS(Sales,SalesRep,K5		
Criteria 1	Sioux		
Criteria 2	PCC		
COUNTIFS	SUMIFS(sum_range, criteria_range1, **criteria1**, [crit		

Figure 496

   8. Type a comma to get the next argument.

Notice that the name of this argument is criteria1.

   9. Click cell K5.

The SUMIFS function will use the criteria Sioux to find only the records that have the SalesRep Sioux.

=SUMIFS(Sales,SalesRep,K5,Customer		·ria	
Sioux			
PCC			
SUMIFS(sum_range, criteria_range1, criteria1, **[criteria_range2**, criteria2],			

Figure 497

   10. Type a comma to get the next argument.

Notice that the name of this argument is criteria_range2.

   11. Type **cus**.

   12. Press Tab.

The SUMIFS function will use the named range, Customer, in the criteria_range2 argument to look for the word PCC.

SUMIFS	=SUMIFS(Sales,SalesRep,K5,Customer,K6	·ria	
Criteria 1	Sioux		
Criteria 2	PCC		
SUMIFS(sum_range, criteria_range1, criteria1, [criteria_range2, **criteria2**],			

Figure 498

   13. Type a comma to get the next argument.

Notice that the name of this argument is criteria2.

   14. Click cell K6.

The SUMIFS function will use the criteria PCC to find only the records that have the Customer PCC.

SUMIFS	3201	SUMIFS for adding with two criteria
Criteria 1	Sioux	
Criteria 2	PCC	

Figure 499

> 15. Press Enter.

We have just added using two criteria and should have the formula result, 3201.

SUMIFS	1448	SUMIFS for adding with two criteria
Criteria 1	Chin	
Criteria 2	PCC	

Figure 500

> 16. Click in cell K5
> 17. Type **Chin**.

You should see the formula result change to 1448.

Notice that in our FV function example (Figure 446 to Figure 463) we used the FV Function Arguments dialog box to help us enter the arguments for a function and in our most recent example of the SUMIFS function (Figure 493 to Figure 499) we used the SUMIFS screen tips to help us enter the arguments for a function. How do you decide whether to use the Function Arguments dialog box or the screen tips to get help entering the arguments for a function? It depends on how much help you need. If you are entering a function for the first time and need a written description of what belongs in each argument, use the Function Arguments dialog box; but if you have used the function many times and know what belongs in each argument, just use the screen tip prompts.

> **Note**: If you have to share your spreadsheet with someone who is using Excel 2003 or earlier, the SUMIFS function will not work, but instead give you a #NAME? error. Here is an alternative formula that will work in versions of Excel 2003 or earlier:
>
> =SUMPRODUCT(--(SalesRep=K5),--(Customer=K6),Sales)
>
> You can see an example of this formula on the Functions(2) sheet.

We will look at how to use the SUMPRODUCT function later in this section.

Next we want to see how to count with two criteria using the COUNTIFS function.

COUNTIFS for Counting with Two Criteria

Our goal for this formula is to count the number of sales made between $1,000 and $1,500 in the Sales column. Specifically, we want to count the number of sales that are greater than or equal to $1,000 *and* less than $1,500. We can use the COUNTIFS function for counting when there are one or more criteria (up to 127 criteria). In this situation, we have two criteria. The first criterion is that the number must be greater than or equal to $1,000 and the second is that the number must be less than $1,500. *Both* must be TRUE for the COUNTIFS function to count the record.

Back in Figure 312, we saw the COUNTIF function, but that function can count with only one criterion. Because we have two criteria, we cannot use the COUNTIF function. Instead, we will use the COUNTIFS function. The COUNTIFS function was a new function in Excel 2007 and did not exist in earlier versions. So if you were to open a spreadsheet that uses the COUNTIFS is earlier versions, you would get a #NAME! error. A #NAME! error means that the formula sees the word COUNTIFS in the formula, but it does not understand what it means.

Let's take a look at how to get this function to work.

To follow along, open the file named excelisfun-Start.xlsm and navigate to the Functions(2) sheet.

1. Click in cell K8.
2. Type **>=1000**.
3. Press Enter.

COUNTIFS	
Criteria 1	>=1000
Criteria 2	

Figure 501

In Figure 501, we can see the criteria >=1000. Because there is not a single comparative operator for greater than or equal to (as there is in handwritten math), we have to use the two characters, > and =, in succession.

4. In cell K9, enter the criteria **<1500**.
5. In cell K7 and type **=COUNTIFS(s**.
6. Press Tab to accept the Sales name from the drop-down list.

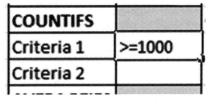

COUNTIFS	=COUNTIFS(Sales,K8
Criteria 1	>=1000
Criteria 2	<1500
COUNTIFS(criteria_range1, criteria1, [c	

Figure 502

Notice that the defined name Sales was entered in as the criteria_range1 argument.

7. Type a comma.
8. Click cell K8 to enter our first criteria into the criteria1 argument.

COUNTIFS	=COUNTIFS(Sales,K8,Sales	g with tv
Criteria 1	>=1000	
Criteria 2	<1500	
COUNTIFS(criteria_range1, criteria1, [criteria_range2, criteria2]		

Figure 503

COUNTIFS	=COUNTIFS(Sales,K8,Sales,K9	g
Criteria 1	>=1000	
Criteria 2	<1500	
FS(criteria_range1, criteria1, [criteria_range2, criteria2], [		

Figure 504

COUNTIFS	30
Criteria 1	>=500
Criteria 2	<1000

Figure 505

9. Type a comma.
10. Type **s**.
11. Press Tab to accept the Sales name from the drop-down list and enter it into to the criteria_range2 argument.

12. Type a comma.
13. Click cell K9 to enter our second criteria into the criteria2 argument.
14. Press Enter.

You should get a count of 26.

As always, the beauty of Excel is in the fact that the formula inputs can be easily changed.

Change your formula inputs and see the magic in action. In Figure 505, I asked the questions: "How many sales were greater than or equal to $500 *and* less than $1,000."

Notice in Figure 505 that we have two criteria and both must be met for the record to be counted. Another way to think of this is as "between" criteria. The sales amount must be between $500 and $1,000. There is a lower end to the interval and an upper end, and in our case the lower end is included in the interval (sales of exactly $500 would be counted), and the upper is not included in the interval (sales of exactly $1000 would *not* be counted). You will see more *between* criteria examples like this later in the book.

Note: There are other ways to count between an upper number and lower number. For example, in the "Array Functions" section of this chapter, you will see that the FREQUENCY function includes the upper end for the interval but not the lower end.

COUNTIFS	=COUNTIFS(Sales,">="&K11,Sales,"<"&K12)			
Criteria 1	1000			
Criteria 2	1500			
COUNTIFS(criteria_range1, criteria1, [criteria_range2, **criteria2**], [c				

Figure 506

Figure 506 shows an alternative for entering criteria into a formula. The advantage of this method is that if other formulas need to look at the actual numbers and need to make a calculation, this method works, just as we did back in Figure 312.

Note: If you have to share your spreadsheet with someone who is using Excel 2003 or earlier, the COUNTIFS function will not work, but instead give you a #NAME? error. Here is an alternative formula that will work in versions of Excel 2003 or earlier:

=SUMPRODUCT(--(Sales>=K11),--(Sales<K12)).

You can see an example of this formula on the Functions(2) sheet.

We will discuss how to use the SUMPRODUCT function later in this chapter.

Next we want to look at how to use the COUNTIF function and a named range to make a small report that shows the number of sales in each region.

COUNTIF Function to Create a Small Report

In our next example, we want to create a report that will show the number of sales we made in each region. This sort of report is called a frequency table. (The word *table* in the phrase *frequency table* does not refer to Table Format Structure or Excel table.)

To follow along, open the file named excelisfun-Start.xlsm and navigate to the Functions(2) sheet.

1. Highlight the range K27:K30.
2. Make sure that K27 is the active cell.

	H	I	J	K	L
25	$512.00				
26	$270.00		Region	COUNTIF	
27	$100.00		West	=COUNTIF(Region,J27	
28	$260.00		MidWest	COUNTIF(range, **criteria**)	
29	$203.50		South		
30	$500.00		East		

Figure 507

3. Type the following formula:
   =COUNTIF(Region,J27)

In Figure 507, we can see that we have entered the named range, Region, into the range argument. By default named ranges are absolute cell references. This is perfect because when we copy our formula down the column we need that range locked so that each of the calculations is looking at the same range. In addition, the relative cell reference, J27, entered into the criteria argument will work perfectly also, because the criteria sits *one cell to the left* for each of the four formulas.

	H	I	J	K	L	
25	$512.00					
26	$270.00		Region	COUNTIF		
27	$100.00		West	24		
28	$260.00		MidWest	24		
29	$203.50		South	27		
30	$500.00		East	=COUNTIF(Region,J30)		

Figure 508

4. To populate all the cells with the formula (copy the formula down), press Ctrl + Enter.
5. To jump to the next corner in the highlighted range, press Ctrl + . (period).
6. To put the formula in Edit mode to verify that the formula is correct, press the F2 key.

In Figure 508, we can see that using named range when absolute cell references are required is convenient because we don't need to worry about locking the cell references; it is done automatically.

Next we want to see how to calculate an average when we have two criteria using the AVERAGEIFS function.

AVERAGEIFS for Averaging with Two Criteria

In our next formula, we want to see how to use the AVERAGEIFS function to answer this question: What is the average number of units sold for the product Bellen in the region West? Here we want to calculate an average, not of all the units sold in the Units column, but of only the units sold that match the criteria Bellen in the Products column *and* West in the Region column. Figure 509 shows how we could use the AVERAGEIFS function to create such a formula. In this example, we use two criteria, but you can have up to 127 criteria.

To follow along, open the file named excelisfun-Start.xlsm and navigate to the Functions(2) sheet.

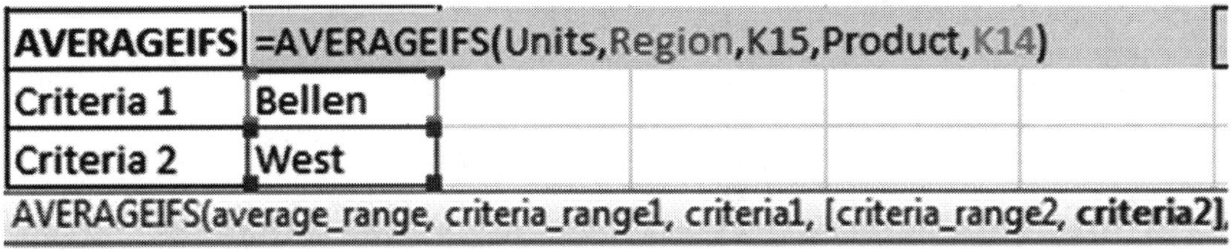

AVERAGEIFS	=AVERAGEIFS(Units,Region,K15,Product,K14)					[
Criteria 1	Bellen					
Criteria 2	West					

AVERAGEIFS(average_range, criteria_range1, criteria1, [criteria_range2, **criteria2**],

Figure 509

> **Note**: If you have to share your spreadsheet with someone who is using Excel 2003 or earlier, the AVERAGEIFS function will not work (you will get a #NAME! error). Instead you could use a formula like this:
>
> =SUMPRODUCT(--(Product=K14),--(Region=K15),Units)/ SUMPRODUCT(--(Product=K14),--(Region=K15)).
>
> We will look at how to use the SUMPRODUCT function later in this section.

In the last few sections, we have been talking about *and* logical tests (where we check to determine whether one criteria and a second criteria are *both* TRUE). But what about *or* criteria (that is, checking to determine whether one or the other is TRUE, but not necessarily both)?

Logical Tests (and/or)

When you have two criteria and both must simultaneously be true for the record/transaction to be used in the calculation, we use the word *and*. For example, we can ask for the following: Add all the sales for Sioux in the SalesRep column *and* PCC in the Customer column. Both criteria must be met with a TRUE for the record/transaction to be used. We call this an *and* logical test. However, when you have two criteria and one or the other can be TRUE for the record/transaction to be used in the calculation, we use the word *or*. Now usually our language gets loose when it gets to *or* statements, so we have to be careful. For example, we could ask the for the following: Add up all the sales for the West and MidWest regions. From our statement, we see the word *and*, but what we really mean is "add all the sales for West in the Region column or MidWest in the Region column." If you think about it, there is no *and* condition where the record can be simultaneously from *both* the West and the MidWest regions. For our *or* question, one or the other criteria can be met for the record/transaction to be used in the calculation.

Figure 510 and Figure 511 show how we can use two functions and the plus symbol to add or count with *or* criteria. In both examples, there are two criteria, and for each record only one of the criteria will be TRUE for each one of the records used in the calculations. The SUMIFS example adds all the sales in the West and MidWest regions, and the COUNTIFS example counts all the sales in the West and MidWest regions. Figure 512 shows how to do an Average function with *or* criteria.

To follow along, open the file named excelisfun-Start.xlsm and navigate to the Functions(2) sheet.

SUMIFS	=SUMIFS(Sales,Region,K17)+SUMIFS(Sales,Region,K18)
OR Criteria 1	West
OR Criteria 2	MidWest

Figure 510

COUNTIFS	=COUNTIFS(Region,K20)+COUNTIFS(Region,K21)
OR Criteria 1	West
OR Criteria 2	MidWest

Figure 511

SUMIFS	40454
OR Criteria 1	West
OR Criteria 2	MidWest
COUNTIFS	48
OR Criteria 1	West
OR Criteria 2	MidWest
Average	=K16/K19
OR Criteria 1	West
OR Criteria 2	MidWest

Figure 512

> Note: If you have to share your spreadsheet with someone who is using Excel 2003 or earlier, three alternative formulas for adding, counting, and averaging with *or* criteria are as follows:
>
> Adding with *or* criteria (substitute for formula in Figure 510):
>
> =SUMIF(Region,K17,Sales)+SUMIF(Region,K18,Sales)
>
> Counting with *or* criteria (substitute for formula in Figure 511):
>
> =COUNTIF(Region,K20)+COUNTIF(Region,K21)
>
> Averaging with *or* criteria (substitute for formula in Figure 512):
>
> =(SUMIF(Region,K17,Sales)+SUMIF(Region,K18,Sales))/(COUNTIF(Region,K20)+COUNTIF(Region,K21))

Later in this chapter, you will see that there are AND and OR functions. In this section, we talked about *or* and *and* criteria. These concepts will help us later when we look at the Filter and Advanced Filter features.

Now you have seen how to use *or* and *and* criteria in formulas that use the COUNTIFS, SUMIFS, and AVERAGEIFS functions. In versions of Excel 2003 and earlier, these functions did not exist, and so one common method for adding and counting with more than one criterion was to use the SUMPRODUCT function. Let's take a look at how this function works.

SUMPRODUCT (to multiply and then add in succession)

The SUMPRODUCT function allows us to take two or more columns of numbers and first multiply the numbers and then add them. For example, if we have 3, 4, 5 in one column and 2, 1, 2 in another column, the SUMPRODUCT would do this: $3 * 2 + 4 * 1 + 5 * 2 = 6 + 4 + 10 = 20$. Notice that the name of the function is SUMPRODUCT. The word SUM means to add, and the word PRODUCT means the result of multiplying. So what the function does is to first multiply the corresponding components in a column, in our example we got $6 + 4 + 10$, then we added the products and got 20. The SUMPRODUCT multiplies and then adds in succession. Let's take a look at an example.

To follow along, open the file named excelisfun-Start.xlsm and navigate to the SUMPRODUCT sheet.

	A	B	C	D
1	Date	Product	PriceOfProduct	Units
2	11/4/2010	Sunset	$21	220
3	11/5/2010	Carlota	$23	202
4	11/6/2010	Carlota	$23	189
5	11/7/2010	Quad	$27	224
6	11/8/2010	Bellen	$22	236
7	11/9/2010	Quad	$27	137
8	11/10/2010	Sunshine	$19	228
9				
10			Total Sales	

Notice that our data set has transaction sales data and shows a column of price for the product and a column of number of units sold for each transaction, but there is no total sales column.

Figure 513

Now imagine that your boss e-mails you and asks you to calculate total sales. What would you do? Most of us would add an extra column and create a formula for the total sales for each transaction by multiplying the price times the units, and then we could add a SUM function to the bottom of the column (see Figure 514 and Figure 515).

	B	C	D	E	F
1	Product	PriceOfProduct	Units		Total Sales
2	Sunset	$21	220		=D2*C2
3	Carlota	$23	202		$4,646
4	Carlota	$23	189		$4,347
5	Quad	$27	224		$6,048
6	Bellen	$22	236		$5,192
7	Quad	$27	137		$3,699
8	Sunshine	$19	228		$4,332
9					$32,884
10		Total Sales			
11					

Figure 514

$21 * 220 = $4,620
$23 * 202 = $4,646
$23 * 189 = $4,347
$27 * 224 = $6,048
$22 * 236 = $5,192
$27 * 137 = $3,699
$19 * 228 = $4,332

Figure 515

If we were required to calculate the total sales, most of us would do this: add an extra column that multiplies the corresponding cells in each column and then add s SUM function at the bottom of the column.

Your boss sees this and says: "No, no! I do not want you to waste space in the spreadsheet with an extra column; I want you to calculate the total sales in cell D10. One cell only!" The SUMPRODUCT function will come to the rescue and make our boss happy and make us look Excel savvy.

Before we see how the amazing SUMPRODUCT works in cell D10, let's look at the two-step process needed to get to our final answer of $32,884. Figure 515 shows use step one, which is to multiply the corresponding elements and get the products (total sale) for each transaction; this is the PRODUCT part of SUMPRODUCT. Figure 516 shows us step two, which is to add all the products we got in step one; this is the SUM part of SUMPRODUCT.

$$\$4,620 + \$4,646 + \$4,347 + \$6,048 + \$5,192 + \$3,699 + \$4,332 = \$32,884$$

Figure 516

Now let's see how to use the SUMPRODUCT function.

Figure 517

1. Click in cell D10.
2. Start your formula with **=SUMPRODUCT(**.

Notice that the screen tip for the SUMPRODUCT says array1, array2, and so on. More on what *array* means in a little bit.

	A	B	C	D	E
1	Date	Product	PriceOfProduct	Units	
2	11/4/2010	Sunset	$21	220	
3	11/5/2010	Carlota	$23	202	
4	11/6/2010	Carlota	$23	189	
5	11/7/2010	Quad	$27	224	
6	11/8/2010	Bellen	$22	236	
7	11/9/2010	Quad	$27	137	
8	11/10/2010	Sunshine	$19	228	
9					
10			Total Sales	=SUMPRODUCT(C2:C8,D2:D8	
11				SUMPRODUCT(array1, [array2]	

3. Highlight the range C2:C8.
4. Type a comma.
5. Highlight the range D2:D8.
6. Press Ctrl + Enter.

Figure 518

D10			fx	=SUMPRODUCT(C2:C8,D2:D8)	
	A	B	C	D	E
1	Date	Product	PriceOfProduct	Units	
2	11/4/2010	Sunset	$21	220	
3	11/5/2010	Carlota	$23	202	
4	11/6/2010	Carlota	$23	189	
5	11/7/2010	Quad	$27	224	
6	11/8/2010	Bellen	$22	236	
7	11/9/2010	Quad	$27	137	
8	11/10/2010	Sunshine	$19	228	
9					
10			Total Sales	$32,884.00	

7. Use the Ctrl + Shift + 4 keyboard shortcut for Currency number formatting.

Imagine how much space you would save if the data set were 500 rows tall!

Figure 519

The SUMPRODUCT function is not limited to just columns. You can sum the products from data in rows, a rectangular range of cells, or even arrays of data, as long as they are the same dimensions. An example of the term same dimensions is summing the products of a 1x3 column and another 1x3 column, or even a 2x3 rectangular range of cells by another 2x3 rectangular range of cells. The term *array* means we can do operations on a range of cells (or an array constant like we saw back in Figure 320). In the example we just worked through, we performed the operations multiply and add on the ranges D2:D8 and C2:C8.

Next we want to take a look at a use for the SUMPRODUCT that you would see in the finance field.

Next we want to look at another example. This example is from economics and finance. It is important in these fields of study to know how to use the SUMPRODUCTS because it is often the case that you have many multiply-column calculations and you do not want to fill up the spreadsheet with lots of extra columns. In Figure 520 and Figure 521, we see two typical finance calculations for estimating the return on a stock. In the Figure 520 example, we have estimated the returns for a single stock and probability for four economic states. To get an estimate of the future return on stock, you have to multiply the probability column by the returns column and then add. The SUMPRODUCT function does this perfectly.

	State of Economy	Prob. Of State of Economy	Stock A Return	
12				
13	Boom	0.030	0.150	
14	Normal	0.250	0.095	
15	Reccession	0.650	0.025	
16	Depression	0.070	-0.160	
17		E(R$_i$)	=SUMPRODUCT(B13:B16,C13:C16)	

Figure 520

	State of Economy	Prob. Of State of Economy	Stock A Return if State Occurs	Stock B Return if State Occurs	Stock C Return if State Occurs
20					
21	Weight	Weight	0.3	0.4	0.3
22	Boom	0.15	0.3	0.45	0.33
23	Good	0.45	0.12	0.1	0.15
24	Poor	0.35	0.01	-0.15	-0.05
25	Bust	0.05	-0.2	-0.3	-0.09
26					
27		Expected Return for Portfolio	=SUMPRODUCT(C22:E25*B22:B25*C21:E21)		

Figure 521

In Figure 521, the calculation is similar except for the calculation is made for more than one stock. In Figure 521, it is important to note that because the arrays are not the same dimensions, we use the * (multiplication symbol) rather than commas. (Why? Because that is just the way they programmed it to work.)

You can try these examples yourself by opening the file named excelisfunStart.xlsm and navigating to the SUMPRODUCT sheet.

Finally, we want to take a look at how the SUMPRODUCT function can be used as a substitute for the functions COUNTIFS and SUMIFS. This is important if you have to share your spreadsheet with people who have Excel 2003 or earlier. As mentioned previously, the COUNTIFS and SUMIFS function will not work and will deliver a #NAME? error rather than a formula result.

Multiple Criteria Counting and Summing for Excel Versions Before 2007

We have already seen how to use COUNTIFS and SUMIFS function to count and add, respectively, when there are two or more criteria. Now we want to see how to do it with the SUMPRODUCT.

You can try these examples yourself by opening the file named excelisfunStart.xlsm and navigating to the SP(2) sheet.

Our goal is to count the number of sales that the SalesRep, Gault, had to the Customer, PCC, using both the COUNTIFS and SUMPRODUCT functions. In Figure 522, you can see that the COUNTIFS function uses four arguments. Each argument is separated by a comma. The first argument (criteria_range1) is the SalesRep range, the second argument (criteria1) has the criteria Gault, the third argument (criteria_range2) is the Customer range, and the fourth argument (criteria2) is the criteria PCC. The beauty of the

COUNTIFS function is that it will find all the records that have a Gault in the SalesRep range *and* a PCC in the Customer range and then count them. The COUNTIFS function is programmed to say TRUE when it finds a Gault and then TRUE a second time when it finds a PCC, and only when there are two TRUEs does it register it as a count of 1. It is as if it says TRUE * TRUE = 1. This means that if we want to simulate this process, but we don't have the COUNTIFS function, we have to get the SUMPRODUCT function to say TRUE * TRUE = 1 every time it finds a Gault and a PCC.

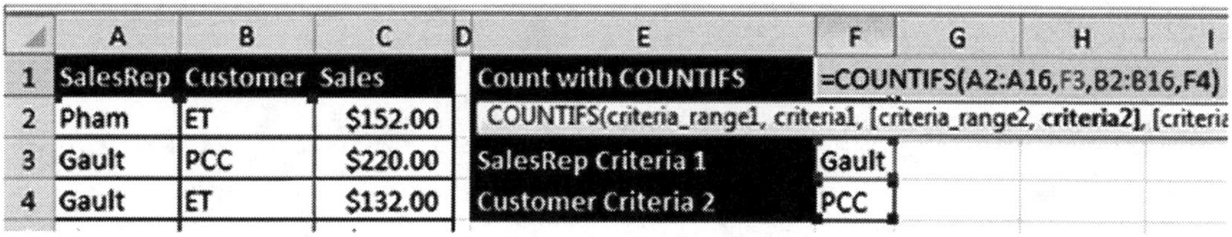

▲	A	B	C	D	E	F	G	H	I
1	SalesRep	Customer	Sales		Count with COUNTIFS	=COUNTIFS(A2:A16,F3,B2:B16,F4)			
2	Pham	ET	$152.00		COUNTIFS(criteria_range1, criteria1, [criteria_range2, criteria2], [criteria				
3	Gault	PCC	$220.00		SalesRep Criteria 1	Gault			
4	Gault	ET	$132.00		Customer Criteria 2	PCC			

Figure 522

Figure 523 shows us our SUMPRODUCT formula for counting with 2 criteria.

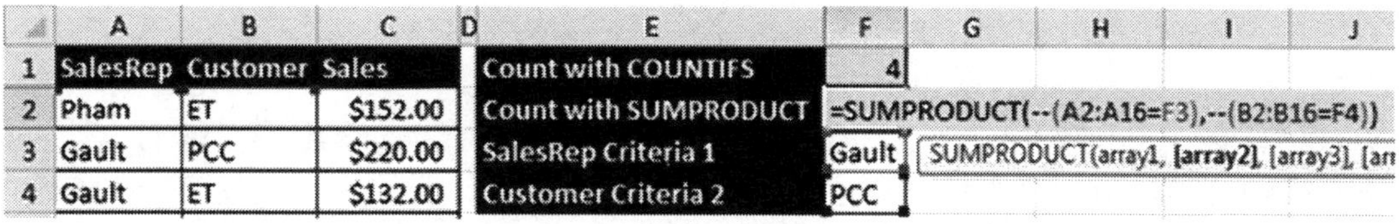

▲	A	B	C	D	E	F	G	H	I	J
1	SalesRep	Customer	Sales		Count with COUNTIFS	4				
2	Pham	ET	$152.00		Count with SUMPRODUCT	=SUMPRODUCT(--(A2:A16=F3),--(B2:B16=F4))				
3	Gault	PCC	$220.00		SalesRep Criteria 1	Gault	SUMPRODUCT(array1, [array2], [array3], [arr			
4	Gault	ET	$132.00		Customer Criteria 2	PCC				

Figure 523

To see why this formula is working let's look at the step-by-step process of how the formula calculates on the next page.

8. First, the formula asks this question: What is in the range of cells, A2:A16?

=SUMPRODUCT(--({"Pham";"Gault";"Gault";"Pham";"Pham"; "Pham";"Gault";"Gault";"Pham";"Gault";"Gault";"Gault"; "Pham";"Gault";"Gault"}="Gault"),--(B2:B16=F4))

Second, the formula answers the question: "Are any of the elements equal to Gault?

=SUMPRODUCT(--({FALSE;TRUE;TRUE;FALSE;FALSE;FALSE; TRUE;TRUE;FALSE;TRUE;TRUE;TRUE;FALSE;TRUE;TRUE}), --(B2:B16=F4))

Third, the double negative converts the TRUEs and FALSEs to 1s and 0s.

=SUMPRODUCT({0;1;1;0;0;0;1;1;0;1;1;1;0;1;1},--(B2:B16=F4))

Fourth, the formula asks this question: What is in the range of cells, B2:B16?

=SUMPRODUCT({0;1;1;0;0;0;1;1;0;1;1;1;0;1;1},--({"ET";"PCC";"ET"; "ET";"PSA";"PCC";"ET";"ET";"PCC";"PCC";"PSA";"PCC";"PCC"; "PCC";"AST"}="PCC"))

Fifth, the formula answers this question: Are any of the elements equal to PCC?

=SUMPRODUCT({0;1;1;0;0;0;1;1;0;1;1;1;0;1;1},--({FALSE;TRUE; FALSE;FALSE;FALSE;TRUE;FALSE;FALSE;TRUE;TRUE; FALSE;TRUE;TRUE;TRUE;FALSE}))

Sixth, the double negative converts the TRUEs and FALSEs to 1s and 0s.

=SUMPRODUCT({0;1;1;0;0;0;1;1;0;1;1;1;0;1;1}, {0;1;0;0;0;1;0;0;1;1;0;1;1;1;0})

Seventh, the 1s and 0s are multiplied.

=SUMPRODUCT({0;1;0;0;0;0;0;0;0;1;0;1;0;1;0})

Eight, the 1s and 0s are added to get an answer of 4.

In Figure 524 you can see the formula comparison between SUMIFS and SUMPRODUCT for adding with two criteria. (Column F has the calculating formula and column G shows the formula that is being used in column F.) The only difference between the adding and counting formulas is that you have to include the Sales range in column C for adding the sales. The logic for adding when there is a sales made by Gault to PCC would be TRUE * TRUE * 220 = 1 * 1 * 220 = 220. And that logic would be repeated for each sale that Gault made to PCC and then those resulting numbers would be added by the SUMPRODUCT function.

	C	D	E	F	G	H	I	J	K
er	Sales		Count with COUNTIFS	4	=COUNTIFS(A2:A16,F3,B2:B16,F4)				
	$152.00		Count with SUMPRODUCT	4	=SUMPRODUCT(--(A2:A16=F3),--(B2:B16=F4))				
	$220.00		SalesRep Criteria 1	Gault					
	$132.00		Customer Criteria 2	PCC					
	$154.00								
	$1,449.00		Sum with SUMIFS	1572	=SUMIFS(C2:C16,A2:A16,F8,B2:B16,F9)				
	$783.00		Sum with SUMPRODUCT	1572	=SUMPRODUCT(C2:C16,--(A2:A16=F8),--(B2:B16=F9))				
	$594.00		SalesRep Criteria 1	Gault					
	$352.00		Customer Criteria 2	PCC					

Figure 524

Note: The COUNTIFS and SUMIFS and AVERAGEIFS functions are faster at calculating the formula result than the SUMPRODUCT equivalents. This matters in large spreadsheets where you have thousands of rows of data. For small spreadsheets, you cannot tell the difference because the formula calculates instantly.

Note: There are many variations on the SUMPRODUCT formulas seen above. In particular, there are many ways to convert TRUEs and FALSEs to 1s and 0s. However, if you have to use SUMPRODUCT, the double-negative method is the fastest calculating method. This matters in large spreadsheets where you have thousands of rows of data. Here is a list of some of the variations you might see in the working world for the counting example:

4	=COUNTIFS(A2:A16,F3,B2:B16,F4)
4	=SUMPRODUCT(--(A2:A16=F3),--(B2:B16=F4))
4	=SUMPRODUCT((A2:A16=F3)*(B2:B16=F4))
4	=SUMPRODUCT((A2:A16=F3)*1,(B2:B16=F4)*1)
4	=SUMPRODUCT((A2:A16=F3)^1,(B2:B16=F4)^1)
4	{=SUM((A2:A16=F3)*(B2:B16=F4))}
4	=SUMPRODUCT((A2:A16=F3)+0,(B2:B16=F4)+0)

For more detail about calculations on arrays, see the "Array Functions" section, later in this chapter.

In the next section, we look at one of the most commonly used functions in Excel: the IF function.

IF Function (for putting one of two items in a cell or formula)

We already saw how to use the IF function to put one of two words or one of two numbers into a cell back in Figures 333 to 347. (If you did not read those pages, you should go back and read them now.) A visual summary of those pages is presented in Figure 525 and Figure 526.

	A	B	C	D	E	F	G	H	I
1	Sales	Expenses	Profit Hurdle	Question	Pass Hurdle = Bonus	Formula from E column			
2	$500	$392	$100	Is 500 -392 > 100 TRUE or FALSE?	TRUE	Logical Formula: =A2-B2>C2		value_if_ true	value_if_ false
3	$500	$392	$100	Is 500 -392 > 100, Yes or No?	Yes	IF function that puts one of two words in a cell: =IF(A3-B3>C3,H3,I3)		Yes	No
4	$500	$392	$100	Is 500 -392 > 100, 10 or 0?	$10.00	IF function that puts one of two numbers in a cell: =IF(A4-B4>C4,H4,I4)		$10.00	$0.00

Figure 525

	A	B	C	D	E	F	G	H	I
1	Sales	Expenses	Profit Hurdle	Question	Pass Hurdle = Bonus	Formula from E column			
2	$500	$700	$100	Is 500 -700 > 100 TRUE or FALSE?	FALSE	Logical Formula: =A2-B2>C2		value_if_ true	value_if_ false
3	$500	$700	$100	Is 500 -700 > 100, Yes or No?	No	IF function that puts one of two words in a cell: =IF(A3-B3>C3,H3,I3)		Yes	No
4	$500	$700	$100	Is 500 -700 > 100, 10 or 0?	$0.00	IF function that puts one of two numbers in a cell: =IF(A4-B4>C4,H4,I4)		$10.00	$0.00

Figure 526

The purpose of the IF function is to put one of two items into a cell (or formula). Because the IF function must choose between one of two items, it requires a logical test that comes out to be TRUE or FALSE. If the logical test comes out to be TRUE, the first item will be put into the cell; if it comes out to be FALSE, the second item will be put into the cell. To review what we saw earlier in the book, let's look at three formulas:

- Logical formula
- IF function to put one of two words in a cell
- IF function to put one of two numbers in a cell

To follow along, open the file named excelisfun-Start.xlsm and navigate to the IF(2) sheet.

In Figure 527, we can see a list of employees in column A, the employee's sales in column B, the bonus hurdle in cell B9, and the bonus amount in cell B10. We will create our three formulas in columns C to E.

	A	B	C	D	E
1			Logical Formula or logical_test	IF used to put 1 of 2 words in cell	IF used to put 1 of 2 numbers in cell
2	Employee	Sales	Bonus: TRUE or FALSE	Bonus: "Yes" or "No"	Bonus Amount
3	Rod Barbaria	$20,382	=B3>=B$9		
4	Elinore Cromedy	$19,504			
5	Twanda Spruce	$21,579			
6	Darius Raffety	$12,117			
7	Frida Vickerson	$26,081			
8					
9	Bonus Hurdle	$20,000			
10	Bonus Amount If Hurdle Equaled or Passed	$750			

Figure 527

In column C we want to create a logical formula that will say TRUE when the employee's sales or equal to or exceed the bonus hurdle and FALSE when they do not.

1. On the IF(2) sheet, highlight the range C3:C7 with C3 in the active cell, then type the following formula:
   =B3>=B$9

In Figure 527, you can see that the formula looks one cell to the left (relative cell reference) at the employee's sales and then asks whether it is greater than or equal to the bonus hurdle in cell B$9 (row reference absolute/locked when copying across the rows). We use the two symbols >= together so that the employee gets the bonus if his or her sales are bigger than the $20,000 hurdle, or if the employee's sales are exactly equal to $20,000.

	A	B	C	D	E
1			Logical Formula or logical_test	IF used to put 1 of 2 words in cell	IF used to put 1 of 2 numbers in cell
2	Employee	Sales	Bonus: TRUE or FALSE	Bonus: "Yes" or "No"	Bonus Amount
3	Rod Barbaria	$20,382	TRUE		
4	Elinore Cromedy	$19,504	FALSE		
5	Twanda Spruce	$21,579	TRUE		
6	Darius Raffety	$12,117	FALSE		
7	Frida Vickerson	$26,081	=B7>=B$9		

Figure 528

2. To populate the highlighted cells with the formula, press Ctrl + Enter.
3. To jump to the next corner of the highlighted range, press Ctrl + . (period).
4. To put the cell into Edit mode and verify that the formula is correct, press the F2 key.
5. To exit Edit mode, press the Esc key.

	A	B	C	D	E
1			Logical Formula or logical_test	IF used to put 1 of 2 words in cell	IF used to put 1 of 2 numbers in cell
2	Employee	Sales	Bonus: TRUE or FALSE	Bonus: "Yes" or "No"	Bonus Amount
3	Rod Barbaria	$20,382	TRUE	=IF(B3>=B$9,"Yes","No")	
4	Elinore Cromedy	$19,504	FALSE	IF(logical_test, [value_if_true], [value_if_...	
5	Twanda Spruce	$21,579	TRUE		
6	Darius Raffety	$12,117	FALSE		
7	Frida Vickerson	$26,081	TRUE		

Figure 529

6. Highlight the range D3:D7 with D3 as the active cell, then type the following formula:
   =IF(B3>=B$9,"Yes,""No")

The formula in Figure 529, =IF(B3>=B$9,"Yes,""No"), is read as "if two cells to the left is greater than or equal to the number in cell B$9, then put a Yes in the cell, otherwise put a No." Notice that the logical_test for our IF function is the same as for the logical formula we just created (Figure 527); namely, are the employee's sales (relative cell reference) greater than or equal to the bonus hurdle in cell B$9 (locked when copying across the rows)? But instead of putting a TRUE or FALSE in each cell, the IF function will put the words Yes or No into each cell. Notice also that we typed the formula inputs Yes and No into our formula (this is called hard-coding).

Earlier in this chapter (Figure 340), we did a similar formula for a bonus, but instead of typing the values into the formula, we put the Yes and No into cells and referred to then with cell references. In our example here, because we are never going to change the wording, it is okay to hard-code the formula inputs into our formula.

	Employee	Sales	Bonus: TRUE or FALSE	Bonus: "Yes" or "No"	Bonus Amount
2	Employee	Sales	TRUE or FALSE	"Yes" or "No"	Amount
3	Rod Barbaria	$20,382	TRUE	Yes	
4	Elinore Cromedy	$19,504	FALSE	No	
5	Twanda Spruce	$21,579	TRUE	Yes	
6	Darius Raffety	$12,117	FALSE	No	
7	Frida Vickerson	$26,081	TRUE	=IF(B7>=B$9,"Yes","No")	
8					
9	Bonus Hurdle	$20,000			

Figure 530

7. To populate all the cells with the formula, press Ctrl + Enter.
8. Verify that the formula is correct.

Notice that the IF function puts one of two words into each cell.

	A	B	C	D	E	F
1			Logical Formula or logical_test	IF used to put 1 of 2 words in cell	IF used to put 1 of 2 numbers in cell	
2	Employee	Sales	Bonus: TRUE or FALSE	Bonus: "Yes" or "No"	Bonus Amount	
3	Rod Barbaria	$20,382	TRUE	Yes	=IF(B3>=B$9,B$10,0)	
4	Elinore Cromedy	$19,504	FALSE	No		
5	Twanda Spruce	$21,579	TRUE	Yes	IF(logical_test, [value_if_true], [value_if_false])	
6	Darius Raffety	$12,117	FALSE	No		
7	Frida Vickerson	$26,081	TRUE	Yes		

Figure 531

9. Highlight the range D3:D7 with D3 as the active cell, then type the following formula:
   =IF(B3>=B$9,B$10,0)
10. Enter the formula into all the cells and then verify that it is correct.

The formula in Figure 531 is read as "if three cells to the left is greater than or equal to the number in cell B$9, then put the number in cell B$10 in the cell; otherwise put a 0." Notice that the logical_test is the same as our last two formulas. Also notice that this IF function puts one of two numbers into the cell.

Note: Highlighting a range, entering a formula into the active cell, and using Ctrl + Enter to populate all the cells with the formula is a substitute for entering the formula and copying it down the column.

In Figure 532, you can see that Rod, Twanda, and Frida all have TRUE, Yes, and $750 in their row because their sales are greater than or equal to $20,000.

Employee	Sales	Bonus: TRUE or FALSE	Bonus: "Yes" or "No"	Bonus Amount
Rod Barbaria	$20,382	TRUE	Yes	$750
Elinore Cromedy	$19,504	FALSE	No	$0
Twanda Spruce	$21,579	TRUE	Yes	$750
Darius Raffety	$12,117	FALSE	No	$0
Frida Vickerson	$26,081	TRUE	Yes	$750
Bonus Hurdle	$20,000			
Bonus Amount If Hurdle Equaled or Passed	$750			

Figure 532

In Figure 533, you determine whether we change the formula inputs, and all of our formulas update: Only Twanda and Frida got the bonus.

Employee	Sales	Bonus: TRUE or FALSE	Bonus: "Yes" or "No"	Bonus Amount
Rod Barbaria	$20,382	FALSE	No	$0
Elinore Cromedy	$19,504	FALSE	No	$0
Twanda Spruce	$21,579	TRUE	Yes	$500
Darius Raffety	$12,117	FALSE	No	$0
Frida Vickerson	$26,081	TRUE	Yes	$500
Bonus Hurdle	$21,000			
Bonus Amount If Hurdle Equaled or Passed	$500			

Figure 533

Figure 534 shows the screen tip for the IF function.

IF(logical_test, [value_if_true], [value_if_false])

Figure 534

A summary of the IF functions arguments are as follows:

- The logical_test argument requires a comparative statement using any of the comparative operators as seen in Figure 535. In addition, the logical_test will interpret any nonzero number as TRUE and the number 0 (zero) as FALSE. Still further, the logical_test will accept logical functions such as AND or OR (more on that later).
- The [value-if-true] argument is the item you want to put in the cell (or formula) if the logical_test evaluates to TRUE. This can be a word/ text, a number, a formula, or even an array.
- The [value-if-false] argument is the item you want to put in the cell (or formula) if the logical_test evaluates to FALSE. This can be a word/ text, a number, a formula, or even an array.

Note: You can have up to 64 nested IF functions. You'll learn how to nest IF functions later.

Comparative Operators
> Greater Than
>= Greater Than Or Equal To
< Less Than
<= Less Than Or Equal To
= Equal To
<> Not Equal To

Figure 535

Next we want to see how to use the IF function to check to determine whether two column totals are equal, or in balance.

To follow along, open the file named excelisfun-Start.xlsm and navigate to the IF(3) sheet.

IF Function (to check whether two columns are in balance)

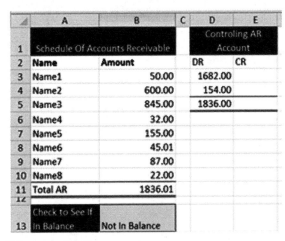

Figure 536

1. In the IF(3) sheet, click in cell B13 and create the following formula:
   =IF(B11=D5,"In Balance","Not In Balance")

Notice that our comparative operator is an equal sign and that we are putting one of two phrases or text strings into the cell.

2. To put the formula into the cell, press Enter.

	A	B	C	D	E
1	Schedule Of Accounts Receivable			Controling AR Account	
2	Name	Amount		DR	CR
3	Name1	50.00		1682.00	
4	Name2	600.00		154.00	
5	Name3	845.00		1836.00	
6	Name4	32.00			
7	Name5	155.00			
8	Name6	45.01			
9	Name7	87.00			
10	Name8	22.00			
11	Total AR	1836.01			
12					
13	Check to See If In Balance	Not In Balance			

Figure 537

The formula result is "Not In Balance." This is because there is a one penny discrepancy in cell B8. The 45.01 should be 45.00.

3. Enter the number **45** into cell B8 and the IF function should deliver the text string "In Balance" to cell B13.

Next we want to see how to use the IF function to add a column of data to a data set.

To follow along, open the file named excelisfun-Start.xlsm and navigate to the IF(4) sheet.

OR Function

Figure 538 shows our data set. In column C our goal is to put the word Out in every record (row) where there is a Pro5 *or* Pro6 and the word In for all other records. Notice that we are putting one of two words into a cell, a perfect job for the IF function.

	A	B	C	D	E
			IN/OUT		
1	Sale	Product	House		Out
2		10	Pro1			Pro5
3		19	Pro5			Pro6
4		15	Pro6		

Figure 538

Before we can use our IF function, though, we must first see how to use the OR function, which is one of several logical functions that deliver TRUEs or FALSEs to a cell or formula. Let's first see how the OR function works by itself.

	A	B	C	D	E
			IN/OUT		
1	Sale	Product	House		Out
2		10	Pro1	=OR(B2=E$2,B2=E$3)		Pro5
3		19	Pro5	OR(logical1, [logical2], [logical3], ...)		Pro6
4		15	Pro6		

Figure 539

1. On the IF(4) sheet, click in cell C2 and create the following formula:
   =OR(B2=E$2,B2=E$3)

In Figure 539, we can see that the OR function lets us enter two logical formulas or logical tests into one function separated by a comma. (The OR screen tip calls them logical1, logical2, and so on.) The first logical test is B2=E$2 (one cell to the left equal to whatever is in E$2), and the second logical test is B2=E$3 (one cell to the left equal to whatever is in E$3). If one or the other of these logical formulas evaluates to TRUE, the OR function will put a TRUE into the cell.

	A	B	C	D	E
			IN/OUT		
1	Sale	Product	House		Out
2	10	Pro1	FALSE		Pro5
3	19	Pro5	TRUE		Pro6
4	15	Pro6	TRUE		
5	5	Pro1	FALSE		
6	3	Pro6	TRUE		
7	18	Pro2	FALSE		
8	5	Pro2	FALSE		

Figure 540

2. To enter the formula into cell C2 and keep the cell selected, press Ctrl + Enter.
3. To copy the formula down the column (across the rows), double-click the fill handle with the crosshair cursor.

Nesting Functions

In Figure 540, we can see that for every record that has a Pro 5 or Pro 6 the OR function delivered a TRUE to the cell and for every record that is not Pro 5 or Pro 6 it put a FALSE. Now, because we want to replace the words TRUE and FALSE in the cell with the words Out or In, respectively, we can simply use our OR function in the first argument of the IF function. This process is called **nesting functions** because one function is inside another function. (You already saw this once with the SUM and LARGE functions.) Let's take a look at how to nest the OR function inside the IF function.

	A	B	C	D	E
			IN/OUT		
1	Sale	Product	House		Out
2	10	Pro1	=OR(B2=E$2,B2=E$3)		Pro5
3	19	Pro5	TRUE		Pro6
4	15	Pro6	TRUE		

Figure 541

4. With the column still selected and C2 as the active cell, press the F2 key to put the formula in Edit mode.
5. Carefully, click after the first equal sign but before the OR function. You should see a flashing insertion cursor.

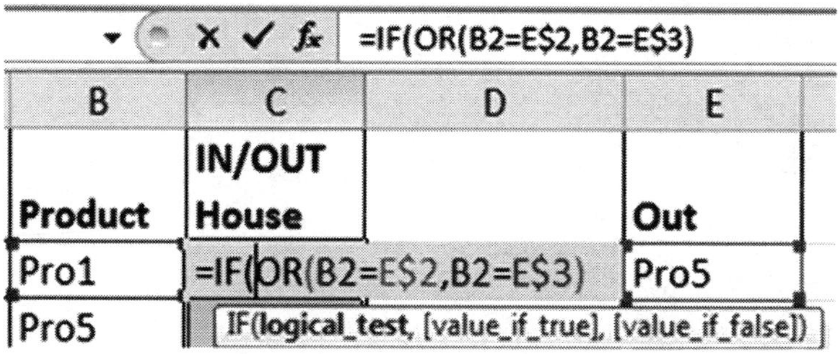

	▼	○ ✕ ✓ *fx*	=IF(OR(B2=E$2,B2=E$3)	
B	**C**	**D**	**E**	

B	C	D	E
	IN/OUT		
Product	**House**		**Out**
Pro1	=IF(OR(B2=E$2,B2=E$3)		Pro5
Pro5	IF(**logical_test**, [value_if_true], [value_if_false])		

Figure 542

6. Type **IF(**.

Notice the screen tip shows up and indicates in bold that the OR function is already placed in the logical_test argument.

Figure 542 shows, in bold, the logical_test argument. Remember, all that is required for the logical_test argument is a TRUE or FALSE. Because that is what the OR function delivers, the OR function is a perfect input for this argument.

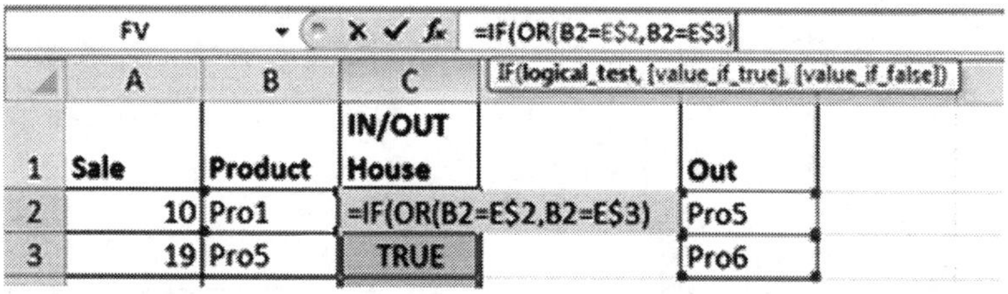

	FV	▼	○ ✕ ✓ *fx*	=IF(OR(B2=E$2,B2=E$3)	
	A	B	C	IF(**logical_test**, [value_if_true], [value_if_false])	

	A	B	C		E
1	Sale	Product	**IN/OUT** **House**		**Out**
2	10	Pro1	=IF(OR(B2=E$2,B2=E$3)		Pro5
3	19	Pro5	TRUE		Pro6

Figure 543

7. Carefully, click at the end of the formula in the formula bar. You should see a flashing insertion cursor.

In Figure 543 we have decided to use the formula bar to edit our formula instead of the cell. Why? Because it is safer to edit a formula in the formula bar because you can avoid inadvertently clicking in a cell and incorrectly inserting cell references into the formula.

fx   =IF(OR(B2=E$2,B2=E$3),"Out","In")

IF(logical_test, [value_if_true], [**value_if_false**])

Figure 544

8. Finish the formula as shown in Figure 544.
9. To populate all the cells with the edited formula, press Ctrl + Enter.

▲	A	B	C	D	E
			IN/OUT		
1	Sale	Product	House		Out
2	10	Pro1	In		Pro5
3	19	Pro5	Out		Pro6
4	15	Pro6	Out		
5	5	Pro1	In		
6	3	Pro6	Out		
7	18	Pro2	In		
8	5	Pro2	In		
9	8	Pro5	Out		
10	13	Pro1	In		

Figure 545

Figure 545 shows us the finished product: using the IF and OR function together to create a column of data in a data set.

Next we want to see how to use the IF and AND function to analyze customers' credit ratings.

AND Function

In the preceding example, you saw how the OR function took two logical tests and if one or the other or both evaluated to TRUE the OR function delivered a TRUE to the cell or formula. The AND function is similar, except all logical tests must evaluate to TRUE for the AND function to deliver a TRUE. The AND function, like the OR function, is considered a logical functions because it delivers a TRUE or a FALSE.

To follow along, open the file named excelisfun-Start.xlsm and navigate to the IF(5) sheet.

In Figure 546, we can see the Customers listed in column A, Net Worth listed in column B, Ave Yearly Sales in column C, and Credit Score listed in column D. Our goal is to use the hurdles in cells B11, B12, and B13 to determine whether we should extend credit (make loans) to the customer. For a customer to qualify for credit, he or she must meet the following three tests:
- Net worth >= 100,000
- Ave yearly sales >= 500,000
- Credit score > 3

All three tests must evaluate to TRUE for credit to be extended to the customer. In essence, there are three logical formulas that all must evaluate to TRUE. This is the perfect job for the AND function because it will allow us to enter the three logical formulas into one function separated by a commas. (The AND screen tip calls them logical1, logical2, and so on.) Let's take a look at how to enter the AND function into column E of our Customer Credit Analysis spreadsheet.

	A	B	C	D	E	F	G	H
1			Customer Credit Analysis					
2	Customer	Net Worth	Ave Yearly Sales	Credit Score	Pass Hurdles?	Extend Credit?		
3	PCC	100,000	1,500,000	4	=AND(B3>=B$11,C3>=B$12,D3>B$13)			
4	WFMI	1,000,000	5,000,000	2	AND(logical1, [logical2], [logical3], [logical4], ...			
5	FM	250,000	1,250,000	3.5				
6	AMZ	6,000,000	35,000,000	3.5				
7	EIF	95,000	52,000	5				
8	ME	125,000	95,000	5				
9								
10		Hurdles						
11	Net Worth	100,000						
12	Ave Yearly Sales	500,000						
13	Credit Score	3						
14								

Figure 546

1. On the IF(5) sheet, highlight the range E3:E8 with E3 as the active cell, and then type the following formula:
   =AND(B3>=B$11,C3>=B$12,D3>B$13)

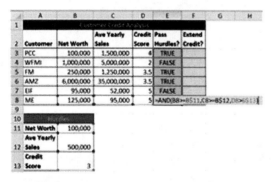

Figure 547

2. To populate all the cells with the formula, press Ctrl + Enter.
3. Verify that the formula is correct.

IF Function (to analyze customer creditworthiness)

In Figure 547, we can see that we got TRUEs and FALSEs. But what if we want Extend Credit and No Credit instead? Because we want one of two items in each cell, we can use the IF function. Also, because the first argument in the IF function, logical_test, requires a TRUE or FALSE, we can put our AND function into the logical_test argument and it will work just fine. Figure 548 shows what this formula would look like.

	A	B	C	D	E	F	G	H	I
1			Customer Credit Analysis						
2	Customer	Net Worth	Ave Yearly Sales	Credit Score	Pass Hurdles?	Extend Credit?			
3	PCC	100,000	1,500,000	4	TRUE	=IF(AND(B3>=B$11,C3>=B$12,D3>B$13),			
4	WFMI	1,000,000	5,000,000	2	FALSE	"Extend Credit","No Credit")			
5	FM	250,000	1,250,000	3.5	TRUE	IF(logical_test, [value_if_true], [value_if_false])			
6	AMZ	6,000,000	35,000,000	3.5	TRUE				
7	EIF	95,000	52,000	5	FALSE				
8	ME	125,000	95,000	5	FALSE				
9									
10		Hurdles							
11	Net Worth	100,000							
12	Ave Yearly Sales	500,000							
13	Credit Score	3							

Figure 548

After you enter the formula as seen in Figure 548 into column F, you should have a formula that says whether a particular customer should be given credit. See Figure 549.

			Customer Credit Analysis			
	Customer	Net Worth	Ave Yearly Sales	Credit Score	Pass Hurdles?	Extend Credit?
	PCC	100,000	1,500,000	4	TRUE	Extend Credit
	WFMI	1,000,000	5,000,000	2	FALSE	No Credit
	FM	250,000	1,250,000	3.5	TRUE	Extend Credit
	AMZ	6,000,000	35,000,000	3.5	TRUE	Extend Credit
	EIF	95,000	52,000	5	FALSE	No Credit
	ME	125,000	95,000	5	FALSE	No Credit

Figure 549

Next we want to see how to use the IF function to put one of two numbers into a formula.

To follow along, open the file named excelisfun-Start.xlsm and navigate to the IF(6) sheet.

IF Function (for commission calculation)

In Figure 550, we can see column A has the sales rep's names, column B has their sales amount, column C has the IF function that is delivering the number 0.03 (formatted this would be 3%) or 0.0 (zero) to each cell based on a sales hurdle of $7,000. Notice that our logical_test for the IF function uses only the comparative operator >; this is why Carlo, (name 3) got a zero. (I guess the payroll guy is mean – if you get exactly on the hurdle, you still don't get a bonus.) Our goal is to calculate the dollar value of each commission earned. However, notice that the current IF function is not doing that; it is only delivering either a 0.0 or a 0.03. The 0 and the 0.03 are both commission rates; and because the formula for the dollar value of each commission earned is CommissionRate * Sales, we can use the IF function as a formula element in our CommissionRate * Sales formula. The formula would look something like =IF(B2>E$2,E$4,0) * Sales.

	A	B	C	D	E
1	Name	Sales	Comission		Hurdle
2	Cleo Gajate	$5,018	=IF(B2>E$2,E$4,0)		$7,000
3	Lane Haruta	$5,651	0		Com Rate
4	Carlo Warrenfeltz	$7,000	0		0.03
5	Dick Thackaberry	$9,623	0.03		
6	Lurlene Caira	$9,008	0.03		
7	Cleotilde Metting	$5,220	0		

Figure 550

Figure 551 and Figure 552 show the formula and formula result that will work for column C.

	A	B	C	D	E
1	Name	Sales	Comission		Hurdle
2	Cleo Gajate	$5,018	=IF(B2>E$2,E$4,0)*B2		$7,000
3	Lane Haruta	$5,651	0		Com Rate
4	Carlo Warrenfeltz	$7,000	0		0.03
5	Dick Thackaberry	$9,623	0.03		

Figure 551

	C2			f_x	=IF(B2>E$2,E$4,0)*B2	
	A	B	C	D		E
1	Name	Sales	Comission			Hurdle
2	Cleo Gajate	$5,018	$0			$7,000
3	Lane Haruta	$5,651	$0			Com Rate
4	Carlo Warrenfeltz	$7,000	$0			0.03
5	Dick Thackaberry	$9,623	$289			
6	Lurlene Caira	$9,008	$270			
7	Cleotilde Metting	$5,220	$0			
8	Porsche Artola	$5,417	$0			
9	Aurelio Broody	$6,436	$0			
10	Win Aydt	$8,407	$252			
11	Collin Mesteth	$5,815	$0			

Figure 552

To see how the IF function delivers one of two numbers to a formula, click in cell C10 and run Evaluate Formula. (Click the Formula tab, click the Evaluate Formula button in the Formula Auditing group; alternatively, use the keyboard shortcut Alt, T, U, F.) Figure 553 to Figure 559 show the evaluation process and how the IF function is delivering one of two numbers to a formula. Figure 557 explicitly shows the IF function delivering a number to the formula.

Evaluation:

= IF(B10>E$2,E$4,0)*B10

Figure 553

Evaluation:

= IF(8407>E$2,E$4,0)*B10

Figure 554

Evaluation:

= IF(8407>7000,E$4,0)*B10

Figure 555

Evaluation:

= IF(TRUE,E$4,0)*B10

Figure 556

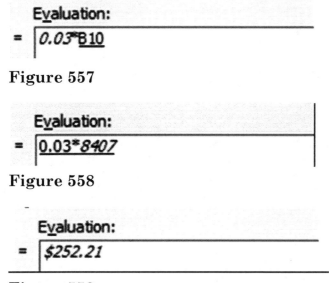

Evaluation:

= | 0.03*B10

Figure 557

Evaluation:

= | 0.03*8407

Figure 558

Evaluation:

= | $252.21

Figure 559

Next we want to look at another type of commission formula calculation that involves more than one hurdle and more than one commission rate. In the process of doing this, you will also learn about how to nest an IF function inside another IF function.

Nesting IF Functions

In the preceding example, we calculated the commission given a single hurdle of $7,000 and a single commission rate of 0.03. Each employee either got a 0 commission on sales or a 0.03 commission on sales. As shown in Figure 561 in the range A1:C4, there are three commission rates in this example. Employees will either get a 0, a 0.02, or a 0.03 commission on sales. This time there are three commission rates rather than just two. When we had just two, we needed just one IF function. Now that there are one of three items that need to go into the cell or formula, we will have to use two IF functions in one formula. This is called **nesting IF functions**. The rule is this: Whatever number of items that could possibly go in the cell or formula, you will always need one fewer IF functions. Figure 560 sums up this rule.

One of two items in cell or formula: 1 IF function in formula
One of three items in cell or formula: 2 IF functions in formula
One of four items in cell or formula: 3 IF functions in formula
Etc...

Figure 560

	A	B	C	E
1	Rule For Commission	Hurdle	Com. Rate	
2	$0 <= Sales < $5,000	$0	0.00	
3	$5,000 <= Sales < $7,000	$5,000	0.02	
4	Sales >= $7,000	$7,000	0.03	
5				
6	Name	Sales	Comission	
7	Mike Tello	$5,018		← We need 0.02 because $5,000 <= $5,018 < $7,000
8	Samuel George	$4,125		← We need 0.00 because $0 <= $4,125 < $5,000
9	Jeff Pannell	$7,000		← We need 0.03 because $7,000 >= $7,000
10	Bruce Urrutia	$3,012		← We need 0.00 because $0 <= $3,012 < $5,000
11	Keith Reno	$9,558		← We need 0.03 because $9,558 >= $7,000
12				

H ◄ ► H IF(6) **IF(7)** VLOOKUP(1) ◄

Figure 561

Now take a look at Figure 561. In cell C7, Mike will get a commission rate of 0.02 because his sales are between $5,000 and $7,000. But be careful with the word *between*! Because we need categories that do not overlap, we must be careful in how we define our upper and lower limits for each commission rate. In our example, we will include the lower limit and exclude the upper limit for each category, except the last category which will have an open upper limit. For example, the category that Mike's sales fall within can be expressed in math terms this way:

$$\$5,000 <= \mathbf{\$5,018} < \$7,000$$

For a second example, we can see that Keith will get a 0.03 commission because

$$\mathbf{\$9,558} >= \$7,000$$

Although commissions are calculated many different ways and are always defined by contract, if at all possible it is beneficial to set up categories that include the lower limit and exclude the upper limit (except for the last category, which is open ended) because many of Excel's built-in functions (like VLOOKUP, in our next section) are set up to interpret categories this way. In addition, we must make sure that we list all the possible categories. This may seem self-evident, but it is not uncommon that people build commission formulas and leave out some possible scenarios. And finally, it is helpful to list the categories in ascending order (from smallest to biggest). If we set up our categories this way, our nested IF formulas and VLOOKUP-type formulas will be much easier to create.

Our next Excel Efficiency-Robust Rule is as follows:

Rule 33: When setting up categories for formulas that use the IF or VLOOKUP functions, follow these rules (if possible): 1) The lower limit is included in the category, but the upper limit is not (for example, $5,000 <= Sales < $7,000). 2) All possible categories are included. 3) Categories are organized in ascending order. These rules can be stated in formal language; the categories are mutually exclusive and collectively exhaustive and are organized in ascending order.

Now let's see how to create this nested IF formula.

To follow along, open the file named excelisfun-Start.xlsm and navigate to the IF(7) sheet.

	A	B	C	D
1	Rule For Commission	Hurdle	Com. Rate	
2	$0 <= Sales < $5,000	$0	0.00	
3	$5,000 <= Sales < $7,000	$5,000	0.02	
4	Sales >= $7,000	$7,000	0.03	
5				
6	Name	Sales	Comission	
7	Mike Tello	$5,018	=IF(B7>=B$4,C$4,	
8	Samuel George		IF(logical_test, [value_if_true], [value_if_false])	
9	Jeff Pannell	$7,000		

Figure 562

1. On the IF(7) sheet, click in the cell C7 and create the first part of the following formula:
   =IF(B7>=B$4,C$4,

In Figure 562, we can read the formula so far this way: "If the sales (one cell to my left) are greater than or equal to the $7,000 (cell B$4), then put the commission rate 0.03 (cell C$4)." But now what do we put for the value_if_false if there are two possibilities left? Whenever we have more than one item that could go into the value_if_false, we must put another IF function. It is also important to notice that because we are in the value_if_false argument and we have already asked the question Sales >= $7,000, it means that we have excluded that category from further consideration. This is why when we do the next IF function, we do not have to ask $5,000 <= Sales < $7,000, we only have to ask Sales >= $5,000.

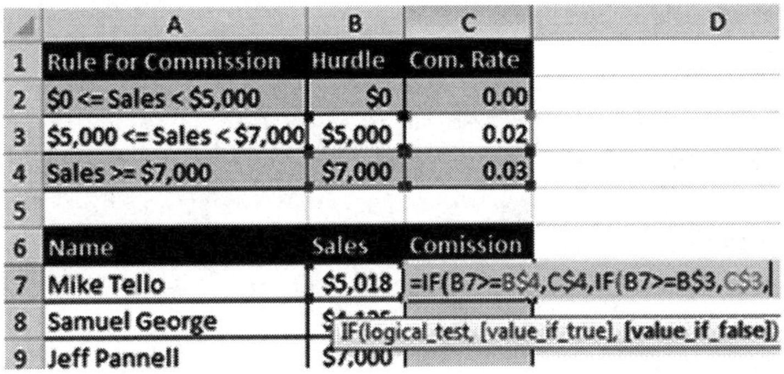

	A	B	C	D
1	Rule For Commission	Hurdle	Com. Rate	
2	$0 <= Sales < $5,000	$0	0.00	
3	$5,000 <= Sales < $7,000	$5,000	0.02	
4	Sales >= $7,000	$7,000	0.03	
5				
6	Name	Sales	Comission	
7	Mike Tello	$5,018	=IF(B7>=B$4,C$4,IF(B7>=B$3,C$3,	
8	Samuel George		IF(logical_test, [value_if_true], [value_if_false])	
9	Jeff Pannell	$7,000		

Figure 563

2. Now add the second IF function so that the formula looks like this:
   =IF(B7>=B$4,C$4,IF(B7>=B$3,C$3,

Notice that the open parenthesis after the second IF function is a green color. This is to help distinguish between the two IF functions.

In Figure 563, notice that we started our formula by looking at the largest hurdle first. When stringing IF functions together in a formula like this, it is usually most efficient to start with the biggest number and work your way down through the smaller numbers without skipping any categories. It is also important to notice that because we are in the second value_if_false argument and we have already asked the questions Sales >= $7,000 and $5,000 <= Sales < $7,000, it means that we have excluded those categories from further consideration. Because there is only one option left, namely, 0.0%, all we need to do now is enter that cell in the second value_if_false argument.

```
=IF(B7>=B$4,C$4,IF(B7>=B$3,C$3,C$2))
```
`ical_test, [value_if_true], [value_if_false])`

Figure 564

3. Because we only have one option left, we can simply put the cell reference C$2 into the second value_if_false argument.
4. Type a close parenthesis.

In Figure 564, you can see that when you type a close parenthesis it appears in a green color. The open and close parenthesis of the second IF are both a green color to help identify that they belong to the second IF function.

▲	A	B	C	D
1	Rule For Commission	Hurdle	Com. Rate	
2	$0 <= Sales < $5,000	$0	0.00	
3	$5,000 <= Sales < $7,000	$5,000	0.02	
4	Sales >= $7,000	$7,000	0.03	
5				
6	Name	Sales	Comission	
7	Mike Tello	$5,018	0.02	
8	Samuel George	$4,125	0	
9	Jeff Pannell	$7,000	0.03	
10	Bruce Urrutia	$3,012	0	
11	Keith Reno	$9,558	=IF(B11>=B$4,C$4,IF(B11>=B$3,C$3,C$2))	
12				

Figure 565

5. Type a close parenthesis for the first IF function; it should appear in a black color.
6. Copy the formula down and then verify that the formula is correct.

Sales	Comission
$5,018	$0.02
$4,125	$0.00
$7,000	$0.03
$3,012	$0.00
$9,558	=IF(B11>=B$4,C$4,IF(B11>=B$3,C$3,C$2))*B11

Figure 566

7. With the formula still in Edit mode, add "times one cell to my left" to the end of the formula.
8. To populate all the cells with the edited formula, press Ctrl + Enter.

Name	Sales	Comission
Mike Tello	$5,018	$100.36
Samuel George	$4,125	$0.00
Jeff Pannell	$7,000	$210.00
Bruce Urrutia	$3,012	$0.00
Keith Reno	$9,558	$286.74

Figure 567

In Figure 567, you can see our finished column of commission calculations.

	A	B	C	D
19				
20	Rule For Commission	Hurdle	Com. Rate	
21	$0 <= Sales < $2,000	$0	0	
22	$2,000 <= Sales < $3,000	$2,000	0.01	
23	$3,000 <= Sales < $4,000	$3,000	0.02	
24	$4,000 <= Sales < $5,000	$4,000	0.03	
25	$5,000 <= Sales < $7,000	$5,000	0.04	
26	Sales >= $7,000	$7,000	0.05	
27				
28	Name	Sales	Comission	
29	Mike Tello	$5,018	=IF(B29>=B$26,C$26,IF(B29>=B$25,C$25,	
30	Samuel George	$1,000	IF(B29>=B$24,C$24,IF(B29>=B$23,C$23,	
31	Jeff Pannell	$7,000	IF(B29>=B$22,C$22,C$21)))))*B29	
32	Bruce Urrutia	$3,012	$60.24	
33	Keith Reno	$9,558	$477.90	

Figure 568

In Figure 568, you can see an example of a formula used for a typical column of commission calculations. Because we have six categories, the formula requires five nested IF functions. However, this formula can be easily replaced with the VLOOKUP function.

In the next section, we want to take a look at another one of the most commonly used functions in Excel: the VLOOKUP function.

Lookup Functions

In this section, we look at a category of functions that are called **lookup functions**. You will learn about the VLOOKUP, MATCH, and INDEX functions. In essence, lookup functions all take an item, look it up in some sort of table (like a traditional tax table), and return an item to the cell or formula that contains the lookup function. Think of a commission table where we look up a commission rate or a customer table where we look up a customer balance. (The word *table* in the phrases *tax table* or *commission table* or *customer table* does not necessarily refer to table format structure or Excel table.) We will start by looking at one of the most common lookup functions, the VLOOKUP.

VLOOKUP (for looking up values)

Before we look at how the VLOOKUP function works, let's see how to do a lookup task manually, without the VLOOKUP function. This will help you to understand and appreciate the VLOOKUP function much better!

To follow along, open the file named excelisfun-Start.xlsm and navigate to the VLOOKUP(1) sheet.

F	G	H	I	J	K	L	M
its	COGS	Sales	Sales Category		to help understand VLOOKUP	Category Lower Limit	Sales Category
7	$70.00	$154.00			0 <= Sales < 100	$0.00	Subpar
61	$610.00	$1,342.00			100 <= Sales < 500	$100.00	OK
6	$48.00	$114.00			500 <= Sales < 750	$500.00	Good
61	$564.25	$1,281.00			750 <= Sales < 1000	$750.00	Great
8	$64.00	$152.00			Sales >= 1000	$1,000.00	Exceptional
59	$649.00	$1,357.00					
19	$190.00	$418.00					

Figure 569

In Figure 569, you can see the Sales field in column H and the Sales Category field in column I. Our goal is to assign a sales category to each sale. For example, because the first sale is $154, we need to assign the sales category OK to the cell I2 because the sale amount of $154 falls *between* $100 and $500. Now the word between has to be defined carefully so that we don't have overlapping categories or so that we don't double count. Our between will mean "greater than or equal to $100 and less than $500," or said in math symbols, $100 <= Sales Amount < $500. Notice when we write it in math symbols, it should be easier to understand how the categorization works because the <= Sales Amount < phrase sits between the two numbers. Notice that on the left the "greater than" part (open part of the symbol) points toward the Sales Amount and on the right side the "less than" part (closed part of the symbol) points toward the Sales Amount. In addition, the number on the left is the only one that has the equal sign. Now for some people this will seem obvious, but for some of us math-challenged people (that want to get this right), breaking it down in simple terms like this helps *a lot*.

Now, what about the second number, $1,342? What category should we put in cell I3? In Figure 569, you can see all the math categories in column K and all the sales categories associated with each math category in column M. So, looking through the math categories from top to bottom, we select the last category because $1,342 >= $1,000, and thus the sales category Exceptional should be put into cell I3.

What about the third number, $144, as shown in Figure 570? To categorize this number, let's do it again manually, but this time we will do it exactly like the VLOOKUP function would do it so that we understand how VLOOKUP does its magic:

1. With cell I4 selected, we look at the $144 sales number and remember it.
2. We look over to the lookup table (black range L2:M6), which has these characteristics. (The word *table* in the phrase *lookup table* does not refer to table format structure or Excel table.)

- The lookup table is vertically oriented. (This is why there is a V in front of LOOKUP.)
- The first column has numbers, which must be sorted smallest to biggest (ascending).
- The second column has the sales categories that could be delivered to a cell.

3. With the number $144 in our head, we look through the first column of the lookup table from top to bottom and when we see the first number that is bigger than $144, we jump back up one row.

- In our case, we looked at $0, then at $100, then when we get to $500, we say, "$500 is the first bigger number we see (as compared to $114)," and so we jump back to the row with the $100.

4. Once we know that the $144 amount belongs on the $100 row, we jump over to the second column and grab the sales category OK and remember it.
5. We put the sales category OK into the cell I4.

That process is how the VLOOKUP works. (Actually, it does something called a binary search, but the method described above is an awesome metaphor that makes it easy to understand how VLOOKUP does what it does.) Now let's create our VLOOKUP formula.

	E	F	G	H	I	J	K	L	M	N	O
1	Customer Units		COGS	Sales	Sales Category		to help understand VLOOKUP	Category Lower Limit	Sales Category		
2	FRED	7	$70.00	$154.00	OK		0 <= Sales < 100	$0.00	Subpar		
3	FM	61	$610.00	$1,342.00	Exceptional		100 <= Sales < 500	$100.00	OK		
4	DDH	6	$48.00	$114.00			500 <= Sales < 750	$500.00	Good		
5	T	61	$564.25	$1,281.00			750 <= Sales < 1000	$750.00	Great		
6	AST	8	$64.00	$152.00			Sales >= 1000	$1,000.00	Exceptional		
7	ET	59	$649.00	$1,357.00							
106	SFWK	19	$190.00	$418.00							

Lookup Table

Figure 570

VLOOKUP Function (to assign a category to a sales number)

The VLOOKUP function will replace the task of manually assigning categories. In short, the VLOOKUP function will look at a value and assign the correct sales category from our lookup table. Now let's enter our VLOOKUP function into cell I2 and then copy our formula down the whole column.

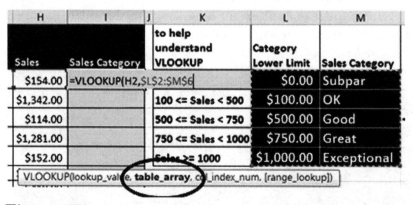

H	I	J	K	L	M
Sales	Sales Category		to help understand VLOOKUP	Category Lower Limit	Sales Category
$154.00	=VLOOKUP(H2		0 <= Sales < 100	$0.00	Subpar
$1,342.00			100 <= Sales < 500	$100.00	OK
$114.00			500 <= Sales < 750	$500.00	Good
$1,281.00			750 <= Sales < 1000	$750.00	Great
$152.00			Sales >= 1000	$1,000.00	Exceptional

VLOOKUP(**lookup_value**, table_array, col_index_num, [range_lookup])

Figure 571

1. On the VLOOKUP(1) sheet, in the cell I2, type **=VLOOKUP(**.
2. Click cell H2.

In Figure 571, you can see that the first argument is lookup_value. This is the value that VLOOKUP will use for assigning a category. In essence, this is the item VLOOKUP puts into its brain before it goes over to the lookup table and tries to find the correct sales category.

H	I	J	K	L	M
Sales	Sales Category		to help understand VLOOKUP	Category Lower Limit	Sales Category
$154.00	=VLOOKUP(H2,$L$2:$M$6			$0.00	Subpar
$1,342.00			100 <= Sales < 500	$100.00	OK
$114.00			500 <= Sales < 750	$500.00	Good
$1,281.00			750 <= Sales < 1000	$750.00	Great
$152.00			Sales >= 1000	$1,000.00	Exceptional

VLOOKUP(lookup_value, **table_array**, col_index_num, [range_lookup])

Figure 572

3. Type a comma.
4. Select the range L2:M6. This range is our lookup table.
5. Press the F4 key one time to lock the references and make them absolute. Because the lookup table would be locked no matter where we copy it, we make it absolute.

In Figure 572, you can see that the second argument is table_array. This is our lookup table, where the first column ($0, $100, $500, $750, $1000) is used as our lookup column, and the second column (Subpar, OK, Good, Great, Exceptional) contains the values to return to the cell.

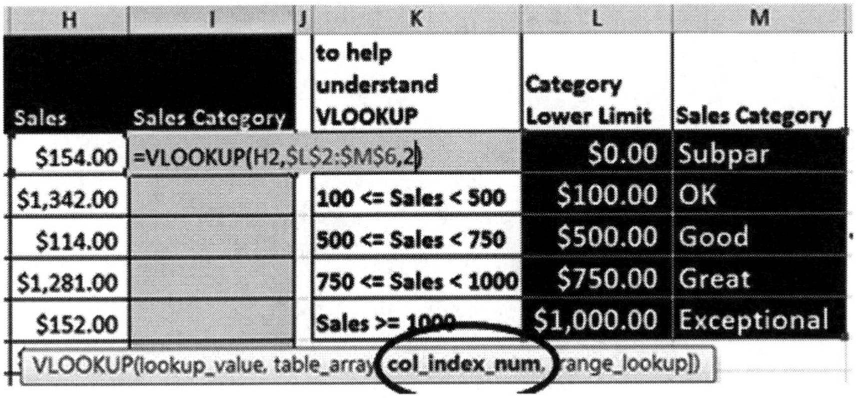

H	I	J	K	L	M
Sales	Sales Category		to help understand VLOOKUP	Category Lower Limit	Sales Category
$154.00	=VLOOKUP(H2,$L$2:$M$6,2)			$0.00	Subpar
$1,342.00			100 <= Sales < 500	$100.00	OK
$114.00			500 <= Sales < 750	$500.00	Good
$1,281.00			750 <= Sales < 1000	$750.00	Great
$152.00			Sales >= 1000	$1,000.00	Exceptional

VLOOKUP(lookup_value, table_array, **col_index_num**, range_lookup])

Figure 573

6. Type a comma.
7. Type the number **2**.
8. Type a close parenthesis.

In Figure 573, you can see that the third argument is col_index_num. We put a 2 because the values we want to return to the cell are in the second column of our table_array. (Later we will see examples of where we return values from the third and fourth columns of the table_array.)

In Figure 573, you can also see that the fourth argument is [range_lookup]. The square brackets around this argument means that it is an optional argument depending on whether you want the default setting. Because the default setting is for a lookup table that has numbers sorted in ascending order (just like we have), we do not need to put anything in this argument. Later when we do an exact match VLOOKUP, we will have to add a 0 in this fourth argument.

Note: When we omit the [range_lookup] argument for VLOOKUP this means we are doing an approximate match on a column that is sorted ascending and we are trying to find the biggest value that is less than or equal to the lookup value. Now, for some of us, that is hard to understand. I always shake my head when I read the Excel help on this topic. This is why I always think of it as looking down the sorted column until it bumps into a value bigger than the lookup value, then it jumps back one row and takes that row. This conceptual trick will help us when we study the MATCH function later on.

The [range_lookup] argument for VLOOKUP is similar to the [match_type] argument for the MATCH function:
- Omitted and it does an approximate match.
- Put a 0 (zero) and it does an exact match (more on exact matches shortly).

H	I	J K	L	M
		to help understand	Category	
Sales	Sales Category	VLOOKUP	Lower Limit	Sales Category
$154.00	OK	0 <= Sales < 100	$0.00	Subpar
$1,342.00	Exceptional	100 <= Sales < 500	$100.00	OK
$114.00	OK	500 <= Sales < 750	$500.00	Good
$1,281.00	Exceptional	750 <= Sales < 1000	$750.00	Great
$152.00	OK	Sales >= 1000	$1,000.00	Exceptional
$1,357.00	Exceptional			
$418.00	=VLOOKUP(H106,$L$2:$M$6,2)			

Figure 574

9. Press Ctrl + Enter to enter the formula and keep the cell selected.
10. Double-click the fill handle to copy the formula down to cell I106.
11. Verify that the last cell contains the correct formula.

In Figure 574, some rows have been hidden so that we can see the last formula in cell I106. The last formula looks good because it is still looking one cell to the left (relative cell reference) and it is still looking at the lookup table in the locked range $L$2:$M$6 (absolute cell reference). That is exactly 105 formulas that each delivers the correct sales category!

Next we want to take a closer look at all the details of the VLOOKUP function.

Now let's take a closer look at the VLOOKUP's arguments. Figure 575 shows the screen tip for the VLOOKUP function.

VLOOKUP(lookup_value, table_array, col_index_num, [range_lookup])

Figure 575

- The lookup_value argument is the "number that we are looking up."
    Not case sensitive (Tom = tom = tOM).
    Cannot be longer than 255 characters.
    Can be a number, text, logical value, or a name or reference that refers to a one of these.
- The table_array argument is the lookup table and can contain one or more columns.
    The first column is the lookup column.

The column with the values to return can be in any of the columns (1, 2, 3, and so on).

If you are doing an approximate match, the first column must be sorted smallest to biggest (ascending).

If you are doing an exact match, the first column does not need to be sorted.

- The col_index_num argument is a number (1, 2, 3, and so on) that represented the column in the table_array that has the value to return to the cell.

- The [range_lookup] argument tells the VLOOKUP function whether you are doing an approximate match or an exact match when looking up a value.

  Approximate match means that the values in the first column of table_array has gaps. For example, if the first column has the numbers $0, $100, $500, $750, $1,000, and we give the VLOOKUP the number $154 as the lookup_value, it "will fit into the gap between $100 and $500" and will be assigned to the $100 row.

  If you are doing an approximate match, the first column must be sorted smallest to biggest (ascending).

  For approximate match, the [range_lookup] argument can be omitted. The square brackets mean that if the argument is omitted it will assume the default setting, which is approximate match. If you wanted to explicitly list this argument, you could put in 1 or TRUE.

  If the lookup_value is smaller than the first value in the first column of the table_array , you get a #N/A error.

  If the lookup_value is bigger than all the values in the first column of the table_array , the last value will be returned.

  Examples of table_arrays that have gaps are tax tables, commission tables and grade tables. (The word *table* does not refer to table format structure or Excel table.)

  Exact match means that the values in the first column of table_array have no gaps. For example, if our first column has the numbers $0, $100, $500, $750, $1,000, exact match would return an item only if the lookup_value was $0, $100, $500, $750, or $1,000. With an exact match, it will not find values between the numbers.

  If you are doing an exact match, the first column does not need to be sorted.

  For exact match, the [range_lookup] argument requires a 0 or FALSE.

  If the lookup_value is not in the first column of the table_array , you get a #N/A error.

If there are duplicates in the first column, VLOOKUP will choose the first one listed.

Examples of table_arrays that have no gaps are invoice/product tables and customer data tables. (The word *table* does not refer to table format structure or Excel table.)

Now we want to look at four common examples of how to use the VLOOKUP function.

VLOOKUP Function (to help calculate commissions earned)

In Figure 576, we can see the nested IF formula used for calculating commissions that we saw in the preceding section. This formula is way to big! The VLOOKUP is a much better solution for this problem. However, before we can use our VLOOKUP for this commission calculation, we have to make sure that our categories are set up correctly. Recall our rules for setting up categories:

- The lower limit is included in the category, but the upper limit is not (for example, $5,000 <= Sales < $7,000).
- All possible categories are included.
- The categories are organized in ascending order.

All of these must be true to use our VLOOKUP function to do an approximate match lookup.

	A	B	C	D	E
1	VLOOKUP to calculate Commission Earned				
2	Rule For Commission	Hurdle	Com. Rate		
3	$0 <= Sales < $2,000	$0	0		
4	$2,000 <= Sales < $3,000	$2,000	0.01		
5	$3,000 <= Sales < $4,000	$3,000	0.02		
6	$4,000 <= Sales < $5,000	$4,000	0.03		
7	$5,000 <= Sales < $7,000	$5,000	0.04		
8	Sales >= $7,000	$7,000	0.05		
9				IF(logical_test, [value_if_true], [value_if_false])	
10	Name	Sales	Comission	Comission	
11	Mike Tello	$5,018		=IF(B11>=B$8,C$8,IF(B11>=B$7,	
12	Samuel George	$1,000		C$7,IF(B11>=B$6,C$6,IF(B11>=B$5,	
13	Jeff Pannell	$7,000		C$5,IF(B11>=B$4,C$4,C$3)))))*B11	
14	Bruce Urrutia	$3,012		$60.24	
15	Keith Reno	$9,558		$477.90	

Figure 576

To follow along, open the file excelisfun-Start.xlsm and navigate to the VLOOKUP(2) sheet.

⊿	A	B	C	D
1	VLOOKUP to calculate Commission Earned			
2	Rule For Commission	Hurdle	Com. Rate	
3	$0 <= Sales < $2,000	$0	0	
4	$2,000 <= Sales < $3,000	$2,000	0.01	
5	$3,000 <= Sales < $4,000	$3,000	0.02	
6	$4,000 <= Sales < $5,000	$4,000	0.03	
7	$5,000 <= Sales < $7,000	$5,000	0.04	
8	Sales >= $7,000	$7,000	0.05	
9				
10	Name	Sales	Comission	Comission
11	Mike Tello	$5,018	=VLOOKUP(B11,$B$3:$C$8,2)	
12	Samuel George	VLOOKUP(lookup_value, table_array, col_index_num, [ran		
13	Jeff Pannell	$7,000		$350.00

Figure 577

1. On the VLOOKUP(2) sheet, click in cell C11 and create the following formula:

   =VLOOKUP(B11,$B$3:$C$8,2)

In Figure 577, we can see that we used a relative cell reference for the employee's sales number in the lookup_value argument, an absolute cell reference for the table_array argument, and a 2 for the col_index_num because the value we want to return to our formula is the commission rate.

	A	B	C	D
10	Name	Sales	Comission	Comission
11	Mike Tello	$5,018	0.04	$200.72
12	Samuel George	$1,000	0	$0.00
13	Jeff Pannell	$7,000	0.05	$350.00
14	Bruce Urrutia	$3,012	0.02	$60.24
15	Keith Reno	$9,558	=VLOOKUP(B15,$B$3:$C$8,2)	

Figure 578

2. Enter the formula.
3. Copy it down the column.
4. Verify that it worked.

In Figure 578 notice that the VLOOKUP is delivering a commission rate to each cell. This is not what we want. We really want the rate times the sales number.

Sales	Comission	Comission
$5,018	0.04	$200.72
$1,000	0	$0.00
$7,000	0.05	$350.00
$3,012	0.02	$60.24
$9,558	=VLOOKUP(B15,$B$3:$C$8,2)*B15	

Figure 579

5. With the formula in Edit mode, change to formula to this:
   =VLOOKUP(B15,$B$3:$C$8,2)*B15

	Name	Sales	Comission	Comission
10				
11	Mike Tello	$5,018	$200.72	$200.72
12	Samuel George	$1,000	$0.00	$0.00
13	Jeff Pannell	$7,000	$350.00	$350.00
14	Bruce Urrutia	$3,012	$60.24	$60.24
15	Keith Reno	$9,558	$477.90	$477.90

Figure 580

6. Populate the edited formula into the column by pressing Ctrl + Enter.
7. Apply the Currency number formatting with the Ctrl + Shift + 4 keyboard shortcut.

In Figure 580, we can see that the VLOOKUP function and our nested IF formula both give us the same answer, but the VLOOKUP is much more efficient.

Next we want to see how to use the VLOOKUP function to assign a grade.

VLOOKUP Function (to assign a grade)

	A	B	C	D
1		VLOOKUP to assign a grade		
2	Rule For Grade	Score		Grade
3	0 <= Sales < 90	0	Fail	F
4	90 <= Sales < 110	90	Below Ave.	D
5	110 <= Sales < 130	110	Ave.	C
6	130 <= Sales < 150	130	Above Ave.	B
7	150 <= Sales < 160	150	High Ach.	A
8	Sales >= 160	160	Top	A+
9				
10	Name	Sales	Grade	
11	Leah Gamboa	118	=VLOOKUP(B11,$B$3:$D$8,3)	
12	Patrick Dahlberg	88		
13	Kristen Sharpe	147		
14	Sean Mullens	53		
15	Gina Coronado	143		
16	Daisy Shepherd	168		
17				

Figure 581

On the V(3) sheet, in the range C11:C16, enter the following formula:

=VLOOKUP(B11,$B$3:$D$8,3)

Notice that because the grade is in the third column of the lookup table (table_array), we use a **3** in the col_index_num argument.

Name	Sales	Grade
Leah Gamboa	118	C
Patrick Dahlberg	88	F
Kristen Sharpe	147	B
Sean Mullens	53	F
Gina Coronado	143	B
Daisy Shepherd	168	A+

Figure 582

After you enter the VLOOKUP function into the range and verify that the formula is correct, you should see these grades.

Next, we want to see how to use the Data Validation feature and the VLOOKUP function to complete an invoice.

Data Validation and VLOOKUP (to complete an invoice)

In Figure 583, we can see that in cell A10 there is a drop-down list with product IDs. The goal is to create that drop-down list using the Data Validation List feature and then use the VLOOKUP function to look up the product name and price based on the item selected from the drop-down list. For example, in Figure 583 we can see when we select Pro-187 we get the name Sunshine and the price $22, whereas if we select Pro-901 we get the name Sunbell and the price $24.

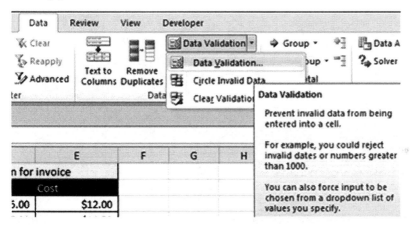

	A	B	C	D	E
1	VLOOKUP to look up product information for invoice				
2	ProductID	Name	Description	Price	Cost
3	Pro-650	Bellen	20 meters - 2	$25.00	$12.00
4	Pro-643	Carlota	20 meters - 3	$27.00	$14.50
5	Pro-187	Sunshine	30 meters	$22.00	$11.00
6	Pro-901	Sunbell	35 meters	$24.00	$13.00
7	Pro-711	Sunset	45 meters	$23.00	$12.00
8					
9	ProductID	Name	Price	Units	Total
10	Pro-187 ▾	Sunshine	$22.00	2	$44.00
11	Pro-650				
12	Pro-643				
13	Pro-187				
	Pro-901				
	Pro-711				
14					

	A	B	C	D	E
1	VLOOKUP to look up product information for invoice				
2	ProductID	Name	Description	Price	Cost
3	Pro-650	Bellen	20 meters - 2	$25.00	$12.00
4	Pro-643	Carlota	20 meters - 3	$27.00	$14.50
5	Pro-187	Sunshine	30 meters	$22.00	$11.00
6	Pro-901	Sunbell	35 meters	$24.00	$13.00
7	Pro-711	Sunset	45 meters	$23.00	$12.00
8					
9	ProductID	Name	Price	Units	Total
10	Pro-901 ▾	Sunbell	$24.00	2	$48.00
11	Pro-650				
12	Pro-643				
13	Pro-187				
	Pro-901				
14	Pro-711				

Figure 583

To follow along, open the file named excelisfun-Start.xlsm and navigate to the V(4) sheet.

Figure 584

1. On the V(4) sheet, click in cell A10.
2. On the Data tab, Data Tools group, click the Data Validation icon.
3. In the drop-down, click Data Validation.

The keyboard shortcut is Alt, D, L.

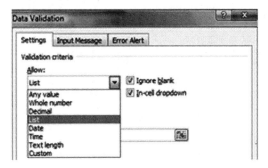

Figure 585

    4. In the Allow text box, select List from the drop-down.
    5. Press Tab to move to the Source text box.

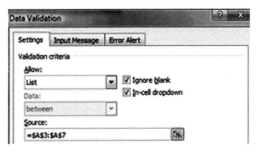

Figure 586

    6. With your cursor in the Source text box, select the range A3:A7 with your selection cursor.

Notice that Absolute References are put into the Source text box during this process. (This becomes important only if you are copying the cell; because we are not, we do not need to worry about it.)

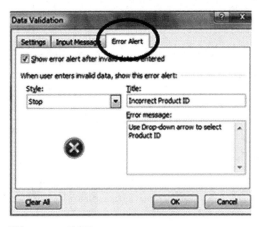

Figure 587

    7. Click the Error Alert tab.
    8. In the Title text box, type something like **Incorrect Product ID**.

9. In the Error message text box, type something like **Use drop-down arrow to select Product ID**.

10. Click the OK button.

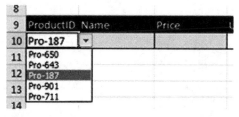

Figure 588

11. In cell A10, select Pro-187 from the drop-down list.

Figure 589

12. In cell A10, type **Pro-111**.

13. Press Enter.

Notice the Message box.

14. Click Cancel in the Message box.

	A	B	C	D	E
1	VLOOKUP to look up product information for invoice				
2	ProductID	Name	Description	Price	Cost
3	Pro-650	Bellen	20 meters - 2	$25.00	$12.00
4	Pro-643	Carlota	20 meters - 3	$27.00	$14.50
5	Pro-187	Sunshine	30 meters	$22.00	$11.00
6	Pro-901	Sunbell	35 meters	$24.00	$13.00
7	Pro-711	Sunset	45 meters	$23.00	$12.00
8					
9	ProductID	Name	Price	Units	Total
10	Pro-187	=VLOOKUP($A10		2	
11		VLOOKUP(lookup_value, table_array, col_index_num, [range_lookup			

Figure 590

15. In cell B10, begin the formula with **=VLOOKUP($A10**.

Notice that we locked the column reference A because when we copy this formula across the columns to cell C10, we need the formula to still be looking at the ProductID in cell $A10.

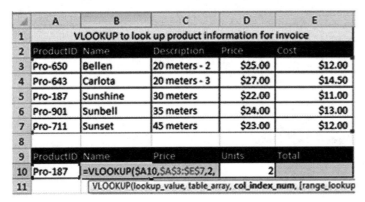

	A	B	C	D	E
1		VLOOKUP to look up product information for invoice				
2	ProductID	Name	Description	Price	Cost
3	Pro-650	Bellen	20 meters - 2	$25.00	$12.00
4	Pro-643	Carlota	20 meters - 3	$27.00	$14.50
5	Pro-187	Sunshine	30 meters	$22.00	$11.00
6	Pro-901	Sunbell	35 meters	$24.00	$13.00
7	Pro-711	Sunset	45 meters	$23.00	$12.00
8					
9	ProductID	Name	Price	Units	Total
10	Pro-187	=VLOOKUP($A10,$A$3:$E$7		2	
11		VLOOKUP(lookup_value, **table_array**, col_index_num, [range_lookup			

Figure 591

16. Type a comma.
17. Highlight the table_array (lookup table) in the range A3:E7.
18. Press the F4 key to lock both the column and row references.

Note: The lookup table usually is an absolute cell reference because no matter where you copy the formula you will always need to be looking at the same range of cells for the lookup table.

	A	B	C	D	E
1		VLOOKUP to look up product information for invoice				
2	ProductID	Name	Description	Price	Cost
3	Pro-650	Bellen	20 meters - 2	$25.00	$12.00
4	Pro-643	Carlota	20 meters - 3	$27.00	$14.50
5	Pro-187	Sunshine	30 meters	$22.00	$11.00
6	Pro-901	Sunbell	35 meters	$24.00	$13.00
7	Pro-711	Sunset	45 meters	$23.00	$12.00
8					
9	ProductID	Name	Price	Units	Total
10	Pro-187	=VLOOKUP($A10,$A$3:$E$7,2,		2	
11		VLOOKUP(lookup_value, table_array, **col_index_num**, [range_lookup			

Figure 592

19. Type a comma.
20. Type a **2**.

Notice that we are typing a 2 because the second column in the lookup table contains the names that we want to return to cell B10.

21. Type a comma to get to the [range-lookup] argument.

⊿	A	B	C	D	E	
1	VLOOKUP to look up product information for invoice					
2	ProductID	Name	Description	Price	Cost	
3	Pro-650	Bellen	20 meters - 2	$25.00	$12.00	
4	Pro-643	Carlota	20 meters - 3	$27.00	$14.50	
5	Pro-187	Sunshine	30 meters	$22.00	$11.00	
6	Pro-901	Sunbell	35 meters	$24.00	$13.00	
7	Pro-711	Sunset	45 meters	$23.00	$12.00	
8						
9	ProductID	Name	Price	Units	Total	
10	Pro-187	=VLOOKUP($A10,$A$3:$E$7,2,		2		
11			VLOOKUP(lookup_value, table_array, col_index_num, [range_lookup])			
12				TRUE - Approximate match	Approx	
13				FALSE - Exact match		

Figure 593

Notice that the [range-lookup] argument has a drop-down menu that has two options. We have already used the approximate match option because we had gaps in-between elements in the first column of the lookup table. Here we do not have gaps. We want the VLOOKUP to look up an exact match.

If you look at the ProductID column (first column of lookup table) in Figure 593, you can see that we have all ProductIDs listed. There is no such thing as a ProductID that would fit in between any two other ProductIDs. So it does not make any sense to do an approximate match. However, we could do an approximate match if we had sorted the ProductID column alphabetically (ascending). But in our case the Description column is sorted to show the shorter-range boomerangs on top, so we cannot sort the first column. In general, anytime the first column of the lookup table has all the values listed (there are no gaps where items could fit between any other two items), it is best to use the exact match option in the fourth argument of the VLOOKUP function.

9	ProductID	Name	Price	U
10	Pro-187	=VLOOKUP($A10,$A$3:$E$7,2,0)		

Figure 594

   22. Type a **0** (zero) in the [range-lookup] to indicate that you want exact match.

In Figure 594 you can see that we typed 0 (zero) into the [range-lookup] argument. FALSE works also. Because FALSE = 0, you can put either one in to indicate that you want an exact match. The reason that I always choose 0 (zero) rather than FALSE is that it involves fewer keystrokes.

9 ProductID Name Price Units
10 Pro-187 Sunshine Sunshine
11

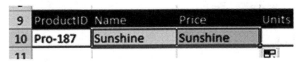

Figure 595

23. Enter the formula into cell B10 and then copy it to cell C10.

Notice that both cells have the product name Sunshine.

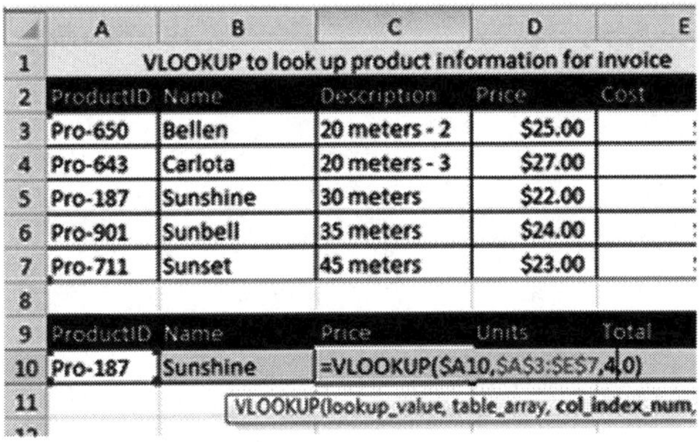

A B C D E
1 VLOOKUP to look up product information for invoice
2 ProductID Name Description Price Cost
3 Pro-650 Bellen 20 meters - 2 $25.00
4 Pro-643 Carlota 20 meters - 3 $27.00
5 Pro-187 Sunshine 30 meters $22.00
6 Pro-901 Sunbell 35 meters $24.00
7 Pro-711 Sunset 45 meters $23.00
8
9 ProductID Name Price Units Total
10 Pro-187 Sunshine =VLOOKUP($A10,$A$3:$E$7,4,0)
11 VLOOKUP(lookup_value, table_array, col_index_num,

Figure 596

24. Click in cell C10.
25. Press the F2 key to put the cell in Edit mode.
26. Using your fingers to count, determine which column in the lookup table has the price information.
27. Enter the number that represents the Price column into the col_index_num argument in the VLOOKUP function.
28. Press Tab two times.

Price Units Total
22 2 =C10*D10

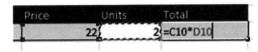

Figure 597

29. In cell E10, enter the following formula:
    two cells to the left times one cell to the left
30. Press Enter.

9 ProductID Name Price
10 Pro-187 nshine 22
11

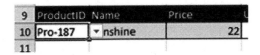

Figure 598

31. Click in cell A10.

Notice that the drop-down arrow blocks the Product name.

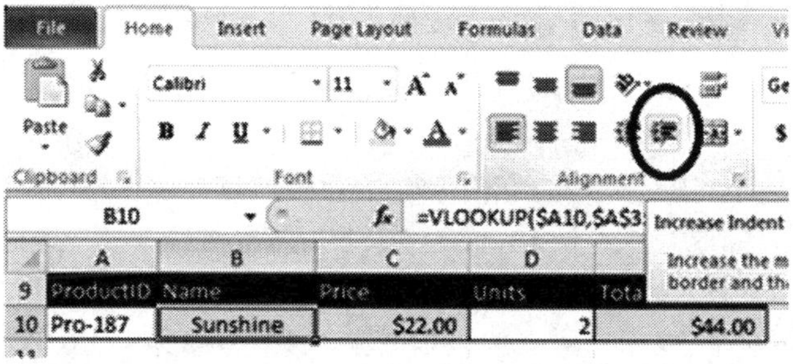

9	ProductID	Name	Price	Units	Tota
10	Pro-187	Sunshine	$22.00	2	$44.00

B10   fx =VLOOKUP($A10,$A$3

Increase Indent

Increase the m
border and th

Figure 599

32. Click in cell B10.
33. On the Home tab in the Alignment group, click the Increase Indent button two times.
34. Click in cell C10.
35. Apply Currency number formatting with the Ctrl + Shift + 4 keyboard shortcut.

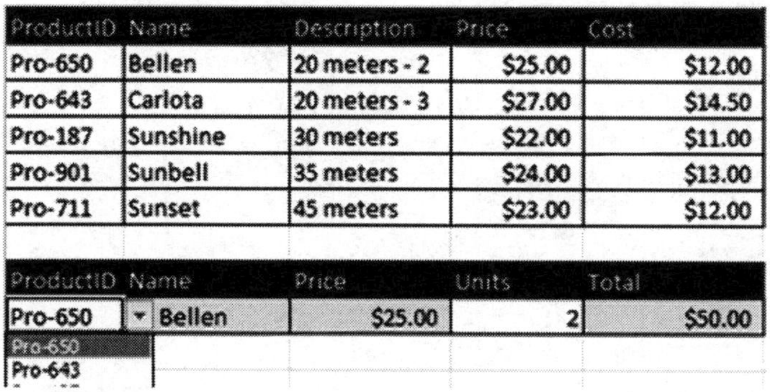

ProductID	Name	Description	Price	Cost
Pro-650	Bellen	20 meters - 2	$25.00	$12.00
Pro-643	Carlota	20 meters - 3	$27.00	$14.50
Pro-187	Sunshine	30 meters	$22.00	$11.00
Pro-901	Sunbell	35 meters	$24.00	$13.00
Pro-711	Sunset	45 meters	$23.00	$12.00

ProductID	Name	Price	Units	Total
Pro-650 ▾	Bellen	$25.00	2	$50.00
Pro-650				
Pro-643				

Figure 600

36. Test the formulas by selecting a different value in cell A10.

It is important to note that if there are duplicates in the first column, the VLOOKUP, and other lookup functions, will find only the first one listed.

Next we want to look at how to create the same type of formula for looking up product information, but instead of having to edit the col_index_num argument by hand, we will see how to use the MATCH function.

MATCH Function with VLOOKUP (to do a two-way lookup)

The MATCH function tells you what the relative position an item is in a list. For example, in Figure 601, you can see that the word Price is the fourth field name, and that the word Name is the second field name. If you tell the MATCH function to look up the word Price in the range A15:E15, it will return the number 4 because Price is the fourth item in the range A15:E15. In this situation, the MATCH function will be perfect for telling us which column the Name or Price is in for our VLOOKUP function. It will help us to create a more efficient formula than the one we saw back in Figure 596. You can think of this as a two-way lookup because 1) we are looking up a ProductID to tell us which row in the data set we need and 2) we are looking up a field name to tell us which column in the data set we need. First let's see how to get the MATCH function to work.

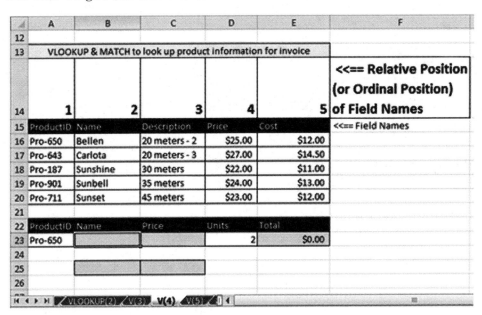

Figure 601

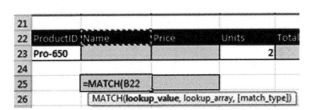

Figure 602

1. On the V(4) sheet, click in B25 and begin the formula with this:
    =MATCH(B22

Notice that the first argument for the MATCH is the same as for the VLOOKUP.

	A	B	C	D	E
15	ProductID	Name	Description	Price	Cost
16	Pro-650	Bellen	20 meters - 2	$25.00	$12.00
17	Pro-643	Carlota	20 meters - 3	$27.00	$14.50
18	Pro-187	Sunshine	30 meters	$22.00	$11.00
19	Pro-901	Sunbell	35 meters	$24.00	$13.00
20	Pro-711	Sunset	45 meters	$23.00	$12.00
21					
22	ProductID	Name	Price	Units	Total
23	Pro-650			2	$0.00
24					
25		=MATCH(B22,$A$15:$E$15			
26		MATCH(lookup_value, **lookup_array**, [match_type])			

Figure 603

2. Type a comma.
3. Select the range A15:E15.
4. Press the F4 key to lock the range.

Note: The lookup_array argument can be either horizontal or vertical. (Ours is horizontal.)

=MATCH(B22,$A$15:$E$15,0

Figure 604

5. Because we are doing an "exact match" (looking up a word in a list that is not sorted), we enter a **0** (zero) in the third argument.

	A	B	C	D	E
15	ProductID	Name	Description	Price	Cost
16	Pro-650	Bellen	20 meters - 2	$25.00	$12.00
17	Pro-643	Carlota	20 meters - 3	$27.00	$14.50
18	Pro-187	Sunshine	30 meters	$22.00	$11.00
19	Pro-901	Sunbell	35 meters	$24.00	$13.00
20	Pro-711	Sunset	45 meters	$23.00	$12.00
21					
22	ProductID	Name	Price	Units	Total
23	Pro-650			2	$0.00
24					
25		2	4		
26					

Figure 605

6. Use Ctrl + Enter to put the formula in cell B25.
7. Copy the formula to C25.

Notice that the relative position of the words Name and Price are displayed. These will represent our column numbers for our lookup table.

	A	B	C	D
21				
22	ProductID	Name	Cost	
23	Pro-650			
24				
25			2	5
26				

Figure 606

8. Test the MATCH function by typing **Cost** into cell C22.

The formula result in C25 should be 5.

	A	B	C	D	
15	ProductID	Name	Description	Price	Cost
16	Pro-650	Bellen	20 meters - 2	$25.00	
17	Pro-643	Carlota	20 meters - 3	$27.00	
18	Pro-187	Sunshine	30 meters	$22.00	
19	Pro-901	Sunbell	35 meters	$24.00	
20	Pro-711	Sunset	45 meters	$23.00	
21					
22	ProductID	Name	Cost	Units	Tota
23	Pro-650	=VLOOKUP($A23,$A$16:$E$20,B25,0)			
24		VLOOKUP(lookup_value, table_array, col_index_num,			
25			2	5	

Figure 607

9. Create the VLOOKUP formula in cell B23 but instead of typing in the col_index_num, refer to the MATCH function formula result two cells *below*:
   =VLOOKUP($A23,$A$16:$E$20,B25,0)
10. Press Ctrl + Enter.
11. Copy the formula to C23.

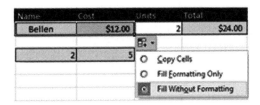

Name	Cost	Units	Total	
Bellen	$12.00	2	$24.00	
	2	5		

○ Copy Cells
○ Fill Formatting Only
◉ Fill Without Formatting

Figure 608

12. After you copy the formula, click the drop-down arrow on the smart tag and point to Fill Without Formatting.

	ProductID	Name	Cost	Units	Total	
22	ProductID	Name	Cost	Units	Total	
23	Pro-901 ▾	Sunbell	$13.00	2	$26.00	
24	Pro-650					
25	Pro-643 / Pro-187		2	5		
26	Pro-901 / Pro-711					
27						

Figure 609

13. To test the VLOOKUP, change the ProductID in cell A23 to Pro-901.

	ProductID	Name	Price	Units	Total
22					
23	Pro-901	Sunbell	$24.00	2	$48.00
24					
25		2	4		
26					
27					

Figure 610

14. Because this is an invoice and we don't want cost, but instead we want price, change the word in cell C22 to **Price**.

In Figure 610 we have our invoice working well, but if the column numbers of 2 and 4 in the range B25:C25 are not desirable, we can simply copy the MATCH formula in cell B25 and paste it into the VLOOKUP formula in cell B23.

Figure 611

15. Click in cell B25.
16. To put the cell in Edit mode, press the F2 key.
17. With your I-beam cursor, select the formula.
18. To copy the formula press Ctrl + C.
19. To get out of Edit mode, click the Esc key.

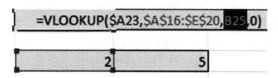

Figure 612

20. Click in cell B25.
21. To put the cell in Edit mode, press the F2 key.
22. To select the B25, double-click it. (This is a fast method for selecting the cell reference.)

	A	B	C	D	E	
15	ProductID	Name	Description	Price	Cost	<<
16	Pro-650	Bellen	20 meters - 2	$25.00	$12.00	
17	Pro-643	Carlota	20 meters - 3	$27.00	$14.50	
18	Pro-187	Sunshine	30 meters	$22.00	$11.00	
19	Pro-901	Sunbell	35 meters	$24.00	$13.00	
20	Pro-711	Sunset	45 meters	$23.00	$12.00	
21						
22	ProductID	Name	Price	Units	Total	
23	Pro-901	=VLOOKUP($A23,$A$16:$E$20,MATCH(B22,$A$15:$E$15,0),0)				
24		VLOOKUP(lookup_value, table_array, **col_index_num**, [range_lookup				
25		2	4			

Figure 613

23. To paste the copied MATCH function into the col_index_num, press Ctrl + V. It should look like this Figure 6.13.
24. Press Ctrl + Enter.
25. Copy the formula to cell C23.
26. Click the drop-down arrow on the smart tag and point to Fill Without Formatting.

27. To remove the content and formatting from the cells B25:C25, highlight the range B25:C25.
28. Go to the Home tab, Edit group, and click the Eraser icon and click Clear All (keyboard = Alt, E, A, A).

Figure 614

	A	B	C	D	E	
21						
22	ProductID	Name	Price	Units	Total	
23	Pro-643	Carlota	$27.00	2	$54.00	
24	Pro-650					
25	Pro-643					
	Pro-187					

Figure 615

29. Test it one last time.

> Note: The VLOOKUP and MATCH are in a category of functions called Lookup. Whereas the VLOOKUP looks up a value and returns a value from a cell, the MATCH looks up a value and returns the relative position of an item in a cell.

Next we want to look at how to use data validation list with the VLOOKUP and MATCH functions to retrieve customer information. However, unlike our invoice example, the data will not be on the same sheet as the lookup functions and data validation list.

VLOOKUP (to retrieve customer information from a different sheet)

Sometimes you have a data set with customer information and you want to be able to look up a customer ID and retrieve all the customer information in the customer record. This is the exact same situation as with our Invoice example, and as a result we can use our VLOOKUP and MATCH formula and a Data Validation List to solve this problem. However, because the data is on a different sheet, it is most efficient to name the ranges that we will use in our formulas using the Defined Name feature. Although we could just use sheet references for the VLOOKUP and MATCH, the Data Validation List feature will not work at all unless you use a defined name. Let's take a look at how to do this.

To follow along, open the file named excelisfun-Start.xlsm and navigate to the V(5) sheet.

Defined Name for Data Validation List and VLOOKUP and MATCH Functions

In Figure 616, you can see the template that we will use to retrieve the customer data on the V(5) sheet. In Figure 617, you can see the customer table on the CTable sheet, which contains data down to row 37 (not pictured).

To complete the example, we will need to name these three ranges from the CTable sheet using the Defined Name feature:

- The range C4:C37 will be given the defined name AccountDV and will be used for the Data Validation drop-down list.
- The range C4:G37 will be given the defined name CustomerDataV and will be used as the table_array (lookup table) argument for the VLOOKUP function.
- The range C3:G3 will be given the defined name ColumnNumM and will be used as the lookup_array (lookup range) argument for the MATCH function.

	A	B	C	D	E
1	Data Validation, VLOOKUP & MATCH to lookup customer information when data is on different sheet.				
2	Account#		Fname	Lname	Balance	E-mail
3					
4					
5					
6					

Figure 616

	A	B	C	D	E	F	G
1							
2							
3			Account#	Fname	Lname	Balance	E-mail
4			1258-DaDo-7418	Danielle	Dowell	$4,191.56	DaDo@gmail.com
5			1258-ViHo-1321	Victor	Horvath	$3,676.61	ViHo@gmail.com
6			1258-HoSh-4750	Howard	Shah	$7,350.44	HoSh@gmail.com
7			1258-MaKo-6449	Mark	Koehler	$1,367.36	MaKo@gmail.com
8			1258-DeSt-7389	Debbie	Stephen	$3,196.24	DeSt@gmail.com
9			1258-KuWe-1748	Kurt	Weckerly	$7,052.93	KuWe@gmail.com
10			1258-GuSu-6102	Guy	Sur	$1,445.17	GuSu@gmail.com
11			1258-OdLa-8740	Odessa	Lauria	$7,812.45	OdLa@gmail.com
12			1258-ElRh-4436	Elinor	Rhames	$6,225.46	ElRh@gmail.com
13			1258-NoSu-2274	Nova	Sumler	$4,749.54	NoSu@gmail.com

Figure 617

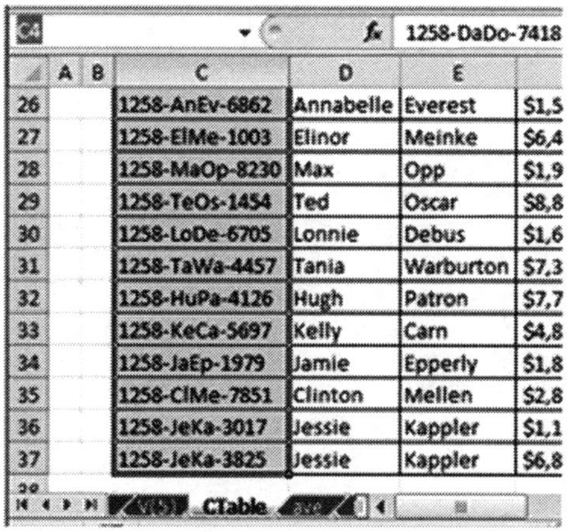

Figure 618

1. On the CTable sheet, click in cell C4.
2. To highlight the column with Account#, press Ctrl + Shift + Down Arrow.
3. On the left side of the formula bar, click in the Name box to select the cell reference C4.

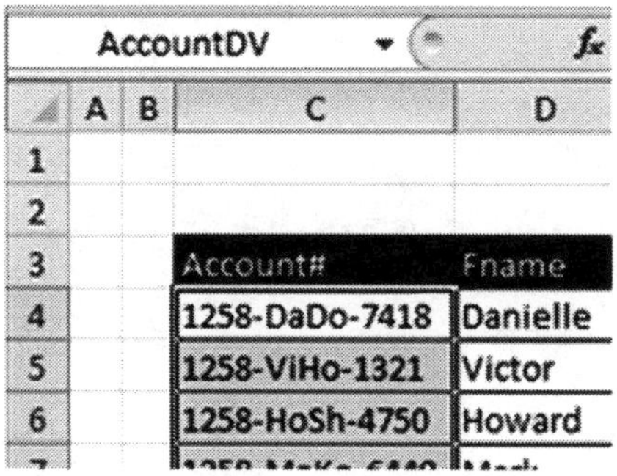

Figure 619

4. Type **AccountDV**.
5. Press Enter to register the name.

This defined name will be used for our Data Validation drop-down list.

Next we want to highlight the customer table and name it for the VLOOKUP function. But we have to be careful because the field names cannot be used in the table_array argument in the VLOOKUP function. We also want to see a series of keyboard shortcuts that will allow us to highlight the table without the field names.

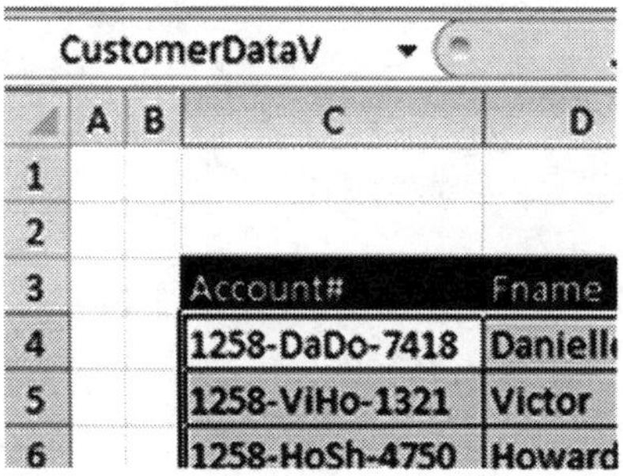

Figure 620

6. Click in cell C4.
7. Hold Ctrl and Shift down, and then tap the Right Arrow key once, and then tap the Down Arrow key once (to highlight the table without the field names).
8. Click in the Name box.
9. Type **CustomerDataV**.
10. Press Enter to register the name.

This defined name will be used in the table_array argument in the VLOOK-UP function.

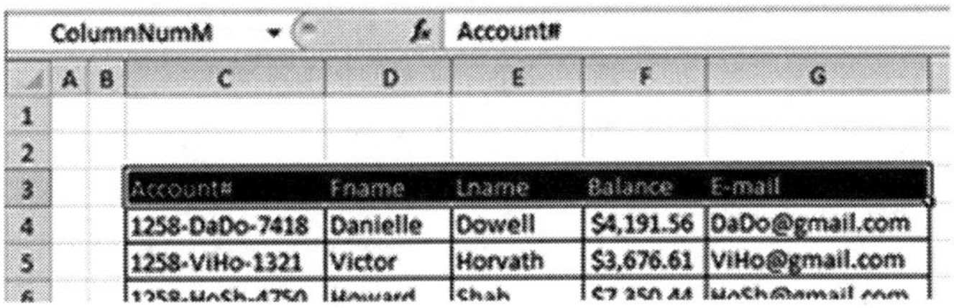

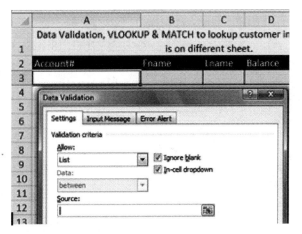

Figure 621

11. Name the range C3:G3 **ColumnNumM**.
12. Press Enter.
13. This defined name will be used in the lookup_array argument in the MATCH function.

14. On the sheet V(5) sheet, click in A3.
15. To open Data Validation, use the Alt + D + L keyboard shortcut. Alternatively, you can go to the Data tab, Data Tools group, and click the Data Validation button.
16. In the Allow text box, select List.
17. To move the cursor to Source text box, press the Tab key.

Figure 622

Our source is the list of Account#s from the data set on the CTable, which is the range that we named AccountDV.

18. To open up the Paste Name dialog box and insert the defined name into the Source text box, press the F3 key.
19. Double-click the name AccountDV. (You might see a slightly different list of names.)

Figure 623

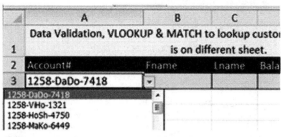

Figure 624

You should now see a Data Validation drop-down list in A3.

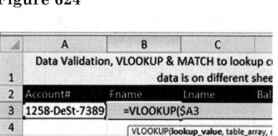

Figure 625

20. Click in A3.
21. Click the Increase Indent button twice.
22. Begin the formula with **=VLOOKUP($A3**.

Notice that the column reference is locked because when we copy the formula across the columns we need VLOOKUP to always look at the Account# in the A column.

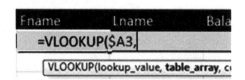

Figure 626

23. Type a comma.

Notice that the screen tip is asking for the table_array. We have the defined name CustomerDataV that will go into this argument.

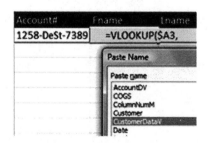

Figure 627

24. To open up the Paste Name dialog box, press the F3 key.
25. Double-click the defined name CustomerDataV.
26. Click OK.

2	Account#	Fname	Lname	Balance	E-r
3	1258-DeSt-7389	=VLOOKUP($A3,CustomerDataV,			
4		VLOOKUP(lookup_value, table_array, **col_index_num**,			
5					

Figure 628

27. Type a comma to get to the next argument.

In Figure 628, we can see a screen tip for the VLOOKUP function. We also can see that the VLOOKUP is expecting us to enter the third argument, col_index_num. Now, we know from our last invoice example that we can put a MATCH function into the col_index_num and the formula will work like a charm. Last time we did this, we first did the MATCH function in a separate cell and then we copied and pasted the MATCH into the col_index_num argument. But this time we want to type out the whole formula in one shot instead of doing it in two steps. It seems like this would be hard, but if you watch the screen tips carefully, they will help guide you through this nested formula process. The key is to watch the screen tips as we start to create the MATCH part of the formula.

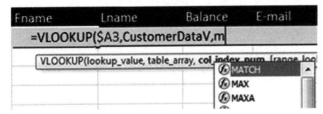

Figure 629

28. Type the letter M.

Notice that the drop-down menu for functions is highlighting the MATCH function.

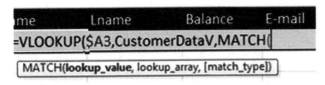

Figure 630

29. To accept the MATCH function from the drop-down and insert it into the function, press the Tab key.

Notice that the screen tip has changed to show the MATCH screen tip.

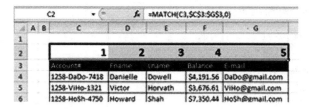

Figure 631

Before we go further with this nested formula, it is wise to go back and look at the data set to remind yourself of what the goal is for using the MATCH function.

In Figure 6.31, you can see that the relative position of the field names also tells us the column number that the VLOOKUP function will need in its col_index_num argument.

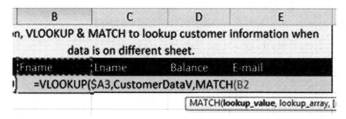

Figure 632

30. For the lookup_value for MATCH, click *one cell above.*

Looking back at Figure 631, you can see that our goal is to get MATCH to deliver the number 2.

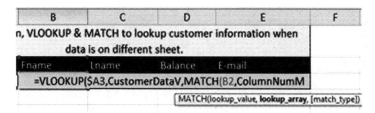

Figure 633

31. Type a comma.
32. Paste the defined name ColumnNumM in the lookup_array argument.

Remember that this name is the range C3:G3, as shown in Figure 631.

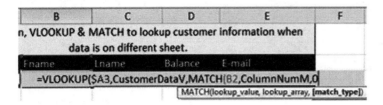

Figure 634

33. Type a comma.
34. Type **0** (zero) because we are doing an exact match.

Notice that the MATCH screen tip is still showing.

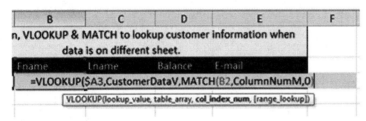

Figure 635

35. Type a close parenthesis.

Notice that the VLOOKUP screen tip is back.

Notice that the MATCH function is sitting in the col_index_num argument for the VLOOKUP function.

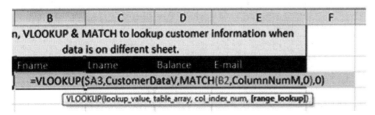

Figure 636

36. Type a comma.
37. Type **0** (zero) because we are doing an exact lookup in the VLOOK-UP's fourth argument.
38. Type close parenthesis.

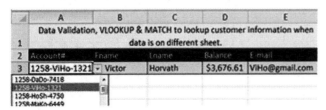

Figure 637

39. Enter the formula and copy it through the range B3:E3.
40. Be sure to use the smart tag Fill Without Formatting.
41. Test your formula by using the drop-down in cell A3, but also by changing the values on the CTable.

> **Note**: Just as in our invoice example, you can think of this as a two-way lookup because the formula in the range B3:E3 uses the Account# to decide which row we need in the customer table and uses the field name to decide which column we need in the customer table. A visual for this idea of a two-way lookup when retrieving customer information is shown in Figure 638. Figure 639 shows you the formula, and Figure 638 shows you the visual concept of a two-way lookup. This idea of a two-way lookup is important because, often, tax tables, commission tables, or shipping rate tables are setup in a two-way lookup format. (The word *table* does not necessarily refer to table format structure or Excel table.) Later, when we look at the INDEX function, you will see an alternative method for doing two-way lookup.

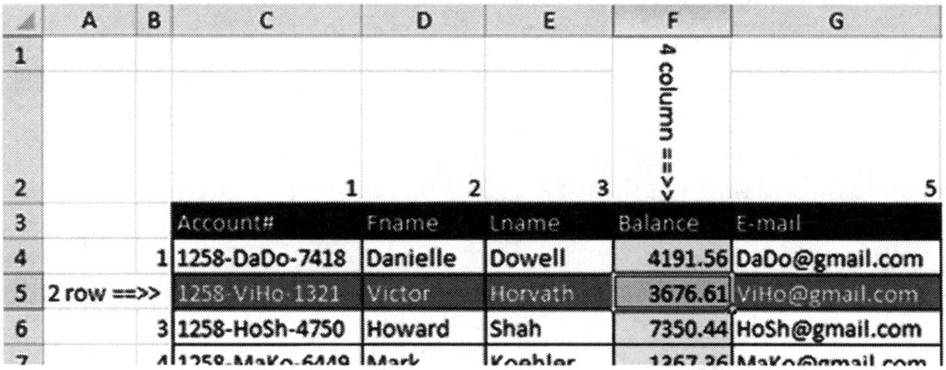

Figure 638

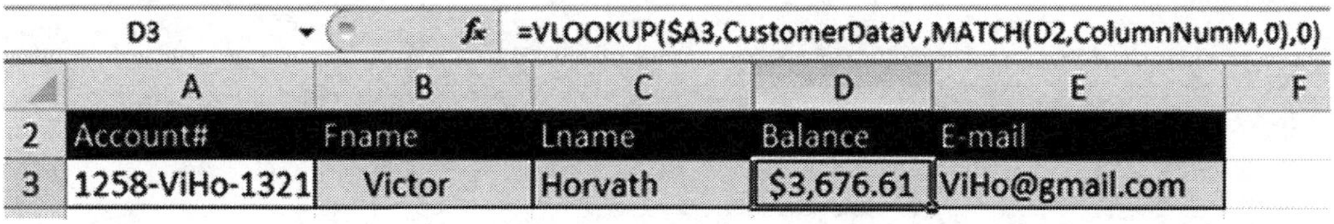

Figure 639

Next we want to look at a great use for the MATCH function that involves checking to determine whether a particular item already exists in a master list.

MATCH Function (to check whether item is in master list)

In Figure 640, our goal is to create a formula in the New Item column (column D) that will find all the names in the Current List column (column C) that are not in the Master List column (column A).

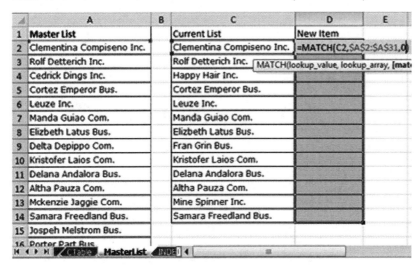

Figure 640

1. Select the MasterList sheet.
2. Highlight the range D2:D14 with the active cell being D2.
3. Create the following formula:
   =MATCH(C2,$A$2:$A$31,0)

A	B	C	D
1 **Master List**		**Current List**	**New Item**
2 Clementina Compiseno Inc.		Clementina Compiseno Inc.	1
3 Rolf Detterich Inc.		Rolf Detterich Inc.	2
4 Cedrick Dings Inc.		Happy Hair Inc.	#N/A
5 Cortez Emperor Bus.		Cortez Emperor Bus.	4
6 Leuze Inc.		Leuze Inc.	5
7 Manda Guiao Com.		Manda Guiao Com.	6
8 Elizbeth Latus Bus.		Elizbeth Latus Bus.	7
9 Delta Depippo Com.		Fran Grin Bus.	#N/A
10 Kristofer Laios Com.		Kristofer Laios Com.	9
11 Delana Andalora Bus.		Delana Andalora Bus.	10
12 Altha Pauza Com.		Altha Pauza Com.	11
13 Mckenzie Jaggie Com.		Mine Spinner Inc.	#N/A
14 Samara Freedland Bus.		Samara Freedland Bus.	13
15 Jospeh Melstrom Bus.			

Figure 641

4. To populate all the cells with our formula, press Ctrl + Enter.

The #N/A errors tell us that MATCH could not find the relative position of the item in the list because *they are not in the list*. In this case, an error is just what we want!

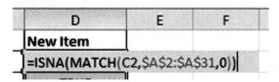

Figure 642

5. With the range still highlighted, press the F2 key to put the cell in Edit mode and put the ISNA function around the MATCH.

The ISNA function will return TRUE to the cell if it finds an #N/A error and FALSE if it does not find an #N/A error.

6. Press Ctrl + Enter.

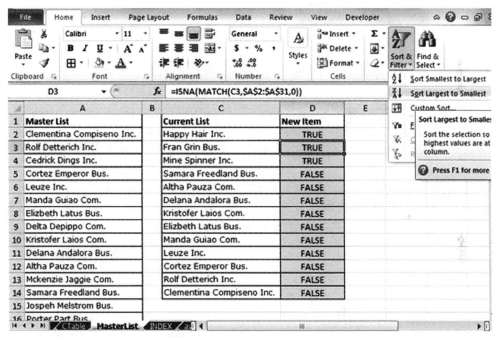

Figure 643

7. Select the single cell D3. *Do not highlight the whole column before sorting!*
8. Sort using the Z to A button in the Edit group in the Home tab. (More on how to sort later.)

In Figure 643, we can see that the ISNA and MATCH function together with sorting Z to A accomplished our goal of finding the names in the current list that are not in the master list. Now that the names are grouped together, we can copy and paste them into the master list.

> Note: We did not have to use the ISNA function to accomplish our goal. We could have simply sorted Z to A, and all the error values (and the new names) would have come to the top.

Note: If our goal were reversed, namely we want to find all the items in our current list that are in the master list, we could use a formula like this: =ISNUMBER(MATCH(C2,$A$2:$A$31,0)).

So far we have looked at the lookup functions VLOOKUP and MATCH, but now we want to learn about the INDEX function. The INDEX is very versatile and can solve some lookup problems that the VLOOKUP cannot solve. For example, INDEX will allow us to look up an item in a column to the left of the lookup column; you will see how to do this and two other amazing lookup tricks in the next section.

INDEX and MATCH Functions (for two-way lookup)

Back in Figure 638 and Figure 639, you saw how to do a two-way lookup using the VLOOKUP and MATCH. Now we want to see how to do the same thing with the INDEX and MATCH functions. But why do we have to learn a different method do accomplish the same task? You don't! But I am showing you both for two reasons:

- The VLOOKUP method we looked at is great because most working people and many job interviews use the VLOOKUP function almost exclusively and so it is a must to know how to use VLOOKUP.
- But the INDEX and MATCH combination is much more powerful and can be applied in many more situations than the VLOOKUP, and so you must learn this method so that your Excel toolkit is complete.

To start, let's look at the end result we need for a two-way lookup that involves commission rates. In Figure 644 and Figure 645, we can see that to look up the commission rate, we need a row number and a column number.

The person's sales will get us the row number and the product that he or she sold will get us the column number. The great thing about the INDEX is that it is specifically set up to take a row number and column number. The syntax for the INDEX looks like this:

=INDEX(array, row_num, [column_num])

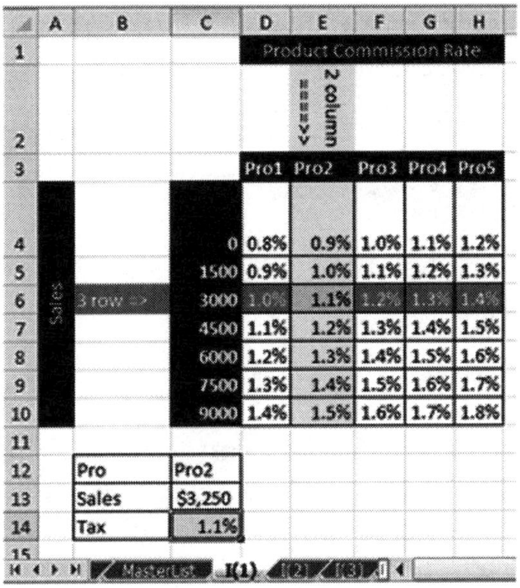

Figure 644

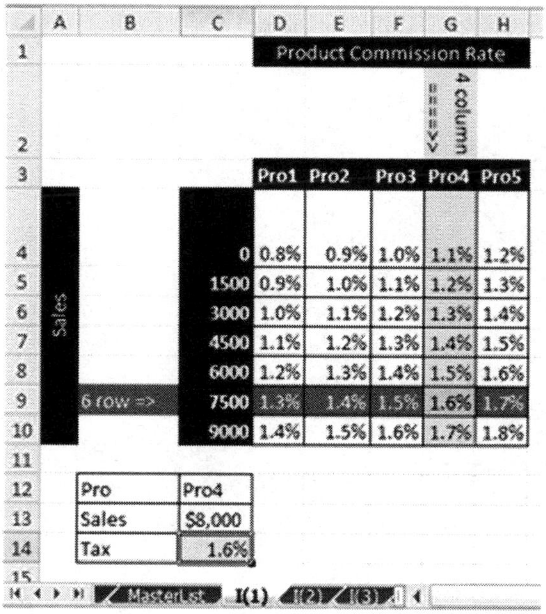

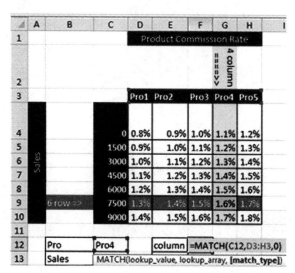

Figure 645

This means that in the example in Figure 644 we can tell the INDEX to look at the array (lookup table) D4:H10 and then give it the row number (row_num) and column number (column_num) and it will find the intersecting value. Our knowledge of the MATCH function will help us to get the column or row number. Let's take a look at how to do this.

To follow along, open the file named excelisfun-Start.xlsm and navigate to the I(1) sheet.

1. On the I(1) sheet, click in F12 and create the formula to find the column number for the product:

   =MATCH(C12,D3:H3,0)

Notice that the third argument for MATCH, match_type, is a 0 (zero) because we are doing an exact match lookup.

Notice that the lookup_array is horizontal.

2. Press Enter.

Figure 646

	A	B	C	D	E	F	G	H	I
1					Product Commission Rate				
2							####### 4 column >>		
3					Pro1	Pro2	Pro3	Pro4	Pro5
4				0	0.8%	0.9%	1.0%	1.1%	1.2%
5				1500	0.9%	1.0%	1.1%	1.2%	1.3%
6	Sales			3000	1.0%	1.1%	1.2%	1.3%	1.4%
7				4500	1.1%	1.2%	1.3%	1.4%	1.5%
8				6000	1.2%	1.3%	1.4%	1.5%	1.6%
9	6 row =>			7500	1.3%	1.4%	1.5%	1.6%	1.7%
10				9000	1.4%	1.5%	1.6%	1.7%	1.8%
11									
12		Pro	Pro4		column	4			
13		Sales	$8,000		row	=MATCH(C13,C4:C10)			
14		Tax	MATCH(lookup_value, lookup_array, [match_type])						

Figure 647

3. In F13, create the formula to find the row number for the sales:
   =MATCH(C13,C4:C10)

Notice that the third argument for MATCH, match_type, is omitted. Because we are doing an approximate match lookup.

Notice that the lookup_array is vertical.

4. Press Enter.

	A	B	C	D	E	F	G	H	I
3					Pro1	Pro2	Pro3	Pro4	Pro5
4				0	0.8%	0.9%	1.0%	1.1%	1.2%
5				1500	0.9%	1.0%	1.1%	1.2%	1.3%
6	Sales			3000	1.0%	1.1%	1.2%	1.3%	1.4%
7				4500	1.1%	1.2%	1.3%	1.4%	1.5%
8				6000	1.2%	1.3%	1.4%	1.5%	1.6%
9	6 row =>			7500	1.3%	1.4%	1.5%	1.6%	1.7%
10				9000	1.4%	1.5%	1.6%	1.7%	1.8%
11									
12		Pro	Pro4		column	4			
13		Sales	$8,000		row	6			
14		Tax	=INDEX(D4:H10,F13,F12)						
15			INDEX(array, row_num, [column_num])						
			INDEX(reference, row_num, [column_num], [area_num])						

Figure 648

5. Click in C14.
6. Create this formula:
   =INDEX(D4:H10,F13,F12)

7. The three arguments we will use are as follows:
   - array = D4:H10
   - row_num = F13
   - column_num = F12

In Figure 648 notice two things:
- Notice we can see that the INDEX screen tip has two options. The second one has four arguments and is for situations when you have more than one lookup table. Because we have only one lookup table, we will use the first option.
- Notice also that the array argument is the lookup table, but unlike the VLOOKUP function, the first column with the lookup values that determine the row number is not included in the array.

| Pro4 | | column | 4 |
| $8,000 | | row | 6 |

=INDEX(D4:H10,MATCH(C13,C4:C10),MATCH(C12,D3:H3,0))

INDEX(array, row_num, [column_num])

Figure 649

Finally, to put it all together (as you saw how to do back in Figures 611 to 613), we can copy and paste the MATCH functions from cells F13 and F12 into the row and column arguments to get the formula seen in Figure 649.

In the last few figures, you have learned something very powerful about the MATCH function. With MATCH, you can *look up* something in any direction! Because Excel only has two directions, horizontal and vertical, this will come in very handy when we have unusual lookup situations that VLOOKUP cannot handle like "Lookup Left" and "Lookup Above" (our next two examples). The MATCH function has another aspect that the VLOOKUP does not: It has three options in the third argument, match_type, that gives it more flexibility than the VLOOKUP function. Here is how all three argument elements work for match_type:
- 0 = Exact match.
- Omitted = Approximate match on a lookup_array that is sorted ascending and we are trying to find the biggest value that is less than or equal to the lookup_value. (looking through range until it sees a value bigger than the lookup_value, and then jumping back one row).
- -1 = Approximate match on a lookup_array that is sorted descending and we are trying to find the smallest value that is greater than or equal to the lookup_value. (looking through range until it sees a value smaller than the lookup_value, and then jumping back one row).

Next we want to do a Lookup Left with the INDEX and MATCH functions.

INDEX and MATCH (for one-way lookup to the left)

Looking at Figure 650, we can see the Lookup Left problem. If we are selling boomerangs and a customer comes in and asks says, "I want a boomerang that flies 30 meters," we want to select the *Flying Range is 30* from the drop-down in cell E3 and have the formulas in cells F3 and G3 retrieve the product and price. The problem is that if we take the phrase Flying Range is 30 and look that up in the Description column (column C) how are we going to retrieve a value from the Description column (column A)? VLOOKUP won't do this. The key here is to recognize that the Description column and Product column have the same number of cells in each of them. Once we see that, we can use the INDEX and MATCH function to retrieve an item in a column (Product column) to the left of the lookup column (Description column).

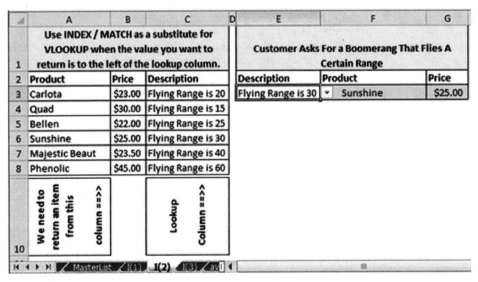

Figure 650

To follow along, open the file excelisfun-Start.xlsm and navigate to the I(2) sheet.

Looking at Figure 651, we can see that the INDEX function uses only two of its arguments. (Notice that the INDEX screen tip shows square brackets around the [column_num] argument, which means this argument can be omitted from the formula.) The two arguments being used are as follows:

- array = column that contains the items to be retrieved = A3:A8 = Product column.
- row_num = MATCH($E3,$C$3:$C$8,0) = relative position of lookup item Flying Range is 30.

The formula will work in both F3 and G3.

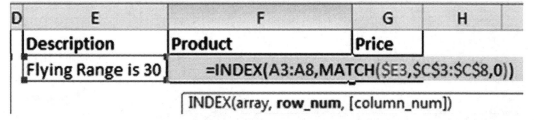

D	E	F	G	H	
	Description	Product	Price		
	Flying Range is 30	=INDEX(A3:A8,MATCH($E3,$C$3:$C$8,0))			
		INDEX(array, **row_num**, [column_num])			

Figure 651

Testing our formula, we see that the Lookup Left formula works fine.

	A	B	C	D	E	F	G
1	Use INDEX / MATCH as a substitute for VLOOKUP when the value you want to return is to the left of the lookup column.				Customer Asks For a Boomerang That Flies A Certain Range		
2	Product	Price	Description		Description	Product	Price
3	Carlota	$23.00	Flying Range is 20		Flying Range is 15	Quad	$30.00
4	Quad	$30.00	Flying Range is 15		Flying Range is 20		
5	Bellen	$22.00	Flying Range is 25		Flying Range is 15		
					Flying Range is 25		
					Flying Range is 30		

Figure 652

Next we want to look at a similar type of problem: Lookup Above.

To follow along, open the file excelisfun-Start.xlsm and navigate to the I(3) sheet.

INDEX and MATCH (for one-way lookup above)

The goal of the formula seen in Figure 653 is to retrieve the vendor's name with the lowest bid. The formula that can be entered into G3 and copied down the column is as follows:

=INDEX($B$2:$E$2,MATCH(F3,B3:E3,0))

The aspects of the formulas are as follows:
- The Low Bid column (F column) contains the MIN function and is finding the low bid for each product listed in column A.
- The array argument for INDEX = Vendor names in range $B$2:$E$2 = row that contains the items to be retrieved. (Each new cell in the row is a new column / same row.)
- Square brackets around the [column_num] argument for INDEX means that this argument can be omitted. In our example the array argument contains the range $B$2:$E$2, which has the columns B, C, D, E. So, really, we need a column number (col_num). But because the range for the array argument does not contain both rows and columns (meaning it is a one-way array), we simply put either the row_num or column_num into the row_num argument. If that is confusing, just

think of it this way: If it is a one-way array, just put the number into the row_num argument.

- The row_num argument for INDEX = MATCH(F3,B3:E3,0) = column number.

(The MATCH is finding the column number for the low bid that corresponds to the vendor with the lowest bid.)

	A	B	C	D	E	F	G	H	I
1	Use INDEX, MIN & MATCH to find vendor name with low bid								
2	Products/ Vendors	Vendor1	Vendor2	Vendor3	Vendor4	Low Bid	Vendor for Low Bid		
3	Product1	$47.63	$58.77	$59.76	$42.00	$42.00	=INDEX($B$2:$E$2,MATCH(F3,B3:E3,0))		
4	Product2	$48.36	$38.10	$52.94	$55.81	$38.10	Vendor2		
5	Product3	$43.61	$32.11	$42.37	$59.74	$32.11	Vendor2		
6	Product4	$47.06	$43.89	$49.22	$33.67	$33.67	Vendor4		

Figure 653

Wow! That was a lot about lookup functions. We covered some great tips about the VLOOKUP, MATCH, and INDEX functions.

Next we want to look at the ROUND function for accuracy in certain calculations.

ROUND Function

Knowing how to round a number to a certain digit is important for calculations that involve tax, payroll, and invoicing. The standard rule for rounding is as shown in Figure 654.

Rules For Rounding:
1) Choose 'position you want to round to'
2) Look at decimal to right of 'position you want to round to': if >= 5, add 1 to 'position you want to round to' if < 5, add 0 to 'position you want to round to'
3) Drop all decimals to right of 'position you want to round to'
Example of how rounding works for a tax calculation => $127.33 * 0.0145 = 1.846285 'position you want to round to' is 2 places to right of decimal (penny) 6 >= 5 1.846285 becomes 1.85

Figure 654

To follow along, open the file named excelisfun-Start.xlsm and navigate to the ROUND sheet.

Many people use Excel for calculations that involve tax, payroll, and invoicing and therefore are required to round. The good news is that Excel has a built-in function called ROUND that will make rounding automatic. However, a common mistake is to try and round the tax, payroll, or invoicing calculations with number formatting such as Currency or by decreasing the decimals. In Figure 655, you can see such a mistake. You can add the tax amounts yourself and see that $1.85 + $3.74 + $2.88 + $3.53 = $12.00, *not* $11.99.

C4			f_x	=B4*B$1	
	A	B	C	D E	F
1	Tax Rate	0.0145			
3	Employee	Before Tax	Tax (column not rounded)	After Tax	
4	Sioux	$127.33	$1.85	$125.48	Value in C4 = 1.846285 is formatted to look like: $1.85
5	Sue	$257.87	$3.74	$254.13	Value in C5 = 3.739115 is formatted to look like: $3.74
6	Jo	$198.35	$2.88	$195.47	Value in C6 = 2.876075 is formatted to look like: $2.88
7	Joe	$243.19	$3.53	$239.66	Value in C7 = 3.526255 is formatted to look like: $3.53
8	Totals	$826.74	$11.99	$814.75	<<==Incorrect total because tax calculations were not rounded correctly
10			$1.85 + $3.74 + $2.88 + $3.53 = $12.00, NOT $11.99.		

Figure 655

Recall from our earlier discussion about number formatting, formulas do not see formatting and so the SUM function in cell C8 is adding the unformatted numbers, not the formatted numbers that we see on the surface of the spreadsheet. To remedy this, we must edit our tax calculation and add use the ROUND function as shown in Figures 656 and 657.

	A	B	C	D
1	Tax Rate	0.0145		
3	Employee	Before Tax	Tax (column not rounded)	After Tax
4	Sioux	$127.33	=B4*B$1	$125.48
5	Sue	$257.87	$3.74	$254.13
6	Jo	$198.35	$2.88	$195.47
7	Joe	$243.19	$3.53	$239.66
8	Totals	$826.74	$11.99	$814.75

Figure 656

	A	B	C	D
1	Tax Rate	0.0145		
3	Employee	Before Tax	Tax (column not rounded)	After Tax
4	Sioux	$127.33	=ROUND(B4*B$1,2)	
5	Sue	$257.87	$3.74	$254.13
6	Jo	$198.35	$2.88	$195.47
7	Joe	$243.19	$3.53	$239.66
8	Totals	$826.74	$12.00	$814.74

Figure 657

In Figure 656, we see the incorrect formula for the range C4:C7. In Figure 657, we see the correct formula for the range C4:C7. We put a 2 (two) in the second argument in the ROUND function because we were rounding to the penny. After you add the ROUND function to the calculation, you can see that the SUM functions in cells C8 and D8 are correct. In this example, we are adding the tax calculations using the SUM function. If we were not using our tax calculations (formula result) in any subsequent formula, number formatting would be sufficient and we would not need to use the ROUND function.

Does one penny difference really matter? Well, a few pennies are not a big deal (unless a customer or employee discovers the error and no longer trusts that you can make accurate calculations).

You want to use the ROUND function in certain scenarios, including the following:

- You are required to round like with money involved with invoices, taxes, or payroll; there are no partial pennies.
- The formula calculation involves multiplying or dividing numbers that contain decimals (numbers that are being added or subtracted should already be rounded properly).
- The formula calculation result will be used in a subsequent formula (like SUM function for adding a column of tax calculations).

	C26			f_x	=ROUND(B26,2)	
	A	B	C	D	E	F
			ROUND			ROUND function 2nd argument
		Number	function			
25	Example	To Round	rounds	Formula		'position you want to round to'
26	Round to penny	12.555	12.560	Formula in C26 =ROUND(B26,2)	2	positive rounds to right of decimal
27	Round to dollar	12.500	13.000	Formula in C27 =ROUND(B27,0)	0	0 (zero) rounds to integer (ones position)
28	Round to thousands position	58900.000	59000.000	Formula in C28 =ROUND(B28,-3)	-3	negative rounds to left of decimal

Figure 658

One final note about the ROUND function: In some calculations, it might seem like the ROUND function would be required, but it may not be required. An estimate for a budget is an example. Often, when the columns for total expenses in a budget are off by a few pennies, it is not that important because no money will actually change hands. Whereas with a paycheck, tax form, or invoice, money is changing hands and so it usually matters that you make the correct rounding in your calculation. However, the finally judgment is up to you.

Our next Excel Efficiency-Robust Rule is as follows:

Rule 34: Use ROUND function when 1) you are required to round (like with money), 2) you are multiplying or dividing numbers with decimals, or 3) you will use the formula result in subsequent calculations.

Next we want to look at how to make average calculations in Excel.

Averaging with AVERAGE, MEDIAN, and MODE Functions

The reason that we have averages is so that we can have one number that will represent all the numbers in a data set. An average is a typical value that we can use in discussions, reports, and for comparative purposes. For example, an average score on a test is a useful number for comparing how well you did on the test; an average miles/gallon for a car is a useful number for advertising; and the median house price in a neighborhood can be a useful guide for making a purchase decision.

For most of us, we only know about one type of average. But there are many. In particular, there are three types of averages that are of great use in business. The three averages we will look at are as follows:

- **Average** for calculating arithmetic mean: SUM/COUNT

  Example: For calculating an average score on a test.

  Good for most number data sets that don't have a few outliers (really big or small values).

  Function to use: AVERAGE

- **Median** for finding the value in the middle of a sorted list

  Example: For real estate values, it is better to calculate the median because the average might be too large if you have a few $1,000,000 houses. A few values would pull the average up away from a more fairly representative middle value or typical value.

  Good for when there are a few unusually large or small values and the rest of the data is clustered around some middle value.

  Function to use: MEDIAN.

- **Mode** for finding the value that occurs most often

  Example: When you are counting survey data for customer preferences for a soft drink and the categories are Below Par, OK, Good, Great.

  Good when you need an average for counting situations.

  When data is being counted, it is not possible to calculate the arithmetic mean because the sum/count always equals 1.

  Function to use for numbers: MODE.

  Function to use for words: COUNTIF.

  There is also the new Excel 2010 functions MODE.MULT (returns multiple modes) and MODE.SNGL (same as MODE), which are beyond the scope of this book.

AVERAGE Function

To follow along, open the file named excelisfun-Start.xlsm and navigate to the AVE sheet.

In Figure 659, you can see that the AVERAGE function can look at a range of numbers and calculate the average. In the data set, the 0 score for Shelia is included in the average calculation, but the blank nonscore for Tom is not included. When calculating, the AVERAGE function will include zeros and ignore blanks.

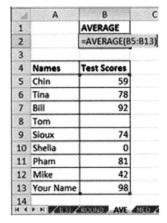

In Figure 660, you can see the algorithm for how the AVERAGE function calculates an average: (SUM of all numbers)/COUNT of all numbers). Once the average is calculated to be 65.5, the 65.5 is considered the typical value that can then be used for comparative purposes. In Figure 659, you can clearly see that Your Name is well above average!

Figure 659

	A	B	C
1		AVERAGE	
2		65.5	
3			
4	Names	Test Scores	
5	Chin	59	
6	Tina	78	
7	Bill	92	
8	Tom		
9	Sioux	74	
10	Shelia	0	
11	Pham	81	
12	Mike	42	
13	Your Name	98	
14			

(D/E columns: SUM 524, COUNT 8, SUM/COUNT = 524/8 65.5)

Figure 660

MEDIAN Function

To follow along, open the file named excelisfun-Start.xlsm and navigate to the MED sheet.

In Figure 662, you can see that the MEDIAN function can look at a range of numbers and calculate the median; which is to say, it will find the value that sits in the middle of a sorted list. (In the figure, the numbers are sorted, but they do not have to be.) The data set we are using is sorted, but the MEDIAN function will work perfectly with sorted or not-sorted number lists. Also, just as with the AVERAGE function, if there were zeros or blanks, the MEDIAN function would include the zeros in the calculation, but ignore blanks.

But why would a real estate agent want to use the MEDIAN function rather than the AVERAGE function? In Figure 662, you can see that the median is $312,500, whereas the average is $560,467. Because there are two houses worth more than a million dollars, the average gets pulled up by the two really big values. The real estate agent wants to use the typical value that more fairly represents the value of most of the houses in the neighborhood and so she chooses the median! Whenever you have a data set that has a few unusually large or small values, the MEDIAN function is the way to go.

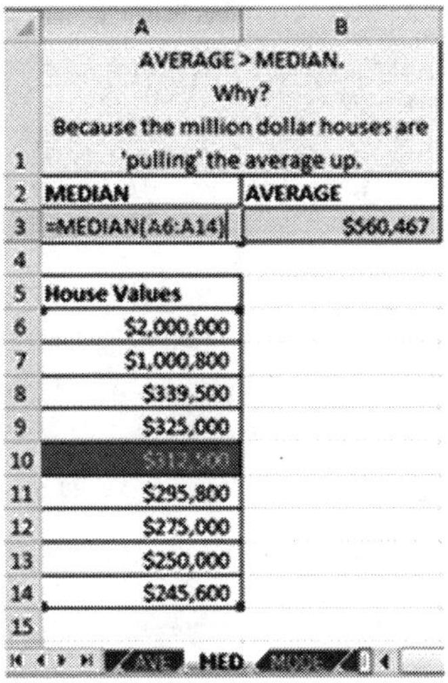

Figure 661

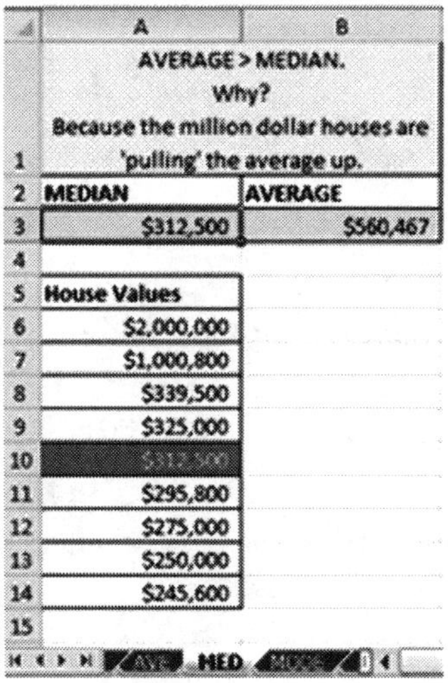

Figure 662

In the preceding example, we had an odd number of data points and so it is easy to find the one in the middle. But what if we have a data set with an even number of data points? As shown in Figure 663, the MEDIAN function will add the two middle values and divide by 2.

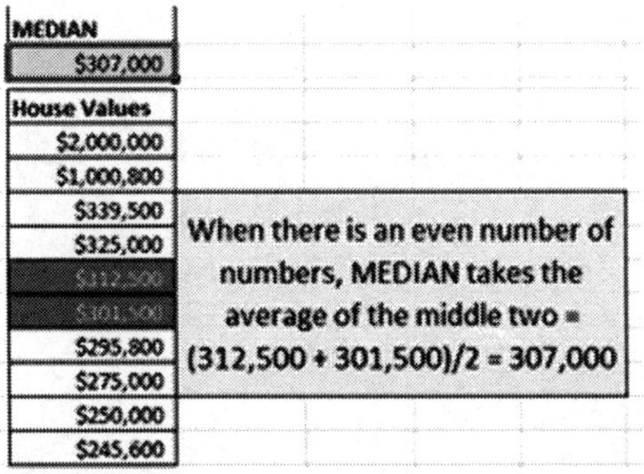

Figure 663

MODE Function

To follow along, open the file named excelisfun-Start.xlsm and navigate to the MODE sheet.

In our example for the MODE function, we will consider the survey results from 100 people who were asked to rate a new soda pop. They were given four categories (Great, Good, OK, and Below Par) and asked to choose one category for their response. In the Figure 664, you can see that the COUNTIF function was used in the range C6:C9 to count the categories (words) in the Survey Results column (range A13:A112). Because the category Below Par had the largest count at 42, it is considered the typical value. Sometimes, however, the survey results are not given with word categories, but instead they use a number equivalent for the word category. In our case Great = 4, Good = 3, OK = 2, Below Par = 1. If numbers are given rather than words, the MODE function can be used to find the typical value, or, value that occurs most often. In Figure 665, you can see the MODE function in cell A3 is looking in the range B13:B112 and has determined that the number one (1) occurs most often. The number one corresponds to the Below Par category, and therefore Below Par is considered the typical value. If you are asking why we can't just use the AVERAGE function to calculate the typical value, the reason is that the SUM/COUNT = 42/42 = 1. Anytime you have categories that you are counting, the AVERAGE function will always calculate to one (1). This is why it is great that there is more than one type of average!

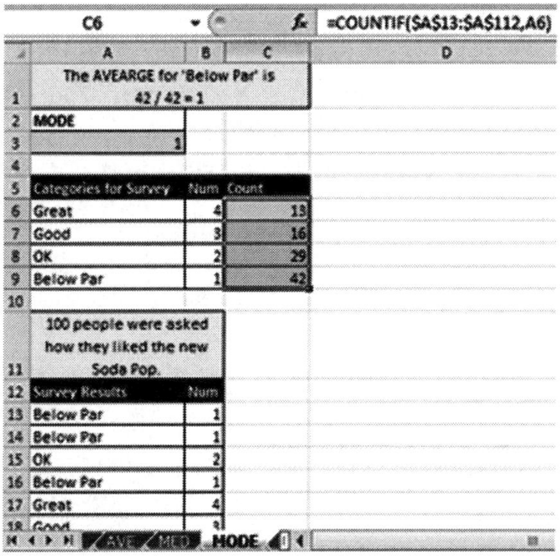

Figure 664

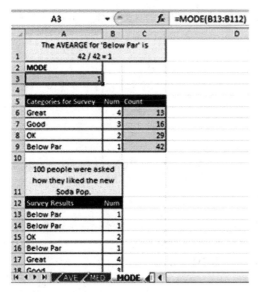

Figure 665

> **Note**: Just as with the AVERAGE function, if there were zeros or blanks, the MODE function would include the zeros in the calculation, but ignore blanks.

> **Note**: If there is more than one mode, meaning that two values have the same count, the MODE function will not pick this up. In cases like that, it is best to use the COUNTIF function. The new Excel 2010 function MODE.MULT can deal with more than one mode, but it is beyond the scope of this book.

Next we would like to take a look at the RANK function and also the new compatibility functions that exist in Excel 2010.

New Excel 2010 Functions (RANK.EQ and RANK.AVE) and Earlier Version Compatibility Function (RANK)

Ranking numbers is sometimes important. For example, you may be interested in finding the three days that had the top sales. In Figure 666, our goal will be to rank the sales numbers first place to seventh place and find the three days with the largest sales (first, second, third). In Figure 667, you can see a list of three RANK functions appears after you begin typing a RANK formula in a cell: RANK.AVE, RANK.EQ, and RANK with a yellow warning triangle. In Excel 2007 and earlier versions, RANK was the only ranking function available. Starting in Excel 2010,

A	B	C
1 Date	Sales	RANK
2 11/19/2010	$9,349	
3 11/20/2010	$9,316	
4 11/21/2010	$15,850	
5 11/22/2010	$15,973	
6 11/23/2010	$15,973	
7 11/24/2010	$12,435	
8 11/25/2010	$16,783	

Figure 666

there are now the three RANK functions (as shown in Figure 667). The reason that Microsoft put the older RANK function at the bottom of the list (with a warning triangle) is because they wanted to de-emphasis it in hopes that you will not use it. All functions that show the yellow warning triangle are called **compatibility functions** and are included in Excel so that older spreadsheets that contain the function will still work. The new RANK.EQ

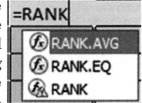

Figure 667

function is intended to be the replacement for the older RANK function. You will see how to use all three, but in Excel versions Excel 2010 or later, you only need RANK.EQ and RANK.AVE. First, let's see how to use RANK. EQ.

RANK.EQ Function

To follow along, open the file named excelisfun-Start.xlsm and navigate to the RANK sheet.

	A	B	C	D	E
1	Date	Sales	RANK.EQ	RANK	RANK.AVE
2	11/19/2010	$9,349	=RANK.EQ(B2		
3	11/20/2010	$9,316	RANK.EQ(number, ref, [order])		

Figure 668

1. In C2 create the first part of the formula:
   =RANK.EQ(B2

The number argument requires the number that you want to rank.

	A	B	C	D	E
1	Date	Sales	RANK.EQ	RANK	RANK.AVE
2	11/19/2010	$9,349	=RANK.EQ(B2,$B$2:$B$8		
3	11/20/2010	$9,316	RANK.EQ(number, ref, [order])		

Figure 669

2. Type a comma.
3. Highlight the range B2:B8.
4. To lock the range, press the F4 key.

The ref argument requires all the numbers in the list.

)	$9,349	=RANK.EQ(B2,$B$2:$B$8,		
)	$9,316	RANK.EQ(number, ref, [order])		
)	$15,850			0 - Descending
)	$15,973			1 - Ascending

Figure 670

5. Type a zero so the biggest number gets first place.
6. Type a close parenthesis and copy the formula down the column.

RANK.AVE Function

In Figure 671, you can see that after we copy the RANK.EQ function down the column, the largest value gets a one (1) for first place. You can also see in Figure 671 that the columns for the RANK and RANK.AVE functions are completed and the only difference between the functions is how they handle ties. The Excel 2010 RANK.EQ and the compatibility function RANK both give equivalent rankings of second place and then the next position is given fourth place. The RANK.AVE assigns an average rank of (second + 3rd) / 2 = 2.5.

	A	B	C	D	E
1	Date	Sales	RANK.EQ	RANK	RANK.AVE
2	11/19/2010	$9,349	6	6	6
3	11/20/2010	$9,316	7	7	7
4	11/21/2010	$15,850	4	4	4
5	11/22/2010	$15,973	2	2	2.5
6	11/23/2010	$15,973	2	2	2.5
7	11/24/2010	$12,435	5	5	5
8	11/25/2010	$16,783	1	1	1

Figure 671

RANK.AVE, RANK.EQ, and RANK are not the only new and old compat-ibility functions in Excel 2010. A few other examples are PRECENTILE, QUARTILE, and BINOMDIST functions (all statistical functions).

In the preceding example, you saw how to assign first for the biggest value. But what if you need to assign first for the smallest value, like in timing an assembly process in a manufacturing business? Figure 672 shows an example of this. Notice that the third argument (order) of the RANK.AVE function contains a one (1) for ascending order.

X ✓ fx	=RANK.AVG(G2,$G$2:$G$8,1)	
G	RANK.AVG(number, ref, [order])	
Assembling Product Times (Hours)	**RANK.AVE**	
5.5	;$2:$G$8,1)	
4.85	2.5	
4.55	1	
6.05	7	
5.1	5	
5.05	4	
4.85	2.5	

Figure 672

Next we need to look at an amazing feature called Goal Seek.

Goal Seek

To follow along, open the file excelisfun-Start.xlsm and navigate to the GS sheet.

Goal Seek is an amazing feature that will allow us to go backward through a formula calculation. Usually we type a formula input into a cell and then watch the formula change. Goal Seek will let us do the opposite: We will tell the formula what the answer is and we will watch the formula input change (sort of like going backward through the formula). In Figure 673, you can see the formula for total revenue is using the cell reference B3, which is units sold. If we want to know how many units we have to sell to make $500,000 revenue, we could just change the value is cell B3 manually. It may take us a few tries, but eventually we would find the formula input that would make the formula calculate to $500,000. With Goal Seek we just tell the following formula: I want you to calculate to $500,000 by chang-ing the formula input and units sold. Goal Seek will iterate back and forth until it finds the right units sold to get us our $500,000! In Figure 673, you can see that Goal Seek is found in the Data tab, Data Tools group, What-If

Analysis drop-down arrow. When we open the Goal Seek dialog box (shown in Figure 674)

- The Set Cell text box is a reference to the cell with the formula that we want to get an answer for. In our case, we want the formula in cell B4 evaluate to $500,000.
- The To Value text box must contain the answer we want the formula to evaluate to (type this value in). Notice that there is no "collapse text box" button (blue grid square with red diagonal-pointing arrow button) that would enable us to link this to a cell.
- The "By changing cell" is the reference to the formula input. This is the cell that contains the formula input (a *number* typed into a cell). In our case, it is the units sold cell.

Figure 675 show the result that Goal Seek got us. Revenue is $500,000, and the formula input, units sold, got changed to 20,000. This means that the answer to our original question is this: We must sell 20,000 units to reach $500,000 in revenue.

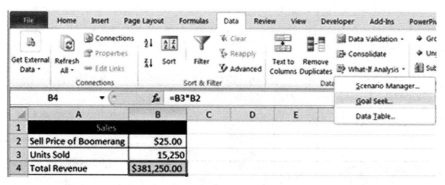

Figure 673

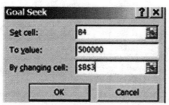

Figure 674

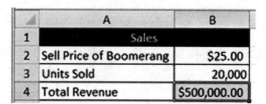

Figure 675

Goal Seek is a powerful feature that allows us to find exactly the formula result we want! Next we want to look at the basics of array formulas.

Array Formulas

The word *array* simply means more than one item. **Array formulas** are formulas that do operations on ranges of cells (arrays) rather than single-cell references. For example, in Figure 676 you can see a normal (nonarray) formula that does the operation subtraction on the single-cell references D2 and C2. That is, one number minus another single number. Whereas in Figure 677 you can see an array formula that does the operation subtraction on the range of cells D13:D19 and C13:C19. That is, seven numbers minus seven other numbers. Because the definition of an array is a collection of more than one item, when we subtract seven numbers from seven other numbers, we call it an array formula. What? No one ever taught me this when I was learning math in school! Well, we might not have learned it in school, but we are going to learn it when we learn Excel because array formulas can help to create compact, efficient spreadsheets. Not only that, but sometimes it is difficult to make our calculation without an array formula. That means that the two benefits of array formulas are as follows:

- Create compact spreadsheets that use less spreadsheet real estate
- Create spreadsheet solutions that would otherwise be difficult to make without array formulas

Now we want to take a closer look at the example shown in Figures 676 and 677 to see how to create our first array formula, which will create a compact spreadsheet.

	A	B	C	D	E
1	Date	Product	COGS	Sales	Gross Profit
2	9/13/10	Mchn 2	7,740	21,500	=D2-C2
3	7/17/10	Mchn 3	9,460	21,500	12,040
4	7/30/10	Mchn 4	4,350	15,000	10,650
5	8/27/10	Mchn 5	4,350	15,000	10,650
6	9/25/10	Mchn 6	14,785	31,458	16,673
7	8/28/10	Mchn 7	4,176	14,400	10,224
8	7/29/10	Mchn 8	8,859	29,532	20,673
9					
10				Total	94,670
11					

Figure 676

	A	B	C	D	E
12	Date	Product	COGS	Sales	
13	9/13/10	Mchn 2	7,740	21,500	
14	7/17/10	Mchn 3	9,460	21,500	
15	7/30/10	Mchn 4	4,350	15,000	
16	8/27/10	Mchn 5	4,350	15,000	
17	9/25/10	Mchn 6	14,785	31,458	
18	8/28/10	Mchn 7	4,176	14,400	
19	7/29/10	Mchn 8	8,859	29,532	
20					
21	Total Gross Profit			=SUM(D13:D19-C13:C19)	
22					

Figure 677

Array Formulas Use Less Spreadsheet Real Estate

The goal is the same in both Figure 676 and Figure 677; namely, we need to calculate the total gross profit for our data set. Gross profit is the profitability measure that takes the sales and subtracts the cost of goods sold (COGS). In Figure 676, the strategy for accomplishing the goal is to add an extra column that calculates the gross profit for each transaction. Then in cell E10 we used the SUM function to add all the sales. Our total gross profit is $94,670. In Figure 677, the strategy for accomplishing the goal is to not add an extra column, but instead subtract the entire COGS column from the Sales column inside a SUM function. The calculated answer for this formula is $94,670 (not pictured). The difference in strategy is simple: The array formula method in Figure 677 takes up less space in the spreadsheet than the adding an extra column method in Figure 676. Not only that, but the array formula method performs the exact same individual calculations that the adding an extra column method does, but instead of doing the calculations in the individual cells, it does an array of calculations in a single cell. We now want to see how to create this array formula and how an array of calculations can be done in a single cell.

To follow along, open the file named excelisfun-Start.xlsm and navigate to the Array(1) sheet.

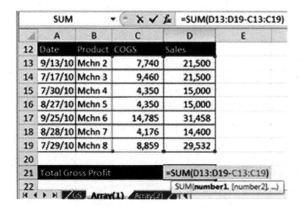

1. On the Array(1) sheet, click in F12 and create the following formula:
=SUM(D13:D19-C13:C19)
2. To put the array formula into the cell, press Ctrl + Shift + Enter.

Figure 678

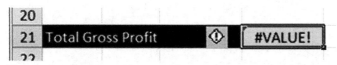

Figure 679

If you do not press Ctrl + Shift + Enter, you will get a #VALUE! Error.

	D21			f_x	{=SUM(D13:D19-C13:C19)}	
	A	**B**	**C**		**E**	
12	Date	Product	COGS	Sales		
13	9/13/10	Mchn 2	7,740	21,500		
14	7/17/10	Mchn 3	9,460	21,500	Curly	
15	7/30/10	Mchn 4	4,350	15,000	Brackets	
16	8/27/10	Mchn 5	4,350	15,000		
17	9/25/10	Mchn 6	14,785	31,458		
18	8/28/10	Mchn 7	4,176	14,400		
19	7/29/10	Mchn 8	8,859	29,532		
20						
21	Total Gross Profit			94,670		

Figure 680

If you press Ctrl + Shift + Enter your array formula will be entered and you will see curly brackets at the beginning and end of the array formula in the formula bar.

These curly brackets are automatically put in by Excel and are a signal to the spreadsheet user that this is an array formula.

In Figure 680, you can see that we have used Ctrl + Shift + Enter to put the array formula into the cell and that curly brackets were automatically placed at the beginning and end of the array formula.

Here are two important rules about array formulas:

- When putting an array formula into a cell you must use the keystrokes Ctrl + Shift + Enter. This is the signal from you to Excel that the formula you are putting in the cell is an array formula. When you press Ctrl + Shift + Enter, you are telling Excel "I am putting an array formula into a cell." If you do not press Ctrl + Shift + Enter, you will either get 1) the wrong answer or 2) a #VALUE! error.
- After you press Ctrl + Shift + Enter to put the array formula into the cell, Excel will automatically place curly brackets at the beginning and end of the formula. This is the signal from Excel to you that the formula is an array formula. These curly brackets cannot be typed in, but instead they are put in automatically after you press Ctrl + Shift + Enter.

Now we want to look at how this array formula does an array of calculations in a single cell. To do this we will run the Evaluate Formula feature on cell D21. (Select cell D21 and perform the keyboard shortcut Alt, T, U, F).

Evaluate Formula

Reference: Evaluation:
'Array(1)'!$D$21   =   SUM(D13:D19-C13:C19)

Figure 681

Evaluate Formula

Reference: Evaluation:
'Array(1)'!$D$21   =   SUM({13760;12040;10650;10650;16673;10224;20673})

Figure 682

Evaluate Formula

Reference: Evaluation:
'Array(1)'!$D$21   =   94,670

Figure 683

In Figure 682, you can see that our operation on an array (D13:D19-C13:C19) actually calculates an array of answers. This means that array formulas always do two things: 1) They perform operations on arrays, and 2) they deliver an array of answers. In Figure 683, you can see that the SUM function adds the array of answers. The Evaluate Formula feature does not actually show all the steps in how the total is calculated. No problem, Figure 684 simulates exactly how our array formula calculates. If you compare this to the adding an extra column method as shown in Figure 685, you can see that in both methods all the individual gross profit calculations are made. It is just with our array formula we use up much less spreadsheet real estate. Now, in some cases, the requirements of your project dictate that you should show all the individual calculations in a column. In that case, use the adding an extra column method. Otherwise, if spreadsheet real estate should be conserved, use the array formula method.

21,500 - 7,740 = 13,760
21,500 - 9,460 = 12,040
15,000 - 4,350 = 10,650
15,000 - 4,350 = 10,650
31,458 - 14,785 = 16,673
14,400 - 4,176 = 10,224
29,532 - 8,859 = 20,673

Figure 684

	A	B	C	D	E
1	Date	Product	COGS	Sales	Gross Profit
2	9/13/10	Mchn 2	7,740	21,500	=D2-C2
3	7/17/10	Mchn 3	9,460	21,500	12,040
4	7/30/10	Mchn 4	4,350	15,000	10,650
5	8/27/10	Mchn 5	4,350	15,000	10,650
6	9/25/10	Mchn 6	14,785	31,458	16,673
7	8/28/10	Mchn 7	4,176	14,400	10,224
8	7/29/10	Mchn 8	8,859	29,532	20,673
9					
10				Total	94,670

Figure 685

With regard to the array formula that we just created, we want to see how we can make an improvement to it by using the SUMPRODUCT function rather than the SUM function.

SUMPRODUCT (to avoid Ctrl + Shift + Enter)

Earlier, when we discussed SUMPRODUCT, all the formulas we did contained operations on arrays. (If you really want to learn about the concept of array formula, go back and reread that section.) In the formula we just did, we subtracted two ranges of cells *and then added*. Anytime you have an array that needs to be added, it is usually more efficient to use the SUM-PRODUCT function because it does not require Ctrl + Shift + Enter.

	A	B	C	D	E	F
23	Date	Product	COGS	Sales		
24	9/13/10	Mchn 2	7,740	21,500		
25	7/17/10	Mchn 3	9,460	21,500		
26	7/30/10	Mchn 4	4,350	15,000		
27	8/27/10	Mchn 5	4,350	15,000		
28	9/25/10	Mchn 6	14,785	31,458		
29	8/28/10	Mchn 7	4,176	14,400		
30	7/29/10	Mchn 8	8,859	29,532		
31						
32	Total Gross Profit			=SUMPRODUCT(D24:D30-C24:C30)		
33				SUMPRODUCT(**array1**, [array2], [array3], ...)		

Figure 686

In Figure 686, you can see that we have re-created the same formula in cell D32, but instead of using the SUM function, we used the SUMPRODUCT function. The reason that the SUMPRODUCT does not require the Ctrl + Shift + Enter is because its arguments allow arrays. As shown in the screen tip in Figure 686, the actual name of the argument is array1, array2, and so on. We simply put our array of calculations (D24:D30-C24:C40) into the array1 argument and the SUMPRODUCT will add all the differences in the array. Anytime you see a function that has an argument with the name array, you can create arrays in that argument and it does not require Ctrl + Shift + Enter. (INDEX and LOOKUP are other functions that can handle arrays.) Notice in Figure 687 that the formula has been entered without Ctrl + Shift + Enter and it calculates the correct answer. (You can tell because there are no curly brackets at the beginning and end of the formula.) Using SUMPRODUCT to avoid using Ctrl + Shift + Enter is helpful because it makes it like most other formulas, which do not require Ctrl + Shift + Enter; and it makes it more user friendly, not only for us, but for others who may use the spreadsheet and may not know about the array formulas.

D32 =SUMPRODUCT(D24:D30-C24:C30)

	A	B	C	D	E	F
23	Date	Product	COGS	Sales		
24	9/13/10	Mchn 2	7,740	21,500		
25	7/17/10	Mchn 3	9,460	21,500		
26	7/30/10	Mchn 4	4,350	15,000		
27	8/27/10	Mchn 5	4,350	15,000		
28	9/25/10	Mchn 6	14,785	31,458		
29	8/28/10	Mchn 7	4,176	14,400		
30	7/29/10	Mchn 8	8,859	29,532		
31						
32	Total Gross Profit			94,670		
33						

GS | Array(1) | Array(2)

Figure 687

Now we want to look at an example of a calculation that is difficult to make without array formulas.

Array Formulas as the Only Efficient Option

In Figure 688, we have a data set from a manufacturing company in columns A and B. The location of the manufacturer is in column A and the time in minutes for assembling a product in column B. The manager wants you to calculate the average, minimum, maximum, and mode times for each location. This means that our formulas must isolate only the records (rows) for each location. For example, for the Seattle average time, we need to look at only the Seattle records. For the average calculation, this is easy because we can just use the AVERAGEIF function (as seen back in the AVERAGEIF section of the book). But for the remaining three calculations, there is no built-in function that will do all this. In addition, three further parameters exist for this project:

- We do not want to sort the data set and create subtotal formulas because we want to be able to add new records to the bottom of the table.
- We do not want to use a PivotTable because we want the data to automatically update without having to refresh the PivotTable and because there is no MODE function in a PivotTable.
- Although there is something called Database functions (not covered in this book), this method would not match our required setup that Seattle, Oakland, and SF be located as row labels in the formula range and because there is no MODE Database function.

What do we do in this circumstance? Array formulas will come to our rescue! Let's take a look at how to do this.

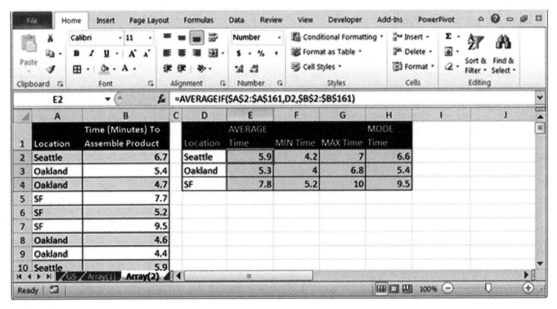

Figure 688

To follow along, open the file named excelisfun-Start.xlsm and navigate to the Array(2) sheet.

	A	B	C	D	E	F
		Time (Minutes) To Assemble			AVERAGE	
1	Location	Product		Location	Time	MIN Time MAX
2	Seattle	6.7		Seattle	5.9	=MIN(
3	Oakland	5.4		Oakland	5.3	MIN(number1
4	Oakland	4.7		SF	7.8	

Figure 689

1. On the Array(2) sheet, click in cell F2 and type the following:
   =MIN(

In Figure 689, you can see the MIN function. This function can find the smallest value from a group of values. However, we cannot just highlight the entire range of times in column B. Instead, we need to limit the values in column B to just those that are associated with the word Seattle in column A. If we were to put it into plain language, we would say the following:

If the word *Seattle* is in column A, please take the number from column B and use it in the MIN function; otherwise, say FALSE and don't use the number from column B.

From our knowledge of the IF function, we should guess that this is the perfect use for the IF function. The one difference from our earlier study of the IF function is that when we use it this time, the IF function will not deliver just a single item, but instead it will deliver an array of items. By nesting our IF function inside the MIN function, the IF function can deliver the array of times that are associated with the Seattle location.

D	E	F	G	H
	AVERAGE			MODE
Location	Time	MIN Time	MAX Time	Time
Seattle	5.9	=MIN(IF(		
Oakland	5.3		IF(logical_test [value_if_true], [v	
SF	7.8			

Figure 690

2. Type **IF(**.

Notice that the screen tip for the IF function appears. When you are nesting functions, this feature is convenient because it helps us keep track of where we are in the formula.

	A	B	C	D	E	F	G
		Time (Minutes) To Assemble			AVERAGE		M
1	Location	Product		Location	Time	MIN Time MAX Time	Ti
2	Seattle	6.7		Seattle	5.9	=MIN(IF($A$2:$A$161	
3	Oakland	5.4		Oakland	5.3	IF(logical_test [valu	
4	Oakland	4.7		SF	7.8		

Figure 691

3. Click in cell A2.
4. To highlight down to the bottom of the Location column press Ctrl + Shift + Down-Arrow.
5. To lock the range of cells, press the F4 key.

Notice that the F4 key not only adds the $ signs to lock the range, but it also jumps the screen back up to where the formula is being created.

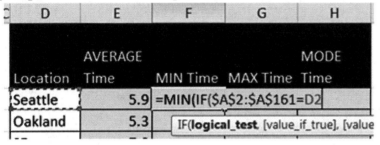

Figure 692

6. Type an equal sign.
7. Click the criteria cell, D2.

In the logical_test argument of the IF function (Figure 692), we have asked this question: Are any of the values in the array (A column) equal to "Seattle"? We accomplish this by using the comparative operator, the equal sign. This means that our "operation on an array" is not subtraction as in our preceding example, but instead it is the operation "are you equal." This meets our definition of an array formula: to do an operation on an array. If we evaluate just this logical test, $A$2:$A$161=D2, we would see this:

{TRUE;FALSE;FALSE;FALSE;FALSE;FALSE;FALSE;FALSE;TRUE;FALSE;FALSE;FALSE;FAL SE;FALSE;FALSE;FALSE;FALSE;FALSE;TRUE;FALSE;FALSE;FALSE;TRUE;FALSE;TRUE;FA LSE;FALSE;TRUE;FALSE;FALSE;TRUE;FALSE;FALSE;TRUE;FALSE;TRUE;FALSE;FALSE;FA LSE;FALSE;TRUE;FALSE;FALSE;FALSE;FALSE;FALSE;FALSE;FALSE;TRUE;FALSE;FALSE; TRUE;TRUE;FALSE;TRUE;TRUE;FALSE;TRUE;FALSE;TRUE;FALSE;FALSE;FALSE;TRUE;FA LSE;TRUE;TRUE;FALSE;TRUE;FALSE;FALSE;FALSE;FALSE;FALSE;TRUE;TRUE;FALSE;FA LSE;FALSE;FALSE;FALSE;FALSE;TRUE;FALSE;FALSE;FALSE;TRUE;FALSE;FALSE; FALSE;FALSE;FALSE;FALSE;TRUE;TRUE;FALSE;FALSE;FALSE;FALSE;FALSE;FALSE;FALS E;FALSE;FALSE;FALSE;FALSE;FALSE;TRUE;TRUE;FALSE;TRUE;TRUE;TRUE;FALSE;FALS E;FALSE;TRUE;FALSE;TRUE;FALSE;FALSE;FALSE;FALSE;FALSE;TRUE;FALSE;TRUE;FALS E;TRUE;TRUE;FALSE;TRUE;FALSE;FALSE;FALSE;FALSE;TRUE;TRUE;FALSE;FALSE;FALS E;TRUE;TRUE;TRUE;FALSE;FALSE;FALSE;TRUE;FALSE;FALSE;FALSE;FALSE;FALSE;FALS E;FALSE;TRUE;TRUE;TRUE;TRUE}

The TRUEs represent the rows where the word Seattle is located.

B	C	D	E	F	G	H	I
Time (Minutes) To Assemble Product		Location	AVERAGE Time	MIN Time	MAX Time	MODE Time	
6.7		Seattle	5.9	=MIN(IF($A$2:$A$161=D2,$B$2:$B$161			
5.4		Oakland	5.3	IF(logical_test, **[value_if_true]**, [value_if_false])			
4.7		SF	7.8				

Figure 693

8. Type a comma.
9. Highlight the range B2:B161.
10. Lock the range of cells by pressing F4.

The value_if_true argument will pick up all the times that are associated with Seattle.

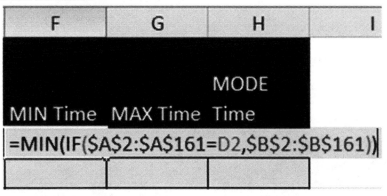

Figure 694

We do not need to put anything into the value_if_false argument because the IF function will automatically put a FALSE in for us if we leave the argument empty.

11. Type a close parenthesis on the IF.
12. Type a close parenthesis on the MAX.

In Figure 694 we can see the completed array formula. When it calculates, the IF function will deliver an array of values to the MIN functions that will look like this:

=MIN({6.7;FALSE;FALSE;FALSE;FALSE;FALSE;FALSE;FALSE;5.9;FALSE;FALSE;FALSE;FAL
SE;FALSE;FALSE;FALSE;FALSE;FALSE;6.7;FALSE;FALSE;FALSE;4.2;FALSE;6.3;FALSE;FAL
SE;6.4;FALSE;FALSE;6.9;FALSE;FALSE;4.4;FALSE;6.6;FALSE;FALSE;FALSE;FALSE;6.2;FALS
E;FALSE;FALSE;FALSE;FALSE;FALSE;FALSE;4.4;FALSE;FALSE;5.2;5.7;FALSE;6.1;6.7;FALSE
;6.7;FALSE;6.1;FALSE;FALSE;FALSE;4.2;FALSE;7;6.1;FALSE;6.3;FALSE;FALSE;FALSE;FALS
E;FALSE;5.7;5.7;FALSE;FALSE;FALSE;FALSE;FALSE;FALSE;FALSE;6;FALSE;FALSE;FALSE;
6.8;FALSE;FALSE;FALSE;FALSE;FALSE;FALSE;6.9;6.3;FALSE;FALSE;FALSE;FALSE;FALSE;
FALSE;FALSE;FALSE;FALSE;FALSE;FALSE;FALSE;5.6;4.8;FALSE;5.7;5.2;6.5;FALSE;FALSE;F
ALSE;5.5;FALSE;4.2;FALSE;FALSE;FALSE;FALSE;FALSE;4.6;FALSE;5;FALSE;6.5;4.3;FALSE;5
;FALSE;FALSE;FALSE;FALSE;6.6;6.6;FALSE;FALSE;FALSE;6.4;5.4;6.5;FALSE;FALSE;FALSE;
7;FALSE;FALSE;FALSE;FALSE;FALSE;FALSE;FALSE;6.6;6.8;6.6;4.9})

The MIN function ignores the FALSEs and then finds the smallest number from all numbers in the array.

F2			f_x {=MIN(IF($A$2:$A$161=D2,$B$2:$B$161))}				
A	B	C	D	E	F	G	
	Time (Minutes) To Assemble				AVERAGE		M
Location	Product		Location	Time	MIN Time	MAX Time	Tir
Seattle	6.7		Seattle	5.9	4.2		
Oakland	5.4		Oakland	5.3	4		
Oakland	4.7		SF	7.8	5.2		

Figure 695

13. To enter the array formula, press Ctrl + Shift + Enter.

The formula bar shows us that the curly brackets are present, which means we entered the array formula correctly.

You can then copy the formula down.

f_x {=MAX(IF($A$2:$A$161=D2,$B$2:$B$161))}				
D	E	F	G	H
	AVERAGE			MODE
Location	Time	MIN Time	MAX Time	Time
Seattle	5.9	4.2	7	
Oakland	5.3	4	6.8	
SF	7.8	5.2	10	

Figure 696

14. Using the same techniques, enter the formula for the MAX calculation.

f_x {=MODE(IF($A$2:$A$161=D2,$B$2:$B$161))}				
D	E	F	G	H
	AVERAGE			MODE
Location	Time	MIN Time	MAX Time	Time
Seattle	5.9	4.2	7	6.6
Oakland	5.3	4	6.8	5.4
SF	7.8	5.2	10	9.5

Figure 697

15. Using the same techniques, enter the formula for the MODE calculation.

Figure 698

Our last requirement is that we need to be able to add records to the bottom of the table and have our formulas update. To do this, we will remember that the Excel Table feature can provide us with dynamic ranges.

16. To create an Excel table, click in cell B2 and use the keyboard shortcut Ctrl + T.
17. Click OK in the Create Table dialog box.

			f_x	{=MIN(IF($A$2:$A$162=D2,$B$2:$B$162))}			
B		C	D	E	F	G	H
Time (Minutes) To Assemble Product	▾		Location	AVERAGE Time	MIN Time	MAX Time	MODE Time
6.7			Seattle	5.8	3	7	6.6
5.4			Oakland	5.3	4	6.8	5.4
4.7			SF	7.8	5.2	10	9.5

Figure 699

18. Click in cell A162 and type **Seattle**.
19. Click in cell B163 enter 3.

The formulas should update as shown in Figure 699.

Notice in the formula bar that the A column range of cells now extends to row 162.

That is quite a feat we just pulled off in Excel: a completely dynamic update after we entered a new record.

Next we want to look at array functions.

Array Functions

There are a number of special functions in Excel called **array functions**. They are called array functions because

- They are entered into a range of cells (array).
- They return an array of values (more than one value).
- They require the keystroke Ctrl + Shift + Enter to put the function into the range of cells, not just Enter like nonarray formulas or functions.

Some example of array functions are the FREQUENCY, TRANSPOSE, LINEST, MMULT, and MODE.MULT functions. In this book, we look at the FREQUENCY and TRANSPOSE array functions. Let's first look at the FREQUENCY function.

The FREQUENCY function is a convenient way to count numbers in categories that have a lower and upper limit. In Figure 700, we can see a data set of sales numbers in column A. Our goal is to count how many sales numbers fall into each category (categories are in column C). In our first category, we need to count how many sales are less than or equal to $250. In our second category, we need to count how many sales are between $250 and $500.

	E2	▾	f_x	{=FREQUENCY(A2:A14,D2:D5)}	
	A	B	C	D	E
1	Sales		Category	Upper Limit	Frequency
2	$249.99		Sales <= $250	250	2
3	$250.00		$250 > Sales <= $500	500	4
4	$250.01		$500 > Sales <= $750	750	1
5	$450.00		$750 > Sales <= $1,000	1000	5
6	$500.00		Sales > $1,000		1
7	$499.99				
8	$500.01				
9	$800.00				
10	$900.00				
11	$850.00				
12	$800.00				
13	$1,000.00				
14	$2,000.00				

Figure 700

However, we must be careful about how the interval for this category is defined. There is a lower end to the interval and an upper end, and in our case the lower end is *not* included in the interval (sales of exactly $250 will *not* be counted) and the upper is included in the interval (sales of exactly $500 will be counted). This sort of setup can be thought of as "between" criteria. A similar between criteria is used in the third and fourth categories. The final category will count all the sales above $1,000. These categories are automatically created by the FREQUENCY function when you give it the upper limits for each category (as shown in column D). Notice that the first category counts everything below or equal to the first upper limited listed, the middle three categories use a between criteria, and the final category is always everything above the last upper limit listed. This means that the FREQUENCY function will always deliver one more frequency result than there are upper limits given.

> **Note**: The "between" criteria that the FREQUENCY function creates (including the upper end to interval but not the lower end) differs from the between criteria that we discussed with regard to COUNTIFS earlier in this book and from the between criteria that we discuss in Chapter 6, "Data Analysis Features) (which do not include upper end to interval but do include the lower end).

Now let's put the FREQUENCY function to use.

To follow along, open the file named excelisfun-Start.xlsm and navigate to the Array(3) sheet.

B	C	D	E	F	G
	Category	Upper Limit	Frequency		
	Sales <= $250	250	=FREQUENCY(		
	$250 > Sales <= $500	500	FREQUENCY(**data_array**, bins_array)		
	$500 > Sales <= $750	750			
	$750 > Sales <= $1,000	1000			
	Sales > $1,000				

Figure 701

1. Highlight the range E2:E6.

> **Note**: The FREQUENCY function requires that you select a range of cells because it will return an array of values. You can't just select a single cell; otherwise, you will not get the correct answer.

2. In the active cell, E2, type the following:
   =FREQUENCY(

In Figure 701, we can see that the FREQUENCY function has two arguments. The data_array argument needs that range with the raw data, and the bins_array needs the upper limits for each category.

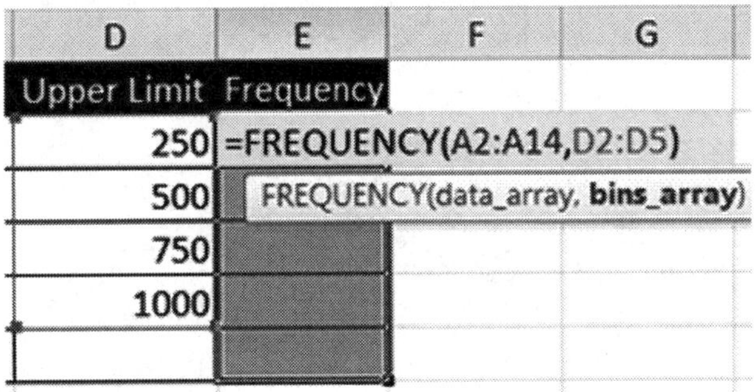

D	E	F	G
Upper Limit	Frequency		
250	=FREQUENCY(A2:A14,D2:D5)		
500	FREQUENCY(data_array, **bins_array**)		
750			
1000			

Figure 702

3. For the data_array argument, select the range A2:A14.
4. Type a comma.
5. For the bins_array argument, select the range D2:D5.

Note: When the size of the bins_array argument is one cell smaller than the size of the range we selected to enter the FREQUENCY function. This is because of the last category that is automatically created (discussed earlier).

Note: We do not need to lock the cell references with the F4 key. In array functions, the ranges are automatically locked when we press Ctrl + Shift + Enter.

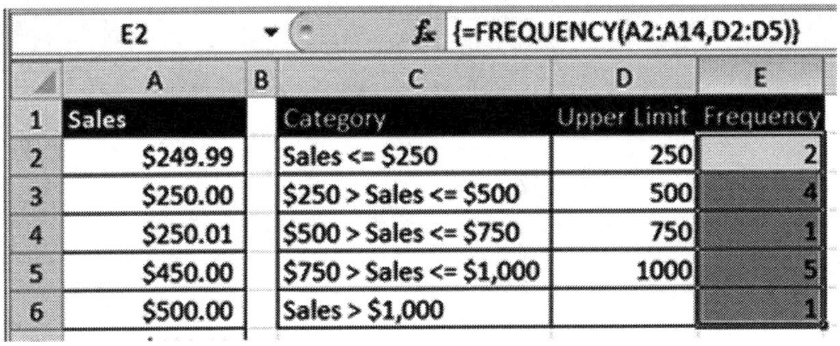

	E2	▾	f_x	{=FREQUENCY(A2:A14,D2:D5)}	

	A	B	C	D	E
1	Sales		Category	Upper Limit	Frequency
2	$249.99		Sales <= $250	250	2
3	$250.00		$250 > Sales <= $500	500	4
4	$250.01		$500 > Sales <= $750	750	1
5	$450.00		$750 > Sales <= $1,000	1000	5
6	$500.00		Sales > $1,000		1

Figure 703

6. Press Ctrl + Shift + Enter to enter the array function into the selected range with the keystrokes.

In the formula bar, notice the curly brackets are automatically added.

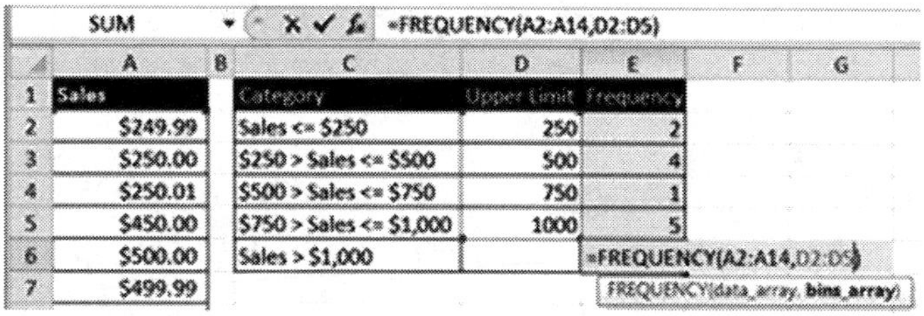

Figure 704

7. Click in cell E6 and press the F2 key to put the cell into Edit mode.

Notice that the range of cells A2:A14 is the same in all cells even though we did not use the F4 key to lock the cells references.

> **Note**: Because the FREQUENCY array function was entered into a range of cells with Ctrl + Shift + Enter, if you want to delete it, you must highlight the entire range E2:E6 and then press the Delete key. This is true of all array functions and formulas that are entered into a range of cells with Ctrl + Shift + Enter.

The FREQUENCY function is a convenient way to count numbers in categories that have a lower and upper limit. The key is to remember that the first and last categories differ slightly and that the number of cells that must be selected to enter the functions is one more than the number of upper limits.

Next we want to look at the TRANSPOSE function.

Transposing a Range of Cells with the TRANSPOSE Array Function

All the way back in Figure 15, you saw how to transpose a range of cells using a keyboard shortcut. In this section, we transpose a range of cells with the array function TRANSPOSE. The difference between the two methods is that with the keyboard shortcut method the data is not linked, but with the TRANSPOSE function the data will be linked. When the ranges of cells are linked, if you change any data in the source range, the linked transposed range will automatically update.

Here's a reminder: The goal of transposition is to flip the row and column headers so that they become column and row headers, respectively. Figures 705 and 706 show how row headers become column headers.

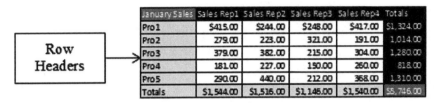

January Sales	Sales Rep1	Sales Rep2	Sales Rep3	Sales Rep4	Totals
Pro1	$415.00	$244.00	$248.00	$417.00	$1,324.00
Pro2	279.00	223.00	321.00	191.00	1,014.00
Pro3	379.00	382.00	215.00	304.00	1,280.00
Pro4	181.00	227.00	150.00	260.00	818.00
Pro5	290.00	440.00	212.00	368.00	1,310.00
Totals	$1,544.00	$1,516.00	$1,146.00	$1,540.00	$5,746.00

Figure 705

Become Column Headers

January Sales	Pro1	Pro2	Pro3	Pro4	Pro5	Totals
Sales Rep1	$415.00	279.00	379.00	181.00	290.00	$1,544.00
Sales Rep2	$244.00	223.00	382.00	227.00	440.00	$1,516.00
Sales Rep3	$248.00	321.00	215.00	150.00	212.00	$1,146.00
Sales Rep4	$417.00	191.00	304.00	260.00	368.00	$1,540.00
Totals	$1,324.00	1,014.00	1,280.00	818.00	1,310.00	$5,746.00

Figure 706

Now let's see how to use the TRANSPOSE function.

To follow along, open the file named excelisfun-Start.xlsm and navigate to the Array(4) sheet.

For this example, there will be two steps:
1. We will use Paste Special to transpose the formatting.
2. We will use the TRANSPOSE function to link and transpose the data.

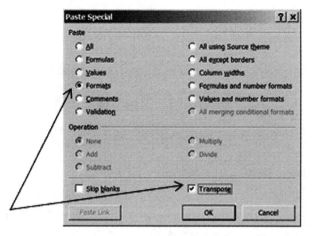

Figure 707

1. On the Array(4) sheet, highlight the range A1:F7.
2. Press Ctrl + C to copy the range.
3. Click in cell A10.
4. Press Ctrl + Alt + V to open the Paste Special dialog box.
5. Enable the Formats radio button and check the Transpose check box.

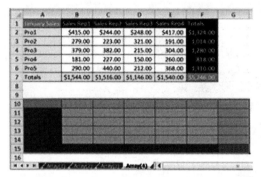

Figure 708

6. Click OK.

This figure shows how the formatting should be transposed.

In Figure 708, notice that the Paste Special selected a range that has six rows and seven columns. This is the exact transposition of the original range, which has seven rows and six columns. This is perfect because the TRANSPOSE array function requires that we select a transposed range before we enter it. If we had not used Paste Special first, we would have had to select the transposed range manually before we entered our formula.

7. In the active cell in the highlighted range, type the following formula:

   =TRANSPOSE(A1:F7)

8. Press Ctrl + Shift + Enter to enter this function.

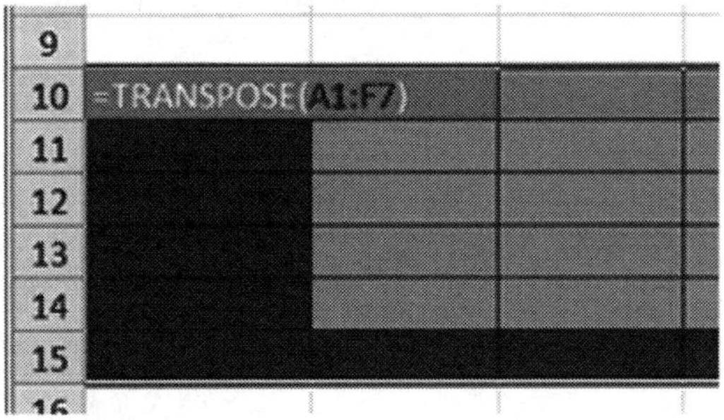

Figure 709

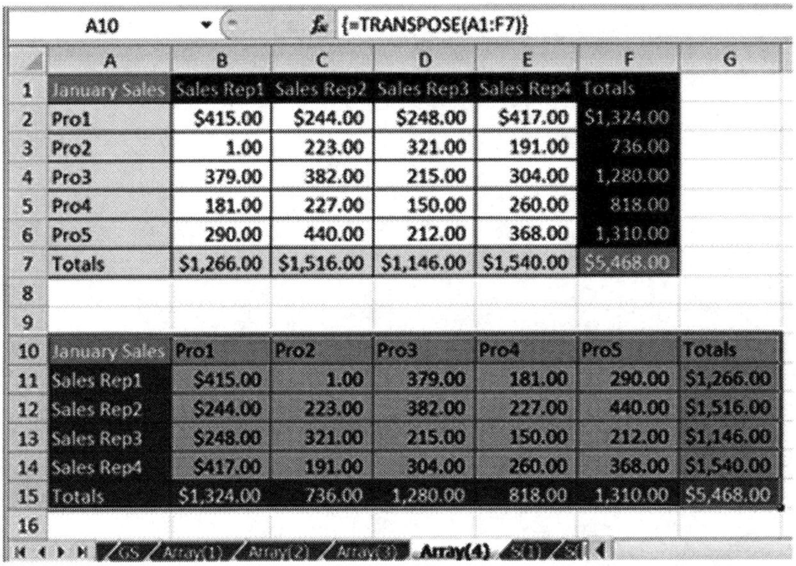

	A	B	C	D	E	F	G
1	January Sales	Sales Rep1	Sales Rep2	Sales Rep3	Sales Rep4	Totals	
2	Pro1	$415.00	$244.00	$248.00	$417.00	$1,324.00	
3	Pro2	1.00	223.00	321.00	191.00	736.00	
4	Pro3	379.00	382.00	215.00	304.00	1,280.00	
5	Pro4	181.00	227.00	150.00	260.00	818.00	
6	Pro5	290.00	440.00	212.00	368.00	1,310.00	
7	Totals	$1,266.00	$1,516.00	$1,146.00	$1,540.00	$5,468.00	
8							
9							
10	January Sales	Pro1	Pro2	Pro3	Pro4	Pro5	Totals
11	Sales Rep1	$415.00	1.00	379.00	181.00	290.00	$1,266.00
12	Sales Rep2	$244.00	223.00	382.00	227.00	440.00	$1,516.00
13	Sales Rep3	$248.00	321.00	215.00	150.00	212.00	$1,146.00
14	Sales Rep4	$417.00	191.00	304.00	260.00	368.00	$1,540.00
15	Totals	$1,324.00	736.00	1,280.00	818.00	1,310.00	$5,468.00
16							

Figure 710

You should see the curly brackets added in the formula bar.

9. Change the data in cell B3 to **$1.00** and you should see that the linked range updates perfectly.

Array formulas are amazing and have many uses. This section and the "SUMPRODUCT (to multiply and then add in succession)" section should give you a good foundation for creating your own array formulas.

Our next Excel Efficiency-Robust Rule is as follows:

> *Rule 35: Array formulas do operations on arrays (ranges of cells as opposed to single cells). Array formulas are great because they can help in two ways: 1) Array formulas can help to create compact, efficient spreadsheets because they use less spreadsheet real estate, and 2) there are some calculations that cannot be made at all unless you use an array formula. When entering an array formula, you must*

use the keystrokes Ctrl + Shift + Enter. After you press Ctrl + Shift + Enter, Excel automatically puts curly brackets at the beginning and end of the formula. When you will be adding the values from an array, it is usually more efficient to use the SUMPRODUCT function because it does not require Ctrl + Shift + Enter. Some functions such as FREQUENCY are array functions and must be entered with Ctrl + Shift + Enter.

Now let's take a quick look at errors that we might encounter in Excel.

Errors

So far in this book, you have seen a few different types of errors. Figure 711 describes some common Excel errors and identifies where in this book you can see examples of these errors.

Error Message	Description of Error	Examples in boo
######	Column width not wide enough to display data (value), or negative date or time.	Figure 10 and Figure 162
#NAME?	Text in a formula that is not a built-in function or a Excel Defined Name.	Figure 458
#N/A	Not Available/ No Answer. Like when a lookup function cannot find what you are looking for.	Figure 641
#REF!	Formula is using cell reference that has been deleted, or other invalid cell reference.	Figure 444
#VALUE!	Invalid operator or argument type in a formula, or array formula was not entered with Ctrl + Shift + Enter.	Figure 445 and Figure 679
#NUM!	Invalid numeric values in a formula or function, or an iterative function like IRR cannot find an answer, or the number is too big or small (number must be between (-10^307 and 10^307).	None
#DIV/0!	Formula divides by zero.	None
Circular		None

Figure 711

In the next chapter, we want to switch gears away from formulas and functions and look at the data analysis features in Excel, such as sort, filtering, and PivotTables.

DATA ANALYSIS FEATURES

In this chapter, we discuss the built-in data analysis features: Sort, Subtotal, PivotTable, Filter, and Advanced Filter. But what is data analysis? Let's review what we already know. **Data analysis** is the process of taking raw data and converting it to information that can be used to make decisions. In this book so far we have done a lot of data analysis. For example, in Chapter 3, "Data in Excel," you saw how to take raw data and convert it into information using the SUMIFS function and a PivotTable. You also saw some great examples of data analysis done with various functions in (Figure 91, Figure 408, and Figure 409). In addition to showing some examples of data analysis, we also discussed many aspects of what data is, how data is stored in Excel, and some of the characteristics of data.

A review of the points made in Chapter 3 follows here:

- **Raw data**

  Always store raw data in Excel in the smallest possible pieces and store it in a single cell. For example, the raw data Seattle, WA 98106 should be stored in three separate cells. Seattle in one cell, WA in one cell, 98106 in one cell. This is so that we can easily search for all the Seattle entries or all the WA entries in our spreadsheet. If raw data is not kept in the smallest possible pieces, it is hard to do data analysis.

- **Information**

  Information is raw data organized in a way so that it provides useful information for decision making. For example, if you take a list of all the transactional sales from last year and summarize them to show how much each customer bought, you can easily find the top three customers.

- **Table format structure**

  None of the data analysis features (Sort, Subtotal, PivotTable, Filter, and Advanced Filter) work unless your data is set up in a table format structure.

  Table format structure (also called list or database structure) means that the data has these characteristics:

    • Field names (column headers) are in first row of data set and are formatted differently than raw data (like bold). Fields are the variables such as Date, Customer Name, Sales, and so on.

- Records are in rows. Records are one collection of variable data such as an individual sales transaction or an individual customer's information.
- No blanks inside data set (field names or variable data). This is not 100% mandatory, but if you have blanks it can make data analysis more difficult.
- The data set is surrounded by either blank cells or column/row headers.

- **Excel Table feature**

  To use the Excel Table feature, your data must have the table format structure.

  The advantages of converting the data set into an Excel Table are as follows:
  - Add a table style.
  - Add an automatic filtering/sorting feature.
  - Create dynamic ranges.
  - Add new records to the bottom of the table.

- **Number formatting as façade**

  Number formatting in Excel is like paint on a house; the number formatting sits on top of the actual number. The actual number is in the cell and the formatting is what we see with our eyes. This is important because formulas and some data analysis features will react to the number in the cell and not to the number formatting.

- **How data is aligned in Excel**

  To more easily track down problems with raw data, it is important to know how Excel aligns data by default:
  - Numbers are aligned right.
  - Text or words are aligned left.
  - Logical TRUE or FALSE data is aligned center.

Table Format Structure

The data analysis features (Sort, Subtotal, PivotTable, Filter, and Advanced Filter) do not work unless you have the data set in a table format structure. As discussed in the preceding list, field names must be the first row of the data set and formatted differently than raw data, records must be in rows, no blanks are permitted in data sets, and the data set must be surrounded by either blank cells or column/row headers. If the data is not set up this way, it is extremely hard, if not impossible, to use the built-in features to do data analysis.

Sort Feature

The Sort feature will sort a list of words or values. You can sort A to Z or Z to A. An A to Z sort means that the smallest numbers or earliest letters in the alphabet will come to top of the column. A Z to A sort means that the largest numbers or latest letters in alphabet will come to top of the column. When you sort a data set, all the records are shuffled so that the data set is in a certain order. The Sort buttons can be found in two different locations in the ribbon. In Figure 712, you can see that the Sort buttons are in the Sort & Filter group on the Data tab, and in Figure 713, you can see that the Sort buttons can also be found in the Editing group on the Home tab.

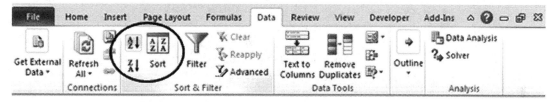

Figure 712

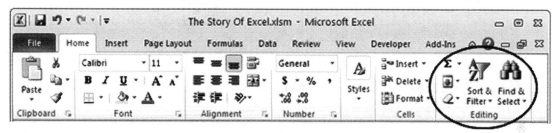

Figure 713

The most important point to remember when sorting is to select *only one cell* in the column you want to sort before clicking the Sort button. (Technically, the rule is that one cell or all the cells must be selected, but selecting all the cells would be a waste of time.) Now let's learn how to sort.

To follow along, open the file named excelisfun-Start.xlsm and navigate to the S(1) sheet.

The goal with our first sort example is to sort a list of sample times for an assembly process and show the shortest times at the top of the data set. In Figure 714, notice that there is a field name at the top that has a bold formatting and that there are times (in minutes) in the column below the field name. The data to be sorted are numbers, and so if we click the A to Z button, the smallest numbers will come to the top. This is exactly what we want because we are interested in the quickest times.

Sorting Numbers in a Single Column A to Z (smallest to biggest)

1. Click the S(1) sheet.
2. Click in cell A3. (Don't worry if the data set in the workbook is not in the same order when you start this exercise.)
3. On the Data tab, Sort & Filter group, click the A to Z button.

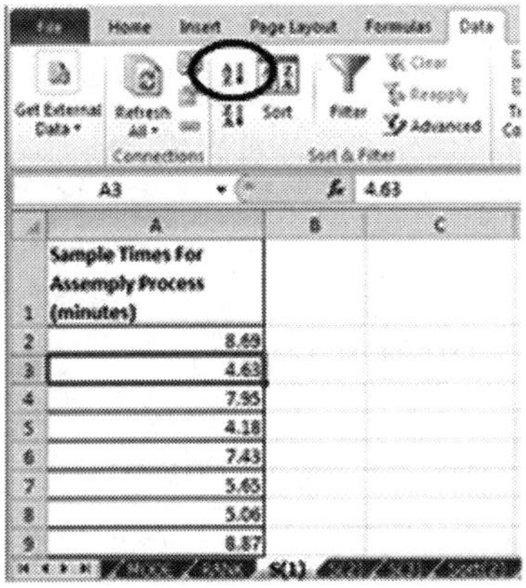

Figure 714

Notice that the smallest numbers come to the top.

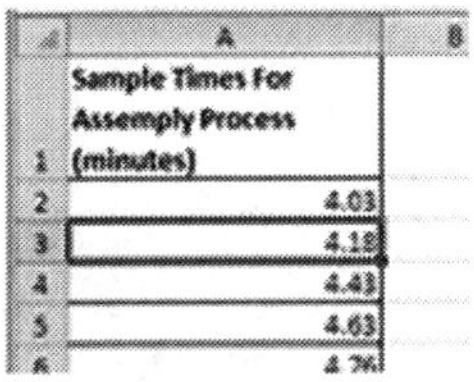

Figure 715

Sorting Numbers in a Data Set with More Than One Column A to Z (smallest to biggest)

In our next example, we want to take a look at how to sort a data set with more than one column. In Figure 716, you can see that our data set has assembly times in the first column and quality rating in the second column. Our goal is to sort the entire data set based on the assembly times. This means that if we sort and the time of 4.18 minutes moves near the top, the associated rating of 4 stars that is part of that record (row) must also move up the list. In Figure 716, you can see this record highlighted in black. Just as with sorting for a single column of values, sorting a data set with more than one column requires that you click *one cell only* in the column you want to sort before clicking the Sort button.

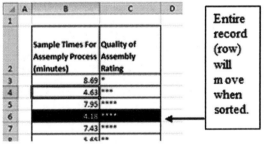

Figure 716

To follow along, open the file named excelisfun-Start.xlsm and navigate to the S(2) sheet.

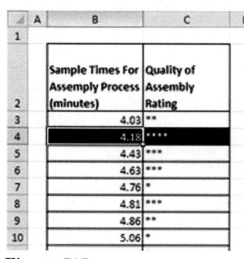

Figure 717

1. Click the S(2) sheet.
2. Click in cell B4. (Don't worry if the data set in the workbook is not in the same order when you start this exercise.)
3. On the Data tab, Sort & Filter group, click the A to Z button.

Notice that after you sort A to Z on the Time column, the entire record (row) for the 4.18 time moves.

Sorting Z to A by Using Right-Click

In Excel 2007 and later, you can use right-click to sort a data set.

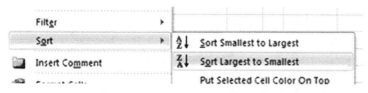

Figure 718

1. Right-click cell B3.
2. Point to Sort.
3. On the submenu point to Z to A.

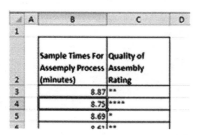

Figure 719

Sorting Z to A brings the largest numbers to the top.

Sorting Words A to Z

When you sort a column with words, the column is sorted alphabetically.

To follow along, open the file named excelisfun-Start.xlsm and navigate to the S(3) Sheet.

	A	B	C	D	E	F	G
1	Customers	Address	City	State	Zip	E-mail	
2	Zeiss, Son	4817 13th St.	Tacoma	WA	981112	DTT@yahoo.com	
3	Ghrist, Annita	313 173rd Blvd.	Kent	WA	981215	FSO485@gmail.com	
4	Dahnke, Georgeann	316 66th Blvd.	Kent	WA	981244	RWN@fun.edu	
5	Herry, Bryon	4358 23rd St.	Kent	WA	981225	LGQ756@gmail.com	
6	Dillaman, Darius	965 151st St.	Kent	WA	981162	MJG@yahoo.com	
7	Hudnell, Rod	3789 4th Blvd.	Seattle	WA	981152	IGJ150@gmail.com	
8	Scrabeck, Keren	2977 66th Lane	Seattle	WA	981171	EBA@gmail.com	
9	Chukes, Hal	7726 66th Ave.	Tacoma	WA	981118	MGF675@fun.edu	

Figure 720

1. Click the S(3) sheet, and then click in cell C3. (Don't worry if the data set in the workbook is not in the same order when you start this exercise.)
2. Sort A to Z.

	A	B	C	D	E	F	G
1	Customers	Address	City	State	Zip	E-mail	
2	Ghrist, Annita	313 173rd Blvd.	Kent	WA	981215	FSO485@gmail.com	
3	Dahnke, Georgeann	316 66th Blvd.	Kent	WA	981244	RWN@fun.edu	
4	Herry, Bryon	4358 23rd St.	Kent	WA	981225	LGQ756@gmail.com	
5	Dillaman, Darius	965 151st St.	Kent	WA	981162	MJG@yahoo.com	
6	General, Marlin	7900 173rd Lane	Kent	WA	981266	KFP@yahoo.com	
7	Lomasney, Lavenia	4047 15th Ave.	Kent	WA	981228	HHU@fun.edu	
8	Zeiser, Keren	4907 13th Ave.	Kent	WA	981232	FRF676@yahoo.com	
9	Hudnell, Rod	3789 4th Blvd.	Seattle	WA	981152	IGJ150@gmail.com	
10	Scrabeck, Keren	2977 66th Lane	Seattle	WA	981171	EBA@gmail.com	
11	Jayson, Dane	3392 23rd St.	Seattle	WA	981131	CLU@fun.edu	

Figure 721

Sorting a column A to Z that contains words will sort the column like a dictionary read from the front to back. If you use the Z to A button, the column will appear like a dictionary read back to front.

Hierarchy for Sort When the Column Has Mixed Data

In the previous few examples, we sorted columns with just numbers or just words. What happens if the column has words and numbers and other mixed data? The hierarchy for sorting A to Z when we have mixed data is as follows:

1. Numbers
2. Text/words
3. FALSE
4. TRUE
5. Errors
6. Blanks

(To sort blanks you have to highlight the whole column, not just one cell. Blanks are always sorted to the bottom whether or not you do A to Z or Z to A).

Sorting A to Z, numbers are first, then words, then FALSE, and so on. If you sort Z to A, the order is reversed. Let's take a look at an example.

To follow along, open the file named excelisfun-Start.xlsm and navigate to the S(4) Sheet.

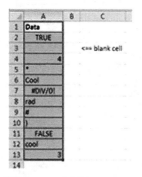

Figure 722

1. Click the S(4) Sheet.
2. Because we have a blank that we want to sort, we must highlight the whole column, so we must select the range A1:A13.
3. Sort A to Z.

Figure 723

After we sort A to Z, you should see what is shown in Figure 723.

Notice that numbers come to the top, then characters that are not letters, then words, then FALSE, then TRUE, then errors, and finally blanks.

Why did the # sign come before the * sign and why the cool before the Cool? The sort is based on the hierarchy of ASCII characters in Excel. For example, the ASCII number for c (lowercase) is 99, whereas the ASCII number for C (uppercase) is 67.

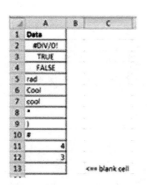

Figure 724

If you sort Z to A, the sort order is reversed, but notice that the blank is still at the bottom.

Now that you have seen how to sort a column with mixed data, are there any real-world example of when this would prove useful? Let's look at two great examples that leverage the uses of the hierarchy for sorting.

Sorting Blanks to Bottom to Remove Unwanted Records (A to Z)

In Figure 725, you can see the top part of a data set that has blanks in the Invoice # and Sales fields (columns). These blanks rows are extra rows that we do not want. So our goal is to quickly delete all the rows. We will group all the blanks together using the Sort feature, and then we can delete the rows with blanks.

To follow along, open the file named excelisfun-Start.xlsm and navigate to the S(5) sheet.

1. Click the S(5) Sheet.
2. Click in cell A1.
3. Highlight the whole data set using the Ctrl + * (asterisk on the number pad) keyboard shortcut.

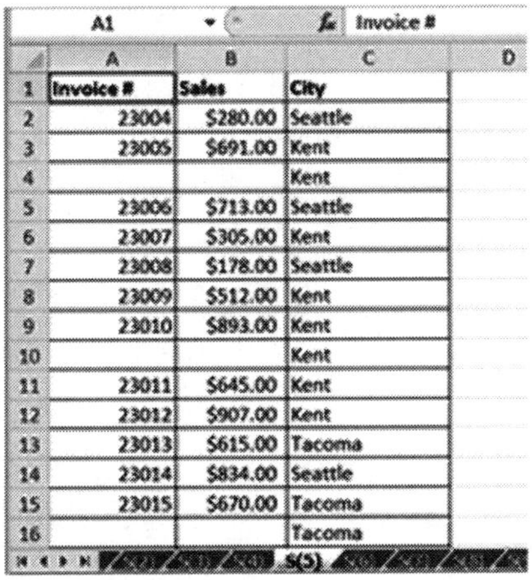

Figure 725

4. Right-click the selected area and point to Sort, and then click A to Z, or press Alt, A, S, A.

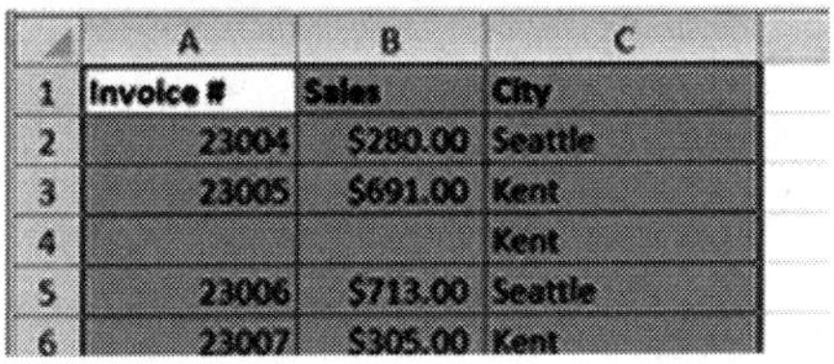

Figure 726

Notice that because we choose Sort A to Z, the invoice number sequence remains intact.

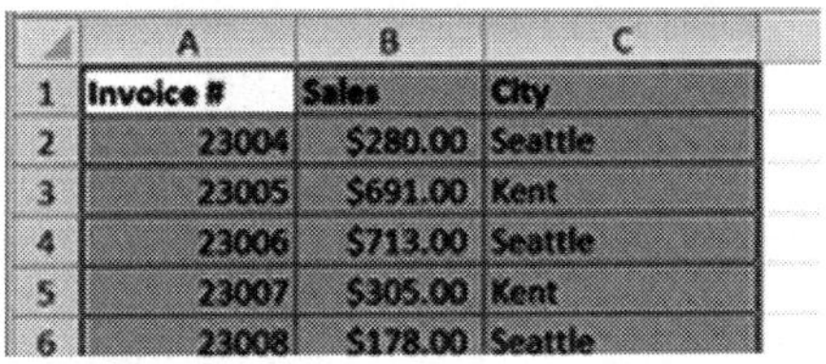

Figure 727

The bottom of the table shows that all the blanks have been sorted to the bottom of the data set.

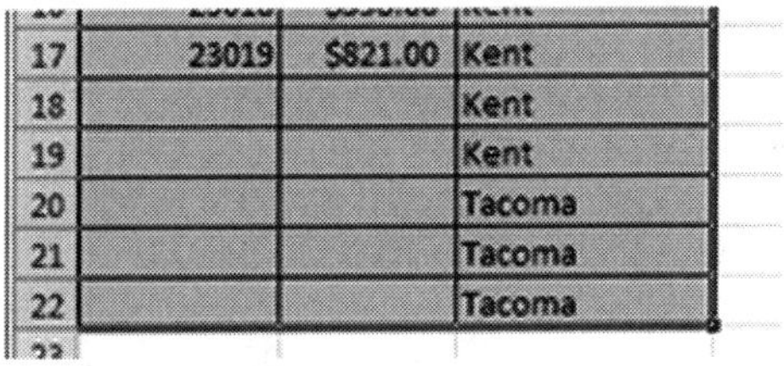

Figure 728

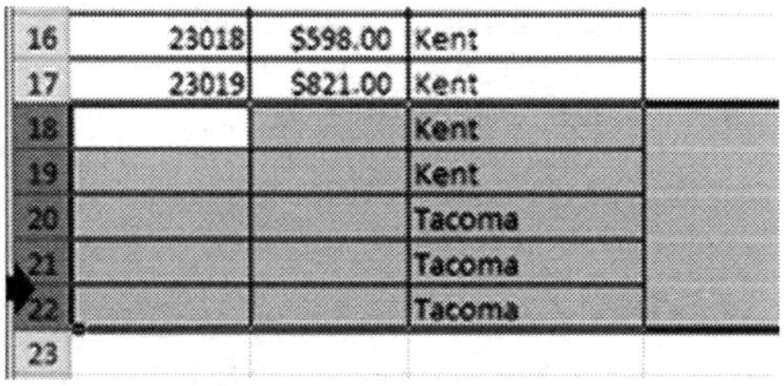

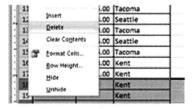

Figure 729

Figure 730

Figure 731

Figure 732

5. To highlight the rows with blanks, point to the row header 18, and when you see the horizontal-pointing black cursor, click and drag down to row 22.

6. Point to the row header 19 and the right-click, and then on the submenu click Delete.

Warning: If you see the dialog box shown in Figure 731, it is because you did not right-click the row header, but instead you right-clicked a cell/s.

7. If you see this, press the Esc key and start over, or click the Entire Row option button in the Delete dialog box.

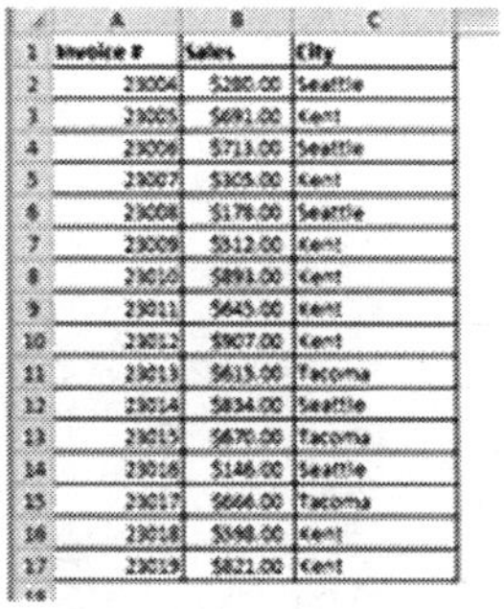

The amended data set should look like Figure 732.

It is important to note that if there had been cell content in rows 18 to 22 to the right of the data set (data or formulas not part of the data set), it would have been deleted when we deleted the rows.

In our example, we had no data anywhere else in the spreadsheet, and so deleting the rows was an efficient method. In our next example, you will see what to do if you need to delete some records and you have data to the right of the data set in the same rows as the ones you need to delete. Instead of deleting rows (like we just did), we will delete cells.

Sorting #N/A Errors to the Top to Remove Prospective Customers Who Are Already in the Master List

Back in Figure 640, you saw how to use the MATCH function to determine whether an item in one list was not in a second list. In Figure 733, you can see that column A has a list of prospective customers, column B has our MATCH function where the #N/A error means the prospective customer is not in the master list, and column D has the master list. The numbers that the MATCH function are delivering to column B show the relative position of the prospective customer's name in the master list and thus means that this prospective customer has already become a customer. Because the #N/A error means that the prospective customer is not in the master list, we still need to make contacts to try to persuade the prospective customer to become a customer. Therefore, our goal is to sort the #N/A errors to the top and then remove the records that have a number in the Is Name in Master List? column. However, unlike the preceding example, we cannot delete the rows because there is master list information in column D. Let's take a look at how to do this.

	A	B	C	D
1	Prospective Customers	Is Name In Master List?		Master List
2	Acquaviva Company	=MATCH(A2,$D$2:$D$12,0)		Manfre Company
3	Degen Company	2		Degen Company
4	Grabenstein Company	#N/A		Farthing Company
5	Haecker Company	10		Blose Company
6	Rana Company	#N/A		Spafford Company

Figure 733

To follow along, open the file named excelisfun-Start.xlsm and navigate to the S(6) sheet.

	A	B	C	D
1	Prospective Customers	Is Name In Master List?		Master List
2	Acquaviva Company	#N/A		Manfre Company
3	Grabenstein Company	#N/A		Degen Company
4	Rana Company	#N/A		Farthing Company
5	Shiroma Company	#N/A		Blose Company
6	Wootton Company	#N/A		Spafford Company
7	Yarrington Company	#N/A		Tarnowski Company
8	Haecker Company	10		Alameda Company
9	Spafford Company	5		Prestwich Company
10	Degen Company	2		Rommel Company

Figure 734

1. Click the S(6) sheet, and then click in cell B3.
2. Sort Z to A.

Figure 735

The sort result should look like Figure 735.

3. Highlight the range A8:B10.

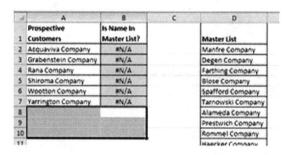

Figure 736

4. On the Home tab, Editing group, click the drop-down arrow next to the Eraser icon and click Clear All.

The keyboard shortcut is Alt, E, A, A.

	A	B	C	D
1	Prospective Customers	Is Name In Master List?		Master List
2	Acquaviva Company	#N/A		Manfre Company
3	Grabenstein Company	#N/A		Degen Company
4	Rana Company	#N/A		Farthing Company
5	Shiroma Company	#N/A		Blose Company
6	Wootton Company	#N/A		Spafford Company
7	Yarrington Company	#N/A		Tarnowski Company
8				Alameda Company
9				Prestwich Company
10				Rommel Company
11				Haecker Company

Figure 737

The records are removed without interfering with the data set in column D.

Clear All is an important feature in Excel because it removes cell content (names and functions in our example) and formatting.

Sorting with Keyboard Shortcuts

If you do sorting a lot, keyboard shortcuts can make you more efficient:
- With a cell selected in the column you want to sort A to Z, use Alt, H, S, S or Alt, A, S, A.
- With a cell selected in the column you want to sort Z to A, use Alt, H, S, O or Alt, A, S, D

Next we want to take a look at how the Sort buttons can cause an accidental sort of field names with the raw data.

Using the Sort Dialog Box When Field Names Are Accidentally Sorted with Raw Data

In Figure 738, you can see our data set before sorting, and in Figure 739 you can see our data set after we sorted with the Sort A to Z button. Because the field name and raw data are all words, the field name gets sorted with the rest of the data. If the field name were a word and the rest of the data were numbers, this would not happen. We can get around this problem by using the Sort dialog box.

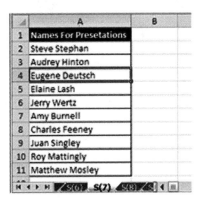

Figure 738

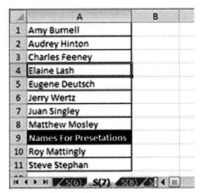

Figure 739

To follow along, open the file named excelisfun-Start.xlsm and navigate to the S(7) sheet.

1. Click the S(7) sheet.
2. Click in cell A4.
3. On the Data tab, Sort & Filter group, click the Sort button. (You can also use the keyboard shortcut Alt, D, S.)

Figure 740

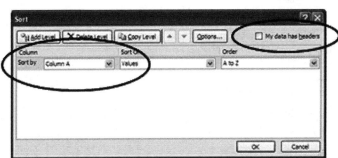

Figure 741

When a data set has words for both the field name and the data, the Column - Sort By drop-down *might* show the column rather than the field name (in our example column A) and the My Data Has Headers check box *might not* be checked (Figure 741).

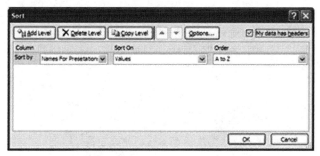

Figure 742

If you check the My Data Has Headers check box, the field name will appear in the Column Sort By drop-down.

4. Select A to Z in the Order drop-down.

Notice that the Column-Sort By drop-down is what determines the column for sorting.

5. Click OK.

Names For Presetations
Amy Burnell
Audrey Hinton
Charles Feeney

Figure 743

The list is now sorted A to Z.

In the preceding example, we sorted A to Z to see who would do their presentation first. But what if we do not want to do it alphabetically, but instead we want to do it in a random order? In the next example, you will learn how to randomly sort a column or data set.

Randomly Sort a Data Set

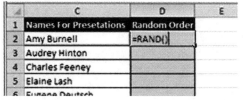

Figure 744

In Figure 744, we have an alphabetic list of presenter names. We want to randomize these names so that the presentation order is random.

We can accomplish this by adding a new column and using the RAND function. The RAND function is an argumentless function that generates random numbers between 0 and 1 (not including 1) that are 15 digits long. The 15 digits can be formatted to show only a few of the digits, and the number in the cell will still retain its 15 digits for the sorting purpose. (See the "Formatting as Façade" section in Chapter 3 for more information about number formatting).

Let's take a look at how to randomly sort using the RAND function.

1. On the S(7) sheet, click in cell D2 and type the following formula

   =RAND()

2. Press Ctrl + Enter to enter function into cell.

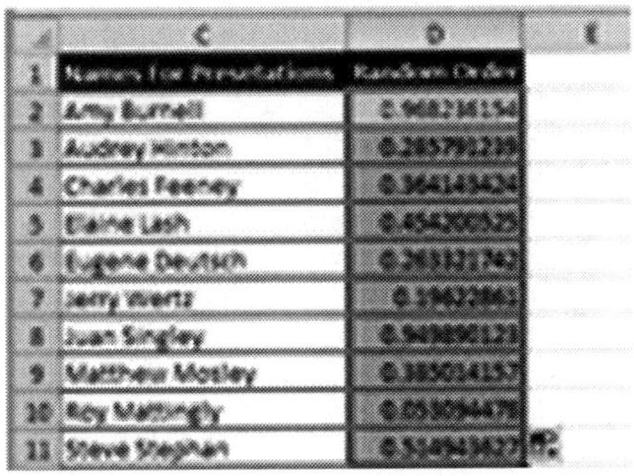

Figure 745

3. Double-click the fill handle to copy the formula down the column.
4. To randomly sort the names, sort the Random Order column A to Z. (Either A to Z or Z to A can be used.)

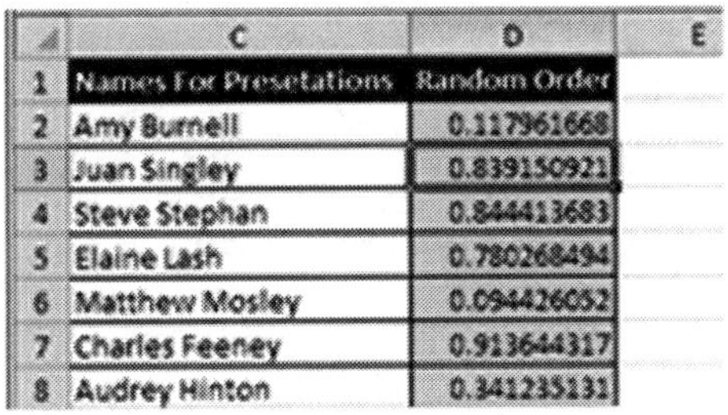

Figure 746

Notice that the names are randomly sorted.

In Figure 746, you can see that the numbers are not sorted A to Z even though we sorted that column. The reason comes from the fact that the RAND function is a volatile function that recalculates every time you take an action in the spreadsheet. This means that the action of sorting causes the RAND function to recalculate, and so by the time the Random Order column is sorted, the numbers have already changed to something different.

Next we want to take a look at how to sort left to right.

Sorting Left to Right

In Figure 747, you can see some sample data that is oriented horizontally. The Sort feature can handle this if you click the Options button in the Sort dialog box and select Sort Left to Right.

To follow along, open the file named excelisfun-Start.xlsm and navigate to the S(8) sheet.

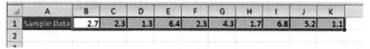

	A	B	C	D	E	F	G	H	I	J	K
1	Sample Data	2.7	2.3	1.3	6.4	2.3	4.3	1.7	6.8	5.2	1.1
2											

Figure 747

Figure 748

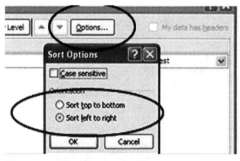

1. On the S(8) sheet, select the range B1:K1. (Do not select the A1, the row header for the data set.)
2. To open the Sort dialog box, press Alt, D, S.
3. Click the Options button.
4. Select the dialog button for Sort Left to Right.
5. Click OK on the Sort Options dialog box.
6. Click OK on the Sort dialog box.

You should see that the numbers are now sorted.

Next we want to take a look at how to sort by color.

Sorting by Color

Sometimes people code elements of a field with color and then want to group those colors together. Since Excel 2007, sorting by color has been a part of the Sort feature. In Figure 749, you can see a list of dates that have been coded by color. To sort and bring the color date records to the top, we can use the Sort dialog box.

	A	B	C	
1	Date	Customer	Sales	E-m
2	1/15/2011	Cust1	$492.00	CJP
3	1/16/2011	Cust2	$270.00	HTS
4	1/17/2011	Cust3	$626.00	DZ
5	1/18/2011	Cust4	$175.00	JPJ
6	1/19/2011	Cust5	$796.00	IQH
7	1/20/2011	Cust6	$588.00	OD
8	1/21/2011	Cust7	$610.00	NZI
9	1/22/2011	Cust8	$665.00	NU
10	1/23/2011	Cust9	$560.00	CZL
11	1/24/2011	Cust10	$519.00	PYL

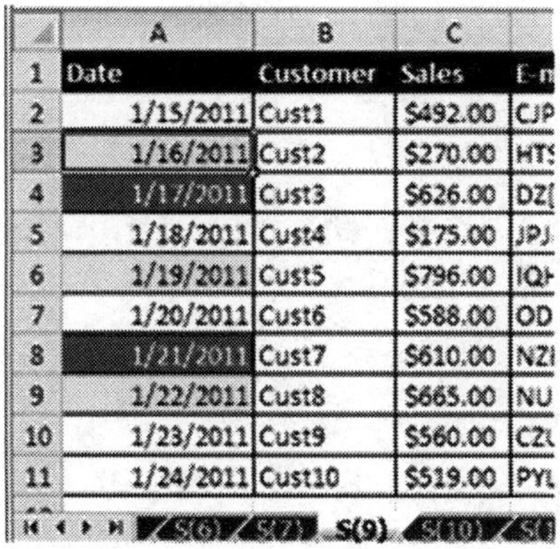

Figure 749

To follow along, open the file named excelisfun-Start.xlsm and navigate to the S(9) Sheet.

1. Click the S(9) sheet.
2. Click in cell A3.
3. To open the Sort dialog box, press Alt, D, S.

Figure 750

4. From the Column-Sort By drop-down, select the Date field.
5. From the Sort On drop-down, select Cell Color.

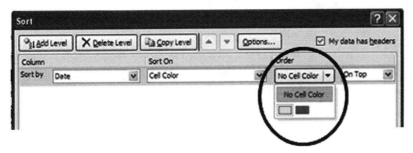

Figure 751

6. For Order, use the Color drop-down arrow and select yellow.

Figure 752

7. Using the Add Level button, add a level for Red, as shown in this Figure 752.
8. Click OK.

In Figure 752, notice that the Add Level button can be used to add more than one level of sorting.

	A	B	C	
1	Date	Customer	Sales	E-mail
2	1/16/2011	Cust2	$356.00	HTS@c
3	1/19/2011	Cust5	$664.00	IQH@c
4	1/22/2011	Cust8	$126.00	NUR@i
5	1/17/2011	Cust3	$548.00	DZ[@o
6	1/21/2011	Cust7	$392.00	NZE@c
7	1/15/2011	Cust1	$254.00	CJP@o
8	1/18/2011	Cust4	$824.00	JPJ@o
9	1/20/2011	Cust6	$328.00	ODL@c
10	1/23/2011	Cust9	$203.00	CZU@c
11	1/24/2011	Cust10	$414.00	PYL@o

Figure 753

The yellow and red records come to the top.

Next we want to take a look at how to add more than one level of sorting to a data set.

Sorting on More Than One Field

In Figure 754, look at the Region and the SalesRep field. In the Region field, all the East records are grouped together (sorted); then within the East records, the SalesRep field is sorted. When this configuration occurs, we say that the Region field is the **major sort** and the SalesRep field is the **minor sort**. To accomplish this sort of sorting result, we have to be careful about the order in which we sort the fields.

	A	B	C	D	E	F	G	H
1	Date	Product	Region	SalesRep	Customer	Units	Sales	COGS
2	1/20/11	Carlota	East	Chin	ET	59	$1,357.00	$649.00
3	1/29/11	Bellen	East	Chin	AST	50	$1,100.00	$500.00
4	1/21/11	Quad	East	Chin	FM	58	$1,566.00	$841.00
5	1/26/11	Bellen	East	Chin	KPSA	17	$374.00	$170.00
6	1/17/11	Quad	East	Franks	HII	62	$1,674.00	$899.00
7	1/18/11	Bellen	East	Franks	DFGH	20	$440.00	$200.00
8	1/14/11	Carlota	East	Franks	JAQ	34	$782.00	$374.00
9	1/6/11	Sunshine	East	Franks	PSA	54	$1,026.00	$432.00
10	1/23/11	Quad	East	Franks	PCC	44	$1,188.00	$638.00
11	1/11/11	Quad	East	Franks	ITW	14	$378.00	$203.00
12	1/9/11	Carlota	East	Franks	WSD	38	$874.00	$418.00
13	1/18/11	Sunshine	East	Franks	AA	24	$456.00	$192.00
14	1/17/11	Quad	East	Gault	SFWK	43	$1,161.00	$623.50
15	1/20/11	Bellen	East	Gault	PSA	10	$220.00	$100.00
16	1/10/11	Sunset	East	Gault	TRU	27	$567.00	$249.75

Figure 754

Using Icon Sort Buttons, Sort the Major Sort Field Last

To follow along, open the file named excelisfun-Start.xlsm and navigate to the S(10) sheet.

	A	B	C	D	E	F	G	H	I
1	Date	Product	Region	SalesRep	Customer	Units	Sales	COGS	
2	1/1/11	Quad	East	Sioux	AA	16	$432.00	$232.00	
3	1/2/11	Bellen	South	Gault	KBTB	24	$528.00	$240.00	
4	1/2/11	Quad	West	Pham	AST	30	$810.00	$435.00	
5	1/2/11	Bellen	West	Pham	SFWK	19	$418.00	$190.00	

Figure 755

1. Click the S(10) Sheet.
2. Click in cell D3.
3. Sort A to Z.

	A	B	C	D	E	F	G	H	I
1	Date	Product	Region	SalesRep	Customer	Units	Sales	COGS	
2	1/3/11	Carlota	MidWest	Chin	FM	20	$460.00	$220.00	
3	1/8/11	Quad	West	Chin	HII	16	$432.00	$232.00	
4	1/9/11	Bellen	South	Chin	WSD	26	$572.00	$260.00	
5	1/10/11	Sunshine	South	Chin	TRU	30	$570.00	$240.00	

Figure 756

4. Click in cell C3. This cell is in the *major sort field*.
5. Sort A to Z.

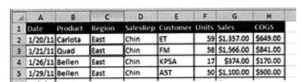

	A	B	C	D	E	F	G	H
1	Date	Product	Region	SalesRep	Customer	Units	Sales	COGS
2	1/20/11	Carlota	East	Chin	ET	59	$1,357.00	$649.00
3	1/21/11	Quad	East	Chin	FM	58	$1,566.00	$841.00
4	1/26/11	Bellen	East	Chin	KPSA	17	$374.00	$170.00
5	1/29/11	Bellen	East	Chin	AST	50	$1,100.00	$500.00

Figure 757

Our data set is now sorted by SalesRep within Region.

In Figure 757, you can see that we have sorted the data set by two fields or columns. But what if we want to sort by three fields? For example, what if we want to sort by Customer within SalesRep within Region? No problem: If you are doing it with the Sort buttons, we would sort the Customer field first, then the SalesRep field, and finally the Region field. Notice that because the Region field is the major sort, we sorted that field last. Now let's see how to do this same three-field sort with the Sort dialog box.

Using the Sort Dialog Box, Select the Major Sort Field as the First Level

To sort by Customer within SalesRep within Region, we would use the Add Level button in the Sort dialog box and make sure that the major sort was listed as the first level, as shown in Figure 758.

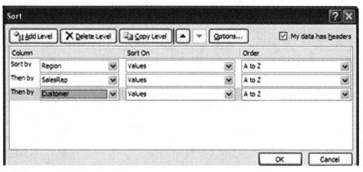

Figure 758

Rules for Sorting More Than One Field
- Using icon Sort buttons, sort the major sort field last.
- Using the Sort dialog box, select the major sort field as the first level.

Our next Excel Efficiency-Robust Rule is as follows:

Rule 36: The three main keys to sorting are as follows: 1) When using the Sort button to sort a column, select only one cell in the column before clicking the sort button. 2) When sorting more than one field using sort buttons, sort the major sort field last. 3) When sorting more than one field using the Sort dialog box, select the major sort field as the first level.

Next we want to take a look at how to use our "sorting more than one field" technique with the data analysis Subtotal feature to create an amazing summary report.

Subtotal Feature

The Subtotal feature enables us to take a data set and quickly summarize it into a compact report. Then you can print the report or copy and paste the report to a different sheet before removing the subtotals and reverting back to the original data set. In Figure 759, you can see a data set with raw transactional data, and in Figure 760, you can see a compact report created with the Subtotal feature. To get from the raw transactional data to the subtotaled report in Figure 760, we have to complete the follow steps:

1. Sort the Region field so that we can add subtotals at each change in Region.
2. Tell the Subtotal feature the following:
   - We want subtotals at each change in Region. (The Excel Subtotal feature will automatically insert a row and add subtotals.)
   - Select the Sum option for adding.
   - Tell it that we want to add the numbers in the three fields: Units, Sales, COGS.
   - Collapse all the raw data so that we only see the subtotals.
3. When you have finished printing or copying the subtotaled report, you remove subtotals to revert back to the original data set.

The most important step in all of these is that you must sort your data *before* adding subtotals. If you do not sort before adding subtotals, the result is a chaotic mess.

	A	B	C	D	E	F	G	H	I
1	Date	Product	Region	SalesRep	Customer	Units	Sales	COGS	
2	1/1/11	Quad	East	Sioux	AA	16	$432.00	$232.00	
3	1/2/11	Bellen	South	Gault	KBTB	24	$528.00	$240.00	
4	1/2/11	Quad	West	Pham	AST	30	$810.00	$435.00	
5	1/2/11	Bellen	West	Pham	SFWK	19	$418.00	$190.00	
6	1/3/11	Sunshine	East	Pham	FM	38	$722.00	$304.00	
7	1/3/11	Carlota	MidWest	Chin	FM	20	$460.00	$220.00	
8	1/3/11	Sunset	South	Pham	WSD	23	$483.00	$212.75	
9	1/3/11	Sunshine	South	Sioux	PCC	6	$114.00	$48.00	
10	1/4/11	Sunset	MidWest	Sioux	BBT	29	$609.00	$268.25	
11	1/5/11	Sunset	South	Pham	TTT	57	$1,197.00	$527.25	
12	1/5/11	Sunshine	West	Franks	ET	12	$228.00	$96.00	
13	1/5/11	Carlota	West	Franks	ITTW	60	$1,380.00	$660.00	
14	1/6/11	Sunshine	East	Franks	PSA	54	$1,026.00	$432.00	
15	1/6/11	Sunshine	South	Smith	QT	40	$760.00	$320.00	

Figure 759

1 2 3		A	B	C	D	E	F	G	H
	1	Date	Product	Region	SalesRep	Customer	Units	Sales	COGS
+	32			East Total			1076	$24,901.00	$12,023.25
+	57			MidWest Total			723	$15,688.00	$7,245.50
+	85			South Total			891	$19,802.00	$9,278.00
+	110			West Total			911	$24,766.00	$10,195.00
-	111			Grand Total			3601	$85,157.00	$38,741.75

Figure 760

To follow along, open the file named excelisfun-Start.xlsm and navigate to the ST(1) sheet.

Subtotals to Summarize Data by Region (sum calculation)

In Figure 761, we see our data set that is not sorted and does not have subtotals. Our goal is to add subtotals for the fields Units, Sales, and COGS for each one of the four regions (East, MidWest, South, West).

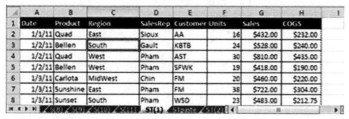

Figure 761

1. On the ST(1) sheet, click in the cell C3.
2. On the Data tab, Sort & Filter group, click the A to Z button.

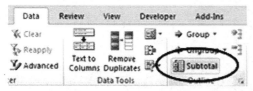

Figure 762

The Region field must be sorted for the Subtotal feature to work properly.

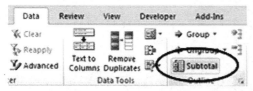

Figure 763

3. On the Data tab, Outline group, click the Subtotal button. Alternatively, you can use the Alt, A, B keyboard shortcut to bring up the Subtotal dialog box.

4. In the At Each Change In drop-down, use the drop-down arrow to select the Region field. This tells the Subtotal feature where to insert rows and create subtotals.

5. In the Use Function drop-down, use the drop-down arrow to select the SUM function. This tells the Subtotal feature what sort of calculation will be made for each subtotal.

6. In the Add Subtotal To area, check or uncheck and use the scrollbar until there are check marks next to the fields Units, Sales, and COGS. This tells the Subtotal feature upon which fields to use the SUM function.

Figure 764

The remaining three check boxes should remain the same as in this figure.

7. Click OK.

1 2 3		A	B	C	D	E	F	G	COC
	1	Date	Product	Region	SalesRep	Customer	Units	Sales	CO(
	2	1/1/11	Quad	East	Sioux	AA	16	$432.00	
	3			East Total			16	$432.00	
	4	1/2/11	Bellen	South	Gault	KBTB	24	$528.00	
	5			South Total			24	$528.00	
	6	1/2/11	Bellen	West	Pham	SFWK	19	$418.00	
	7	1/2/11	Quad	West	Pham	AST	30	$810.00	
	8			West Total			49	$1,228.00	
	9	1/3/11	Carlota	MidWest	Chin	FM	20	$460.00	
	10			MidWest Total			20	$460.00	
	11	1/3/11	Sunset	South	Pham	WSD	23	$483.00	
	12			South Total			23	$483.00	
	13	1/3/11	Sunshine	East	Pham	FM	38	$722.00	
	14			East Total			38	$722.00	
	15	1/3/11	Sunshine	South	Sioux	PCC	6	$114.00	

Figure 765

Figure 765 shows what it looks like if you did not sort before adding subtotals. If this is what your spreadsheet looks like, click the Subtotals button again and click the Remove All button and start over.

	A	B	C	D	E	F	G	H
1	Date	Product	Region	SalesRep	Customer	Units	Sales	COGS
2	1/1/11	Quad	East	Sioux	AA	16	$432.00	$232.00
3	1/3/11	Sunshine	East	Pham	FM	38	$722.00	$304.00
4	1/6/11	Sunshine	East	Franks	PSA	54	$1,026.00	$432.00
5	1/9/11	Bellen	East	Pham	EPP	40	$880.00	$400.00
6	1/9/11	Carlota	East	Franks	WSD	38	$874.00	$418.00
7	1/9/11	Sunshine	East	Smith	PCC	42	$798.00	$336.00
8	1/10/11	Carlota	East	Pham	AA	63	$1,449.00	$693.00
9	1/10/11	Quad	East	Smith	DFR	17	$459.00	$246.50
10	1/10/11	Sunset	East	Gault	TRU	27	$567.00	$249.75
11	1/10/11	Sunset	East	Smith	MBG	17	$357.00	$157.25
12	1/11/11	Quad	East	Franks	ITW	14	$378.00	$203.00
13	1/11/11	Quad	East	Smith	BBT	49	$1,323.00	$710.50
14	1/14/11	Carlota	East	Franks	JAQ	34	$782.00	$374.00

Figure 766

If you did sort before adding subtotals, you should see what is shown in Figure 766.

Notice that we can't see any subtotals!

We must scroll down to see our subtotals.

	A	B	C	D	E	F	G	H
28	1/23/11	Quad	East	Pham	WT	22	$594.00	$319.00
29	1/26/11	Bellen	East	Chin	KPSA	17	$374.00	$170.00
30	1/28/11	Sunset	East	Smith	ZAT	36	$756.00	$333.00
31	1/29/11	Bellen	East	Chin	AST	50	$1,100.00	$500.00
32			**East Total**			1076	$24,901.00	$12,023.25
33	1/3/11	Carlota	MidWest	Chin	FM	20	$460.00	$220.00
34	1/4/11	Sunset	MidWest	Sioux	BBT	29	$609.00	$268.25

Figure 767

8. Using the vertical scrollbar or the roller wheel on your mouse, scroll down to row 32.

In Figure 767, at row 32, you can see what "At each change in" means. Row 32 marks the point where the sorted data changes from East to MidWest. This is the point where the Subtotal feature does the following:

- Inserts a new row
- Adds the words East Total
- Shows subtotals for the three fields Units, Sales, and COGS

	A	B	C	D	E	F	G	H
107	1/28/11	Carlota	West	Smith	LOP	15	$345.00	$165.00
108	1/28/11	Sunset	West	Chin	FM	62	$1,302.00	$573.50
109	1/30/11	Sunshine	West	Gault	DFR	49	$931.00	$392.00
110			**West Total**			911	$24,766.00	$10,195.00
111			**Grand Total**			3601	$85,157.00	$38,741.75
112								

Figure 768

If you scroll down to row 112, you can see the last subtotal for the West field and a Grand Total.

Next we want to take a look at how to collapse the spreadsheet and show just the subtotals.

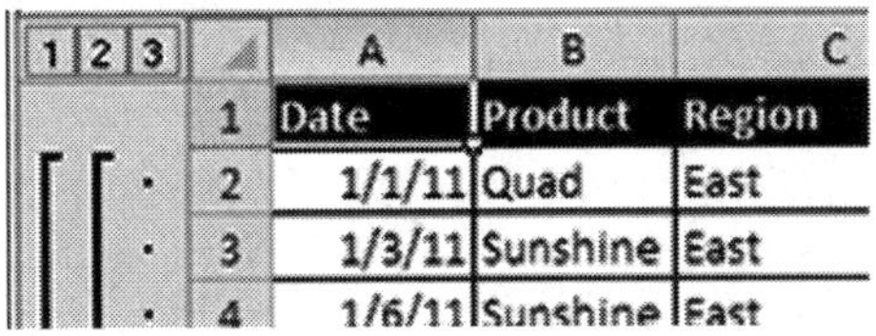

Figure 769

> 9. To jump to the top of the data set, use the keyboard shortcut Ctrl + Home.

Notice that in the upper-left corner of the spreadsheet you can see the numbers 1, 2, 3. These are called Outline buttons.

In Figure 769, you can see Outline buttons. These Outline buttons perform these tasks:
- Click the 3 Outline button to see all raw data and subtotals.
- Click the 2 Outline button to see the subtotals and the grand total. The rows with raw data are hidden.
- Click the 1 Outline button to just the grand total. The rows with raw data and the subtotals are hidden.

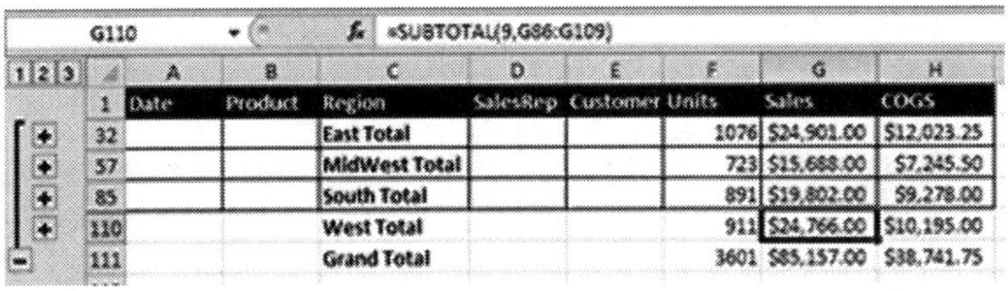

Figure 770

> 10. Click the 2 Outline button and you will see that the raw data in rows is hidden and all that remains are the subtotals!

In Figure 770, notice that in the region field the Subtotal feature added the labels East Total, MidWest Total, and so on. Later you will learn how these labels are removed when we remove subtotals; and in a different situation (when we create averaging subtotals), you will learn how these labels will display the word Average rather than Total. Next let's look at how the Subtotal feature hides the raw data rows.

Selecting Visible Cells Only (copy, paste)

In Figure 770, you can see the rows 1, 32, 85, 110, and 111. The Subtotal feature hides all the rows with the raw data. This is great because we can only see our subtotals and printing a report is easy. However, if we want to copy our report and paste it onto another sheet, the copy and paste process will also copy and paste all the hidden rows. If that is not what we want, we must use what is called the "select visible cells only" option *before* copying and pasting. There are three ways to invoke "select visible cells only":

- **Method 1**
1. Select the table range.
2. Press the F5 key to open Go To dialog box.
3. Click the Special button.
4. Select the dialog button for the Visible Cells Only.
5. Click OK.
- **Method 2**
1. Select the table range.
2. Press Alt + ; (Alt and semicolon key).
- **Method 3**
1. Go to the Home tab, Editing group, and click the Find & Select button.
2. From the drop-down menu, click the Go to Special item.
3. Select the dialog button for the Visible Cells Only.
4. Click OK.

Now let's see how to paste our subtotaled report onto a new sheet.

	A	B	C	D	E	F	G	H
1	Date	Product	Region	SalesRep	Customer	Units	Sales	COGS
32			East Total			1076	$24,901.00	$12,023.25
57			MidWest Total			723	$15,688.00	$7,345.50
85			South Total			891	$19,802.00	$9,278.00
110			West Total			911	$24,766.00	$10,195.00
111			Grand Total			3601	$85,157.00	$38,741.75
112								
113								

Figure 771

1. Select cell A1.
2. To highlight the whole table, press Ctrl + * (the asterisk on the number pad, or Ctrl + Shift + 8).

	A	B	C	D	E	F	G	H
1	Date	Product	Region	SalesRep	Customer	Units	Sales	COGS
32			East Total			1076	$24,901.00	$12,023.25
57			MidWest Total			723	$15,688.00	$7,345.50
85			South Total			891	$19,802.00	$9,278.00
110			West Total			911	$24,766.00	$10,195.00
111			Grand Total			3601	$85,157.00	$38,741.75
112								

Figure 772

3. To select the visible cells only, press Alt, ; (semicolon).
4. To copy the visible cells, press Ctrl + C.

In Figure 772, you can see that the only cells selected are the visible cells only. However, it is hard to visually decipher that just the visible cells are selected. If you look closely, you can see a slight white line between each of the cells that are visible. It is not until we copy our "Visible Cells Only" selection that we can tell definitively that only the visible cells are selected.

After you copy the visible cells, you will see the dancing ants outline around each visible range.

	A	B	C	D	E	F	G	H
1	Date	Product	Region	SalesRep	Customer	Units	Sales	COGS
2			East Total			1076	########	########
3			MidWest Total			723	########	########
4			South Total			891	########	########
5			West Total			911	########	########
6			Grand Total			3601	########	########

Figure 773

5. Click the STpaste sheet.
6. Click in A1.
7. To paste, press Ctrl + V.

Notice the ### signs in column G and H. These indicate that the columns are not wide enough.

In Figure 773, the pound signs in column G and H mean that the columns are not wide enough to display the cell content. To change the width of both columns at the same time, we need to select both columns and then double-click between the G column header and the H column header.

8. Point to the G column header, and when you see the downward-pointing black-arrow, click and drag to the H column header.

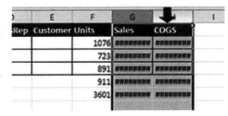

Figure 774

Both columns should be selected.

9. Point in-between the G and H column header, and when you see the horizontal-pointing double arrow with vertical bar cursor, double-click to Best Fit both columns.

Figure 775

	A	B	C	D	E	F	G	H
1	Date	Product	Region	SalesRep	Customer	Units	Sales	COGS
2			East Total			1076	$24,901.00	$12,023.25
3			MidWest Total			723	$15,688.00	$7,245.50
4			South Total			891	$19,802.00	$9,278.00
5			West Total			911	$24,766.00	$10,195.00
6			Grand Total			3601	$85,157.00	$38,741.75

Figure 776

The subtotaled numbers should appear on the new sheet, and you can format it and do any page setup as you see fit (Figure 777).

Now we want to take a closer look at how the Subtotal feature did its magic.

1 2 3		A	B	C	D	E	F	G	
	1	Date	Product	Region	SalesRep	Customer	Units	Sales	
+	32			East Total			1076	$24,901.00	
+	57			MidWest Total			723	$15,688.00	
+	85			South Total			891	$19,802.00	
+	110			West Total			911	$24,766.00	
−	111			Grand Total			3601	$85,157.00	

Figure 777

   10. Click back on the ST(1) sheet.
   11. Click in cell G110.

Notice that the SUBTOTAL function is in the formula bar.

> **Note**: In Figure 777, notice in the formula bar that the SUBTOTAL functions was put in automatically. The 9 in the first argument tells the function to add. Because the Subtotal feature puts this function in automatically, we do not really need to learn much about it. However, if you are curious, Figure 778 shows a list of the first argument numbers for the SUBTOTAL function.

11 Functions for SUBTOTAL function					
Function_num (includes hidden values)	Function_num (ignores hidden values)	What you see in Subtotal "Use function" drop-down		Function	What it does
1	101	Average		AVERAGE	Calculates arithmetic mean
2	102	Count Numbers		COUNT	Counts numbers
3	103	Count		COUNTA	Counts non empty cells
4	104	Max		MAX	Finds largest value
5	105	Min		MIN	Finds smallest value
6	106	Product		PRODUCT	Multiplies
7	107	Stdev		STDEV	Standard Deviation for a sample
8	108	Stdevp		STDEVP	Standard Deviation for a population
9	109	Sum		SUM	Adds
10	110	Var		VAR	Variation for a sample
11	111	Varp		VARP	Variation for a population

Figure 778

In our next example, you will learn how to use the Subtotal feature to calculate averages rather than sums.

Subtotals to Summarize Data by Region (average calculation)

As shown in Figure 779, the current subtotals show the calculation for adding. Our goal is to change the calculation from adding to averaging.

	G110		fx	=SUBTOTAL(9,G86:G109)				
123	A	B	C	D	E	F	G	H
1	Date	Product	Region	SalesRep	Customer	Units	Sales	COGS
32			East Total			1076	$24,901.00	$12,023.25
57			MidWest Total			723	$15,688.00	$7,245.50
85			South Total			891	$19,802.00	$9,278.00
110			West Total			911	$24,766.00	$10,195.00
111			Grand Total			3601	$85,157.00	$38,741.75

Figure 779

1. With cell G110 still selected, open the Subtotal dialog box with Alt, A, B.

When the dialog box opens, you should still see the same settings as when we did our summing calculations.

2. Using the Use Function drop-down arrow, select Average. Keep all other settings the same.
3. Notice that there is a check in the Replace Current Subtotals check box.
4. Click OK.
5. Click the 2 Outline button to collapse the raw data and see only the subtotals. (Figure 781)

In Figure 780, you can see the Replace Current Subtotals check box. Because our goal is to remove the sum calculation and replace it with an average calculation, it is very important that this option is checked.

Figure 780

Later you will see an example where we want to add cumulative calculations to our subtotal report, and in that upcoming instance, we will uncheck this.

	G110		fx	=SUBTOTAL(1,G86:G109)				
123	A	B	C	D	E	F	G	H
1	Date	Product	Region	SalesRep	Customer	Units	Sales	COGS
32			East Average			35.86667	$830.03	$400.78
57			MidWest Average			30.125	$653.67	$301.90
85			South Average			33	$733.41	$343.63
110			West Average			37.95833	$1,031.92	$424.79
111			Grand Average			34.29524	$811.02	$368.97

Figure 781

Looking in the formula bar in Figure 781, notice that the first argument of the SUBTOTAL function is 1.

In Figure 781, you can see our Average Subtotal Report. Most of us never think of subtotals consisting of anything but a sum calculation, but as you can see, the Subtotal feature has 11 different functions that allow us great latitude in what sorts of reports we can create. Notice also that the labels in the Region field now show the word Average rather than Total. Next we want to take a look at how to remove subtotals and revert back to the original data set.

Removing Subtotals

After we have copied the subtotaled data set, we can remove the subtotals and restore the data set to its original state.

Figure 782

6. With cell G110 still selected, open the Subtotal dialog box with Alt, A, B.
7. Click the Remove All button in the lower-left corner.
8. Click OK.

Alt Keyboard Shortcut Distinction

If you do a lot of subtotals and need to remove subtotals often, use the keyboard shortcut Alt, A, B, R. However, unlike most Alt keyboard shortcuts, *for this one you must hold the Alt key during the whole sequence.* So this means you hold the Alt key while tapping each letter key in sequence. The reason this is different from most Alt keyboard shortcuts is because the last R (for Remove All) is in a dialog box, whereas the other letters come from either the ribbon elements or pre-Excel 2007 menu elements.

	A	B	C	D	E	F	G	H
1	Date	Product	Region	SalesRep	Customer	Units	Sales	COGS
2	1/1/11	Quad	East	Sioux	AA	16	$432.00	$232.00
3	1/3/11	Sunshine	East	Pham	FM	38	$722.00	$304.00
4	1/6/11	Sunshine	East	Franks	PSA	54	$1,026.00	$432.00

Figure 783

The data set should be returned to its original state.

Subtotal to Count Words

Next we want to take a look at how to do subtotals that count words. Our goal is to count how many sales each sales representative made. To accomplish this, we will do the following:

1. Sort the SalesRep field.
2. Tell the Subtotal feature to do the following:
- Select the SalesRep field in the At Each Change In drop-down.
- Use the Count option. (The Count option in subtotals is like the COUNTA function, which can count text entries.)
- Check the SalesRep field for Add Subtotal To area.
- Collapse all the raw data so that we see only the subtotals.

1. Sort the SalesRep field.
2. Select the SalesRep field for At Each Change In.
3. Select Count in the Use Function drop-down.
4. Check the SalesRep field in the Add Subtotal To area.
5. Click OK.
6. Click the 2 Outline button to collapse and hide the raw data and see only the subtotals.

Figure 784

Notice that our At Each Change In and Add Subtotal To options are both using the same field: SalesRep.

	A	B	C	D	E	F	G	H
1	Date	Product	Region	SalesRep	Customer	Units	Sales	COGS
17			Chin Count	15				
35			Franks Count	17				
52			Gault Count	16				
71			Pham Count	18				
90			Sioux Count	18				
112			Smith Count	21				
113			Grand Count	105				

D90 = =SUBTOTAL(3,D72:D89)

Figure 785

The subtotals should look like Figure 785.

Next we want to take a look at how to add subtotals within subtotals. For our example, you will learn how to add subtotals for each sales representative's sales within each region.

Subtotals Within Subtotals: Summarize Sales Representative's Sales Within Each Region

In Figure 786, you can see a list of SalesRep's sales with each region created using the Subtotal feature. Notice that there are four Outline buttons in the upper-left corner: 1, 2, 3, 4. Four Outline buttons means that there are two separate subtotals, one for Region and one for SalesRep. This sort of subtotaling is the same sort of adding with two criteria that you saw in Chapter 5, "Formulas and Functions," when we were looking at the SUMIFS function and talked about the difference between an *and* and an *or* logical test. For example, in Figure 786, in cell G6, we are adding the sales numbers for transactional records that meet the two criteria: 1) the word East is in the Region field, *and* 2) the word Chin is in the SalesRep field. But as you will see, doing this sort of "adding with two criteria" is more easily done with the Subtotal feature than with formulas.

	A	B	C	D	E	F	G	H
1	Date	Product	Region	SalesRep	Customer	Units	Sales	COGS
6				Chin Total			$4,397.00	
15				Franks Total			$6,818.00	
22				Gault Total			$3,721.00	
28				Pham Total			$4,943.00	
31				Sioux Total			$1,329.00	
37				Smith Total			$3,693.00	
38			East Total				$24,901.00	
43				Chin Total			$3,494.00	
48				Franks Total			$2,095.00	
53				Gault Total			$1,285.00	
58				Pham Total			$3,198.00	
62				Sioux Total			$2,303.00	
68				Smith Total			$3,313.00	
69			MidWest Total				$15,688.00	
74				Chin Total			$2,227.00	
78				Franks Total			$3,029.00	
81				Gault Total			$2,040.00	

Figure 786

The trick to this sort of setup is that we have to use the Sort feature two times and then after the sorting is done we have to use the Subtotal dialog box twice. That means we must take four total actions, and the order in which we complete these actions is crucial. The order of how we accomplish this is as follows:

1. Sort the SalesRep field A to Z.
2. Sort the Region field A to Z.
3. The "At Each Change In" Sales subtotal is done for Region field.
4. The "At Each Change In" Sales subtotal is done for SalesRep field. Make sure the Replace Current Subtotals check box is *not* checked!

The way I remember the order of how to do this "double subtotal" is that I think of the order for sorting as right to left, and then the order of the subtotal is the opposite (left to right). Another way to envision it is to see SalesRep, Region, Region, SalesRep, where the first two are for the sort and the last two are for the subtotal. Let's take a look at how to do this.

To follow along, open the file named excelisfun-Start.xlsm and navigate to the ST(2) sheet.

1. Click the sheet ST(2) sheet.
2. Click in cell D3.
3. Sort A to Z.
4. Click in cell C3.
5. Sort A to Z.

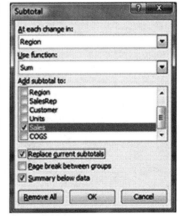

The sort should look like Figure 787.

	A	B	C	D	E	F	G	H
1	Date	Product	Region	SalesRep	Customer	Units	Sales	COGS
2	1/20/11	Carlota	East	Chin	ET	59	$1,357.00	$649.00
3	1/21/11	Quad	East	Chin	FM	58	$1,566.00	$841.00
4	1/26/11	Bellen	East	Chin	KPSA	17	$374.00	$170.00
5	1/29/11	Bellen	East	Chin	AST	50	$1,100.00	$500.00
6	1/6/11	Sunshine	East	Franks	PSA	54	$1,026.00	$432.00
7	1/9/11	Carlota	East	Franks	WSO	38	$874.00	$418.00
8	1/11/11	Quad	East	Franks	ITW	14	$378.00	$203.00
9	1/14/11	Carlota	East	Franks	JAQ	34	$782.00	$374.00

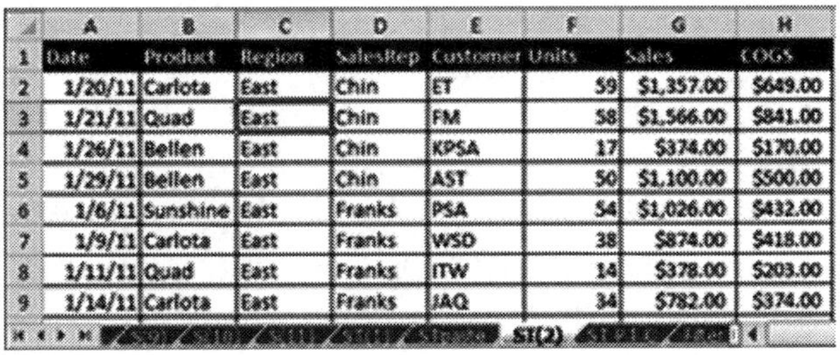

Figure 787

6. To open the Subtotal dialog box, press Alt, A, B.
7. Select the Region field for At Each Change In.
8. Select SUM in the Use Function drop-down.
9. Check the Sales field in the Add Subtotal To area.
10. Click OK.

Figure 788

11. To open the Subtotal dialog box a second time, press Alt, D, B.
12. Select the SalesRep field for At Each Change In.
13. Select SUM in the Use Function drop-down.
14. Check the Sales field in the Add Subtotal To area.

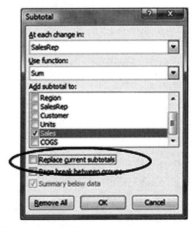

Figure 789

15. Make sure the Replace Current Subtotals check box is *not* checked!
16. Click OK.
17. Click the 3 Outline button in the upper-left corner.

	A	B	C	D	E	F	G	H
1	Date	Product	Region	SalesRep	Customer	Units	Sales	COGS
6				Chin Total			$4,397.00	
15				Franks Total			$6,818.00	
22				Gault Total			$3,721.00	
28				Pham Total			$4,943.00	
31				Sioux Total			$1,329.00	
37				Smith Total			$3,693.00	
38			East Total				$24,901.00	
43				Chin Total			$3,494.00	
48				Franks Total			$2,095.00	
53				Gault Total			$1,285.00	
58				Pham Total			$3,198.00	
62				Sioux Total			$2,303.00	
68				Smith Total			$3,313.00	
69			MidWest Total				$15,688.00	
74				Chin Total			$2,227.00	
78				Franks Total			$3,029.00	

Figure 790

The Report should look like Figure 790.

In Figure 790, you can see the power of the Subtotal feature. Very quickly we can create a summary report from a transactional data.

Our next Excel Efficiency-Robust Rule is this:

> *Rule 37: The three main keys for subtotaling are as follows: 1) Sort the fields before using the Subtotal feature. 2) At Each Change In determines where the new rows will be inserted, and Add Subtotal To determines which column will get the SUBTOTAL function. 3) If doing more than one subtotal, be sure to uncheck Replace Current Subtotals check box.*

There is another Excel data analysis feature called a PivotTable that can do everything that the Subtotal feature does and much more. So why do we even have to learn about subtotals? Well, because you may have a boss who insists on using the Subtotal feature or you might have a job interview Excel test that asks you to complete a subtotal. And occasionally, some people prefer the Subtotal feature over the PivotTable feature.

Next we will look at the PivotTable feature.

PivotTable Feature

For summarizing data, there are few more powerful Excel features than a PivotTable! And what makes them so powerful is that they are so easy. If we look at the "double subtotal" we did in Figure 790, we remember that we had do a double sort and then a double subtotal, and we had to remember the exact order in which we did each

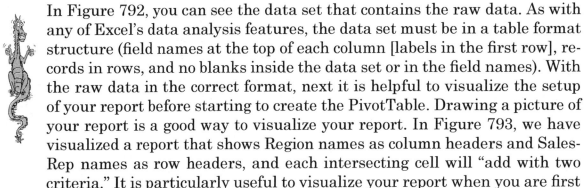

Sum of Sales	Region				
SalesRep	East	MidWest	South	West	Grand Total
Chin	4,397	3,494	2,227	2,004	12,122
Franks	6,818	2,095	3,029	1,608	13,550
Gault	3,721	1,285	2,040	4,374	11,420
Pham	4,943	3,198	1,953	9,788	19,882
Sioux	1,329	2,303	4,787	4,166	12,585
Smith	3,693	3,313	5,766	2,826	15,598
Grand Total	24,901	15,688	19,802	24,766	85,157

Figure 791

sort and subtotal. Now look at Figure 791. In Figure 791, we have the same summarized data (Region and SalesRep), except the information is presented in a table format instead of listed vertically as with the subtotals. But the real benefit of the report in Figure 791 is that with a PivotTable we can create it in four clicks! That is fast. That is the kind of report creation time that gets you noticed at your job. We also want to relate what we learn in this next section to what we have been learning about "adding with two criteria." Why? Because the PivotTable method will be easier than both the Subtotal feature and some of the formula options that we learned about in Chapter 5 (more about the comparison between a PivotTable and formulas later). Now before we create this report, we want to think about the structure of our PivotTable report before we create it. Why? Because most people in the world who use Excel think that creating PivotTables is hard. This perception is *false*. Creating PivotTables is *really easy* if you think about the structure of the report, before you do it. So let's take a look at the structure of the report that the PivotTable feature creates.

PivotTables Are Easy to Make!

In Figure 792, you can see the data set that contains the raw data. As with any of Excel's data analysis features, the data set must be in a table format structure (field names at the top of each column [labels in the first row], records in rows, and no blanks inside the data set or in the field names). With the raw data in the correct format, next it is helpful to visualize the setup of your report before starting to create the PivotTable. Drawing a picture of your report is a good way to visualize your report. In Figure 793, we have visualized a report that shows Region names as column headers and Sales-Rep names as row headers, and each intersecting cell will "add with two criteria." It is particularly useful to visualize your report when you are first learning how to use the PivotTable feature because it will help you to pinpoint which fields from the data set you will use and where you will place the fields when you are creating the PivotTable. From our visualization in Figure 793, we can notice the following:

- We will use the three fields: SalesRep, Region, and Sales.
- The Region field will be used as a column header or "column label."
- The SalesRep field will be used as a row header or "row label."
- The Sales field will be in the area where the row and column labels intersect (called **values**).

It is also helpful to see that this is the classic problem of "adding with two criteria." In this example, we want to find all transactional records that have the word Gault in the SalesRep field *and* the word MidWest in the Region field to add the associated sales figures from the Sales field. The PivotTable will prove to be the fastest way to accomplish "adding with two criteria" as compared to the Subtotal feature or the SUMIFS function.

	A	B	C	D	E	F	G	H	I
1	Date	Product	Region	SalesRep	Customer	Units	Sales	COGS	
2	1/1/11	Quad	East	Sioux	AA	16	$432.00	$232.00	
3	1/2/11	Bellen	South	Gault	KBTB	24	$528.00	$240.00	
4	1/2/11	Quad	West	Pham	AST	30	$810.00	$435.00	
5	1/2/11	Bellen	West	Pham	SFWK	19	$418.00	$190.00	
6	1/3/11	Sunshine	East	Pham	FM	38	$722.00	$304.00	
7	1/3/11	Carlota	MidWest	Chin	FM	20	$460.00	$220.00	
8	1/3/11	Sunset	South	Pham	WSD	23	$483.00	$212.75	
9	1/3/11	Sunshine	South	Sioux	PCC	6	$114.00	$48.00	
10	1/4/11	Sunset	MidWest	Sioux	BBT	29	$609.00	$268.25	

Figure 792

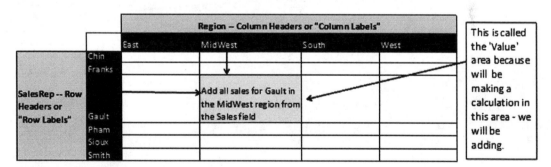

Figure 793

Finally, looking back at Figure 791, you can see what the final PivotTable report will look like. Now that we have the structure of the report in the back of our mind, creating the PivotTable with four clicks will be a breeze.

To follow along, open the file named excelisfun-Start.xlsm and navigate to the PTData sheet.

Creating a PivotTable in Four Clicks.

1. On the PTData sheet, click in cell C2.

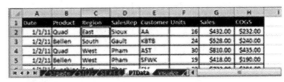

Figure 794

As with the other Excel Data Analysis features, you must click in only one cell before creating your PivotTable.

2. Go to the Insert tab, Tables group, and click the Pivot-Table drop-down arrow, and then click the PivotTable button.

Figure 795

Instead of the ribbon method, you can use the keyboard shortcut to start a PivotTable: Alt, N, V, T.

This one-step Create Pivot-Table dialog box replaces a three-step dialog box in Excel 2003.

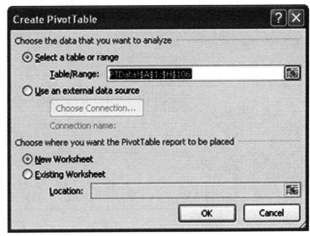

Because our data set had the proper table format structure, the Table/Range is correct.

By default the option button for New Worksheet is selected. We do want our PivotTable on a new sheet.

3. Click OK.

Figure 796

The next page has a picture of what you will see after clicking the OK button.

Figure 797 shows us what we see after we click the OK button in the Create PivotTable dialog box; namely, the PivotTable Creation User Interface. The main parts of this user interface are listed here:

- **PivotTable Tools Options tab and Design tab**: These ribbon tabs show only when you have a cell inside the PivotTable selected.

- **PivotTable Field List**: The top part shows list of field names from the original data set, and the bottom part shows the Column Labels, Row Labels, Values, and Report Filter areas.

> **Note**: If the field list does not appear (#2 in Figure 797), click in the PivotTable area to automatically show the field list or right-click PivotTable area and click Show Field List.

- **PivotTable area (area where PivotTable will appear)**: Notice the check mark; this relates to the PivotTable Field List and visually indicates that if you check the Field Name check box the field will appear in the PivotTable. Notice that there is a picture of a report that looks like our visualization (see Figure 793).
- **Creating the PivotTable**: Just click and drag the field name, and then drop the field name in desired area.

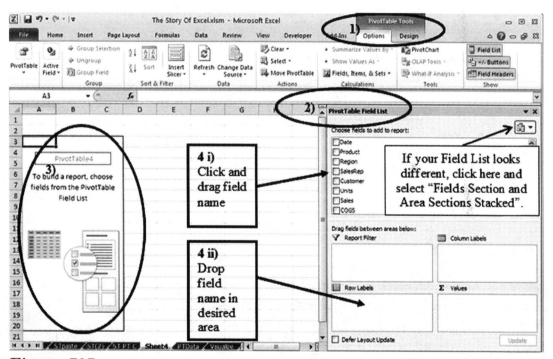

Figure 797

From Figure 797, it is important to recognize that because we already sketched out our PivotTable (see Figure 793), this PivotTable Creation User Interface is simple: We just click the field we want, drag it to the appropriate Column Labels, Row Labels, or Values area, and our PivotTable will be done!

Note: This PivotTable Creation User Interface is designed for the user to simply check the check boxes in the PivotTable Field List. The problem with this method is that the fields do not always automatically populate to the correct area. Therefore, when we create our PivotTable, we will click and drag and drop our fields to the correct area. If you do use the check boxes, by default text fields will show up in the Row Labels area and numeric fields will show up in the Values area.

4. To name the sheet with the PivotTable, double-click the Sheet1 sheet. (Your sheet may say Sheet 2 or some other-numbered sheet.)
5. Type PT(1).
6. Press Enter to register the sheet name.

Figure 798

Now that we have named the sheet, we want to drag and drop the fields to create our PivotTable.

7. Click the SalesRep field name. Hold the click and drag it toward the Row Labels area.

Figure 799

Your cursor will look like the cursor in Figure 800 after you click and start to drag. Notice that when you click and drag the SalesRep field and the cursor is above the field list your cursor shows a "don't circle." This "don't circle" means that you cannot drop it here.

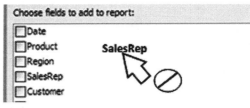

Figure 800

Notice that when you click and drag the SalesRep field and the cursor is above the Row Labels area your cursor shows a small picture of a Pivot-Table with the row header (Row Label) area highlighted in blue. This cursor icon means that you can let go of the mouse (let go of your held click) and the SalesRep field will drop in this area.

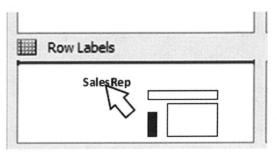

Figure 801

Figure 802

You should see that the SalesRep field has a check mark in the field list and is bold.

The SalesRep field should appear in the Row Labels area in the bottom part of the PivotTable Field List.

A list with each SalesRep's name listed only one time (a unique list) should appear in the PivotTable Area (worksheet).

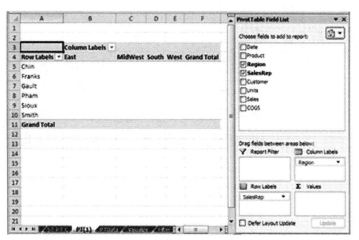

Figure 803

8. Drag the Region field from the field list to the Column Labels area.

Notice that the Pivot-Tables looks like the "visualization" we made back in Figure 793.

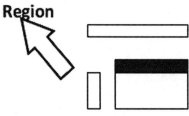

Figure 804

Notice that when you dropped the Region field into the Column Labels area, your cursor looked like Figure 804.

The blue means that the field will drop into the Column Labels area.

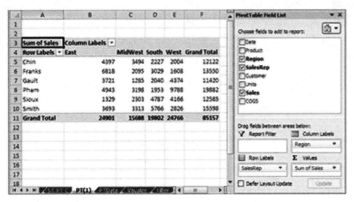

Figure 805

9. Drag the Sales field from the field list to the Values area.

Sum of Sales should appear in the Values area and in cell A3. This indicates that the calculation being made is done with the SUM function. This is the default calculation for a field that contains only numbers.

Notice that when you dropped the Sales field into the Values area, your cursor looked like Figure 806.

The blue means that the field will drop into the Values area.

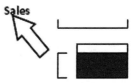

Figure 806

In Figure 805, you can see our basic PivotTable. This is just as we visualized it back in Figure 793. Now, we still have some formatting and other changes that we can make to enhance our PivotTable, but if you are in a hurry to create this sort of report, then creating this PivotTable in only four clicks is a lifesaver. But was it really four clicks? Well, if you don't name the sheet and you count the keyboard shortcut as one click, it is really four clicks. Let's review the clicks we used to create this PivotTable:

1. Alt, N, V, T.
2. Drag the SalesRep field to the Row Labels area.
3. Drag the Region field to the Column Labels area.
4. Drag the Sales field to Values area.

Now that is fast! Just for comparison, go back Figure 410 and look at how long it took us to do a similar report with the SUMIFS functions. Then compare our PivotTable report to Figure 790 and look how long it took us to do a similar report with the Subtotal feature. All you can say is that Pivot-Tables *rule!* So why do we even have the SUMIFS function and the Subtotal feature? As mentioned previously, some people prefer the Subtotal feature, and as for functions, there are a number of reasons you may want to use them and not a PivotTable. Here are a few:

- Functions automatically update when the underlying data (formula inputs) change. PivotTables do not automatically update (although all you have to do to have it update is to right-click the PivotTable and click the submenu item Refresh).
- Functions are much more versatile. PivotTables sometimes cannot be constructed to accomplish the goal at hand.
- PivotTables can increase file size.

However, for the type of report that we just created, PivotTables are fast and efficient.

Next we want to take a look at how to change the report layout, format the PivotTable, change the calculation from adding to averaging, pivot our PivotTable, and create a PivotChart from our PivotTable.

Changing the Report Layout to Show Field Names Rather Than Generic Labels

Look back at Figure 805 and notice that in the PivotTable above the SalesRep's names and Region names are the generic labels Row Labels and Column Labels, respectively. It is usually more informative to have the field names showing rather than these generic labels. It is easy to make this change by changing the report layout, as shown in Figure 807.

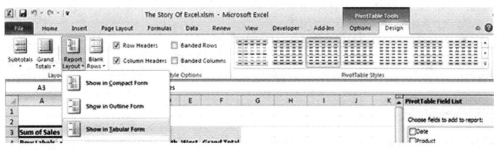

Figure 807

Sum of Sales	Region				
SalesRep	East	MidWest	South	West	Grand Total
Chin	4397	3494	2227	2004	12122
Franks	6818	2095	3029	1608	13550
Gault	3721	1285	2040	4374	11420
Pham	4943	3198	1953	9788	19882
Sioux	1329	2303	4787	4166	12585
Smith	3693	3313	5766	2826	15598
Grand Total	24901	15688	19802	24766	85157

Figure 808

The report should look like Figure 808.

1. With a cell inside the PivotTable selected, go to the PivotTable Tools Design tab, Layout group, and click the Report Layout drop-down arrow, and then click the Show in Tabular Form item.

Style Formatting

1. With a cell inside the Pivot-Table selected, go to the PivotTable Tools Design tab, PivotTable Styles group, and click the More drop-down arrow.
2. Select the second style called Pivot Style Light 1. (Hover cursor over style and read the screen tips.)

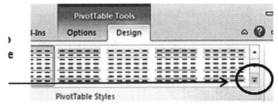

Figure 809

The report should look like Figure 810.

In Figure 810, we selected a rather plain style. Obviously, you can select whatever style you prefer.

Sum of Sales	Region				
SalesRep	East	MidWest	South	West	Grand Total
Chin	4397	3494	2227	2004	12122
Franks	6818	2095	3029	1608	13550
Gault	3721	1285	2040	4374	11420
Pham	4943	3198	1953	9788	19882
Sioux	1329	2303	4787	4166	12585
Smith	3693	3313	5766	2826	15598
Grand Total	24901	15688	19802	24766	85157

Figure 810

3. Add some fill color to the field names in cells B3 and A4 using the Fill Color button in the Font group on the Home tab.
4. Add some fill color to cell A3. (This cell contains a label that states what function is being used in the Values area.)

	A	B	C	D	E	F
1						
2						
3	Sum of Sales	Region				
4	SalesRep	East	MidWest	South	West	Grand Total
5	Chin	4397	3494	2227	2004	12122
6	Franks	6818	2095	3029	1608	13550
7	Gault	3721	1285	2040	4374	11420
8	Pham	4943	3198	1953	9788	19882
9	Sioux	1329	2303	4787	4166	12585
10	Smith	3693	3313	5766	2826	15598
11	Grand Total	24901	15688	19802	24766	85157

Figure 811

The field names we formatted in Figure 811 are the only PivotTable elements where we will not use the built-in PivotTable style formatting features (like our layout and styles we have previously applied). The rest of the elements are more efficiently formatted using the built-in PivotTable style formatting features. For example, in our next example, we will use the Value Field Settings dialog box to apply number formatting.

Number Formatting

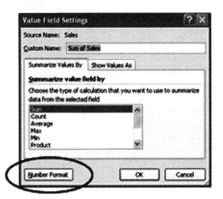

Figure 812

1. Because we must have a cell selected in the Values area of the PivotTable to open the Value Field Settings dialog box, click in cell C6.
2. Right-click cell C6 and click the submenu item Value Field Settings.
3. When the Value Field Settings dialog box appears, click the Number Formatting button.

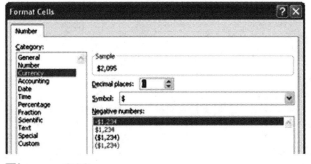

Figure 813

4. Select the Currency number formatting and reduce the decimals to zero.
5. Click OK on the Format Cells dialog box.
6. Click OK on the Value Field Settings dialog box.

In Figures 812 and 813, notice that we accessed the Format Cells dialog box through the Number Formatting button in the Value Field Settings dialog box. It is important to do it this way because any number formatting applied through the Value Field Settings dialog box is permanent even if you change the PivotTable (as you learn to do later). If you were to simply right-click a cell in the PivotTable and open the Format Cells dialog box and change the number formatting that way, the number formatting would be applied to the cells only and not to the entire field. When you add number formatting to the entire field, it remains formatted throughout any pivoting action (as you'll see how to later).

Sum of Sales	Region				
SalesRep	East	MidWest	South	West	Grand Total
Chin	$4,397	$3,494	$2,227	$2,004	$12,122
Franks	$6,818	$2,095	$3,029	$1,608	$13,550
Gault	$3,721	$1,285	$2,040	$4,374	$11,420
Pham	$4,943	$3,198	$1,953	$9,788	$19,882
Sioux	$1,329	$2,303	$4,787	$4,166	$12,585
Smith	$3,693	$3,313	$5,766	$2,826	$15,598
Grand Total	$24,901	$15,688	$19,802	$24,766	$85,157

Figure 814

The finished report should look like Figure 814.

Next we want to look at how to change the calculation from adding to averaging. We will use the Value Field Settings dialog box to accomplish this.

Changing the Calculation from Adding to Averaging

1. Right-click cell C6 and click the submenu item Value Field Settings.
2. When the Value Field Settings dialog box appears, in the Summarize Value Field By list, select Average.
3. Click OK

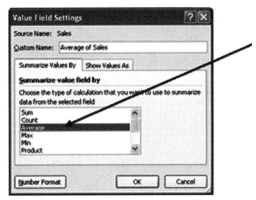

Figure 815

The PivotTable should look like Figure 816.

3	Average of Sales	Region				
4	SalesRep	East	MidWest	South	West	Grand Total
5	Chin	$1,099	$874	$557	$668	$808
6	Franks	$852	$524	$1,010	$804	$797
7	Gault	$620	$321	$1,020	$1,094	$714
8	Pham	$989	$800	$651	$1,631	$1,105
9	Sioux	$665	$768	$598	$833	$699
10	Smith	$739	$663	$824	$707	$743
11	Grand Total	$830	$654	$733	$1,032	$811

Figure 816

The same 11 functions that are available with the Subtotal feature are also available with the PivotTable feature (see Figure 817).

11 Functions available in a PivotTable		
What you see in Value Field Settings dialog box	Function	What it does
Average	AVERAGE	Calculates arithmetic mean
Count Numbers	COUNT	Counts numbers
Count	COUNTA	Counts non empty cells
Max	MAX	Finds largest value
Min	MIN	Finds smallest value
Product	PRODUCT	Multiplies
Stdev	STDEV	Standard Deviation for a sample
Stdevp	STDEVP	Standard Deviation for a population
Sum	SUM	Adds
Var	VAR	Variation for a sample
Varp	VARP	Variation for a population

Figure 817

Next we want to take a look at how to "pivot" the PivotTable.

Pivoting the PivotTable

Average of Sales	Region ▼				
SalesRep ▼	East	MidWest	South	West	Grand Total
Chin	$1,099	$874	$557	$668	$808
Franks	$852	$524	$1,010	$804	$797
Gault	$620	$321	$1,020	$1,094	$714
Pham	$989	$800	$651	$1,631	$1,105
Sioux	$665	$768	$598	$833	$699
Smith	$739	$663	$824	$707	$743
Grand Total	$830	$654	$733	$1,032	$811

Figure 818

Imagine that you have created the report as shown in Figure 818, and then your boss comes in and says that you have created the report backward! She goes on to say that she wants the SalesRep names as column headers and the Region as row headers. You, of course, look over your shoulder and say, "Oh, you mean like this, boss?" and you quickly pivot the report to match your boss's request and with two clicks generate the report as shown in Figure 819. Your boss, not knowing anything about PivotTables falls out of character and says, "Wow! That was so quick!" The action of switching row labels and column labels is called **pivoting the PivotTable** and is the reason that the PivotTable feature is called "pivot table." Now let's see how easy it is to pivot.

Average of Sales	SalesRep ▼						
Region ▼	Chin	Franks	Gault	Pham	Sioux	Smith	Grand Total
East	$1,099	$852	$620	$989	$665	$739	$830
MidWest	$874	$524	$321	$800	$768	$663	$654
South	$557	$1,010	$1,020	$651	$598	$824	$733
West	$668	$804	$1,094	$1,631	$833	$707	$1,032
Grand Total	$808	$797	$714	$1,105	$699	$743	$811

Figure 819

1. Make sure that the PivotTable Field List is showing. (Right-click PivotTable and click Show Field List.)

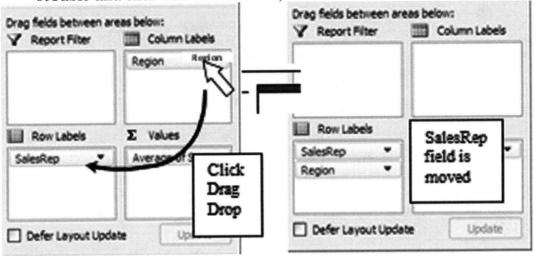

Figure 820

2. Select a cell in the PivotTable.
3. In the Column Label area, click the Region field name, hold click, drag to the Row Labels area below the SalesRep field, and then release the click.

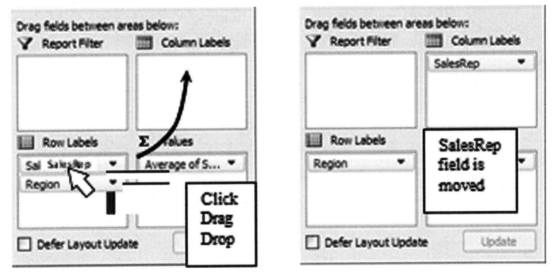

Figure 821

4. In the Row Label area, click the SalesRep field name, hold click, drag up to the Row Labels area, and then release the click.

The PivotTable should look like Figure 819.

Next we want to take a look at how to create a vertically oriented PivotTable that is similar to the Subtotal feature.

Listing Two Fields in Row Labels Area (similar to the Subtotal feature)

If you want your PivotTable to show all data vertically (just like the Subtotal feature), it can be accomplished by dragging the two field names to the Row Labels area. Figure 822 shows what the Row Labels and Values areas would look like in the PivotTable Field List, and Figure 823 shows what the finished report would look like. If you look at the subtotal report we created back in Figure 790, you will see that the PivotTable feature enables us to create the same report, but with much less effort.

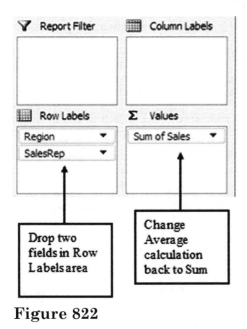

Figure 822

Region	SalesRep	Sum of Sales
East	Chin	$4,397
	Franks	$6,818
	Gault	$3,721
	Pham	$4,943
	Sioux	$1,329
	Smith	$3,693
East Total		**$24,901**
MidWest	Chin	$3,494
	Franks	$2,095
	Gault	$1,285
	Pham	$3,198
	Sioux	$2,303
	Smith	$3,313
MidWest Total		**$15,688**
South	Chin	$2,227
	Franks	$3,029
	Gault	$2,040
	Pham	$1,953
	Sioux	$4,787
	Smith	$5,766
South Total		**$19,802**
West	Chin	$2,004
	Franks	$1,608
	Gault	$4,374
	Pham	$9,788
	Sioux	$4,166
	Smith	$2,826
West Total		**$24,766**
Grand Total		**$85,157**

Figure 823

Now suppose your boss asks for the summary report as shown in Figure 823, except she only wants to see the SalesRep detail for the MidWest region and none of the others. This sort of report is easy to create using the +/- collapse buttons next to each Region field name. Let's take a look at how to create this report next.

Collapsing PivotTable Row Labels

In Figure 824, you can see a +/– collapse button next to the East region field name. Just like with the Subtotal feature, you can click the – collapse button to collapse the SalesRep detail and show only the subtotal for the East region. When the field is collapsed, the – collapse button becomes a + collapse button. Clicking the + collapse button will expand the SalesRep detail.

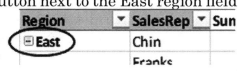

Figure 824

However, the process of clicking the +/– collapse button can be a little tricky. The important thing to remember is that you cannot click a +/– collapse button until you see the white diagonal-pointing arrow, as shown in Figure 825.

Region	SalesRep	Sun
⊟ East	Chin	
	Franks	

Figure 825

Clicking the East, South, and West – collapse button with the white diagonal-pointing arrow will produce the report shown in Figure 826.

If you wanted to revert back to the fully expanded report, you click the East, South, and West + collapse button with the white diagonal-pointing arrow to produce the report shown back in Figure 823.

Region	SalesRep	Sum of Sales
⊞ East		$24,901
⊟ MidWest	Chin	$3,494
	Franks	$2,095
	Gault	$1,285
	Pham	$3,198
	Sioux	$2,303
	Smith	$3,313
MidWest Total		$15,688
⊞ South		$19,802
⊞ West		$24,766
Grand Total		$85,157

Figure 826

Now, what if you need a report that shows only the MidWest and South regions and none of the others? For this we can use the Filter feature available in each field in a PivotTable.

Filtering a Field in a PivotTable

If our goal is create a report for just the MidWest and South regions, we can use the Filter feature that can be accessed through the drop-down arrow next to each field name in the PivotTable.

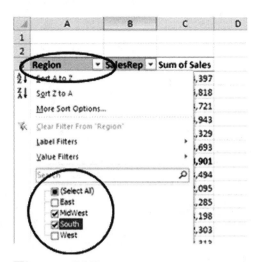

Figure 827

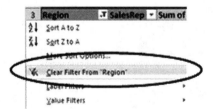

Figure 829

1. Click the drop-down arrow next to the Region field name in cell A3.
2. At the bottom of the submenu, uncheck the East and West regions.

The filtered report should look like Figure 828.

Notice the drop-down arrow next to the Region field name now appears with a "Filter Symbol" icon. This visually indicates that the field has been filtered.

Region	SalesRep	Sum of Sales
⊟MidWest	Chin	$3,494
	Franks	$2,095
	Gault	$1,285
	Pham	$3,198
	Sioux	$2,303
	Smith	$3,313
MidWest Total		$15,688
⊟South	Chin	$2,227
	Franks	$3,029
	Gault	$2,040
	Pham	$1,953
	Sioux	$4,787
	Smith	$5,766
South Total		$19,802
Grand Total		$35,490

Figure 828

3. To remove the filter, click the Filter Symbol icon and from the submenu click Clear Filter from Region.

After you remote the filter, the report should look like the one shown back Figure 823.

The Filter feature can do many more amazing things, too. You will learn more about the Filter feature in the "Filter Feature" section, later in this chapter.

Next we want to take a look at how to add three or more fields to our Pivot-Table.

Listing Three or More Fields in the PivotTable

With a PivotTable, you are always just one click and drag away from adding a new field to the PivotTable. In Figures 830 and 831, you can see that we dragged two fields to the Row Labels area and one field to the Column Labels area. The report in Figure 831 shows us the sum of sales given three criteria: 1) Region, 2) SalesRep, and 3) Product. This sort of PivotTable demonstrates the amazing power of the Pivot-Table feature because if we had to create this report with a formula (adding with three criteria), it would take much longer.

Figure 830

Sum of Sales		Product					
Region	SalesRep	Bellen	Carlota	Quad	Sunset	Sunshine	Grand Total
East	Chin	$1,474	$1,357	$1,566			$4,397
	Franks	$440	$1,656	$3,240		$1,482	$6,818
	Gault	$418		$1,161	$2,142		$3,721
	Pham	$2,178	$1,449	$594		$722	$4,943
	Sioux		$897	$432			$1,329
	Smith			$1,782	$1,113	$798	$3,693
East Total		$4,510	$5,359	$8,775	$3,255	$3,002	$24,901
MidWest	Chin		$460	$1,647		$1,387	$3,494
	Franks		$575			$1,520	$2,095
	Gault	$616		$270	$399		$1,285
	Pham	$2,134				$1,064	$3,198
	Sioux	$1,232			$1,071		$2,303
	Smith	$352		$1,593		$1,368	$3,313
MidWest Total		$4,334	$1,035	$3,510	$1,470	$5,339	$15,688
South	Chin	$726				$1,501	$2,227
	Franks		$1,058	$1,971			$3,029
	Gault	$528		$1,512			$2,040
	Pham				$1,953		$1,953
	Sioux	$1,650		$675	$1,911	$551	$4,787
	Smith	$242	$3,795			$1,729	$5,766
South Total		$3,146	$4,853	$4,158	$3,864	$3,781	$19,802
West	Chin			$702	$1,302		$2,004
	Franks		$1,380			$228	$1,608
	Gault		$230	$3,213		$931	$4,374
	Pham	$6,584		$810	$2,394		$9,788
	Sioux	$770	$414	$1,728		$1,254	$4,166
	Smith	$726	$345	$1,755			$2,825
West Total		$8,080	$2,369	$8,208	$3,696	$2,413	$24,766
Grand Total		$20,070	$13,616	$24,651	$12,285	$14,535	$85,157

Figure 831

Now that we have added three fields to our PivotTable, what if we want to remove some of the fields?

Removing Fields from PivotTables

To remove a field from the PivotTable, simply uncheck the check box next to the field name in the PivotTable Field List. Unchecking is accomplished by clicking a check mark. In Figure 832, you can see that the Product field has a check mark. When you click the check mark next to the Product field, the check mark is removed (see Figure 834). After you removed the Product field, your report should look like the one in Figure 833.

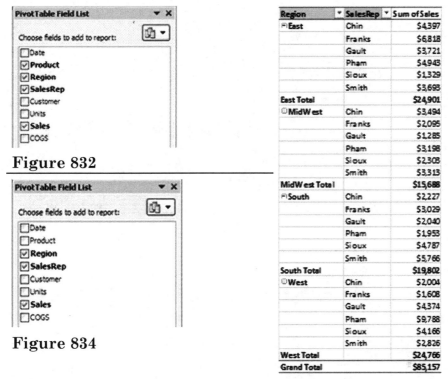

Figure 832

Figure 834

Region	SalesRep	Sum of Sales
East	Chin	$4,397
	Franks	$6,818
	Gault	$3,721
	Pham	$4,943
	Sioux	$1,329
	Smith	$3,693
East Total		$24,901
MidWest	Chin	$3,494
	Franks	$2,095
	Gault	$1,285
	Pham	$3,198
	Sioux	$2,303
	Smith	$3,313
MidWest Total		$15,688
South	Chin	$2,227
	Franks	$3,029
	Gault	$2,040
	Pham	$1,953
	Sioux	$4,787
	Smith	$5,766
South Total		$19,802
West	Chin	$2,004
	Franks	$1,608
	Gault	$4,374
	Pham	$9,788
	Sioux	$4,166
	Smith	$2,826
West Total		$24,766
Grand Total		$85,157

Figure 833

Next, we want to take the report from Figure 833 and make a PivotChart from it.

PivotChart Feature

In Figure 833, you can see all the summarized numbers, but it is hard to quickly see "which SalesRep has the biggest number in each region." Charts are visual presentations of quantitative data that allow the viewer to quickly see patterns and answer questions such as these:

- Which SalesRep has the most sales in each region?
- In which region did each SalesRep have the most sales?

In this section, we look at how easy it is to create a PivotChart from Pivot-Table. In Chapter 7, "Charts," we examine charts in more detail.

Our goal is to use the PivotTable in Figure 833 to make a PivotChart that allows us to quickly see patterns and recognize trends. Then we will pivot the PivotTable and see how the PivotChart changes to interpret the new PivotTable.

1. With the PivotTable still showing as in Figure 833, click in a cell inside the PivotTable.
2. Click the PivotTable Tools Options tab.
3. Click the PivotChart button in the Tools group.

Figure 835

4. On the right side of the Insert Chart dialog box, select the chart type Column.
5. On the left side, select the first column type: Clustered Column.
6. Click OK.

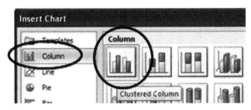

Figure 836

When the PivotChart pops out, you should see something like Figure 837.

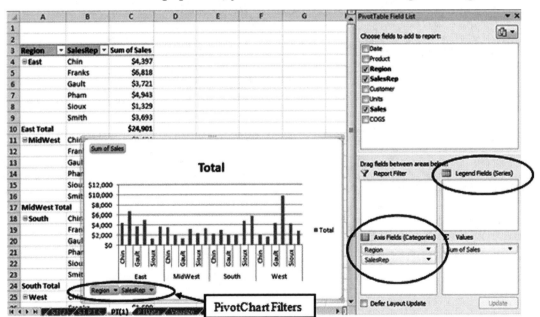

Figure 837

In Figure 837, you can see that the chart exactly reflects the layout of the PivotTable. In the PivotTable, you can see the East region, and then within that you can see each SalesRep name. The same is true on the horizontal axis of the chart. This is important to take note of because later when we "pivot" the PivotTable, the PivotChart will also pivot. Also notice that the

PivotChart has filters directly on the chart (a huge improvement over Excel 2007, which required you to use the Analyze task pane). Still further, notice that because we have the PivotChart selected, the PivotTable Field List area names have changed so that Row Labels has become Axis Fields (Categories) (Horizontal Axis) and Column Labels has become Legend Fields (Series) (Vertical Axis).

Next we want to change the size of the chart to show all the SalesRep names.

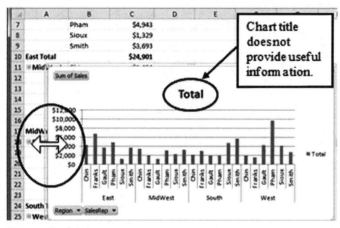

Figure 838

7. Point to the middle of the left edge of the chart; the edge is a translucent color. When you see a white double-headed horizontal-pointing arrow, click and drag to the left to expand the chart.

When you can see all the SalesReps names, you have stretched the chart far enough.

Look at the chart in Figure 838. You can see a chart tile that says Total. Because that title does not provide useful information, we want to change it to read January 2001 Sales.

Figure 839

8. Click the title to select it. You can tell that the title is selected when you see the lined outline with translucent circles in each corner.
9. Type **January 2001 Sales**.
    Notice that as you type the letters to not appear in the title, but instead they appear in the formula bar.
10. Press Enter.

With just the preceding three steps, you can change the title of any chart.

After changing the title, the chart should look like Figure 840.

Notice the Region and SalesRep field names on the PivotChart and on the PivotTable are available for filtering. It does not matter which one you use for filtering, because if the PivotChart is filtered, the Pivot-Table will be filtered also, and vice versa.

Figure 840

This is because they are connected. Anything you do to one will be done to the other.

If we filter the Region field as shown in Figure 841, the resultant PivotTable and PivotChart will appear as shown in Figure 842. To return the chart to its unfiltered state, you can use the Clear Filter from Region button, as shown back in Figure 829, or you can use the Select All option, as shown in Figure 843.

Figure 841

Figure 843

Figure 842

Next we want to take a look at how the PivotChart changes when we "pivot" the PivotTable.

Pivoting PivotTables and PivotCharts

Figure 844 shows the PivotChart and PivotTable before we perform a pivot. Figure 844 shows the PivotChart and PivotTable after we drag the Sales-Rep field to the Legend Fields (Series). Notice that we have two totally different charts. Each chart provides a visual answer to a different question. Here are the questions the each chart answers:

- **The chart in Figure 844 answers this question**: Which SalesRep has the most sales in each Region?
- **The chart in Figure 845 answers this question**: In which region did each SalesRep have the most sales?

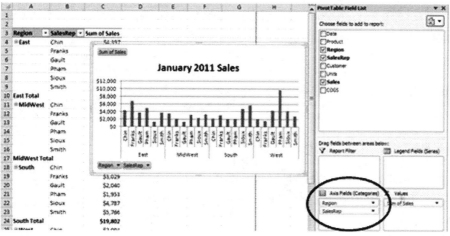

Figure 844

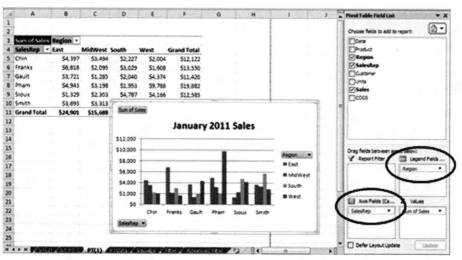

Figure 845

The fact that the chart changes anytime the PivotTable changes and vice versa is the most amazing aspect of the PivotChart feature. This powerful feature enables you to summarize and analyze data quickly. Creating reports quickly and accurately is a skill that helps to get and keep jobs. Bosses and co-workers love people who have this skill!

Next we want to look at how to take daily transactional sales data and group it into monthly sales totals using a PivotTable.

Grouping Dates

Often we are given a data set that has daily transactions and we are required to create a report that summarizes the data by month or quarter or week. In Figure 846, you can see a data set that contains daily transactional records from January to June 2001. In Figure 847, you can see a PivotTable that was created in about eight clicks that took all 1,227 rows of data from Figure 846 and grouped the Date field by month and then added all the sales from the Sales field by Region and Month. What is so amazing about this is that if we were to create this report with formulas, it would take *a lot* more effort and time. Let's take a look at how easy it is to create this report.

	A	B	C	D	E	F	G	H	I
1	Date	Product	Region	SalesRep	Customer	Units	Sales	COGS	
2	1/23/11	Quad	West	Sioux	DFR	23	$621.00	$333.50	
3	1/18/11	Sunshine	West	Pham	TTT	65	$1,235.00	$520.00	
4	6/19/11	Sunset	West	Pham	FM	47	$987.00	$434.75	
5	6/13/11	Quad	MidWest	Smith	PLOT	24	$648.00	$348.00	
6	4/6/11	Sunshine	South	Pham	JAQ	58	$1,102.00	$464.00	
7	3/2/11	Quad	West	Franks	ET	22	$594.00	$319.00	
8	3/24/11	Quad	East	Smith	JAQ	8	$216.00	$116.00	
9	2/27/11	Sunshine	South	Smith	ET	29	$551.00	$232.00	
10	6/19/11	Carlota	West	Chin	ZAT	55	$1,265.00	$605.00	
11	5/17/11	Carlota	MidWest	Franks	ZAT	39	$897.00	$429.00	
12	4/11/11	Sunshine	MidWest	Pham	DFGH	49	$931.00	$392.00	
13	2/15/11	Carlota	MidWest	Pham	KBTB	63	$1,449.00	$693.00	

Figure 846

Sum of Sales	Region				
Date	East	MidWest	South	West	Grand Total
Jan	$38,438	$47,995	$49,374	$36,487	$172,294
Feb	$37,044	$39,134	$31,851	$34,005	$142,034
Mar	$35,064	$38,162	$41,283	$37,155	$151,664
Apr	$43,693	$29,520	$40,505	$43,495	$157,213
May	$35,750	$39,905	$47,170	$45,793	$168,618
Jun	$37,706	$45,037	$46,967	$39,288	$168,998
Grand Total	$227,695	$239,753	$257,150	$236,223	$960,821

Figure 847

To follow along, open the file excelisfun-Start.xlsm and navigate to the PT-Data(2) sheet.

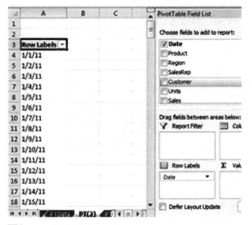

Figure 848

1. On the PTData(2) sheet, click in any cell inside the data set.
2. Use this keyboard shortcut to create a PivotTable: Alt, N, V, T.
3. To accept the settings in the Create PivotTable dialog box, click OK or just press the Enter key.
4. Rename the sheet **PT(2)**.
5. In the PivotTable Field List, drag the Date field to the Row Labels area.

You should see all the dates listed in chronological order.

> **Note:** If we were to drag the Sales field to the Values area, we would have a Daily Sales Report!

Figure 849

6. Select any cell in the Date field inside the emerging PivotTable.
7. Right-click, and on the submenu point to Group.

Notice that there is an Ungroup option that you can use if you decide to ungroup.

8. In the Grouping dialog box, click the Months and Years categories with the diagonal-pointing white-arrow. Be sure that both are selected.

9. Click OK.

In Figure 850, we see that we selected both Months and Year. It is usually a good idea to do this even if you only have data for one year. This is because if you do have data for more than one year and you *do not*

Figure 850

select both Months and Years, all the January data for multiple years will be grouped together, and this is rarely the desired result. If you *do* have only one year's data and you group by both Months and Years, it is easy enough to uncheck the Years group in the PivotTable Field List.

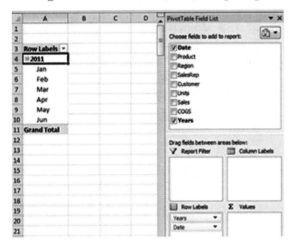

Figure 851

The PivotTable and the PivotTable Field List should show two fields related to the Date. The Date field contains the months, and the Years field contains the years.

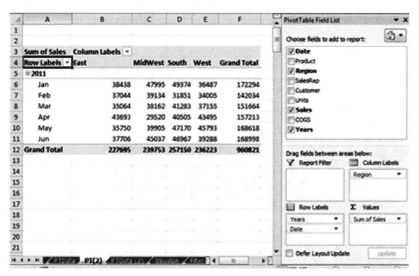

Figure 852

    10. Drag the Region field to the Column Labels area.
    11. Drag the Sales field to the Values Labels area.

In Figure 852, you can see the basics of our report are done. And we did it in only eight clicks. Here is a summary of the amazing eight clicks for creating a PivotTable that groups dates by months and adds sales with the two criteria Month and Region:

    a. Press Alt, N, V, T.
    b. Press Enter.
    c. Drag the Date field to the Row Columns area.
    d. Right-click the Date field in the PivotTable.
    e. Click Years. (Months is selected by default.)
    f. Click OK.
    g. Drag the Region field to the Column Labels area.
    h. Drag the Sales field to the Values Labels area.

This process is particularly amazing if you compare it to how one might do it with formulas. Let's look at how we would do this with formulas next.

Here are the steps we would have to take to create a similar report using formulas:

    a. Type row and column labels into cells.
    b. Create formula like this:
        =SUMPRODUCT(–(TEXT('PTData (2)'!$A$2:$A$1227, "mmm")=$A2),–('PTData (2)'!$C$2:$C$1227=B$1), 'PTData (2)'!$G$2:$G$1227)
    c. Copy the formula through the range of cells.
    d. Type **Grand Total** labels.
    e. Add the SUM function for the grand totals.

To see this example, open the file named excelisfun-Start.xlsm and navigate to the FormulaS sheet. Figure 853 shows the end result of the steps to create this formula report.

	B2			f_x	=SUMPRODUCT(--(TEXT('PTData (2)'!$A$2:$A$1227,"mmm")=$A2),--('PTData (2)'!$C$2:$C$1227=B$1),'PTData (2)'!$G$2:$G$1227)			
	A	B	C	D	E	F	G	H
1		East	MidWest	South	West	Grand Total		
2	Jan	$38,438	$47,995	$49,374	$36,487	$172,294		
3	Feb	$37,044	$39,134	$31,851	$34,005	$142,034		
4	Mar	$35,064	$38,162	$41,283	$37,155	$151,664		
5	Apr	$43,693	$29,520	$40,505	$43,495	$157,213		
6	May	$35,750	$39,905	$47,170	$45,793	$168,618		
7	Jun	$37,706	$45,037	$46,967	$39,288	$168,998		
8	Grand Total	$227,695	$239,753	$257,150	$236,223	$960,821		

Figure 853

The one advantage to a formula like this is that it will automatically update if the source data was changed. For more about this sort of formula, look back at the SUMPRODUCT function in Chapter 5.

Now back to our PivotTable.

Now let's format the report by 1) adding Currency number formatting to the sales numbers, 2) changing the layout, 3) changing the style, and 4) adding fill color to the field names.

	A	B	C	D	E	F
1						
2						
3	Sum of Sales	Column Labels				
4	Row Labels	East	MidWest	South	West	Grand Total
5	2011					
6	Jan	$38,438	$47,995	$49,374	$36,487	$172,294
7	Feb	$37,044	$39,134	$31,851	$34,005	$142,034
8	Mar	$35,064	$38,162	$41,283	$37,155	$151,664
9	Apr	$43,693	$29,520	$40,505	$43,495	$157,213
10	May	$35,750	$39,905	$47,170	$45,793	$168,618
11	Jun	$37,706	$45,037	$46,967	$39,288	$168,998
12	Grand Total	$227,695	$239,753	$257,150	$236,223	$960,821

Figure 854

12. To add the Currency formatting, right-click cell B6 and click the submenu item Value Field Settings.
13. When the Value Field Settings dialog box appears, click the Number Formatting button.
14. Select the Currency number formatting and reduce the decimals to zero.
15. Click OK on the Format Cells dialog box.
16. Click OK on the Value Field Settings dialog box.

The report should look like Figure 855.

	A	B	C	D	E	F	G
1							
2							
3	Sum of Sales		Region ▾				
4	Years ▾	Date ▾	East	MidWest	South	West	Grand Total
5	⊟2011	Jan	$38,438	$47,995	$49,374	$36,487	$172,294
6		Feb	$37,044	$39,134	$31,851	$34,005	$142,034
7		Mar	$35,064	$38,162	$41,283	$37,155	$151,664
8		Apr	$43,693	$29,520	$40,505	$43,495	$157,213
9		May	$35,750	$39,905	$47,170	$45,793	$168,618
10		Jun	$37,706	$45,037	$46,967	$39,288	$168,998
11	Grand Total		$227,695	$239,753	$257,150	$236,223	$960,821

Figure 855

17. To change the layout, select a cell inside the PivotTable, and then go to the PivotTable Tools Design tab, Layout group, and click the Report Layout drop-down arrow, and then click the Show in Tabular Form item.

	A	B	C	D	E	F	G
1							
2							
3	Sum of Sales		Region ▾				
4	Years ▾	Date ▾	East	MidWest	South	West	Grand Total
5	⊟2011	Jan	$38,438	$47,995	$49,374	$36,487	$172,294
6		Feb	$37,044	$39,134	$31,851	$34,005	$142,034
7		Mar	$35,064	$38,162	$41,283	$37,155	$151,664
8		Apr	$43,693	$29,520	$40,505	$43,495	$157,213
9		May	$35,750	$39,905	$47,170	$45,793	$168,618
10		Jun	$37,706	$45,037	$46,967	$39,288	$168,998
11	Grand Total		$227,695	$239,753	$257,150	$236,223	$960,821

The report should look like Figure 856.

Figure 856

18. To change the style, select a cell inside the PivotTable, and then go to the PivotTable Tools Design tab, PivotTable Styles group, and click the More drop-down arrow.

19. Select the second style: Pivot Style Light 1 (read screen tips).

Sum of Sales	Region ▾				
Date ▾	East	MidWest	South	West	Grand Total
Jan	$38,438	$47,995	$49,374	$36,487	$172,294
Feb	$37,044	$39,134	$31,851	$34,005	$142,034
Mar	$35,064	$38,162	$41,283	$37,155	$151,664
Apr	$43,693	$29,520	$40,505	$43,495	$157,213
May	$35,750	$39,905	$47,170	$45,793	$168,618
Jun	$37,706	$45,037	$46,967	$39,288	$168,998
Grand Total	$227,695	$239,753	$257,150	$236,223	$960,821

Figure 857

20. To remove the Year field, uncheck the Year field in the PivotTable Field List.

21. Add some fill color to the field names in cells B3 and A4 using the Fill Color button in the Font group on the Home tab.

22. Add some fill color to cell A3. (This cell contains a label that states what function is being used in the Values area.)

In Figure 857, you can see that the Grouping feature in a PivotTable can group dates by month. However, it is also possible to group by quarters and weeks.

In Figure 858, you can see how it might be done by weeks. For grouping by weeks, the important thing to remember is to set the Starting At date box to a Monday and the Number of Days box set at 7.

Figure 858

Next we want to look at what happens to a PivotTable if there are blanks in the fields of the original data set or if there are nondates in a Date field.

Blanks in Data Sets

Blanks in data sets can cause problems. As mentioned at the beginning of this chapter, properly set up data sets should not have blanks. In Figure 859, you can see that cell G6 in the Sales column for the data set contains a blank. If you did not notice this and you created a PivotTable using the Sales field in the Values area, the default function would be Count rather than Sum (see Figure 860). If you want to change the PivotTable calculation to Sum, you just right-click the Values area in the PivotTable, point to Values Field Settings, and then change the function from Count to Sum. However, sometimes blanks are not desirable, and so when you see the PivotTable calculation default to the function Count, that is your signal to go back and check the data set for blanks or other non-numeric data in the Sales field. In essence, the PivotTable is programmed to default to Count when there is a data mismatch; namely, there was numeric data and empty cells in a single field. Another situation where a data mismatch can cause problems with a PivotTable is with Date fields. We take a look at this next.

To follow along, open the file excelisfun-Start.xlsm and navigate to the PT-Data(3) sheet.

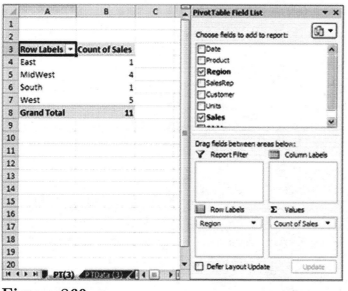

Figure 859

Figure 860

Words in Date Field

If you have a blank or a word/text in a Date field, two common problems can occur:

- Dates will not be sorted in chronological order in the PivotTable.
- You cannot group the dates.

To follow along, open the file excelisfun-Start.xlsm and navigate to the PT-Data(4) sheet.

In Figure 861, you can see a data set that contains a Date field that contains no blanks. The Date field looks like it should work perfectly in the PivotTable. But in Figure 863, you can see a PivotTable made with the Date field in the Row Labels area. If you look closely, you can see that the record with the date 6/10/11 is not sorted correctly and is located at the top of the row labels. When you see dates not sorted properly in a PivotTable, it usually means that there is a problem with the data. If you did not see that the dates were not sorted properly, and you went ahead and tried to group the Date field, you would get an error dialog box as shown in Figure 864. Notice that there are no empty cells in the Date field. So although a blank would cause the same error dialog box as shown in Figure 864, that is not the cause of the problem in this case. It is more than likely cause by a data mismatch. From the "Date Number Formatting" section in Chapter 3, you know that dates are numbers, and from the "Data Alignment" section the same chapter, you know that numbers by default are aligned to the right. A quick way to track down a problem in a field with dates is to expand the column width, as shown in Figure 862. The dates that are aligned left are dates stored as text and must be replaced with dates that are serial numbers. (Date serial numbers are discussed in full detail in the "Date Number Formatting" section of Chapter 3.)

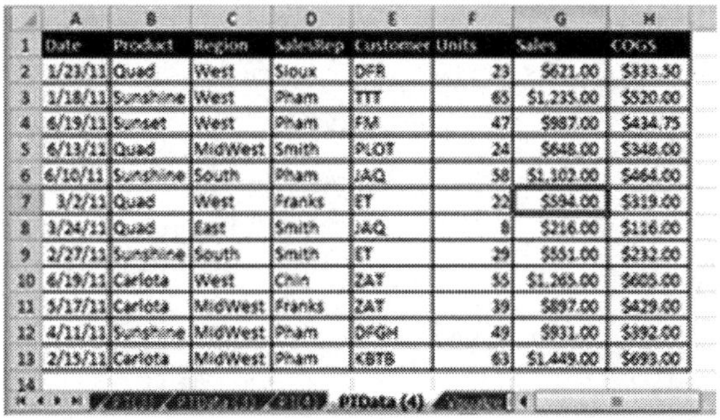

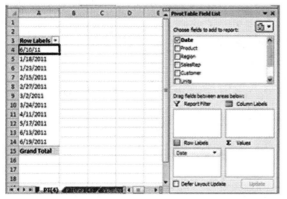

Figure 861

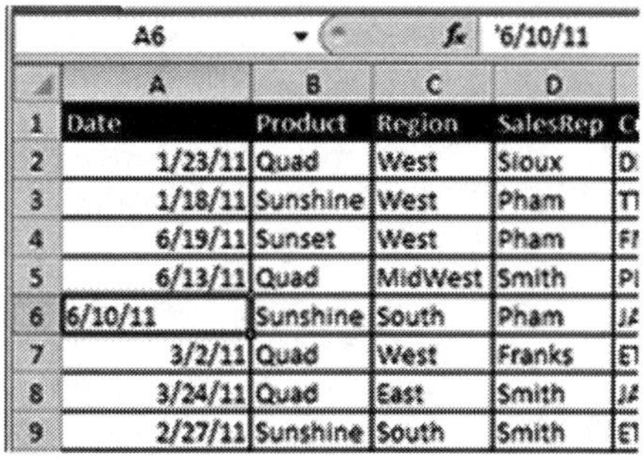

Figure 862

Figure 863

Figure 864

Next we want to take a look at how to use the Report Filter area in the PivotTable Field List.

Amazing Report Filter Area

What if your boss asks you to create and print out the following five reports that show sales for each of the products that the company sells, as shown in Figure 865? Would you have to create each report individually? No, you wouldn't, not if you know how to use the Report Filter in a PivotTable. In essence, all a Report Filter does is to filter the whole report to show only sales for a single product. When the filter is changed, the whole report updates and shows the sales for the selected product.

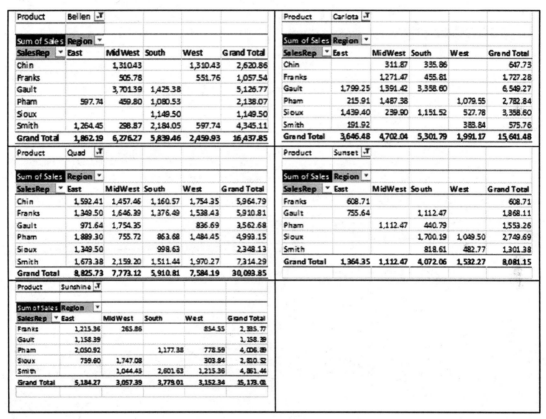

Figure 865

To follow along, open the file named excelisfun-Start.xlsm and navigate to the PT(5) sheet.

	A	B	C	D	E	F
1						
2						
3	Sum of Sales	Region ▼				
4	SalesRep ▼	East	MidWest	South	West	Grand Total
5	Chin	1,592.41	3,079.76	1,496.43	3,064.78	9,233.38
6	Franks	3,173.57	3,689.50	1,832.30	2,944.74	11,640.11
7	Gault	4,684.92	6,847.16	5,896.45	836.69	18,265.22
8	Pham	4,753.87	3,815.37	3,562.38	3,342.59	15,474.21
9	Sioux	3,548.50	1,986.98	4,999.84	1,881.12	12,416.44
10	Smith	3,129.75	3,502.52	7,115.73	4,649.98	18,397.98
11	Grand Total	20,883.02	22,921.29	24,903.13	16,719.90	85,427.34
12						
13						
14						

Figure 866

1. Click the PT(5) sheet, and then click in cell A3.

Notice that a PivotTable has already been created from the data on the PTData(5) sheet.

Notice that the Region field has been dropped into the Columns Labels area, the SalesRep field has been dropped into the Rows Labels area, and the Sales field has been dropped into the Values Labels area.

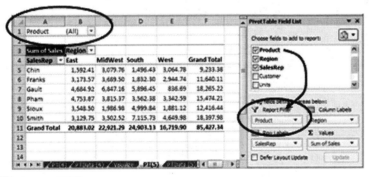

Figure 867

2. Drag the Product field from the PivotTable Field List to the Report Filter area.

Notice that the Report Filter appears in cells A1 and B1 and by default shows "All" of the sales.

3. In cell B1, click the drop-down arrow.
4. On the submenu, click Bellen.
5. Click OK.

Figure 868

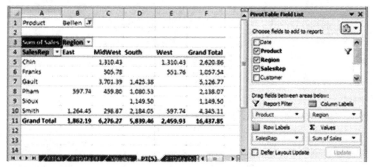

Figure 869

After you select the product Bellen in the Report filter, the report is filtered to show only sales for the Bellen product by SalesRep and Region.

Notice that the PivotTable is adding with the three criteria: Product, Region, and SalesRep.

In Figure 869, you can see our report for the product Bellen, but before we press Print and filter the report for the next product, it is best to do some page setup first.

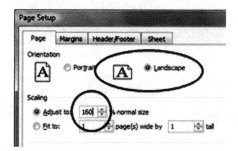

6. Open Page Setup dialog box using Alt, P, S, P.
7. On the Page tab, click the dialog button for Landscape and change the Scaling Adjust To to 160 in the % Normal Size text box.
8. On the Margins tab, check Center on Page Horizontal.
9. Click OK in the Page Setup dialog box.

Figure 870

After you have done page setup, you can print the first report using Ctrl + P. After the first report is printed, you can use the Report Filter drop-down arrow in cell B1 to filter the report to show the next product and then use Ctrl + P to print. Within a few clicks, you will have printed all five reports.

Next we want to take a look at how to create these five reports, each on a separate sheet with just a few clicks!

Creating Five Reports with One Click Using the Show Report Filter Pages Feature

Now, what if your boss wants the five reports each on a separate sheet? Would you have to make five separate PivotTables, creating each one by hand? The answer is no! We can create the PivotTable on one sheet and then use the Show Report Filter Pages feature to create five PivotTable reports, each on a separate sheet. And the amazing thing is all the formatting and page setup that you created on the first PivotTable will carry over to the five new PivotTable reports. Let's take a look at how to do this.

1. Create your PivotTable with at least one field dropped into the Report Filter area. (You can use the one on the PT(5) sheet.)

2. Make sure that the field dropped into the Report Filter area shows All.

	A	B	C	D	E	F
1	Product	(All)				
2						
3	Sum of Sales	Region				
4	SalesRep	East	MidWest	South	West	Grand Total
5	Chin	1,592.41	3,079.76	1,496.43	3,064.78	9,233.38
6	Franks	3,173.57	3,689.50	1,832.30	2,944.74	11,640.11
7	Gault	4,684.92	6,847.16	5,896.45	836.69	18,265.22
8	Pham	4,753.87	3,815.37	3,562.38	3,342.59	15,474.21
9	Sioux	3,548.50	1,986.98	4,999.84	1,881.12	12,416.44
10	Smith	3,129.75	3,502.52	7,115.73	4,649.98	18,397.98
11	Grand Total	20,883.02	22,921.29	24,903.13	16,719.90	85,427.34

Figure 871

3. With a cell inside the PivotTable selected, go to the PivotTable Tools Options tab, and on the far left in the PivotTable group, click the Options drop-down arrow and from the submenu click Show Report Filter Pages.

Figure 872

4. When the Show Report Filter Pages dialog box appears, select the field Product and then click OK.

Immediately, five new sheets will appear to the left of the sheet with the PivotTable (Figure 874).

Figure 873

Figure 874

Each new sheet will be named the actual product name, and each will have a new PivotTable with the formatting and page setup from the original PivotTable.

Amazing!

Next we want to take a look at visualization tool called a Slicer.

Slicer Feature in Excel 2010

The Slicer in an amazing new feature in Excel 2010 that creates a great-looking user interface for the Report Filter feature. A Slicer is just a fancy filter that is easier to use than the Filter drop-down arrows. The Slicer can be used for any field in the field list. In our example, we will add a Slicer (filter) for the PivotTable Report Filter. In Figure 875, you can see that the Report Filter is small and not very obvious. If we add a Slicer, it will be easier for the user to filter the report.

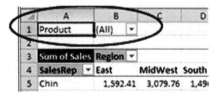

Figure 875

Figure 876 shows that adding a Slicer can be accomplished by going to the PivotTable Tools Options tab, Sort & Filter group, clicking the Insert Filter drop-down arrow, and then clicking Insert Slicer. Figure 877 shows that we have checked the Product check box to insert a Slicer for the Product field.

Figure 876

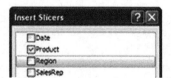

Figure 877

Figure 878 shows that if you click a single item in the Slicer Field List, the report will be filtered for that item only. Figure 879 shows that if you hold the Ctrl key while you click Slicer field names you can filter by multiple items. The Clear Filter and Show All Records button is in the upper-right corner of the Slicer Field List.

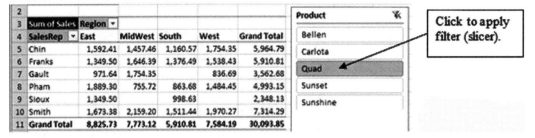

Figure 878

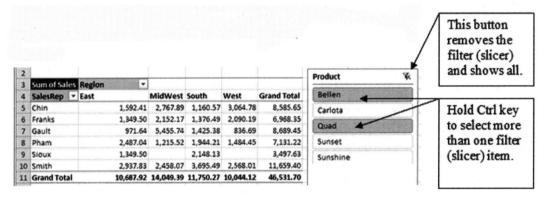

Figure 879

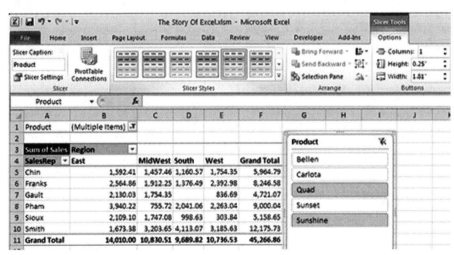

Figure 880

Figure 880 shows that the Slicer can be easily formatted by
- Clicking Slicer
- Going to the Slicer Tools Options tab and selecting a format

Figure 881 shows that you can add slicers for each field, format each slicer, and even size them by clicking edge and dragging to the desired size.

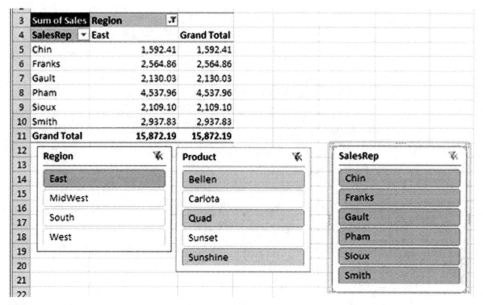

3	Sum of Sales	Region	.T	
4	SalesRep ▾	East		Grand Total
5	Chin		1,592.41	1,592.41
6	Franks		2,564.86	2,564.86
7	Gault		2,130.03	2,130.03
8	Pham		4,537.96	4,537.96
9	Sioux		2,109.10	2,109.10
10	Smith		2,937.83	2,937.83
11	Grand Total		15,872.19	15,872.19

Figure 881

Next we want to take a look at how to use a PivotTable to create a Frequency Distribution Report, a Percentage of Total Report, a Running Total Report, and a report that shows three calculations for the same field.

Frequency Distribution Reports

Frequency distribution. What's that? **Frequency distribution** is just a fancy way of saying "count." Frequency distributions are common reports that simply count items in a given set of categories. For example, in Figure 883, the categories are product names, and the frequency is simply a count of the number of products from the Product field in Figure 882. We can see that there are 24 Bellen products sold, 21 Carlota products sold, and so on. The key thing to remember is that we have categories and we are counting the number of items in each category. In Figure 884, you can see a slightly different set of categories. The categories are grouped numbers, and the frequency is simply a count of the number of sales from the Sales field in Figure 882 that fall into each category. For example, 12 sales were made in the category $0 >= Sales < $250, 22 sales were made in the category $250 >= Sales < $500, and so on. It is important to note that we are counting between a lower amount and an upper amount, where the lower amount is included in the interval, and the upper amount is *not* included in the interval (so that we do not double count). Back in the "COUNTIFS Function" section of Chapter 5, you saw this same kind of counting numbers that were between a lower and upper amount. (You'll also see this again in the "Advanced Filter Feature" section of this chapter and the Histograms section of Chapter 7.) When we have a lower and upper amount that defines the category we are using "between" criteria (between lower and upper).

Let's take a look at the steps necessary to create these PivotTables.

	A	B	C	D	E	F	G	H
1	Date	Product	Region	SalesRep	Customer	Units	Sales	COGS
2	1/12/11	Quad	East	Gault	TTT	36	$971.64	$522.00
3	1/11/11	Quad	East	Smith	HII	62	$1,673.38	$899.00
4	1/6/11	Quad	East	Franks	FM	50	$1,349.50	$725.00
5	1/3/11	Carlota	South	Gault	MBG	59	$1,415.41	$649.00
6	1/16/11	Carlota	MidWest	Franks	JAQ	53	$1,271.47	$583.00
7	1/24/11	Sunshine	West	Pham	ITTW	41	$778.59	$328.00
8	1/10/11	Bellen	MidWest	Smith	HHH	13	$298.87	$130.00
9	1/24/11	Quad	South	Smith	TTT	56	$1,511.44	$812.00
10	1/13/11	Sunshine	East	Gault	WT	50	$949.50	$400.00
11	1/25/11	Sunshine	MidWest	Smith	PSA	26	$493.74	$208.00
12	1/10/11	Bellen	East	Pham	HII	26	$597.74	$260.00
13	1/29/11	Sunset	South	Gault	TRU	53	$1,112.47	$490.25
14	1/17/11	Quad	East	Pham	DFR	43	$1,160.57	$623.50

Figure 882

Product ▼	Frequency
Bellen	24
Carlota	21
Quad	29
Sunset	12
Sunshine	19
Grand Total	**105**

Figure 883

Sales ▼	Frequency
0-250	12
250-500	22
500-750	16
750-1000	14
1000-1250	21
1250-1500	15
1500-1750	5
Grand Total	**105**

Figure 884

To follow along, open the file excelisfun-Start.xlsm and navigate to the PT-Data (6) Sheet.

Creating Product Frequency Tables

Product ▼	Frequency
Bellen	24
Carlota	21
Quad	29
Sunset	12
Sunshine	19
Grand Total	**105**

Figure 885

1. On thePTData(6) sheet, click in one cell inside the data set.
2. To create a PivotTable, use Alt, N, V, T.
3. Press Enter to place the PivotTable on a new sheet.
4. Drag the Product field to the Row Labels area.
5. Drag the Product field to the Values area.
6. Notice that we dragged the Products field to both the Row Labels area and the Values area.
7. Click in cell B3 and type **Frequency**.
8. Format the PivotTable as you see fit.
9. Double-click the sheet and type **PT(6)**, and then press Enter.

Creating Sales Frequency Tables

Sales ▼	Frequency
0-250	12
250-500	22
500-750	16
750-1000	14
1000-1250	21
1250-1500	15
1500-1750	5
Grand Total	**105**

Figure 886

1. On thePTData(6) sheet, click in one cell inside the data set.
2. To create a PivotTable, use Alt, N, V, T.
3. Press Enter to place the PivotTable on a new sheet.
4. Drag the Sales field to the Row Labels area.
5. Right-click the Sales field in Row Labels area and click Grouping.
6. In the Grouping dialog box, type **0** in the Starting At box, type **1750** in the Ending At box, and type **250** in By box.
7. Click OK in the Grouping dialog box.
8. Drag the Sales field to the Values area.

Notice that we dragged the Sales field to both the Row Labels area and the Values area.

9. Click in cell B3 and type **Frequency**.
10. Format the PivotTable as you see fit.
11. Double-click the sheet and type **PT(7)**, and then press Enter.

Next we want to take a look at how to create reports that show a percentage of total.

Percentage of Total to Show Employee Performance

In Figure 887, you can see our transactional data. In Figure 888, you can see that our report shows the sales number for each employee and the percentage of total sales that each employee made. The steps for creating this PivotTable are listed below.

To follow along, open the file excelisfun-Start.xlsm and navigate to the PT-Data(7) sheet.

	A	B	C	D	E	F	G	H	I
1	Date	Product	Region	SalesRep	Customer	Units	Sales	COGS	
2	1/12/11	Quad	East	Gault	TTT	36	$971.64	$522.00	
3	1/11/11	Quad	East	Smith	HII	62	$1,673.38	$899.00	
4	1/6/11	Quad	East	Franks	FM	50	$1,349.50	$725.00	
5	1/3/11	Carlota	South	Gault	MBG	59	$1,415.41	$649.00	
6	1/16/11	Carlota	MidWest	Franks	JAQ	53	$1,271.47	$583.00	

Figure 887

Creating Percentage of Total Reports

1. On the PTData(7) sheet, click in one cell inside the data set.
2. To create a PivotTable, use Alt, N, V, T; then press Enter to place the PivotTable on a new sheet.
3. Drag the SalesRep field to the Row Labels area.
4. Drag the Sales field to the Values area.
5. Right-click the Sales field in the PivotTable and click Value Field Settings. In the Value Field Settings dialog box, click the Number Formatting button. Then select Currency and click OK on the Format Cells dialog box, and then click OK on the Value Field Settings dialog box.
6. Now, for a second time, drag the Sales field to the Values area. You should see the Sales field listed two times, one on top of each other. The second Sales field should say Sum of Sales2.

    Notice that we dragged the Sales field to the Values area twice!
7. Right-click the Sum of Sales2 field in the PivotTable and click Value Field Settings. In the Value Field Settings dialog box, click the Show Values As tab.

SalesRep ▼	Sum of Sales	Performance
Chin	$9,233.38	10.81%
Franks	$11,640.11	13.63%
Gault	$18,265.22	21.38%
Pham	$15,474.21	18.11%
Sioux	$12,416.44	14.53%
Smith	$18,397.98	21.54%
Grand Total	$85,427.34	100.00%

Figure 888

8. From the Show Values As box drop-down arrow, select the % of Column Total, and then click OK.
9. Click in cell C3 and type **Performance**.
10. Format the PivotTable as you see fit.
11. Double-click the sheet and type **PT(8)**, and then press Enter.

Next we want to take a look at how to create reports that show a running total.

Running Totals

In Figure 889, you can see a small data set that has transactional sales data for a week. Our goal is to show the daily totals in the first column and the running total or cumulative total in the second column. Figure 890 shows the Daily Running Total Report. The steps for creating this PivotTable are listed below.

To follow along, open the file excelisfun-Start.xlsm and navigate to the PT-Data(8) sheet.

	A	B	C	D	E	F	G	H	I
1	Date	Product	Region	SalesRep	Customer	Units	Sales	COGS	
2	1/1/11	Bellen	West	Franks	PSA	24	$551.76	$240.00	
3	1/1/11	Carlota	East	Smith	MBG	8	$191.92	$88.00	
4	1/2/11	Sunshine	West	Sioux	TTT	16	$303.84	$128.00	
5	1/2/11	Sunset	South	Sioux	KPSA	58	$1,217.42	$536.50	
6	1/2/11	Bellen	South	Smith	KBTB	17	$390.83	$170.00	
7	1/3/11	Quad	West	Chin	TTT	23	$592.78	$319.00	

Figure 889

Date ▼	Sum of Sales	Running Total
1/1/11	743.68	743.68
1/2/11	2,505.87	3,249.55
1/3/11	3,250.73	6,500.28
1/4/11	1,494.30	7,994.58
1/5/11	5,692.56	13,687.14
1/6/11	3,249.56	16,936.70
Grand Total	16,936.70	

Figure 890

Creating Running Total Reports

1. On the PTData(8) sheet, click in one cell inside the data set.
2. To create a PivotTable, use Alt, N, V, T; then press Enter to place the PivotTable on a new sheet.
3. Drag the Date field to the Row Labels area.
4. Drag the Sales field to the Values area.
5. Right-click the Sales field in the PivotTable and click Value Field Settings. In the Value Field Settings dialog box, click the Number Formatting button. Then select Number (check Use 1000 Separator (,)) and click OK in the Format Cells dialog box, and then click OK in the Value Field Settings dialog box.
6. Now, for a second time, drag the Sales field to the Values area. You should see the Sales field listed two times, one on top of each other. The second Sales field should say Sum of Sales2.

Notice that we dragged the Sales field to the Values area twice!

7. Right-click the Sum of Sales2 field in the PivotTable and click Value Field Settings. In the Value Field Settings dialog box, click the Show Values As tab.
8. From the Show Values As box drop-down arrow, select Running Total In, and then from the Base Field List select the Date field and click OK.
9. Click in cell C3 and type **Running Total** (or you could have named it in the dialog box in step 7 and 8).
10. Format the PivotTable as you see fit.
11. Double-click the sheet and type **PT(9)**, and then press Enter.

Next we want to take a look at how to a report that shows three calculations for the same field.

Showing Three Calculations for the Same Field: AVERAGE, MAX, MIN

If you have a huge data set and you need to calculate the average, maximum, and minimum values by sales representative, a fast way to accomplish this is with a PivotTable. Figure 891 shows us our data set, and Figure 892 shows us the finished report. For the average, we are calculating with one criterion. This means, we are not calculating an average for all the data points, but instead we are calculating six different averages, one for each sales rep. And the same is true for the max and min calculations. With a few clicks, we can make 6 x 3 = 18 calculations. The formula alternative to a PivotTable would be much more complicated to accomplish. This is an example of why some people say that "PivotTables are the most powerful feature in Excel." The steps for creating this PivotTable are listed below.

To follow along, open the file excelisfun-Start.xlsm and navigate to the PT-Data(9) sheet.

	A	B	C	D
1	Date	SalesRep	Sales	
2	1/12/11	Gault	$971.64	
3	1/11/11	Smith	$1,673.38	
4	1/6/11	Franks	$1,349.50	
5	1/3/11	Gault	$1.415.41	

PT(10) PTData (9)

Figure 891

SalesRep	Average of Sales	Max of Sales	Min of Sales
Chin	$1,025.93	$1,592.41	$311.87
Franks	$895.39	$1,646.39	$242.91
Gault	$794.14	$1,471.36	$146.93
Pham	$736.87	$1,487.38	$215.91
Sioux	$827.76	$1,439.40	$239.90
Smith	$766.58	$1,673.38	$137.94
Grand Total	$813.59	$1,673.38	$137.94

Figure 892

Creating AVERAGE, MAX, MIN Reports

1. On the PTData(9) sheet, click in one cell inside the data set.
2. To create a PivotTable, use Alt, N, V, T; then press Enter to place the PivotTable on a new sheet.
3. Drag the SalesRep field to the Row Labels area.
4. Drag the Sales field to the Values area three times. You should see the field names Sum of Sales, Sum of Sales2, and Sum of Sales3.
5. Right-click the Sum of Sales field in the PivotTable and click Value Field Settings. In the Summarize Value Field By tab, select the Average calculation. Using the Number Formatting button, change the number formatting to Currency and then click OK in the Format Cells dialog box. Click OK in the Value Field Settings dialog box.
6. Right-click the Sum of Sales2 field in the PivotTable and click Value Field Settings. In the Summarize Value Field By tab, select the Max calculation. Using the Number Formatting button, change the number formatting to Currency, and then click OK in the Format Cells dialog box. Click OK in the Value Field Settings dialog box.
7. Right-click the Sum of Sales3 field in the PivotTable and click Value Field Settings. In the Summarize Value Field By tab, select the Min calculation. Using the Number Formatting button, change the number formatting to Currency, and then click OK in the Format Cells dialog box. Click OK in the Value Field Settings dialog box.
8. Format the PivotTable as you see fit.
9. Double-click the sheet and type **PT(10)**, and then press Enter.

When Source Data Changes, PivotTables Update Only *After* You Refresh

One downside of PivotTables as compared to formulas is that PivotTables do not automatically update when the source data changes. However, PivotTables are easily "updatable" by right-clicking anywhere in the PivotTable and clicking the Refresh item in the submenu. Let's look at an example.

In Figure 893, you can see the data set and you can see that the sale by Gault on 1/12/11 in cell C2 is equal to $971.64. Figure 894 you can see a PivotTable that we have created. In cell B6, you can see that the total sales for Gault are $18,265.22. Now let's see what happens when we change the source data. In Figure 895, you can see that we have deleted the number in cell C2. If we had used formulas, anything looking at that cell would have automatically updated. But now look at Figure 896, where you can see the PivotTable has not updated. It still has the same total sales for Gault of $18,265.22. But really, it is not a problem, because in Figure 897, you can see that by right-clicking and clicking the Refresh item in the submenu, the PivotTable will update. Figure 898 shows the updated PivotTable.

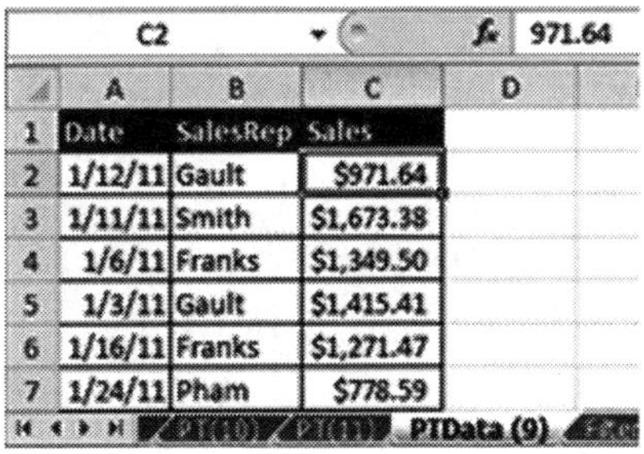

Figure 893

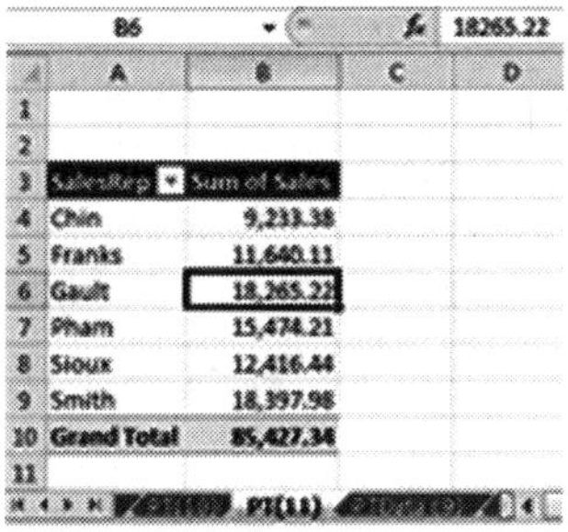

Figure 894

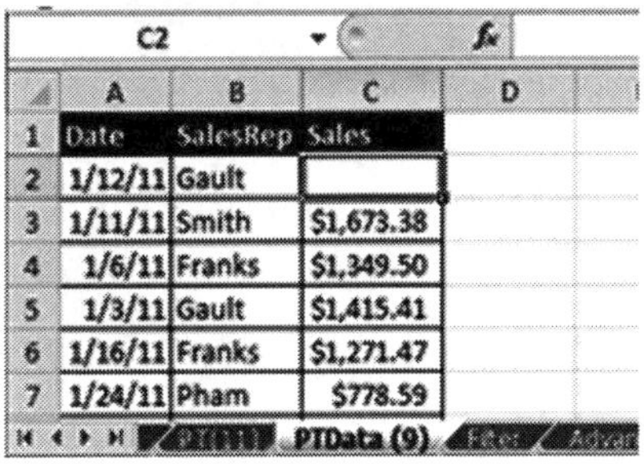

Figure 895

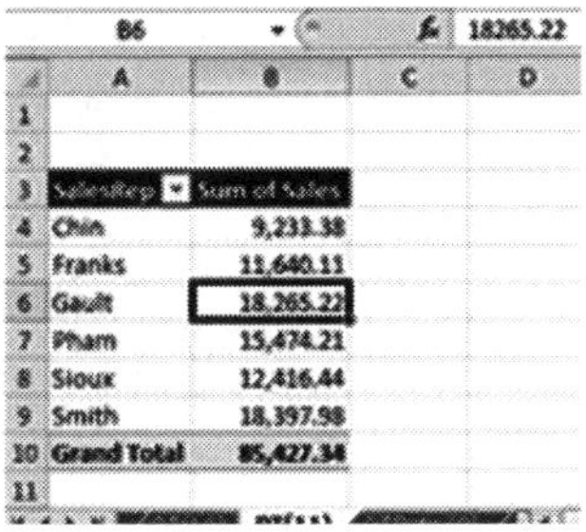

Figure 896

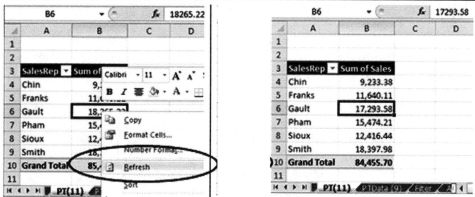

Figure 897   **Figure 898**

The rule of thumb for when to use PivotTables and when to use formulas for summary reports is this: If the data is continually changing, it may be better to use a formula solution rather than a PivotTable solution. If you look back to Chapter 5, you will see some formulas that can be used to create summary reports. In addition, PivotTables are more limited than formulas in what they can do. For example, there are only 11 functions available in a PivotTable, whereas there are about 400 functions available for formulas.

Our next Excel Efficiency-Robust Rule is as follows:

> *Rule 38: PivotTables are amazing for creating summary reports. Key points are as follows: 1) Row and column labels determine the shape of the PivotTable, values contain the fields that will be calculated upon, and the Report Filter can filter the whole PivotTable. 2) Creating and "pivoting" the report is done by clicking and dragging fields to the location you want. 3) Value field settings allow you to change the formatting, function, or calculation.*

Next we want to look at the Filter feature in Excel.

Filter Feature

As with any of Excel's data analysis features, to use the Filter feature, the data set must be in a table format structure (field names at the top of each column [labels in row 1], records in rows, and no blanks inside the data set or in the field names).

The Filter feature is great when you want to extract a small set of records from a large data set. For example, in Figure 899, you can see a large transactional data set that contains a field named Product that contains the names of the products sold for each transaction.

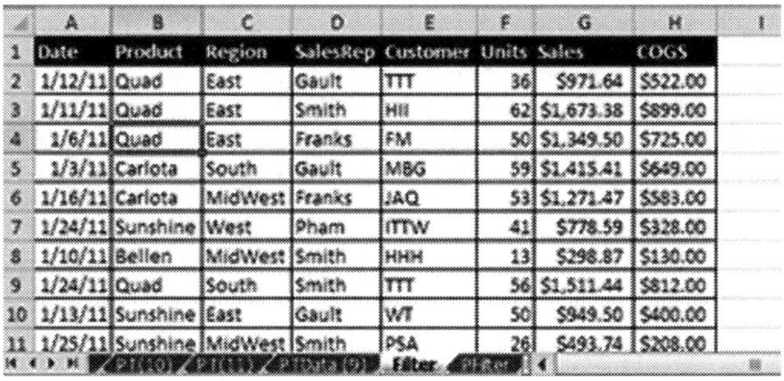

Figure 899

If our goal is to extract all the transactions where a Quad product was sold, the Filter feature can accomplish this with just a few clicks. Figure 900 shows the filtered results where the criterion for filtering is Quad.

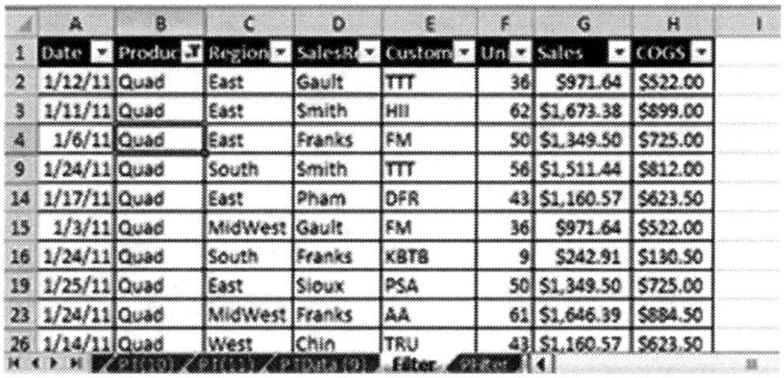

Figure 900

Now some of you are saying, "Hey, can't we just do this sort of thing with the Sort feature?" Well, you could. But here's the difference:

- When you sort on a field, the records are ordered either numerically or alphabetically and all the records remain showing.
- When you filter on a field, all records that match the criterion/criteria remain showing and all other records are *hidden*.

What is fabulous about the fact that the Filter feature "hides" records that do not match the criterion/criteria is that this makes it easy to copy and paste to another location. Although there are other methods of extracting records based on criteria (advanced array formulas and the Advanced Filter feature), the Filter feature is by far the easiest and for this reason many everyday Excel users prefer to use the Filter feature for extracting records.

Now let's see how to turn on the Filter feature and then use it to extract records.

To follow along, open the file named excelisfun-Start.xlsm and navigate to the Filter sheet.

Turning on the Filter Feature

Here are three ways to turn on the Filter feature:
- On the Data tab, Sort & Filter group, click the Filter button.
- Use keyboard shortcuts:
    - Ctrl + Shift + L (Excel 2007/2010 keyboard shortcut)
    - Alt, D, F, F (Excel 2003 keyboard shortcut)
    - Alt, A, T (Excel 2007/2010 keyboard shortcut)
- Convert data in a table format structure to an Excel table using the following:
    - Ctrl + T (Excel 2007/2010 keyboard shortcut)
    - Ctrl + L (Excel 2003 keyboard shortcut)

The advantage of the ribbon method is that it is easy to remember to go to the Data tab and look for the Filter button. The advantage of the keyboard shortcuts is that they are fast. From the three keyboard shortcuts, you should select the keyboard shortcut that easiest to remember. I always found it easy to remember Alt, D, F, F because I could remember D for *data* and F for *filter*. The advantage of converting the data set to an Excel table is that the ranges become dynamic.

The ribbon method and the keyboard methods are toggles. **Toggle** means that the method works to turn the filter on or turn the filter off.

Now let's take a look at filtering with one criterion.

Filtering with One Criterion

Our goal is to filter a data set to only show records that contain the Quad product in the Product field.

	A	B	C	D	E	F	G	H	I
1	Date	Produc	Region	SalesR	Custom	Uni	Sales	COGS	
2	1/12/11	Quad	East	Gault	TTT	36	$971.64	$522.00	
3	1/11/11	Quad	East	Smith	HII	62	$1,673.38	$899.00	
4	1/6/11	Quad	East	Franks	FM	50	$1,349.50	$725.00	
5	1/3/11	Carlota	South	Gault	MBG	59	$1,415.41	$649.00	
6	1/16/11	Carlota	MidWest	Franks	JAQ	53	$1,271.47	$583.00	
7	1/24/11	Sunshine	West	Pham	TTW	41	$778.59	$328.00	

Figure 901

1. On the Filter sheet, click in cell B2.
2. Turn on the Filter feature using Alt, D, F, F.

You should see drop-down arrows at the top of each field.

3. Click the drop-down arrow in the Product field.
4. Uncheck the Select All check box.
5. Check the Quad check box.
6. Click OK.

Figure 902

	A	B	C	D	E	
1	Date ▼	Produc ▼	Region ▼	SalesR ▼	Custom ▼	
2	1/12/11	Quad	East	Gault	TTT	
3	1/11/11	Quad	East	Smith	HII	
4	1/6/11	Quad	East	Franks	FM	
9	1/24/11	Quad	South	Smith	TTT	
14	1/17/11	Quad	East	Pham	DFR	

Figure 903

Only the records for Quad are showing.

In Figure 903, three things tell us that the data set is filtered:
- The row headers are colored blue.
- Some of the row headers are not showing because they are hidden. For example, rows 5-8 and 10-13 are hidden.
- The drop-down arrow for the Product field has changed from a drop-down arrow icon to a filter icon.

That is filtering with one criterion. But what if you are required to show records based on two criteria?

Filtering with "And" Criteria

The Filter feature enables you to apply more than one filter at a time. For example, if you are required to show only the records that contain the word Quad in the Product field *and* the word South in the Region field, you just apply both filters, and the data set will reflect the fact that each record showing will meet both criteria.

	A	B	C	D	E	F	G	H
1	Date ▼	Produc ▼	Region ▼	SalesR ▼	Custom ▼	Un ▼	Sales ▼	COGS ▼
9	1/24/11	Quad	South	Smith	TTT	56	$1,511.44	$812.00
16	1/24/11	Quad	South	Franks	KBTB	9	$242.91	$130.50
47	1/17/11	Quad	South	Franks	SFWK	42	$1,133.58	$609.00
50	1/26/11	Quad	South	Sioux	ITW	20	$539.80	$290.00
82	1/26/11	Quad	South	Sioux	QT	17	$458.83	$246.50
89	1/10/11	Quad	South	Chin	PLOT	43	$1,160.57	$623.50
100	1/3/11	Quad	South	Pham	WSD	32	$863.68	$464.00
107								

Figure 904

1. Make sure that the Product field is filtered to show only the Quad product.
2. Click the drop-down arrow in the Region field.
3. Uncheck the Select All check box.
4. Check the South check box.
5. Click OK.

In Figure 904 you can see that each transactional record that is showing has the word Quad in the Product field *and* the word South in the Region field. Each record shows both criteria.

It is easy to apply more than two criteria. By just adding new filters to new fields, the data set can be filtered with more than two criteria.

Next we want to look at *or* criteria.

Filtering with "Or" Criteria

If our goal is to show records that have the word Quad *or* Sunshine in the Product field *and* the word South in the Region field (as shown in Figure 905), we can accomplish this easily with the Filter feature.

	A	B	C	D	E	F	G	H	I
1	Date	Produc	Region	SalesR	Custom	Un	Sales	COGS	
9	1/24/11	Quad	South	Smith	TTT	56	$1,511.44	$812.00	
16	1/24/11	Quad	South	Franks	KBTB	9	$242.91	$130.50	
22	1/6/11	Sunshine	South	Smith	TRU	53	$1,006.47	$424.00	
41	1/13/11	Sunshine	South	Pham	WFMI	62	$1,177.38	$496.00	
47	1/17/11	Quad	South	Franks	SFWK	42	$1,133.58	$609.00	
50	1/26/11	Quad	South	Sioux	ITW	20	$539.80	$290.00	
72	1/9/11	Sunshine	South	Smith	AA	22	$417.78	$176.00	
82	1/26/11	Quad	South	Sioux	QT	17	$458.83	$246.50	
89	1/10/11	Quad	South	Chin	PLOT	43	$1,160.57	$623.50	
93	1/18/11	Sunshine	South	Smith	ET	62	$1,177.38	$496.00	
100	1/3/11	Quad	South	Pham	WSD	32	$863.68	$464.00	
107									

Figure 905

Figure 906

1. Make sure that the Region field is filtered to show only the South region.
2. Click the drop-down arrow in the Product field.
3. Uncheck the Select All check box.
4. Check the Quad and the Sunshine check boxes.
5. Click OK.

As shown in Figure 905, you can see that for any single transactional record the word Quad *or* the word Sunshine is showing *and* the word South is showing in the Region field.

Now that we have filtered our data, what about copying it to another sheet? Let's take a look at how to do that next.

Filtering to Extract Records from Data Sets

Now that we have our filtered data set, we can either analyze the data in place or we can copy and paste it to a new location. And the great thing about copying and pasting with the Filter feature is that, unlike the Subtotal feature, you can simply copy and paste. (We don't have to use Select Visible Cells Only before copying and pasting as we had to do with the Subtotal feature.)

1. Click in cell B1.
2. To select the filtered data, press Ctrl + * (asterisk on the number pad).
3. To copy, use Ctrl + C.

Notice that the dancing ants only surround the filtered records.

4. Click in cell A1 on the PFilter sheet.
5. To paste the filtered data, press Ctrl + V.

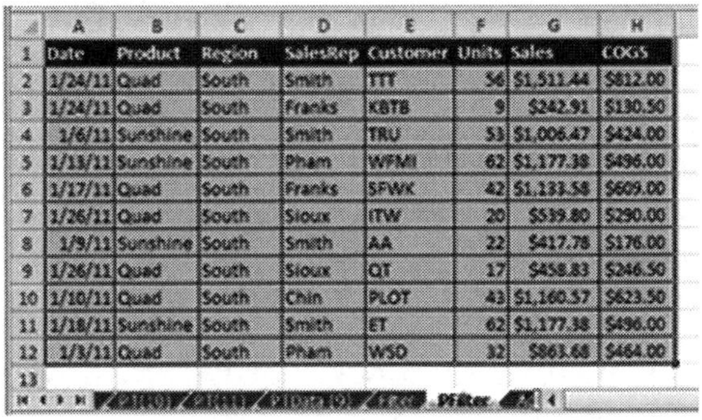

Figure 907

Next we want to take a look at how to remove the filter and see the entire data set.

Removing Applied Filters

To remove all filters, go to the Data tab, Sort & Filter group, and click the Clear button.

Next we want to take a look at how to right-click a data set to accomplish a filter.

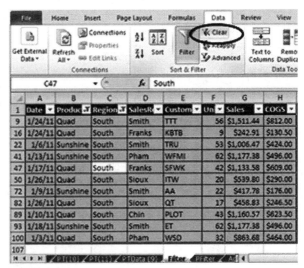

Figure 908

Right-Click Filtering

If our goal is to filter the data set to show just the East region, we can right-click a cell in the Region field that contains the word East and point to Filter on the first submenu and then click Filter by Selected Cell's Value from the second submenu (as shown in Figure 909). From the submenu shown in Figure 909, notice that we can also filter by color, font color, and icon (from Conditional Formatting; more on this later).

Figure 909

Next we want to see some amazing filters that were added in the Excel 2007 version that make filtering certain types of data and formatting much easier than in earlier versions.

Filtering on Cell Fill Color

Sometimes people add fill color to cells to mark them as important. In Figure 910, you can see a data set that contains records, and some of the elements in the Product field have the fill color red applied. In Excel 2007 and later, it is easy to filter to show only the records that contain the fill color red in the Product field. Let's take a look at how to do this.

To follow along, open the file named excelisfun-Start.xlsm and navigate to the FilterC sheet.

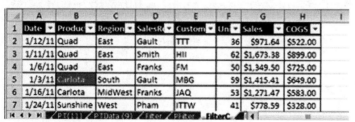

Figure 910

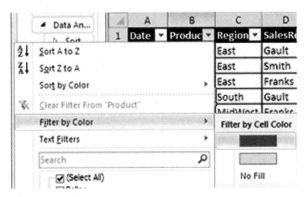

Figure 911

1. On the FilterC sheet, click the drop-down arrow in the Product field.
2. Point to Filter by Color on the submenu.
3. Click the color you want to filter by on the sub-submenu.
4. Click OK.

Figure 912 shows the results.

	A	B	C	D	E	F	G	H	I
1	Date	Produc	Region	SalesR	Custom	Un	Sales	COGS	
5	1/3/11	Carlota	South	Gault	MBG	59	$1,415.41	$649.00	
11	1/13/11	Sunshine	South	Pham	WFMI	62	$1,177.38	$496.00	
18	1/8/11	Quad	West	Smith	BBT	26	$701.74	$377.00	
21	1/28/11	Carlota	MidWest	Pham	PLOT	62	$1,487.38	$682.00	
49									

Figure 912

Next we want to look at the Below Average and Top Five filters for fields that contain values.

Filtering Below Average Values

If your goal is to show only the records where the sales figure is below average, Excel 2007 and later versions have an easy built-in filter to accomplish this. As long as the field you want to filter contains a numeric value, this special filter is available. Here is how to apply this filter.

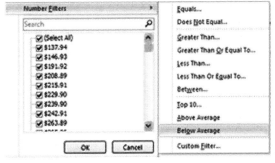

Figure 913

1. On the Filter sheet, click the drop-down arrow in the Sales field.
2. Point to Number Filters on the submenu.
3. Click the Below Average on the sub-submenu.
4. Click OK.

In Figure 914, you can see the results, and you can also see that the average value was calculated in cell K1.

	B	C	D	E	F	G	H	I	J	K
1	Produc	Region	SalesR	Custom	Un	Sales	COGS		Average	$813.59
7	Sunshine	West	Pham	ITTW	41	$778.59	$328.00			
8	Bellen	MidWest	Smith	HHH	13	$298.87	$130.00			
11	Sunshine	MidWest	Smith	PSA	26	$493.74	$208.00			
12	Bellen	East	Pham	HII	26	$597.74	$260.00			
16	Quad	South	Franks	KBTB	9	$242.91	$130.50			
18	Sunset	East	Gault	WSD	7	$146.93	$64.75			
20	Carlota	West	Smith	DFR	16	$383.84	$176.00			
21	Bellen	MidWest	Gault	WFMI	28	$643.72	$280.00			

Figure 914

Filtering Top Five Sales

In Figure 914, you can see all the records with sales values below the average. But what if we want to filter to see records at the opposite end of the spectrum; namely, the top five sales records? Let's take a look at how to do this.

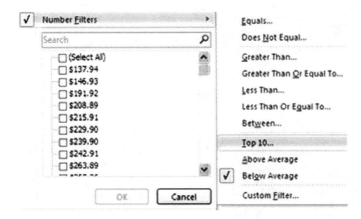

Figure 915

1. Click the drop-down arrow in the Sales field.
2. Point to Number Filters on the submenu. Notice that the Number Filters item has a check mark and the sub-submenu shows that Below Average has a check mark (which means that the Below Average filter has been previously selected).
3. Click the Top 10 on the sub-submenu.
4. Selecting the Top 10 will supplant the Below Average filter.

Figure 916

5. When the Top 10 AutoFilter dialog box appears, change the 10 to a 5.
6. Click OK.

B	C	D	E	F	G	H	I
Product	Region	SalesRe	Custom	Un	Sales	COGS	
Quad	East	Smith	HII	62	$1,673.38	$899.00	
Quad	South	Smith	TTT	56	$1,511.44	$812.00	
Quad	MidWest	Franks	AA	61	$1,646.39	$884.50	
Quad	West	Franks	PLOT	57	$1,538.43	$826.50	
Quad	East	Chin	YTR	59	$1,592.41	$855.50	

Figure 917

The top five sales records are displayed and can be analyzed or copied and pasted to a new sheet.

But the numbers are not sorted!

Figure 918

When the Filter is applied, it is easy to apply a sort on top of a filter.

7. Click the filter icon in cell G1 and then click Sort Largest to Smallest.

B	C	D	E	F	G	H	I
Product	Region	SalesRe	Custome	Uni	Sales	COGS	
Quad	East	Smith	HII	62	$1,673.38	$899.00	
Quad	MidWest	Franks	AA	61	$1,646.39	$884.50	
Quad	East	Chin	YTR	59	$1,592.41	$855.50	
Quad	West	Franks	PLOT	57	$1,538.43	$826.50	
Quad	South	Smith	TTT	56	$1,511.44	$812.00	

Figure 919

Figure 919 shows that a filter and sort can be applied simultaneously.

8. To clear all filters, use the keyboard shortcut Alt, A, C.

In addition to special filters for numbers, there are special filters for fields that contain text. Next let's see how to search for a street within a street address.

Filtering Words/Text

In Figure 920, you can see a data set that contains customer information. If our goal is search for customers who are located on 66th Blvd. *or* 151st St. in the city of Kent, we can accomplish this easily with text filters. Now let's see how this is done.

To follow along, open the file named excelisfun-Start.xlsm and navigate to the FilterT sheet.

	A	B	C	D	E	F	G
1	Customers	Address	City	Sta	Zip	E-mail	
2	, Aier	3557 1st St.	Seattle	WA	981147	JNV@yahoo.com	
3	Acero, Natisha	6281 173rd St.	Tacoma	WA	981317	HDT641@fun.edu	
4	Bruess, Natisha	7149 1st Ave.	Seattle	WA	981335	YSE222@fun.edu	
5	Chukes, Hal	7726 66th Ave.	Tacoma	WA	981118	MGF675@fun.edu	
6	Dahnke, Georgeann	316 66th Blvd.	Kent	WA	981244	RWN@fun.edu	
7	Dillaman, Darius	965 151st St.	Kent	WA	981162	MJG@yahoo.com	
8	Durtschi, Dane	7582 4th Lane	Tacoma	WA	981177	KVC@gmail.com	

Figure 920

Figure 921

1. On the FilterT sheet, click the drop-down arrow in the City field.
2. Uncheck the Select All check box.
3. Check the Kent check box.
4. Click OK.

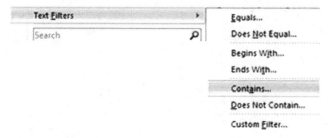

Figure 922

1. Click the drop-down arrow in the Address field.
2. Point to Text Filters on the submenu.
3. Click Contains on the sub-submenu.

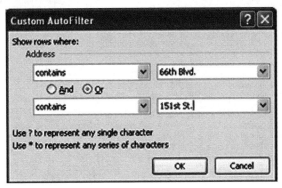

Figure 923

4. From the first drop-down, select Contains.
5. In the top-right combo box (you can type or select from drop-down), type **66th Blvd.**
6. Click the Or option button.
7. From the bottom-left drop-down, select Contains.
8. In the bottom-right combo box type **151st St.**
9. Click OK.

In Figure 923, note two things:

- Typing carefully is important. For example, make sure to get the spaces and periods in the correct place. If you do not type the correct text, you may get a filter that shows no records (because there are no matches for the mis-typed elements).
- This is an *or* criteria search. As we have discussed a number of times already in this book, *or* means it can find a match for one or the other, or both. In our case, we can never get both because none of the addresses list both 66th Blvd. and 151st St. in a single cell.

	A	B	C	D	E	F
1	Customers	Address	City	Sta	Zip	E-mail
6	Dahnke, Georgeann	316 66th Blvd. 151st St.	Kent	WA	981244	RWN@fun.edu
7	Dillaman, Darius	965 151st St.	Kent	WA	981162	MJG@yahoo.com
14	Herry, Bryon	4358 66th Blvd.	Kent	WA	981225	LGQ756@gmail.com

Figure 924

You should see three records that match our filtering criteria.

10. To clear all filters, press Alt, A, C.

Next we want to look at date filters.

Filtering Dates

The most amazing new type of filter that is available in Excel 2007 and later is the date filter. If you click a filter drop-down arrow for a field that contains a date (Date number formatting with serial number), you will see an amazing list of options for dates. Figure 925 shows some of the amazing date filters. Figure 926 shows a data set on the sheet FilterD that contains dates for the years 2009 and 2010. Figure 927 shows a Last Week Filter. And finally, Figure 928 shows the results of a Last Week Filter (because the filter was performed on the date 2/18/2010).

To try this (you will have to experiment yourself because dates will be different), open the file named excelisfun-Start.xlsm and navigate to the FilterD sheet.

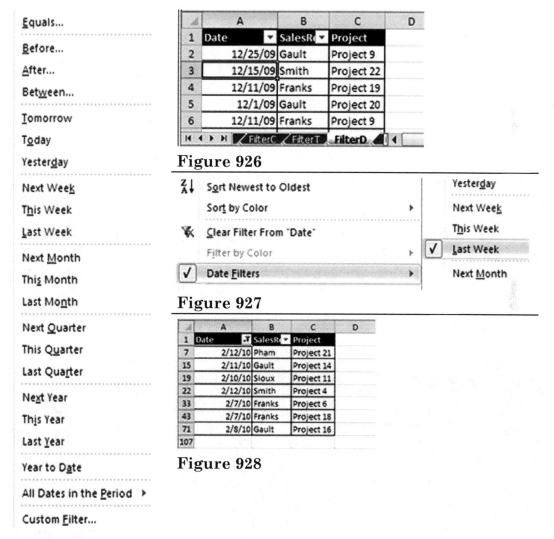

Figure 926

Figure 927

Figure 928

Figure 925

The date filters can be particularly helpful for sales data when you are in a hurry to analyze data from the last quarter or last month.

Next we want to take a look at how the Filter feature can help with making function calculations.

Filtering Records to Add or Average with Multiple Criteria

If our goal is to filter and show just the records for the SalesRep Gault and then add his sales, we can accomplish this easily by using the Excel Table feature and the Totals Row option. Let's take a look at how to accomplish this task.

To follow along, open the file excelisfun-Start.xlsm and navigate to the FilterSales sheet.

1. On the FilterSales sheet, click in cell C4.
2. Convert the data set to an Excel table using Ctrl + T.

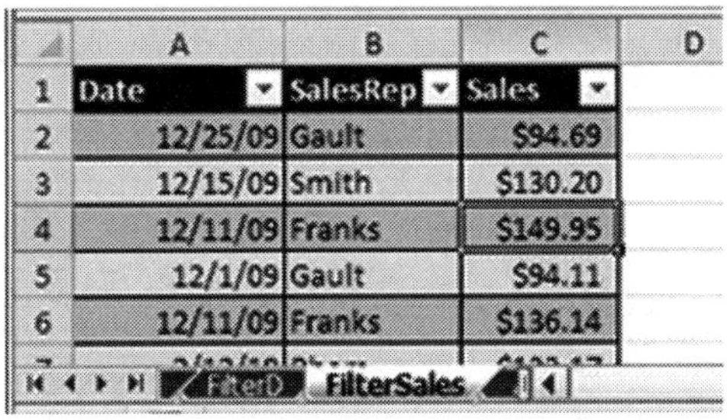

	A	B	C	D
1	Date	SalesRep	Sales	
2	12/25/09	Gault	$94.69	
3	12/15/09	Smith	$130.20	
4	12/11/09	Franks	$149.95	
5	12/1/09	Gault	$94.11	
6	12/11/09	Franks	$136.14	

Figure 929

3. With cell C4 still selected, go to the Table Tools Design tab, and in the Table Style Options area, check the Total Row check box.

Figure 930

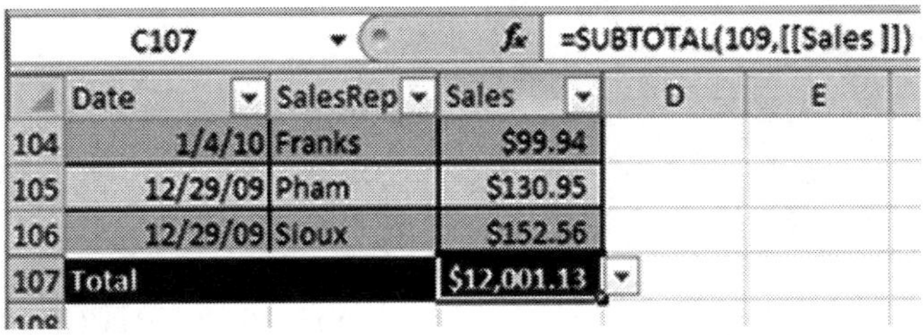

	C107		f_x	=SUBTOTAL(109,[[Sales]])	
	Date	SalesRep	Sales	D	E
104	1/4/10	Franks	$99.94		
105	12/29/09	Pham	$130.95		
106	12/29/09	Sioux	$152.56		
107	Total		$12,001.13		
108					

Figure 931

4. Click in cell C107 and notice that by adding a Total Row, the SUBTOTAL function is showing.

Notice also that because we have scrolled down a long ways, the columns headers that usually show column letters are now showing the field names (great feature!).

Figure 932

5. Click the drop-down arrow in the SalesRep field.
6. Uncheck the Select All check box.
7. Check the Gault check box.
8. Click OK.

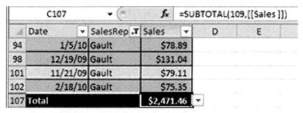

Figure 933

The SUBTOTAL function reflects the fact that the data is filtered.

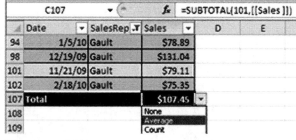

Figure 934

9. Using the drop-down arrow in cell C107, you can change the function to AVERAGE.

As discussed in the "Subtotal Feature" and "PivotTable Feature" sections of this chapter, there are 11 functions available from this drop-down arrow list.

Our next Excel Efficiency-Robust Rule is as follows:

Rule 39: The Filter feature enables you to show records based on criteria. You can do or and and criteria as well as use special built-in filters for dates, numbers, and text. The fastest way to extract the records of interest is to 1) filter, 2) copy, 3) paste in a new location.

Next we want to look at an alternative method of filtering using the Advanced Filter feature.

Advanced Filter Feature

The Advanced Filter feature is great when your goal is to extract records from a data set based on some criteria and place them somewhere else on the same sheet, a different sheet, or in a different workbook. Also, Advanced Filter is good when you are extracting records based on complex criteria. As with all the data analysis features in Excel, Advanced Filter requires that the data set must be in a table format structure (field names at the top of each column [labels in row 1], records in rows, and no blanks inside the data set or in the field names).

Advanced Filter is different from the Filter feature in these ways:
- Advanced Filter does not use filter drop-down arrows for filtering.
- Criteria for the Advanced Filter are placed in cells in the spreadsheet.
- To run Advanced Filter, you use the Advanced Filter dialog box
- Advanced Filter enables you to extract records and paste them in a new location, while keeping the original data set intact (not filtered and no records hidden).

The Advanced Filter feature can be invoked one of three ways:
- Alt, A, Q (Excel 2001/2010). (This one is the fastest.)
- Alt, D, F, A (Excel 2003; easy to remember because D = *data*, F = *filter*, A = *advanced*).
- Go to the Data tab, Sort & Filter group, and click the Advanced button (see Figure 935).

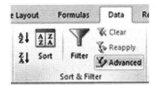

Figure 935

Now let's see how to do an advanced filter to extract records to a new location based on one filtering criterion.

Before we extract our records using the Advanced Filter feature, we want to take note of a few things in Figure 936:
- The data set is in the range A9:D18, and the field names for the data set are in the range A9:D9.
- The criteria area is in the range A3:D4, and the field names for the criteria range are in the range A3:D3. These field names *must be spelled exactly the same as the field names in the data set and must have no extra spaces*. The word Bellen is under the field name Product and will

tell the Advanced Filter feature to only extract records where the word Bellen is in the Product field.

- Cell A22 is designated as the starting point for the extract area. This area is where the extracted records will be placed after running the Advanced Filter feature. The field names from the data set and any records that match the criteria in the criteria range will be extracted and placed in this area.
- The Advanced Filter dialog box has the following:

  Action dialog buttons
  - Filter the List, In-Place (hides records just like the Filter feature)
  - Copy to Another Location (we will do this)

  A **List Range** text box that contains the data set range

  A **Criteria Range** text box contains the criteria range

  A **Copy To** text box that contains the first cell of the extract range

To follow along, open the file named excelisfun-Start.xlsm and navigate to the AF(1) sheet.

Extracting Records with One Criterion

Our goal is to extract all the records for the Bellen product. As shown in Figure 936, the Criteria area has the field names in the range A3:D3, and the criterion Bellen is in cell B4. The single criterion Bellen will be used to determine which records to extract.

Figure 936

1. On the AF(1) sheet, click in A10.
2. Open the Advanced Filter dialog box using Alt, A, Q.
3. The List Range box should automatically have the data set range A9:D18.
4. Click the Copy to Another Location option button.
5. Click in the Criteria Range text box and then select A3:D4.
6. Click in the Copy To text box and select cell A22.
7. Click OK.

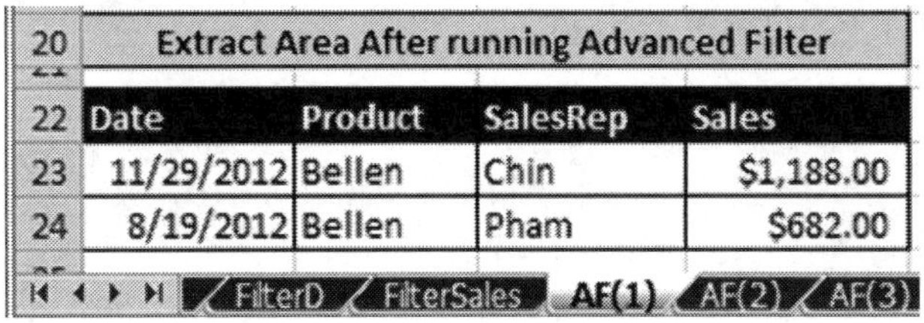

20	Extract Area After running Advanced Filter			
22	Date	Product	SalesRep	Sales
23	11/29/2012	Bellen	Chin	$1,188.00
24	8/19/2012	Bellen	Pham	$682.00

H ◄ ► H　FilterD　FilterSales　**AF(1)**　AF(2)　AF(3)

Figure 937

The field names from the data set and the records that have the word Bellen in the Product field should be extracted and placed in the extract range, leaving the original data set intact.

In Figure 937 you can see that two records had the criterion Bellen in the Product field, and as a result they were extracted.

Next we want to take a look at how to extract records with two criteria on the same line (*and* criteria).

Extracting Records with Two Criteria (*and* criteria is on one line)

Our goal is to extract all the records for the Sunset product where the sales were greater than $1,000. In Figure 938, the criteria Sunset is entered in cell B4 and >500 in cell D4. Because the criteria are entered on the same line (same row), both conditions must be met for a record to be extracted. This is an *and* criteria situation, as you have seen numerous times so far in this book.

For some of us, the criteria >500 may seem confusing. As mentioned earlier in the book, symbols like > are called comparative operators. > is the greater than comparative operator. The trick to understanding this is to see that the small side of the > is pointing toward the 500 and the big side is pointing toward the "other thing," where the "other thing" is all the sales in the Sales field. So this means that if the big side points to a number in the column that is bigger than 500, it says TRUE. For example, the number in D13 is $1,239, so this would lead to 1,239>500, which is TRUE.

Because we have two criteria on the same line in our criteria range, we have to get two TRUEs for any single record to extract the record. As an example, because B13 contains Sunset *and* D13 contains $1,239, we get two TRUEs for a single record and therefore the record is extracted (see Figure 939).

To follow along, open the file named excelisfun-Start.xlsm and navigate to the AF(2) sheet.

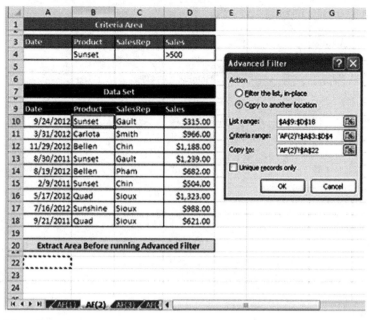

Figure 938

1. On the AF(2) sheet, click in B10.
2. Open the Advanced Filter dialog box using Alt, A, Q.
    The List Range text box should automatically have the data set range A9:D18.
3. Click the Copy to Another Location option button.
4. Click in the Criteria Range text box, and then select A3:D4.
5. Click in the Copy To text box, and then select A22.
6. Click OK.

In Figure 939, you can see that two records had the criteria Sunset in the Product field *and* >500 in the Sales field, and as a result they were extracted.

20	Extract Area After running Advanced Filter		
22	Date	Product	SalesRep	Sales
23	8/30/2011	Sunset	Gault	$1,239.00
24	2/9/2011	Sunset	Chin	$504.00

Figure 939

Next we want to take a look at how to extract records with two criteria on different lines (or criteria).

Extracting Records with Two Criteria (*or* criteria is on two lines)

Our goal is to extract all the records for the Carlota or Bellen product. In Figure 940, the criteria Carlota is entered in cell B4 and Bellen in cell B5. Because the criteria are entered on different lines (different rows or same column), one criterion or the other must be meet for a record to be extracted. This is an *or* criteria situation, as you have seen numerous times so far in this book.

To follow along, open the file named excelisfun-Start.xlsm and navigate to the AF(3) sheet.

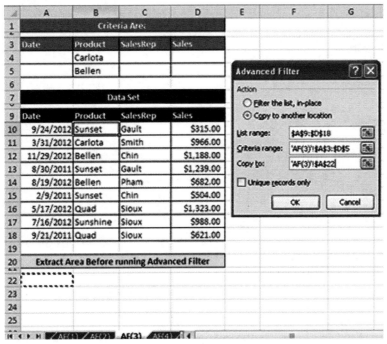

Figure 940

     1. On the AF(3) sheet, click in B10.
     2. Open the Advanced Filter dialog box using Alt, A, Q.

The List Range text box should automatically have the data set range A9:D18.

     3. Click the Copy to Another Location option button.
     4. Click in the Criteria Range text box, and then select A3:D5.
     5. Click in the Copy To text box, and then select A22.
     6. Click OK.

In Figure 941 you can see that three records had the criteria Carlota *or* Bellen in the Product field, and as a result they were extracted.

20	Extract Area After running Advanced Filter			
22	Date	Product	SalesRep	Sales
23	3/31/2012	Carlota	Smith	$966.00
24	11/29/2012	Bellen	Chin	$1,188.00
25	8/19/2012	Bellen	Pham	$682.00

Figure 941

Next we want to take a look at how to extract records with *and* and *or* criteria.

Extracting Records with "And" and "Or" Criteria

Our goal is to extract all the records for the Quad product where the sales were greater than $1,000 *or* the Bellen product where the sales were greater than $1,000. In Figure 942, in the Criteria area, you can see that Quad and >1000 are in row 4 (same line) and then on a different line Bellen and >1000 are in row 5. This indicates that every time the Advanced Filter feature sees a records that contains Quad in the Product field *and* ">1000" in the Sales field *or* it sees a record that contains Bellen in the Product field *and* >1000 in the Sales field, the records will be extracted. Figure 943 shows that two records meet the criteria, and as a result they are extracted to the extract area.

To follow along, open the file named excelisfun-Start.xlsm and navigate to the AF(4) sheet and use figures 942 and 943 as your instructional guide.

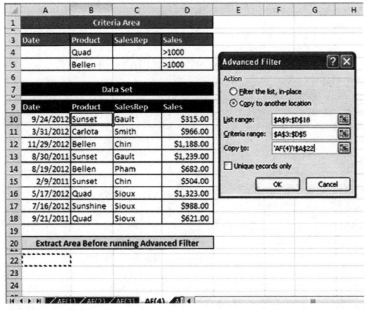

Figure 942

20	Extract Area After running Advanced Filter			
22	Date	Product	SalesRep	Sales
23	11/29/2012	Bellen	Chin	$1,188.00
24	5/17/2012	Quad	Sioux	$1,323.00

K ◀ ▶ H   AF(3)   AF(4)   AF(5) ◀

Figure 943

Next we want to look at how to use *and* criteria that requires us to find values between an upper and lower value.

Extracting Records with "Between" Criteria

Our goal is to extract records where the sales amount is between $900 and $1,200. Our interval of interest has a lower limit of $900 and an upper limit of $1,200, where the lower limit is included in the interval (values of exactly $900 will be extracted) and the upper limit is *not* included (values of exactly $1,200 will not be extracted). We saw this sort of "between" criteria back in Chapter 5. For our Advanced Filter example, notice that the Sales field had to be included twice in the Criteria area. This indicates that when we use *between* criteria, we are also using *and* criteria. Figure 945 shows that two records had sales figures between $900 and $1,200.

To follow along, open the file named excelisfun-Start.xlsm and navigate to the AF(4) sheet and use figures 944 and 945 as your instructional guide.

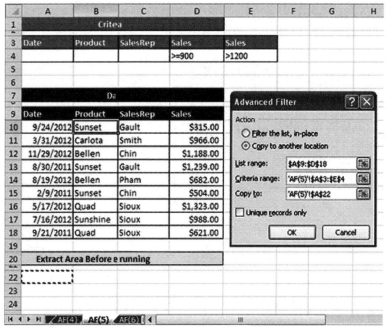

Figure 944

20	Extract Area After running Advanced Filter			
22	Date	Product	SalesRep	Sales
23	8/30/2011	Sunset	Gault	$1,239.00
24	5/17/2012	Quad	Sioux	$1,323.00

Figure 945

Next we want to look at how to extract records when we have dates in a field.

Extracting Records with Date Criteria

Our goal is extract records that are between 2/1/2011 and 5/31/2011; However, unlike the preceding example, both the lower limit and upper limit will be included in the data extract. Our interval of interest has a lower limit of 2/1/2011 and an upper limit of 5/31/2011, where the lower and upper limits are included in the interval. (Dates of exactly 2/1/2011 and 5/31/2011 will be extracted.) Because we are doing a *between* criteria data extract, the field name Date must be listed twice. Notice in Figure 946 the criteria is entered as >=2/1/2001 and <=5/31/2011. Advanced Filter will interpret this as all the dates between 2/1/2011 and 5/31/2001, inclusive. As we have discussed earlier, because there is no single character for the comparative operators greater than or equal to we must use the two characters >=. Similarly, for less than or equal to we must use the two characters <=. Notice in each case that the equal sign always comes second. Figure 947 shows that three records meet the criteria and therefore are extracted.

To follow along, open the file named excelisfun-Start.xlsm and navigate to the AF(6) sheet and use figures 946 and 947 as your instructional guide.

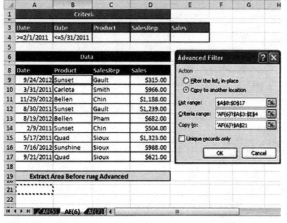

Figure 946

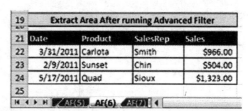

Figure 947

With this knowledge of how to set up *or*, *and*, *between* and Date criteria for the Advanced Filter feature, you have the basic building blocks for even more complex criteria setups.

Next we want to take a look at how to extract records to a new sheet.

Extracting Records to a New Sheet

So far, we have extracted records from a data set on a sheet to that same sheet. Extracting records to a new sheet is exactly the same, except instead of starting the Advanced Filter from the sheet with the data set, you start the Advanced Filter from the sheet where you want your records to be pasted and you must use sheet references. If you look at Figure 948, you can see that we have a Criteria area and an Extract area. The data set is on the sheet Extract. Our goal is to extract the records with the product name Quad in the Product column from the data set on the sheet named AF(7). Let's take a look at how to do this.

To follow along, open the file named excelisfun-Start.xlsm and navigate to the Extract sheet.

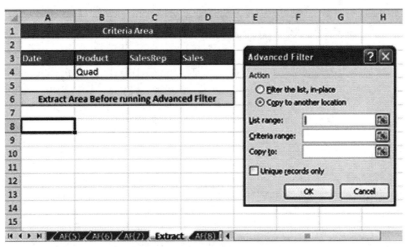

Figure 948

1. On the Extract sheet, and click in A8.
2. Open the Advanced Filter dialog box using Alt, A, Q.
3. Click the Copy to Another Location option button.
4. Click in the List Range text box.

Notice that none of the boxes are filled in (because the cell we selected was not part of a data set).

Notice that the Extract sheet is selected and therefore is visible.

In Figure 948, you can see that we started our Advanced Filter on a sheet without the source data set. To access a data set on a different sheet, we must use sheet references. (You first learned about sheet references back Chapter 5 as we discussed cell references.) Entering sheet references into a box is different from entering cell references in that you are require that you click the sheet with the data set before you select the cell references.

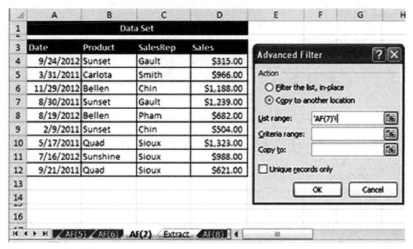

Figure 949

   5. With your cursor in the List Range text box, click the sheet tab named AF(7).

Notice that AF(7) is now the selected sheet and you can see the data set.

Notice that the Extract sheet is now colored white to indicate that it is the sheet we started with.

Notice that the sheet name AF(7) is placed in the List Range text box.

Figure 950

   6. After you have clicked the AF(7) sheet, select the range A3:D12. Be sure to highlight the field names as well as the records.

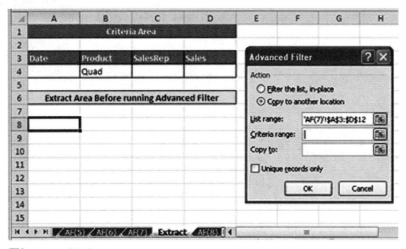

Figure 951

7. Click in the Criteria Range text box.

Notice that as soon as you click in the Criteria Range text box, the Advanced Filter dialog box jumps back the Extract sheet.

8. Select the criteria range A3:D4 on the Extract sheet.
9. Click in the Copy To text box, and then select cell A8 on the Extract sheet.
10. Click OK.

Figure 952

Figure 953 shows the two Quad records that were extracted from the data on the sheet AF(7) and pasted on the sheet Extract.

Next we want to take a look at how Advanced Filter feature can be used to extract unique records from a column of data.

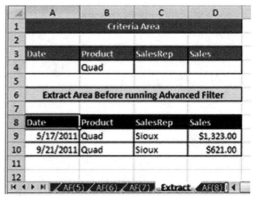

Figure 953

Extracting Unique Records/Items to a New Location (safe method for removing duplicates)

A common problem encountered in the working world is that you are given a huge data set that contains many customer names and the names are repeated many times. If you want a list of customer names where each name is listed only one time (called a unique list), what do you do? You can use the Advanced Filter feature's Unique Records Only feature to extract a unique list of items. In Figure 954, you can see a data set that contains a field named Customer. There are many names and many repeats. Our goal is to extract a unique list and paste it into the E column.

	A	B	C	D	E	F
1	Date	Customer	Sales			
2	1/1/11	Rod Kloer Firm	$621.00			
3	1/9/11	Hal Hinchliff Firm	$1,197.00			
4	1/3/11	Hal Hinchliff Firm	$1,058.00			
5	1/11/11	Shakia Warning Inc.	$1,144.00			
6	1/15/11	Cliff Stalworth Firm	$1,449.00			
7	1/3/11	Jackson Kings LLP	$1,092.00			
8	1/15/11	Jackson Kings LLP	$736.00			
9	1/17/11	Rob Swearegene Company	$567.00			

Extract / AF(8) / TIC / ID(1) / ID(2)

Figure 954

When we run Advanced Filter to extract a unique list of items it is important to remember these facts:

- When you want to extract unique items from a single field (column) that is part of a larger data set, you must remember to highlight just the field you are interested in and not the rest of the data set.
- You must highlight the field name and all the data in the field (column). If you do not highlight the field name, the first item in the list will be treated as a field name, and as a result you will have a single instance of a duplicate. (The first item will be a field name, and the second time Advanced Filter encounters that exact name it will be treated as an entry in the list, and thus you get two equivalent items extracted.)
- The extracted list will contain the field name in the first cell and the unique list below the field name.
- If you want to extract a list of unique records (all fields) to remove duplicates, you would highlight the entire data set and then run the Advanced Filter feature's Unique Records Only feature. If you compare this to the Remove Duplicates feature in Excel, the Remove Duplicates feature removes the duplicates from the original list (permanently altering the original data set), whereas the Advanced Filter feature's

Unique Records Only feature retains the integrity of the original data set and pastes a unique list to a different location.

- When you run the Advanced Filter feature's Unique Records Only feature, you do not need to enter anything in the Criteria Range box, but instead you check the Unique Records Only check box. In essence, this check box is the criteria. However, you could enter criteria and the unique list would be created with that criteria in mind.

To follow along, open the file named excelisfun-Start.xlsm and navigate to the AF(8) sheet.

	A	B	C
1	Date	Customer	Sales
2	1/1/11	Rod Kloer Firm	$621
3	1/9/11	Hal Hinchliff Firm	$1,197
4	1/3/11	Hal Hinchliff Firm	$1,058
5	1/11/11	Shakia Warning Inc.	$1,144
6	1/15/11	Cliff Stalworth Firm	$1,449
7	1/3/11	Jackson Kings LLP	$1,092
8	1/15/11	Jackson Kings LLP	$736
9	1/17/11	Rob Swearegene Company	$567

	A	B	C
99	1/3/11	Marcel Mittelsteadt Firm	$253.0
100	1/23/11	Lashon Yerhot Manufacturers	$475.0
101	1/21/11	Lashon Yerhot Manufacturers	$528.0
102	1/4/11	Marcel Mittelsteadt Firm	$1,210.0
103	1/26/11	Shakia Warning Inc.	$266.0
104	1/27/11	Cliff Stalworth Firm	$315.0
105	1/22/11	Lashon Yerhot Manufacturers	$506.0
106	1/25/11	Marcel Mittelsteadt Firm	$1,232.0
107			

Figure 955

1. On the AF(8) sheet and click in B1.
2. To select the column of data, use the Ctrl + Shift + Down Arrow keyboard shortcut.

3. With the range B1:B106 selected, open the Advanced Filter dialog box using Alt, A, Q.

The List Range text box should automatically contain the range B1:B106.

4. Click the Copy to Another Location option button.
5. Click in the Copy To text box, and then select cell E1 on the Extract sheet.
6. Check the Unique Records Only check box.

Figure 956

Notice that we left the Criteria Range text box empty. The "criteria" for this data extract will come from the fact that we checked the Unique Records Only check box.

8. Click OK.

Figure 957 shows the results of our Advanced Filter feature's Unique Records Only feature. Figure 958 shows an example of what a company might do with a list of unique customers. In this case, the COUNTIFS function is being used to count the number of sales each customer had over $1,000. For more about the COUNTIFS function see Chapter 5.

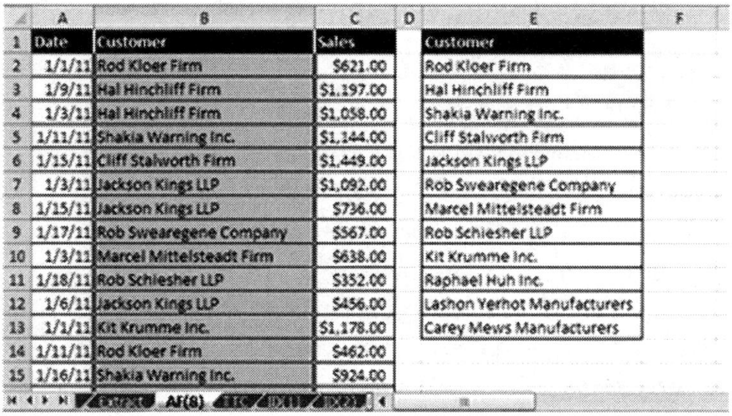

	A	B	C	D	E
1	Date	Customer	Sales		Customer
2	1/1/11	Rod Kloer Firm	$621.00		Rod Kloer Firm
3	1/9/11	Hal Hinchliff Firm	$1,197.00		Hal Hinchliff Firm
4	1/3/11	Hal Hinchliff Firm	$1,058.00		Shakia Warning Inc.
5	1/11/11	Shakia Warning Inc.	$1,144.00		Cliff Stalworth Firm
6	1/15/11	Cliff Stalworth Firm	$1,449.00		Jackson Kings LLP
7	1/3/11	Jackson Kings LLP	$1,092.00		Rob Swearegene Company
8	1/15/11	Jackson Kings LLP	$736.00		Marcel Mittelsteadt Firm
9	1/17/11	Rob Swearegene Company	$567.00		Rob Schiesher LLP
10	1/3/11	Marcel Mittelsteadt Firm	$638.00		Kit Krumme Inc.
11	1/18/11	Rob Schiesher LLP	$352.00		Raphael Huh Inc.
12	1/6/11	Jackson Kings LLP	$456.00		Lashon Yerhot Manufacturers
13	1/1/11	Kit Krumme Inc.	$1,178.00		Carey Mews Manufacturers
14	1/11/11	Rod Kloer Firm	$462.00		
15	1/16/11	Shakia Warning Inc.	$924.00		

Figure 957

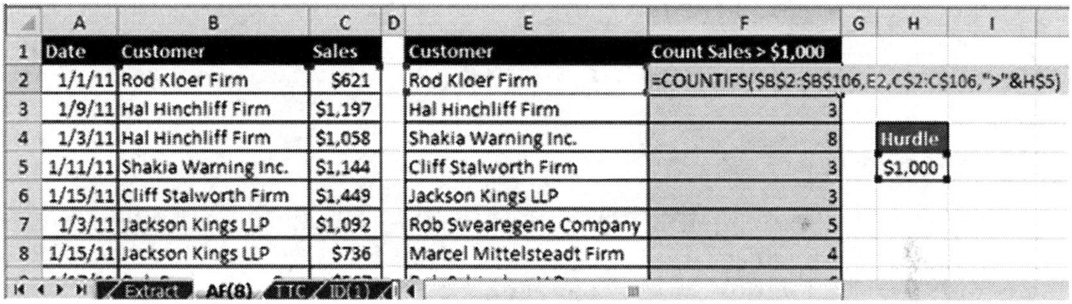

	A	B	C	D	E	F	G	H
1	Date	Customer	Sales		Customer	Count Sales > $1,000		
2	1/1/11	Rod Kloer Firm	$621		Rod Kloer Firm	=COUNTIFS($B$2:$B$106,E2,C$2:C$106,">"&H$5)		
3	1/9/11	Hal Hinchliff Firm	$1,197		Hal Hinchliff Firm	3		
4	1/3/11	Hal Hinchliff Firm	$1,058		Shakia Warning Inc.	8		Hurdle
5	1/11/11	Shakia Warning Inc.	$1,144		Cliff Stalworth Firm	3		$1,000
6	1/15/11	Cliff Stalworth Firm	$1,449		Jackson Kings LLP	3		
7	1/3/11	Jackson Kings LLP	$1,092		Rob Swearegene Company	5		
8	1/15/11	Jackson Kings LLP	$736		Marcel Mittelsteadt Firm	4		

Figure 958

One last note about the Advanced Filter feature: Every time you run Advanced Filter, an Excel defined name is created for the Criteria and Extract ranges. For more about the Defined Name feature, see Chapter 5. Figure 959 shows a small part of the list of the defined names created from the advanced filters that we ran in this chapter. Criteria is the defined name used for the Criteria area and Extract is the defined named used for the Extract area. The reason that defined names are created is so that Excel can remember where your criteria and extract ranges are.

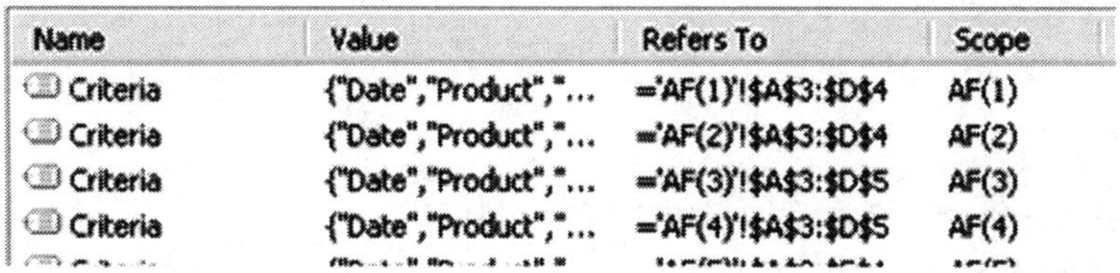

Name	Value	Refers To	Scope
Criteria	{"Date","Product","...	='AF(1)'!$A$3:$D$4	AF(1)
Criteria	{"Date","Product","...	='AF(2)'!$A$3:$D$4	AF(2)
Criteria	{"Date","Product","...	='AF(3)'!$A$3:$D$5	AF(3)
Criteria	{"Date","Product","...	='AF(4)'!$A$3:$D$5	AF(4)

Figure 959

These defined names are convenient if you run many advanced filters on the same sheet. For example, you may have five different sets of criteria that you want to run. The process for this is simple: 1) Type your criteria into Criteria area, 2) run the Advanced Filter feature, 3) cut and paste extracted records to a new area, 4) and then repeat the process. Remember, though, if you are running multiple advanced filter extracts on the same sheet, clear the Data Extract area before running the next Advanced Filter.

Our next Excel Efficiency-Robust Rule is this:

> *Rule 40: Advanced Filter is great for extracting records and placing them in a new location while keeping the original data set intact. The three distinct areas for Advanced Filter are data set, Criteria area, and Extract area. The field names in the data set and the Criteria area must be exactly the same. When using or criteria, place criteria on different lines. When using and criteria, place the criteria on the same lines. When creating between criteria, repeat field names on same row. Advanced Filter can also be used to extract a unique list.*

Now that you have seen the amazing power of Advanced Filter for extracting records, we next want to look at the Text to Column feature for separating data into individual cells.

Text to Columns Feature

The Text to Columns feature can take data in a single cell and separate it into multiple cells. For example, in Figure 960 you can see that each cell has a first and last name in a single cell. For data analysis purposes, this is inefficient. If we need to sort the last names, it would be very difficult to do so without having each last name in its own individual cell. The Text to Column feature can easily take these names and separate them out into individual cells. The key will be something called a delimiter. A **delimiter** is just a certain character (such as a space, a comma, a tab, or other characters) that separates the pieces of raw data. In Figure 960, the delimiter that separates the first and last name is a space. So, if we tell the Text to Column feature, "Hey, our data uses the delimiter space," it will break apart all the data in a column based on the fact that we told it "space." You can think of the delimiter as the trigger that can break data apart into smaller pieces. This is amazing because if you have a list of 200 names, it would take a long time to do it by hand, whereas the Text to Column feature can do it in just a few clicks.

To break apart raw data separated by delimiters we must use the Text to Column Wizard. This wizard has three steps:

1. How is the data separated? (The wizard asks for the data type.)

- Delimited (characters such as spaces, commas, tabs, or other)
- Fixed (an actual width for the column size)

2. Select the specific delimiter that separates the data or the width that determines the data.
3. Format the columns or skip (remove) columns.

> **Note**: Although we will not do a fixed-width example, all that is required is that in step 2 you click to say how wide each data piece is.

To follow along, open the file named excelisfun-Start.xlsm and navigate to the TTC(1) sheet.

Separating First and Last Name from One Cell into Two Cells

Our goal in this example is to use the Text to Column Wizard with the delimiter "space" to break apart the first and last name into individual cells.

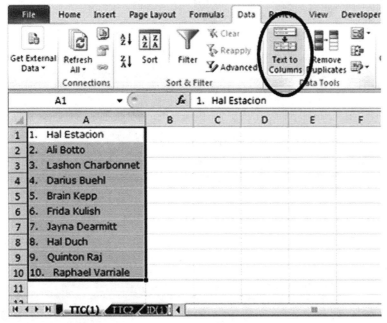

Figure 960

1. On the TTC(1) sheet, select the range A1:A10.
2. Go to the Data Tab, Data Tools group, and click the Text to Column button (or use Alt, A, E).

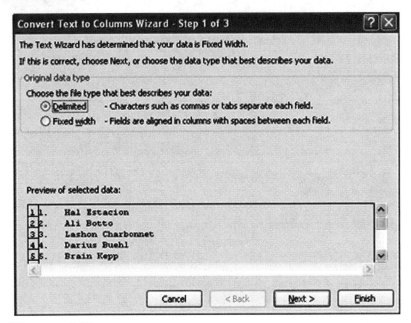

Figure 961

3. In step 1 of the wizard, select the Delimited option button. (Delimited just means characters such as a space or a comma or a tab.)

Notice the preview at the bottom; all the data is still together.

4. Click Next.

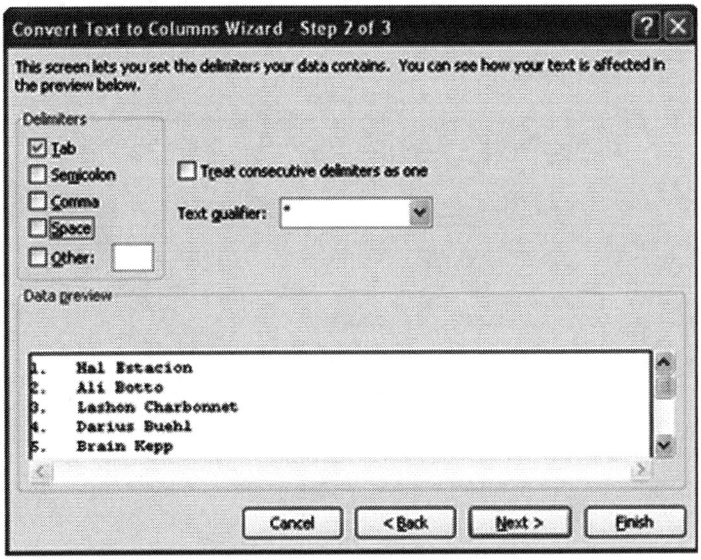

Figure 962

In step 2 of the wizard, notice the preview at the bottom; all the data is still together.

Notice that the delimiters could be Tab, Semicolon, Comma, Space, or Other. The Other option is great because you can type whatever character is required.

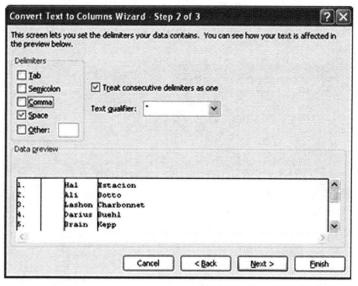

Figure 963

5. Uncheck the check box for Tab.
6. Check the Space check box.

Notice the preview at the bottom has changed; you can know see a preview of what the Text to Column feature will do. This is important because if the preview does not look correct, you can click Cancel and start over.

7. Click Next.

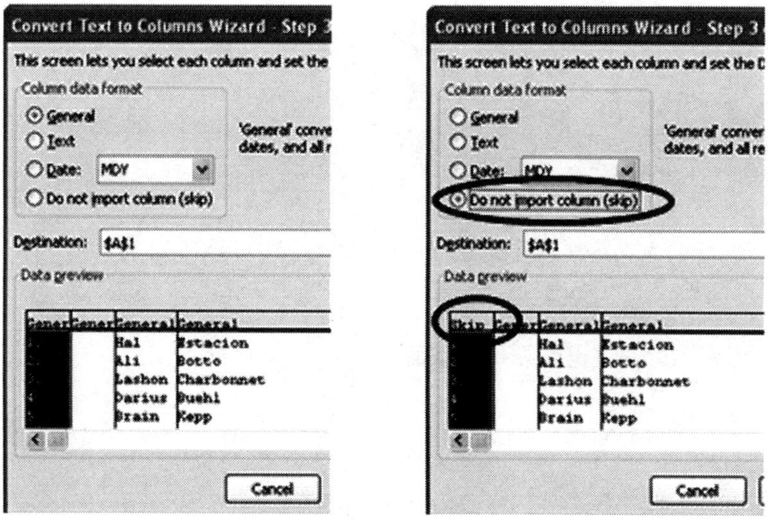

Figure 964

In step 3 of the wizard, we can format the columns or skip (remove) a given column.

8. Click to highlight the second column.
9. Click the Do Not Import Column option button.
10. Make sure that it says Skip at the top of the second column. (If it does not, repeat step 9.)

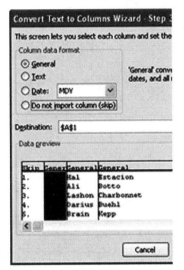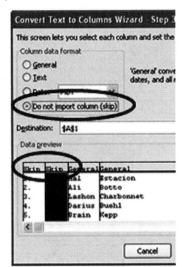

Figure 965

Notice that you have the option in this step to Format the columns with General, Text, or Date number formatting.

11. Click to highlight the second column.
12. Click the Do Not Import Column option button.
13. Make sure that it says Skip at the top of the second column.

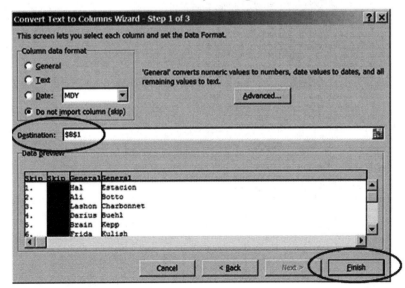

Figure 966

14. To keep the source data, click in the Destination box and change the cell reference to **$B$1**

15. Click the Finish button.

	A	B	C	D
1	1. Hal Estacion	Hal	Estacion	
2	2. Ali Botto	Ali	Botto	
3	3. Lashon Charbonnet	Lashon	Charbonnet	
4	4. Darius Buehl	Darius	Buehl	
5	5. Brain Kepp	Brain	Kepp	
6	6. Frida Kulish	Frida	Kulish	
7	7. Jayna Dearmitt	Jayna	Dearmitt	
8	8. Hal Duch	Hal	Duch	
9	9. Quinton Raj	Quinton	Raj	
10	10. Raphael Varriale	Raphael	Varriale	

Figure 967

Figure 967 shows that the first and last names have been placed in the B and C columns. Thus the name "Text" to "Columns."

Separating First and Last Name from 1 Cell into 2 Cells (formula)

Sometimes people like to separate first and last names with a formula. This is beneficial if the names in the column are continually changing and you want the formulas to automatically extract the first and last name. Figures 968 and 969 show examples for how this could be done if there were a first name and last name separated by a space in each cell.

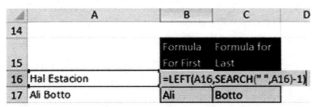

To follow along, open the file named excelisfun-Start.xlsm and navigate to the TTC(1) sheet and use figures 968 and 969 as your instructional guide.

Figure 968

In brief, the formula for extracting the first name works because

- The SEARCH function looks at cell A16 and tries to find the first space. (Double quote, space, double quote is Excel language for space.) When it finds that space, it tells you how many characters in from the left that space is. In our example, it tells us that the space is the fourth character in from the left. Because 4 is 1 too many, we subtract 1 to get our 3.
- The LEFT function looks at cell A16 and extracts a certain number of characters from the left. In our example, we tell the LEFT function to extract the 3 left characters, and it extracts Hal.

	A	B	C	D	E
14					
15		Formula For First	Formula for Last		
16	Hal Estacion	Hal	=REPLACE(A16,1,SEARCH(" ",A16),"")		
17	Ali Botto	Ali	Botto		

Figure 969

In brief, the formula for extracting the last name works because
- The SEARCH function looks at cell A16 and tries to find the first space. When it finds that space, it tells you how many characters in from the left the space is. In our example it tells us that the space is the fourth character in from the left.
- The REPLACE function looks at cell A16 and gets rid of (replaces) the characters from the position 1 to 4 and replaces them with a blank. (Double quote, double quote is Excel language for blank.) In our example, the REPLACE removes Hal and puts in its place a blank, and it extracts the remaining characters, which are Estacion.

Next we want to see that sometimes you may need to run Text to Column twice to get the desired results.

Separating Full Address from One Cell into Four Cells

In Figure 970, you can see that column A contains addresses. The problem is that if we need to do any sort of data analysis, such as sorting by ZIP code, it is very hard to do unless we have each ZIP code in its own individual cell. Text to Columns can help us in this situation. However, if we look at Figure 970, we can't see a consistent pattern of delimiters that will allow us to separate out the Address, City, State and ZIP code into four cells. If we decide to use spaces as the delimiter (as we did in the last example), we could end up with six items in individual cells rather than our desired four items. In this situation, we can run the Text to Column feature one time with the delimiter as a comma and then a second time with the delimiter as a space. Running the wizard twice will yield our desired result of the data broken into four cells.

To follow along, open the file named excelisfun-Start.xlsm and navigate to the TTC(2) sheet.

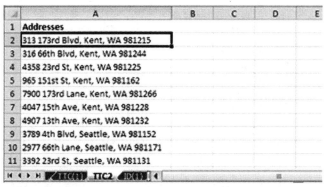

Figure 970

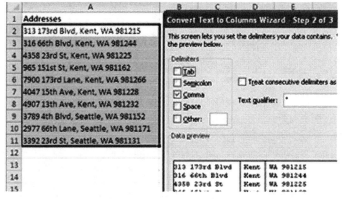

Figure 971

1. On the TTC(2) sheet, select the range A2:A11.
2. Open the Text to Column Wizard: Alt, A, E.
3. In step 1 of the wizard, click the Delimited option button.
4. Click Next.
5. In step 2 of the wizard, uncheck Tab and check Comma.
6. Because we are not skipping or formatting any columns, click the Finish button.

	A	B	C	D	E
1	Addresses				
2	313 173rd Blvd	Kent	WA 981215		
3	316 66th Blvd	Kent	WA 981244		
4	4358 23rd St	Kent	WA 981225		
5	965 151st St	Kent	WA 981162		

Figure 972

In Figure 972, you can see that the address and city data separated out perfectly, but the state and ZIP code did not. If we run the Text to Column Wizard with a space delimiter, we can break apart state and ZIP code into individual cells. But before we do that, take a closer look at the data in column C in Figure 972. If you look closely, you can see that a space occurs before each state abbreviation. We can get rid of that in step 3 of the wizard by skipping that column.

1. Select the range C2:C11.
2. Open the Text to Column Wizard: Alt, A, E.
3. In step 1 of the wizard, click the Delimited option button.
4. Click Next.
5. In step 2 of the wizard, uncheck Comma and check Space.
6. Click Next.

4	A	B	C	D
1	**Addresses**	**City**	**State**	**Zip Code**
2	313 173rd Blvd	Kent	WA	981215
3	316 66th Blvd	Kent	WA	981244
4	4358 23rd St	Kent	WA	981225
5	965 151st St	Kent	WA	981162
6	7900 173rd Lane	Kent	WA	981266
7	4047 15th Ave	Kent	WA	981228
8	4907 13th Ave	Kent	WA	981232
9	3789 4th Blvd	Seattle	WA	981152
10	2977 66th Lane	Seattle	WA	981171
11	3392 23rd St	Seattle	WA	981131

Figure 973

7. In step 3 of the wizard, click to highlight the first column.
8. Click the Do Not Import Column dialog button.
9. Make sure that it says Skip at the top of the first column. (If it does not, repeat step 8.)
10. Click the Finish button.

In Figure 973, you can see that the raw data are in individual cells and field names have been typed in.

Here are two other points about the Text to Columns feature:

- After you run the Text to Columns feature, you should look at the data, even if you just skim the data, because if the data does not have the same pattern of delimiters throughout the entire data set, you may have some rows where there are fewer or more columns of data than the most of the other rows. This is usually caused by bad data entry or anomalies in the data.
- Sometimes after running the Text to Columns Wizard, if you copy and paste some other data in the spreadsheet and the other data have the same delimiter as the one that you used in the Text to Column Wizard, the paste will automatically do Text to Column, meaning that when you paste, instead of the data going into a single cell, it will go into multiple cells. The fix for this is to save the file, close the file, and then open the file. Then copy and paste will work normally again.

Our next Excel Efficiency-Robust Rule is as follows:

Rule 41: Text to Columns is great for breaking apart data in a single cell that is separated by delimiters and placing it into multiple cells. A delimiter is a character such as a space, a comma, or a tab. Sometimes you have to run the Text to Columns feature more than once to get the data broken apart correctly.

Next we want to look at how to import data into Excel.

Importing Data

Because data can be stored in many different ways, it is important to know how to get outside data into Excel. This section covers the following import data topics:

- Importing from a different Excel workbook
- Importing comma-separated or tab-separated data
- Importing data from Access
- Stock Quote web queries

Importing Data from a Different Excel Workbook

What if you want to import data from one workbook to another? There are two ways to do this:

- You can copy and paste the data from one workbook to another.
- You can use the Get External Data feature. This method will allow the data to be refreshed.

Copy and Paste

For the copy and paste method, here are the keyboard shortcuts to copy a range of data from one open workbook to another:

1. Select the range of data.
2. To copy, use Ctrl + C.
3. To switch to the second workbook, use Ctrl + Tab. (This keyboard shortcut switches between two open Excel workbooks.)
4. Select cell A1, and then to paste use Ctrl + V.

Using the Get External Data Feature

	A	B	C	D	E
1	ProductID	Product	Description	Supplier	Suggested Price
2	Be-BF-001	Bellen	20 meter Juggler	Gel Booms	24
3	Ca-BF-002	Carlota	20 meter Trick Catch	Gel Booms	25
4	Su-BF-003	Sunshine	30 meter Accuracy	Gel Booms	27
5	Ma-BF-004	Majestic Beaut	40 Meter Aussie Round	Gel Booms	32
6	Ya-BF-005	Yanaki	25 meter Beginner	Colorado	22
7	As-BF-006	Aspen	15 meter Reversable	Colorado	29
8	Ea-BF-007	Eagle	50 Meter Aussie Round	Roger Perry	45
9	Vr-BF-008	Vrang	Traditional	Channel Craft	15
10					

Figure 974

In Figure 974, you can see a Products sheet in the workbook named Products.xlsm, and in Figure 975 you can see the workbook named excelisfun-Start.xlsm. If our goal is to import the data from the Products.xlsm workbook (the source workbook) into the excelisfun-Start.xlsm workbook (the destination workbook) and allow automatic updates, we can use the Get External Data feature in Excel.

To follow along, open the file named excelisfun-Start.xlsm and navigate to the ID(1) sheet. You will have also had to have access to the file Products. xlsm.

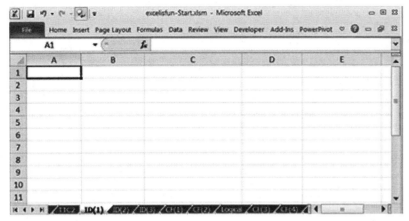

Figure 975

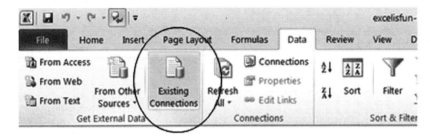

Figure 976

1. In the workbook, excelisfun-Start.xlsm, on the ID(1) sheet, select cell A1.
2. On the far-left side of the Data tab, Get External Data group, click the Existing Connections button.

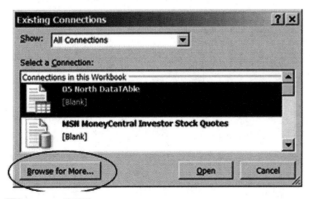

Figure 977

3. When the Existing Connections dialog box appears, click the Browse for More button.

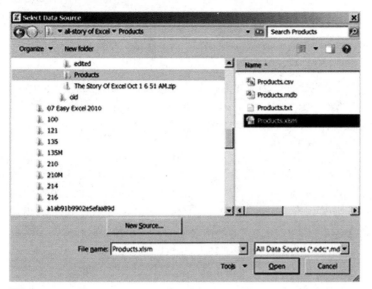

Figure 978

4. When the Select Data Source dialog box appears, navigate to the folder that contains the file Products.xlsm.
5. Then on the right, select the file Products.xlsm.
6. Click the Open button.

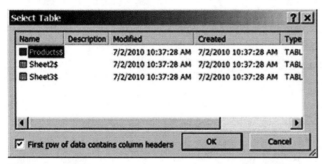

7. Select the Products$ sheet.
8. Click OK in the Select Table dialog box.
9. Click OK in the Import Data dialog box.

Figure 979

Figure 980

Notice that the data is placed in cell A1 as an Excel table. Notice the Refresh All button that can be used to update the destination workbook whenever something is changed in the source workbook.

Next we want to take a look at how to import data from comma-separated or tab-separated data.

Importing Comma-Separated or Tab-Separated Data

It is important to be able to import comma-separated data (often with the file extension .csv) or tab-separated data (often with the file extension .txt) because many programs/applications, such as databases, can only export data into these file formats. Because Excel can import this type of data, it is an indirect way to get data from one system (foreign database) into another (Excel).

Just as you saw with the Text to Columns feature, sometimes there are delimiters that separate data. Comma-separated data has a comma delimiter, and tab-separated data has a tab delimiter. Because of this, when we use the Get External Data feature to import comma- or tab-separated data, the steps are exactly the same as you saw for the Text to Columns feature. The only difference is that the three-step wizard is called the Text Import Wizard rather than the Text to Columns Wizard.

To import any data separated by a delimiter, complete the following steps:
1. Go to the Data tab and click the Get External Data button.
2. Click the From Text button in the Get External Data drop-down (see Figure 981).
3. Follow the same steps as in the "Text to Column Feature" section of this chapter.

Figure 981

Next we want to take a look at how to import data from Access (Microsoft's database program).

Importing Data from Access

If you have data stored in an Access database table or query, it is easy to import it into Excel. Let's take a look at how to do this.

To follow along, open the file named excelisfun-Start.xlsm and navigate to the ID(1) sheet. You will have also had to have access to the file Products.mdb.
1. On the ID(2) sheet, select cell A1.
2. Go to the Data tab and click the Get External Data button.
3. Click the From Access button in the Get External Data drop-down.
4. When the Select Data Source dialog box appears, navigate to the file named Product.mdb and open it.

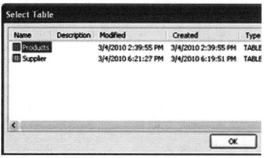

5. When the Select Table dialog box appears, select the Products table (shown in this figure).
6. Click OK in the Select Table dialog box.
7. Click OK in the Import Data dialog box.

Figure 982

	A	B	C	D	E
1	ProductID	Product	Description	Supplier	Suggested Price
2	Be-BF-001	Bellen	20 meter Juggler	Gel Booms	24
3	Ca-BF-002	Carlota	20 meter Trick Catch	Gel Booms	25
4	Su-BF-003	Sunshine	30 meter Accuracy	Gel Booms	27
5	Ma-BF-004	Majestic Beaut	40 Meter Aussie Round	Gel Booms	32
6	Ya-BF-005	Yanaki	25 meter Beginner	Colorado	22
7	As-BF-006	Aspen	15 meter Reversable	Colorado	29
8	Ea-BF-007	Eagle	50 Meter Aussie Round	Roger Perry	45
9	Vr-BF-008	Vrang	Traditional	Channel Craft	15
10					
11					

Figure 983

In Figure 983, you can see the results of importing the Access database table. Anytime the data in the Access table changes, you can use the Refresh button on the Data tab to update the table.

Next we want to take a look at how to get stock data from the Internet using a Stock Quote web query.

Using the Stock Quote Web Query

	A	B	C	D	E	F	G
1			Stock Gain and Loss Table				
2		Price Paid		Historic	Stock	Current	
	Stocks	6/1/2007	Quantity	Value	Value Now	Value	Gain Loss
3	GOOG	$500.397	100	$50,039.70		$0.00	-100.0%
4	MFST	$30.590	100	$3,059.000		$0.00	-100.0%
5	YHOO	$28.780	100	$2,878.000		$0.00	-100.0%
6	WFMI	$41.670	100	$4,167.000		$0.00	-100.0%
7	C	$54.510	100	$5,451.000		$0.00	-100.0%
8	BAC	$50.780	100	$5,078.000		$0.00	-100.0%
9	DELL	$27.300	100	$2,730.000		$0.00	-100.0%
10							

Figure 984

Using a built-in Stock Quote web query, we can get current market stock value for publicly traded companies. In addition, the stock quotes will update whenever the stock markets are open if we use the Refresh button in the Data tab. Figure 984 shows a range with information about stocks that we bought on 6/1/2007. We would like to add the current value for these stocks into the E column so that every time we use the Refresh button the stock quotes and calculations based on the stock quotes will update.

To follow along, open the file named excelisfun-Start.xlsm and navigate to the ID(3) sheet.

1. On the ID(3) sheet, select A13.
2. Go to the Data tab and click the Get External Data button.
3. Click the Existing Connections button in the Get External Data group.
4. In the Existing Connections dialog box, scroll down and click the MSN MoneyCentral Investor Stock Quotes (first picture below) query. (If you cannot find it, ask your systems administrator for help.)

5. Click the Open button in the Existing Connections dialog box.

6. Click Properties in the Import Data dialog box (second picture to right).
7. Uncheck the Adjust Column Width box.
8. Click OK in the External Data Range Properties dialog box.
9. Click OK in the Import Data dialog box.

10. When the Enter Parameter Value dialog box (third picture to right) appears, click in the text box and then select the cells A3:A9.
11. Check the Use This Reference for Future Refreshes check box.
12. Click OK on the Enter Parameter Value dialog box.

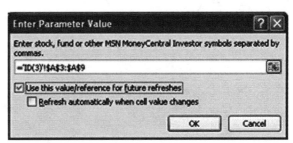

Figure 985

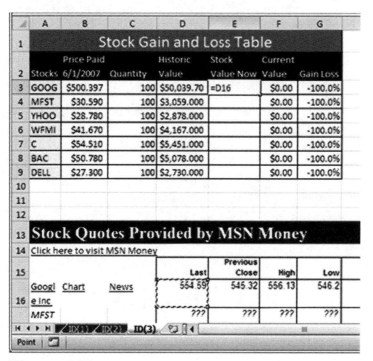

Figure 986

13. Click in cell E3.
14. Type an equal sign.
15. Click cell D16.
16. To enter the formula, press Ctrl + Enter.
17. Copy the formula down the column.

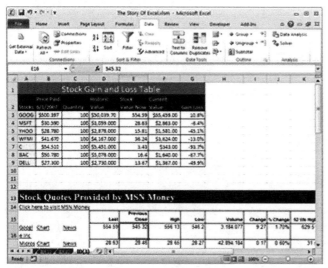

Figure 987

Any time the stock market is open, you can right-click the web query range and point to Refresh, and the entire Stock Gain and Loss Table will update.

Now that was a lot about data analysis. Over the past 60 pages, we talked about the data analysis features in Excel:

- Sort
- Subtotal
- PivotTable
- Filter
- Advanced Filter
- Text to Columns
- Importing data

In the next chapter, we take a detailed look at charts.

7

Charts, also known as graphs, are visual portrayals of quantitative data (number data). Charts help to visualize the data so that you can see patterns or trends more easily than if we you were to simply look at the range of numbers.

Into The Wind Sales				
	Jan	Feb	Mar	Total
Toys	500	6,898	13,893	21,291
Boomerangs	9,079	6,933	11,545	27,557
Kites	9,721	5,367	15,064	30,152
Total	19,300	19,198	40,502	79,000

Figure 988

For example, Figure 988 shows us a report that shows the sales for each item by month. If our goal is to articulate the message "kite sales were twice as big as toy sales," then using the pie chart (Figure 989) does a better job than the report with just numbers and labels. With the pie chart, we can quickly recognize that the kite piece of the pie is *much* bigger than the toy piece of the pie! It is this sort of visual immediacy that makes charts such a powerful way to deliver your message.

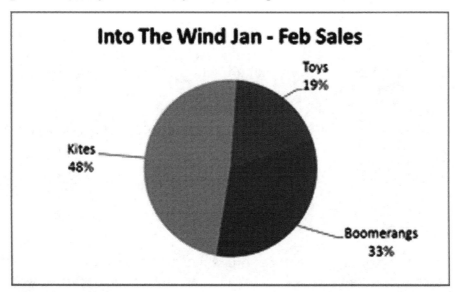

Figure 989

Chart Junk

However, when making charts in Excel, the number one rule to follow is this:

Eliminate all chart junk.

Chart junk is a term from Edward Tufte, the great data visualization author. Chart junk represents chart elements that do not contribute to your message or are misleading. Figure 990 is a great example of a chart filled with chart junk.

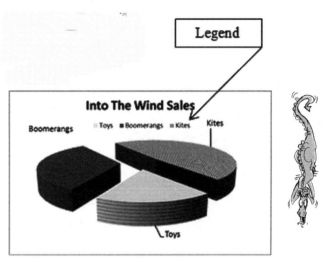

Figure 990

Figure 990 has the following chart junk problems:
- The pie chart should not be shown as a 3D pie because this distorts the percentages. This is misleading and is not an honest portrayal of data. In the example, the toy sales number looks artificially large.
- The legend (colored boxes with the item names) is unnecessary because it adds duplicate labels.
- The different patterns for each pie piece add unnecessary busyness to the chart.
- The fact that the percentages are not shown in the chart could be misleading.
- The use of the "warm color" yellow and the "cool color" blue and the fact that there are horizontal lines and vertical lines all further contribute to a cluttered chart.

Next we want to take a look at how the Excel charting feature sees data as categories or series.

Categories and Series

Before we get started with how to create charts, we want to look at how Excel interprets data when you make charts. This is important because how you setup your data in the cells on the worksheet determines where the data will be placed in the chart.

	Jan	Feb	Mar	
Toys	500	2,150	8,893	◀ These are called 'Categories' and will appear in the horizontal axis.
Boomerangs	4,000	6,933	9,545	◀ The numbers 500, 2,150, 8,893 are called the 'Toys Series'.
Kites	9,721	5,367	15,064	◀ The numbers 4,000, 6,933, 9,545 are called the 'Boomerangs Series'.

◀ The numbers 9,721, 5,367, 15,064 are called the 'Kites Series'.

These labels will appear in the color coded 'Legend'

Figure 991

Figure 991 shows the data for the chart, and Figure 992 shows the finished chart. In Figures 991 and 992, we want to take note of these examples of how Excel interprets data from the cells for a column chart:

- The numbers 500, 2,150, 8,893 are called the Toys *series values* and will appear as blue columns in a column chart.
- The column header labels Jan, Feb, and Mar are called the *categories* and will appear in the horizontal axis.
- The row header labels Toys, Boomerangs, and Kites are called *series names* and will appear in the legend.

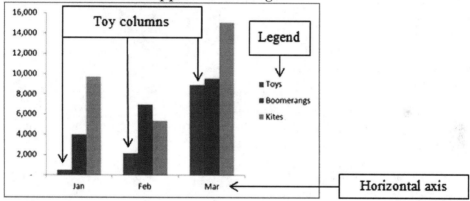

Figure 992

Note three other things about categories and series values:

- If the number of columns is greater than or equal to the number of rows, the column header labels will appear on the horizontal axis. If there are more rows than columns, the row headers will appear on the horizontal axis.
- If you create a chart and want to switch the labels on horizontal axis with the labels in the legend (series and category orientation), go to the Chart Tools Design tab, Data group, and click the Switch Row/Column button.
- When you have X-Y data, the X is called series and the Y is called category (more later).

Now it's time to take a look at the various chart types.

Chart Types

Choosing the right chart type can be the difference between an effective chart and an ineffective chart. In addition, sometimes your data dictates the exact type of chart that you must use (for example, when you have X and Y data points). The following subsections describe some of the charts available in Excel and when to use them.

Pie Charts

Pie charts are for when you have parts that make up a whole, or categories of numbers, and you add to get a total. The total amount will be the whole pie, and the pieces of the pie will be the individual categories.

When you make pie charts, you highlight the cells with the individual numbers. Never highlight the total numbers. This chart is good for when you want to see percentages or proportions.

2D pie charts do not distort the percentages or proportions.

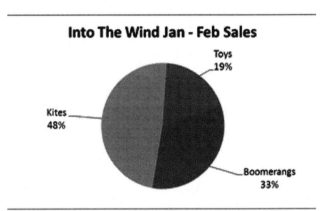

Figure 993

When you have more than six pie pieces, it is useful to select the pie within pie/column charts to avoid "cluttered" pie charts.

3D pie charts do not present an honest visual presentation because they distort the percentages or proportions.

Column Charts

Column charts are good for when you have a range of source data (often created with a PivotTable) with row and column header labels and you want to show how a group of categories did within a second category (such as items sold within a month).

The row labels from the source data range will appear in the

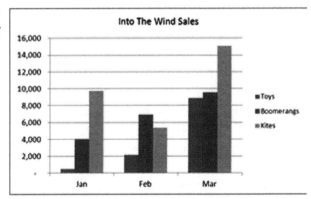

Figure 994

legend, and the column headers will appear on the horizontal axis. Column charts show difference based on column heights across categories. Hint: Column charts have vertical bars, and bar charts have horizontal bars.

Histograms

Histograms are a special type of column chart where the horizontal categories are grouped numbers, such as 0 up to 10, 10 up to 20, 20 up to 30, and so on.

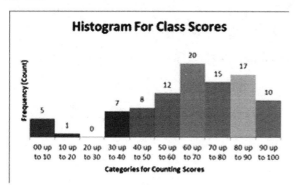

The "gap width" between columns is zero. This is to visually indicate that there are no values possible between categories. The height of each column is the number of scores (in our example) counted in that category.

Figure 995

Bar Charts

Bar charts are very similar to column charts, except that the bars are horizontal rather than vertical. Bar charts are good for emphasizing differences across categories.

Like Column Charts, the source data can come from a range of numbers that have row headers (legend) and column headers (categories). Visually it is easier to decipher the differences between bar lengths when they are oriented horizontally rather than vertically. Hint: Column charts have vertical bars, and bar charts have horizontal bars.

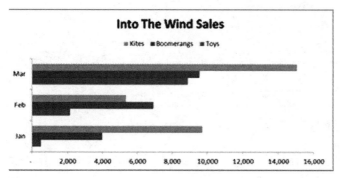

Figure 996

Stacked Bar or Column Charts

Stacked bar charts are good for when you want to see bars compared across categories, but within each bar you can see a color coding that indicates the amount of the bar that came from each legend name.

Like the column or bar charts, the source data can come from a range of numbers that have row headers (legend) and column headers (categories). Hint: Column charts have vertical bars, and bar charts have horizontal bars.

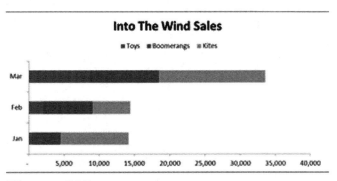

Figure 997

Line Charts

Line charts are good for showing up or down trends across categories. Line charts have a non-numeric category for the horizontal axis and a numeric category or variable for the vertical axis. Even if the horizontal axis contains a variable like year, which is a number, it is considered a non-numeric category because the distance between each new category is always the same.

This is in stark contrast to an X-Y scatter chart, where there are two numeric variables. Line charts have only one numeric variable, and it is listed on the vertical axis.

Like the column or bar charts, the source data can come from a range of numbers that have row headers (legend) and column headers (categories).

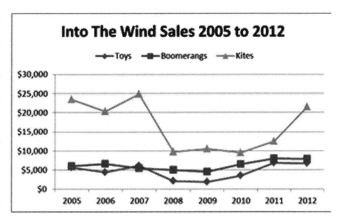

Figure 998

Remember X-Y scatter charts and line charts are not the same. Line charts have one numeric variable, whereas X-Y scatter charts have two numeric variables.

X-Y Scatter Charts

X-Y scatter charts are for when you have two numeric variables and you want to plot an X value or independent value on the horizontal axis and a Y value or dependent value on the vertical axis.

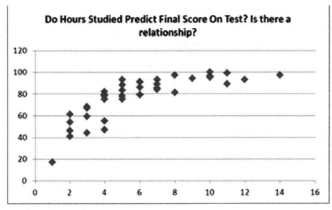

Figure 999

When setting up the data in the worksheet, the X values should be in the first column with a series name in the first row, and the Y values should be in the second column with a series name in the first row.

This gives each row in the data set an X value and a Y value. Excel plots these by moving left or right on the horizontal axis by the X distance and then up or down the vertical axis by the Y distance.

Remember X-Y scatter charts and line charts are not the same. Line charts have one numeric variable, whereas X-Y scatter charts have two numeric variables.

Our next Excel Efficiency-Robust Rule is as follows:

Rule 42: The two rules for charts are 1) Choose the best chart type that matches the data type and the particular message you are delivering, and 2) eliminate chart junk.

Next we cover the general guidelines for creating and formatting charts.

Creating and Formatting Charts

Creating and formatting charts can be accomplished with these general steps:
1. Highlight range with labels (categories) and numeric data (series).
2. Select the chart type:
   a. Go to Insert tab, Charts group, and select your preference from the Chart Type drop-down list.
   b. The F11 key will create the default chart on a new sheet.
   c. Alt, F1 will create the default chart on the current sheet.
3. Look at chart elements such as columns, pie pieces, axes, and legends to determine whether they need to be changed to enhance your visual message.

4. Select chart element to format with one of these three methods:
   a. Click Chart Element.
   b. Once the chart is selected, use arrow keys to cycle through the chart elements.
   c. Go to Chart Tools Layout or the Format tab, Current Selection group (far left), and select Chart Element from drop-down list.
5. To format elements of the chart (such as change column color, change axis interval length, change legend placement, and so on), do the following:
   a. After selecting Chart Element, use Ctrl + 1 to open the Format Chart Element dialog box.
   b. After selecting Chart Element, right-click and point to the Format element item on the submenu.
   c. Use any of the Chart Tools ribbon tabs or the formatting options in the Home tab.

Note: If the chart is not selected, the context-sensitive Chart Tools ribbon tabs will not appear.

Now I'm sure you want see how to make each one of the charts listed earlier (Figures 993 to 999). We'll start with a pie chart.

Pie Charts

In Figure 1000, we can see a range that shows the amount for each funding source. Our goal is to visualize the data so that we see how much each item contributes to the total and show the percentages for each item. Anytime you have a situation where there are parts that make up a whole or total or you want to show percentages of the total, you can use a pie chart. Because we are creating a pie charts, the labels in column A will be the category names for the legend, the numeric values in column B will be the series values that create the pieces of the pie, and the word *Amount* in cell B1 (directly above the numeric values) will be become the series name. (This name becomes important if you edit the source range later.)

To follow along, open the file named excelisfun-Start.xlsm and navigate to the C(1) sheet.

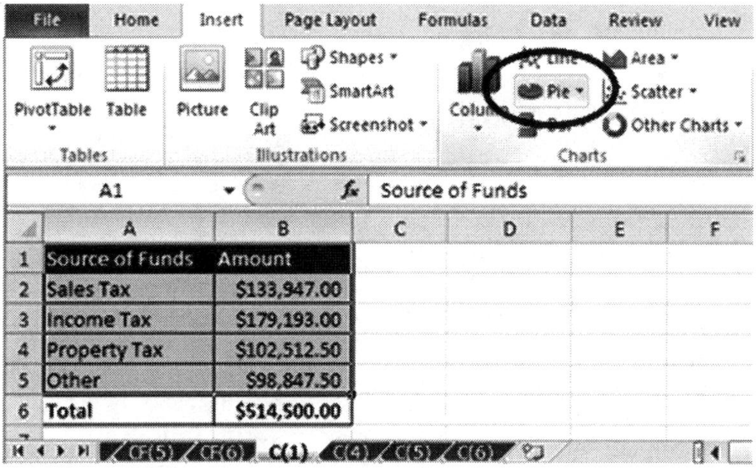

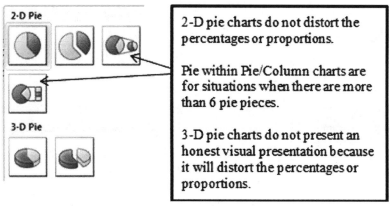

Figure 1000

1. On the sheet C(1) sheet, highlight the range A1:B5.
    Do not highlight totals when making a pie chart.
2. Go to Insert tab, Charts group, and click the Pie Chart drop-down list.

2-D Pie

2-D pie charts do not distort the percentages or proportions.

Pie within Pie/Column charts are for situations when there are more than 6 pie pieces.

3-D Pie

3-D pie charts do not present an honest visual presentation because it will distort the percentages or proportions.

Figure 1001

3. Select the first pie chart (first option in the first row).

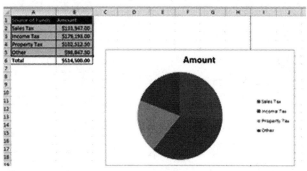

Figure 1002

The chart gets placed on top of the current sheet. This chart still needs a good title and it needs to show percentage labels.

Linking Chart Labels to Cells

In Figure 1003, you can see the words *Source of Funds* in cell A1. Our goal is to link the chart title to this cell so that if we change the contents of cell A1, the chart title will update. Linking chart elements can be done by creating formulas in the formula bar.

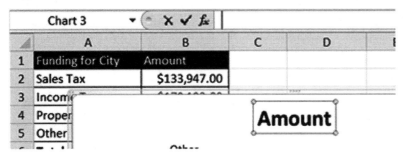

Figure 1003

4. To link the chart title to cell A1, click the chart title. Make sure that you see the translucent circles at each corner of the chart title.
5. Click in the formula bar. The cursor should be flashing (as shown in this figure).
6. Type an equal sign.

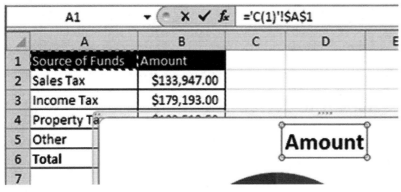

Figure 1004

7. Click in cell A1.

You should see the following formula in the formula bar: ='C(1)'!$A$1

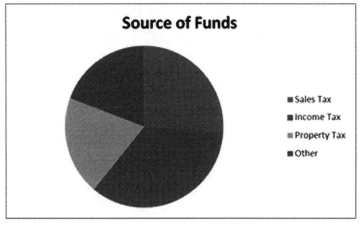

Figure 1005

8. Press Enter to put the formula into the chart title.

The chart should look like Figure 1005.

Adding Chart Data Labels

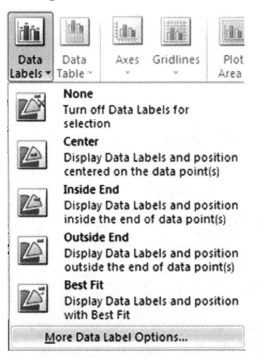

Figure 1006

9. With the chart selected, go to the Chart Tools Layout tab, Labels group, and click the Data Labels drop-down arrow, and then click More Data Label Options in the drop-down list.

10. With the Label options tab selected on the left, check the check boxes for Category Name, Value, Percentage, and Show Leader Lines.

11. Click the Close button.

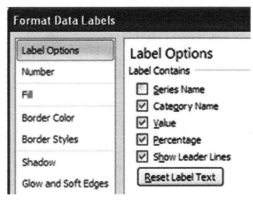

Figure 1007

12. Now we have chart junk because the category names are listed twice.

13. To delete the legend, click it to select it, and then press the Delete key.

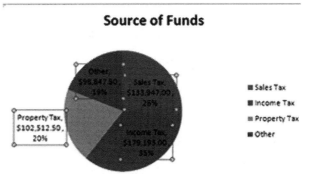

Figure 1008

14. To select a single data label object, click the label once, wait one second, and then click it a second time. This is called a *slow double-click*.

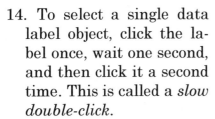

Figure 1009

15. To move the data label outward and show the leader line, point to the edge of the data label until you see the move cursor (four-way-pointing thin black arrow with a larger white diagonal-pointing arrow on top), and then click and drag the label outward.

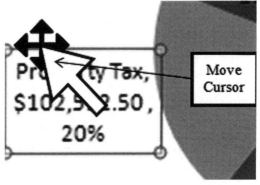

Figure 1010

16. Repeat this for each label.

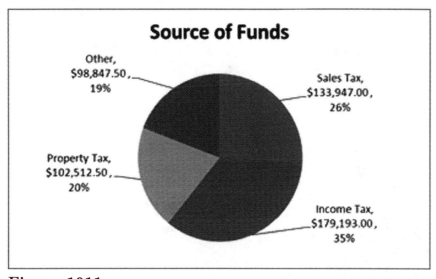

Figure 1011

The chart should look something like Figure 1011.

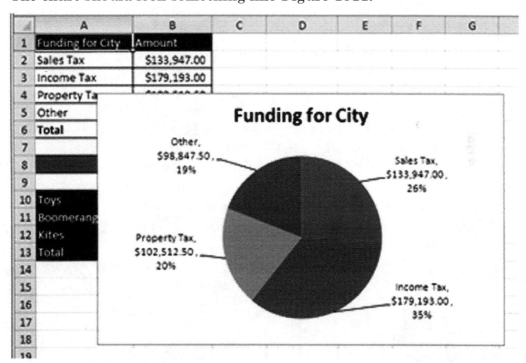

Figure 1012

17. Type **Funding for City** in cell A1, the chart title will update because it is linked to cell A1.

Moving Charts

Because a chart is considered an object, we can move the chart like we move any other object. The key is to point to the outside edge of the chart and when you see the move cursor, we can click, hold, and drag. Figure 1013 shows an example of the move cursor. (It is not really that big.)

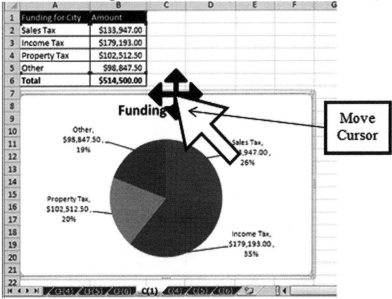

Figure 1013

Printing Charts

Figure 1013 shows that the chart has been placed on the worksheet. Printing can be accomplished by using the keyboard shortcut Ctrl + P. However, when you have a chart on a sheet, Printing can do one of two things:

- If *only* the chart is selected (your cursor is not selecting a cell in the worksheet), Figure 1014 shows you what would print out.
- If a cell is selected in the worksheet, Figure 1015 shows you what would print out.

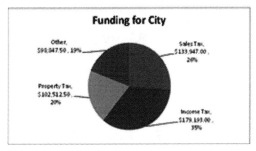

Figure 1014

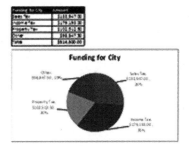

Figure 1015

For full details of how to complete page setup before printing, see Chapter 4, "Style Formatting and Page Setup."

Next we want to see how to change a chart style.

Changing Chart Styles

In Figure 1016, we can see it takes two steps to change the chart style:
1. Select the chart.
2. Go to Chart Tools Design tab and select Style from the Chart Styles group.

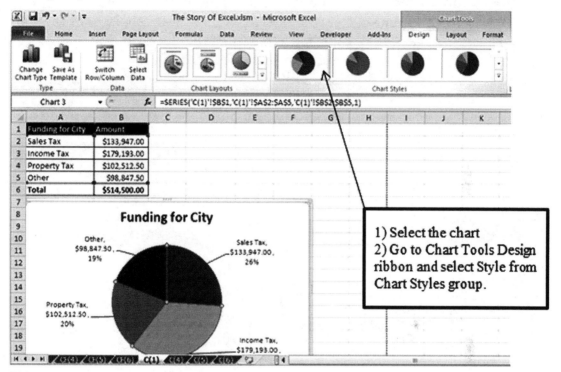

Figure 1016

Next we want save a chart template and set the default chart.

Saving Chart Templates

When you create a chart that you may want to use in other situations, you can save the chart as a template as follows:

1. Select the chart.
2. Go to Chart Tools Design tab, Type group, and click the Save as Template button (see Figure 1017).
3. Name the file and click the Save button (see Figure 1018).
4. To use the template for a chart, select cells in worksheet, and then go to Insert tab and click the Create Chart dialog Launcher in the lower-right corner of the Charts group (see Figure 1019).
5. Select the Template Folder tab on the left side of the Change Chart Type dialog box.(see Figure 1020).
6. Select desired template under My Templates header (see Figure 1020)

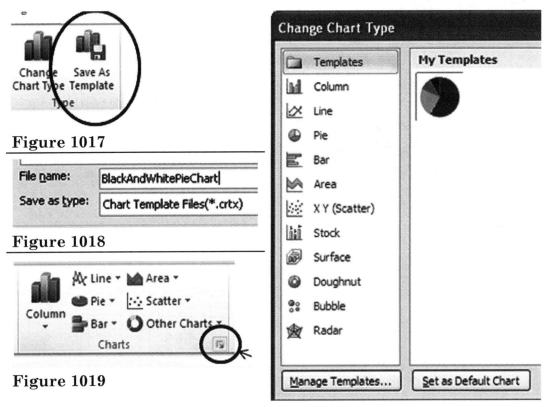

Figure 1017

Figure 1018

Figure 1019

Figure 1020

Setting Default Charts

Setting the default chart is important if you want to be able to create complete charts with a keyboard shortcut (as discussed more fully in the next section). In Figure 1020, you can see that the Change Chart Type dialog box has a Set as Default Chart button in the lower-right corner. To set the default chart, complete these steps:

1. Select a chart in the Change Chart Type dialog box.
2. Click the Set as Default Chart button in the lower-right corner.

Next we want to create complete charts with a keyboard shortcut.

Keyboard Shortcuts to Create Complete Charts

After setting the default chart to your preference (or keeping the default column chart), you can select the source data in the worksheet and use these one-click chart-creation keyboard shortcuts:

- To create the default chart from the selected data and place the chart on top of the worksheet with the source data, press Alt+F1.
- To create the default chart from the selected data and place the chart as a new sheet, press F11.

Next you'll learn how to create a column chart.

Column Charts

In Figure 1021, a range shows us what the sales were for each item within each month. Our goal is to visualize the data so that we see the differences between the months for each item sold. Whenever you want to look at differences across categories, you can use a column chart. Because we are creating a column chart, the labels in column A will appear in the legend, the labels in the range B2:D2 will appear on the horizontal axis, and the numeric values will determine the height of the columns.

To follow along, open the file named excelisfun-Start.xlsm and navigate to the C(2) sheet.

	A	B	C	D	E
1		Into The Wind Sales			
2		Jan	Feb	Mar	Total
3	Toys	500	2,150	8,893	11,543
4	Boomerangs	4,000	6,933	9,545	20,478
5	Kites	9,721	5,367	15,064	30,152
6	Total	14,221	14,450	33,502	62,173
7					

CF(4) / CF(5) / CF(6) / C(1) / C(2) / C(3)

Figure 1021

1. On the C(2) sheet, highlight the range A2:D5. (Do not highlight totals.)
2. Go to Insert tab, Charts group, and click the Column Chart drop-down list, and then click the first item: Clustered Column.

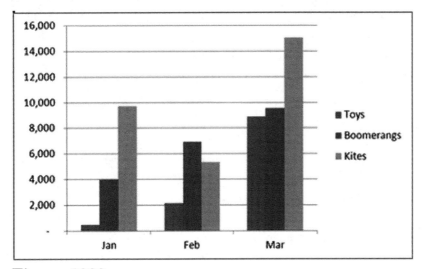

Figure 1022

With this column chart, we can see the differences in sales for each item across the three months.

We can notice trends like the fact that sales are going up over the three months except for the one drop in kite sales for the month of February.

Next we want to add a chart title.

3. To add a chart title, go to Chart Tools Layout tab, Labels group, and click the Chart Title dropdown list, and then click Above Chart.

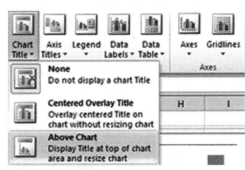

Figure 1023

4. To link the chart title to cell A1, click the chart title. Make sure that you see the translucent circles at each corner of the chart title.

5. Click in the formula bar, type an equal sign, and then click in cell A1.

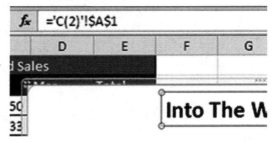

Figure 1024

6. The following formula should be in the formula bar:
    ='C(2)'!$A$1

7. Press Enter to put the formula into the chart title.

Figure 1025 shows the finished column chart.

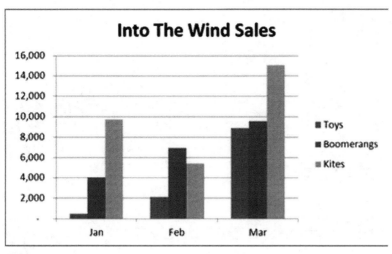

Figure 1025

Next we want to look at a special column chart called a histogram.

Histograms

Histograms are a special type of column chart where the horizontal categories are grouped numbers, such as 0 up to 10, 10 up to 20, 20 up to 30, and so on, and where the gap width between each column is zero. The "zero gap width" visually indicates that there are no values possible between categories.

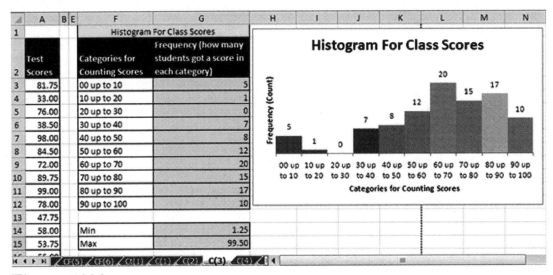

Figure 1026

Figure 1026 shows an example of when a histogram is perfect for visualizing data. The scores for a student test are in column A, and we need to count how many students got a score in the categories:

- From 90 up to (but not including) 100. In math symbols, it would be as follows:

   $90 >= Score < 100$

- From 80 up to (but not including) 90. In math symbols it would be as follows:

   $80 >= Score < 90$

- Etc.

For example, we can see the following:

- Ten students got a score in the category 90 up to 100, which means those 10 students got a score in the 90s.
- Seventeen students got a score in the category 80 up to 90, which means those 17 students got a score in the 80s.

Note: We saw this same sort of "between" criteria for counting in Chapter 5, "Formulas and Functions," in the "COUNTIFS (for counting with two criteria)" section and in the "Frequency Distribution" and the "Advanced Filter" sections of Chapter 6, "Data Analysis Features."

You can see how useful a chart like this can be. The keys for deciding when to use a histogram are as follows

- There are grouped number categories with an upper and lower limit.
- The categories do not overlap, and therefore there are no gaps between the columns.

Now let's see how to create this chart.

To follow along, open the file named excelisfun-Start.xlsm and navigate to the C(3) sheet.

	A	B	C	D	E	F	G	H	I	J
1						Histogram For Class Scores				
2	Test Scores		Lower	Upper		Grouped Number Categories	How Many Students Got A Score In Each Category			
3	81.75		0	10		00 up to 10	=COUNTIFS($A$3:$A$97,">="&C3,$A$3:$A$97,"<"&D3)			
4	33.00		10	20		10 up to 20	COUNTIFS(criteria_range1, criteria1, [criteria_range2, **criteria2**], [c			
5	76.00		20	30		20 up to 30	0			
6	38.50		30	40		30 up to 40	7			
7	98.00		40	50		40 up to 50	8			
8	84.50		50	60		50 up to 60	12			
9	72.00		60	70		60 up to 70	20			
10	89.75		70	80		70 up to 80	15			
11	99.00		80	90		80 up to 90	17			
12	78.00		90	100		90 up to 100	10			

Figure 1027

1. On the C(3) sheet click in cell G3 and create the following formula:

=COUNTIFS($A$3:$A$97,">="&C3,$A$3:$A$97,"<"&D3)

To remind yourself how to create this formula and what it means, look back to Figure 312 and Figure 506 and then re-read those sections.

2. Copy the formula in cell G3 into the range G3:G12.

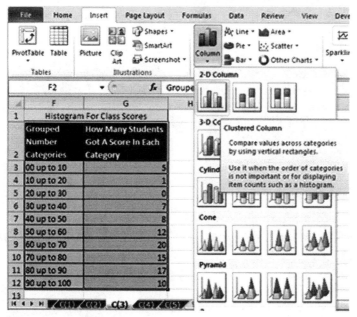

3. Select the range F2:G12.

4. Go to Insert tab, Charts group, and click the Column chart drop-down list, and then click the first item: Clustered Column.

5. Immediately click the legend and press the Delete key.

Figure 1028

6. To format the columns, click a single time on one of the columns so that all the columns are selected. You can tell that all the columns are selected because all the columns have translucent circles in each corner.

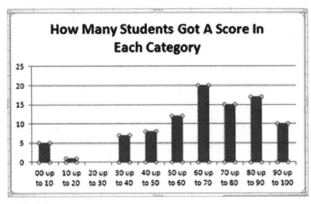

Figure 1029

The chart should look like the one in Figure 1029.

In Figure 1029, you can see that all the columns are selected. You select all columns by clicking one of the columns (clicking a single time). When all the columns are selected, you can format them collectively, like change the color and change the gap width. If you want to format a single column and none of the rest, you just click one time, wait a moment, and then click a second time (slow double-click). With our columns selected, we are going to change the color and gap width.

Just as with the Format Cells dialog box for formatting cells, the Format Chart Element dialog boxes can be opened with the keyboard shortcut Ctrl + 1.

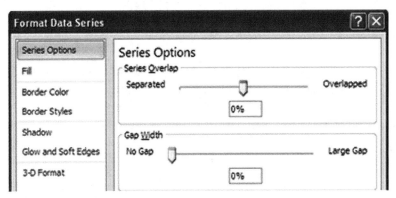

Figure 1030

7. Press Ctrl + 1 to open the Format Data Series dialog box.
8. With the Series tab (on left) selected, change the gap width to 0 (zero) by sliding the Gap Width bar.

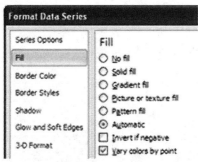

Figure 1031

9. With the Fill tab (on left) selected, check the Vary Colors by Point check box.
10. Click the Close button.

Figure 1032

11. To add data labels (values, height of column), right-click the columns and click Add Data Labels.

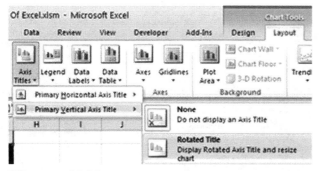

Figure 1033

12. Next, go to Chart Tools Layout tab, Labels group, and click the axis titles, and then on the submenu point to Primary Vertical Axis Title, and then on the submenu click Rotated Title.
13. Immediately type the words **Frequency of Count**, and then press Enter. (Flip to the next page for a larger view of the resulting chart)

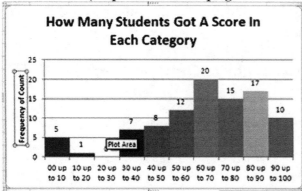

In Figure 1034, we can see the vertical axis title.

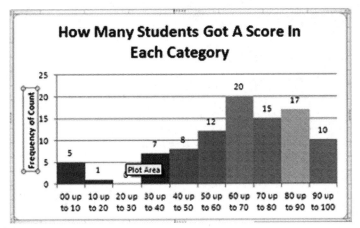

Figure 1034

The keys to creating labels when you are not linking them to the cells (as we did earlier) are to follow these three steps:

    a. Add a label.

    b. Immediately type label words.

    c. Press Enter.

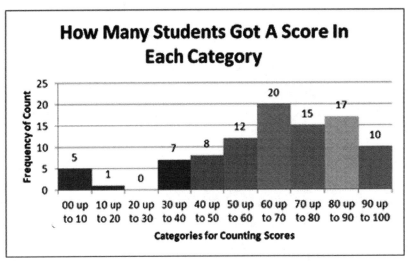

Figure 1035

14. Go to Chart Tools Layout tab, Labels group, and click the axis titles, and then on the submenu point to Primary Horizontal Axis Title, and then on the submenu click Title Below Axis.

15. Immediately type the words **Categories for Counting Scores**, and then press Enter.

Figure 1035 shows us our finished histogram. Next we want to take a look at a bar chart.

Bar Charts

Bar charts are similar to column charts except that the bars are horizontal rather than vertical. This gets confusing sometimes because how people speak about column and bar charts is not always consistent. In Excel, this is the difference:

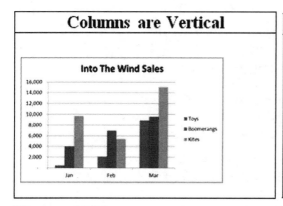

Figure 1036

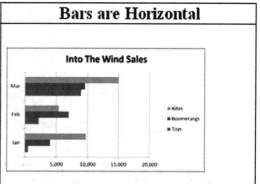

Figure 1037

Column and bar charts are both good for visualizing data when you want to show differences across categories. However, the column chart will tend to show up and down movement across the categories or trends better than a bar chart, and the bar chart will tend to show differences across categories better than a column chart. Further, like column charts, the bar chart is great for data sets that have row and column headers (PivotTables often summarize data in this form). One last distinction: The bar chart is great when you have category labels that are really long.

Let's take a look at how to create a bar chart.

To follow along, open the file named excelisfun-Start.xlsm and navigate to the C(4) sheet.

1. On the C(4) sheet, highlight the range A2:D5. (Do not highlight totals.)
2. Go to Insert tab, Charts group, and click the Bar Chart drop-down list, and then click the first item: Clustered Bar.
3. To add a chart title, go to Chart Tools Layout tab, Labels group, and click the Chart Title drop-down list, and then click Above Chart.
4. To link the chart title to cell A1, click in the formula bar, type an equal sign, and click in cell A1.

The following formula should be in the formula bar:

='C(4)'!$A$1

5. Press Enter to put the formula into the chart title.
6. Click the Legend and press Ctrl + 1 to open the Format Legend dialog box.

7. To place the legend at the top of the chart, click the Top dialog box (see Figure 1038).

8. Click Close.

9. The finished chart should look like Figure 1039.

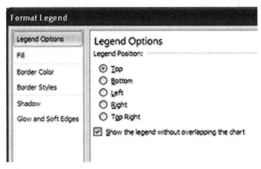

Figure 1038

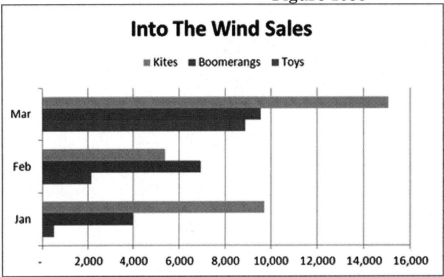

Figure 1039

Next we want to look at creating a stacked chart from our clustered chart.

Copying Charts and Changing Chart Types

The Change Chart Type option is great for when you want to create different charts from the same set of data. Here are the steps to create five charts:

    a. Create your first chart 1.

    b. Click outer edge of chart and press Ctrl + C to copy the chart

    c. Click in a cell and press Ctrl + V to paste a copy of the chart.

    d. With the second chart still selected, go to the Chart Tools Design tab and click the Change Chart Type button from Type group, and then select a new chart type.

    e. Repeat steps 3 and 4 three more times to create all five charts.

In Figure 1040, that chart was created from the chart shown in Figure 1039 by just copying, pasting, and then changing the chart type!

Stacked Bar or Column Charts

Stacked bar charts are good for when you want to see bars compared across categories, but within each bar you can see a color coding that indicates the amount of the bar that came from each legend name (see Figure 1040). This stacked option is available for both a column chart and a bar chart. The great thing about this sort of chart is that it is like getting two charts in one: 1) The bar or column shows the total for the category item (in Figure 1040, it shows the total for the month), and 2) then within the column you get a color coding for the items listed in the legend.

Now we want to see how to create a stacked bar chart from the bar chart we made in the previous example.

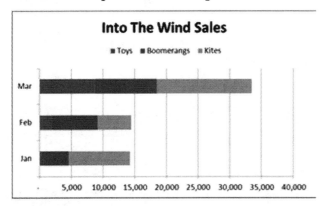

Figure 1040

1. On the C(4) sheet, select the bar chart as shown in Figure 1039 (the one you just created).
2. To copy the chart, press Ctrl + C.
3. Click in cell E23 and press Ctrl + V to paste the copied chart.
4. Go to the Chart Tools Design tab and click the Change Chart Type button from Type group.
5. Scroll down and select the second option for bar charts: Stacked Bar.
6. Click OK.

The chart should look like Figure 1040.

Now let's look at a line chart.

Line Charts

Line charts are good for showing up or down trends across categories. Line charts have a non-numeric category for the horizontal axis and a numeric category or variable for the vertical axis. Line charts have only one numeric variable, and it is listed on the vertical axis. Even if the horizontal axis contains a variable like year, which is a number, it is considered a non-numeric category because the distance between each new category is always the same (see Figure 1041). This is in stark contrast to an X-Y scatter chart (next example), which always has two numeric variables.

Line charts have *one* numeric variable (vertical only).	X-Y scatter charts have *two* numeric variables (horizontal and vertical)

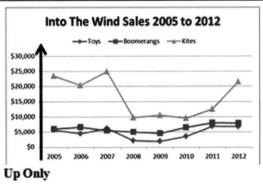

Up Only	Out and Up
Figure 1041	**Figure 1042**

Line charts have categories that are equidistant on the horizontal axis and a numeric variable on the vertical axis that determines how high the line is above the horizontal axis.	X-Y scatter charts have a numeric variable on the horizontal axis that determines how far out to go on the horizontal axis *and then* from that point the numeric variable on the vertical axis determines how far up the vertical axis to move.

One other important note about line charts: Like the column or bar charts, the source data can come from a range of numbers that have row headers (legend) and column headers (categories).

Now let's create a line chart.

To follow along, open the file named excelisfun-Start.xlsm and navigate to the C(5) sheet.

1. On the C(5) sheet, highlight the range A2:I5.

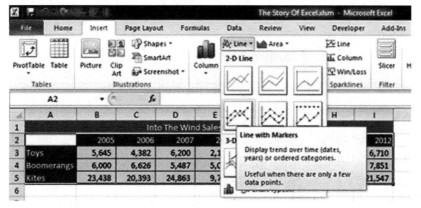

Figure 1043

2. Go to Insert tab, Charts group, and click the Line Chart drop-down list, and then click the first item in the second row called: Line with Markers.

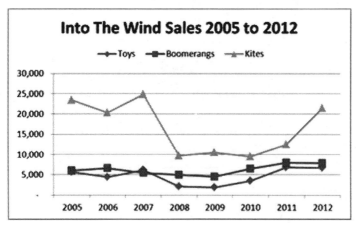

Figure 1044

3. To add a chart title, go to Chart Tools Layout tab, Labels group, and click the Chart Title drop-down list, and then click Above Chart.
4. To link the chart title to cell A1, click in the formula bar, type an equal sign, and then click in cell A1.

You should see this formula in the formula bar:

   ='C(5)'!$A$1

5. Press Enter to put the formula into the chart title.
6. Click the legend and press Ctrl + 1 to open the Format Legend dialog box.
7. To place the legend at the top of the chart, click the Top option button.
8. Click Close.

Notice in Figure 1044 that we are not sure whether the vertical axis is in units or in dollars. It is always important to label axes so that there is no confusion. Remember, if your visual message is to be understood quickly, you don't want the viewer getting tripped up asking questions like "what's that?" In this chart, we can probably get away with not labeling the horizontal axis with a Years label, but we must indicate that the vertical axis is in dollars. We will do this with the Currency number format.

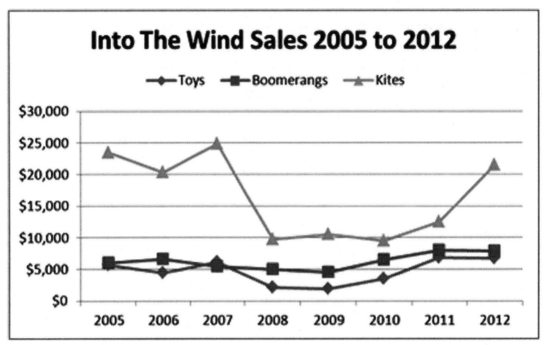

Figure 1045

1. To add Currency number formatting to the vertical axis, click the axis to select it.
2. To open the Format Axis dialog box, press Ctrl + 1
3. On the left, click the Number tab.
4. Select Currency number formatting and show 0 (zero) decimals.
5. Click Close.

Next we want to look at an X-Y scatter chart.

X-Y Scatter Charts

X-Y scatter charts are for when you have two numeric variables and you want to plot an X value (independent value) on the horizontal axis and a Y value (dependent value) on the vertical axis. When setting up the data in the worksheet, the X values should be in the first column of the data set, and the Y values should be in the second column (see Figures 1048 and 1049). This gives each row in the data set a pair of values (X value and a Y value). Excel will plot each pair of values by moving on the horizontal axis (left or right) by the X distance and then moving on the vertical axis (up or down) by the Y distance. We can use the X-Y scatter chart in one of two ways:

- We can show the paired points on the chart with an estimated line that reflects the pattern of the points (see Figure 1046).

Or

- We show the paired points on the chart with a line that connects all the points (see Figure 1047).

Also, remember from our earlier discussion: X-Y scatter charts and line charts are not the same. Line charts have one numeric variable, whereas X-Y scatter charts have two numeric variables.

X-Y Scatter with Points and Estimated Line (Trendline)	X-Y Scatter with Points and Line Through Points

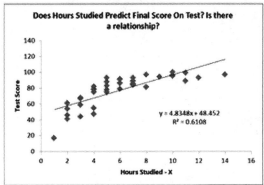 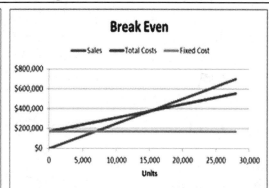

Figure 1046	Figure 1047

Hours Studied - X	Student Scores On Final - Y
5	88
4	82
2	61
4	78
8	81
1	17
11	89
11	99

Figure 1048

Units	Sales	Total Costs	Fixed Cost
0	$0	$171,563	$171,563
3,500	87,500	219,688	171,563
7,000	175,000	267,813	171,563
10,500	262,500	315,938	171,563
14,000	350,000	364,063	171,563
17,500	437,500	412,188	171,563
21,000	525,000	460,313	171,563
24,500	612,500	508,438	171,563
28,000	700,000	556,563	171,563

Figure 1049

Now let's see how to create these two X-Y scatter charts.

Trendlines

Figure 1050 shows the chart we are trying to create. On the horizontal axis (x axis), we will plot the number of hours that each student studied for the final, and on the vertical axis (y axis), we will plot the score that the student earned on the final. For example, if a particular student studied 8 hours and earned an 81 on the final, to plot this point, Excel would count 8 out the horizontal axis (x axis) and then count 81 up the vertical axis (y axis). Excel repeats this for every paired set of numbers to plot all the points (see Figure 1050). The advantage of this visual presentation of the raw data is that we can determine whether any trend in the data may suggest a relationship between the number of hours studied and the score on the final test. From this example, it looks like the trend is "the more you study, the higher the score." Said a different way, if the hours studied goes up, the final score goes up. Because this is an up-up relationship, we call it a direct relationship. There are other relationships, such as indirect, that would be an up-down relationship. (For example, as the number of police goes up, crime goes down.) Here we will only look at direct relationships.

After you have plotted your paired points, it is easy to add a trendline, called a linear regression line, and the algebraic equation that goes with it, with just a few clicks.

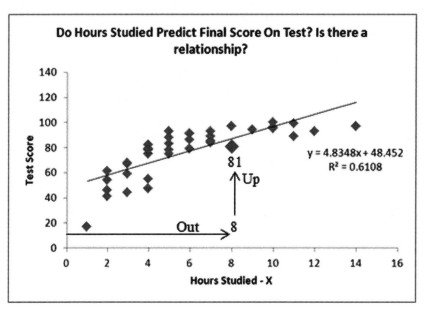

Figure 1050

Now let's see how to create this chart. To follow along, open the file named excelisfun-Start.xlsm and navigate to the C(6) sheet.

1. On the C(6) sheet, highlight the range A2:B40.

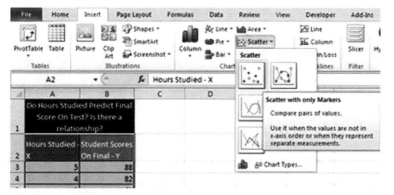

Figure 1051

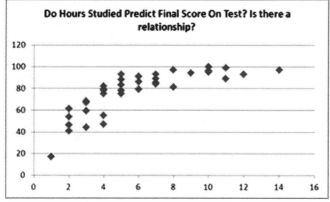

Figure 1052

2. Go to Insert tab, Charts group, and click the Scatter Chart dropdown list, and then click the first item in the first row: Scatter with Only Markers.

3. To link the chart title to cell A1, highlight the default chart title formula in the formula bar, click in cell A1, and press Enter.

4. To change the font size of the chart title, right-click the chart title, click Font, change the font size to 12 in the Font combo box, and then click OK.

5. To delete legend, click the legend and press the Delete key.

The chart should look like Figure 1052 at this point.

6. To add a vertical axis title and link it to cell B2, go to Chart Tools Layout tab, Labels group, and click the axis titles, and then on the submenu point to Primary Vertical Axis Title, and then on the submenu click Rotated Title.

7. To link the axis title to cell B2, click in the formula bar, type an equal sign, click in cell B2, and press Enter.

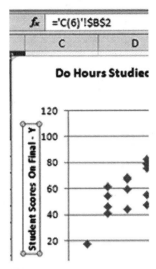

Figure 1053

When the label is selected you should see your formula in the formula bar.

8. To add a horizontal axis title and link it to cell A2, go to Chart Tools Layout tab, Labels group, and click the axis titles, and then on the submenu point to Primary Vertical Axis, and then on the submenu click Title Below Axis.

9. To link the axis title to cell A2, click in the formula bar, type an equal sign, click in cell A2, and press Enter.

Figure 1054

10. To add our trendline, right-click any one of the paired points, and then click Add Trendline.

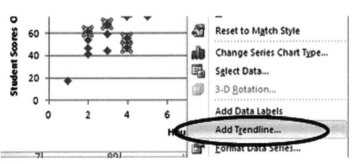

Figure 1055

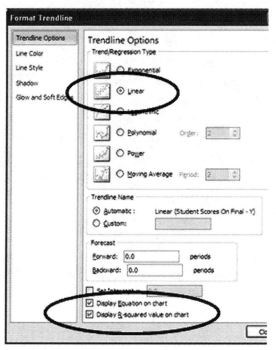

11. When the Format Trendline dialog box appears, click the dialog button for Linear, and then check the Display Equation on Chart and the Display R-Squared Value on Chart check boxes.

The line created is done by a mathematical process called least squares method. This equation gives use the general math equation y = mx + b.

R-squared is a measure that shows the amount of influence x has on y (not causation).

Figure 1056

12. To remove the horizontal gridlines (background gray lines), click the gridlines, and when you see that they are selected, press the Delete key.

13. To move the equation and R-square, click the edge of the label and drag it to a new location.

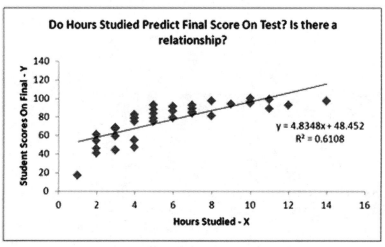

The finished chart should look like Figure 1057.

Figure 1057

Next we want to see how to create an X-Y scatter chart for a break-even analysis.

Break-Even Analysis

Another way to use an X-Y scatter chart is to plot the lines and run a line through all the points. A common business use of this type of chart is a break-even chart, where the horizontal axis (x axis) shows the units sold and the horizontal axis (y axis) shows dollars for both sales and costs (revenue and expenses). A break-even chart shows a line for sales and a line for total costs and the intersection of the two (crossover) shows the break-even point, or the point at which profit is zero. In Figure 1058, we can see those two lines plus a horizontal line for the fixed costs. Everything to the left of the crossover point shows the region where profits are below zero (loss), and everything to the right of the crossover point shows the region where profits are above zero (profit). Just as with the chart we did in the preceding example, the x values must be in the first column, and the y values go in the columns to the right of the x values. (Notice in our figure that we have three columns to the right; all three of these columns will be separate y values.) The steps for creating this chart are listed below.

To follow along, open the file named excelisfun-Start.xlsm and navigate to the C(7) sheet.

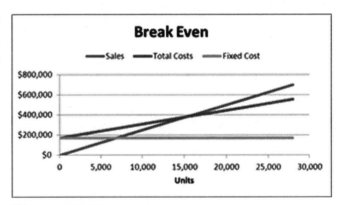

Figure 1058

1. On the C(7) sheet, highlight the range A1:D10.
2. Go to Insert tab, Charts group, and click the Scatter Chart drop-down list, and then click the first item in the second row: Scatter with Smooth Lines.

Units	Sales	Total Costs	Fixed Cost
0	$0	$171,563	$171,563
3,500	87,500	219,688	171,563
7,000	175,000	267,813	171,563
10,500	262,500	315,938	171,563
14,000	350,000	364,063	171,563
17,500	437,500	412,188	171,563
21,000	525,000	460,313	171,563
24,500	612,500	508,438	171,563
28,000	700,000	556,563	171,563

Figure 1059

3. To add a chart title go to Chart Tools Layout tab, Labels group, and click the Chart Title drop-down list, and then click Above Chart.

4. Type the words **Break Even**, and then press Enter.
5. To move the legend, click the legend, press Ctrl + 1 to open the Format Legend dialog box, and then click the option button for Top. Click Close.
6. To add a horizontal axis title and link it to cell A2, go to Chart Tools Layout tab, Labels group, and click the Axis Titles, and then on the submenu point to Primary Vertical Axis, and then on the submenu click Title Below Axis.
7. Type the word **Units** and press Enter.
8. Both axes should have the correct number formatting because the chart will pick up the number formatting from the cells.

The chart should look like Figure 1058.

Next we want to see how to add two different chart types to one chart.

Two Chart Types in One Chart

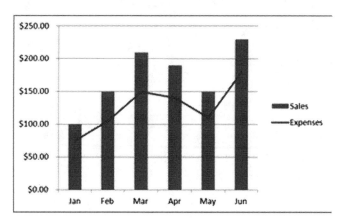

Sometimes using just one chart type is not enough to articulate your desired message. For example, in Figure 1060, we can see a line chart type is being used for expenses, and the column chart type is being used for the revenue.

Figure 1060

Combining these two charts together does two things: reduces the clutter in the chart and helps to more effectively deliver a message. In essence, the solid columns show the revenues (backbone of any business) while the trending line shows how expenses are changing over time.

Selecting/Editing Source Data for a Chart

Figure 1060 shows two chart types in one chart. The columns represent the sales figures, and the line represents the expenses. To see how to create this chart, we are going to start with an existing chart that has sales data only, and then we will "add source data" to add the expense values, and finally we will change the chart type. Although there are several ways to create a chart like this, we want to learn important tricks that will help us when we get to more complicated charts:

- To edit the source ranges for the legend names, or the data on the horizontal axis (categories), or the data on the vertical axis (series), go to Chart Tools Design tab, Data group, and click the Select Data button. The Select Data Source dialog box enables you to add, delete, or edit the data source. For many advanced charts, this provides the real power because you get to decide what elements go into the chart and where they go.
- We can change the chart type for one data series in the chart by selecting the data series, going to the Chart Tools Design tab, Type group, and clicking the Change Chart Type button. For many advanced charts, this provides the real power because you are not limited to the built-in templates.

To follow along, open the file named excel-isfun-Start.xlsm and navigate to the C(8) sheet.

Figure 1061

1. On the C(8) sheet, select the chart.
2. To edit the source ranges, go to Chart Tools Design tab, Data group, and click the Select Data button.

In the Select Data Source dialog box, notice that the left side allows you to Add, Edit, or Remove Series Values; and the *right side* allows you to Edit the Horizontal Categories.

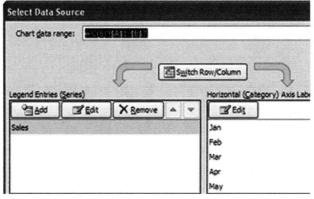

Figure 1062

3. Click the Add button.

Figure 1063

4. Click in the Series Name field and then click in cell C1.

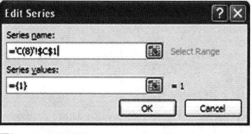

Figure 1064

5. Highlight the default value in the Series Values field.

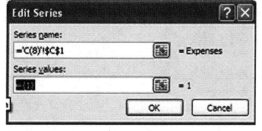

Figure 1065

6. With the default value in the Series Values field highlighted, press the Delete key.

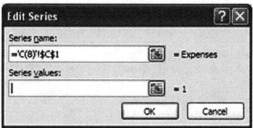

Figure 1066

7. With the default value removed from the Series Values field, select the range C2:C7.
8. Click OK in the Edit Series dialog box.
9. Click OK in the Select Data Source dialog box.

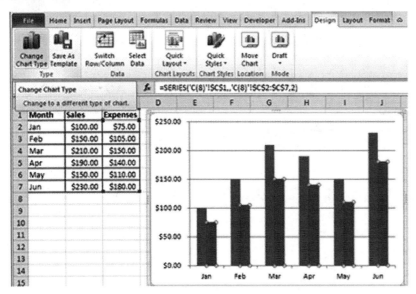

Figure 1067

10. With the Expense columns selected, our goal is to change the Chart Type. Go to Chart Tools Design tab, Type group, and click the Change Chart Type button.
11. From the Change Chart Type dialog box, select a line chart.
12. Click OK.

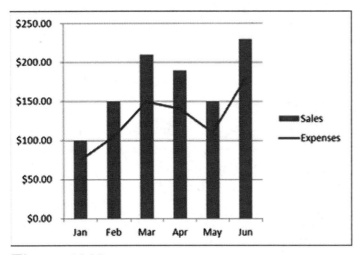

Figure 1068

The finished Chart Should look like Figure 1068

The last thing we want to look at in this charting section is a new feature in Excel 2010 called sparklines.

Sparklines

Sparklines are an amazing new feature in Excel 2010 that enable you to make charts in cells (another amazing visualization trick that I first saw from the quantitative chart master Edward Tufte). Figure 1069 shows sparklines in the range B1:G1 that reflect the sales data in the range B3:G7. Each one of the cells in the range B1:G1 contains a chart that reflects the sales data in the column. In addition, the cell charts are dynamic. So, as the source data changes, the sparklines will update. There is even a Sparkline Tools Design tab from which you can format the sparklines. Amazing!

	A	B	C	D	E	F	G	H
1								
2		Bellen	Carlota	Sunshine	Aspen	Sunset	Quad	
3	Day 1	$141	$179	$188	$196	$150	$174	
4	Day 2	$174	$155	$129	$123	$129	$189	
5	Day 3	$177	$163	$160	$136	$178	$190	
6	Day 4	$168	$182	$121	$175	$171	$168	
7	Day 5	$121	$178	$197	$175	$194	$144	
8								

Figure 1069

To follow along, open the file named excelisfun-Start.xlsm and navigate to the C(9) sheet.

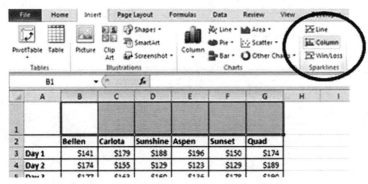

Figure 1070

1. On the C(9) sheet, select the range B1:G1.
2. Go to Insert tab, Sparklines group, and click the Column button as shown in Figure 1070.
3. In the Data Range field in the Create Sparklines dialog box, select B3:G7.
4. Click OK.

Your cell charts should look like Figure 1069.

5. To remove sparklines, select the cells with the sparklines, right-click, and select Clear Selected Sparklines.

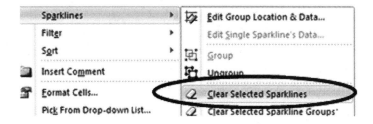

Figure 1071

Figure 1072 shows an example of the same data with a line cell chart and various formatting elements applied from the Sparkline Tools Design tab.

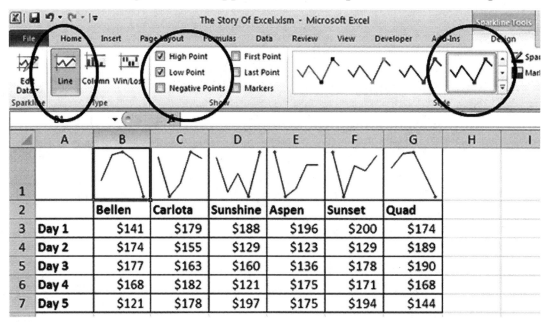

	A	B	C	D	E	F	G	H	I
1									
2		Bellen	Carlota	Sunshine	Aspen	Sunset	Quad		
3	Day 1	$141	$179	$188	$196	$200	$174		
4	Day 2	$174	$155	$129	$123	$129	$189		
5	Day 3	$177	$163	$160	$136	$178	$190		
6	Day 4	$168	$182	$121	$175	$171	$168		
7	Day 5	$121	$178	$197	$175	$194	$144		

Figure 1072

Wow! That was a lot about visualizing quantitative data with charts and sparklines.

Next we want to look at the Conditional Formatting feature in Excel, which we cover in the next chapter.

CONDITIONAL FORMATTING

The Conditional Formatting feature allows you to add formatting to cells based on a condition such as "item is a duplicate" *or* "value is above average" or "value is in top 10%," or other criteria. Figure 1073 shows an example of each of these conditions.

⊿	A	B	C	D	E	F
1	Hilights Duplicates		Above Average		Top 10%	
2	Customer		Sales		Sales	
3	Rod Kloer Firm		3.04		3.04	
4	Hal Hinchliff Firm		19.41		19.41	
5	Hal Hinchliff Firm		18.87		18.87	
6	Shakia Warning Inc.		6.9		6.9	
7	Cliff Stalworth Firm		11.37		11.37	
8	Jackson Kings LLP		18.89		18.89	
9	Jackson Kings LLP		18.59		18.59	
10	Rob Swearegene Company		7.36		7.36	
11	Marcel Mittelsteadt Firm		13.05		13.05	
12	Rob Schiesher LLP		4.29		4.29	
13	Jackson Kings LLP		11.24		11.24	
14						

Figure 1073

In Figure 1073, each one of these conditions is really a question or logical test that either comes out TRUE or FALSE. For example, consider these questions:

- Is this item in the list a duplicate?
- Is this value in the list above the average value?
- Is this value in the list in the top 10% of values?

The answer to each one is either TRUE or FALSE. For conditional formatting, if the answer to the question is TRUE, the formatting will be applied. If the answer to the question is FALSE, the formatting will be *not* be applied.

Figure 1074 illustrates this idea.

	A	B	C	D	E	F	G	H
1	Hilights Duplicates			Above Average			Top 10%	
2	Customer			Sales			Sales	
3	Rod Kloer Firm	FALSE		3.04	FALSE		3.04	FALSE
4	Hal Hinchliff Firm	TRUE		19.41	TRUE		19.41	TRUE
5	Hal Hinchliff Firm	TRUE		18.87	TRUE		18.87	FALSE
6	Shakia Warning Inc.	FALSE		6.9	FALSE		6.9	FALSE
7	Cliff Stalworth Firm	FALSE		11.37	FALSE		11.37	FALSE
8	Jackson Kings LLP	TRUE		18.89	TRUE		18.89	FALSE
9	Jackson Kings LLP	TRUE		18.59	TRUE		18.59	FALSE
10	Rob Swearegene Company	FALSE		7.36	FALSE		7.36	FALSE
11	Marcel Mittelsteadt Firm	FALSE		13.05	TRUE		13.05	FALSE
12	Rob Schiesher LLP	FALSE		4.29	FALSE		4.29	FALSE
13	Jackson Kings LLP	TRUE		11.24	FALSE		11.24	FALSE

Figure 1074

So, the whole idea behind conditional formatting is a TRUE/FALSE logical test. We talked about logical tests earlier in this book in Chapter 5, "Formula and Functions." There, you learned about logical formulas and the IF function. Conditional formatting is the third great example of how useful logical tests are. Basically, if you can think of a question or a logical test, you can use it to apply formatting conditionally. We will discuss two ways to apply conditional formatting:

- Built-in Conditional Formatting features
- Logical formulas stored in memory (in the Conditional Formatting dialog box) that apply conditional formatting

We will start with the built-in conditional formatting features.

Built-in Conditional Formatting

Applying conditional formatting with built-in conditional formatting rules (logical tests) will take three easy steps:

1. Highlight the range with values.
2. Go to Home tab. In the Styles group, click the Conditional Formatting button and select the built-in feature you want from the drop-down list.
3. Select the formatting to apply in the Conditional Formatting dialog box and click OK.

The amazing thing about the built-in conditional formatting rules is that there are so many of them. Similar to the Filter feature you learned about in Chapter 6, "Data Analysis Features," in Excel 2007 and later versions, there are hundreds of built-in rules that take just a few clicks to apply. We will look at five common conditional formatting rules. Figures 1075 to 1079 show how to apply these five common conditional formatting rules:

- Is this item in the list a duplicate?
- Is this value in the list above the average value?
- Is this value in the list in the top 10% of values?
- What rank does it have by icon?
- What rank does it has by horizontal bar length?

To follow along, open the file named excelisfun-Start.xlsm and navigate to the CF(2) sheet.

The following five figures do not have written steps, but instead have a visual picture of what range to select and what button to click.

Highlighting Duplicates

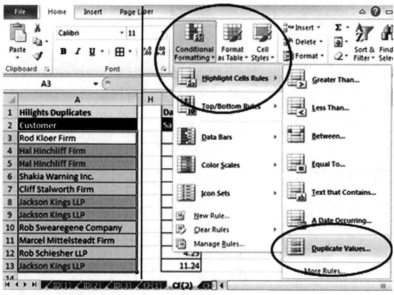

Figure 1075

Highlighting Values That Are Greater Than the Average

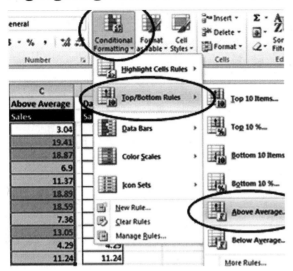

Figure 1076

Highlighting Values That Are in the Top 10%

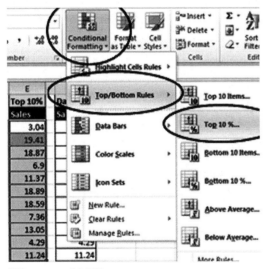

Figure 1077

Icons

Rank values as high, medium, or low with colored arrow icons.

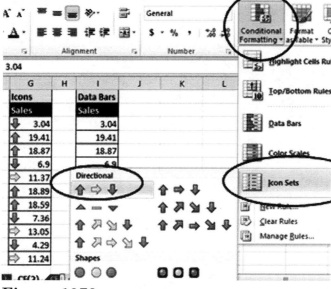

Figure 1078

Data Bars

Rank values, biggest to smallest, by horizontal bar length.

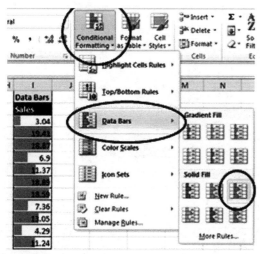

Figure 1079

As you can see there are thousands of possibilities with the built-in conditional formatting options. However, the real power of conditional formatting comes from using logical formulas to apply conditional formatting. Let's take a look at how to do this next.

Logical Formulas

Formulas that evaluate to only TRUE or FALSE are called logical formulas. Logical formulas can be used to apply conditional formatting. However, if you can find a built-in feature to accomplish your conditional formatting goal, it is almost always easier to use the built-in feature than it is to construct a TRUE/FALSE logical formula. Nevertheless, in situations where there is no built-in conditional formatting option, logical formulas can accomplish your conditional formatting goals. Logical formulas have been discussed earlier in the book, in Chapter 5 (Figures 298 to 302, Figures 333 to 348, and Figures 525 to 547).

Figure 1080 shows a summary of what we have already learned about logical formulas. Column A shows the comparative operators that can be used in logical formulas, column E shows the formula results, and column F shows the logical formula. We will use logical formulas similar to these to apply our conditional formatting. However, unlike the logical formulas in Figure 1080, which are stored in cells on the face of the spreadsheet, when we create logical formula to apply conditional formatting, we will use the Conditional Formatting dialog box to enter our formulas and they will be stored in memory. It will be as if the logical formula were created in a cell and copied down a column, except it will all be behind the scenes, stored in memory. For our first example, we will see how to add a fill color of yellow to all the sales numbers that took place on a specified date.

	A	B	C	D	E	F
1	Comparative Operators		1st number	2nd number	Logical Formula Result	Logical Formula
2	> Greater Than		34	43	FALSE	=C2>D2
3	>= Greater Than Or Equal To		34	34	TRUE	=C3>=D3
4	< Less Than		500	100	FALSE	=C4<D4
5	<= Less Than Or Equal To		Jo	Joe	FALSE	=C5=D5
6	= Equal To		Jo	Jo	TRUE	=C6=D6
7	<> Not Equal To		Jo	Jo	FALSE	=C7<>D7
8						

Figure 1080

Highlighting a Cell Based on Another Cell's Value

Our goal is to start with the sales numbers listed in the column B (Figure 1081) and add a fill color of yellow to all the sales numbers that took place on 3/7/2011 (see Figure 1082).

	A	B	C
1	Highlight Cell Based on another Cells Value		
2	**Date to Highlight**	3/7/2011	
3			
4	Date	Sales	
5	3/7/2011	$8,336.00	
6	3/11/2010	$9,894.00	
7	3/7/2011	$11,686.00	
8	3/11/2010	$7,599.00	
9	3/7/2011	$9,609.00	
10	3/9/2010	$11,210.00	
11	3/9/2010	$12,561.00	
12	3/7/2011	$7,125.00	
13	3/9/2010	$11,140.00	

Figure 1081

	A	B	C
1	Highlight Cell Based on another Cells Value		
2	**Date to Highlight**	3/7/2011	
3			
4	Date	Sales	
5	3/7/2011	$8,336.00	
6	3/11/2010	$9,894.00	
7	3/7/2011	$11,686.00	
8	3/11/2010	$7,599.00	
9	3/7/2011	$9,609.00	
10	3/9/2010	$11,210.00	
11	3/9/2010	$12,561.00	
12	3/7/2011	$7,125.00	
13	3/9/2010	$11,140.00	

Figure 1082

To follow along, open the file named excelisfun-Start.xlsm and navigate to the CF(3) sheet.

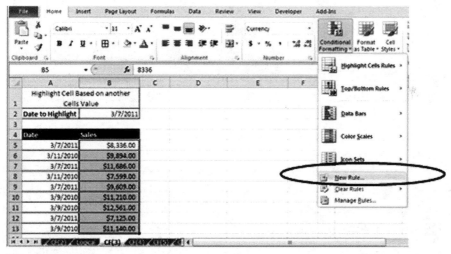

Figure 1083

1. On the CF(3) sheet, highlight the range B5:B13. Be sure that the active cell (white cell in highlighted range) is B5.

2. Go to Home tab. In the Styles group, click the Conditional Formatting button and select New Rules from the drop-down list. The New Formatting Rule dialog box will appear.

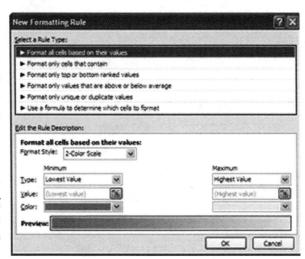

The Conditional Formatting Rules Manager dialog box can be opened more quickly with the Alt, O, D keyboard shortcut.

Figure 1084

3. From the Select a Rule Type list, click Use a Formula to Determine Which Cells to Format. This will open the Conditional Formatting Rules Manager dialog box.

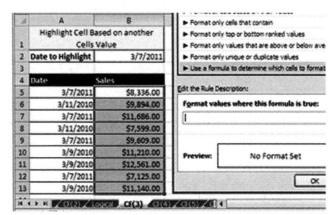

4. When the Conditional Formatting Rules Manager dialog box appears, click in the Format Values Where This Formula Is True text box.

Figure 1085

Before you build your formula, note where the active cell in the selected range is, because you must build your formula from the point of view of the active cell. This is because, even though the formula is put into the dialog box, it is as if it were put into the cell and copied down the selected range to give us our TRUEs and FALSEs.

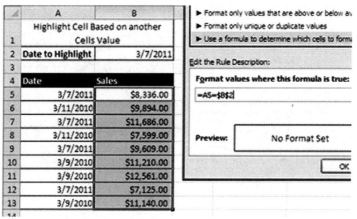

Figure 1086

5. Click cell A5.

By default, an absolute cell reference is entered into the Format Values Where This Formula Is True text box.

6. To convert the absolute cell reference to a relative cell reference, press the F4 key three times.

7. Type an equal sign.
8. Click cell B2.

If you need to brush up on how to use cell references in formulas, see the "Cell References" section of Chapter 5.

In Figure 1086, notice that the formula is in the dialog box. Also notice that the active cell is B5. Although the logical formula is sitting in the dialog box, it is as if it is really sitting in cell B5. In memory, cell B5 is going to get a TRUE or a FALSE depending on the formula result. Further, because the A5 is a relative cell reference and B2 is an absolute cell reference, when the formula is copied down the column in memory, each cell will be told whether the date that sits one cell to the left is equal to 3/7/2011. In this way, each sales number in the highlighted range will get a TRUE or FALSE and thus be formatted, or not formatted, respectively. Now that we have our logical formula, we need to tell it what sort of formatting to apply when the formula evaluates to TRUE.

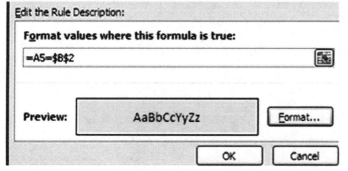

Figure 1087

9. Click the Format Button.
10. When the Format Cells dialog box appears, click the Fill tab and select the color yellow.
11. Click OK on the Format Cells dialog box.
12. Click OK on the New Formatting Rule dialog box.

The sales numbers that are associated with the date 3/7/2011 should now be highlighted.

If you change the date in B2 to 3/9/2010, the conditional formatting will change.

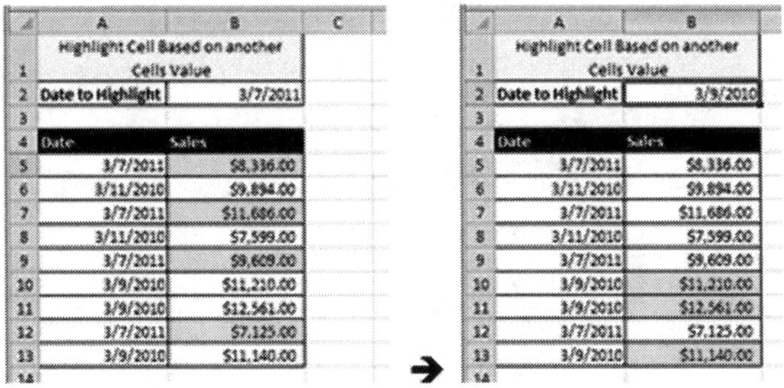

Figure 1088

Because the logical formulas for conditional formatting are stored in memory, it can sometimes be hard to grasp what is actually going on. If we take the same formula that we used in the Formatting Rule dialog box and place it into an actual range of cells in the spreadsheet, it will help us to understand what is occurring.

13. Select the range D5:D13 with the active cell as D5.

14. Create the following formula: **=A5=$B$2**

15. To populate all the cells with the formula, press Ctrl + Enter.

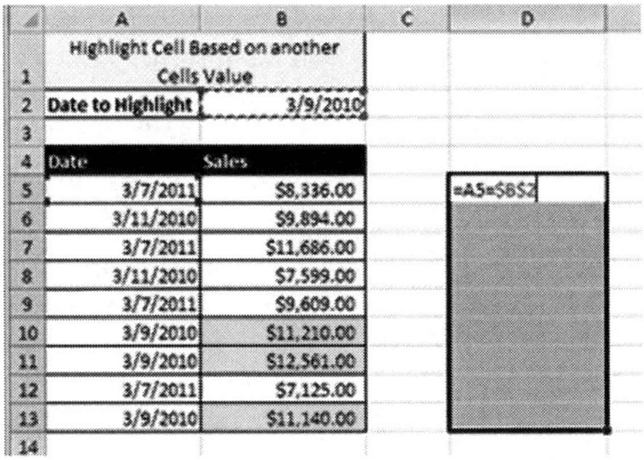

Figure 1089

The TRUE and FALSE formula results that we see in these cells are the same as the TRUE and FALSE formula results that the conditional formatting feature stores in memory.

In Figure 1090, we can see that the individual cells for the sales numbers have formatting applied, but what if we want the whole row to get formatted conditionally? With a slight amendment to our formula, we can easily accomplish this.

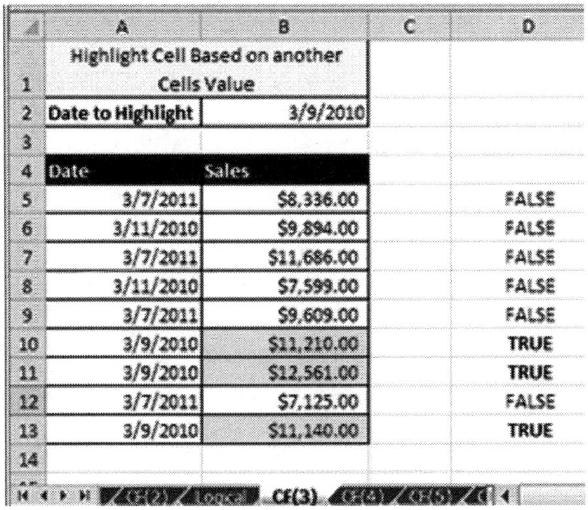

Figure 1090

Highlighting a Whole Row for an Exact Value

Our goal is to apply conditional formatting that will highlight the whole row when the date column contains a date that matches the date in cell B2. Figure 1091 shows the table before applying conditional formatting, and Figure 1092 shows the table after applying conditional formatting.

	A	B	C
1	Highlight Whole Row for an exact value		
2	Date to Highlight	3/7/2011	
3			
4	Date	Sales	
5	3/7/2011	$8,336.00	
6	3/11/2010	$9,894.00	
7	3/7/2011	$11,686.00	
8	3/11/2010	$7,599.00	
9	3/7/2011	$9,609.00	
10	3/9/2010	$11,210.00	
11	3/9/2010	$12,561.00	
12	3/7/2011	$7,125.00	
13	3/9/2010	$11,140.00	
14			

Figure 1091

	A	B	C
1	Highlight Whole Row for an exact value		
2	Date to Highlight	3/7/2011	
3			
4	Date	Sales	
5	3/7/2011	$8,336.00	
6	3/11/2010	$9,894.00	
7	3/7/2011	$11,686.00	
8	3/11/2010	$7,599.00	
9	3/7/2011	$9,609.00	
10	3/9/2010	$11,210.00	
11	3/9/2010	$12,561.00	
12	3/7/2011	$7,125.00	
13	3/9/2010	$11,140.00	
14			

Figure 1092

	A	B	C	D	E	F
1	Highlight Whole Row for an exact value					
2	Date to Highlight	3/7/2011				
3						
4	Date	Sales				
5	3/7/2011	$8,336.00		=$A5=$B$2		
6	3/11/2010	$9,894.00				
7	3/7/2011	$11,686.00				
8	3/11/2010	$7,599.00				
9	3/7/2011	$9,609.00				
10	3/9/2010	$11,210.00				
11	3/9/2010	$12,561.00				
12	3/7/2011	$7,125.00				
13	3/9/2010	$11,140.00				

To follow along, open the file named excelisfun-Start.xlsm and navigate to the CF(4) sheet.

Figure 1093

Sometimes it is easier to create the Logical Formula in the cells before you create it in the New Formatting Rule dialog box.

1. On the CF(4) sheet, highlight the range D5:E13 with D5 as the active cell.
2. Create the following formula: **=$A5=$B$2**
3. To populate all the cells with the formula, press Ctrl + Enter.

If you need to brush up on how to use cell references in formulas (that is, what $A5 and $B$2 mean), see the "Cell References" section in Chapter 5.

We can see that because the Cell Reference $A5 had the column reference locked and not the row, our formula works perfectly!

4	Date	Sales		
5	3/7/2011	$8,336.00	TRUE	TRUE
6	3/11/2010	$9,894.00	FALSE	FALSE
7	3/7/2011	$11,686.00	TRUE	TRUE
8	3/11/2010	$7,599.00	FALSE	FALSE
9	3/7/2011	$9,609.00	TRUE	TRUE
10	3/9/2010	$11,210.00	FALSE	FALSE
11	3/9/2010	$12,561.00	FALSE	FALSE
12	3/7/2011	$7,125.00	TRUE	TRUE
13	3/9/2010	$11,140.00	FALSE	FALSE

Figure 1094

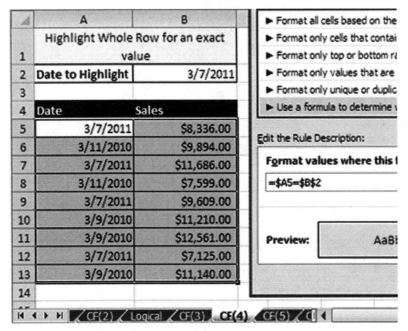

Figure 1095

4. Highlight the range A5:B13.
5. To open the New Rules dialog box, press Alt, O, D.
6. When the Conditional Formatting Rules Manager dialog box appears, click the New Rule button.
7. When the New Formatting Rule dialog box appears, from the Select a Rule Type list, click Use a Formula to Determine Which Cells to Format.
8. In the Format Values Where This Formula Is True field, create the following formula: **=$A5=$B$2**
9. Click the Formatting button and add a yellow fill color.
10. Click OK three times.

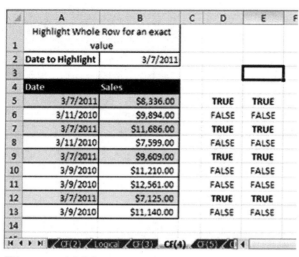

	A	B	C	D	E	F
1	Highlight Whole Row for an exact value					
2	Date to Highlight	3/7/2011				
3						
4	Date	Sales				
5	3/7/2011	$8,336.00		TRUE	TRUE	
6	3/11/2010	$9,894.00		FALSE	FALSE	
7	3/7/2011	$11,686.00		TRUE	TRUE	
8	3/11/2010	$7,599.00		FALSE	FALSE	
9	3/7/2011	$9,609.00		TRUE	TRUE	
10	3/9/2010	$11,210.00		FALSE	FALSE	
11	3/9/2010	$12,561.00		FALSE	FALSE	
12	3/7/2011	$7,125.00		TRUE	TRUE	
13	3/9/2010	$11,140.00		FALSE	FALSE	
14						

The end result should look like Figure 1096.

Figures 1097 and 1098 show the next two examples.

Figure 1096

Highlighting a Whole Row for an Approximate Value

To follow along, open the file named excelisfun-Start.xlsm and navigate to the CF(5) sheet.

The formula used for the range A5:B13 is as follows:
   =VLOOKUP($B$2,$A$5:$A$13,1)=$A5

The goal is that when any value is entered into cell B2, the respective row in the tax table is highlighted.

	A	B	C	D	E
1	Highlight Whole Row for an aproximate value				
2	Income	$5,555.00			
3					
4	Upper Value For Tax	Tax Rate			
5	$0.00	0.00%		FALSE	FALSE
6	$500.00	0.50%		FALSE	FALSE
7	$1,000.00	1.00%		FALSE	FALSE
8	$2,000.00	1.25%		FALSE	FALSE
9	$3,000.00	1.75%		FALSE	FALSE
10	$5,000.00	2.00%		TRUE	TRUE
11	$10,000.00	3.00%		FALSE	FALSE
12	$20,000.00	4.00%		FALSE	FALSE
13	$30,000.00	5.00%		FALSE	FALSE
14					

Select a Rule Type:
► Format all cells based on their values
► Format only cells that contain
► Format only top or bottom ranked values
► Format only values that are above or below ave
► Format only unique or duplicate values
► Use a formula to determine which cells to format

Edit the Rule Description:

Format values where this formula is true:

=VLOOKUP($B$2,$A$5:$A$13,1)=$A5

Preview: AaBbCcYyZz

OK

Figure 1097

If you need to brush up on how to use cell references in formulas (if, for example, you've forgotten what $A5 and $B$2 mean), see the "Cell References" section of Chapter 5.

For more about how the VLOOKUP function works, see "Lookup Functions" section of Chapter 5. In brief, what the VLOOKUP is doing is looking up the $5,555 number in the range A5:A13 and finding the closest match, which is the number $5.000. The VLOOKUP function then delivers the number $5,000 to the formula and asks this question: For this row, does the value in the A column equal $5,000? For row 10, the formula is evaluated this way for both cell A10 and B10:

=VLOOKUP($B$2,$A$5:$A$13,1)=$A5
=5000=5000
TRUE

Highlighting Weekends or Holidays

To follow along, open the file named excelisfun-Start.xlsm and navigate to the CF(6) sheet.

The formula used for the range A5:B16 is as follows:
=NOT(NETWORKDAYS($A5,$A5,$G$5:$G$11))

The goal is to highlight holidays and weekends.

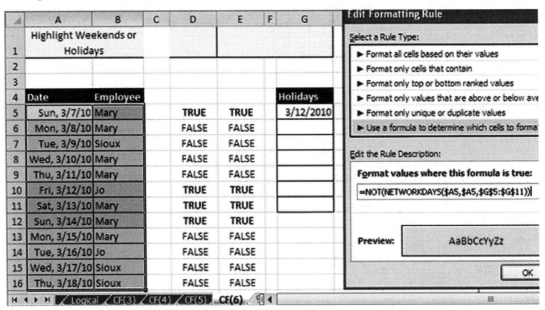

Figure 1098

The logical formula in this example uses two functions that we have not looked at before: NETWORKDAYS and NOT. The NETWORKDAYS function looks at a start and end date and a series of holiday dates and then counts the number of workdays. The NETWORKDAYS function works when the weekend is considered Saturday and Sunday.

You might now be asking, "Yeah, but what if you have days off during the traditional workweek?" Easy: For days other than Saturday or Sunday, use the new Excel 2010 function NETWORKDAYS.INTL. In our example, because the start and end date are the same day, the NETWORKDAYS function will deliver only a 1 (yes, it is a workday) or a 0 (no, it is not a workday). Because logical functions, such as the IF, OR, and AND functions (described earlier in the book) and the NOT function can interpret a 1 as TRUE and a 0 as FALSE, we can use the NOT function to tell us which days are weekends or holidays. The two possible results for our formula are as follows:

NOT(1) = NOT(TRUE) = FALSE = It is a workday = Will not get the formatting

NOT(0) = NOT(FALSE) = TRUE = It is not a workday = Will get the formatting

So, as you can see, you can use many amazing tricks to automatically highlight data with the Conditional Formatting feature.

Our next Excel Efficiency-Robust Rule is this:

Rule 43: Whether with the built-in features or logical formulas, conditional formatting always comes down to building a logical statement that evaluates to TRUE (formatting applied) or FALSE (formatting not applied).

Next we want to look at the Find and Replace and Go To features in Excel.

9

FIND AND REPLACE AND GO TO FEATURES

Inevitably, you'll sometimes need to find all the occurrences of an item and replace them with something new. For example, in Figure 1099, we can see that the name Sue is repeated numerous times in column A. If our goal is to find all the occurrences of Sue and replace them with Sioux, we can do this with the Find and Replace feature. Find and Replace can find and replace text, numbers, or even formula elements. The Find and Replace feature is found in the Editing group on the Home tab. The keyboard shortcuts for Find and Replace feature and the Go To feature are as follows:

- Find = Ctrl + F
- Find and Replace = Ctrl + H
- Go To = F5

To follow along, open the file excelisfun-Start.xlsm and navigate to the F&R&GoTo sheet.

	A	B	C	D	E	F
1	Names	Sales	Sales	Sales	Sales	
2	Sue	86	53	96	91	
3	Sue	0	79	128	98	
4	Joe	72	54	129	105	
5	Joe	61	125	0	94	
6	Phil	120	112	127	90	
7	Frank	121	0	95	60	
8	Chin	96	107	125	63	
9	Frank	50	111	75	127	
10	Chin	94	57	0	67	
11	Sue	76	75	71	104	
12	Phil	107	0	87	94	
13	Phil	50	64	95	0	
14	Chin	0	51	62	68	
15						

Figure 1099

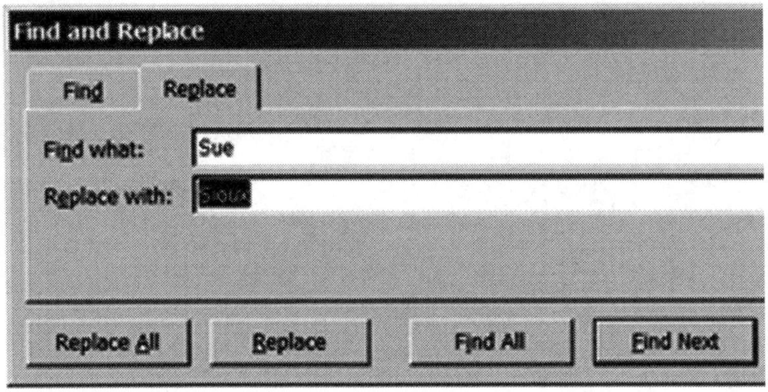

Figure 1100

1. On the F&R&GoTo sheet, highlight the range A2:A14.
2. Press Ctrl + H to open the Find and Replace dialog box use.
3. Type **Sue** in the Find What text box and type **Sioux** in the Replace With field.
4. Click the Replace All button.
5. Click Close.

> **Note**: If you want to be more cautious, you can use the Find Next and Replace buttons to look at each occurrence. This can prevent mistakes like replacing the verb sue with Sioux if your file has such a case. You can also use the Options button to search Case Sensitive or Match Entire Cell Contents.

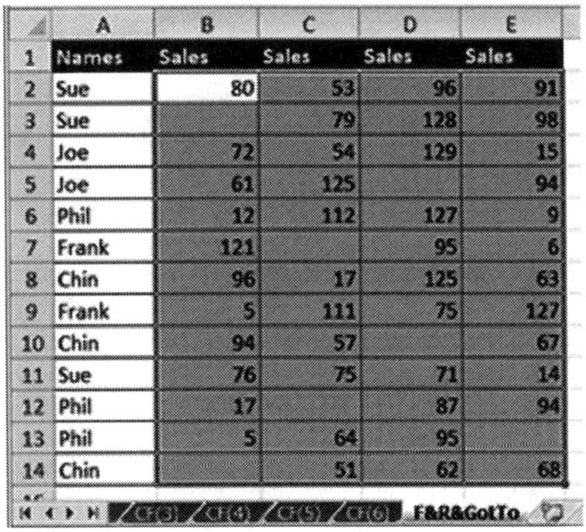

	A	B	C	D	E
1	Names	Sales	Sales	Sales	Sales
2	Sue	80	53	96	91
3	Sue		79	128	98
4	Joe	72	54	129	15
5	Joe	61	125		94
6	Phil	12	112	127	9
7	Frank	121		95	6
8	Chin	96	17	125	63
9	Frank	5	111	75	127
10	Chin	94	57		67
11	Sue	76	75	71	14
12	Phil	17		87	94
13	Phil	5	64	95	
14	Chin		51	62	68

Figure 1101

6. To replace all the zeros with blanks, highlight the range B2:E14 and open the Find and Replace by pressing Ctrl + H.
7. Click the Options button and then check the Match Entire Cell Contents check box.
8. Type **0** in the Find What field and leave the Replace With field empty.
9. Click the Replace All button.
10. Click Close.

You can see the result in this figure.

In Figure 1101, we saw how to remove all the zeros and replace them with blanks. This trick is good when you have zeros in cells and they are being used by the AVERAGE function and you need to remove them so that they are not used in the Average calculation. Now what if you actually have blanks and you want to put the word None in each blank cell? Let's take a look at how to do this next.

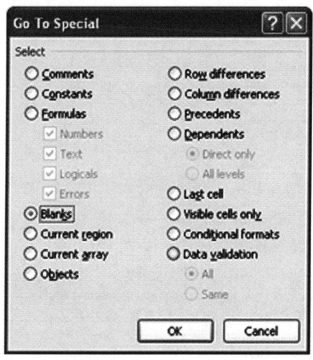

Figure 1102

11. To replace all the blanks with the word *None*, highlight the range B2:E14 and open the Go To feature by pressing the F5 key.
12. When the Go To dialog box appears, click the Special button.
13. Click the Blanks option button.

In Figure 1102, we can see the Go To Special dialog box. This Go To feature will highlight all the "special" items that you select. In our example, we will highlight all the blank cells and then enter our items. But notice some of these other options:

- **Constants**: Will highlight all cells that do not contain a formula (if, for instance, you want to format them).
- **Formulas**: Will highlight all cells that contain a formula (if, for instance, you want to protect them)
- **Objects**: Will highlight all objects (if, for instance, you want to delete them)
- **Conditional Formats**: Will highlight all cells that contain a conditional format (if, for instance, you want to remove them)
- **Data validation**: Will highlight all cells that contain a data validation (if, for instance, you want to remove them)

	A	B	C	D	E	F
1	Names	Sales	Sales	Sales	Sales	
2	Sioux	86	53	96	91	
3	Sioux		79	128	98	
4	Joe	72	54	129	15	
5	Joe	61	125		94	
6	Phil	12	112	127	9	
7	Frank	121		95	6	
8	Chin	96	17	125	63	
9	Frank	5	111	75	127	
10	Chin	94	57		67	
11	Sioux	76	75	71	14	
12	Phil	17		87	94	
13	Phil	5	64	95		
14	Chin		51	62	68	
15						

Figure 1103

1. With all the blank cells highlighted, type **None** in the active cell.
2. Then to enter the text into all the cells, press Ctrl + Enter.

	A	B	C	D	E	F
1	Names	Sales	Sales	Sales	Sales	
2	Sioux	86	53	96	91	
3	Sioux	None	79	128	98	
4	Joe	72	54	129	15	
5	Joe	61	125	None	94	
6	Phil	12	112	127	9	
7	Frank	121	None	95	6	
8	Chin	96	17	125	63	
9	Frank	5	111	75	127	
10	Chin	94	57	None	67	
11	Sioux	76	75	71	14	
12	Phil	17	None	87	94	
13	Phil	5	64	95	None	
14	Chin	None	51	62	68	
15						

Figure 1104

The sheet should look like Figure 1104.

Appendix

Excel Efficiency-Robust Rules

Now that we are at the end of this book, I must confess that I could have included significantly more material here. However, it is not possible to put everything in one book. So, see you in the next book for more!

I hope you have learned a lot about how to build efficient and robust Excel solutions and, as important, how to have *fun* with Excel. If you have learned even some of the foundations of Excel from this book, you can be the hero in any workplace, "excel" in any Excel job interview, and slay any Excel dragons that your boss demands that you face!

The next few pages review the 43 Excel Efficiency-Robust Rules, thus summarizing much of what you have learned in this book and providing a quick reminder of how to optimize all your Excel experiences:

Rule 1: Excel sheets are rectangles with columns (letters) that move left to right and rows (numbers) that move up and down. A firm understanding of this will help us later to build formulas that are efficient and robust. (page 3)

Rule 2: Always name sheets (double-click the sheet tab, type the name, press Enter) with an easy-to-understand name so that navigation through the workbook and formulas with sheet references are easy to understand. (page 3)

Rule 3: Learn keyboard shortcuts because they are fast! (page 23)

Rule 4: If we are the ones designing the spreadsheet, we always want a way to double-check to determine whether our calculation or data analysis is correct. (page 31)

Rule 5: Excel is literal about how it sees data. Spaces matter in Excel. "Tina" is different from " Tina". (page 33)

Rule 6: When investigating a problem with a formula, it is efficient to check the formula first to determine whether the formula is correct, and then to work backward through the formula's inputs to determine whether any of the raw data is creating the problem. The keyboard shortcut F2 puts a cell into Edit mode and places the cursor at the end of the formula. (page 33)

Rule 7: PivotTables are amazing for summarizing data. As long as you can visualize the summary table and see the row labels or column labels before you begin creating the PivotTable, PivotTables are not hard to do! (page 40)

Rule 8: To use Excel's data analysis features, such as Sorting and PivotTables, you have to store your raw data with a table format structure, which requires that you have: 1) field names in first row, 2) records in rows, 3) blank cells surround outside edge of table, 4) no blank cells, columns, or rows inside table. (page 43)

Rule 9: The Excel Table feature converts a table of data stored with the table format structure into an Excel-like database that has advantages such as dynamic ranges. (page 49)

Rule 10: Number formatting can make the surface of the spreadsheet look different from what is actually there, in the cells. For example, you can format the number 10.255 to look like it is the number 10. (60)

Rule 11: Formulas do not "see" formatting. When formulas calculate, they do not look at the formatted numbers, but instead they look at the actual number that sits in the cell. In terms of our house metaphor, formulas do not look at the façade of the house; they look at the inside of the house. The lone dreaded exception to this rule is if someone has enabled the Precision as Displayed option. (page 61)

Rule 12: When entering dates, Excel uses Date number formatting for the surface of the spreadsheet, but underneath is a serial number that enables us to do date math. Examples of serial numbers are 1 for 1/1/1900, 2 for 1/2/1900, and so on. Examples of date math are "Days Between Two Dates = Later Date – Earlier Date" and "Loan Maturity Date = Loan Issue Date + Number of Days Loan Is Outstanding." (page 65)

Rule 13: If a formula input will never change, just type the number into the formula; otherwise, if a formula input will change, put it in a cell and refer to it in a formula with a cell reference. This leads to efficient formula creation. (page 69)

Rule 14: When you enter time into Excel, enter hour, minutes, seconds separated by colons, then a space, then AM or PM. Excel uses Time number formatting for the surface of the spreadsheet, but underneath is a serial number that allows us to do time math. Time serial numbers are between 0 and 1 and represent the proportion of one 24-hour day. For example, the time 6:00 AM represents the number 0.25 or 6/24. Two useful time formulas are "Proportions of 24 Hour Day = Later Time – Earlier Time" and "Hours Worked = 24 * (Later Time – Earlier Time)." (page 70)

Rule 15: 8.8% is not a number. 8.8% is a formatted symbolic representation of the number 0.088. (page 71)

Rule 16: If you type .03 in cell, and then apply the Percentage number formatting, you get 3.0%. (page 74)

Rule 17: If you type 3 in a cell, and then apply the Percentage number format, you get 300.0%. (page 75)

Rule 18: If you preformat the cells with Percentage number formatting and type a .03 or a 3 into a cell, you get 3.0%. (page 76)

Rule 19: Always be sure to determine whether you have enough decimals showing when you are using Percentage number formatting. (77)

Rule 20: Number formatting is on top (what you see), and the numbers are underneath (what Excel uses for calculations). (page 78)

Rule 21: Avoid adding alignment formatting to data because the default alignment (numbers = right, text = left, logical values = centered) can help us to quickly track down data problems. (page 87)

Rule 22: Center Across Selection is a good alternative to the commonly used Merge and Center because it has fewer drawbacks (like cut and paste problems with Merge and Center). You can apply Center Across Selection from the Horizontal option on the Alignment tab in the Format Cells dialog box. (page 92)

Rule 23: Borders must be applied in the proper sequence: 1) style, 2) color, 3) preview diagram. A single line above and a double line below the last number in a report is a visual indicator that the number is the "bottom line." (page 96)

Rule 24: Always use Print Preview before you print so that you can determine what page setup must be done to create a professional-looking report. (page 99)

Rule 25: When building formulas, if the formula input can change, put it into a cell and refer to it with a cell reference in all formulas. Said a different way: If the formula input can change, don't type it into a formula. This leads to efficient formula creation. (page 123)

Rule 26: Numbers that don't change (for example, 12 months or 24 hours) can be type directly into a formula. (page 124)

Rule 27: Learn the math order of operations so that you can create accurate formulas. (page 151)

Rule 28: The four types of cell references are relative, absolute, mixed with column locked, and mixed with row locked. When creating formulas with cell references that you will copy to other cells, ask two questions of every cell reference in your formula to figure out which of the four cell references you need. Q1: What do you want the cell reference to do when you copy it across the columns or horizontally? Q2: What do you want the cell reference to do when you copy it across the rows or vertically? This leads to efficient formula creation. (page 176)

Rule 29: To save time in formula creation and to create spreadsheets that are easy to use, formula inputs should be put into an assumption table created with these rules in mind: 1) Labels in the formula range and assumption table are parallel, 2) the assumption table is set off to the side and distinctly formatted, and 3) formula inputs are unambiguously labeled. (page 188)

Rule 30: The rules for efficient formula creation are: 1) If a formula input can vary, put it into a cell and refer to it in your formula with a cell reference; 2) label all formula inputs; 3) if a formula input does not vary, type it directly into the formula; 4) learn how to use all four types a cell references effectively; 5) orient your assumption table so that the labels in the formula range and assumption table are parallel. (page 188)

Rule 31: Use cell ranges in formulas whenever possible. For example, use the formula =SUM(A2:A7) rather than =A2+A3+A4+A5+A6+A7 because it is faster to create, it allows structural updates (like inserting rows or deleting cells), and it can handle inconsistent data (like numbers and words in same column). (page 207)

Rule 32: Use the Insert Functions dialog box to find functions and use the function Help to learn how to use a specific function. (page 217)

Rule 33: When setting up categories for formulas that use the IF or VLOOKUP functions, follow these rules (if possible): 1) The lower limit is included in the category, but the upper limit is not (for example, $5,000 <= Sales < $7,000). 2) All possible categories are included. 3) Categories are organized in ascending order. These rules can be stated in formal language; the categories are mutually exclusive and collectively exhaustive and are organized in ascending order. (page 265)

Rule 34: Use ROUND function when 1) you are required to round (like with money), 2) you are multiplying or dividing numbers with decimals, and 3) you will use the formula result in subsequent calculations. (page 310)

Rule 35: Array formulas do operations on arrays (ranges of cells as opposed to single cells). Array formulas are great because they can help in two ways: 1) Array formulas can help to create compact, efficient spreadsheets because they use less spreadsheet real estate, and 2) there are some calculations that cannot be made at all unless you use an array formula. When entering an array formula, you must use the keystrokes Ctrl + Shift + Enter. After you press Ctrl + Shift + Enter, Excel automatically puts curly brackets at the beginning and end of the formula. When you will be adding the values from an array, it is usually more efficient to use the SUMPRODUCT function because it does not require Ctrl + Shift + Enter. Some functions such as FREQUENCY are array functions and must be entered with Ctrl + Shift + Enter. (page 338)

Rule 36: The three main keys to sorting are as follows: 1) When using the Sort button to sort a column, select only one cell in the column before clicking the sort button. 2) When sorting more than one field using sort buttons, sort the major sort field last. 3) When sorting more than one field using the Sort dialog box, select the major sort field as the first level. (page 359)

Rule 37: The three main keys for subtotaling are as follows: 1) Sort the fields before using the Subtotal feature. 2) At Each Change In determines where the new rows will be inserted, and Add Subtotal To determines which column will get the SUBTOTAL function. 3) If doing more than one subtotal, be sure to uncheck Replace Current Subtotals check box. (page 373)

Rule 38: PivotTables are amazing for creating summary reports. Key points are as follows: 1) Row and column labels determine the shape of the PivotTable, values contain the fields that will be calculated upon, and the Report Filter can filter the whole PivotTable. 2) Creating and "pivoting" the report is done by clicking and dragging fields to the location you want. 3) Value field settings allow you to change the formatting, function, or calculation. (page 419)

Rule 39: The Filter feature enables you to show records based on criteria. You can do or and and criteria as well as use special built-in filters for dates, numbers, and text. The fastest way to extract the records of interest is to 1) filter, 2) copy, 3) paste in a new location. (433)

Rule 40: Advanced Filter is great for extracting records and placing them in a new location while keeping the original data set intact. The three distinct areas for Advanced Filter are data set, Criteria area, and Extract area. The field names in the data set and the Criteria area must be exactly the same. When using or criteria, place criteria on different lines. When using and criteria, place the criteria on the same lines. When creating between criteria, repeat field names on same row. Advanced Filter can also be used to extract a unique list. (page 448)

Rule 41: Text to Columns is great for breaking apart data in a single cell that is separated by delimiters and placing it into multiple cells. A delimiter is a character such as a space, a comma, or a tab. Sometimes you have to run the Text to Columns feature more than once to get the data broken apart correctly. (page 456)

Rule 42: The two rules for charts are 1) Choose the best chart type that matches the data type and the particular message you are delivering, and 2) eliminate chart junk. (page 471)

Rule 43: Whether with the built-in features or logical formulas, conditional formatting always comes down to building a logical statement that evaluates to TRUE (formatting applied) or FALSE (formatting not applied). (page 521)

3D cell reference 198
3D charts
  Avoiding 466

A
A1
  Jump to 13
Above average
  Highlighting 510
Absolute reference 156, 160
Access
  Importing from 460
Accounting format 56
Adding through sheets 198
Address
  Separating 454
Ad-hoc analysis 405
Adjusting
  Width 93
Advanced filter 434
  Two criteria - AND 436
  Two criteria - mixed 439
  Two criteria - OR 438
Alignment 78
AND 258
Ants
  Dancing 6
Argument 27
Array formulas 320
  vs. SUMPRODUCT 324
Array functions 332
Arrow keys
  for formula entry 151
  Formula entry 19
  Navigating 14

Arrows
  Sheet navigation 3
Assumption tables 185
Aunt Sally 145
AutoComplete
  Trouble 49
AVERAGE 217, 312
  Highlighting above 510
  in pivot table 416
  vs. median or mode 311
AVERAGEIF 218
AVERAGEIFS 238
Averaging
  Multiple criteria 238
  without zeroes 218
Axis
  Number format 494

B
Backing in to answer 318
Balancing columns 254
Bar charts 469, 489
  Tiny 511
Bar vs. column 489
  Default chart 467
Behind cells
  See 72
Below average
  Filtering 426
Blank rows 41
Blanks
  in pivot data 402
  Replacing all 526
  Selecting all 523
  Sorting to bottom 348
Bold 89

Borders 94
Break apart data 448
Break-Even analysis 500
Built-In functions 206

C

Car payments 221
Carlberg, Conrad 146
Categories
  Assigning 271
Category
  for X-Y 467
Cell references 1, 155
Cell styles 114
  Create new 116
Center
  Across selection 90
Centering 78
  when printed 109
Chart
  Bar 469
  Changing style 479
  Column 468, 481
  Combining two types 501
  Creating 471
  Data labels 475
  Histograms 469
  Junk 466
  Line 470
  Linked labels 474
  Moving 478
  Multiple 490
  Pie 468
  Printing 478
  Scatter 471
  Shortcuts 481
  Source data 501
  Stacked 470
  Templates 480
  Tiny 505
  Types 468

  X-Y 471
Charting
  Pivot chart 391
Charts
  Adding 97
  Data 467
Clear all 351
Color
  Fill or font 92
  Filtering by 425
  part of cell 511
  Sorting by 355
Color coding 21
Column
  Charts 481
  Select 13
Column charts 468
Column vs. bar
  Default chart 467
Column width 8
Columns 1
  Rearranging with sort 355
Columns in balance 254
Combination charts 501
Comma separated
  see CSV
Comma style 93
Commission calculation 261
Comparative operators 132, 253
Compare 2 lists
  Using match 300
Compounded rate 209
Condition
  Adding 26
Conditional formatting 507
  Built-In 508
  Formulas 512
Convert to number 87
Copy formulas
  Using fill handle 20
Copying
  Page setup 107

Copying data 7
Copying from workbooks 457
Count with 1 condition 136
COUNTA 229
COUNTIF 136, 236
COUNTIFS 234
    vs. SUMPRODUCT 236
Counting numbers 83
Counting words 229
Create table 113
Creating
    Charts 471
Creditworthiness 260
Criteria
    Multiple 231
    with SUMIFS 26
Crosshair cursor 20
CSV
    Importing 460
Ctrl
    Flyout menu 9
    Noncontiguous 92
Ctrl+Enter 16
Ctrl+Shift+Enter 321
Curly brackets 322
Currency
    Formatting with formula 139
Current region 6

D

Daily sales report 397
Dancing
    Ants 6
Dark vs. light 93
Data
    Importing 457
    vs. information 25
Data alignment 78
Data bars 511
Data labels
    Charts 475

Data validation 294
Database
    Excel as 43
Date
    Formatting 61
    Math 62
    on each page 103
    seeing serial number 64
Dates
    Adding to 65
    Filtering 431
    Grouping in pivot table 396
    with words 403
Decimals
    Increase 59
    Permanently remove 61
Defined names 224
    for VLOOKUP 292
    from selection 227
    Manager 226
Dialog launcher 100
DIV/0! error 339
DOLLAR 139
Dollar signs
    Formatting in table 55
Dollar signs in reference 156
Double line 96
Double negative
    in SUMPRODUCT 247
Dropdown list 294
Dropdowns
    Hiding 113
Duplicates
    Highlighting 509
    Remove with filter 445
Dynamic ranges 45

E

Edit
  Links 198
Edit mode 21
Edit source data
  for charts 501
Efficiency rules
  Recap 527
Efficient formulas 188
Enter key
  Direction 203
Error checking 86
Errors 339
  Sorting to top 350
Evaluate formula 142
Excel rules
  Recap 527
External data 457
Extract records
  Advanced filter 435
  Remove duplicates 445
  to new sheet 441
  with filter 424

F

F4 key 157
Façade 57
Field list
  Pivot tables 377
Field names disappear
  After sort 352
Fill handle
  Copy formulas 20
Filter dropdowns
  Hiding 113
Filtering 420
  Adding after 432
  Advanced 434
  Averaging after 432
  Below average 426
  Between 440

by Color 425
Date criteria 441
Dates 431
Removing 424
Right-Click 425
to extract 424
Top 10 427
with and 422
with dropdowns 421
with or 423
Words 427
Find 523
Finishing typing
  Automatically 49
Fitting
  to 1 page wide 109
Flipping data 11
Font size 91
Footer 101
Format cells dialog 90
Formatted
  Version of number 59
Formatting
  Clear all 351
  Conditionally 507
  Date 61
  Percentages 72
  Style 90
  Time 65
  with table styles 113
Formula auditing 142
Formula auditing mode 72
Formula copy
  Using fill handle 20
Formula input rules 187
Formulas
  3 ways to enter 151
  5 types 120
  5 ways to enter 202
  Creating 120
  Defined 119
  Efficient 188

Elements 120
Entering many at once 252
Inputs 123
Selecting all 525
Table nomenclature 51
Using ranges 203
FREQUENCY 332
Frequency distribution
  Charting 484
  using FREQUENCY 332
  with pivot table 412
Function
  Finding 208
  Nesting 256
Functions
  Help 215
Future value 208
FV 208

G

Gap width 486
General format
  Keyboard shortcut 68
Get external data 457
Go to 523
Go to special 525
Goal seek 318
Green triangle 86
Group mode 107
  Damaging 107
  Exiting 107

H

Hash signs 8
Header 101
  Worksheet name 102
Headings
  Repeating 110
Help
  Function 215

Hiding
  Dropdowns 113
Highlight column 13
Highlighting
  Approximate value 519
  Based on other cell 512
  Holidays 520
  Shortcuts 15
  Weekends 520
  Whole row 517
Histograms 469, 483
Holidays
  Highlighting 520
House payments 221

I

Icons
  Adding 511
IF 148, 248
  Nesting functions 264
  vs. VLOOKUP 268
  with and 258
  with or 255
Importing
  Data 457
INDEX
  with MATCH 302
Input values
  not changing 69
Inputs
  Formulas 123
Insert function dialog 208
Interest rates
  Entering 213
Interface 1
Investment value 208
ISNA 301
Italics 89

J

Joining text 132
Junk
  on charts 466

L

LARGE 141
Large spreadsheets
  Page setup 107
Largest value 225
Largest values 141
Left to right
  Sort 355
Left vs. right 78
Light vs. dark 93
Line charts 470, 492
Linking
  to workbook 195
  to worksheet 191
Links
  Edit 198
Lists
  Compare 2 300
Loan payments 221
Locking a reference 156
Logical formula 131
Lookup
  see VLOOKUP

M

MATCH 286
  vs. VLOOKUP 291
  with INDEX 302
Math operators 123
MAX 225
  in pivot table 416
Median 311, 312
Merge
  Drawbacks 91

MIN 228
  in pivot table 416
Minus-Minus
  in SUMPRODUCT 247
Mixed data
  Sorting 347
Mixed reference 169
Mode 311, 314
Moving
  Charts 478
Moving data 5
Multiplication table 176

N

N/A error 339
  Sorting to top 350
Name
  Separating first and last 449
  Separating with formula 453
  Worksheets 2
NAME? error 339
Names
  Defined 224
  from selection 227
Navigate
  Worksheets 2
Navigating
  Shortcuts 15
Nesting functions 256
  IF 264
Noncontiguous 92
NUM! error 339
Number
  vs. format 57
Number format
  in chart axis 494
Number signs 8
Numbers
  Text 79

O

One cell
  Selecting only 113
Operators
  Comparative 132
  Comparative 132, 253
  Math 123
OR 255
Order of operations 144

P

Page breaks
  Viewing 107
Page numbers
  at bottom 101
Page setup 98
  Copying to new sheet 107
  Multiple pages 105
Parsing data 448
Paste name 294
Percentage of total 414
Percentages 70
  Decimals 77
  Entering 74
  Formatting 72
  Pre-Formatting 76
Pie charts 465, 468
Pivot chart 391
  Pivoting 395
Pivot tables
  % of total 414
  3 or more fields 390
  After data change 418
  Average 416
  Blanks in data 402
  by Weeks 402
  Calculation function 384
  Checkmarks vs. dragging 378
  Collapsing 388
  Creating 376
  Date field problems 403

Drawbacks 418
  Easy 374
  Field list missing 39
  Filtering 388
  Four areas 377
  Grouping dates 396
  Max 416
  Number formatting 383
  Percentage of total 414
  Pivoting 385
  Replicating 408
  Report filter 405
  Running totals 415
  Show field names 381
  Slicers 408
  Style formatting 382
  vs. formulas 419
  vs. subtotals 387
  vs. SUMIFS 34
  vs. SUMIFS 34, 380
  vs. SUMPRODUCT 399
PMT 221
Positioning charts 97
Pound signs 8
Print area
  Advantages 107
Print preview 99
Printing
  Charts 478
  Entire workbook 104
  Noncontiguous 106
  Preparing to 99
  Selection 104
Proportion decrease 159

Q

QAT
  Adding icons 4
Quick access toolbar
  Adding icons 4

R

Railroad track 68
Rainbow coding 21
RAND function 354
Random sort 353
Range finder 21
Ranges 203
RANK 316
Ranking 316
REF! error 206, 339
Reference 1
Region
　Current 6
Relative reference 156, 158
Remove duplicates
　Advanced filter 445
Removing
　Subtotals 369
Rename
　Worksheets 2
Repeat on each page 103
Repeating
　Headings 110
REPLACE 454, 523
Report filter
　Pivot tables 405
　Showing all 408
Ribbon 1
　Appearance 3
　Explained 4
　Hide 4
　Size 3
Right vs. left 78
Right-Click key 10
ROUND 308
Rounding 308
Row vs. column
　Default chart 467
Rows 1
Rows to repeat 110
Running totals 415

S

Scatter charts 471, 494
Scenarios 189
Screen tips 22
SEARCH 454
See behind spreadsheet 72
Select
　Column 13
Select all 5
Selecting
　Blanks 525
　Shortcuts 15
Selecting one cell
　vs. all cells 113
Selection cursor 20
Series
　for X-Y 467
Set up 1
Sheet navigation arrows 3
Sheet references 191
Shortcut
　for A1 13
　to SUM 15
Shortcuts 5
Show formulas mode 72
Show report filter 408
Slicers 409
SMALL 141
Small charts 505
Smallest value 228
Smart tag 8
　Error check 87
Sorting 42, 343
　Appears wrong 347
　Blanks to remove 348
　by Color 355
　Errors 350
　Field names 352
　Hierarchy 346
　Left to right 355
　Many columns 344
　Mixed data 347

Multiple fields 357
Random sequence 353
Right-Click 345
Shortcuts 351
Smallest to biggest 344
Using AZ or ZA 358
Words 346
Spaces
Calculation problems 33
Sparklines 505
Spearing formula 198
Special cells
Selecting 525
Splitting data 448
Square dot
see Fill handle
Squint method 93
Stacked charts 470, 490
Status bar
Point vs edit 28
Sum 31
Stay in cell 16
Stock quotes
via web query 461
Style
Formatting 90
Styles 112
Cell 114
SUBTOTAL
Arguments 367
Filtered data 433
Subtotals
Adding 360
Averaging 368
Copying only 365
Count words 370
Gone wrong 362
Removing 369
Show only 364
Two levels 371
vs. pivot table 387

SUMIFS 26, 183, 231
Compatibility 2003 30
vs. pivot table 380
SUMPRODUCT 240
Minus-Minus 247
Replacing COUNTIFS 244
vs. array formulas 324
Surface
Under 72
Switch data 11

T
Table 44
Formulas 51
Name 52
Shortcut 113
Table structure 40
Tabs 2
Ribbon 4
Templates
Charts 480
Text
Numbers 79
Text formatting
on formulas 121
Text to columns 448
Time
Entering 70
Formatting 65
seeing fraction 69
Subtracting 67
Tiny charts 505
ToolTips 22
Top 10
with filter 427
Top 10%
Highlighting 510
Traffic lights
Adding 511
Transpose 11, 336
Transposing

using TRANSPOSE 336
Trendlines 494, 498
Tufte, Edward 466, 505
Two-Way lookup 286, 302

U
Under
  Surface 72
Undo 64

V
Validation list
  Defined names 292
VALUE! error 339
Variable label 138
Verifying results 31
View
  Second 194
Visible cells 365
VLOOKUP 268
  Above 307
  Other sheet 291
  to left 306
  vs. MATCH 290

W
Web query 461
Weekends
  Highlighting 520
Weeks
  Grouping by 402
Widen column 12
Width
  Adjusting 93
  Chart columns 486
  Column 8
Words in date field 403
Workbook references 191

Worksheet
  Insert 8
  Names 2
  Navigate 2
  Tabs 2
Worksheet name
  in header 102
Wrap text 115

X
X-Y charts 471, 494

Y
Yes or no 248

EVERY FRIDAY
Watch two Excel super-heroes
Duke it Out

MrExcel
vs.
Excel Is Fun

in the

DUELING EXCEL PODCASTS

 ## Mike "ExcellsFun" Girvin
&
Bill "MrExcel" Jelen

See that there are many different ways to solve any Excel problem. Watch as Bill and Mike offer innovative ways to solve common Excel problems. Become more efficient with Excel in five minutes a week!

More fun than watching the Jersey Shore!

GTLD - Gym, Tan, Laundry, DuelingExcel

http://www.youtube.com/user/ExcellsFun

http://learnmrexcel.wordpress.com

Mike Gel Girvin on "ExcelisFun"

Over 1,000 Excel Videos!

Every Topic In This Book
Explained By The Author
Mike 'ExcelisFun' Girvin

http://www.youtube.com/user/ExcelisFun